Conservation of Exploited Species

The use of wildlife for food and other human needs poses one of the greatest threats to the conservation of biodiversity. Wildlife exploitation is also critically important for subsistence and commerce to many people from a variety of cultures. This book brings together international experts to examine interactions between the biology of wildlife and the divergent goals of people involved in hunting, fishing, gathering and culling wildlife. Reviews of theory show how sustainable exploitation is tied to the study of population dynamics, with direct links to reproductive rates, life histories, behaviour, and ecology. This information is used to predict the impacts of exploitation on population conservation. As such theory is rarely put into effective practice to achieve sustainable use and successful conservation, *Conservation of Exploited Species* explores the many reasons for failure and considers remedies to tackle them, including scientific issues such as how to incorporate uncertainty into estimations, as well as social and political problems that stem from conflicting goals in exploitation.

JOHN D. REYNOLDS is a Reader in Evolutionary Ecology at the University of East Anglia, UK. His research focuses on the evolution of reproductive behaviour and life histories, with an emphasis on implications for conservation of marine and freshwater fishes. He is a co-author of a textbook *Marine Fisheries Ecology* (2001) and is co-editing *The Handbook of Fish and Fisheries* (2002). He was awarded the FSBI medal of the Fisheries Society of the British Isles in 2000.

GEORGINA M. MACE is the Director of Science at the Institute of Zoology, Zoological Society of London, UK. Her research concerns extinction risk assessment and she has had extensive involvement with the IUCN in developing systems for classifying species in Red Lists of threatened species. She has co-edited *Creative Conservation* (1994) and *Conservation in a Changing World* (1999), and is currently a co-editor of the journal *Animal Conservation*. She was awarded the Order of the British Empire in 1998 in recognition of her contributions to conservation science.

KENT H. REDFORD is Director of Biodiversity Analysis at the Wildlife Conservation Society, New York, USA. His research interests focus on effects of human use on biodiversity conservation, parks and protected areas and also on wildlife use by indigenous peoples. He has co-edited *Neotropical Wildlife Use and Conservation* (1991), *Conservation of Neotropical Forests* (1992) and *Parks in Peril* (1998).

JOHN G. ROBINSON is Senior Vice-President and Director of International Conservation at the Wildlife Conservation Society, New York, USA. His research examines impacts of hunting on wildlife, particularly in tropical forests. He has worked on the IUCN's Sustainable Use Initiative and has co-edited *Neotropical Wildlife Use and Conservation* (1991) and *Hunting for Sustainability in Tropical Forests* (1999).

Conservation Biology

Conservation biology is a flourishing field, but there is still enormous potential for making further use of the science that underpins it. This series aims to present internationally significant contributions from leading researchers in particularly active areas of conservation biology. It focuses on topics where basic theory is strong and where there are pressing problems for practical conservation. The series includes both single-authored and edited volumes and adopts a direct and accessible style targeted at interested undergraduates, postgraduates, researchers and university teachers. Books and chapters will be rounded, authoritative accounts of particular areas with the emphasis on review rather than original data papers. The series is the result of a collaboration between the Zoological Society of London and Cambridge University Press. The series editor is Professor Morris Gosling, Professor of Animal Behaviour at the University of Newcastle upon Tyne. The series ethos is that there are unexploited areas of basic science that can help define conservation biology and bring a radical new agenda to the solution of pressing conservation problems.

Published Titles

1. *Conservation in a Changing World* (1998), edited by Georgina Mace, Andrew Balmford and Joshua Ginsberg 0 521 63270 6 (hardback), 0 521 63445 8 (paperback)
2. *Behaviour and Conservation* (2000), edited by Morris Gosling and William Sutherland 0 521 66230 3 (hardback), 0 521 66539 6 (paperback)
3. *Priorities for the Conservation of Mammalian Diversity* (2000), edited by Abigail Entwistle and Nigel Dunstone 0 521 77279 6 (hardback), 0 521 77536 1 (paperback)
4. *Genetics, Demography and Viability of Fragmented Populations* (2000), edited by Andrew G. Young and Geoffrey M. Clarke 0 521 78207 4 (hardback), 0 521 79421 8 (paperback)
5. *Carnivore Conservation* (2001), edited by John L. Gittleman, Stephan M. Funk, David W. Macdonald and Robert K. Wayne 0 521 66232 X (hardback), 0 521 66537 X (paperback)

Conservation of Exploited Species

Edited by

JOHN D. REYNOLDS
University of East Anglia

GEORGINA M. MACE
Institute of Zoology, London

KENT H. REDFORD
Wildlife Conservation Society, New York

and

JOHN G. ROBINSON
Wildlife Conservation Society, New York

PUBLISHED BY THE PRESS SYNDICATE OF THE UNIVERSITY OF CAMBRIDGE
The Pitt Building, Trumpington Street, Cambridge, United Kingdom

CAMBRIDGE UNIVERSITY PRESS
The Edinburgh Building, Cambridge CB2 2RU, UK
40 West 20th Street, New York NY 10011-4211, USA
10 Stamford Road, Oakleigh, VIC 3166, Australia
Ruiz de Alarcón 13, 28014 Madrid, Spain
Dock House, The Waterfront, Cape Town 8001, South Africa

http://www.cambridge.org

First published 2001

Printed in the United Kingdom at the University Press, Cambridge

Typeface FFScala 9.75/13pt   *System* Poltype® [VN]

A catalogue record for this book is available from the British Library

Library of Congress Cataloguing in Publication Data

Conservation of exploited species / edited by John D. Reynolds ... [et al.].
     p.   cm.
Includes bibliographical references.
ISBN 0 521 78216 3 (hardback) – ISBN 0 521 78733 5 (pb.)
1. Wildlife conservation.   2. Wildlife utilization.   I. Reynolds, John D., Ph.D.
QL82.C668 2002   2001025712

ISBN 0 521 78216 3 hardback
ISBN 0 521 78733 5 paperback

Contents

Contributors

STEVEN R. BEISSINGER
Ecosystem Sciences Division
Department of Environmental Science,
  Policy & Management
University of California
Berkeley, CA 94720-3110
USA

BARNEY DICKSON
Africa Resources Trust
World Conservation Monitoring Centre
219 Huntingdon Road
Cambridge CB3 0DL
UK

NICHOLAS K. DULVY
Department of Marine Sciences and
  Coastal Management
Ridley Building
University of Newcastle-Upon-Tyne
Newcastle-Upon-Tyne NE1 7RU
UK

STEINAR ENGEN
Department of Mathematics and
  Statistics
Norwegian University of Science and
  Technology
N-7034 Trondheim
Norway

JOHN E. FA
Durrell Wildlife Conservation Trust
Les Augrès Manor
Trinity
Jersey JE3 5BP
UK

PETER FEINSINGER
Department of Biological Sciences
Northern Arizona University
Flagstaff, AZ 86011
USA

JENNIFER A. GILL
School of Biological Sciences
University of East Anglia
Norwich NR4 7TJ
UK

GORDON C. GRIGG
Department of Zoology and
  Entomology
The University of Queensland
Brisbane, QLD 4072
Australia

ANNE GUNN
Department of Resources, Wildlife and
  Economic Development
Government of the Northwest
  Territories
Box 1320
Yellowknife, NT, X1A 3S8
Canada

JON HUTTON
Africa Resources Trust
World Conservation Monitoring Centre
219 Huntingdon Road
Cambridge CB3 0DL
UK

SIMON JENNINGS
Centre for Environment, Fisheries
  and Aquaculture Science
Lowestoft Laboratory
Pakefield Road
Lowestoft NR33 0HT
UK

MICHEL J. KAISER
School of Ocean Sciences
University of Wales-Bangor
Menai Bridge,
Gwynedd LL59 5EY
UK

HANNA KOKKO
Department of Zoology
University of Cambridge
Downing Street
Cambridge CB2 3EJ
UK

RUSSELL LANDE
Division of Biology 0116
University of California San Diego
9500 Gilman Drive
La Jolla, CA 92093
USA

RICHARD LAW
Department of Biology
University of York
PO Box 373
York YO10 5YW
UK

DON R. LEVITAN
Department of Biological Science
Florida State University
Talahassee, FL 32306
USA

JAN LINDSTRÖM
Department of Zoology
University of Cambridge
Downing Street
Cambridge CB2 3EJ
UK

DONALD LUDWIG
Departments of Mathematics and
  Zoology
University of British Columbia
Vancouver
British Columbia, V6T 1Z2
Canada

GEORGINA M. MACE
Institute of Zoology
The Zoological Society of London
Regent's Park
London NW1 4RY
UK

ROBERT M. MAY
Zoology Department
Oxford University
Oxford OX1 3PS
UK

E.J. MILNER-GULLAND
Renewable Resources Assessment
  Group
T.H. Huxley School of Environment,
  Earth Sciences and Engineering
Imperial College
8 Princes Gardens
London SW7 1NA
UK

CARLOS A. PERES
School of Environmental Sciences
University of East Anglia
Norwich NR4 7TJ
UK

CHARLES M. PETERS
Institute of Economic Botany
The New York Botanical Garden
Bronx, NY 10458
USA

CHRISTOPHER W. PETERSEN
College of the Atlantic
105 Eden Street
Bar Harbor, ME 04609
USA

ANTHONY R. POPLE
Department of Zoology and
  Entomology
The University of Queensland
Brisbane, QLD 4072
Australia

ANDRÉ E. PUNT
School of Aquatic and Fishery Sciences
Box 355020
University of Washington
Seattle, WA 98195-5020
USA

ANDY PURVIS
Department of Biology
Imperial College
Silwood Park
Ascot SL5 7PY
UK

ESA RANTA
Integrative Ecology Unit, Division of
  Population Biology
Department of Ecology and Systematics
University of Helsinki
PO Box 17
FIN-00014
Finland

KENT H. REDFORD
International Conservation Programs,
Wildlife Conservation Society
2300 Southern Boulevard
Bronx, NY 10460
USA

JOHN D. REYNOLDS
School of Biological Sciences
University of East Anglia
Norwich NR4 7TJ
UK

JOHN G. ROBINSON
International Conservation Programs
Wildlife Conservation Society
2300 Southern Boulevard
Bronx, NY 10460
USA

BERNT-ERIK SÆTHER
Department of Zoology
Norwegian University of Science and
  Technology
N-7034 Trondheim
Norway

STEVEN SANDERSON
Wildlife Conservation Society
2300 Southern Boulevard
Bronx, NY 10460
USA

ANTHONY D.M. SMITH
CSIRO Marine Research
GPO Box 1538
Hobart, TAS 7001
Australia

WILLIAM J. SUTHERLAND
School of Biological Sciences
University of East Anglia
Norwich NR4 7TJ
UK

PAUL R. WADE
Office of Protected Resources, NOAA,
National Marine Fisheries Service,
National Marine Mammal Laboratory
7600 Sand Point Way NE
Seattle, WA 98115
USA

Foreword

We do not know, to within 10%, how many distinct species of eukaryotic species (broadly, plants, animals and fungi) have been named and recorded. The total is roughly 1.5 million, but problems with synonyms, and other problems associated with the lack of a synoptic database, prevent an exact answer. The total number of eukaryotic species alive on Earth today is much less well known, with reasonable estimates ranging from 5 million to 15 million, and numbers as low as 3 million or as high as 100 million or more being defensible. Given these lamentable uncertainties, it is not surprising that we have very little idea of exactly how many species – mainly small invertebrates – became extinct last year.

We do know, however, that for some well-studied groups, particularly birds and mammals, rates of documented extinction over the past century ran roughly 100 to 1000 times faster than the average background rates of extinction over the half-billion year sweep of the fossil record. And four different methods of projecting extinction rates over the coming centuries – all four beset with approximations and extrapolations – suggest a further acceleration by a factor of 10 or more. This puts us clearly on the breaking tip of a sixth great wave of extinctions, fully comparable with the Big Five mass extinctions in the fossil record.

What are the causes of the loss of those species who enjoy the dubious honour of a tombstone of certified extinction over the past 100 years or so? Three main causes are usually identified: excessive exploitation by humans, loss of habitat, and effects of the introduction of alien species (including infectious diseases). Often two, or all three, of these factors are implicated.

This brings us to the present book. It derives from a meeting focused on the conservation of species which are imperilled by 'overexploitation' or 'overharvesting'.

The question immediately arises (see Ludwig, Chapter 2): under what circumstances is it possible, with good management, to exploit a species for human purposes without endangering it? I think that, as for so much else in biology, Darwin had the essentials of the answer. Three fundamental observations underpin *The Origin of Species*. The first is that there is heritable (genetically based) variation within all natural populations. The second is that all natural populations have the inherent reproductive capacity to increase, generation to generation, were resources not limiting. But various factors do limit population growth, leading to a 'struggle for existence' among progeny. Thirdly, when external conditions change, those offspring who – within the population's variability – are best adapted to the changed environment are more likely to survive. This, over time, leads to changes in the gene pool and eventually to new species.

Darwin's second point says yes, it is in principle possible to substitute human exploitation for other mortality factors, harvesting a potential surplus. Such a harvest is, of course, only sustainable if it is not so high that death rates exceed the inherent, resource-unlimited birth rate.

But such harvesting represents, for the species in question, an environmental change. So Darwin's third point suggests that exploitation, even when at sustainable levels, is likely to result in genetic changes in the population. A colourful example, widely cited in Darwin's day but rarely found in today's texts, is the high incidence of crabs with a striking skull-like pattern on their shells, found in a bay in Japan. Fishermen's superstitious discarding of such ill-omened individuals from their catch appears to have produced this phenomenon, which might even have helped the crab population to persist. More commonly, however, such exploitation-induced changes can threaten the species' persistence. Several better-documented cases of significant changes in exploited species' gene pools are discussed in the present volume.

These questions are pursued in diverse ways – some theoretically, others through detailed examples – in this book. There is much devilment in the details. For a start, although most would agree that all natural populations have birth and/or death rates that depend, to some extent, on population density, we rarely have a precise understanding of these density-dependent factors. Yet simple ideas about maximising sustainable yields tacitly assume we indeed know how birth and death rates change as population numbers are lowered by harvesting.

Even if techniques – no matter how heuristic – can be developed to assess maximum levels of harvesting that are sustainable, further complications arise and are important. For one thing, environmental stochasticity causes population fluctuations. Sustainable harvesting in such fluctuating environments presents complications that undercut simple ideas about 'maximum sustainable yield' (MSY); precautionary approaches are necessary. For another thing, heterogeneity in the spatial distribution of the exploited population – sometimes in the form of protected areas – offers other kinds of complication. Yet again, the species under discussion may be embedded in a complex web of interactions among species, so that harvesting a particular species not only can endanger other species, but can even threaten the target species in a way that conventional single-species methods would not anticipate. All these difficulties are exemplified in this volume.

These biological questions about conserving exploited species are only a beginning. Economic, political and social questions usually pose more serious barriers to sustainable management.

For starters, it is too often assumed that overexploitation of a potentially sustainable resource is always a 'tragedy of the commons'. Were there a single owner of the resource, rationality would indicate maximising the *sustainable* yield, or some appropriately sophisticated latter-day variant. But in a 'commons', it is in each exploiter's interest to take as much as possible, until the resource is either extinguished or dwindles to the point where the yield is not worth its cost; any exploiter exercising restraint, in the cause of sustainability, will be disadvantaged, and the Gadarene – but remorselessly logical – rush to collective collapse will continue. This is indeed the case for exploitation based on natural populations – such as most fish populations, or many softwoods – that have an intrinsic growth rate, r (per capita birth rate minus death rate, at low density) exceeding the inflation-corrected economic discount rate, δ (usually taken to be around 5–7%). In this event, the solution is to construct an effective political mechanism such that there is a sole owner/manager. In principle, examples are the International Whaling Commission or the many fisheries consortia such as the International Council for the Exploration of the Sea (ICES). In practice, even for $r > \delta$, things go wrong either because short-term social and political considerations override the regulatory authorities' advice, or because the regulatory mechanisms (aimed at controlling the harvesting via quotas, licences or other means) are badly designed or not enforced, or both.

But all this is irrelevant for resources where intrinsic population growth rates are simply less than the discount rate, $r < \delta$; this applies, for example, to most whale species, and to many hardwoods such as mahogany. Here economic realities conflict with sustainability even when there is a truly effective sole owner. If the sustainable return is below the economic discount rate, accountancy suggests liquidating the biological stock, and reinvesting the consequent money elsewhere. There is still much unhelpful confusion in the conservation movement about this distinction between $r > \delta$ and $r < \delta$. In the latter case, the conflict is really about an appropriate long-term definition of δ. Should it be set purely by economic considerations, or should ethical or other arguments (possible preservation of ecological services which are not counted in conventional economic balance sheets) require us not to discount the future, thus putting $\delta = 0$?

Ultimately, however, it is the social and political pressures from growing populations that constrain essentially all choices about conservation. In developing countries, these pressures are compounded by legitimate aspirations to the material comforts of the developed world, vividly conveyed by global media in a shrinking world. In the developed world itself, ever more prodigal patterns of consumption counterbalance lower levels of population growth (one rough calculation suggests that, in terms of environmental impact, one newborn in the USA equals 30–40 newborns in many developing countries). So, as many chapters in this book make clear, any effective plan for the conservation of an endangered species must be based not only on sound understanding of its ecology but even more on untidy social and political realities.

A critic could dismiss much of this book as 'touchy-feely' sentiment. Maybe we can grievously simplify the marvellously diverse ecological systems whose function we do not yet understand, and which built the biosphere as a place where life can flourish, without extinguishing ourselves as an unintended consequence. Maybe the world of the cult movie *Bladerunner* is sustainable. Maybe fears of disasters – new plagues from careless exploitation of other animals (HIV from hunting our cousins, the chimpanzees, is a forewarning), loss of various amenities from carelessly introduced aliens (waterweeds, from the equator to the Norfolk Broads), climate change and all its many consequences – can be magicked away by our technological cleverness. So long as the motivation for conservation is pinned primarily on our human interests, on preservation of endangered species for our sustainable use or aesthetic pleasure, I think the basis is shaky. I prefer a motivation that endows biological diversity, and its constituent species, with their own inherent rights: a motivation based on our role as the uniquely self-conscious species that is causing the problems, and accepts the responsibilities of stewardship. But this motivation has its own shakiness, not least because it is more easily sustained from the privileged luxuries of a developed-world life.

Robert M. May
Oxford University

Preface

Exploitation poses special problems for conservation. Individuals are usually removed directly from populations and this is intentional, rather than a by-product of other human activities. Although 'exploitation' is often used synonymously with 'harvesting', the comfort implied by the latter term is belied by the fact that many species have become extinct as a result of commercial and non-commercial activities. Whatever term one uses, many species are threatened by this activity and many populations have been reduced to a fraction of their former size.

In theory, the intensity of some forms of exploitation is manageable. In practice, however, controlling exploitation usually proves difficult. Conservation of exploited populations thus raises particular biological and social questions. For example, because the response of populations may be directly tied to one factor – elevated mortality – there are direct links to the study of population dynamics, reproductive rates, life histories and ecology. Furthermore, 'conservation' in the context of exploitation clearly means different things to different people. Some people wish to conserve their ability to profit from animal 'resources', with little concern about long-term declines in populations or impacts on ecosystems. Other people are more interested in minimising risks of extinctions of targeted species and minimising impacts on ecosystem function. While these goals may come into conflict with one another, there may also be pragmatic reasons for them to reinforce one another, as in the case of populations that may not survive unless they are exploited for some economic benefit.

This book has arisen from a meeting that we organised in London on 9 and 10 December 1999. The speakers who contributed these chapters focused primarily on biological issues in conservation of exploited species, but many also explored various social dimensions.

In Part I of this book two chapters set the scene of exploitation as a conservation issue. First, Georgina Mace and John Reynolds consider differing goals of exploitation, ranging from preservation to sustainable use to 'hit-and-run'. Donald Ludwig then examines biological and social dimensions that answer the question of whether we can exploit sustainably. His review of the basic biological principles that underlie the theory of sustainable exploitation provides a foundation for the more detailed treatments that appear elsewhere in the book, as does his discussion of the 'tragedy of the commons' and important economic principles such as discounting.

Part II explores various population-based approaches to sustainable exploitation. André Punt and Anthony Smith review the death and reincarnation of the classical concept of maximum sustainable yield. This review is concerned with fisheries, but the concepts are general, concerning targets for populations and yields, reference points and the precautionary principle. Russ Lande, Bernt-Erik Sæther and Steinar Engen examine the particular problems faced by exploitation of fluctuating populations. They aim for a target different from most models of exploitation – maximum yields prior to extinction – and suggest how this might be achieved. E. J. Milner-Gulland examines the importance of spatial structure in the conservation of exploited species, including the spatial behaviour of the hunters as well as the hunted. In the final chapter in this section, Paul Wade reviews novel quantitative methods for dealing with uncertainty in population assessments of exploited populations. First, he raises serious concerns about the fundamental methods of statistical inference that the editors of this volume and most of our readers were taught and still use! Then he explores exciting new ways of incorporating uncertainty into parameter estimation and decision theory.

Part III examines taxonomic differences in responses of populations to exploitation. John Reynolds, Simon Jennings and Nicholas Dulvy consider how life histories affect population trends of exploited fish species. These questions are becoming increasingly relevant as conservationists express concern about impacts of fisheries. Andy Purvis reviews similar issues with mammals, including a comparative analysis of relationships between life histories and threatened status of a wide variety of species. Steven Beissinger reviews the importance of international trade for bird conservation. This exemplifies problems faced by many species threatened by exploitation for use as pets, rather than being killed outright as sources of food. Beissinger presents a sophisticated model for calculating sustainable yields, as well as recommendations to guide the international trade. In the fourth chapter in this section, John Fa and Carlos Peres then review how tropical hunting compares between Africa and South America. Hunting for bushmeat is the number one threat to many species in Africa, and the projections based on human population growth make for sobering reading. In the final chapter in this section, Charles Peters offers lessons from the plant kingdom. Of course, plants deserve far more than one chapter, but the subject matter has a strong bias towards animals, and indeed, towards vertebrates, as the content of this book suggests. In this chapter, Charles draws interesting comparisons between plants and animals.

In Part IV we have six topics that range from individuals to communities. William Sutherland and Jennifer Gill examine the role of animal behaviour in determining responses of populations to exploitation. Christopher Petersen and Don Levitan then focus on one particular process that is usually driven by behaviour, the Allee effect, whereby inverse density dependence can cause populations to decline sharply once they reach a low density. Hanna Kokko, Jan Lindström and Esa Ranta examine the role of life histories within populations in determining yields and population changes. They include a consideration of which age classes and sexes should be taken, in terms of reducing impacts on populations and yields. Nearly all forms of exploitation are selective within populations. Richard Law considers how such selectivity, combined with heritability estimates for specific traits, can cause evolutionary changes within species. The final two chapters of this section scale up from population changes to community impacts. Michel Kaiser and Simon Jennings examine the evidence for changes in marine, freshwater and terrestrial communities due to trophic interactions. Kent Redford and Peter Feinsinger then consider more subtle processes that can affect communities due to disruptions in symbioses, such as plant–pollinator interactions.

Part V brings us more squarely into the realm of human social considerations that are encountered when conservation meets sustainable use. Gordon Grigg and Anthony Pople's review of management of Australian kangaroos shows how the largest sustainable hunting programme in the world is governed by conflicting goals ranging from pest control to resource exploitation. Anne Gunn's review of conservation and resource use in Arctic ecosystems shows how a range of difficult issues are tackled, from biological uncertainty to distrust of administrators by aboriginal peoples. Local concerns also feature prominently in Jon Hutton and Barney Dickson's review of conservation through resource use in Africa. These authors scoff at the idea of being able to find parameters for many of the biological models discussed elsewhere in this book as they search for pragmatic solutions to local problems. This brings us to Steven Sanderson's discussion of the politics involved in conserving exploited species. The political advice he offers demands to be taken seriously by any biologist who wishes to translate research into action.

In Part VI John Robinson offers some final thoughts on the goals of conservation. We need to understand that different people have different objectives if we are to make progress in improving the conservation of exploited species.

Readers of this book will thus see some divergent viewpoints over these issues, amid a heavy dose of biological considerations. We hope that this airing of the biological and social dimensions of exploitation will help lead towards an appreciation of alternative attitudes to the use of wildlife, and ways of solving conservation problems.

ACKNOWLEDGEMENTS

We thank the Zoological Society of London and the Wildlife Conservation Society for funding the conference that led to this book. We appreciate the invitation from Morris Gosling and Bill Sutherland to tackle this project, and we thank Linda DaVolls and Deborah Body for helping to organise the meeting.

John Reynolds
Georgina Mace
Kent Redford
John Robinson

PART I

Setting the scene

1

Exploitation as a conservation issue

GEORGINA M. MACE & JOHN D. REYNOLDS

People have exploited wildlife throughout their history and even in ancient times this activity is known to have caused the extinction of many species. Today's exploitation pressures are massively more severe than in the past for several reasons. The human population now exceeds 6 billion globally, and people impact on every part of the Earth's land surface and increasingly on the oceans and atmosphere. Current estimates suggest that about 40% of all the earth's primary productivity is harnessed for human use (UNEP, 2000). As Figure 1.1 illustrates, rapid population growth is a feature most evident in the last century and growth is expected to continue for hundreds of years into the future (UN, 1998). These high population numbers are permitted by our technological developments, which enable us to exploit natural resources with rapidly increasing levels of efficiency, against which the natural defences of wild species are hopelessly inadequate. Alongside this, progress in transportation and communications allows people to travel further and occupy more areas that once provided refuges for wild species.

The result of escalating human populations and increased intensity of our consumption of natural resources is that exploitation (or harvest) of wildlife represents a major threat to many of the world's plant and animal species. For birds and mammals it is second in importance only to habitat degradation as a cause of threat (WCMC, 1992; Hilton-Taylor, 2000) (Figure 1.2). Various forms of exploitation have been implicated in species declines, including commercial and subsistence hunting, extraction, collecting activities and the impacts of trade. These population declines can have severe economic and social impacts in activities ranging from subsistence hunting of bushmeat to large-scale commercial fisheries. In Figure 1.3 we present decline data for some marine species; these kinds of trajectory are now common among terrestrial plants and animals, although we rarely have adequate data to document them so closely. Attitudes to continuing declines of once widespread species are quite different in the

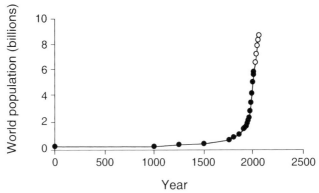

Figure 1.1. World population trends for humans, including projections to the year 2050. Shaded circles are past population estimates and open circles are future projections. (From UN, 1998.)

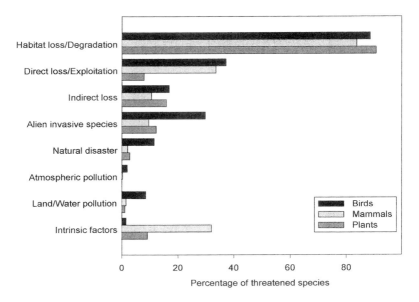

Figure 1.2. The major threatening processes affecting birds, mammals and plants listed in the IUCN *Red List of Threatened Species* (Hilton-Taylor, 2000).

conservation and resource management literature. While declines may be regarded by resource managers as an inevitable consequence of a managed harvest, conservationists may see them as a serious threat to populations (Mace & Hudson, 1999). Here we explore this dichotomy of views in a little more detail to ask when declines should become a conservation issue.

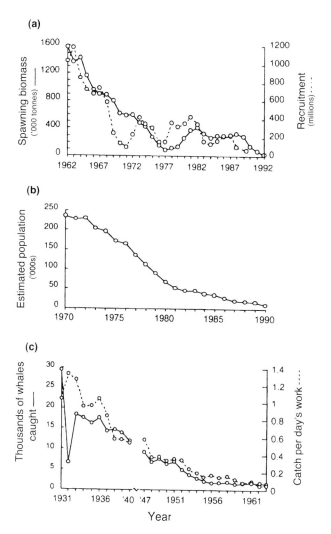

Figure 1.3. Population declines of three species of exploited animals. (a) Northern cod stock *Gadus morhua* off eastern Canada. Spawners are at least seven years old and recruits are three years old. (b) Western Atlantic bluefin tuna *Thunnus thynnus*; (c) blue whales *Balaenoptera musculus* in the Antarctic. Numbers caught are shown by the solid line and numbers caught per hunter-day's work are shown by the broken line. (Figure and original references from Reynolds & Jennings, 2000, with permission from Cambridge University Press.)

Broadly speaking, this book asks why overexploitation occurs, and what might be done about it. We should be heartened by the fact that sustainable exploitation is central to much current conservation policy. The *World Conservation Strategy* (IUCN/UNEP/WWF, 1980) and its successor, *Caring for the Earth* (IUCN/UNEP/WWF, 1991) emphasise the way in which sustainable human livelihoods will depend upon prudent use of natural resources, including wild species. In understanding the dynamics of harvesting, we can draw on experience from a long history of research into sustainable exploitation. This work has led directly to many of the key concepts that feature in modern theories of ecology and population biology (for a review, see Milner-Gulland & Mace, 1998). Given the extent of this effort, one might wonder how we could run into problems with overexploitation. There are two obstacles. First, despite extensive research into methods for harvesting natural populations in a sustainable manner, there are still many biological difficulties in estimating key parameters and predicting the consequences of management regimes. Secondly, even if we can get the biology right, there are usually severe difficulties in implementing and enforcing management plans. Thus, conservation of exploited species represents a considerable biological and social challenge.

In this chapter we ask three questions about the conservation of exploited species: (1) what are the goals of exploitation? (2) Why is sustainable exploitation so difficult? (3) What are the characteristics of vulnerable species? We conclude with a brief set of suggestions for successful conservation of exploited species.

WHAT ARE THE GOALS OF CONSERVATION AND EXPLOITATION?

Goals for conservation and exploitation can be divided into those that relate to our attitudes to nature, and those that determine what it is we are trying to sustain.

Attitudes to nature

At the broadest level, people vary in their attitudes to nature and natural resources. These views can be presented along a continuum which encompasses two extreme positions. On the one hand, we characterise a 'preservationist' attitude, where the goal is to preserve nature in its current state (or perhaps a historical state). This attitude views exploitation by humans as artificial and undesirable. On the other hand, we characterise a 'hit-and-run' attitude, where the goal is to maximise returns from nature, with no desire to maintain or sustain any natural resources. Clearly, to most people,

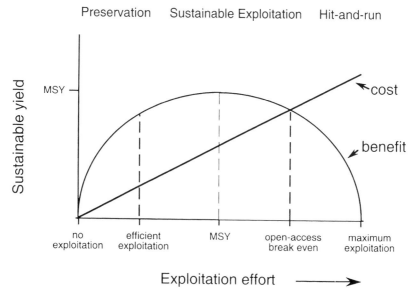

Figure 1.4. Attitudes to nature, shown across the top of the figure, reflect differing goals of exploitation. Exploitation effort increases along the x-axis, ranging from 'no exploitation' stemming from a 'preservation' goal at one end of the continuum to 'maximum exploitation' stemming from a 'hit-and-run' goal at the other. The y-axis measures the sustainable yield that results from any level of exploitation of a population. MSY, maximum sustainable yield.

these extreme positions are both absurd and indefensible, but the continuum between them is real and an important backdrop against which to consider sustainable use.

A schematic diagram (Figure 1.4) illustrates these attitudes superimposed on a simple, classic formulation that relates costs and benefits to exploitation effort. Here, as exploitation effort increases, the yield first increases as a consequence of reduced density dependence in smaller populations leading to higher productivity. Yield then declines as the population becomes too small (for a review, see Ludwig, Chapter 2). Maximum sustainable yield (MSY) is achieved at an intermediate level of exploitation. However, the costs of exploitation increase linearly with the level of exploitation. Levels of exploitation below MSY may result in lower yields but the investment required to exploit the resource is lower and there is a point of 'maximum efficiency' where the difference between cost and benefit is maximised (Figure 1.4). At levels of exploitation above MSY there are declining benefits and increasing costs. The level of exploitation at which costs equal benefits is the break-even point, where any further increase in exploitation will result in net losses. This may be characteristic of exploitation of open-access resources. A 'hit-and-run' attitude to nature may lead to maximum exploitation whereby one 'liquidates the resource' and invests the profits to maximise economic gain from an extinct population, as discussed by Donald Ludwig (Chapter 2). Obviously, people with such goals cannot be considered conservationists, but conservationists need to understand them if they are to win the argument with their own goals.

Figure 1.4 thus shows how different goals ranging from preservation to hit-and-run can be met by different amounts of exploitation. These goals need to be set out clearly before we can debate the success or failure of conservation programmes that involve exploited species.

What are we trying to sustain?

The second kind of goal relates to what, exactly, we are trying to sustain. Are we interested in sustaining populations, species, ecosystems or human communities? These differing goals are discussed in the closing chapter of this book by John Robinson, who notes that different goals are implicit in different species' harvesting programmes, but these are rarely made explicit. Yet they affect the currencies that are plotted in Figure 1.4. For economists, the yield and costs curves might represent money; to a member of the Yuqui of Bolivia, the gain curve might represent kilograms of bushmeat and the loss might represent time and energy; a community ecologist might view the functions as gains or losses in biodiversity.

Most of these differing goals are covered by different chapters in this book. Maximisation of yields from single species has been the traditional goal of temperate fisheries, as reviewed by André Punt & Anthony Smith (Chapter 3). Thus the dome-shaped function in Figure 1.4 is usually measured in biomass of species X harvested over the long term, which is usually considered in terms of about a decade. Extinction almost never enters into the equation. In contrast, Russ Lande and his co-authors (see Chapter 4) confront extinction directly and suggest that the most prudent and long-term goal is to maximise the cumulative harvest before extinction occurs. In their analyses the yield curve thus explicitly refers to sustainability over thousands of years – far longer than any commercially based natural resource managers would consider relevant.

Perhaps the target species and the revenues and products to be gained from it are not the currency of interest. Many biologists are more concerned about communities and ecosystems. Michel Kaiser & Simon Jennings (Chapter 16) describe the wide variety of responses that communities may undergo in response to reductions in targeted species. Some measure of biodiversity might therefore replace the single-species yield curve in Figure 1.4, though its relationship with exploitation effort will not be straightforward. Some marine food webs have proved to be quite resilient against the loss of individual species, whereas others have shown dramatic effects, as have various freshwater and terrestrial communities. Kent Redford & Peter Feinsinger (see Chapter 17) have a similar currency in mind, though they are concerned with processes that are more subtle than the predator–prey relationships usually considered in 'multispecies' approaches to exploitation. They consider the potential for dramatic effects of processes resulting, for example, from disruptions to interactions between plants and pollinators, or frugivorous birds and the plants that rely on them for dispersal. Hence their metaphor of a 'half-empty forest' – the species are still there for the time-being, but their interactions are disrupted in ways that may reduce populations in the future.

Goals based on human social and economic development may be a long way from the objectives of single-species or ecosystem sustainability. Two authors (Ludwig, Chapter 2; Sanderson, Chapter 21) discuss this issue in general terms but Jon Hutton & Barney Dickson (Chapter 20) explicitly assess the success of southern African conservation strategies for large mammals in terms of the livelihoods and economic consequences for the human communities involved. Indeed, they evaluate the success of various programmes on the basis of economics rather than direct measures of plant or animal population sizes, and objectives in that chapter can be achieved without maintaining species diversity. However, from a pragmatic viewpoint, the authors argue that we will lose species anyway, and present their case as the best from among difficult possibilities.

We believe that disagreements over goals cause most of the debates about sustainable exploitation, especially for charismatic species. As Steven Sanderson makes clear, this is a political discourse that cannot be ignored. We do not seek to resolve what the goals of sustainable exploitation could or should be. Rather we point out that the lack of clarity has led to unproductive debates that have compared the merits of apples versus oranges.

WHY IS SUSTAINABLE EXPLOITATION SO DIFFICULT?

Problems that hamper efforts to exploit wild populations sustainably can be divided into limits to biological knowledge and limits to control.

Limits to knowledge

Theoretical models of exploitation include some of the most sophisticated models of population dynamics that have been produced. Fisheries biologists and terrestrial ecologists routinely produce age-structured models that can incorporate a huge number of parameters concerning life histories, behaviour and ecology. Yet we never seem to know enough.

Parameter estimation is a troubling issue for many authors in this book. John Reynolds and collaborators (Chapter 7) resort to using simple life history characteristics to develop 'rules of thumb' for predicting responses of understudied fish populations to exploitation. William Sutherland & Jennifer Gill (Chapter 12) worry about the effect of density dependence on measurements of rates of population increase, and Jon Hutton & Barney Dickson (Chapter 20) rule out measuring population parameters for most African mammals that are subject to hunting. But there are more optimistic contributions to the problems of parameter estimation, and especially progress with methods for dealing with uncertainty. Paul Wade (Chapter 6) shows how we can incorporate uncertainty directly into parameter estimation as well as in making management recommendations. So, if we cannot measure all of the parameters we would like, at least we should work towards formal procedures for admitting this uncertainty into our analyses.

Another limit to knowledge involves the status of the population and the rate at which it is being exploited. Direct censuses of most exploited populations are extremely difficult, time-consuming, and expensive. One might think that counting caribou in an Arctic environment would be relatively straightforward, but Anne Gunn (Chapter 19) shows that the costs and practical issues involved make this impossible. While large-scale activities such as commercial fisheries provide large-scale data and funding for research, this is the exception rather than the rule.

Even if we can estimate our model parameters and census the populations, it is often very difficult to predict the future with any confidence. Environmental stochasticity is a fact of life for most animal populations, as illustrated for kangaroos by Gordon Grigg & Anthony Pople (Chapter 18), and for caribou by Anne Gunn (Chapter 19). Russ Lande and colleagues (Chapter 4) show how stochasticity can be successfully incorporated into models, but the problems of projecting into the future remain. This severely hampers long-term forecasts and management advice.

Limits to control

The 'tragedy of the commons' looms large in most discussions of the difficulty of controlling exploitation of wild populations. Understandable self-interest leads individuals to exploit wild populations well beyond the MSY towards the break-even point (Figure 1.4). Thus we overexploit in the present rather than leaving individuals and their offspring to be exploited by others.

There are also mismatches between human and biological scales, both spatial and temporal, which can make exploitation risky. For example, political and economically driven management plans are likely to operate on a cycle length of a few years at most, whereas the precautionary approaches discussed by Russ Lande and co-authors (Chapter 4) require much longer time scales. Even more problematic for reliable implementation is the fact that these precautionary methods would call for irregular and hard-to-predict periods when no exploitation would be permitted. Lande *et al.* discuss this problem and possible approaches to dealing with it, but it is clear that such methods will be vulnerable to the difficulty of reducing or stopping exploitation when human needs preclude such an approach.

Spatial mismatches also create risk-prone situations for certain species. In marine environments especially, but in terrestrial environments as well, species may range over areas controlled by different management authorities. Under these circumstances, the species will always be vulnerable to the lowest standard of management. Another spatial risk factor demonstrated by E. J. Milner-Gulland (Chapter 5) occurs when the distribution of hunters relative to that of the prey has a significant impact on the species' vulnerability that would not be detected without detailed records and sophisticated analyses.

Ultimately, limits to control are about social and political context and the implementation of regulations and plans. Various social and economic factors can increase problems with enforcement. Gordon Grigg & Anthony Pople (Chapter 18) describe the difficulties and tensions when dealing with a species that can be viewed as a pest or a resource, and yet is at the same time a focus for concern of animal welfare groups. Anne Gunn's case study of caribou (Chapter 19) shows how cultural tensions and differences can jeopardise what could be relatively straightforward management issues. The problems of distrust and poor communication between authorities, scientists, managers and hunters is a general one, though especially clearly presented in this case. Jon Hutton & Barney Dickson (Chapter 20) also emphasise the importance of community involvement in management decisions and they especially make the case that there should be direct and transparent links between economic gains from the species and benefits to the community. In this context, Steven Sanderson's analysis of the politics of exploitation is especially significant (Chapter 21). These chapters reflect a strong emphasis over the past decade towards the development of institutions that match temporal and spatial scales of conservation goals.

WHICH SPECIES ARE VULNERABLE TO OVEREXPLOITATION?

There are many ways to design a vulnerable species. A low rate of population productivity associated with a 'slow' life history is an obvious trait that hampers the ability of populations to withstand exploitation. This is shown in theoretical analyses by Hanna Kokko and collaborators (Chapter 14), and by comparative studies reviewed for mammals by Andy Purvis (Chapter 8), birds in the pet trade studied by Steven Beissinger (Chapter 9), tropical plants by Charles Peters (Chapter 11) and for fishes by John Reynolds and collaborators (Chapter 7).

The spatial structure of populations can also be important, as shown by E. J. Milner-Gulland (Chapter 5). This may determine rates of dispersal, and has ramifications for efforts to protect species within reserves. It is also important for the economics of capture. Thus species living within easy reach of human settlements, or which are aggregated at predictable places and times, will be more readily targeted. Milner-Gulland's analyses of wild pigs in North Sulawesi also provide a nice demonstration of the problems encountered by species that are taken as 'by-catches', i.e. which are taken opportunistically or accidentally when other species are the intended target. This can be a serious issue, since such by-catch species continue to be captured even after their population sizes are too small to be worth while targeting directly. Similar concerns are raised for a variety of taxa by Michel Kaiser & Simon Jennings (Chapter 16), William Sutherland & Jennifer Gill (Chapter 12), and John Reynolds *et al.* (Chapter 7).

A number of additional aspects of behaviour can render species especially vulnerable to over-exploitation. Among the behaviours reviewed by William Sutherland & Jennifer Gill, the potential for Allee effects, covered in detail by Christopher Petersen & Don Levitan (Chapter 13), are particularly worrying. For example, populations of sessile marine invertebrates such as abalone can be reduced to densities that are too low for successful fertilisation. Thus details of behaviour may be critical to the success or failure of populations.

All of the characteristics of vulnerability discussed above are in some way bound up in economics. A particularly difficult problem is faced by species that suffer from the economics of supply and demand placing a higher price on their heads as they become rarer. This is well illustrated by species such as rhinoceros and tigers, for which the economic incentives are enormous, and it is also characteristic of species that are the focus of collectors, as shown by Steven Beissinger in his review of the wild bird trade (Chapter 9). The likelihood of such species actually being hunted to extinction is much greater than for other comparable species because hunting effort continues to increase as they become rarer.

The chapters in this book also highlight a set of risky processes. Once a population is influenced by one of these, a series of events may be set in train that threaten the population or its community, yet such processes are hard to halt and reverse. Allee effects, mentioned above and by several chapters in this book, are one of the best-known examples. With the inverse density dependence characteristic of Allee effects, populations that are reduced to low densities suffer declines in reproductive rate and therefore decline more quickly. Genetic changes may also be hard to reverse. For example, Richard Law (Chapter 15) discusses the strong likelihood that fisheries that target the largest individuals in a population will cause the evolution of reduced adult size. Worryingly, however, the selection pressures for reduced size are unlikely to be reversed if fishing pressures are relaxed. Under the best circumstances, recovery to the original size is therefore likely to be delayed and may in fact never occur.

Asymmetries between population changes and recovery are found elsewhere. For example, some food chains and habitats that are altered by the effects of exploitation may never recover once the structure and species composition are greatly altered (see Kaiser & Jennings, Chapter 16) and loss of specific pollinators through overexploitation can lead to irreversible declines or even extinctions of a mutualistic plant species (see Redford & Feinsinger, Chapter 17).

SUGGESTIONS FOR CONSERVATION OF EXPLOITED SPECIES

Here are some simple rules and advice that we have picked up from the authors in this book which should limit the chances that exploitation will jeopardise a species or its associated community.

- *Be clear about your objectives*
  As we have argued at the beginning, and John Robinson argues at the end, we must be clear about what we are trying to conserve before we can suggest how to go about it, how to judge our success and how to adapt to new circumstances.
- *Get the biology right, if you can*
  It is important to understand the basic biology and natural history of the

target species. Particularly significant are the fundamental life history parameters relating to mortality and fecundity, but harvesting programmes can also benefit by considering how individuals of different ages and sex should be targeted (see Peters, Chapter 11; Sutherland & Gill, Chapter 12; Kokko *et al.*, Chapter 14; Law, Chapter 15; Kaiser & Jennings, Chapter 16). If possible, such information should be considered in a spatial context and especially in relation to the places where exploitation is targeted (see Milner-Gulland, Chapter 5).

- *Use whatever information is available*
We will never know everything we want to know about biology, but useful generalisations can still be made through experience with similar taxa and similar exploitation regimens. If you can't build a Rolls-Royce model, you can still make educated guesses based on rules of thumb. Closely related taxa and general associations can provide useful guidance (see Reynolds *et al.*, Chapter 7; Purvis, Chapter 8).

- *Be precautionary*
Since we do not know everything and cannot predict the future with certainty, we must be precautionary. This is a guiding principle for most policies of resource exploitation, as discussed, for example, by André Punt & Anthony Smith (Chapter 3).

- *Embrace uncertainty*
Uncertainty in all its various forms poses special problems to managers, and there is no longer any excuse for ignoring it (see Wade, Chapter 6). Uncertainty can be embraced at many levels: from parameter estimation to choice of model to selection of management programmes.

- *Monitor the hunters and the hunted*
Effective monitoring will inform changes that should be made to management in response to unforeseen consequences. Thus management should be adaptive (see Ludwig, Chapter 2; Punt & Smith, Chapter 3; Wade, Chapter 6).

- *Involve everyone concerned with the exploitation*
Conservation that ignores people is an oxymoron. We make no apologies for slanting this book towards biology, because we think this is an interesting and important part of conservation. But getting the biology right will solve nothing if we do not consider carefully the motivations of the people who are exploiting the species, and the political context in which this occurs. Steven Sanderson (Chapter 21) tackles this issue head-on. However, these issues also loom large throughout the book, especially in discussions by Donald Ludwig, John Fa & Carlos Peres, Gordon Grigg & Anthony Pople, Anne Gunn, and

John Robinson. These authors all show how the best attempts at scientifically based management are doomed to failure if no attention is paid to getting the right systems in place, involving the right local interests and stakeholders, and dealing with alternative kinds of benefit and cost and priorities and goals.

REFERENCES

Hilton-Taylor, C. (2000). The IUCN *Red List of Threatened Species*. IUCN, Gland, Switzerland.

IUCN/UNEP/WWF (World Conservation Union/United Nations Energy Programme/Worldwide Fund for Nature) (1980). *World Conservation Strategy: Living Resource Conservation for Sustainable Development*. IUCN, Gland, Switzerland.

IUCN/UNEP/WWF (World Conservation Union/United Nations Energy Programme/Worldwide Fund for Nature) (1991). *Caring for the Earth: A Strategy for Sustainable Living*. IUCN, Gland, Swizerland.

Mace, G. M. & Hudson, E. J. (1999). Attitudes toward sustainability and extinction. *Conservation Biology*, **13**, 242–246.

Milner-Gulland, E. J. & Mace, R. (1998). *Conservation of Biological Resources*. Blackwell Science, Oxford.

Reynolds, J. D. & Jennings, S. (2000). The role of animal behaviour in marine conservation. In *Behaviour and Conservation*, ed. L. M. Gosling & W. J. Sutherland, pp. 238–257. Cambridge University Press, Cambridge.

UN (1998). United Nations Population Division, *World Population Growth*. (Website: http://www.undp.org/popin/wdtrends.htm)

UNEP (United Nations Environment Programme) (2000). *Global Biodiversity Assessment 2000*. Cambridge University Press, Cambridge.

WCMC (World Conservation Monitoring Centre) (1992). *Global Diversity: Status of the Earth's Living Resources*. Chapman & Hall, London.

WCMC (World Conservation Monitoring Centre) (2000). *Global Biodiversity: Earth's Living Resources in the 21st Century*. World Conservation Press, Cambridge.

2

Can we exploit sustainably?

DONALD LUDWIG

The history of management of renewable resources has shown little evidence of sustainability (Ludwig *et al.*, 1993). Can we do better? I shall review some of the main themes in the theory of renewable resource management and attempt to explain why management in practice has not been successful, in spite of all the theory. A proper understanding of this complicated phenomenon involves much more than ecology or conservation biology in their present forms.

Conservation biology is a relatively new science that has been developed in response to widespread concern about human impacts on natural systems. It appears to many biologists that we are in a state of crisis (Ehrlich, 1997). This urgency has not been felt so strongly in other disciplines. Hence the field of conservation science has been dominated by biological investigations. That is a source of strength, since biological and physical processes underlie all others, and hence they must be accorded primary focus. It is also a source of weakness, since human activities and motivations are largely beyond the ken of biological theories. Theories of conservation biology stop short of an explanation of the dominant phenomenon, which is a steady erosion of habitats and consequently of species diversity. Due to my own limitations, the present treatment is no exception to this rule. I have tried to provide some hints about the directions that proper explanations of our lamentable record of conservation might take, but these are a poor substitute for a properly grounded explanation.

Scientific investigation may play only a minor role in the conservation of resources. Even where there is substantial scientific information, prudent conservation policies are by no means assured. Sutherland & Reynolds (1998) pointed out that peat bogs have been destroyed in Britain over the last few centuries despite the fact that the state of the bogs and the reasons for their decline were perfectly clear. Another good example is the depletion of English oak during the Napoleonic Wars. Even though it was recognised that the future of the nation might well depend upon it, the British

Admiralty was unable to ensure adequate supplies of ship's timber for the Royal Navy and for merchant shipping (Albion, 1926).

More recently, there is alarming evidence of worldwide overexploitation of marine fisheries, in spite of well developed theories of management. Although total catch levels for marine fisheries have been relatively stable in recent decades, a trophic analysis of the data shows that landings from global fisheries have shifted from large piscivorous fishes towards invertebrates and planktivores (Pauly *et al.*, 1998). This shift can be quantified through assignment of a fractional trophic level to each species depending upon the composition of the diet. These trophic levels range from a value of 1 for primary producers to over 4.6 for a few top predators such as tuna (Scombridae) in open water and groupers (Epinephilinae) and snappers (Lutjanidae) among bottom fishes. In the Northwest Atlantic the mean trophic level is now below 2.9. There is not much room for further decreases, since most fish have trophic levels between 3 and 4. Indeed, many fisheries now rely on invertebrates, which tend to have low trophic levels. Global trends appear to show a decline of 0.1 trophic level per decade. It is likely that a continuation of present trends will lead to widespread fisheries collapses. These trends cast doubt on the idea that we can estimate future catches by extrapolating from present trends.

RESOURCE MANAGEMENT MODELS OF SUSTAINABLE USE

The simplest goal of resource management is maintenance of steady conditions. The best objective of this type is sustainable yield or maximum sustainable yield, which is discussed immediately below. Like most simple and direct approaches to complex problems, it is quite unworkable. Somewhat better performance is obtained by a policy of proportional harvesting, where the harvest fluctuates up and down with the size of the exploited population. Finally, there is the idea of bionomic equilibrium, which is the result of unrestricted access to the resource rather than of a conscious policy. This idea is also too simple to be generally applicable, but it does capture the most prominent feature of commercial resource extraction: the overcapitalisation of the industry and consequent overexploitation of the resource. Rather than restraining this practice, governments typically encourage it through subsidies. These theories were developed in the context of fisheries, but similar principles apply to any renewable resource. Reed (1991) has written an interesting essay on the history and significance of early work by Scott Gordon (1954) and Schaefer (1954).

CONSTANT QUOTA

A prominent ideal in resource management is a sustainable yield, or even a maximum sustainable yield (MSY). The underlying notion of population dynamics is that per capita reproduction at a given time depends only on the population size. Competition for food or space decreases the per capita growth rate as the population size increases. If the population is not exploited, the population will reach a size at which births are just balanced by deaths: the 'carrying capacity' of the environment. At lower population sizes, there is a surplus of births over deaths. If exploitation removes this 'surplus production' then the population size will remain constant and the yield will be steady. One may then ask how the yield will vary with the population size and find the size at which the yield is a maximum.

I shall denote the population size by N and assume that the logistic model applies, where the net growth rate before harvesting is given by

$$g(N) = rN(1 - N/K). \tag{2.1}$$

Here r is the per capita growth rate at low densities and K is the carrying capacity. If the population is harvested at a steady rate H, then it satisfies

$$\frac{dN}{dT} = rN(1 - N/K) - H. \tag{2.2}$$

The dynamics are illustrated in Figure 2.1. This symmetrical yield curve can be compared with other shapes that are possible, depending on the underlying form of density dependence (Sutherland & Gill, Chapter 12). If H is not too large, then there will be an interval $N_1 < N < N_2$ where $g(N) > H$, and hence the net population growth after harvesting will be positive. If the population starts within or above that interval, it will approach N_2. If it starts below N_1, it will decrease towards zero. Note that 'sustainable' has acquired a slightly different meaning in this context: the sustainability applies only if the population never drops below N_1. I denote the maximum of $g(N)$ by $H_{MSY} = rK/4$ and the point at which the maximum is attained by $N_{MSY} = K/2$. Since the yield can be maintained if $H < H_{MSY}$, that is the MSY. If $H = H_{MSY}$, then $N_1 = N_2 = N_{MSY}$, and sustainability applies only if the population never drops below N_{MSY}. If $H > H_{MSY}$, the population will always decrease towards zero: the yield is not sustainable. Moreover as H approaches H_{MSY} from below, then the points N_1 and N_2 approach N_{MSY}. The yield is sustainable only if we can ensure that N never falls below N_1.

This feature illustrates the sort of trade-off that always seems to occur

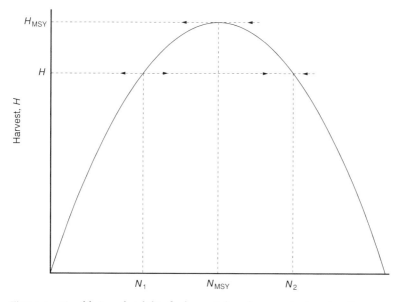

Figure 2.1. Equilibria and stability for harvests based on constant quotas. For harvest rates below H_{MSY} there is a stable equilibrium at $N = N_2$, but there is no non-zero equilibrium if $H > H_{MSY}$.

when one attempts to maximise one quantity: some other aspect of the situation deteriorates. In this case, the stability of the yields suffers as the yield is pushed closer to the maximum, since variations and fluctuations are always present. This point appears more clearly below where random dynamics are assumed. There is a conflict between maximisation and sustainability: the higher we set the harvest rate, the more fragile is the sustainability we seek to preserve. There is no margin for error if $H = H_{MSY}$ and $N = N_{MSY}$. If environmental variation should temporarily decrease the per capita growth rate, a policy based upon the previously observed population growth rate may be unsustainable. If environmental variation should temporarily increase the net growth rate, our desire to maximise returns may lead us to set the harvest rate too high to be sustained over the longer term. A policy of maximisation of the sustainable yield can succeed only if information about changing conditions is readily available, and if it is possible to make quick adjustments to changing conditions. However, for many natural populations it is difficult to monitor or control the harvest rate because harvesting activities may cause deaths that are not recorded as part of the harvest.

There are many other difficulties with the preceding approach (see also

Punt & Smith, Chapter 3). The most serious theoretical problem is that one must somehow determine H_{MSY} from data about the population. Hilborn & Walters (1992, pp. 10–13) maintained that 'You cannot determine the potential yield from a fish stock without overexploiting it.' The underlying reason is that statistical methods are unreliable where extrapolation is required. Any attempt to estimate H_{MSY} without harvesting in excess of that value requires such extrapolation.

The most serious practical difficulty with the idea of MSY is the inability to control or limit harvests when there are large commercial interests at stake (Larkin, 1977). Hilborn & Walters (1992, pp. 10–13) maintained that 'The hardest thing to do in fisheries management is to reduce fishing pressure.' Caughley & Sinclair (1994, p. 289) refer to a 'symbiotic relationship in management'. Often the resource is owned by the public, and the government sets up an agency to regulate private exploiters. The symbiosis occurs when the regulators take the attitude that they and the commercial harvesters are actually part of a team that jointly owns the resource. The theoretical and practical effects reinforce each other: the inability of scientists to make confident predictions of collapse is often regarded as a justification for taking large harvests and even for increasing harvests. The steady decline in population size (the 'one way trip' in Hilborn's terminology) makes it impossible to provide reliable estimates of future yields.

PROPORTIONAL (CONSTANT EFFORT) HARVESTING

A somewhat more sophisticated idea than maintaining a constant quota is to use proportional harvesting. That means to take a constant fraction of the population during each harvest cycle. The actual size of the harvest will fluctuate with population size. If E denotes the exploitation rate, then

$$H = EN. \tag{2.3}$$

Then the condition for a steady population size is

$$E = r(1 - N/K). \tag{2.4}$$

For each value of E between 0 and r, the corresponding value of N is given by

$$N = K(1 - E/r). \tag{2.5}$$

The maximum yield is obtained when $N = K/2$, and hence $E_{MSY} = r/2$. Figure 2.2 illustrates the dynamics in the case of a fixed exploitation rate. Note that E determines the slope of the line $H = EN$. In contrast to the case

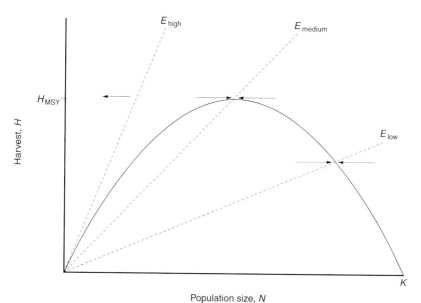

Figure 2.2. Equilibria for proportional (constant effort) harvesting (H). A constant fraction of the population (N) is removed, rather than a constant absolute amount, as in Figure 2.1. The dashed lines have slope E, corresponding to a constant exploitation rate. If $E < r$, there is a single stable equilibrium (e.g. E_{low} and E_{medium}). However, if $E > r$, there is no non-zero equilibrium (E_{high}). The arrows indicate population trajectories.

where yields are fixed, this system always approaches its stable equilibrium as long as E is fixed below r. Since the MSY value of E is usually far lower than r, there would appear to be less danger of precipitating a collapse with a system of control of the exploitation rate. The desirable properties of this system have been shown by Hilborn (1985).

On the other hand, the theoretical and practical problems that were described for the constant yield case are undiminished in this case: in fact they may be worse. Whereas harvests are straightforward to measure, the exploitation rate must be measured indirectly. The usual surrogate is some index of harvesting 'effort' on the part of humans. Regulations are usually restrictions on effort, such as gear limitations or closed seasons. This results in an arms race between the exploiters and the regulators (Hilborn *et al.*, 1995). The exploiters have an incentive to find more effective ways of harvesting the population without violating the regulations. The result is likely to be an unrecognised rise in the exploitation rate, although the measured 'effort' is constant. Under these circumstances, statistical attempts to estimate the optimal exploitation rate are actually tracking a moving target.

ECONOMIC THEORIES OF SUSTAINABLE USE

Dynamic theory: optimal control and discounting

For many of us the field of natural resource management or 'mathematical bioeconomics' began with the work of Clark (1973a,b, 1976, 1990). Clark developed a dynamic theory that applied methods of control theory to determine optimal exploitation trajectories in a state space that might include such variables as the population size or age composition and a level of investment. Clark's theory applies to a private owner of a renewable resource asset, who uses standard economic cost–benefit analysis. Clark showed that under certain simplifying assumptions the optimal control typically has a 'bang-bang' character. That is, the control variable (fishing effort) is either at a maximum or a minimum (determined by constraints) rather than at intermediate levels. Box 2.1 provides a simplified version of the theory.

The 'optimal' management of a natural resource is generally assumed to consist in the maximisation of a discounted sum of net economic returns (Clark, 1976). Discounting (discount factor < 1) weights future returns less heavily than present returns, and small discount factors correspond to a short time horizon. There is considerable controversy over the appropriate choice of discount factor and even whether discounting is appropriate for natural resources (Heal, 1997; Sutherland & Gill, Chapter 12). The theory shows that, for each value of the discount factor, there is an optimal value of the stock size. Under appropriate assumptions, the optimal strategy is to harvest down to the optimal size if the stock is above, and not to harvest at all if the stock is below the optimal size. Figure 2.3 shows how the optimal stock size S depends upon the discount factor α as well as the per capita growth rate. If α is too small, there is no positive optimal stock size. The theory implies that the optimal strategy is to harvest the stock to extinction in that case.

This last result is Clark's most famous and far-reaching observation: it is 'economically rational' to exploit populations to the point of extinction. The extinction or collapse of exploited populations has been an enduring paradox of resource management. Why do industries destroy resources in spite of their dependence upon them? Informal discussions of this topic were given by Clark (1990) in his Preface and Introduction, based upon more thorough treatments by Clark (1973a,b) and in subsequent works. Clark pointed out that foregone harvests may be considered as investments in the future resource. Such investments must be compared with other potential investments. If a higher return is available from other investments than

Box 2.1 A simplified version of Clark's dynamic theory

A dynamic theory allows for the possibility of changes in population size and exploitation rate from one year to another. If s_t is the population size after exploitation in year t, then we assume that the population before exploitation in the following year is given by

$$N_{t+1} = G(s_t). \tag{2.6}$$

In order to simplify the theory, we shall identify the net return with the number of individuals harvested:

$$R_i = N_i - s_i \tag{2.7}$$

The present value of the resource is defined as

$$V_p = R_0 + \alpha R_1 + \alpha^2 R_2 + \ldots, \tag{2.8}$$

where α is a discount factor applied to future returns. One way to arrive at the discounting formula is to ask how large a loan one might be able to repay with returns from the resource. Interest must be paid on future payments, and hence they must be appropriately discounted.

Theory shows that this discounted sum is maximised if a feedback control strategy is adopted to hold the population after harvest at a certain level S (Clark, 1990, p. 230). This can be obtained as follows: equation 2.8 takes the form

$$V_p = N_0 - s_0 + \alpha(G(s_0) - s_1) + \alpha^2(G(s_1) - s_2) + \ldots, \tag{2.9}$$

The choice of population sizes must satisfy $0 \leq s_t \leq N_t$. The sum V_p is maximised by maximising with respect to the choices of $s_0, s_1, \ldots$ Hence each optimal s satisfies

$$G'(s) = 1/\alpha. \tag{2.10}$$

The root of this equation will be denoted by S. This relationship is plotted in Figure 2.3. At the level $N = S$, the net return from an additional unit of harvest is exactly balanced by the decrease in discounted future returns due to population depletion. The decrease in future returns is interpreted as the 'shadow price' of the resource. One may think of the problem as one of investment. If a unit of harvest is worth more than the shadow price, then one should take the harvest. If the shadow price is higher than the net return, one should invest in the future population. A similar result holds for populations that fluctuate stochastically.

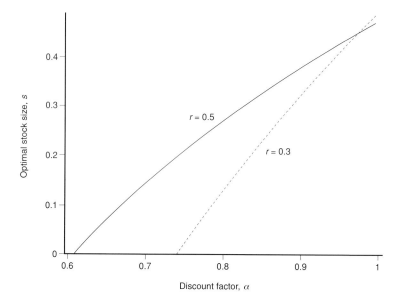

Figure 2.3. Optimal stock size (s) versus discount factor (α). Here the recruitment function $G(s) = s\exp(0.5(1-s))$. The solid curve corresponds to $r = 0.5$, and the dashed curve corresponds to $r = 0.3$. In each case, there is a minimum discount factor below which the optimal stock size is zero.

from growth in the natural population, then it is 'economically rational' to liquidate the natural population and invest the proceeds elsewhere. Natural populations with low growth rates are unlikely to survive the competition with other forms of investment. Forests are the pre-eminent example of natural resources that are poor investments, since growth rates are low or moderate and returns on investment generally are delayed for many decades. Returns are by no means certain, since many natural or human-created hazards may destroy the value of forests before they can be harvested.

Low growth rates correspond to long times to realise returns on investments. Hence preservation of resources depends upon a long time horizon for decision-making. In the competition for political or financial influence, short-term benefits have obvious advantages. Human decision-making often shows strong influence of the short term, as when people build on flood plains or unstable mountain slopes. People who are destitute do not have the freedom to consider the long term. The application of economic discounting to long time periods or to life support systems has been severely criticised (Heal, 1997). Clark's contribution was to show the dire consequences of 'business as usual' in the exploitation of renewable resources.

Age-structured resources

The preceding arguments can be extended to populations with age structure (Clark, 1990). Forests are the most obvious example. The optimal strategy in this case is to harvest trees at the end of an optimal rotation period. The rotation period depends upon the discount rate: Clark (1990, p. 272) provides a table. Optimal rotation periods for Douglas fir *Pseudotsuga menziesii* may be as long as 100 years if the discount rate is zero, but they drop to 49 years if the discount rate is 10%. The long interval between harvests suggests that investments in replanting or silviculture will be difficult to justify on economic grounds. Indeed, in British Columbia there are large areas classified as 'Not Sufficiently Restocked', presumably because logging companies did not think the investment worth while. More recently, legislation has required proper silvicultural practices (including proper road building) to safeguard the future resource. But forestry faces the same difficulty as any other commercial exploitation of a slowly regenerating resource: investments are difficult to justify using the customary economic discounting. As Clark pointed out for the case of whaling, even the sole owner may have little or no incentive to conserve the resource.

In contrast to fishery problems, it is not difficult to make an inventory of forest resources, so population estimation is much simpler. However, the estimation of future values of the resource is extremely difficult. For some species and areas, we lack experience of the history of even a single rotation. In some cases, it is known that the first rotation or two may not be a reliable guide to future performance (Plochmann, 1968). It is unreasonable to expect that biomass and associated nutrients can be removed from the system over long periods without eventually impoverishing the soil and hence the capacity for regrowth.

There are other difficulties related to the age structure of the forest. A traditional goal of forestry has been achieving a 'regulated forest', which has equal proportions in all age classes within the rotation period. However, the original old growth has larger volume and is more valuable than later rotations. Hence there is a possibility of 'fall down', where early harvests have greater values than later ones (Ludwig, 1993). The temptation is to overcut the old growth and remove the profits. This has been the history of forestry all over the world (Repetto & Gillis, 1988; Vincent, 1992; World Commission on Forests and Sustainable Development, 1999).

ECONOMIC RATIONALITY AND THE FALLACY OF DRAWING POLICY IMPLICATIONS

Interpretation of economic studies often makes a leap from optimisation exercises to policy implications. Clark (1973a,b) pointed out that 'economically rational' behaviour (maximisation of discounted net returns) may lead to extinction of the population under exploitation. Clark did not advocate such behaviour in that publication and he has assured me that it was never his intention to draw such an implication. But such a leap appears in Clark *et al.* (1979), which I describe in the next section. They stated at the very end of their work:

> Finally, the policy implications of our study are sufficiently clear from a qualitative viewpoint. On the one hand, the analysis supports the accepted belief that excessive capitalization is likely to occur during the initial development of a common-property resource, although a certain degree of over-capitalization is now shown to be generally acceptable. On the other hand, the analysis shows that extreme policies of stock rehabilitation (e.g., fishing moratoria), may be unwarranted unless the stock has become very severely depleted. The less transferable are capital assets, the more important this latter consideration becomes. (Along these lines, it is clear that non-transferability of labor would have similar implications.) The application of these findings to explicit resource-management problems will require additional research.

This passage illustrates not only the leap to policy implications (over-capitalisation is now shown to be generally acceptable) but also an emphasis upon financial values rather than the values of conservation (fishing moratoria are extreme). The conflict between finances and conservation was perhaps not as obvious in 1979 as it is now. But now we should ensure that management reflects the goals of society as a whole rather than the goals of a privileged few.

Some hints of better ways are provided by Ostrom *et al.* (1999). They indicated that the usual economic assumptions that 'all individuals are selfish, norm-free, and maximizers of short-run results' are not supported when 'individuals face a public good or CPR [common pool resource] problem and are able to communicate, sanction one another, or make new rules.' They pointed out that 'Promoting institutional diversity related to how diverse peoples cope with CPRs may be as important for our long-run survival as the protection of biological diversity.'

Another indication that there may be more effective ways of managing for sustainability is provided by Hastings & Botsford (1999). They showed that a system of reserves can produce yields as high as with a constant exploitation rate, but with far superior ability to avoid overexploitation when population sizes are uncertain, and when harvest rates are variable.

INVESTMENT PATTERNS

Bionomic equilibrium

Theories of sustained yield and constant exploitation rate are incomplete, since they fail to take account of the behaviour of the human exploiters. The fundamental result about human behaviour was obtained by Scott Gordon (1954). He assumed a model where the exploitation rate was determined by the economic returns to exploiters. I choose units so that the unit price of the harvest is 1. Effort will be equated with the exploitation rate and is assumed to bear a unit cost c. Thus the cost of effort is measured in units of the population. If access to the resource is unrestricted, more exploiters will enter the system and hence the exploitation rate will increase as long as there is a net return from the harvest: that is, as long as $EN(E) > cE$, where $N(E) = K(1 - E/r)$ is determined from the condition of equilibrium under a constant exploitation rate. Cancelling E from each side of this condition, we see that the exploitation rate will increase as long as $K(1 - E/r) > c$. Eventually $K(1 - E/r)$ will come close to c. The corresponding level of exploitation rate is $E_c = r(1 - c/K)$, and the corresponding population size is $N_c = K(1 - E_c/r)$. The yield is $rN_c(1 - N_c/K) = cE_c$. That is the point of 'bionomic equilibrium'. At that point, the population is so depleted that nobody obtains a net economic return. The dynamics are illustrated in Figure 2.4.

Although the model used by Scott Gordon (1954) is simple, the research is very important as it illustrates the 'tragedy of the commons'. Scott Gordon concluded that the underlying cause of the lack of economic return was the open access feature: anybody could exploit the population. Positive returns are only possible if access is restricted. As was pointed out by Clark (1990), Scott Gordon's results have a number of important implications. The net return may vary from one individual exploiter to another. As the population is depleted and returns decrease, those individuals who are able to realise larger returns from other enterprises will tend to leave for these other enterprises. Eventually only individuals who are less efficient at other enterprises will remain. This may cause social problems as well as financial difficulties for the entrepreneurs and the lenders from whom they borrowed to set up in business. Scott Gordon had already pointed out how the immobility of fishermen and their tendency towards risk-taking behaviour may also depress returns below the bionomic equilibrium. Governments often

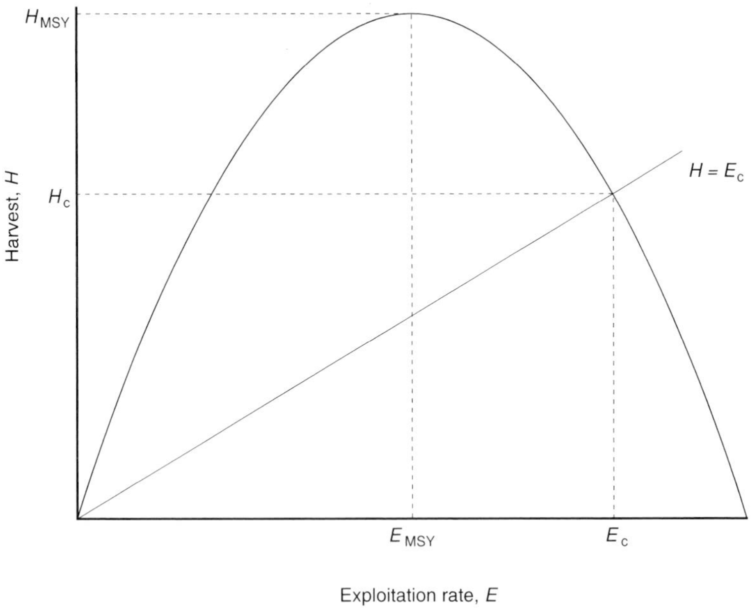

Figure 2.4. The solid curve shows harvest (H) versus exploitation rate (E). The solid line shows the cost, which is cE. In the units shown, the return exceeds the cost when the solid curve lies above the solid line. Effort increases until $E = E_c$ and $H = H_c$.

subsidise continued exploitation in order to relieve social pressures and pressures from influential constituents. The result is a steady downward trend in net returns from exploitation, even dropping below the bionomic equilibrium predicted by Scott Gordon. The phenomenon of overcapitalisation and government subsidisation of destruction of resources is not confined to fisheries. Repetto & Gillis (1988) detailed numerous examples of government subsidisation of overexploitation of forests under a wide variety of political systems. Systems of ecological accounting show the costs of such practices, yet they continue unabated. However, Ostrom *et al.* (1999) pointed out that results such as Scott Gordon's do not apply where local groups are able to develop controls over access to common pool resources.

Scott Gordon's result, though fundamental, is only theoretical. As Hilborn & Walters (1992) pointed out, there has been surprisingly little study of the actual investment behaviour of fishermen, except for Lane (1988). Hilborn & Walters devoted a chapter of their book to the behaviour of fishing fleets, and recommended modelling and game playing to get a feeling for the likely patterns of behaviour.

Theory of irreversible investment

As Scott Gordon had already recognised, a major factor in the decline of fisheries has been overinvestment in vessels and processing facilities. Once such investments have been made, the marginal costs of harvesting may be relatively small. Hence there is an incentive to continue harvesting even when populations are severely depleted. These investments are essentially irreversible: there is little use for fishing vessels other than for fishing. If investment were completely reversible, then the theories described above would apply, but the theory for irreversible investment is quite different. If one views the problem of investment as one of control, there are two states (the amount of investment and the size of the exploited population) and two control variables (the rate of investment and the amount of fishing effort). This greatly complicates the theory.

The deterministic theory is provided by Clark et al. (1979). I shall give only a brief outline here, since the main issues are well summarised by Clark (1990) and Charles & Munro (1985). The assumption is that the exploitation rate (effort) is constrained by the capital invested in vessels and processing capacity. There is no upper limit on the rate of investment, but investment can decrease only through depreciation. Clark et al. assume that the fishery begins with an unexploited population at equilibrium with no investment in the fishery. They find an optimal solution to the problem of maximising the discounted net income subject to the constraint that investment may decrease no faster than the depreciation rate. Their solution shows an initial instantaneous investment, which typically far overshoots the capacity required to maintain the fishery in a stable (sustainable) state, and associated high effort. The resulting high exploitation rate causes a decline in the exploited population. Eventually effort is reduced and only part of the fleet capacity is used in order to avoid extinction of the population. No further investment takes place until the population recovers to the optimal population size S described above. At that time there is a second pulse of investment that brings the capacity to the level required to hold the population at the size S. Afterwards investment just balances depreciation.

It is noteworthy that a policy of overcapitalisation is optimal according to the criterion of maximising discounted net income. This is because the immediate gains from a rapid harvest of the population (initially assumed to be at carrying capacity) outweigh later losses when the population is allowed to recover.

A stochastic version of the theory of irreversible investment was given by Charles (1983); a simplified account is in Charles & Munro (1985). The main conclusion is that the qualitative form of the optimal control is similar to the deterministic optimal control. If the deterministic control is implemented in a feedback form, there is little reduction in yield as compared with the optimal stochastic control. However, as for the simpler harvesting models described below, the behaviour of the solution is quite different if there is substantial stochastic variation. Simulations show that the fleet capacity fluctuates much as the population size does. The fleet often overinvests in response to high population sizes, but then has excess capacity later on. Thus, although overcapacity is an initial transient phenomenon in the deterministic case, stochastic fluctuations cause a continual cycling between undercapacity and overcapacity.

As Clark *et al.* (1979) pointed out, the initial overshooting effect may be exaggerated if there is a 'scramble competition' among several firms, all of which have access to the resource. This effect may be even more severe if we realise that the capability of the vessels does not decay exponentially, as Clark *et al.* assumed for reasons of mathematical simplicity. In fact these vessels may continue for years to operate at near capacity (Stump & Batker, 1996). As I pointed out (Ludwig, 1998), neglect of complications in population dynamics may result in grossly optimistic estimates of future returns. Such overestimates may also lead to overinvestment.

None of the economic analyses take into account the political influence wielded by the industry and the fishermen themselves and the government subsidies that are a consequence. As Repetto & Gillis (1988) pointed out, governments seldom can resist subsidising declining or overcapitalised industries. This contributes to the 'ratchet effect' pointed out by Caddy & Gulland (1983), where there is overinvestment during favourable periods but the harvest continues during unfavourable periods. A Worldwatch report estimates worldwide subsidies of fishing fleets at over $50 billion per year (Weber, 1994, cited by Stump & Batker, 1996).

STOCHASTIC MODELS

Stochastic theories with perfect information

Hilborn *et al.* (1995) provided abundant evidence that large fluctuations are common in exploited populations. Early stochastic harvesting theories were provided by Jaquette (1972), Reed (1974) and Gleit (1978). May *et al.* (1978) were concerned about the effects of harvesting upon local stability of the population, as measured by the time to return to equilibrium when displaced from it. I was primarily concerned with the robustness of strategies based upon deterministic models, and modifications of deterministic models to account for possible population collapses (Ludwig, 1979; Ludwig & Varah, 1979). Under the assumption of perfect information, strategies based upon deterministic models perform fairly well for populations subject to moderate stochastic fluctuations. The optimal population size decreases as the size of the fluctuations increases. This difference is only important for the net present value if the fluctuations are large.

There is an important difference between the behaviour of deterministic and stochastic systems (May *et al.*, 1978). In the deterministic case, as described above, there is an optimal population size. If the current population exceeds this, one harvests the population down to the optimum. Alternatively, one foregoes harvests if the population is below the optimum. In either case, deterministic theory concludes that the harvests and returns are steady after an initial period of adjustment. In the stochastic case, the returns will fluctuate, since the population will ordinarily fluctuate above and below the target size (Lande *et al.*, Chapter 4).

May *et al.* (1978) considered a range of possible forms of population dynamics, which vary in the skewness of the stock–recruit relationship. They evaluated the effect of various levels of exploitation rate upon the distribution of yield, in particular its expectation and coefficient of variation. They found a trade-off between high yields and variability of yield, and they posed the choice of exploitation rate as a 'portfolio' problem. They also called attention to difficulties in population assessment and the consequent need for management strategies that are robust with respect to uncertainty.

I (Ludwig, 1980) examined the characteristics of a number of management strategies. Simple notions of sustainability indicate that steady harvests are most desirable. Steady harvests are also important if substantial investments in harvesting capacity or infrastructure are required for exploitation. Such cases are very common, and debt service requires a steady income from the exploitation. If one were to adopt a policy of constant harvests, this would presumably provide a steady stream of benefits, but the consequences for the population under exploitation may be disastrous (May, 1977). One or more years of poor environmental conditions might bring the population to a level at which it cannot replace the harvests, and collapse is then inevitable. May *et al.* (1978) pointed out that, even when populations are managed with a harvest quota system, these quotas are usually reviewed or updated frequently. Hence they felt that 'constant quotas' are not in fact very different from constant effort strategies. On the other hand historical evidence shows that harvests often increase while the population is collapsing. This may be due to a 'ratchet' effect of Caddy & Gulland (1983), referred to above. In view of the many costs involved, it is difficult to imagine an industry starting up and shutting down in response to fluctuations in abundance of the exploited population. I know of no cases in which such a policy has been followed (but see Lande *et al.*, Chapter 4, for some ways to make such a policy more attractive).

A compromise strategy between the optimal bang-bang and a constant harvest might be to use proportional harvesting, as described on p. 20, i.e. a constant fraction of the population taken at each harvest. Such a policy has properties intermediate between the other two. A more systematic account is given by Hilborn & Walters (1992) and Ludwig (1998). Comparisons of a variety of harvesting strategies also appear in Lande *et al.* (1995).

Restraint in harvesting

It was shown in Clark's (1976) classic work that the strategy that maximises the discounted net return has the bang–bang form: harvest if the population is above a target level and do not harvest at all if the population lies below that level. It was shown (Ludwig, 1979; Ludwig & Varah, 1979) that a similar strategy is also optimal for stochastic dynamics. Results (Ludwig, 1980, 1998) confirmed that such strategies are robust in the presence of critical depensation and natural catastrophes. Strategies of an analogous form are also appropriate in case of uncertainty about the population dynamics (Ludwig & Hilborn, 1983), if sustainability of the resource is introduced as a constraint (Ludwig, 1995), or if population estimates are uncertain (Engen *et al.*, 1997). Nevertheless such strategies are not applied. Presumably 'optimal' strategies that call for foregoing harvests when the population is below a certain target level are not followed because the formulation fails to capture the true goals of management.

STATISTICAL PROBLEMS IN POPULATION ASSESSMENT

The works cited above allowed for fluctuations in population abundance, but they did not take into account statistical difficulties in determining the dynamics of exploited populations. Hilborn & Walters (1992) gave a lengthy account of the process of population assessment. Here I shall outline some of the difficulties in assessment that may contribute to management failures. Assessment may be viewed as a statistical problem where data must be collected and analysed in order to provide guidance for decision-making. This is quite different from scientific inference for a number of reasons (Hilborn & Ludwig, 1993; Hilborn *et al.*, 1995). An important obstacle to reliable assessment is the lack of sufficient data of good quality. In cases such as fisheries, tropical mammals, and many other situations described in this book, accurate census of the population under exploitation may be difficult or impossible. Time series of observations may be short or confined to small segments of the population. Data may be biased either intentionally or by a variety of confounding effects such as modifications in equipment or census techniques. Natural populations often go through large fluctuations due to interactions with other species, changes in food supply, or unknown causes. Such fluctuations make it difficult to discern the relationship between population size and recruitment or to arrive at simple characterisations of population dynamics. Analogous difficulties in estimating probabilities of extinction are dealt with elsewhere (Ludwig, 1999).

A second category of difficulty is the lack of replicates or scientific controls. Even many years later, it may be unclear whether exploitation is implicated in a population collapse, or whether the collapse can be blamed solely upon unfavourable environmental conditions. In a strict sense one cannot speak of 'scientific management', since the basic tools of scientific inference are not available for assessment. Scientists working on population assessment try to predict the consequences of future actions, but that may involve extrapolation of observed trends and relationships beyond the region where there are data. Such a procedure is risky under any circumstances. It makes little sense in light of the many difficulties with the data and their statistical treatment.

An inevitable consequence of the difficulties described above is uncertainty about the population dynamics. Biologists now have access to a variety of techniques for confronting such uncertainties (for a review, see Wade, Chapter 6). Is uncertainty about population dynamics important for management? Holling's (1973) paper on resilience emphasised a world view quite different from that of perfectly known systems whose management may be optimised with simple techniques. Holling proposed that many natural systems undergo large rather than small fluctuations, and indeed that the fluctuations are part of the system rather than extraneous to it. This is analogous to Darwin's view that deviations of characteristics of individuals in a population from the population mean or 'ideal type' are not to be ignored, since such deviations constitute the material for natural selection (Mayr, 1982). Holling pointed out that the fluctuations in natural systems could sometimes cause them to deviate from the behaviour they had shown in the past for long periods or permanently. Such changes in behaviour typically occur over short time periods (flips), and their timing is unpredictable.

ADAPTIVE MANAGEMENT

The implications of Holling's view for management are far reaching. A prudent manager should take into account the possibility of sudden changes without much warning, and must base policy upon a variety of possible dynamic regimes. Holling proposed that managers probe or experiment with systems in order to obtain better information about these possibilities and make appropriate plans (Holling, 1978). In order to try to include all of the essential components, Holling devised workshops where experts and practitioners from very diverse fields could plan the experiments. Computers, though quite rudimentary by present standards, were an important tool for communication among the diverse disciplines. The resulting models were never intended to have much predictive value. Their main merit was their suggestiveness: what were the minimum ingredients to obtain the gross qualitative behaviour? Would this behaviour be displayed in more realistic elaborations? Which are the critical areas of uncertainty that we should seek to clarify by means of well-designed experiments?

What sets Holling's ideas apart from more conventional experimental management is the concept of experimenting on the system as a whole, rather than attempting to analyse the individual parts. The attitude is that we will never be able to understand the individual parts well enough to synthesise the overall system behaviour. Moreover, whole-ecosystem experiments may be the only feasible ones. This process was termed 'adaptive management'. Holling's views and their implications were elaborated by Walters (1986).

Experience in implementing adaptive management was surveyed by Halbert (1993), Taylor *et al.* (1997), Walters (1997) and Parma (1998). There are many possible reasons for failure to adopt this approach: it is difficult to communicate such a broad and novel vision beyond the circle of those involved in its conception. Perhaps the greatest difficulty is that the experiments that are contemplated by the method can only be justified if very long-term objectives are adopted, contrary to all past experience. A pay-off from experimentation would require (1) that the experiments result in large improvement in knowledge of the potential behaviour of the system, (2) that the improved knowledge lead to actions substantially different than those that would otherwise be taken, and (3) that these different actions result in large differences in the outcomes. Numerical experiments have shown circumstances in which all three requirements can be met, but only when the economic discount rate is low and rapid learning is possible (Ludwig & Walters, 1982; Ludwig & Hilborn, 1983). The expense of experiments must be measured not only in direct expenditures, but in foregone opportunities. The costs are not only directly financial, but also social and political. If we shut down a fishery in order to see whether the population will increase in abundance, hundreds or thousands of people may lose employment. If we exclude people in developing nations from traditional hunting practices, they may starve. It is very difficult to balance a certain present loss against a merely possible or plausible future gain or loss, based mainly on the hunches of a few 'experts'.

In spite of the lack of actual implementations of adaptive management, it has become a very popular goal of management agencies. Perhaps it is used as a defensive measure by bureaucrats anxious to create an image of change without actually changing very much. Perhaps it is appealing because the other choices seem so bleak.

CONCLUSIONS

The theory and practice of renewable resource management has taken on a new significance with widespread concern about 'sustainable development' and the loss of biodiversity due to overexploitation, destruction of habitats and possibly global warming. The theory of fisheries management has a long history and it is the most sophisticated of any of the theories of natural resource management. This sophistication has not prevented the widespread destruction of the world's fisheries (Ludwig *et al.*, 1993; Pauly *et al.*, 1998). Does this situation imply that more efforts along the same lines are needed, or are more fundamental reassessments and changes required? Clark (1990) ends the Preface to the second edition of his work as follows:

> The principal aim of this book is to clarify the fundamental principles of renewable resource economics. I will have succeeded in this quest to the extent that I can convince readers of the necessity of deliberate resource conservation for the continuation of civilization as we know it, and if I have shown that present practices in resource management, or the lack thereof, need to be drastically revised if this objective is to be achieved. The current state of affairs, in which most professional economists ignore resource limitations and in which most ecologists maintain a proud disdain of economics, must give way to a science of renewable resource management based upon sound principles of bioeconomics. The practical application of these bioeconomic principles will be essential if the vision of sustainable development is to be realized.

I share Clark's deep concern about the possibility of sustaining flows of resources, but I do not believe that construction of a science of renewable resource management is sufficient to achieve sustainability. The history of resource management shows a remarkable lack of progress in solving problems that were evident from the earliest treatments. The main deficiency has been in application of well-understood principles.

ACKNOWLEDGEMENTS

This work was supported in part by grant number A-9239 from the Natural Sciences and Engineering Research Council of Canada. I thank Colin Clark for helpful suggestions.

REFERENCES

Albion, R. G. (1926). *Forests and Sea Power: The Timber Problem of the Royal Navy, 1652–1862.* Anchor Books, Hamden, CT, reprinted in 1965.

Caddy, J. F. & Gulland, J. A. (1983). Historical patterns of fish stocks. *Marine Policy*, **7**, 267–278.

Caughley, G. & Sinclair, A. (1994). *Wildlife Ecology and Management.* Blackwell, Oxford.

Charles, A. T. (1983). Optimal fisheries investment under uncertainty. *Canadian Journal of Fisheries and Aquatic Sciences*, **40**, 2080–2091.

Charles, A. T. & Munro, G. R. (1985). Irreversible investment and optimal fisheries management: a stochastic analysis. *Marine Resource Economics*, **1**, 247–264.

Clark, C. (1973a). Profit maximization and the extinction of animal species. *Journal of Political Economics*, **81**, 950–961.

Clark, C. (1973b). The economics of overexploitation. *Science*, **181**, 630–634.

Clark, C. W. (1976). *Mathematical Bioeconomics. The Optimal Management of Renewable Resources.* Wiley, New York.

Clark, C. W. (1990). *Mathematical Bioeconomics. The Optimal Management of Renewable Resources*, 2nd edn. Wiley, New York.

Clark, C. W., Clarke, F. H. & Munro, G. R. (1979). The optimal exploitation of renewable resource stocks: problems of irreversible investment. *Econometrica*, **47**, 25–47.

Ehrlich, P. (1997). *A World of Wounds: Ecologists and the Human Dilemma.* Ecology Institute, Oldendorf, Germany.

Engen, S., Lande, R. & Sæther, B. E. (1997). Harvesting strategies for fluctuating populations based on uncertain population estimates. *Journal of Theoretical Biology*, **186**, 201–212.

Gleit, A. (1978). Optimal harvesting in continuous time with stochastic growth. *Mathematical Biosciences*, **41**, 111–123.

Halbert, C. L. (1993). How adaptive is adaptive management? *Reviews in Fish Biology and Fisheries*, **1**, 261–283.

Hastings, A. & Botsford, L. W. (1999). Equivalence in yield from marine reserves and traditional fisheries management. *Science*, **284**, 1537–1538.

Heal, G. (1997). Discounting and climate change. *Climatic Change*, **37**, 335–343.

Hilborn, R. (1985). A comparison of harvest policies for mixed stock fisheries. In *Resource management: Proceedings of the Second Ralf Yorque Workshop*, ed. M. Mangel, pp. 75–87. Lecture Notes in Biomathematics no. 61. Springer-Verlag, Berlin.

Hilborn, R. & Ludwig, D. (1993). The limits of applied ecological research. *Ecological Applications*, **3**, 550–552.

Hilborn, R. & Walters, C. J. (1992). *Quantitative Fisheries Stock Assessment*. Chapman & Hall, New York.

Hilborn, R., Walters, C. J. & Ludwig, D. (1995). Sustainable exploitation of renewable resources. *Annual Review of Ecology and Systematics*, **26**, 45–67.

Holling, C. S. (1973). Resilience and stability of ecological systems. *Annual Review of Ecology and Systematics*, **4**, 1–23.

Holling, C. S. (ed.) (1978). *Adaptive Environmental Assessment and Management*. Wiley, Chichester.

Jaquette, D. L. (1972). A discrete-time population-control model. *Mathematical Biosciences*, **15**, 231–252.

Lande, R., Engen, S. & Sæther, B. E. (1995). Optimal harvesting of fluctuating populations with a risk of extinction. *American Naturalist*, **142**, 728–745.

Lande, R., Engen, S. & Sæther, B. E. (1997). Harvesting strategies for fluctuating populations based on uncertain population estimates. *Journal of Theoretical Biology*, **186**, 201–212.

Lane, D. E. (1988). Investment decision making by fishermen. *Canadian Journal of Fisheries and Aquatic Sciences*, **45**, 782–796.

Larkin, P. (1977). An epitaph for the concept of maximum sustained yield. *Transactions of the American Fisheries Society*, **106**, 1–11.

Ludwig, D. (1979). Optimal harvesting of a randomly fluctuating resource. I. Application of perturbation methods. *SIAM Journal of Applied Mathematics*, **37**, 166–184.

Ludwig, D. (1980). Harvesting strategies for a randomly fluctuating population. *Journal du Conseil Permanent pour l'Exploration de la Mer*, **39**, 168–174.

Ludwig, D. (1993). Forest management strategies that account for short-term and long-term consequences. *Canadian Journal of Forest Research*, **23**, 563–572.

Ludwig, D. (1995). A theory of sustainable harvesting. *SIAM Journal of Applied Mathematics*, **55**, 564–575.

Ludwig, D. (1998). Management of stocks that may collapse. *Oikos*, **83**, 397–402.

Ludwig, D. (1999). Is it meaningful to estimate a probability of extinction? *Ecology*, **80**, 298–301.

Ludwig, D. & Hilborn, R. (1983). Adaptive probing strategies for age-structured fish stocks. *Canadian Journal of Fisheries and Aquatic Sciences*, **40**, 559–569.

Ludwig, D. & Varah, J. M. (1979). Optimal harvesting of a randomly fluctuating resource. II. Numerical methods and results. *SIAM Journal of Applied Mathematics*, **37**, 185–205.

Ludwig, D. & Walters, C. J. (1982). Optimal harvesting with imprecise parameter estimates. *Ecological Modelling*, **14**, 273–292.

Ludwig, D., Hilborn, R. & Walters, C. J. (1993). Uncertainty, resource exploitation, and conservation: lessons from history. *Science*, **260**, 17, 36.

May, R. M. (1977). Thresholds and breakpoints in ecological systems with a multiplicity of stable states. *Nature*, **269**, 471–477.

May, R. M., Beddington, J. R., Horwood, J. W. & Shepherd, J. G. (1978). Exploiting natural populations in an uncertain world. *Mathematical Biosciences*, **42**, 219–252.

Mayr, E. (1982). *The Growth of Biological Thought*. Harvard University Press, Cambridge, MA.

Ostrom, E., Burger, J., Field, C. B., Norgaard, R. B. & Policansky, D. (1999). Revisiting the commons: local lessons, global challenges. *Science*, **284**, 278–282.

Parma, A. (1998). What can adaptive management do for our fish, forests, food, and biodiversity? *Integrative Biology*, **1**, 16–26.

Pauly, D., Christensen, V., Dalsgaard, J., Froese, R. & Torres, F. Jr. (1998). Fishing down marine food webs. *Science*, **279**, 860–863.

Plochmann, R. (1968). *Forestry in the Federal Republic of Germany*. Hill Family Foundation Series, School of Forestry, Oregon State University, Corvallis, OR.

Reed, W. J. (1974). A stochastic model for the economic management of a renewable animal resource. *Mathematical Biosciences*, **22**, 313–337.

Reed, W. J. (1991). Bionomics: an essay on the classic papers of H. Scott Gordon, Milner B. Schaefer and Harold Hotelling. *Bulletin of Mathematical Biology*, **53**, 217–229.

Repetto, R. & Gillis, M. (eds.) (1988). *Public Policies and the Misuse of Forest Resources*. Cambridge University Press, Cambridge.

Schaefer, M. B. (1954). Some considerations of population dynamics and economics in relation to the commercial marine fisheries. *Journal of the Fisheries Research Board of Canada*, **14**, 669–681.

Scott Gordon, H. (1954). Economic theory of a common-property resource: the fishery. *Journal of Political Economics*, **62**, 124–142.

Stump, K. & Batker, D. (1996). *Sinking Fast: How Factory Trawlers are Destroying U.S. Fisheries and Marine Systems*. Greenpeace, Washington, DC.

Sutherland, W. J. & Reynolds, J. D. (1998). Sustainable and unsustainable exploitation. In *Conservation Science and Action*, ed. W. J. Sutherland, pp. 90–115. Blackwell Science, Oxford.

Taylor, B., Kremsater, L. & Ellis, R. (1997). *Adaptive Management of Forests in British Columbia*. BC Ministry of Forests – Forest Practices Branch, Victoria, BC.

Vincent, J. R. (1992). The tropical timber trade and sustainable development. *Science*, **256**, 1651–1655.

Walters, C. J. (1986). *Adaptive Management of Renewable Resources*. Macmillan, New York.

Walters, C. J. (1997). Challenges in adaptive management of riparian and coastal ecosystems. *Conservation Ecology*, **1**, 1. (Available on the internet at http://www.consecol.org/vol1/iss2/art1, last visited 12 February 2001.)

World Commission on Forests and Sustainable Development (1999). *Our Forests, Our Future*. Cambridge University Press, Cambridge.

PART II

Population-based approaches

3

The gospel of maximum sustainable yield in fisheries management: birth, crucifixion and reincarnation

ANDRÉ E. PUNT & ANTHONY D. M. SMITH

A traditional key objective for fisheries management is that removals should be as large as possible but nevertheless sustainable in the long term, i.e. that the fishery catch should be equal to the maximum sustainable yield, MSY. MSY has therefore played a very significant role in fisheries management. However, its general use and applicability have been challenged. This chapter provides an overview of some of the arguments against the use of MSY, and of how many of these have been overcome in recent years so that MSY is once again a key concept in fisheries management advice.

Larkin (1977) provided a tongue-in-cheek description of the 'Gospel of MSY' as it is implemented in fisheries as 'any species each year produces a harvestable surplus, and if you take that much, and no more, you can go on getting it forever and ever'. Larkin also noted that MSY-based management involves setting the harvest rate (in fisheries, defined in terms of fishing effort) to that level which produces a catch of MSY 'no more and no less'.

MSY has been, and to some extent remains, a key paradigm in fisheries management science. Fisheries management science itself consists of a wide range of scientific disciplines including biology, ecology, mathematics and even criminology (Stephenson & Lane, 1995). However, the primary purpose of the fisheries scientist is to provide advice (usually to decision-makers) regarding the relative merits of alternative management actions (Punt & Hilborn, 1997). The traditional questions addressed by fisheries scientists have related to levels of 'sustainable' catch and fishing effort, and appropriate selection of fishing gear. That role has expanded over time to include issues such as evaluating marine protected areas and the 'ecosystem impacts' of fishing. Nevertheless, the fundamental role of the fisheries scientist has changed little, and scientists today still provide advice on the implications of different levels of catch and fishing effort.

The concept of MSY has played a central role in fisheries science for over four decades. This is because MSY is simple to explain to non-mathematicians, it is a purely physical measure (i.e. not tied to any economic or social and hence political doctrine), fishing the biomass to below that at which MSY is achieved has been a traditional definition of biological overexploitation, and MSY can (in principle at least) be estimated using limited data and computing resources. Cunningham (1981) argued that, of the traditional objectives of fisheries management, aiming at MSY results in the least decline in effort (and hence the least decline in employment).

The examples used in this chapter are based on the Cape hakes *Merluccius capensis* and *M. paradoxus* off northern Namibia and the west coast of South Africa. The quantitative results presented should, however, be considered to be illustrative only, because the data used are not the most recent. Nevertheless, the qualitative results should be insensitive to including the most recent data.

PROVIDING MANAGEMENT ADVICE IN AN UNCERTAIN WORLD – THE BIRTH OF MSY

The concept of a sustainable yield and hence of the MSY in fisheries appears to have originated in the 1930s (see e.g. Russel, 1931; Hjort *et al.*, 1933; Graham, 1935), a time when mathematical approaches to fisheries management were gaining increasing attention (Smith, 1994). However, in constructing their theory of fishing, these early pioneers of quantitative fisheries science were not unaware of the limitations of their simple models. For example, Russel (1931) noted that 'It appears that the ideal of a stabilised fishery yielding a constant maximum value is impractical', although he also stated that 'the aim of rational exploitation is to get the maximum yield annually, compatible with maintaining stocks at a steady level'.

The 1950s saw the development of two mathematical approaches that could be used to estimate the relationship between fishing mortality and catch under the assumption that the population is in equilibrium. Both approaches attempted to assess the impact of different levels of fishing intensity on changes in population biomass. The first approach, initially proposed by Schaefer (1954), is based on the concept of 'surplus production' – the difference between the increase in biomass due to growth and recruitment to the fishable population, and the loss in biomass due to natural mortality. A surplus arises because density dependence means that growth will be faster, survival will be greater or maturation earlier at stock levels below the unfished biomass (K). The surplus production approach does not, however, attempt to model the various processes (growth, mortality, etc.) that determine surplus production explicitly. Instead, Schaefer's arguments lead to a simple relationship between surplus production (which is the same as sustainable yield) and biomass, with MSY occurring at a biomass B_{MSY} that is half the unfished biomass K (Figure 3.1a). The relationship between biomass and surplus production in Figure 3.1a is based on the assumption that population growth follows a logistic function in the absence of exploitation. Other forms for the surplus production function (see e.g. Fox, 1970) arise from different assumptions in this regard.

A variety of methods exist for estimating MSY using the data traditionally collected from a fishery. Figure 3.1b illustrates the simplest of these. The catch rate (the annual catch C divided by the corresponding fishing effort E) is regressed on the annual fishing effort:

$$(C/E)_y = \alpha - \beta E_y + \varepsilon_y$$

where $(C/E)_y$ is the catch rate for year y, E_y is the fishing effort for year y, α, β are regression coefficients, and ε_y is the residual for year y.

If catch and biomass are related according to the simple (quadratic) relationship in Figure 3.1a and catch rate changes linearly with abundance, it is straightforward to show that MSY is $\alpha^2/4\beta$. The values of the parameters of the curve that relates biomass to catch in Figure 3.1a are determined using an alternative algorithm, based on different assumptions (for details see Butterworth & Andrew, 1984).

The second approach, yield-per-recruit analysis, as outlined in particular by Beverton and Holt in their seminal volume (Beverton & Holt, 1957), is based on consideration of the dynamics of a single year class, where account is taken of changes with age in relative probability of capture, abundance and mass. In simple terms, the lower the fishing mortality, the longer an animal will live and hence the larger it will be if caught. Yield-per-recruit analysis thus allows an examination of the trade-off between allowing fish to grow larger, and the probability that they will die of natural causes before capture. It allows the relationship between fishing intensity and the yield per individual to be determined (Figure 3.2). The fishing mortality rate corresponding to MSY (F_{MSY}) can be determined from this relationship, assuming that recruitment (the number of individuals born) is not affected by changes in stock level. The level of fishing effort corresponding to MSY can then be determined from a relationship between fishing effort and fishing mortality, which is usually assumed to be one of linear proportionality.

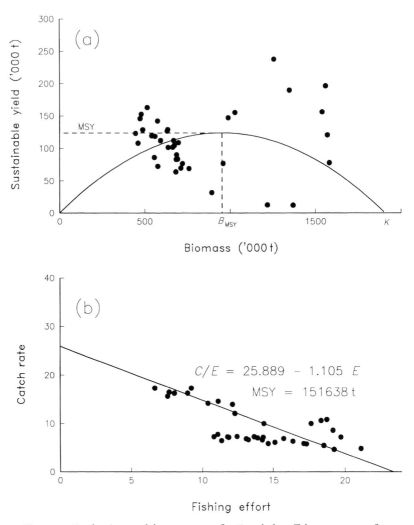

Figure 3.1. Production model assessments for Cape hake off the west coast of South Africa. (a) Equilibrium sustainable yield against population biomass based on the Butterworth–Andrew method. B_{MSY} is the biomass at which MSY is achieved and K is the environmental carrying capacity (unfished equilibrium biomass). The solid dots represent realised sustainable yield in each year (derived using the method of Schaefer (1954)). (b) Application of the catch rate regression method to estimate MSY (see equation 3.1).

The Food and Agriculture Organization (FAO) of the United Nations gave considerable support and emphasis to management based on MSY. For example Sparre & Venema (1992) noted in an FAO manual that 'fish stock assessment may be described as the search for the exploitation level

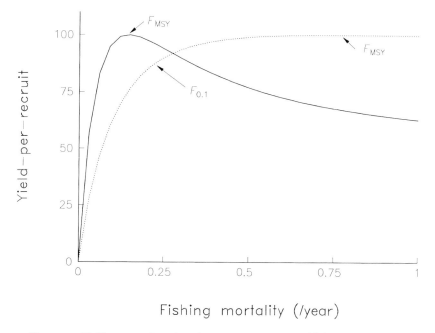

Figure 3.2. Yield per recruit against the instantaneous rate of fishing mortality. F_{MSY} is the level of fishing mortality at which the yield-per-recruit curve is maximised and $F_{0.1}$ is the level of fishing mortality at which the rate of change of yield per recruit is 10% of that at the origin. The dotted line shows a species that grows 10 times as quickly as the species with the solid line.

which in the long run gives the maximum yield in weight from the fishery'. The development of quantitative methods for determining the level of fishing mortality or fishing effort corresponding to MSY, and the support from the FAO, led to the wide adoption of MSY as a management goal (either explicitly or implicitly) in the 1950s, 1960s and even 1970s. Several international fisheries commissions (e.g. the Inter-American Tropical Tuna Commission, the International Commission for the Northwest Atlantic Fisheries and the North Pacific Fur Seal Commission) had adopted MSY as a management goal by the mid 1960s (FAO, 1966). The International Whaling Commission's 'New Management Procedure' (NMP), adopted in 1974, was based explicitly on MSY (Allen & Kirkwood, 1988). MSY was the only reference point explicitly referred to in the 1982 Law of the Sea Convention (Caddy, 1999).

By the mid 1970s, however, MSY as a management goal had moved beyond the intentions of its originators. For example, Holt & Talbot (1978) (cited by Smith, 1994) noted that 'like some other simplified concepts, maximum sustainable yield has become institutionalised in a more absolute and precise role than intended by the biologists who were responsible for its original formulation'.

PROBLEMS WITH MSY – THE CRUCIFIXION OF THE 1970s

The criticisms of the MSY paradigm can be divided into three main categories: the ability to estimate MSY given uncertainty regarding models and data; the appropriateness of MSY as a management goal given other objectives for management; and the ability to implement effectively a harvest strategy based on MSY (i.e. to limit the fishery to actually take the catch according to the harvest strategy rather some larger (or smaller) catch).

Estimation considerations
Surplus production model approach
Schaefer (1954) presented two methods for estimating the parameters of the relationship between sustainable yield and population biomass. One relied on the assumption that the data reflect a population that is in steady state (equilibrium) while the other did not. Unfortunately, the latter method required information on the catchability coefficient (the fraction of the biomass taken per unit effort), while the steady state (equilibrium) method did not. The equilibrium method involves regressing catch per unit effort (CPUE) on fishing effort (Figure 3.1b). Since such data are usually available, this method was applied widely. However, it has two major faults. First, the dependent and independent variables of the regression both involve fishing effort, which leads to some correlation between these variables irrespective of whether the data actually contain any information on the shape of the surplus production function (Sissenwine, 1978; Uhler, 1980). Secondly, the assumption that the resource is in steady state is seldom, if ever, valid.

Figure 3.3 shows relative error distributions for estimates of MSY for Cape hake off northern Namibia, based on the Schaefer (1954) equilibrium method and the method developed by Butterworth & Andrew (1984), which does not assume the population to be in steady state. The distributions were obtained from the results of 10 000 simulations, each of which involved generating an artificial dataset based on a fit of the discrete logistic model to the catch and data for northern Namibian hake (for details, see Punt, 1994). The results of the simulations show that the Schaefer (1954) method can be biased by close to 50%, while the non-equilibrium method is close to unbiased. The quantitative level of bias in Figure 3.3 may too low for most fish

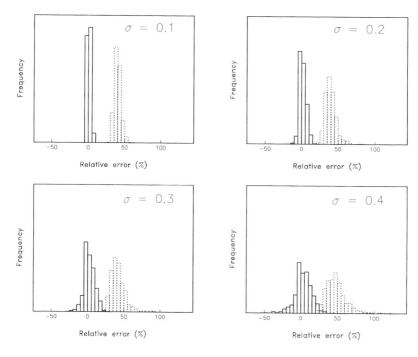

Figure 3.3. Distributions for the relative error of estimates of MSY for Cape hake off northern Namibia. Results are shown for the Schaefer (1954) equilibrium approach (dotted lines) and the Butterworth–Andrew (1984) non-equilibrium approach (solid lines), for four levels of assumed variability, σ, about the relationship between catch per unit effort and abundance.

stocks, as the dataset for northern Namibian hake is very informative. This is because it started with the commencement of substantial harvesting in 1964 and because the stock experienced large changes in both fishing effort and biomass over the period to 1987. Greater levels of bias and variability in estimates of MSY are to be expected for developing fisheries (Smith, 1993), and when effort and biomass do not vary substantially over the period for which data are available (Hilborn, 1979).

Gulland (1961) provided a modification to the Schaefer (1954) method that involved regressing the catch rate for each year on a 'moving average' fishing effort, in an attempt to deal indirectly with the equilibrium assumption. For a given year the moving average is defined by taking a weighted average of the effort for the year concerned and for some previous years. This method has been applied widely (e.g. Fox, 1975) and sadly continues to be. However, the averaging procedure does not remove the problem that the dependent and independent variables are implicitly correlated, a problem which is compounded because fishing effort is itself generally temporally correlated (Roff & Fairbairn, 1980), nor does it resolve the problem that the system is not in steady state (Polacheck *et al.*, 1993). Notwithstanding the problems with the original Schaefer method and its subsequent modifications, this method has been advocated in several stock assessment manuals produced by the FAO (e.g. Gulland, 1965; Sims, 1985; Sparre & Venema, 1992).[1]

Subsequent modifications to the production model approach (e.g. Pella & Tomlinson, 1969; Schnute, 1977; Deriso, 1980; Butterworth & Andrew, 1984; Hilborn, 1990) have resolved some of the problems with the Schaefer (1954) approach. However, estimates of MSY from surplus production models can still be substantially in error. For example, many stock assessments are based on fitting to CPUE data under the assumption that CPUE is linearly proportional to abundance. Unfortunately, the relationship between CPUE and stock abundance is seldom well understood and can differ markedly from that of linear proportionality (see e.g. Cooke & Beddington, 1984; Hilborn & Walters, 1992; Walters & Ludwig, 1994; Hutchings, 1996). It should be noted that some of the problems associated with CPUE as an index of abundance were known decades before models that rely on CPUE came into popular use (see e.g. Kyle, 1928, cited by Russel, 1931).

These problems can be overcome by fitting surplus production models to catch data and estimates of fishing mortality, rather than to catch and effort data (Garcia *et al.*, 1989; Caddy & Defeo, 1996). Estimates of fishing mortality can be obtained using information on the age structure of the catch (see Ricker, 1975; Hilborn & Walters, 1992) or from tagging studies. However, there remain many other sources of error in estimating MSY from surplus production models, including biases in fishing effort and the absence of reliable estimates of catches (owing, for example, to misreporting and discarding).

Yield-per-recruit approach

The yield-per-recruit approach has not suffered quite the same amount of criticism as the surplus production model approach even though the assumptions underlying most yield-per-recruit analyses are unrealistically simple. For example, the common practice of linking the fishing mortality

---

[1] At this point, the first author should confess that he was a co-author of a publication (Butterworth *et al.*, 1989) in which the Schaefer (1954) method was advocated (admittedly in a qualified way).

at which yield per recruit is maximised, F_{max}, to that at which MSY is achieved, F_{MSY}, is based on the assumption that recruitment is independent of spawner stock size for fishing mortalities between 0 and F_{max}. However, analysis of stock and recruitment datasets for many species (e.g. Myers *et al.*, 1994; Myers & Barrowman, 1996) reveals that this assumption is probably invalid for many, if not most, stocks by some amount. The relationship between F_{MSY}, F_{max} and other commonly applied fishing mortality reference points such as $F_{0.1}$, the level of fishing mortality at which the rate of change of yield per recruit is 10% of that at the origin (Gulland & Boerema, 1973; Figure 3.2), has been examined by several authors (e.g. Deriso, 1982, 1987; Clark, 1991, 1993; Mace, 1994; Die & Caddy, 1997; Punt, 2000). F_{max} is almost always the largest (and hence most risky) of the commonly used fishing mortality reference points (Punt, 2000).

F_{MSY} and other commonly used fisheries reference points such as $F_{0.1}$ are usually much larger than F_{crash}, the lowest fishing mortality, which, if fishing continued at that level, would eventually render the resource extinct. For example, based on a simple density-dependent demographic model, Punt (2000) showed that F_{crash} for Cape hake is three times larger than F_{MSY} and $F_{0.1}$. However, F_{MSY} can be quite similar to F_{crash} for stocks for which the stock–recruitment relationship exhibits depensation (Allee effect) or (more generally) for stocks for which recruitment drops off rapidly with reductions in stock size (Cook *et al.*, 1997; Punt, 2000). For example, Punt (2000) shows that F_{max} can exceed F_{crash} substantially for slow-growing, long-lived and unproductive species such as sharks. These species have low values for F_{crash} but are species for which F_{max} can be very large (or even infinite). Punt (2000) shows that F_{max} for school shark *Galeorhinus galeus* is infinite and $F_{0.1}$ is 0.169/year but F_{crash} ranges from 0.088/year to 0.385/year, depending on the assumed level of productivity.

The problem that F_{crash} may be similar to F_{MSY} for some species is exacerbated by uncertainty regarding the estimation of F_{MSY} and current fishing mortality from actual fisheries data. Imprecision in these estimates could lead to the estimate of F_{MSY} greatly exceeding F_{crash} for stocks for which F_{MSY} is really similar to F_{crash}. Unfortunately, F_{MSY} (and F_{crash}) is often poorly estimated using fisheries data because to estimate F_{MSY} accurately requires good information not only on growth rates but also on the shape of the stock–recruitment relationship. The latter is, however, seldom well determined because of uncertainty regarding estimates of spawner stock size and recruitment, and lack of contrast in spawner stock size.

Other problems with yield-per-recruit analysis are that the results can be sensitive to the assumed age-specific selectivity pattern (Goodyear,

1996), the level of natural mortality (Punt, 1994) and any age dependence in natural mortality. Furthermore, the yield-per-recruit curve is often flat near its maximum, so virtually the same yield per recruit can be achieved by fishing intensities markedly lower than F_{max} (e.g. see for example the dotted line in Figure 3.2).

Other considerations

A number of other problems stem from the fact that stock assessments, no matter how complicated, are nevertheless based on simple models of the system being managed. Such problems are not necessarily associated only with MSY-based management, but may be exacerbated if attempts are made to extract the maximum possible sustainable harvest. For example, spatial structure and biological interactions are generally ignored when researchers are conducting stock assessments, owing to lack of data. However, it is well understood that if the population consists of substocks rather than a single homogeneous resource, harvesting may target (and perhaps even extirpate) the more accessible substocks. Unfortunately, few attempts have been made to estimate MSY by taking account of the spatial dynamics of the population (a notable exception being Die *et al.*, 1990).

One implication of model uncertainty is that reality is often (substantially) outside the modelled estimates of uncertainty. This can be seen from the results of retrospective analyses (Sinclair *et al.*, 1991; Mohn, 1993, 1999). Retrospective analysis examines how well a model predicts events that have already been observed. For example, Figure 3.4a shows applications of the Butterworth & Andrew (1984) method to CPUE data for Cape hake off the west coast of South Africa. Results are shown for a range of final years of the assessment from 1978 to 1996. For the years beyond the end of the assessment, the curves correspond to projections to 1996 under the actual catches for the years from the end of the assessment to 1996. This is a clear example of 'retrospective bias', where the estimates of historical and future population sizes change systematically as additional data are included in the assessment. In this case, estimates of resource productivity reduce as the length of the data series is increased (Figure 3.4b). The reasons for retrospective bias will differ among stocks. For Figure 3.4, a key reason appears to be that, as the resource recovered, the frequency with which net liners were used (illegally) to capture small fish declined (D. S. Butterworth, University of Cape Town, personal communication). However, the general cause is that the model is too simple or the data are misleading. Sensitivity tests, although conducted routinely, cannot easily represent uncertainty due to model structure (Sainsbury, 1998).

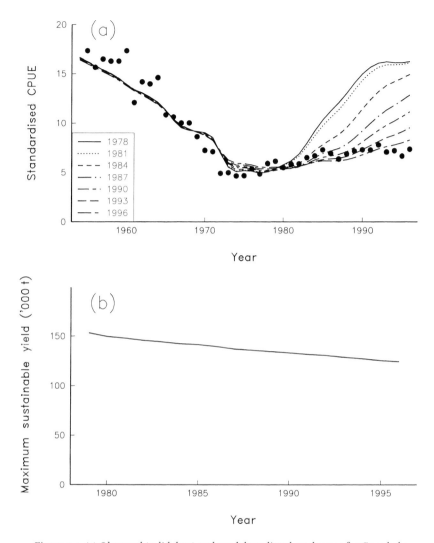

Figure 3.4. (a) Observed (solid dots) and model predicted catch rates for Cape hake off the west coast of South Africa for various choices for the final year of the assessment. The population is projected to 1996 for each assessment. CPUE, catch per unit effort. (b) MSY estimates as a function of the year in which the assessment was conducted.

Attempts to use more complicated (and realistic) models can lead to estimation problems, and worse performance than use of simple models (Ludwig & Walters, 1985).

The International Whaling Commission's management regime based on MSY apparently worked adequately for a few years but, by the late 1970s, problems emerged. These related mainly to the inability to estimate MSY and the current and pre-exploitation stock sizes reliably. The estimates of these quantities could change markedly from one year to another (owing to changes in assessment methodology and dataset choice), which led to wildly fluctuating catch limits (Kirkwood, 1997). This eventually resulted in the replacement of the NMP by a more robust regime.

Is MSY an appropriate goal for fisheries management?

The goal of MSY-based management in its purest form involves adjusting the fishery so that the catch each year is equal to MSY – i.e. a constant catch strategy. Alternatively, one could set the fishing effort (or mortality) to the level at which MSY is achieved, E_{MSY} (F_{MSY}), i.e. a constant effort strategy (see Ludwig, Chapter 2). A constant catch strategy is easy to understand, consistent with the deterministic considerations that underlie the surplus production function, and satisfies the need for constant supplies of catch to markets, and approximately steady income for fishers. Unfortunately, such a strategy also carries considerable risks of overfishing, as it is unresponsive to changes in stock levels (Beddington & May, 1977; Murray, 1993). Attempts to achieve MSY using a constant effort strategy may lead to large interannual variation in catches, because the susceptibility of the stock to natural variability (owing to, for example, recruitment) increases at higher levels of fishing mortality (Sissenwine et al., 1988).

One of the other main criticisms of the MSY paradigm is that it ignores economic and social considerations. For most fisheries, the goal for fishers is dollars not tonnes of fish, and the goal for politicians is jobs and the votes they bring. Managing for MSY does not take any account of the value of the catch or of the costs associated with harvesting, processing and marketing. Bioeconomic modelling (see e.g. Scott Gordon, 1954; Clark, 1973, 1976; Ludwig, Chapter 2) led to concepts such as maximum economic yield (MEY). However, these concepts also have their problems (Cunningham, 1981) and have seldom formed the basis for fisheries management decisions. Discounting of future catches (Clark, 1973) places greater weight on current rather than future catches and hence maximisation of net present value (the sum of discounted future profits) is the 'correct economic objective' (Cunningham, 1981; Ludwig, Chapter 2). For a risky activity such as fishing, discount rates are likely to be high relative to the social discount rate. Unfortunately, future discounting can lead to an inability to achieve conservation-related objectives if the discount rate is high relative to the intrinsic productivity of the stock. For example, some bioeconomic theories that pay little attention to the costs of fishing and the response of price to supply suggest that it is 'optimal' to extirpate resources (such as baleen whales) if the intrinsic growth rate is smaller than the discount rate (Clark, 1973). A more common problem is that fishers often wish to defer reductions in catch (e.g. to achieve recovery from overexploitation) because they can see an immediate loss in profits for what is only the possibility for increased profits in the future. They rate the loss in profit now as not being as valuable as increased profits in the future. This fear may well have a sound basis because once recovery is achieved, it is not uncommon for the decision-makers to allow additional operators to enter the fishery with the net effect that the original participants are no better off than they were earlier.

The biological reference point $F_{0.1}$ (Gulland & Boerema, 1973; see Figure 3.2) is argued to correct for economic factors to some extent. However, this correction, while in the appropriate direction for most fisheries, makes arbitrary assumptions regarding the dynamics of prices and costs (Kaufmann *et al.*, 1999). In the 1970s, the concept of 'optimum yield' was introduced (Roedel, 1975) but unfortunately this meant something different to everyone who ever considered its use (Larkin, 1977; Cunningham, 1981).

The impact of social factors on the ability to implement fisheries management regulations is well known. Many of the risks faced by the fishing industry are social and political rather than biological (or even economic) and governments often look to fisheries to provide a source of income for coastal communities. Unfortunately, attempts to integrate economic and (particularly) social models with those used to provide biological advice on the status of fish populations have been (and continue to be) rather unsuccessful. At the time of writing, only frameworks (e.g. Catanzano & Mesnil, 1995) have been developed for this integration.

Can a management policy based on MSY be implemented effectively?

MSY (and its economic counterparts) arose from theoretical models of fish populations and fisheries. Unfortunately, the implementation of fisheries regulations is much easier in mathematical analyses than it is in the real world, and fisheries management is often described as being more about the management of people than that of fish (see e.g. Anderson, 1987). If MSY were known, setting the catch to MSY could be achieved by setting fishing quotas (or catch limits). However, situations in which multiple species are harvested but quotas are set for single species promote misreporting and discarding of species for which the quota is scarce or already used (Caddy, 1999). Systems based on allocating a proportion of the overall quota to each operator (an individual quota system) can be even worse because fishers who have fully used their allocation might discard excess catches even when many other fishers have hardly caught any of their allocation. In principle, allowing allocations to be transferable resolves this problem. However, for the Australian South East Trawl Fishery at least, fishers have been reluctant to sell or lease quota, so that quota-related discarding occurs even for species for which the total allowable catch (TAC) is underlanded by up to 50% (Tilzey, 1999).

The reality that fisheries management occurs in a political context cannot be ignored. Increases in TACs are far more likely to be acceptable politically (and socially) than reductions, so that the impact of the political process is often to keep catches at unsustainable levels, especially where there is substantial uncertainty. The desire not to reduce catches and fishing effort is perhaps not unexpected, given that the time needed for resources to rebuild frequently exceeds the tenure of the politician who has to make the decision to impose harsh management measures (Corten, 1996; Caddy, 1999). This problem is exacerbated by the tendency to appoint Ministers of Fisheries (or their equivalents) whose electorates include fishing communities.

Overcapacity occurs when there are more fishing vessels (fishing capacity) than are needed to harvest sustainably. It is acknowledged as a (if not the) key problem in achieving effective fisheries management (Mace, 1996, 1997; Garcia & Newton, 1997). Reduction in fishing capacity is both costly and causes social dislocation. However, for most fisheries, fishing mortality increases over time even if the number of vessels and the time they spend fishing remains constant as a result of technological advances such as the use of the Global Positioning System to identify fishing locations (e.g. Robins et al., 1998). Consequently, fishing capacity has to be reduced virtually continuously if fishing mortality is to remain at desired levels. This is difficult to implement and governments themselves often encourage the increases in fishing capacity through, for example, boat-building subsidies.

All of the arguments listed above are based on the assumption that the fishery operates on a single species. In contrast, most fisheries are fundamentally multispecies (both biologically and operationally) in nature and consist of both target and non-target species. It is clear that it is impossible to achieve MSY simultaneously for all species in a multispecies fishery, because for almost any level of fishing intensity some species will be overexploited while others will be underutilised. Setting management regulations to attempt to achieve (single-species) MSY is inconsistent with 'ecosystem management'. This is because the evaluations of MSY ignore the impacts of removal of fish biomass on ecosystem dynamics and function-ing, and the impacts of the use of fishing gear at different levels of intensity on fish habitat (see Kaiser & Jennings, Chapter 16).

THE 1980S AND PRECAUTIONARY MANAGEMENT – THE REINCARNATION OF MSY

Given the problems highlighted above with MSY, and how long ago most of them were identified, one would not expect the term 'MSY' to appear in the scientific literature after roughly 1980 (except, of course, to be criticised as an antiquated and rejected approach to fisheries management). In reality, a recent literature search indicated over 600 uses of MSY in abstracts since 1986. Almost all of the papers concerned aimed to estimate MSY or stock status relative to B_{MSY}, for a wide range of species from whales (Butter-worth & Punt, 1992) to prawns (Wang & Die, 1996).

Why has MSY not been abandoned? The main reason is that MSY has shifted (been reincarnated – defined according to the *Oxford English Dictionary* as 'the formation of new flesh upon or in a wound or sore'!). It has changed from a management target to an 'upper limit'. The fishing mortal-ity at which MSY is achieved, F_{MSY}, provides a logical upper bound for fishing mortality (Caddy & McGarvey, 1996). This is because both biologi-cal and economic (but not necessary social or political) arguments point to fishing mortalities in excess of F_{MSY} being undesirable.

MSY was redefined in the 1980s to reflect uncertainty more appro-priately. For example, in New Zealand, where legislation dictates that TACs must be set to move the resource towards B_{MSY}, two alternative definitions for MSY are used: maximum constant yield (MCY) and maximum average yield (MAY). MCY is defined as 'the maximum constant catch that is es-timated to be sustainable, with an acceptable level of risk, at all possible future levels of biomass' and MAY is defined as the maximum average catch that arises from applying a constant level of fishing mortality (Annala, 1993). The calculation of MAY and MCY is based on models that allow for variability in recruitment. MCY, being independent of the current biomass, is smaller than MAY to allow for the impact of variable recruit-ment. Unfortunately, adequate data are not available to estimate MCY and MAY for most of the stocks for which TACs are set in New Zealand. Therefore, simpler, more empirical, estimation methods are used for many species (for details see Annala *et al.*, 1999).

The 1980s and 1990s also saw the introduction to fisheries manage-ment of three closely linked concepts: fisheries reference points, the precautionary approach and feedback-control decision rules. Each of these has had an important impact on the utility of MSY for fisheries management.

Fisheries reference points

Garcia (1996) defined a (management) reference point to be 'an estimated value derived from an agreed scientific procedure and an agreed model to which corresponds a state of the resource and of the fishery and which can be used as a guide for fisheries management'. A *limit reference point* is used to indicate 'the state of a fishery and/or a resource that is not considered desirable' while a *target reference point* is used to indicate 'the state of a fishery and/or a resource that is considered desirable'. A *threshold reference point* is used to identify 'that a fishery and/or resource is approaching a target and [or] limit reference point'. Note that if a limit reference point is triggered, this does not mean that the species has a high risk of biological extinction; an appropriate response to a limit reference point being triggered would be a reduction in fishing mortality rather than, say, a closure of the whole fishery. If appropriately set, the target probability of triggering a limit reference point should be low but clearly not zero.

Several papers have attempted to define appropriate target and limit reference points (e.g. Mace, 1994; Myers *et al.*, 1994; Caddy & McGarvey, 1996). However, although by no means the only limit reference point in current use, F_{MSY} (ideally not estimated by F_{max}), is increasingly being selected as the fishing mortality-based limit reference point. For example, the UN Fish Stock Agreement (United Nations, 1995) states that F_{MSY} should be used as the minimum standard for limit reference points, while for overexploited stocks, B_{MSY} (see Figure 3.1) can act as a (minimum) rebuilding target. Note that the use of F_{MSY} and B_{MSY} rather than MSY when defining reference points deals with the concerns that MSY is a deterministic concept.

The precautionary approach

The FAO precautionary approach to fisheries management (FAO, 1995) involves *inter alia*:

1 Being more cautious when information is less certain.
2 Not using the absence of information as a reason to postpone or fail to implement conservation and management measures.
3 When developing management plans, taking account of uncertainties relating to the size and productivity of stocks, reference points, stock

condition relative to those reference points, levels and distribution of fishing effort, and impacts on non-target and associated or dependent species.

4 Taking a very cautious approach to the management of newly developing fisheries until sufficient data are available to assess the impact of the fishery on the long-term sustainability of the resource.

5 Defining and implementing limit and target reference points.

6 Defining, in advance, decision rules for stock management.

Feedback control decision rules

Decision rules specify the management actions to take if limit or target reference points are exceeded. More generally, they specify the data to collect, how to analyse those data, and the management actions to take given the results from the analyses (Kirkwood & Smith, 1996; Butterworth *et al.*, 1997; Cochrane *et al.*, 1998). The performances of decision rules are evaluated by simulation. This involves the development of a range of (operating) models that represent the alternative possible dynamics of the system being managed, and can generate data typical of those used when conducting assessments and hence determining management actions. The operating models are then used to represent possible 'real worlds', and the decision rule is used to manage the fishery. The success (or otherwise) of the decision rule is determined by whether it is able to satisfy the (prespecified) objectives for management. The operating models are based on experience with the system being managed as well as on hypotheses related to the future behaviour of the system. The operating models can consider a wide variety of factors, including the behaviour of the fish stock, changes over time in the environment, and the reaction of fishers to management regulations. Butterworth & Punt (1999) reviewed many of the factors considered to date in operating models.

A management plan for a fishery is (generally) a legally binding agreement that describes the access rights, gear restrictions and any decision rule for the fishery. FAO (1995) and the UN Fish Stock Agreement (United Nations, 1995) both emphasise the need not to implement a management plan until it has been shown to perform effectively in terms of its ability to avoid undesirable outcomes. A management plan can be tested using the approach described above only if it involves clearly specified decision rules. The inclusion in management plans of decision rules that have been evaluated by simulation is usually supported by both industry and conservation groups (Cochrane *et al.*, 1998; Smith *et al.*, 1999). The former see decision rules as a form of security against the machinations of the managers, while the latter gain confidence that a set of rules are in place that have been shown to perform adequately (at least within the simulation framework).

Limit reference points play a direct role in the evaluation of management plans in that the performance of a management plan is evaluated *inter alia* in terms of whether the simulated stock triggers the limit reference point an undesirable number of times (Punt *et al.*, 2001). Using B_{MSY} as a limit reference point reintroduces one of the reasons for its original development, namely as a definition of overfishing (Smith, 1994). The role of B_{MSY} as a target reference point (and target reference points in general), within an evaluation of management plans, is questionable. As long as the probability of not dropping below the agreed limit reference point is low, the biological concerns about the stock should have been addressed. What to do once these concerns have been addressed then becomes an economic (and social) rather than a biological issue. However, New Zealand, for example, has legislative obligations to set TACs to move the resource towards B_{MSY}, and B_{MSY} is a natural (and convenient) target. Starr *et al.* (1997) examined the performance of a decision rule for a rock lobster population where the objective for management is to allow a high probability of rebuilding to B_{MSY}.

How does the reincarnation of MSY overcome its previous failings?

There were many criticisms of the use of MSY in fisheries management. It would be naive to believe that all of these have been overcome by the use of F_{MSY} and B_{MSY} as limit rather than target reference points and by developing management plans that include decision rules whose performance has been evaluated by simulation. However, many of the criticisms have been dealt with to a considerable extent. For example, methods of stock assessment based on the assumption that the stock is in equilibrium are used only rarely now. This is illustrated by the conclusion by Polacheck *et al.* (1993) on the basis of a simulation study that 'Under no circumstances should agency staff, conference organizers, reviewers, managers or journal editors accept assessments or publications that are based on effort-averaging or process-error estimators only'.

The adoption of B_{MSY} as a target for fisheries management (as is the case in New Zealand; Annala, 1993) is not equivalent to the previous practice of aiming to stabilise the biomass at B_{MSY} and take a constant catch of MSY. Rather B_{MSY} is interpreted probabilistically, and management measures are set to ensure that the biomass does not drop below B_{MSY} with a preagreed level of probability. During the 1980s and 1990s, there were substantial improvements in the methods used to conduct risk analyses for fisheries (see e.g. Smith *et al.*, 1993; Francis & Shotten, 1997; Punt & Hilborn, 1997). While problems still remain (see e.g. Cordue & Francis, 1994), considerably more confidence can be placed in the methods of risk analysis now being applied. The approach of not basing management regulations (e.g. catch limits) on the 'best' estimate but rather basing them on a lower percentage (than 50) of distributions that allow for estimation uncertainty (see e.g. Punt & Smith, 1999) means that lower harvest levels will be imposed when uncertainty is large.

The evaluation of a management plan should assess whether it is robust both to statistical (data) uncertainty, and to incomplete knowledge of factors such as stock identity and abundance. As such, the evaluation implicitly incorporates points 1 to 4 above. The most thorough evaluation of a management plan was conducted by the Scientific Committee of the International Whaling Commission, which considered the impact of uncertainty related to stock structure, historical catches, biases in abundance estimates and environmental change (Donovan, 1989; Kirkwood, 1997). It is now unusual for assessments (in Australia at least) to be based on a single hypothesis of 'how the world works' and, increasingly, very many scenarios are being considered when researchers are conducting assessments and providing management advice (e.g. Punt *et al.*, 2000). Nevertheless, problems remain in identifying the correct range of hypotheses to consider when one is evaluating a decision rule (although this range is starting to expand considerably) and in assigning weights to different hypotheses. However, it is hard to argue with the comment by Sainsbury *et al.* (2000) that 'If a strategy doesn't work on a simple [operating] model what justification is there for assuming that it will work in the real world'.

One of the major deficiencies of earlier assessments was the reliance on commercial catch rates as an index of stock abundance. While this practice remains reasonably common, fisheries assessments are now often based on 'fishery-independent' methods of indexing abundance.

The greatest challenges to fisheries management remain outside the scientific realm. These include overcapacity, the sharing of resources among different user groups, and the political and social pressure for short-term benefits at the expense of long-term environmental degradation. In essence, the last issue can be considered explicitly by quantifying expected risks. However, ultimately, the selection of the appropriate risk level is a political issue and only with appropriate consultation with all stakeholders and increased ownership and responsibility by stakeholders are major changes in 'acceptable' risk levels likely to occur.

CONCLUSIONS

MSY as a concept has been used in fisheries at least since the 1950s. It has been used variously as a management goal, a harvest strategy, and a biological reference point. The death of MSY as a key concept in fisheries management, as expected from its crucifixion in the 1970s, has clearly been overexaggerated. While achieving a constant catch of MSY is no longer regarded as an appropriate management objective, the notion remains that MSY provides a reference against which exploitation can be measured. It has been reincarnated as the fishing mortality and biomass at which MSY is achieved (F_{MSY} and B_{MSY}) and remains a key concept in fisheries management, where it has now emerged as a limit rather than as a target reference point. This reincarnation of MSY has addressed many of the concerns related to estimation problems, and lack of consideration of stochasticity. We wait with interest to see whether future studies on this subject can argue that the concerns related to the larger problems of ignoring social, economic and ecosystem issues are addressed by the next reincarnation of the ubiquitous concept of MSY!

ACKNOWLEDGEMENTS

We thank Robert Campbell, David Die, Doug Butterworth, Ray Hilborn, Georgina Mace, Tom Polacheck, John Reynolds and Robin Thomson for comments on earlier drafts. We also thank numerous friends and colleagues for the discussions that are summarised in this chapter.

REFERENCES

Allen, K. R. & Kirkwood G. P. (1988). Marine Mammals. In *Fish Population Dynamics*, 2nd edn., ed. J. A. Gulland, pp. 251–269. Wiley, Chichester.

Anderson, L. G. (1987). Expansion of the fishery management paradigm to include institutional structure and function. *Transactions of the American Fisheries Society*, 116, 396–404.

Annala, J. H. (1993). Fishery assessment approaches in New Zealand's ITQ system. In *Proceedings of the International Symposium on Management Strategies for Exploited Fish Populations*, ed. G. Kruse, D. M. Eggers, R. J. Marasco, C. Pautzke & T. J. Quinn II, pp. 791–805. Alaska Sea Grant College Program Report no. 93-02, University of Alaska Fairbanks.

Annala, J. H., Sullivan, K. J. & O'Brien, C. J. (1999). Report from the Fishery Assessment Plenary, April 1999: stock assessments and yield estimates. (Available from the NIWA library, Wellington.)

Beddington, J. R. & May, R. M. (1977). Harvesting natural populations in a randomly fluctuating environment. *Science*, 197, 463–465.

Beverton, R. J. H. & Holt, S. J. (1957). *On the Dynamics of Exploited Fish Populations.* HMSO, London.

Butterworth, D. S. & Andrew, P. A. (1984). Dynamic catch-effort models for the hake stocks in ICSEAF Divisions 1.3 to 2.2. *Collected Scientific Papers of the International Commission for the South East Atlantic Fisheries,* 11, 29–58.

Butterworth, D. S. & Punt, A. E. (1992). Assessments of the East Greenland-Iceland fin whale stock. *Reports of the International Whaling Commission,* 42, 671–696.

Butterworth, D. S. & Punt, A. E. (1999). Experiences in the evaluation and implementation of management procedures. *ICES Journal of Marine Science,* 56, 985–998.

Butterworth, D. S., Punt, A. E., Borchers, D. L., Pugh, J. B. & Hughes, G. S. (1989). *A Manual of Mathematical Techniques for Linefish Assessment.* South African National Scientific Programmes Report no. 160.

Butterworth, D. S., Cochrane, K. L. & De Oliveria, J. A. A. (1997). Management procedures: a better way to manage fisheries? The South African experience. In *Global Trends: Fisheries Management,* ed. E. L. Pikitch, D. D. Huppert & M. P. Sissenwine, pp. 83–90. American Fisheries Society, Bethesda, MD.

Caddy, J. F. (1999). Fisheries management in the twenty-first century: will new paradigms apply? *Reviews in Fish Biology and Fisheries,* 9, 1–43.

Caddy, J. F. & Defeo, O. (1996). Fitting the exponential and logistic surplus yield models with mortality data: some explorations and new perspectives. *Fisheries Research,* 25, 39–62.

Caddy, J. F. & McGarvey, R. (1996). Targets or limits for the management of fisheries? *North American Journal of Fisheries Management,* 16, 479–487.

Catanzano, J. & Mesnil, B. (1995). Economics and biology used in fisheries research or when social and natural sciences try to depict together the object of their research. *Aquatic Living Resources,* 8, 223–232.

Clark, C. W. (1973). The economics of overexploitation. *Science,* 181, 630–634.

Clark, C. W. (1976). *Mathematical Bioeconomics.* Wiley, New York.

Clark, W. G. (1991). Groundfish exploitation rates based on life history parameters. *Canadian Journal of Fisheries and Aquatic Sciences,* 48, 734–750.

Clark, W. G. (1993). The effect of recruitment variability on the choice of a target level of spawning biomass per recruit. In *Proceedings of the International Symposium on Management Strategies for Exploited Fish Populations,* ed. G. Kruse, D. M. Eggers, R. J. Marasco, C. Pautzke & T. J. Quinn II, pp. 233–246. Alaska Sea Grant College Program Report no. 93-02, University of Alaska Fairbanks.

Cochrane, K. L., Butterworth, D. S., De Oliveria, J. A. A. & Roel, B. A. (1998). Management procedures in a fishery based on highly variable stocks and with conflicting objectives: experiences in the South African pelagic fishery. *Reviews in Fish Biology and Fisheries,* 8, 177–214.

Cook, R. M., Sinclair, A. & Stefánsson, G. (1997). Potential collapse of North Sea cod stocks. *Nature,* 385, 521–522.

Cooke, J. G. & Beddington, J. R. (1984). The relationship between catch rates and abundance in fisheries. *IMA Journal of Mathematics Applied in Medicine and Biology,* 1, 391–405.

Cordue, P. L. & Francis, R. I. C. C. (1994). Accuracy and choice in risk estimation for fisheries assessment. *Canadian Journal of Fisheries and Aquatic Sciences*, **51**, 817–829.

Corten, A. (1996). The widening gap between fisheries biology and fisheries management in the European Union. *Fisheries Research*, **27**, 1–15.

Cunningham, S. (1981). The evolution of the objectives of fisheries management during the 1970's. *Ocean Management*, **6**, 251–278.

Deriso, R. B. (1980). Harvesting strategies and parameter estimation for an age-structured model. *Canadian Journal of Fisheries and Aquatic Sciences*, **37**, 268–282.

Deriso, R. B. (1982). Relationship of fishing mortality to natural mortality and growth at the level of maximum sustainable yield. *Canadian Journal of Fisheries and Aquatic Sciences*, **39**, 1054–1058.

Deriso, R. B. (1987). Optimal $F_{0.1}$ criteria and their relationship to maximum sustainable yield. *Canadian Journal of Fisheries and Aquatic Sciences*, **44** (Supplement 2), 339–348.

Die, D. J. & Caddy, J. F. (1997). Sustainable yield indicators from biomass: are there appropriate reference points for use in tropical fisheries? *Fisheries Research*, **32**, 69–79.

Die, D. J., Restrepo, V. R. & Fox, W. W. Jr (1990). Equilibrium production models that incorporate fished area. *Transactions of the American Fisheries Society*, **119**, 445–454.

Donovan, G. P. (ed.) (1989). *The Comprehensive Assessment of Whale Stocks: The Early Years.* Reports of the International Whaling Commission (Special Issue), 11.

FAO (Food and Agriculture Organization) (1966). International fisheries bodies. *FAO (Food and Agriculture Organisation of the United Nations) Fisheries Technical Paper*, **64**.

FAO (Food and Agriculture Organization) (1995). Precautionary approach to fisheries. Part 1: Guidelines on the precautionary approach to capture fisheries and species introductions. *FAO (Food and Agriculture Organization of the United Nations) Fisheries Technical Paper*, **350/1**.

Fox, W. W. (1970). An exponential surplus-yield model for optimizing exploited fish populations. *Transactions of the American Fisheries Society*, **99**, 80–88.

Fox, W. W. (1975). Fitting the generalized stock production model by least-squares and equilibrium approximation. *Fisheries Bulletin US*, **73**, 23–37.

Francis, R. I. C. C. & Shotton, R. (1997). 'Risk' in fisheries management: A review. *Canadian Journal of Fisheries and Aquatic Sciences*, **54**, 1699–1715.

Garcia, S. M. (1996). The precautionary approach to fisheries and its implications for fisheries research, technology, and management: an updated review. *FAO (Food and Agriculture Organization of the United Nations) Fisheries Technical Paper*, **350/2**, 1–75.

Garcia, S. M. & Newton, C. (1997). Current situations, trends and prospects in world capture fisheries. In *Global Trends: Fisheries Management*, ed. E. L. Pikitch, D. D. Huppert & M. P. Sissenwine, pp. 3–27. American Fisheries Society, Bethesda, MD.

Garcia, S., Sparre, P. & Csirke, J. (1989). Estimating surplus production and maximum sustainable yield from biomass data when catch and effort series are not available. *Fisheries Research*, **8**, 13–23.

Goodyear, C. P. (1996). Variability of fishing mortality by age: consequences for maximum sustainable yield. *North American Journal of Fisheries Management*, **16**, 8–13.

Graham, M. (1935). Modern theory of exploiting a fishery, an application to North Sea trawling. *Journal du Conseil, Conseil International pour l'Exploration de la Mer*, **10**, 264–274.

Gulland, J. A. (1961). Fishing and the stocks of fish at Iceland. *Fishery Investigation (Ministry of Agriculture, Fisheries and Food)*, UK, Ser. 2, **23**(4), 1–52.

Gulland, J. A. (1965). Manual of methods for fish stock assessment. Part I. Fish population analysis. *FAO (Food and Agriculture Organization of the United Nations) Fisheries Technical Paper*, **40**.

Gulland, J. A. & Boerema, L. K. (1973). Scientific advice on catch levels. *Fisheries Bulletin, US*, **71**, 325–335.

Hilborn, R. (1979). Comparison of fisheries control systems that utilize catch and effort data. *Journal of the Fisheries Research Board of Canada*, **36**, 1477–1489.

Hilborn, R. (1990). Estimating the parameters of full age-structured models from catch and abundance data. *Bulletin of the International North Pacific Fisheries Commission*, **50**, 207–213.

Hilborn, R. & Walters, C. J. (1992). *Quantitative Fisheries Stock Assessment*. Chapman & Hall, London.

Hjort, J., Jahn, G. & Ottestad, P. (1933). The optimum catch. *Hvalradets Skrifter*, **7**, 92–127.

Hutchings, J. A. (1996). Spatial and temporal variation in the density of northern cod and a review of hypotheses for the stock's collapse. *Canadian Journal of Fisheries and Aquatic Sciences*, **53**, 943–962.

Kaufmann, B., Geen, G. & Sen, S. (1999). *Fish Futures: Individual Transferable Quotas in Fisheries*. Fisheries Economics, Research and Management Pty Ltd, Kiama.

Kirkwood, G. P. (1997). The revised management procedure of the International Whaling Commission. In *Global Trends: Fisheries Management*, ed. E. L. Pikitch, D. D. Huppert & M. P. Sissenwine, pp. 91–99. American Fisheries Society, Bethesda, MD.

Kirkwood, G. P. & Smith, A. D. M. (1996). Assessing the precautionary nature of fishery management strategies. *FAO (Food and Agriculture Organization of the United Nations) Fisheries Technical Paper*, **350/2**, 141–158.

Larkin, P. A. (1977). An epitaph for the concept of maximum sustainable yield. *Transactions of the American Fisheries Society*, **106**, 1–11.

Ludwig, D. & Walters, C. J. (1985). Are age-structured models appropriate for catch-effort data? *Canadian Journal of Fisheries and Aquatic Sciences*, **42**, 1066–1072.

Mace, P. M. (1994). Relationships between common biological reference points used as thresholds and targets of fisheries management strategies. *Canadian Journal of Fisheries and Aquatic Sciences*, **51**, 110–122.

Mace, P. M. (1996). Limited access for Atlantic highly migratory fish stocks: changing the ground rules. *Fisheries*, **21**(4), 20.

Mace, P. M. (1997). Developing and sustaining world fisheries resources. The state of science and management. In *Developing and Sustaining World Fisheries Resources. The State of Science and Management*, ed. D. A. Hancock, D. C.

Smith, A. Grant & J. P. Beumer, pp. 1–20. CSIRO, Collingwood, Victoria.

Mohn, R. K. (1993). Bootstrap estimates of ADAPT parameters, their projection in risk analysis and their retrospective patterns. In *Risk Evaluation and Biological Reference Points for Fisheries Management*, ed. S. J. Smith, J. J. Hunt & D. Rivard, pp. 173–184. Canadian Journal of Fisheries and Aquatic Sciences (Special Publication), **120**.

Mohn, R. K. (1999). The retrospective problem in sequential population analysis: An investigation using cod fishery and simulated data. *ICES Journal of Marine Science*, **56**, 473–488.

Murray, J. D. (1993). *Mathematical Biology*, 2nd edn. Springer-Verlag, Berlin.

Myers, R. A. & Barrowman, N. J. (1996). Is fish recruitment related to spawner abundance? *Fisheries Bulletin, US*, **94**, 707–724.

Myers, R. A., Rosenberg, A. A., Mace, P. M., Barrowman, N. & Restrepo, V. R. (1994). In search of thresholds for recruitment overfishing. *ICES Journal of Marine Science*, **51**, 191–205.

Pella, J. J. & Tomlinson, P. K. (1969). A generalized stock production model. *Bulletin of the Inter-American Tropical Tuna Commission*, **13**, 421–496.

Polacheck, T., Hilborn, R. & Punt, A. E. (1993). Fitting surplus production models: comparing methods and measuring uncertainty. *Canadian Journal of Fisheries and Aquatic Sciences*, **50**, 2597–2607.

Punt, A. E. (1994). Assessments of the stocks of Cape hake *Merluccius* spp. off South Africa. *South African Journal of Marine Science*, **14**, 159–186.

Punt, A. E. (2000). Extinction of marine renewable resources – a demographic analysis. *Population Ecology*, **42**, 19–27.

Punt, A. E. & Hilborn, R. (1997). Fisheries stock assessment and decision analysis: a review of the Bayesian approach. *Reviews in Fish Biology and Fisheries*, **7**, 35–63.

Punt, A. E. & Smith, A. D. M. (1999). Harvest strategy evaluation for the eastern stock of gemfish (*Rexea solandri*). *ICES Journal of Marine Science*, **56**, 860–875.

Punt, A. E., Pribac, F., Walker, T. I., Taylor, B. L. & Prince, J. D. (2000). Stock assessment of school shark *Galeorhinus galeus* based on a spatially-explicit population dynamics model. *Marine and Freshwater Research*, **51**, 205–220.

Punt, A. E., Campbell, R. A. & Smith, A. D. M. (2001). Evaluating empirical indicators and reference points for fisheries management: application to the broadbill swordfish fishery off Eastern Australia. *Marine and Freshwater Research*, in press.

Ricker, W. E. (1975). Computation and interpretation of biological statistics of fish populations. *Bulletin of Fisheries Research Board of Canada*, **191**.

Robins, C. M., Wang, Y.-W. & Die, D. (1998). The impact of global positioning systems and plotters on fishing power in the northern prawn fishery, Australia. *Canadian Journal of Fisheries and Aquatic Sciences*, **55**, 1645–1651.

Roedel, P. M. (ed.) (1975). *Optimum Sustainable Yield as a Concept in Fisheries Management*. Special Publication no. 9. American Fisheries Society, Washington, DC.

Roff, D. A. & Fairbairn, D. J. (1980). An evaluation of Gulland's method for fitting the Schaefer model. *Canadian Journal of Fisheries and Aquatic Sciences*, **37**, 1229–1235.

Russel, E. S. (1931). Some theoretical considerations on the 'overfishing' problem.

Journal du Conseil, Conseil International pour l'Exploration de la Mer, **6**, 1–20.

Sainsbury, K. (1998). Living marine resource assessment for the 21st century: what will be needed and how will it be provided? In *Fishery Stock Assessment Models*, ed. F. Funk, T. J. Quinn II, J. Heifetz, J. N. Ianelli, J. E. Powers, J. F. Schweigert, P. J. Sullivan & C.-I. Zhang, pp. 1–40. Alaska Sea Grant College Program Report no. AK-SG-98-01, University of Alaska Fairbanks.

Sainsbury, K. J., Punt, A. E. & Smith, A. D. M. (2000). Design of operational management strategies for achieving fishery ecosystem objectives. *ICES Journal of Marine Science*, **57**, 731–741.

Schaefer, M. B. (1954). Some aspects of the dynamics of populations important to the management of the commercial marine fisheries. *Bulletin of the Inter-American Tropical Tuna Commission*, **1**, 25–56.

Schnute, J. (1977). Improved estimates from the Schaefer production model: theoretical considerations. *Journal of the Fisheries Research Board of Canada*, **34**, 583–603.

Scott Gordon, H. (1954). Economic theory of a common-property resource: the fishery. *Journal of Political Economy*, **62**, 124–142.

Sims, S. E. (ed.) (1985). Selected computer programs in FORTRAN for fish stock assessment. *FAO (Food and Agriculture Organization of the United Nations) Fisheries Technical Paper*, **259**.

Sinclair, A., Gascon, D., O'Boyle, R., Rivard, D. & Gavaris, S. (1991). Consistency of some Northwest Atlantic groundfish stock assessments. *NAFO Scientific Council*, **16**, 59–77.

Sissenwine, M. P. (1978). Is MSY an adequate foundation for optimum yield? *Fisheries*, **3**, 22–42.

Sissenwine, M. P. (1981). An overview of some methods of fish stock assessment. *Fisheries*, **6**(6), 31–35.

Sissenwine, M. P., Fogarty, M. J. & Overholtz, W. J. (1988). Some fisheries management implications of recruitment variability. In *Fish Population Dynamics*, 2nd edn, ed. J. A. Gulland, pp. 129–152. Wiley, Chicester.

Smith, A. D. M. (1993). Risks of over- and under-fishing new resources. In *Risk Evaluation and Biological Reference Points for Fisheries Management*, ed. S. J. Smith, J. J. Hunt & D. Rivard, pp. 261–267. Canadian Journal of Fisheries and Aquatic Sciences (Special Publication), **120**.

Smith, A. D. M., Sainsbury, K. J. & Stevens, R. A. (1999). Implementing effective fisheries management systems – management strategy evaluation and the Australian partnership approach. *ICES Journal of Marine Science*, **56**, 967–979.

Smith, S. J., Hunt, J. J. & Rivard, D. (ed.) (1993). *Risk Evaluation and Biological Reference Points for Fisheries Management*. Canadian Journal of Fisheries and Aquatic Science (Special Publication), **120**.

Smith, T. D. (1994). *Scaling Fisheries: The Science of Measuring the Effects of Fishing*. Cambridge University Press, Cambridge.

Sparre, P. & Venema, S. C. (1992). Introduction to tropical fish stock assessment. *FAO (Food and Agriculture Organization of the United Nations) Fisheries Technical Paper*, **306/1**.

Starr, P. J., Breen, P. A., Hilborn, R. H. & Kendrick, T. H. (1997). Evaluation of a management decision rule for a New Zealand rock lobster substock. *Marine and Freshwater Research*, **48**, 1093–1101.

Stephenson, R. L. & Lane, D. E. (1995). Fisheries management science: a plea for conceptual change. *Canadian Journal of Fisheries and Aquatic Sciences*, **52**, 2051–2056.

Tilzey, R. D. J. (ed.) (1999). *The South East Fishery 1998. Fishery Assessment Report compiled by the South East Fishery Assessment Group.* Australian Fisheries Management Authority, Canberra.

Uhler, R. S. (1980). Least squares regression estimates of the Schaefer production model: some Monte Carlo simulation results. *Canadian Journal of Fisheries and Aquatic Sciences*, **37**, 1284–1294.

United Nations (1995). Structure and process of the 1993–1995 United Nations Conference on Straddling Fish Stocks and Highly Migratory Fish Stocks. *FAO (Food and Agriculture Organization of the United Nations) Fisheries Circular*, **898**.

Walters, C. J. & Ludwig, D. (1994). Calculation of Bayes posterior probability distributions for key population parameters. *Canadian Journal of Fisheries and Aquatic Sciences*, **51**, 713–722.

Wang, Y.-G. & Die, D. (1996). Stock–recruitment relationships of tiger prawns (*Penaeus esculentus* and *Penaeus semisulcatus*) in the Australian northern prawn fishery. *Marine and Freshwater Research*, **27**, 87–95.

4

Sustainable exploitation of fluctuating populations

RUSSELL LANDE, BERNT-ERIK SÆTHER & STEINAR ENGEN

Harvesting generally accelerates the process of extinction for species with population dynamics that are not chaotic (May *et al.*, 1978), i.e. nearly all species (Ellner & Turchin, 1995). About half of the endangered mammals and a third of the endangered birds around the world are threatened with extinction in part because of hunting and international trade (Groombridge, 1992; Redford, 1992). Nearly half of the commercial fisheries in Europe and the USA were recently classified as overexploited, and there have been many collapses of harvested fish and mammal populations (Ludwig *et al.*, 1993; Hutchings & Myers, 1994; Myers *et al.*, 1997). Some species have been harvested to extinction or near extinction (Groombridge, 1992; Casey & Myers, 1998). Overexploitation and resource collapse may have serious economic and social consequences (see e.g. Hutchings & Myers, 1994; Myers *et al.*, 1997).

Most overexploitation is attributable to the economic factors of unregulated competition (as in open-access fisheries) and to economic discounting of future harvests (Clark, 1990; Ludwig *et al.*, 1993; Lande *et al.*, 1994; Ludwig, Chapter 2). However, stochasticity and uncertainty in population dynamics also have contributed to overexploitation, particularly for coastal fisheries and exploited terrestrial species in developed countries where regulatory agencies exist which in principle should have prevented overharvesting. The historical failure of resource management agencies to exercise sufficient caution to prevent resource collapse or extinction is caused by the dominance of a resource extraction philosophy over a resource conservation philosophy. Even in the face of high stochasticity and uncertainty, this dominance favours continued harvests in the short term to support declining industries over long-term sustainability of resources (Ludwig *et al.*, 1993; Taylor & Dunstone, 1996). Most conservation failures are caused by lack of application of basic ecological principles. Nevertheless, an adequate conceptual and theoretical framework including stochasticity and uncertainty, and detailed studies of the species' ecology, are necessary (but not sufficient) for effective conservation of exploited species.

Here we review and contrast basic goals for exploitation, focusing on long-term sustainability of resources. We explore the consequences of different management strategies for achieving these goals using simple theoretical models that incorporate population fluctuations. Then we investigate two case studies of Scandinavian brown bear and Fennoscandian moose, where the goals differ, to illustrate how principles of optimal harvesting developed from these simple models can be applied more realistically to age-structured populations. Finally, we discuss methods for reducing the variance in animal harvest and the frequency of years with no harvest associated with optimal (threshold) harvesting strategies.

All natural populations fluctuate, with coefficients of variation in estimated annual population sizes usually in the range 20–80% (Pimm, 1991). Deterministic models that neglect this stochastic variation omit an important component of extinction risk in small populations. Most variability in population size is caused by environmental stochasticity, and in small populations demographic stochasticity, owing to chance individual events of reproduction and mortality, also causes significant fluctuations (Shaffer, 1981; Lande, 1993, 1998; Engen *et al.*, 1998). Harvesting strategies derived from deterministic population models, such as maximum sustainable yield, fail to account for fluctuations in population size, which can lead to overexploitation and early collapse or extinction of a population if harvesting continues when the population becomes small (Ludwig, Chapter 2; Punt & Smith, Chapter 3). Uncertainty in population estimates also can cause overexploitation because, when population sizes are overestimated, harvesting quotas will be set too high and the population may be reduced to dangerously low levels.

ANALYTICAL RESULTS FROM DIFFUSION MODELS

Most theory for exploitation of renewable resources relies extensively on simulation models of age- or stage-structured populations (Getz & Haight, 1989). A major challenge in this approach is to obtain reliable estimates of the many parameters in such models (Ludwig & Walters, 1985). Often it may be difficult to know even the correct order of magnitude of essential parameters. This introduces serious problems when interpreting the results of such models and makes it difficult to reach robust general theoretical conclusions. Our approach is first to derive general principles from simple stochastic population models without age structure, and then to apply these principles to more complex age-structured models of particular species to derive optimal harvesting strategies in practice. We show that analytical results obtained from simplified models may provide insight into important processes and suggest guidelines for managing populations that otherwise would have been difficult to obtain.

Stochastic harvesting theory is a few decades old, but only in the past several years has serious attention been devoted to developing general harvesting strategies that include a conservation orientation by accounting for the risk of population collapse or extinction. Factors affecting the risk of population collapse and extinction include stochastic population dynamics, uncertainty in population parameters, and harvesting itself. Previous analyses of the effects of a fluctuating environment on the choice of harvesting strategy have usually assumed a stationary distribution of population size ranging from zero to infinity (Beddington & May, 1977; Reed, 1978). However, with demographic stochasticity and/or an Allee effect (Petersen & Levitan, Chapter 13), no stationary distribution exists and extinction is the eventual fate of all species regardless of whether they are harvested (Lande *et al.*, 1995). Using general diffusion theory (Karlin & Taylor, 1981), we have derived approximate estimates for the time to extinction without assuming a stationary distribution, which can be used to compare different harvesting strategies, including the risk of population collapse or extinction. We focus on general qualitative results derived from simple stochastic population models. Diffusion approximations are most accurate for stochastic processes that change by small increments, and cannot describe the dynamics of populations with high growth rates (e.g. chaotic dynamics) or those subject to major catastrophes that suddenly reduce the population to small numbers. However, even highly fecund species have maximum rates of population growth far below their reproductive potential because of high density-independent mortality (Myers *et al.*, 1995, 1999). Thus vertebrate species with body weights above 1 kg tend to have intrinsic rates of increase less than 0.1 per year (Charnov, 1993), to which diffusion approximations can be accurately applied. Diffusion models also can ade-quately describe the cumulative effects of small or moderate catastrophes by using a suitably large environmental stochasticity (Lande, 1993).

We compare three classical harvesting strategies and one new strategy in terms of their yield statistics and risk of population collapse or extinction (see Figure 4.1). The constant harvest strategy removes a fixed number of individuals, a, each year regardless of the population size. Proportional harvesting removes a fixed fraction, b, of the population each year. This could be accomplished either by harvesting a proportion b of a known population or

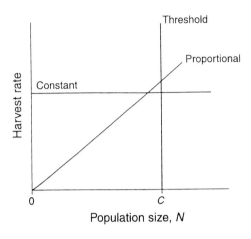

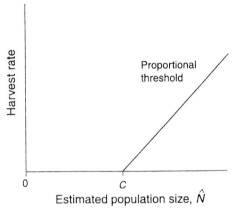

Figure 4.1. Exploitation strategies giving the harvest rate as a function of population size, N, or estimated population size, $\hat{N}$. *Top*: three classical strategies of constant quota, proportional (or constant effort) harvesting and threshold harvesting. *Bottom*: a new strategy of proportional threshold harvesting. See Table 4.1 for formulas. c, threshold population size for harvesting.

by constant effort harvesting of an unknown population (see also Ludwig, Chapter 2). In threshold harvesting the population is exploited at the highest possible rate when it is above a certain size, c, with no harvest when the population is below c. Of these three classical strategies, constant harvest and proportional harvest (constant effort) are the simplest to perform because they require no knowledge of population size, N, whereas threshold harvesting can only be carried out using yearly estimates of population size. To deal with uncertainty in estimated population size, $\hat{N}$, Engen *et al.* (1997)

Table 4.1. Exploitation strategies giving the harvest rate, y, as a function of population size, N, or estimated population size, $\hat{N}$

Strategy	Harvest rate
Constant	$y(N) = a$
Proportional	$y(N) = bN$
Threshold	$y(N) = \begin{cases} 0 & \text{for } N < c \\ y_{\max} & \text{for } N \geq c \end{cases}$
Proportional threshold	$y(\hat{N}) = \begin{cases} 0 & \text{for } \hat{N} < c \\ (\hat{N} - c)q & \text{for } \hat{N} \geq c \end{cases}$

proposed proportional threshold harvesting in which only a fraction, q, of the estimated population above the threshold, $\hat{N} - c$, is harvested each year, with no harvest when the estimated population is below the threshold.

It is important to distinguish the goal of harvesting from the harvesting strategy. Perhaps the most prudent goal is to maximise the expected cumulative harvest over all time before eventual extinction of the population (or before the resource collapses to a specified level). A more aggressive goal is to maximise the mean annual harvest that can be sustained. A range of intermediate or more extreme goals also can be considered. For any given harvesting goal, each type of harvesting strategy in Figure 4.1 and Table 4.1 can be optimised by choosing the best value of its parameter(s). In practice, most commercial or non-commercial exploitation now and in the past has had the stated or unstated goal of short-term maximisation of harvest or profit. Often this is accomplished using a strategy resembling proportional (constant effort) harvesting to maximise the mean annual harvest. In contrast, we focus on long-term goals of resource conservation, using optimal threshold harvesting strategies that minimise the risk of extinction under any harvesting goal. For the goal of maximising the mean annual harvest under the proportional or threshold harvesting strategies we choose intermediate parameter values that produce the local or internal maximum harvest rate, which is sustainable, rather than the extreme parameter values that produce the global maximum harvest rate that would harvest the population to extinction in a single year, which obviously is not sustainable. Thus, in the example in Figure 4.2 with the goal of maximising the annual harvest, $\bar{y}$, the proportional harvesting strategy is optimised at a harvest rate of about $b/r = 0.4$ rather than $b = \infty$, and the threshold strategy is optimised at a threshold of about $c/K = 0.6$ rather than $c = 0$.

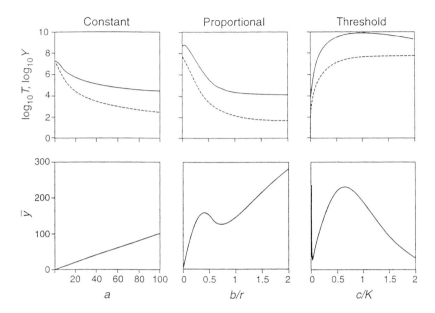

Figure 4.2. Expected cumulative harvest before extinction, $\log_{10} Y$ (solid lines), mean time to extinction, $\log_{10} T$ (dashed lines) and approximate mean annual yield, $\bar{y} \approx Y/T$, as functions of the harvesting parameters for three classical harvesting strategies under constant, proportional, and threshold harvesting strategies (Figure 4.1 and Table 4.1). The population has logistic density dependence. Initial size at the stochastically stable equilibrium or carrying capacity is $K = 10\,000$ with mean intrinsic rate of increase, $\bar{r} = 0.1$ per year, environmental variance in density-independent growth rate of 0.04 and demographic variance of 1.0. *a*, number of individuals removed per year; *b*, the fraction of the population removed per year; *c*, threshold population size for harvesting.

When population sizes are known exactly, for any harvesting goal, the optimal threshold harvesting strategy always produces a higher yield with a lower risk of collapse or extinction than any other strategy (Lande *et al.*, 1995). For populations with a high mean intrinsic rate of increase $\bar{r}$, and little risk of extinction, the optimal threshold harvesting strategy may give only slightly better mean annual yield than the optimal proportional harvesting strategy. However, for populations with low $\bar{r}$, the mean time to extinction may be orders of magnitude larger under optimal threshold harvesting than under optimal proportional or constant or harvesting (Figure 4.2). Evidently, the harvesting rates at small population sizes strongly influence the mean time to extinction. Threshold harvesting allows a population to recover at its maximum natural rate when it is below the threshold (Figure 4.1 and Table 4.1). The main drawback of a threshold harvesting

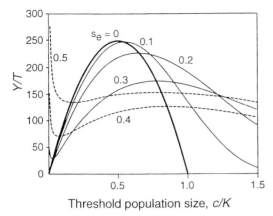

Figure 4.3. Mean annual harvest, $\bar{y} \approx Y/T$, as a function of the threshold for different amounts of environmental standard deviation in population growth rate, s_e. Other parameters as in Figure 4.2.

strategy is that it entails frequent years of no harvest when the population is below the threshold, creating a high variance in annual harvest.

A remarkably general result for the most prudent goal of maximising the expected cumulative harvest before extinction or collapse is that the optimal threshold is equal to the expected carrying capacity or stochastically stable equilibrium population size, K (Lande et al., 1995; Whittle & Horwood, 1995; Ludwig, 1998). This applies for any form of stochastic population dynamics that can be adequately approximated as a diffusion process, i.e. for any form of stochasticity in population growth rate and carrying capacity, and for any form of density dependence, assuming that population sizes are known exactly. An intuitive explanation of this result is that when the population is above K the excess individuals that are harvested would probably have died or not replaced themselves because of density limitation on the population, whereas allowing the population to grow unexploited up to K prolongs its existence and future harvests. This optimal threshold strategy for the most prudent harvesting goal also entails relatively little disturbance to the population and its ecosystem.

The more aggressive goal of maximising the mean annual harvest produces a lower optimal threshold. In most cases (where the harvest is sustainable) the optimal threshold under this goal increases with increasing environmental stochasticity (Lande et al., 1997) and with increasing maximum harvest rate (Sæther et al., 1996a). Thus stochasticity dictates more prudent harvesting than would be suggested by deterministic theory (see Figure 4.3). Limited harvesting capacity, for example limiting the size or capability of a fishing fleet, allows the population to fluctuate above the threshold and reduces the optimal threshold for any harvesting goal, allowing harvesting to occur more frequently over a wider range of population sizes (Lande *et al.*, 1995). Conversely, a large harvesting capacity dictates more cautious threshold harvest strategies with higher thresholds.

Another general result concerns the duration of the final decline to the point of population collapse or extinction. This is derived from the theory of conditional diffusion processes, considering population trajectories after they have last passed a stochastic equilibrium (with sustainable or no harvesting) to when they first reach the specified level of collapse or extinction (Lande *et al.*, 1995). For populations with a positive expected long-run growth rate below a stochastic equilibrium, and initial sizes anywhere near the stochastic equilibrium, the expected duration of the final decline to collapse or extinction, T^*, is much less than the unconditional expected waiting time to extinction, T. In other words, under sustainable harvesting, population trajectories typically spend a relatively long time fluctuating around a stochastic equilibrium and then decline rapidly to collapse or extinction (see Figure 4.4). The expected duration of the final decline is inversely proportional to the long-run growth rate of the population below the stochastic equilibrium. An intuitive explanation of this surprising result is that a population with a high long-run growth rate must experience a series of exceptionally bad years in a row in order to drive it rapidly to collapse or extinction, or else it will recover. The message from this result is that the conservation of even quite abundant and resilient species capable of rapid growth and recovery from population collapses should not be neglected: although extreme collapse or extinction may be a low probability event for such species, when it does occur it will be rapid and immediate conservation measures should be taken.

Substantial uncertainty usually exists in estimated population sizes, with standard errors often in the range 10–50% (Engen *et al.*, 1997). With low or moderate stochasticity and moderate or high uncertainty in population estimates, proportional threshold harvesting produces superior cumulative or average harvests with a lower risk of population extinction or collapse than the three classical harvesting strategies shown in Figure 4.1 (Engen *et al.*, 1997; Lande *et al.*, 1997). This result occurs because harvesting only a fraction, q, of the estimated population above the threshold, $\hat{N} - c$, reduces the risk of overharvesting when the population size is overestimated. The optimal values of the parameters for proportional threshold harvesting depend on the harvesting goal as well as the amounts of stochasticity and uncertainty in the population dynamics. Increasing uncertainty

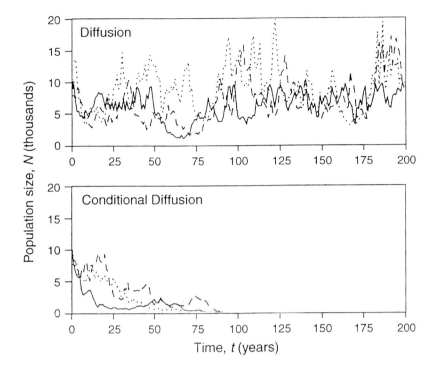

Figure 4.4. Typical trajectories for the unconditional and conditional diffusion processes describing a population exploited optimally under constant (dotted lines), proportional (dashed lines), and threshold (solid lines) strategies. Population parameters are as in Figure 4.2. The unconditional processes have mean times to extinction, T, of the order of 10^7 to 10^9 years (Figure 4.2), whereas the conditional processes have mean times to extinction, T^*, of the order of 100 years.

in population estimates generally dictates more prudent harvesting strategies by increasing the optimal threshold and (possibly) decreasing the proportion harvested of the estimated population above the threshold.

SCANDINAVIAN BROWN BEAR

In Scandinavia the brown bear *Ursus arctos* has been strongly persecuted for several centuries because of its predation on sheep and semi-domestic reindeer. As a result, the bear was probably exterminated in Norway, and by 1930 only about 100 individuals were left in Sweden (Swenson *et al.*, 1995). After successful management actions by the Swedish government, the population has built up, resulting in immigration of individuals into

Norway. Today there are roughly 1000 bears in Sweden and Norway (Swenson *et al.*, 1998). These immigrating bears can cause serious problems in Norway because the livestock breeders now adopt a less intensive husbandry with removal of the large predators, leaving the sheep unattended. In some areas, up to 10% of the ewes may be killed by the immigrating bears, leading to strong political and public pressure for killing individual bears that cause damage for the farmers. In those areas, strong political restrictions will be placed on the size of bear populations, which can easily conflict with the obligations of the International Convention on Biological Diversity to secure viable populations.

We do not advocate hunting of brown bear, but if they are to be hunted it should be done using a strategy that minimises the risk of population collapse or extinction. Previous analyses of the demography of the brown bear based on data from radio-collared individuals demonstrated large uncertainty in several demographic variables (Sæther *et al.*, 1998). Even assuming no density dependence at low population sizes, this resulted in very uncertain predictions of future population sizes. Furthermore, precise estimates of the population size of this shy species are extremely difficult to obtain. Both these types of uncertainty must be considered when suggesting management strategies for this species. To account for such uncertainties, a proportional threshold harvesting strategy has been suggested for the management of the Norwegian brown bear (Tufto *et al.*, 1999). Here we employ a proportional threshold harvesting strategy and compute the smallest possible value of c satisfying the criteria of the World Conservation Union (IUCN) for population viability, $< 10\%$ risk of extinction in 100 years (IUCN, 1994).

The uncertainties in demographic variables were found by parametric bootstrapping from the age-structured model described by Sæther *et al.* (1998). For each bootstrap replicate of the population parameters, a corresponding bootstrap replicate of the threshold c^* was obtained (Tufto *et al.*, 1999), satisfying the criterion that the probability of extinction before 100 years is ≤ 0.10. We used the upper 95% quantile of the distribution of c^*, because this choice will be precautionary since the correct threshold c will be larger than this value in approximately 5% of the realisations of the data. This analysis illustrates two important points (Figure 4.5):

1 When the uncertainty in the population estimates increases, a larger threshold c is necessary if the population is to avoid extinction with the prescribed probability. Thus, accurate population estimation is a prerequisite for removing individuals from such a small population.

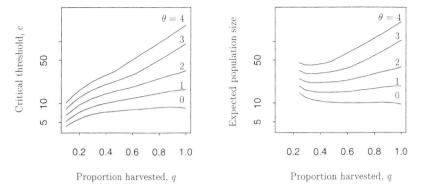

Figure 4.5. The upper 95% quantile of the critical threshold, c, and the expected population size at equilibrium as functions of the proportion harvested, q, for Scandinavian brown bear for different levels of uncertainty in population estimates, θ, the coefficient of variation (standard deviation/mean) of population size caused by random sampling errors. Each line gives the same risk of extinction with approximately 95% confidence. Population parameters are estimated from the southern population described by Sæther *et al.* (1998).

2 The population size where harvest can start depends on q, the proportion of the difference between the estimated population size and the threshold that is removed. Harvest can start at a lower population size for a small q.

This leaves the option for alternative management strategies by varying q and c that will give the same probability of extinction with approximately 95% confidence. For instance, if the goal is to minimise the expected equilibrium population size, this is achieved by having a low q. However, when only inaccurate population estimates are available, the threshold has to be raised considerably to avoid extinction. Then harvesting only an intermediate proportion ($q = 0.35$) gives the smallest expected population size. This example illustrates the importance of including the accuracy in population estimates when suggesting management actions for such small populations. This occurs even when no density dependence is assumed because of the stochastic effects on the population dynamics.

THE FENNOSCANDIAN MOOSE

The moose *Alces alces* is the most important game animal in Fennoscandia, after an almost continuous increase since the Second World War in the number of individuals shot. A maximum was reached in 1982, when more than 170 000 individuals were harvested in Sweden alone. Today nearly 200 000 individuals are shot each year in Finland, Sweden and Norway combined. Obviously, such a harvest represents an enormous value in terms of meat and money. However, large moose populations also represent a cost, for example because of damage to forestry from browsing on commercially important tree species, and accidents from collisions between moose and cars or trains.

Environmental stochasticity strongly influences moose population dynamics (Solberg *et al.*, 1999). Variation in climate, especially summer precipitation (Sæther, 1985; Solberg & Sæther, 1994) and winter snow depth (Sæther *et al.*, 1996b), affects the body mass of the youngest females. The differences in body weight then influence age at maturity because larger females have a higher chance of conceiving as yearlings than do smaller females (Sæther & Heim, 1993). Similar mass-dependent effects of climate variation have also been recorded in other ungulates (Sæther, 1997). In addition, large annual variation is often found in neonatal calf survival in northern populations (Sæther *et al.*, 1996b; Stubsjøen *et al.*, 2000). Thus, environmental stochasticity should be considered when developing management strategies for moose populations. Because this species has a high population growth rate the harvesting goal is to maximise the mean annual yield.

Here we use the general theory of Lande *et al.* (1994, 1995) to explore by simulations of age-structured models how different harvesting strategies affect annual variation in the yield and population size. Our aim is to examine whether the qualitative results obtained from simple diffusion models also are applicable when using complex, but more realistic, models to maximise the mean annual yield with minimum risk of extinction.

We consider an age-structured population with f_i females and m_i males in age class i, where $i = 0, 1, \ldots, 20$. We assume that the change in numbers occurs sequentially in three stages: after reproduction in spring the population is harvested during autumn and individuals die of natural causes during winter. At the end of winter, the remaining individuals move from one age class to the next. We assume that independent climatic factors affect calf survival during winter as well as the proportion of females that reproduce at age two years. These two demographic variables also are affected by two different forms of density regulation (for details see Sæther *et al.*, 2001).

Hunting quotas of Scandinavian moose are specified into numbers of different categories of animals, which results in age- and sex-specific harvest rates. The chosen harvest strategy must therefore give the number of calves, and adult (one-year-old) males and females that should be shot for

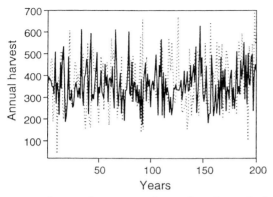

Figure 4.6. Annual variation in the number of animals shot in a rapidly growing moose population harvested according to a threshold (dotted lines) or a proportional (solid lines) strategy. The parameters are assumed to be representative for the population in northern Norway described by Solberg *et al.* (1999). The thresholds that define the optimal strategy are 353 calves, 1425 adult (> 1 year old) females and 296 adult males. The optimal proportions when the population is harvested according to a proportional harvest strategy are 0.481, 0.005 and 0.182 for calves, adult females and males, respectively. For further description, see the text.

the given optimisation criteria. For instance, a proportional harvest strategy requires specification of the proportion of the estimated population that should be removed from each category of individual. Similarly, for threshold harvesting, we must define a threshold for each category. If the estimated number of individuals of a category is above this threshold, we attempt harvesting the difference between the estimated number of animals of the category in the population and the predefined threshold.

To determine the strategy that gives the largest mean annual yield we simulate the process over a large number of years. For a fixed random number seed in the simulations, the mean annual yield is simply a function of the three parameters involved in the definitions of each class of strategy. The numerical maximisation can then be carried out by standard numerical procedures for maximising functions of several variables.

Results from this complex density-dependent age-structured model confirm our main results (Lande *et al.*, 1994, 1995) from analyses of simple diffusion models. In general, threshold harvesting gives a higher mean annual yield and a higher variance in annual yield than does proportional harvesting (Figure 4.6), although when the mean population growth rate is high, as in this example, the differences may not be large. In Figure 4.6, with the goal of maximising the mean annual harvest, the optimal

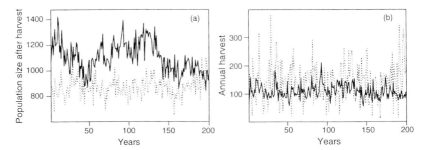

Figure 4.7. Annual variation in (a) population size and (b) the number of animals shot in a moose population harvested according to a threshold (dotted line) or a proportional (solid line) strategy. The parameters are for the population in northern Norway described by Solberg *et al.* (1999), except that calf survival is equal to 0.4. The thresholds that define the optimal strategy are 228 calves, 424 adult (> 1 year old) females and 149 adult males. The optimal proportions when the populations are harvested according to a proportional harvest strategy are 0.15, 0.01 and 0.20 for calves, adult females and males, respectively. For further description, see the text.

threshold strategy produces a mean of 369 and a standard deviation of 121, whereas the optimal proportional strategy produces a mean of 356 and a standard deviation of 89.

Analyses of the population dynamics of ungulates (Sæther, 1997; Gaillard *et al.*, 1998) have shown that calf survival is one of the most variable demographic traits, which often correlates closely to annual variation in the population growth rate. In order to examine how a change in the mean population growth rate would affect the harvest strategy, we decreased the natural calf survival from 0.8 to 0.4 (Figure 4.7). Such low survival rates may occur, for example, in areas where large carnivores prey heavily on moose calves (Larsen *et al.*, 1989; Ballard *et al.*, 1991). Such a reduction resulted in a larger difference in the mean annual yield between threshold and proportional harvesting. This illustrates that threshold harvesting gives a more sustainable exploitation than proportional harvesting, especially for low population growth rates.

Density dependence in a variable environment may strongly influence the choice of harvest strategy (Sæther *et al.*, 1996a). For low calf survival, increasing the strength of density dependence has a larger impact on the age structure under proportional harvesting than under threshold harvesting. The number of animals harvested can be maximised by increasing the number of females in the population, by harvesting mainly adult males and calves.

DISCUSSION

Although large temporal variation features prominently in the dynamics of many exploited populations (Myers *et al.*, 1995; Hofmann & Powell, 1998), it is rarely considered when suggesting sustainable harvesting strategies. Fluctuation in the size of exploited populations affects not only the harvests but also the risk of population collapse or extinction when the population size is low, because of demographic and environmental stochasticity. Stochastic dynamics, as well as uncertainty in population size estimates and population dynamic parameters, may result in inaccurate predictions of the effects of the exploitation on future population sizes. In order to avoid overexploitation it is therefore necessary to account for the effects of stochasticity and uncertainty in determining an optimal harvesting strategy for any harvesting goal. In contrast to most past and current management of renewable resources that focused and focus on short-term goals for maximising harvests, we consider long-term goals of sustainable harvesting that reduce the risk of resource collapse or extinction. Remarkably, we find that threshold strategies, which greatly reduce the risk of resource collapse or extinction, also produce higher expected harvests, but with a higher variance in annual harvest, than other strategies.

From simple analytical models without age structure we derived the following general results. For any harvesting goal, from the most prudent goal of maximising the expected cumulative harvest before eventual extinction to the more aggressive goal of maximising the mean annual harvest, the optimal strategy is threshold harvesting. In threshold harvesting, when the population is above a threshold size it is exploited at the highest possible rate, with no harvest when the population is below the threshold. For any given harvesting goal, a threshold harvesting strategy will produce higher expected yield with a lower risk of population collapse or extinction. For the most prudent goal of maximising the expected cumulative harvest before eventual extinction of a population, with unlimited harvesting capacity and stochasticity in population dynamics obeying a stationary time series, the optimal strategy is threshold harvesting with the threshold at the carrying capacity or stochastically stable equilibrium, $c = K$. This holds regardless of the amount or form of stochasticity or the form of population density regulation. Harvesting only the excess individuals above the carrying capacity has the desirable feature of exploitation with relatively little ecological disturbance. For the more aggressive goal of maximising the mean annual harvest the optimal threshold is lower, but increases with increasing stochasticity. Limited harvesting capacity reduces the optimal threshold under both the goal of maximising the expected cumulative harvest before extinction and that of maximising the mean annual harvest. Thus stochasticity and a high harvesting capacity dictate more cautious threshold strategies, with higher thresholds and more frequent years of no harvest. Uncertainty in population estimates and in population dynamic parameters also leads to the more cautious strategy of proportional threshold harvesting, as has been suggested for the Norwegian brown bear. According to the 'precautionary principle' we should select the harvest strategy minimising the risk that unfortunate events (e.g. extinction) will occur.

Diffusion approximations to simple stochastic population models with density regulation show that threshold harvesting is a more sustainable exploitation strategy than proportional or constant harvest strategies (Lande *et al.*, 1994, 1995, 1997; Sæther *et al.*, 1996a; Engen *et al.*, 1997; see also Whittle & Horwood, 1995). Our analysis of the harvest of moose supports this conclusion even in a far more complex model involving age structure, density dependence and stochasticity in the population dynamics. Threshold harvesting gives a higher mean annual yield than proportional harvesting (Figures 4.2 and 4.3), but the variance in the yield is also higher. This difference becomes larger with increasing environmental stochasticity and with decreasing mean annual growth rate, illustrating that threshold harvesting represents a more sustainable exploitation strategy for populations in a fluctuating environment. This is because there is no harvest in years with small population sizes.

Actual harvesting usually is carried out with a short-term goal such as maximising the mean annual harvest with a strategy resembling proportional (or constant effort) harvesting that does relatively little or nothing to minimise the extinction risk. Long-term goals of sustainable harvesting with minimal extinction risk generally involve threshold harvesting strategies. When thresholds are used, they are typically set too low, at the point of resource collapse or endangerment (Kruse *et al.*, 1993; Smith *et al.*, 1993; Taylor & Dunstone, 1996). The reluctance to apply threshold harvesting strategies reflects a bias in favour of continued harvesting to satisfy short-term economic and political interests at the expense of long-term sustainability of the resource. The commonly used strategies of proportional or constant harvesting allow continued harvesting of even small populations, reducing both mean annual harvests and sustainability of the resource, thereby harming the industries and consumers that may depend on it.

The main drawback of threshold harvesting strategies is that they entail a high variance in annual harvest, with frequent years of no harvest. There are several ways to reduce the variance in annual harvest and the frequency of years with no harvest, while maintaining a low risk of population collapse or extinction (Lande *et al.*, 1994, 1997; Engen *et al.*, 1997). First is to limit the harvesting capacity, which reduces the optimal threshold, allowing harvesting to continue at a reduced rate over a wider range of population sizes, i.e. with fewer years of no harvest. Second is the use of optimal or nearly optimal strategies of proportional threshold harvesting. With substantial uncertainty in population estimates, proportional threshold harvesting will often be the optimal strategy. In many cases the choice of a suboptimally low q will greatly reduce the threshold c, again allowing harvesting to proceed at a reduced rate over a wider range of population sizes with fewer years of no harvest. Thirdly, insurance plans such as storing the harvest or saving profits in good years would help to carry harvesters through years of little or no harvest. Fourthly, income sharing by harvesters that specialise in different resources that fluctuate out of synchrony with each other would reduce the coefficient of variation in annual income. Insurance and diversification schemes are standard methods of reducing economic risk in financially sophisticated industries, such as banking and investment, that deal routinely with high stochasticity and uncertainty. Such concepts could be applied to help promote sustainable harvesting and conservation of fluctuating resources.

CONCLUSIONS

Commonly used strategies for short-term exploitation of biological resources that fail to account for ubiquitous stochasticity and uncertainty in population dynamics are likely to cause overexploitation and may contribute to population collapse or extinction. We review general analytical results from stochastic harvesting theory based on diffusion approximations to simple models without age structure. A range of harvesting goals can be considered, from the most prudent long-term goal of maximising the expected cumulative harvest before eventual extinction of the population, to the more aggressive goal of maximising the mean annual harvest. For any harvesting goal, a threshold harvesting strategy (harvesting at the maximum possible rate when the population exceeds the threshold with no harvest below the threshold) produces the maximum yield with a lower risk of population collapse or extinction than any other strategy. The optimal threshold depends on the harvesting goal, the maximum harvesting capacity, the degree of stochasticity in population dynamics, and the form of population density regulation. With substantial uncertainty in estimated population sizes, a superior strategy is proportional threshold harvesting, in which only a fraction of the estimated population size above the threshold is harvested, with no harvest below the threshold. Stochasticity and uncertainty dictate more conservative approaches for sustainable harvesting. Principles of optimal threshold harvesting can be applied to age-structured populations, as illustrated in examples of harvesting Scandinavian brown bear and Fennoscandian moose. Methods are available for reducing the variance in annual harvest and the frequency of years with no harvest associated with threshold harvesting strategies.

REFERENCES

Ballard, W. B., Whitman, J. S. & Reed, D. J. (1991). Population dynamics of moose in South Central Alaska. *Wildlife Monographs*, **114**, 1–49.

Beddington, J. R. & May, R. M. (1977). Harvesting populations in a randomly fluctuating environment. *Science*, **197**, 463–465.

Casey, J. M. & Myers, R. A. (1998). Near extinction of a large, widely distributed fish. *Science*, **281**, 690–692.

Charnov, E. L. (1993). *Life History Invariants*. Oxford University Press, Oxford.

Clark, C. W. (1990). *Mathematical Bioeconomics. The Optimal Management of Renewable Resources*, 2nd edn. Wiley, New York.

Ellner, S. & Turchin, P. (1995). Chaos in a noisy world: new methods and evidence from time series analysis. *American Naturalist*, **145**, 343–375.

Engen, S., Lande, R. & Sæther, B.-E. (1997). Harvesting strategies for fluctuating populations based on uncertain population estimates. *Journal of Theoretical Biology*, **186**, 201–212.

Engen, S., Bakke, Ø. & Islam, A. (1998). Demographic and environmental stochasticity – concepts and definitions. *Biometrics*, **54**, 840–846.

Gaillard, J.-M., Festa-Bianchet, M. & Yoccoz, N. G. (1998). Population dynamics of large herbivores: variable recruitment with constant adult survival. *Trends in Ecology and Evolution*, **13**, 58–63.

Getz, W. M. & Haight, R. G. (1989). *Population Harvesting*. Princeton University Press, Princeton, NJ.

Groombridge, B. (1992). *Global Biodiversity: Status of the Earth's Living Resources*. Chapman & Hall, New York.

Hofmann, E. E. & Powell, T. M. (1998). Environmental variability effects on marine fisheries: four case histories. *Ecological Applications*, **8**, S23–S32.

Hutchings, J. A. & Myers, R. A. (1994). What can be learned from the collapse of a renewable resource? Atlantic cod, *Gadus morhua*, of New Foundland and Labrador. *Canadian Journal of Fisheries and Aquatic Sciences*, **51**, 2126–2146.

IUCN (World Conservation Union) (1994). *IUCN Red List Categories*. IUCN, Gland, Switzerland.

Karlin, S. & Taylor, H. M. (1981). *A Second Course in Stochastic Processes*. Academic Press, New York.

Kruse, G., Eggers, D. M., Marasco, R. J., Pautzke, C. & Quinn, T. J. II (eds.) (1993). *Proceedings of the International Symposium on Management Strategies for*

Exploited Fish Populations. Alaska Sea Grant College Program report no. 93-02. University of Alaska Fairbanks.

Lande, R. (1993). Risks of population extinction from demographic and environmental stochasticity and random catastrophes. *American Naturalist*, **142**, 911–927.

Lande, R. (1998). Demographic stochasticity and Allee effect on a scale with isotropic noise. *Oikos*, **83**, 353–358.

Lande, R., Engen, S. & Sæther, B.-E. (1994). Optimal harvesting, economic discounting, and extinction risk in fluctuating populations. *Nature*, **372**, 88–90.

Lande, R., Engen, S. & Sæther, B.-E. (1995). Optimal harvesting of fluctuating populations with a risk of extinction. *American Naturalist*, **145**, 728–745.

Lande, R., Sæther, B.-E. & Engen, S. (1997). Threshold harvesting for sustainability of fluctuating resources. *Ecology*, **78**, 1341–1350.

Larsen, D. G., Gauthies, D. A. & Markel, R. L. (1989). Causes and rate of moose mortality in the southwest Yukon. *Journal of Wildlife Management*, **53**, 548–557.

Ludwig, D. (1998). Management of stocks that may collapse. *Oikos*, **83**, 397–402.

Ludwig, D. & Walters, C. J. (1985). Are age-structured models appropriate for catch-effort data? *Canadian Journal of Fisheries and Aquatic Sciences*, **42**, 1066–1072.

Ludwig, D., Hilborn, R. & Walters, C. J. (1993). Uncertainty, resource exploitation and conservation: lessons from history. *Science*, **260**, 17, 36.

May, R. M., Beddington, J. R., Horwood, J. W. & Shepherd, J. G. (1978). Exploiting natural populations in an uncertain world. *Mathematical Biosciences*, **42**, 219–252.

Myers, R. A., Bridson, J. & Barrowman, N. J. (1995). Summary of worldwide spawner and recruitment data. *Canadian Technical Report of Fisheries and Aquatic Sciences*, **2024**, 1–274.

Myers, R. A., Hutchings, J. A. & Barrowman, N. J. (1997). Why do fish stocks collapse? The example of cod in Atlantic Canada. *Ecological Applications*, **7**, 91–106.

Myers, R. A., Bowen, K. G. & Barrowman, N. J. (1999). Maximum reproductive rate of fish at low population sizes. *Canadian Journal of Fisheries and Aquatic Sciences*, **56**, 2404–2419.

Pimm, S. L. (1991). *The Balance of Nature?* University of Chicago Press, Chicago.

Redford, K. H. (1992). The empty forest. *BioScience*, **42**, 412–422.

Reed, W. J. (1978). The steady state of a stochastic harvesting model. *Mathematical Biosciences*, **41**, 273–307.

Sæther, B.-E. (1985). Annual variation in carcass weight of Norwegian moose (*Alces alces*) in relation to climate along a latitudinal gradient. *Journal of Wildlife Management*, **49**, 977–983.

Sæther, B.-E. (1997). Environmental stochasticity and population dynamics of large herbivores: a search for mechanisms. *Trends in Ecology and Evolution*, **12**, 143–149.

Sæther, B.-E. & Heim, M. (1993). Ecological correlates of individual variation in age at maturity of female moose (*Alces alces*): the effects of environmental variability. *Journal of Animal Ecology*, **62**, 482–489.

Sæther, B.-E., Engen, S. & Lande, R. (1996a). Density-dependence and optimal harvesting of fluctuating populations. *Oikos*, **76**, 40–46.

Sæther, B.-E., Andersen, R., Hjeljord, O. & Heim, M. (1996b). Ecological correlates of regional variation in life history of the moose *Alces alces*. *Ecology*, **77**, 1493–1500.

Sæther, B.-E., Engen, S., Swenson, J. E., Bakke, Ø. & Sandegren, F. (1998). Assessing the viability of Scandinavian brown bear *Ursus arctos* populations: the effects of uncertain parameter estimates. *Oikos*, **83**, 403–416.

Sæther, B.-E., Engen, S. & Solberg, E. J. (2001). Optimal harvest of age structured populations of moose *Alces alces* in a fluctuating environment. *Wildlife Biology*, **7**, in press.

Shaffer, M. L. (1981). Minimum population sizes for species conservation. *BioScience*, **31**, 131–134.

Smith, S. J., Hunt, J. J. & Rivard, D. (1993). *Risk Evaluation and Biological Reference Points for Fisheries Management*. Canadian Special Publication of Fisheries and Aquatic Sciences 120. National Research Council and Department of Fisheries and Oceans, Ottawa.

Solberg, E. J. & Sæther, B.-E. (1994). Sexually selected characters as life history traits: annual variation in male body weight and antler size in moose (*Alces alces*). *Journal of Mammalogy*, **75**, 1069–1079.

Solberg, E. J., Sæther, B.-E., Strand, O. & Loison, A. (1999). Dynamics of a harvested Norwegian moose population in a variable environment. *Journal of Animal Ecology*, **68**, 186–204.

Stubsjøen, T., Sæther, B.-E., Solberg, E. J., Heim, M. & Rolandsen, C. M. (2000). Moose (*Alces alces*) survival in three populations in northern Norway. *Canadian Journal of Zoology*, **78**, 1822–1830.

Swenson, J. E., Wabakken, P., Sandegren, F., Bjarvall, A., Franzen, R. & Soderberg, A. (1995). The near extinction and recovery of brown bears in Scandinavia in relation to the bear management policies of Norway and Sweden. *Wildlife Biology*, **1**, 11–25.

Swenson, J. E., Sandegren, F. & Soderberg, A. (1998). Geographic expansion of an increasing bear population: evidence for presaturation dispersal. *Journal of Animal Ecology*, **67**, 819–826.

Taylor, V. J. & Dunstone, N. (1996). *The Exploitation of Mammal Populations*. Chapman & Hall, London.

Tufto, J., Sæther, B.-E., Engen, S., Swenson, J. E. & Sandegren, F. (1999). Harvesting strategies for conserving minimum viable populations based on World Conservation Union criteria: brown bears in Norway. *Proceedings of the Royal Society of London B*, **266**, 961–967.

Whittle, P. & Horwood, J. (1995). Population extinction and optimal resource management. *Philosophical Transactions of the Royal Society of London B*, **350**, 179–188.

5

The exploitation of spatially structured populations

E. J. MILNER-GULLAND

As has been demonstrated elsewhere in this volume, exploitation is a major threat to many species. The effects of exploitation are often discussed with reference to the proportion of the population as a whole that is removed each year, without taking into consideration which particular individuals are being removed and how they are selected. It is increasingly being realised that spatial location is a key determinant of both the ecology and the susceptibility to exploitation of many species. The large conservation literature on the effects of habitat fragmentation and the long-running debates on issues such as reserve size and shape, the effectiveness of corridors, and the problems of small isolated populations demonstrate the general importance of the spatial structure of populations for conservation (Soulé, 1987; Primack, 1993). This recognition is now extending to the literature on the effects of exploitation on populations of harvested species.

In order to predict the behaviour of ecological systems, it is helpful to characterise them using a model. For example, if we wish to predict the effects of a given level of exploitation on a population, we first need to develop a model of the dynamics of that population and its density-dependent response. Very simple models of population dynamics, such as the logistic equation, are sometimes adequate representations of how a population behaves, but generally more realism is needed before a model becomes a useful tool for prediction (Milner-Gulland & Mace, 1998). Realism is often introduced by explicitly modelling the structure of the population, perhaps by breaking the population into different age or size classes, which might be differentially targeted by harvesters, or might have different roles in population dynamics. The spatial location of individuals or of subgroups of the population is often an important component of a population's ecology. Few populations exist for which it is valid to assume that there is no spatial structuring, and the degree of population subdivision affects both evolutionary and ecological processes. In order to be useful, a predictive model must be as simple as possible, while still capturing the essentials of the dynamics of the system. Whether a model to predict the effects of exploitation requires spatial structure depends on the importance of spatial structure to the ecology of the species, or to the behaviour of hunters, in the real world.

In this chapter I first outline the main approaches to modelling spatial structure in ecology and then give an overview of some of the ways in which spatial structure is important for the conservation of exploited species. Two case studies are used to illustrate the different ways in which spatial structure can influence the relationship between the ecology of exploited species and the incentives faced by those who exploit them. Finally, I summarise the important issues that need to be borne in mind when considering the influence of spatial structure on the conservation of exploited species, and how these issues can be addressed.

MODELLING SPATIAL STRUCTURE IN ECOLOGY

The modelling of spatial structure in ecology is a rapidly developing field, excellently reviewed by Keeling (1999). Models that do not include the spatial structure of the population are making the mean field assumption, that the average density over the whole area is the same as the density in the area where any individual is. In this case, the local environment in which an individual exists is ignored, and only the global behaviour of the system is considered. This can work well in some cases where there is much mixing, such as many aquatic systems, but in cases where local interactions are important, adding spatial structure can make the behaviour of a modelled system much more realistic. There is also a thriving literature on the analysis of spatial data in ecology and the search for underlying mechanisms (e.g. Bjørnstad et al., 1999), but here I concentrate on the theoretical modelling aspects.

Much of the early work on modelling spatial structure in biology involved the use of partial differential equations. These have been used to explain structures as diverse as the patterns of animal markings (Murray, 1981) and fish dispersal between harvested and unharvested areas (Clark, 1990). Although these equations can be solved analytically, they soon become too complex for analytical solution as the degree of ecological realism increases. They also make the assumption that space, time and population size are all continuous; in many ecological systems this is not a tenable assumption. Conservation, in particular, often deals with small populations; when the total population size is small and subject to stochastic variation, results obtained from models of populations containing fractions of individuals are misleading.

Metapopulation models are also extremely popular among ecologists and conservation biologists. They divide the population into a number of identical patches, connected by dispersal between the patches. The amount of dispersal between patches must be quite low, or the spatial structure of the system is lost. The original metapopulation model, developed by Levins (1969) and discussed by Gilpin & Hanski (1991), makes quite restrictive assumptions about the relative time scales of interpatch and intrapatch dynamics; patches are assumed to be either at carrying capacity or empty, so that intrapatch population dynamics are not relevant to the dynamics of the system as a whole. This assumption fits the original system of insect patch dynamics well, but is generally not suitable for slower-growing species such as mammals, for which the assumption that a patch is either at carrying capacity or empty is less likely to hold. None the less, there have been applications of this model even to species such as badgers *Meles meles* (which actually fitted the model rather well; Verboom *et al.*, 1991). These models have been used widely in ecology, because of their flexibility and relative simplicity. The models can be made more realistic by allowing the population size in each patch to be below carrying capacity, or by allowing the patches to be different rather than identical (Keeling, 1999); these more complex models are often referred to as patch models.

With the advent of increasingly high-powered computers, there has been a huge increase in the modelling of spatial population dynamics through numerical simulation rather than analytical solution. This allows more complicated, and so more realistic, systems to be modelled. A current major research area is in the use of discrete lattice models; these are models in which space is divided up into a lattice of cells, each of which may contain a single individual or a subpopulation. The cells interact with each other, usually through dispersal between neighbouring cells. Discrete lattice models are simple to visualise, but are none the less very powerful tools that open up many interesting theoretical questions, particularly concerning the scales at which processes happen, and so the size of the lattice that is needed correctly to capture the dynamics of the system (Keeling *et al.*, 1997). Two main kinds of lattice model are used: coupled map lattices, in which the population size in a cell is assumed to be a continuous variable, connected to other cells through a set of coupled equations; and cellular automata models, where the population size is a discrete variable, and there are probabilistic rules connecting the cells. Coupled map lattice models have been used in applications such as insect population dynamics (Hassell *et al.*, 1991), plant growth (Hendry *et al.*, 1996) and crown of thorn starfish *Acanthaster* outbreaks on coral reefs (Green, 1990). However, for conservation applications where small population sizes are important, cellular automata models may be more appropriate, though they are also more computer intensive (Bascompte & Solé, 1996).

APPROACHES TO SPATIAL STRUCTURE IN HARVESTING THEORY AND CONSERVATION

There are two components to exploitation: the ecology of the species being exploited and the decision-making of the people who exploit them. Both of these components need to be taken into account when one is modelling exploitation; only when both are included can answers be found to questions such as 'What will the size of the exploited population be in the long term?' 'How many hunters will there be, and how many individuals will they harvest every year?' When the two components are combined in a model of the system, it is called a bioeconomic model (see Ludwig, Chapter 2). The biological component of the bioeconomic model describes how the population grows, both naturally and under exploitation. The economic component describes how much effort will be put into harvesting the population. This depends both on the biological characteristics of the species and on the the costs of harvesting and the price received for the products of harvesting. Many models express the decision-making of harvesters in monetary terms – they are aiming to maximise their profits. Other influences on decision-making can also be included in the model, such as the user's attitude to uncertainty or the wish to retain the population above a certain size for conservation reasons. More details on bioeconomic modelling can be found in Milner-Gulland & Mace (1998).

Both the ecological and the economic components of a bioeconomic model can be affected by spatial structure. For example, the economic component can be affected by the costs involved in travelling to a location to harvest; the longer it takes to reach a particular area, the costlier this area is to harvest. The ecological component could include the dispersal ability of the species, and so the degree of isolation of a particular subpopulation. Exploiting a species in which dispersal is minimal may lead to localised extinctions as particular areas are harvested, whereas harvesting a species that mixes at a high rate may cause the whole population to decline. Wherever the spatial structure is expressed, either in the ecological or economic components, the effect is to alter the predicted levels of harvesting effort, yield and long-term population size of the harvested species. Below, I discuss three of the main areas in which spatial considerations have been included in harvesting models: harvesting source–sink populations, marine reserves and spatial behaviour of hunters. Then I discuss two case studies, one of which has the spatial structuring on the economic side, the other on the ecological side.

Harvesting source–sink populations

The first people to address the issue of the effects of exploitation on a metapopulation were Tuck & Possingham (1994). Their definition of a metapopulation is two local populations connected by dispersal of juveniles; the internal dynamics of the local populations are modelled, so this is a patch model rather than a Levins metapopulation. Tuck & Possingham assume that the per capita larval production in one population (the source population) is higher than in the other (the sink population). The model shows that the source population should be exploited at a lower rate than if the population was homogeneously mixed, and the sink population at a higher rate. This is because part of the value of the source population to harvesters is its ability to produce recruits for future exploitation. In the extreme case where all the recruits to the population are produced by the source population and none by the sink, the sink should be harvested completely each year (assuming, among other things, that harvesting is costless). Lundberg & Jonzén (1999a) have also addressed this issue, using a similar model. They show that source and sink populations vary in their optimal harvest rates, yields and equilibrium population sizes under harvesting, so that it is important to harvest differently in the two types of area. However, they also show that population densities are not necessarily higher in source populations, and so it can be difficult to tell whether a given population is a source or a sink.

Marine reserves

The main area of current research interest in the conservation of spatially structured harvested populations is marine reserves. Although the theory of reserve design for the conservation of terrestrial species is well developed, it has paid less attention to the potential of reserves as tools for sustainable harvesting (except for suggestions that buffer zones allowing limited traditional harvesting may be useful, but these have yet to be fully explored theoretically). In contrast, the discussion of marine reserves usually has the explicit aim of maintaining or increasing sustainable yields of harvested species.

A large number of papers have been published recently addressing the effects of setting aside no-take areas on the yield and sustainability of fishing, the biology of fish populations and the socioeconomic status of fishers (e.g. Roberts, 1997; Valdes-Pizzini, 1995; Malleret-King, 1998; Mosquera *et al.*, 2000). Although early discussions of the benefits of marine reserves tended to be quite speculative, recent discussions have been based on more theoretical analyses. However, there has still been little theoretical work on the spatial dynamics of the fish populations protected by marine reserves, and on the consequences of spatial structure for the effectiveness of reserves. Generally, the emphasis has instead been on their role as a buffer against uncertainty in the management of fish resources; by setting aside an unharvested area, we recognise that our abilities to predict the effects of harvesting and to manage these resources are limited. Lauck *et al.* (1998) showed, using a simple non-spatial logistic population model, that if actual harvest rates follow a probability distribution around the target harvest rate, and if the variability in harvest rate is high, then overharvesting can occur even when the target harvest rate is low. Although in a deterministic situation, not harvesting a proportion of the population is identical with harvesting the entire population at a lower rate, Lauck *et al.* (1998) demonstrated that when there is a high level of uncertainty in harvest rates, not harvesting a proportion of the population is an effective buffer against overexploitation.

Other authors have emphasised the issues of spatial structure raised by marine reserves (Hatcher, 1995; Guénette & Pitcher, 1999; Lundberg & Jonzén, 1999b). The reason why marine reserves involve issues of spatial structure is that in order for them to work, the reserve must act as a refuge for individuals that would otherwise suffer fishing mortality. This implies that there is not full random mixing in the fish population, otherwise fishing effort could simply move from the closed area to the remainder of the area and have exactly the same effect on the population as before (assuming there is enough space for the vessels to fish unhindered by others and that there is no uncertainty in the level of harvest). Guénette & Pitcher (1999) used a non-equilibrium age-structured population model with random movement of fish between the reserve and the fished area. They showed that, at low transfer rates between the reserve and fished area, yield is lower with the reserve than without it, but that, as transfer rates increase, yield increases with a reserve and surpasses yield in the no-reserve scenario. By using an age-structured model they are able to capture the improvements in recruitment caused by the reserve, because larger fish produce more recruits than do smaller ones. They suggest that future work should include more realistic representations of spatial structure and seasonal changes in fish movement patterns (e.g. fish movement into spawning areas or to deeper water in particular seasons).

Lundberg & Jonzén's (1999b) model includes habitat heterogeneity; they used a very simple model in which there are two different qualities of habitat, one which is fully protected by a marine reserve and another which is fished. They also assume an ideal free distribution of individuals, so that the individuals are distributed such that the fitness in each habitat is equal; thus the poorer quality habitat contains fewer individuals. Their results suggest that the catch and optimal harvest rate are affected only by the quality of the unprotected area, not by the quality of the reserve. When an export of recruits from the reserve to the fished area is included, the quality of the reserve habitat does affect catch rates. Although this is an unrealistically simple model, it does emphasise the requirement to think in more depth about how populations distribute themselves in the environment when one is considering whether marine reserves are effective tools for the conservation of exploited species.

Spatial behaviour of hunters

The previous topics concentrated on the ecological effects of harvesting on population dynamics and so on yield when populations are spatially structured. Marine reserves can also be seen as a way in which the spatial behaviour of fishers can be controlled: the management authority decides where harvesting should take place, and puts regulations in place to enforce this. A more general approach to the problem of the spatial behaviour of harvesters would look at how they choose where to harvest, how this choice can be influenced by managers and how this decision-making process interacts with the spatial ecology of the harvested species. This requires consideration of the incentives that harvesters face: the costs and benefits of harvesting in one area rather than another. The problem has obvious similarities to patch selection in behavioural ecology. There has been much research done on search effort by fishers, assuming that fish are found in identifiable schools and the search process is random (Mangel, 1982; Mangel & Beder, 1985). Extensions could include incorporating learning by fishermen, and modelling clumped distributions of fish aggregations so that the fish population is explicitly spatially structured (Mangel & Beder, 1985), as well as considering the costs and benefits of different searching strategies. Hart (1997) has addressed the costs and benefits of fishing in one area rather than another, with particular reference to the incentives to fish illegally in a closed zone; he has shown, for example, that as the end of a fishing trip becomes closer, there is more incentive to risk entering the closed zone. Although this model is not explicitly spatial, it could easily be extended to include the costs and benefits of travelling to a particular location.

A few authors have looked at the spatial aspects of game hunter behaviour. For example, Hofer et al. (1996) explored the spatial distribution of poachers within the Serengeti National Park, and showed that poaching rates in an area are related to the distance from the boundary of the Park, the suitability of the area for hunting (the density of resident wildlife) and the demand for meat at the periphery of the Park (human population density). Marks (1994) collected data on the frequency of encounters between hunters and wildlife in Zambia, and noted that there has been a marked decrease over time in the frequency of wildlife sightings near settlements, with hunters having to go further to find game. He suggested that this is a result of game avoidance of inhabited areas and an increase in the use of snaring as a hunting technique. Although there has been some work done on the spatial behaviour of hunters, this remains a relatively under-researched area, and one that is as important for understanding the spatial dynamics of exploitation as studying the spatial behaviour of prey populations.

CASE STUDY: RED DEER HINDS ON THE ISLAND OF RUM

This case study is based on a paper by Milner-Gulland et al. (2000). Red deer *Cervus elaphus* on the island of Rum off the west coast of Scotland have been studied in detail since 1971, and so there are detailed individual-based data available on which to base a spatially structured model (Clutton-Brock et al., 1982, 1997). An important consideration in modelling spatially structured populations is the scale at which spatial variation occurs. In the case of the red deer on Rum, the scale is rather small; Milner-Gulland et al. (2000) show that there are differences in fecundity and mortality rates, especially among juveniles, between neighbouring hind groups. This has implications for the management of deer harvesting, because decisions about harvest rates tend to be made at the estate level; if neighbouring groups of hinds are significantly different in their population dynamics, they will also require different harvesting strategies if harvesting is to be optimal.

Red deer population dynamics
Adult male and female red deer have very different behaviour patterns in their use of space (Clutton-Brock et al., 1982); females are typically loyal to

their maternal home range throughout their lives, while males disperse. Males occupy areas different from those of females throughout most of the year. Because of these differences, only females are considered in this case study. Two neighbouring hind groups are modelled, occupying home ranges of 2 km² and 3 km² respectively, a few hundred metres apart. The sizes of the two Rum groups are significantly positively correlated over time, because they are exposed to similar climatic conditions (Grenfell *et al.*, 1998). Juvenile mortality, in particular, is strongly correlated between the groups, because it is strongly affected by the climate. However, although group sizes are correlated, this correlation explains only 31% of the variance, suggesting that the rates of dispersal between subpopulations are not sufficient to allow close entrainment of the dynamics. There are various reasons why two geographically proximate subpopulations of individuals of the same species might show different dynamics. In this case, the differences are likely to be linked to differences in the quality of the forage available to each group; the group with the more variable dynamics has a lower proportion of herb-rich *Agrostis–Festuca* grassland, which is favoured by the females (Clutton-Brock *et al.*, 1987).

There is little migration between the two groups, despite their geographical proximity. Red deer females do not move readily between groups, because of the cohesive nature of group social structure. Over the 22 years during which the deer have been studied, only 32 individuals have been observed moving between the groups, with an average dispersal rate from one subpopulation to the other of 0.73 females/year (Milner-Gulland *et al.*, 2000). Most studies of dispersal among vertebrates, both theoretical and empirical, suggest that density-dependent dispersal is likely to be the norm (Doncaster *et al.*, 1997; McPeek & Holt, 1992). However, in red deer, dispersal rate is not density dependent and does not vary significantly between the two subpopulations. The number of individuals dispersing from a group each year is well described by a Poisson distribution, which suggests that it is a density-independent process (Figure 5.1).

A model for red deer harvesting

The model used to describe the dynamics of the two red deer groups is age structured (Getz & Haight, 1989). Juvenile and adult mortality rates are linearly dependent on group size, but fecundity is independent of group size. Fecundity is assumed to vary from year to year according to a normal distribution, with the mean and variance observed in the Rum groups. Mortality rates are also assumed to be normally distributed, but are correlated between the two groups. Dispersal is assumed to be density

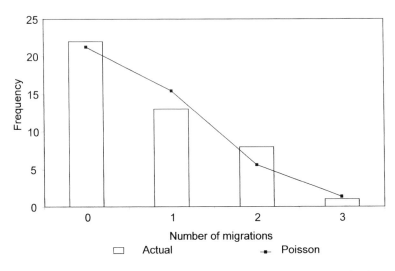

Figure 5.1. The observed number of individuals moving from one group of red deer hinds on the island of Rum, Scotland, to the other in a year, plotted against a Poisson distribution, with the mean number moving taken from the data as 0.727 per year. There is no significant difference between the observed frequency of migrations and the expected frequency under a Poisson distribution ($\chi^2 = 1.52$, not significant). Data are aggregated for both subpopulations, and for the years 1974–1995. (Figure from Milner-Gulland et al., 2000.)

independent and to follow a Poisson distribution. Deer managers are assumed to aim to maximise their profits from culling females. They are assumed to have a strategy of culling a certain proportion of each group each year, and to be able to cull different proportions of the two female groups. In calculating the monetary yield from a particular culling strategy, only the variable costs of deer culling are considered, ignoring the fixed costs of management. These fixed costs are not relevant to the decision-making of a manager when deciding how many of each group to cull, rather than whether to cull at all. The variable costs of culling are assumed to be predominately related to search time, with the costs of searching inversely proportional to group size.

Figure 5.2 shows how the monetary yield from harvesting varies with different harvest rates. The maximum profit can be made by harvesting 10% of the Kilmory Glen group each year and 14% of the Shamhnan Insir group each year. The Shamhnan Insir group is more variable in its fecundity and mortality rates than the Kilmory Glen group, and also has stronger density dependence; the latter enables the population to sustain a higher

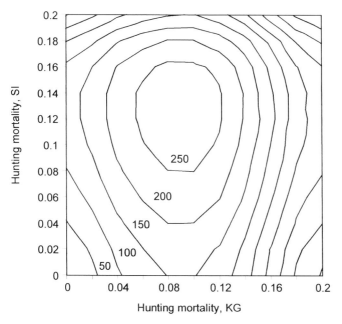

Figure 5.2. The effects of using different rates of harvesting (expressed as the percentage of the population harvested each year) on each hind group, shown as the mean monetary yield per year (in pounds) from harvesting the two groups. Means are calculated over 20 years (after transitional effects have finished) for 100 simulations. There are two groups of hinds: KG, Kilmory Glen; SI, Shamhnan Insir. SI is the more variable population, with stronger density dependence operating. The strategy that maximises monetary yield involves harvesting 10% of the KG population and 14% of the SI population each year. (Figure from Milner-Gulland et al., 2000.)

hunting mortality rate. Variability in vital rates reduces the optimal hunting mortality rates (see Lande et al., Chapter 4). If the model were deterministic, the optimal harvest mortality rates would be 12% and 16%, respectively. The fact that the maximum monetary yield from the Shamhnan Insir group is obtained at a harvest rate 40% higher than that producing the maximum yield in Kilmory might suggest that the harvesters could be losing a substantial proportion of their potential profits by harvesting the two groups at the same rate, rather than considering them separately. However, because the yields are relatively similar over the range of harvesting mortalities in question (10–14%), the actual losses incurred are small; in this case managers harvesting the groups at the same rate still receive 96% of the yield obtainable under differential harvesting.

Lessons from the case study

This case study uses long-term data on the population dynamics of a particular red deer population, so that its detailed predictions are specific to that population. However, the model does give some more general indications for harvesting structured populations:

- Two subpopulations could react very differently to harvesting and have very different vital rates, however close they are geographically. This means that a detailed understanding of the dynamics of harvested populations is needed, if a resource manager is to discern whether there are subpopulations within an area which have sufficiently different dynamics for their optimal harvest rates to be significantly different. Using a single harvest rate may lead to lower yields, or in extreme cases to the loss of one of the subpopulations. An added complication is that the dynamics of neighbouring groups may be correlated through exposure to similar climatic variation, and/or may be linked through migration. These two processes need to be disentangled, as they have different implications for the effects of harvesting pressure on the population: harvesting a group that is not linked to others, but has correlated dynamics due to exposure to the same climatic conditions, has no effect on the rest of the population; harvesting a group that is linked by dispersal to another will affect the rest of the population.
- Dispersal is the key factor determining how closely coupled the subpopulations are; it is particularly important to know whether it is dependent on or independent of density. The model discussed here can be used to show that, at low hunting mortalities, density-independent dispersal is very similar in effect to no dispersal, and so the linkage between the groups is not likely to be significant in determining optimal hunting strategies. However, if the groups were linked by density-dependent migration, as is thought to be more usual among vertebrates, the model shows that the effect would be to even out the density-related differences between the groups, and make the optimal harvest rate in one group much more dependent on the size of the other group.
- The complex social and age structure of this species (and, by extension, many other vertebrate species) means that the predictions of simple theoretical models are not upheld. McPeek & Holt (1992) showed theoretically that when ecological conditions in patches fluctuate in time and space, but with broadly similar ranges in each patch, selection should favour generalist adaptations to this range of ecological

conditions, and a high dispersal propensity. Thus subpopulation differentiation is not likely in these conditions. In the area inhabited by the two hind groups discussed here, ecological conditions fluctuate in space and time over a broadly similar range. However, this population has a rather complex, sex-differentiated social structure, in which life history parameters are strongly determined by age. Female dispersal is rare and density independent, and the dynamics of the two subpopulations are not as closely coupled as might have been expected from their geographical proximity. This case study thus suggests that further theoretical work is required on the spatial dynamics of populations in cases where population structure is complex.

CASE STUDY: WILD PIGS IN NORTH SULAWESI

This case study is based on papers by Clayton *et al.* (1997) and Keeling *et al.* (1999). The study of red deer on Rum emphasised the importance of a detailed knowledge of the ecology of harvested species, to ensure that the spatial structure of harvested populations is taken into account by managers. In this case study, by contrast, the emphasis is on how the spatial distribution of harvested species acts as a cost to harvesters, and how hunter behaviour is determined by the costs of travel to areas where they can hunt. This difference in emphasis is determined by the major processes driving the interaction between harvesters and their prey in each case.

Wild pig population dynamics

Sulawesi contains two endemic wild pig species, the babirusa *Babyrousa babyrussa* and Sulawesi wild pig *Sus celebensis*. The babirusa is found at low densities in primary forest only, and is classified as Endangered by IUCN (World Conservation Union) and protected by Indonesian law. The total babirusa population size is estimated at only around 5000 individuals. The Sulawesi wild pig is found at much higher densities, in both primary and disturbed forest, and is not protected by law or classified as threatened by IUCN. Details of the biology of the babirusa can be found in Clayton (1996), and of the Sulawesi wild pig in Macdonald (1993). The two wild pig species are consumed in the market towns of the eastern tip of North Sulawesi, where the people are predominately Christian, and are rarely consumed elsewhere in the island, where the people are predominately Muslim. There is a single road running through North Sulawesi along

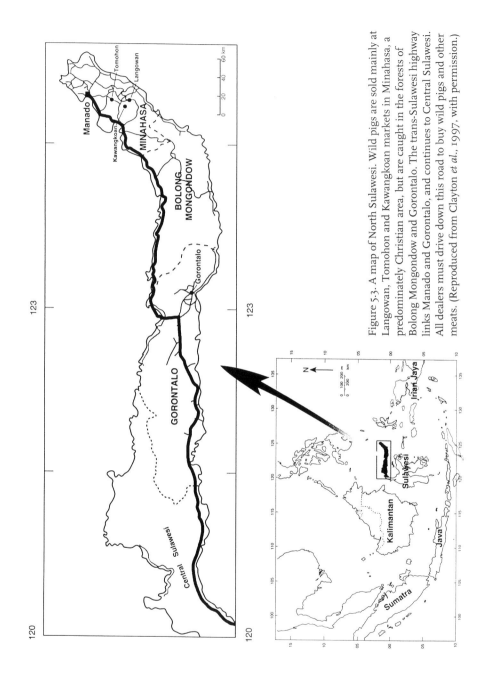

Figure 5.3. A map of North Sulawesi. Wild pigs are sold mainly at Langowan, Tomohon and Kawangkoan markets in Minahasa, a predominately Christian area, but are caught in the forests of Bolong Mongondow and Gorontalo. The trans-Sulawesi highway links Manado and Gorontalo, and continues to Central Sulawesi. All dealers must drive down this road to buy wild pigs and other meats. (Reproduced from Clayton et al., 1997, with permission.)

which dealers travel to the forests to buy wild pigs (Figure 5.3). The dealers also buy other species, such as bats and domestic dogs, but these are less important goods. Hunters snare pigs in the forests, and carry them to the forest edge to sell to the dealers. The dealers are competitive, and the resource is treated as open access. The trade is described in more detail by Clayton & Milner-Gulland (2000). The road was fully tarmacked only in 1992, and there has recently been a massive expansion of the number of hunters and dealers operating in the province, suggesting that the trade is still in disequilibrium. Wild pigs in Sulawesi make an interesting case study for two reasons:

1 Hunting costs vary in a directional manner, increasing as dealers drive further along a single road to collect pigs. The distance that a location is from the market has a major effect on the travel costs of the dealer, and so on the profitability of pig harvesting. The distance that a hunter has to walk from the road into the forest to snare pigs, and the topography of the area he has to walk in, are also major components of the cost of harvesting pigs. This is why it is essential to include a spatial component in any model of wild pig harvesting in North Sulawesi.

2 There are two species of pig hunted together, which are not discriminated between by the methods used to catch them or by consumers, but which have very different population dynamics. One is endangered; the other is not. The fact that hunters and consumers do not distinguish between these two species means that a two-species model is needed to characterise the system properly.

A model of wild pig harvesting

Spatial models can be used to predict the equilibrium distribution of pigs under open access harvesting, and the effect of various management actions on the equilibrium distribution of wild pigs. Clayton *et al.* (1997) used a coupled map lattice model to calculate the equilibrium sizes of the Sulawesi wild pig and babirusa populations under open access harvesting (see p. 89 for a description of coupled map lattice models). The unusual features of the model include the use of the underlying structure of vegetation type and road location as the base for the model, rather than assuming a homogeneous environment – another example of this approach was given by Green (1990). Also, global spatial distributions, not a localised neighbourhood of sites, drive the dynamics, because spatial structure enters the model through the dealers' travel costs. The implementation of the coupled map lattice involves the discretisation of space into a lattice of square cells, each with an area of 4 km². Five variables are assigned to each cell: the type of habitat to be found at the site (i.e. sea, major road, minor road, forest, logged area, etc.), the average costs of snaring and transporting a single pig to market from that site, the number of pigs to be harvested from the site, and the populations of babirusas and of Sulawesi wild pigs at the site. The population dynamics of the two species are represented by coupled differential equations assuming simple logistic growth of the populations. The two species experience identical hunting effort, but have different population dynamics and different catchabilities (babirusas are generally slower growing, found at lower densities and easier to catch than Sulawesi wild pigs).

Harvest costs depend on the cost of transporting a pig along the road, divided by the number of pigs being transported. They also depend on the density of pigs in an area; the lower the density, the more effort it takes to catch one, and so the higher the harvest cost. Unlike in the previous case study, here it is assumed that there is no dispersal of pigs between neighbouring sites. The omission of dispersal is justifiable because harvesting varies slowly over space so that each wild pig would experience little or no variation over its usual home range. Also, this model is concerned with the final equilibrium state while dispersal has a definite temporal scale that would greatly complicate the model. The effect of including dispersal would be a slight reduction in population sizes as wild pigs disperse out of the less hunted areas into those more heavily hunted.

Results of the model

The model predicts that under the current physical and economic circumstances the snaring of wild pigs will increase to such a rate that the babirusa will become extinct over the vast majority of the northern arm of Sulawesi (Figure 5.4). Only a relatively small amount of harvesting is necessary for the babirusa to be wiped out in any one area, whereas this amount of harvesting leaves the Sulawesi wild pig population virtually intact, causing a decline of less than 5%. In order to see whether the range contraction of the babirusa is an inevitable outcome of hunting or whether it is driven by the recent expansion of the road network, making it easier to reach all areas of the island quickly and easily, the model was rerun using the approximate road network from the 1950s; most of today's roads were in place then but their condition was far worse, little better than dirt tracks. As can be seen from Figure 5.5, when the road network is less developed the transport times are greatly increased, with it taking almost four days to reach some areas, the consequence of this being that in many regions babirusas

(a)

(b)

(c)

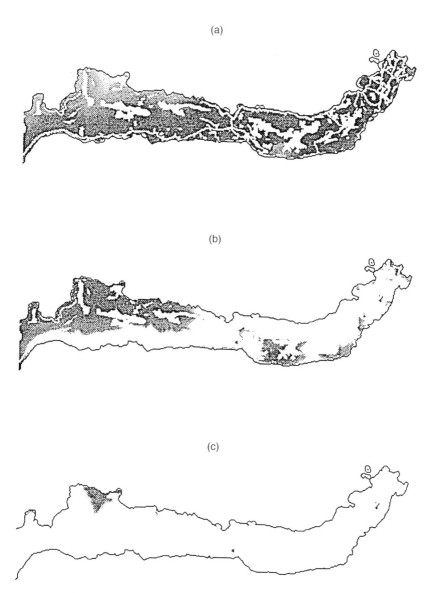

Figure 5.4. Output of the wild pig harvesting model under 1995 parameter values. In the figures, white represents a complete absence, and the sites are then scaled from light grey to black, black corresponding to the maximum sustainable harvest rate or the population being at carrying capacity. (a) The amount of harvesting at each site. (b) The number of Sulawesi wild pigs that can be supported at each site under this harvesting rate. (c) The number of babirusas that can be supported at each site under this harvesting rate. (Reproduced from Clayton *et al.*, 1997, with permission.)

(a)

(b)

(c)

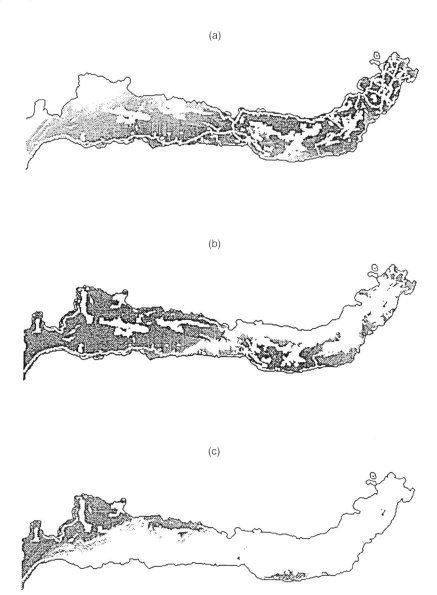

Figure 5.5. Output of the wild pig harvesting model under 1950s road conditions. In the figures, white represents a complete absence, and the sites are then scaled from light grey to black, black corresponding to the maximum sustainable harvest rate or the population being at carrying capacity. (a) The amount of harvesting at each site. (b) The number of Sulawesi wild pigs that can be supported at each site under this harvesting rate. (c) The number of babirusas that can be supported at each site under this harvesting rate. (Reproduced from Clayton *et al.*, 1997, with permission.)

Table 5.1. The effects of the assumptions made in the wild pig harvesting model on its results

The figures given are the equilibrium population sizes of the two species as a percentage of carrying capacity (thus 100 implies that the population is not harvested, while a low number implies that the population is heavily overharvested). The results under the baseline assumptions are shown spatially in Figure 5.4, the results under the 1950s road network are shown in Figure 5.5. Data from Clayton *et al.* (1997).

Situation	Sulawesi wild pig	Babirusa
Baseline assumptions	37	4
Only babirusa hunted	100	100
Only Sulawesi wild pig hunted	43	100
1950s road network	66	31
Meat consumed locally	13	0.2

survive. The areas in which babirusas remain extant correspond fairly well to the regions where the population can be found today, thus supporting the results from the model if it is assumed that the real system is slow to reach equilibrium.

Table 5.1 shows the effect of the major features of the model on its results. First, it is clear that it is the Sulawesi wild pig driving the dynamics of the harvesting, and that, although babirusas suffer the heaviest losses, their presence or absence in an area is virtually irrelevant to hunters' decision-making. Hunting only one of the species reduces the number of individuals that a hunter catches, and so reduces profits. If the two species are hunted separately, then hunting babirusas alone is not economically viable, as the costs outweigh the revenues from hunting. This is shown in Table 5.1 by the babirusa population being at 100% of carrying capacity (i.e. unhunted) if it is hunted alone. On the other hand, the small drop in profits from hunting the Sulawesi wild pig alone leads only to a small decrease in hunting pressure (shown by a small increase in population size from 37% to 43% of carrying capacity). Thus the fact that babirusas are hunted along with Sulawesi wild pigs is the reason why it is worth hunting them at all – a result similar to that found for hunting of rhino and elephant in the Luangwa Valley, Zambia (Milner-Gulland & Leader-Williams, 1992). If, however, Sulawesi wild pigs are hunted alone, without babirusas, the increase in harvesting costs is small, leading to only a small increase in the Sulawesi wild pig population over its size under two-species harvesting. Secondly, one of the most interesting features of this system is the effect of religious taboo on the hunting of wild pigs – in effect it is religious taboos that introduce the spatial element of the system through the need to transport wild pigs to market in the Christian tip of the province. It is clear from the sensitivity analyses that this imposes a substantial cost on the harvesters, allowing the equilibrium population of both species to remain much higher than it would be under the more usual circumstances of meat being hunted principally for local consumption.

Several points emerge from this case study:

- Travel costs have a key influence on the outcome of harvesting. Keeling *et al.* (1999) found that the results are even more sensitive to the time taken for a hunter to walk through the forest to find pigs from the road than to the costs of driving along the road from the forest edge to the market.
- This case study used a digitised map of the province, showing the different vegetation types and topographies of each area, to provide the base for the coupled map lattice model. This use of a heterogeneous underlying physical environment for the model is not common in coupled map lattice models, but it is useful because it enables us to make predictions for the real system. It also opens the way for future modelling work in which changes in habitat availability (through logging and forest clearance) can be included in the model as well as changes in the economic situation.
- If harvesting costs vary spatially, then the least accessible areas can act as refuges for endangered species, by being too costly to harvest. By showing where harvesting costs are highest, the model can predict which areas are likely to hold out longest as refuges for the babirusa. This allows conservation actions to be targeted at areas where babirusas might still survive.

CONCLUSIONS

Spatial population structure can be approached from two angles in the conservation of exploited species – the ecology of the population being hunted and the decision-making of the exploiter. Both are equally important. The two case studies have shown how including a spatial element on either of these sides can improve our understanding of the effects of harvesting on exploited species, and help in the formulation of conservation policy. In the case of the red deer, including the ecological differences between hind groups allowed us to explore the yield improvements that could be obtained by harvesting the groups as separate entities. In the case of the wild pigs, the explicit consideration of spatial heterogeneity and its effect on the economics of harvesting led to predictions about where refuges might exist for the endangered babirusa.

Spatial structure has not had enough attention in the conservation and harvesting literature as yet, from either the ecological or the economic angles. This is true of research into spatial structure in ecology in general, but in mainstream ecology, modelling spatial structure is currently an exciting and expanding field. It is to be hoped that it is only a matter of time before these ideas spill over into the more applied disciplines of conservation and harvesting theory, and there are hopeful signs that this is already happening. The huge amount of recent interest in the theory and practice of marine reserves is one such example. The increasing use of Geographical Information Systems (GIS) will help to make spatial data much more accessible to conservationists and researchers, although a theoretical basis is also needed if GIS work is to move from being merely descriptive to being usefully predictive. The approaches described in this chapter could form part of the foundation of this spatial theory of the conservation of exploited species.

ACKNOWLEDGEMENTS

I am very grateful to Matt Keeling for his comments and advice. The wild pig case study was funded by the Darwin Initiative of the UK Department of the Environment, Transport and the Regions and the People's Trust for Endangered Species.

REFERENCES

Bascompte, J. & Solé, R. V. (1996). Habitat fragmentation and extinction thresholds in spatially explicit models. *Journal of Animal Ecology*, **65**, 465–473.

Bjørnstadt, O. N., Ims, R. A. & Lambin, X. (1999). Spatial population dynamics: analysing patterns and processes of population synchrony. *Trends in Ecology and Evolution*, **14**, 427–432.

Clark, C.W. (1990). *Mathematical Bioeconomics: The Optimal Management of Renewable Resources*. Wiley, New York.

Clayton, L. M. (1996) *Conservation biology of the babirusa in North Sulawesi, Indonesia*. PhD thesis, University of Oxford.

Clayton, L. & Milner-Gulland, E. J. (2000). The trade in wildlife in North Sulawesi, Indonesia. In *Hunting for Sustainability in Tropical Forests*, ed. J. R. Robinson & E. L. Bennett, pp. 473–495. Columbia University Press, New York.

Clayton, L., Keeling, M. & Milner-Gulland, E. J. (1997). Bringing home the bacon: a spatial model of wild pig harvesting in Sulawesi, Indonesia. *Ecological Applications*, **7**, 642–652.

Clutton-Brock, T. H., Guinness, F. E. & Albon, S. D. (1982). *Red Deer: Behaviour and Ecology of Two Sexes.* University of Chicago Press, Chicago.

Clutton-Brock, T. H., Iason, G. R. & Guinness, F. E. (1987). Sexual segregation and density-related changes in habitat use in male and female red deer. *Journal of Zoology*, **211**, 275–289.

Clutton-Brock, T. H., Illius, A. W., Wilson, K., Grenfell, B. T., MacColl, A. D. C. & Albon, S. D. (1997). Stability and instability in ungulate populations: an empirical analysis. *American Naturalist*, **149**, 195–219.

Doncaster, C. P., Clobert, J., Doligez, B., Gustafsson, L. & Danchin, E. (1997). Balanced dispersal between spatially varying local populations: an alternative to the source–sink model. *American Naturalist*, **150**, 425–445.

Getz, W. M. & Haight, R. G. (1989). *Population Harvesting: Demographic Models of Fish, Forest and Animal Resources.* Monographs in Population Biology no. 27. Princeton University Press, Princeton, NJ.

Gilpin, M. & Hanski, I. (1991). *Meta-Population Dynamics: Empirical and Theoretical Investigations.* Academic Press, London.

Green, D. G. (1990). Cellular automata models of crown-of-thorns outbreaks. In *Acanthaster and the Coral Reef: A Theoretical Perspective*, ed. R. Bradbury, pp. 157–166. Lectures in Biomathematics no. 88. Springer-Verlag, Berlin.

Grenfell, B. T., Wilson, K., Finkenstädt, B. L., Coulson, T. N., Murray, S., Albon, S. D., Pemberton, J. M., Clutton-Brock, T. H. & Crawley, M. J. (1998). Noise and determinism in synchronised sheep dynamics. *Nature*, **394**, 674–677.

Guénette, S. & Pitcher, T. J. (1999). An age-structured model showing the benefits of marine reserves in controlling overexploitation. *Fisheries Research*, **39**, 295–303.

Hart, P. J. B. (1997) Controlling illegal fishing in closed areas: the case of mackerel off Norway. In *Developing and Sustaining World Fisheries Resources: The State of Science and Management.* Second World Fisheries Congress, eds. D. A. Hancock, D. C. Smith, A. Grant & J. P. Beumer, pp. 411–414. CSIRO, Canberra.

Hassell, M. P., Comins, H. & May, R. M. (1991). Spatial structure and chaos in insect population dynamics. *Nature*, **353**, 255–258.

Hatcher, B. G. (1995). How do Marine Protected Areas benefit fisheries? *Caribbean Park and Protected Areas Bulletin*, **5**, 9–10.

Hendry, R., McGlade, J. M. & Weiner, J. (1996). A coupled map lattice model of the growth of plant monocultures. *Ecological Modelling*, **84**, 81–90.

Hofer, H., Campbell, K. L. I., East, M. L. & Huish, S. A. (1996). The impact of game meat hunting on target and non-target species in the Serengeti. In *The Exploitation of Mammal Populations*, ed. V. J. Taylor & N. Dunstone, pp. 117–146. Kluwer Academic Publishers, Dordrecht.

Keeling, M. J. (1999). Spatial models of interacting populations. In *Advanced Ecological Theory*, ed. J. McGlade, pp. 64–99. Blackwell Science, Oxford.

Keeling, M. J., Mezic, I., Hendry, R. J., McGlade, J. & Rand, D. A. (1997). Characteristic length scales of spatial models in ecology. *Philosophical Transactions of the Royal Society of London B*, **352**, 1589–1601.

Keeling, M., Milner-Gulland, E. J. & Clayton, L. (1999). Spatial dynamics of two harvested wild pig populations. *Natural Resource Modeling*, **12**, 147–169.

Lauck, T., Clark, C. W., Mangel, M. & Munro, G. R. (1998). Implementing the precautionary principle in fisheries management through marine reserves. *Ecological Applications*, **8**, S72–S78.

Levins, R. (1969). Some demographic and genetic consequences of environmental heterogeneity for biological control. *Bulletin of the Entomological Society of America*, **15**, 237–240.

Lundberg, P. & Jonzén, N. (1999a). Optimal population harvesting in a source–sink environment. *Evolutionary Ecology Research*, **1**, 719–729.

Lundberg, P. & Jonzén, N. (1999b). Spatial population dynamics and the design of nature reserves. *Ecology Letters*, **2**, 129–134.

Macdonald, A. A. (1993). The Sulawesi warty pig. In *Status Survey and Conservation Action Plan: Pigs, Peccaries and Hippos*, ed. W. L. R. Oliver, pp. 15–21. IUCN, Gland, Switzerland.

Malleret-King, D. (1998). No-take zone for coral reef related fisheries management: how do stakeholders perceive the problem? *Institut Français de Recherche en Afrique*, **11**, 24–51.

Mangel, M. (1982). Search effort and catch rates in fisheries. *European Journal of Operational Research*, **11**, 361–366.

Mangel, M. & Beder, H. (1985). Search and stock depletion: theory and applications. *Canadian Journal of Fisheries and Aquatic Science*, **42**, 150–163.

Marks, S. A. (1994). Local hunters and wildlife surveys: a design to enhance participation. *African Journal of Ecology*, **32**, 233–254.

McPeek, M. A. & Holt, R. D. (1992). The evolution of dispersal in spatially and temporally varying environments. *American Naturalist*, **140**, 1010–1027.

Milner-Gulland, E. J. & Leader-Williams, N. (1992). A model of incentives for the illegal exploitation of black rhinos and elephants: poaching pays in Luangwa Valley, Zambia. *Journal of Applied Ecology*, **29**, 388–401.

Milner-Gulland, E. J. & Mace, R. (1998). *Conservation of Biological Resources*. Blackwell Science, Oxford.

Milner-Gulland, E. J., Coulson, T. N. & Clutton-Brock, T. (2000). On harvesting a structured ungulate population. *Oikos*, **88**, 592–602.

Mosquera, I., Côté, I. M., Jennings, S. & Reynolds, J. D. (2000). Conservation benefits of marine reserves for fish populations. *Animal Conservation*, **4**, 321–332.

Murray, J. D. (1981). A pre-pattern formation mechanism for animal coat markings. *Journal of Theoretical Biology*, **88**, 161–199.

Primack, R. (1993). *Essentials of Conservation Biology*. Sinauer, New York.

Roberts, C. (1997). Ecological advice for the global fisheries crisis. *Trends in Ecology and Evolution*, **12**, 35–38.

Tuck, G. N. & Possingham, H. P. (1994). Optimal harvesting strategies for a metapopulation. *Bulletin of Mathematical Biology*, **56**, 107–127.

Soulé, M. E. (1987). *Viable Populations for Conservation*. Cambridge University Press, Cambridge.

Valdes-Pizzini, M. (1995). La Parguera Marine Fishery Reserve: involving the fishing community in planning a Marine Protected Area. *Caribbean Park and Protected Areas Bulletin*, **5**, 2–3.

Verboom, J., Lankester, K. & Metz, J. A. J. (1991). Linking local and regional dynamics in stochastic meta-population models. *Biological Journal of the Linnean Society*, **42**, 39–55.

6

The conservation of exploited species in an uncertain world: novel methods and the failure of traditional techniques

PAUL R. WADE

The conservation and management of exploited species is often difficult and contentious. As reviewed in the opening and closing chapters of this volume, there are several possible management goals for exploited species. These include managing to minimise extinction risk, managing to prevent the depletion of a population to a level below some fraction of its pre-exploitation size, or managing to allow continued exploitation in the foreseeable future. By definition, a species that is exploited has some group of people that is doing the exploiting. These groups, quite understandably, usually insist that some scientific evidence be used to justify any proposed restriction on the level of exploitation that is allowed. Therefore, regardless of the conservation goal, the conservation and management of exploited species usually involves the quantitative analysis of data.

It is well documented that many populations of exploited species have collapsed due to overexploitation. Often this has happened because of a lack of management. However, there are also many examples where populations have collapsed even while they were being 'managed' (Ludwig *et al.*, 1993; Myers *et al.*, 1997). Punt & Smith (Chapter 3) explore some of the causes of these mistakes in fisheries management. Examples exist for other natural resources besides fish populations. The collapse of populations of several whale species in the Antarctic under management quotas set by the International Whaling Commission is one famous example (Allen, 1980).

The causes of these past management failures were many. One primary factor was a failure to recognise fully the uncertainty in available information. Uncertainty about exploited populations can come from many sources, including sampling error, potential biases, 'process' error (environmental variance), model error and sometimes a lack of data on some aspects of populations. However, analysis methods have traditionally incorporated uncertainty from sampling error but not from other potential sources.

A second primary factor was a lack of procedures that could include uncertainty into the decision-making process. Conservation and management involve making decisions. For example, managers have to decide how many animals can be harvested in a given year, and conservationists have to decide whether a species is critically endangered or not (Mace & Lande, 1991). However, even if scientists had gone to the trouble of calculating the sampling error of estimated parameters, few procedures were available that could account for that uncertainty in the decision-making process. Managers often failed to consider uncertainty when making decisions. There was little consideration of the possibility that the inherent uncertainty in their information could lead to incorrect advice. Only recently has a broad consensus emerged that it is important and necessary to explicitly consider uncertainty in the conservation and management of species (Mangel *et al.*, 1996; Flaaten *et al.*, 1998; Akcakaya *et al.*, 2000; Ralls & Taylor, 2000).

Recently, there have been many new developments in how to incorporate uncertainty into quantitative analyses. There has been an increasing movement away from the use of traditional statistics. Many alternative methods, both statistical and non-statistical, have been developed. Many of the alternative methods have at least one common trait – they express uncertainty about an estimated parameter as a distribution. The wider the distribution, the more uncertainty there is about the value of the parameter. It is apparent that many scientists have independently concluded that expressing uncertainty in this way is more useful than traditional statistical methods for conservation issues.

At the same time, there have also been several new developments on how conservation decisions can be made. First is that decision-making procedures have become more explicit and perhaps more formal, compared with previous procedures that were often somewhat *ad hoc*. Secondly, these decision-making procedures incorporate uncertainty into the decision process. These methods, which include procedures such as decision theory and risk analysis, have the common feature that consideration is given to a range of potential outcomes. For example, the potential fate of a population might be predicted for a range of different harvest levels. Thirdly, there is the use of management schemes based on achieving a specified level of performance, where the performance is 'tested' using simulation models.

I first discuss the issue of uncertainty and explain why traditional statistics are thought to be inadequate, and I then describe several of the recent methods that have been developed.

THE ISSUE OF UNCERTAINTY

There are several types of uncertainty that complicate the management of any population. First of all, any data we collect about a population are usually subject to sampling error (also called measurement or observation error). For example, if we estimate the abundance of a population, we get a point estimate of abundance, but it has a confidence limit associated with it which gives an indication of the precision of the estimate. Even under ideal conditions, we will be somewhat uncertain about the exact size of any population we are attempting to manage.

Bias is another problem that potentially affects much of the data we collect about populations. Bias represents a consistent tendency to over- or underestimate a parameter (e.g. Taylor & Wade, 2000). We try to minimise bias through careful sampling procedures, and we usually attempt to correct our estimates for known potential biases. However, even the most careful study can be subject to unknown biases from unforeseen circumstances, and from assumptions that are violated.

Further, there are often many attributes of a population for which we have few or no data. For example, we often have no estimate of the survival rate of a harvested population, and it is rarer still to have estimates of survival by age and sex class. Therefore, we are often forced to make assumptions about the life history of many species. This is often done by making comparisons with related taxa (see e.g. Reynolds *et al.*, Chapter 7).

The fact that the world is a random place is another source of uncertainty when one is managing wild populations. It is generally accepted that most, if not all, wild populations are affected by changes in their environment, and therefore have, for example, 'good' and 'bad' years for survival or reproduction (Lande *et al.*, Chapter 4). This means that even if we knew exactly the average survival rate of a population, it would change from year to year as conditions changed. We refer to this as environmental variance. Modellers (particularly in fisheries stock assessment) and engineers sometimes refer to this as 'process error', to distinguish it from sampling error, meaning that there is some randomness to the process that takes a population from one year to the next.

Finally, when we model a population, another type of uncertainty is the discrepancy between the model and reality, which is termed model error. Some analysis approaches attempt to investigate more than one model, but this source of potential error is often ignored.

In scientific studies, we have classically used standard statistical methods to address issues of uncertainty in our analyses. These standard techniques have included the calculation of confidence limits, and the use of hypothesis and significance tests, such as the calculation of probability (p) values. However, for a variety of reasons, many scientists have become convinced that these standard statistical methods are inadequate for dealing with complex issues of conservation and management. Consequently, there have recently been several new developments in methods for explicitly incorporating various sources of uncertainty into quantitative analyses. Some of these new methods represent novel statistical techniques, while some represent non-statistical methods that have been adapted from other fields, such as engineering.

INCORPORATING UNCERTAINTY

The traditional approach: statistical hypothesis tests and confidence limits
The traditional way in which uncertainty about data has been expressed is through statistics. Standard statistical approaches usually use two types of calculation: (1) hypothesis testing and (2) parameter estimation and confidence limits. Historically, inference has usually focused on hypothesis tests. For example, one checks whether the observed data are consistent with a predetermined null hypothesis, and one either rejects or does not reject the null hypothesis. This traditional approach to statistics is termed frequentist statistics; the name 'frequentist' is used because the statistics are defined by their long-run frequency behaviour under hypothetical repetition of similar circumstances (Bernardo & Smith, 1994). For example, one could ask about the distribution of an estimated parameter if a dataset were collected over and over again (as an aside, note that Reckhow (1990) argued that most ecological data do not fall into this paradigm – e.g., we cannot contemplate collecting ecological time series data more than once). In other words, the statistics that are used are based on long-run performance over hypothetical resampling of data. One characteristic of frequentist statistics is that all the probability statements that are made refer to the probability of observing data for a fixed value of a parameter (this contrasts with Bayesian statistics – see below).

Although these methods represent the standard statistical tools that most scientists are taught, it has been argued that these traditional methods, particularly statistical hypothesis testing, are not the best way to approach science (Howson & Urbach, 1991). It has also been argued that these traditional methods are particularly ill suited to ecology (Reckhow, 1990; Ellison, 1996) and to biological conservation and management (Ludwig, 1994; Hilborn, 1997; Johnson, 1999; Wade, 2000).

Many statisticians have expressed concern about the overemphasis on statistical significance, without enough attention being paid to the actual significance of the difference (the effect size) (Cox, 1977, 1986; McCloskey, 1995). Many biologists and ecologists have expressed the same concern (Matloff, 1991; Yoccoz, 1991; Pearce, 1992; Burnham & Anderson, 1998), and argue that there is an overemphasis on statistical significance rather than biological relevance. Because of this concern, statisticians have proposed placing emphasis on estimation and precision rather than on hypothesis testing (Guttman, 1977; Cox, 1982), and biologists have made this same proposal (Jones & Matloff, 1986; Burnham & Anderson, 1998).

Some statisticians have gone further and concluded that significance tests have little value in science (Guttman, 1985; Jones & Matloff, 1986; Wang, 1993), and this same message has been made by biologists and resource managers (Quinn & Dunham, 1983; McBride *et al.*, 1993; Hilborn, 1997). Some of the main criticisms are that p values may have no relationship with the probability that a null hypothesis is true, and that any null hypothesis can be rejected at any significance level if a large enough sample size is collected (Berger & Berry, 1988; Johnson, 1999). Criticism has also been made that a system that allows only two possible outcomes (reject or not reject) is a poor way to summarise what is known, and it is proposed that decision theory (see below) is a more appropriate tool for science, rather than significance tests (Hilborn, 1997; Howson & Urbach, 1991).

Novel methods for incorporating uncertainty

The dissatisfaction with the standard frequentist approach to statistics, at least by some scientists, can be seen in the increasing use of alternative approaches. Some of these approaches are non-traditional schools of statistical inference, while others are not statistical in nature. All of these approaches purposefully discard the use of traditional hypothesis testing. Most of these methods have the common theme that uncertainty is summarised in the form of a distribution, rather than represented by standard errors and confidence limits. Some of these methods allow incorporating uncertainty from alternative sources, such as specifying likely ranges for environmental variance or unknown potential biases. Finally, some of these approaches also allow for model uncertainty to be incorporated into the results. I briefly describe these alternative methods here.

Akaike's information criterion

As one important example, an increasing number of biologists now use Akaike's information criterion (AIC) for model selection rather than traditional likelihood ratio tests, and a recent book on the subject details the advantages of this approach over the standard hypothesis testing framework (Burnham & Anderson, 1998). Although limited only to the issue of model selection, this development is symbolic of the desire of many scientists for something other than hypothesis testing.

AIC was originally developed from information theory, but it can be viewed as an extension of likelihood theory with a term that penalises the addition of more parameters (Burnham & Anderson, 1998). In brief, a typical problem in model selection would be how many terms (parameters) to include in a multiple regression model. The traditional approach would be to use a stepwise procedure, where each parameter is checked individually to see whether it provides a significantly better fit to the data. In contrast, model selection using AIC is done simultaneously across all models, and the model (or models) with the smallest AIC value is considered the model that the data best support. Advantages over the traditional hypothesis-testing framework are that models no longer have to be nested (i.e. each model does not have to be a sub-model of the most complex model), there is no longer an order in which models are tested (which can influence the final model selection in traditional methods), and model uncertainty is explicitly described (Burnham & Anderson, 1998). Additionally, model uncertainty can be explicitly incorporated into the results by averaging the results across the set of models that provide an adequate fit to the data.

As an example, Caswell *et al.* (1999) used AIC to compare different survival models for North Atlantic right whales *Eubalaena glacialis*, in a mark–recapture analysis using photo identification data. The conservation status of this population is a concern because it is thought to number no more than 300 animals and it experiences human-caused mortality from entanglement in fishing gear and collisions with ships (Knowlton & Kraus, 2000). Caswell *et al.* (1999) found that the best fitting model was a decline in survival over the years of the study (1979–86). Because the suite of models they compared was not nested, they would not have been able to carry out a similar analysis using traditional significance testing procedures. Caswell *et al.* (1999) were able to conclude that the decline in annual survival over the study period had probably contributed to a shift from a stable or increasing population to a declining population, an important finding for this small and highly endangered population.

Probability distributions (Bayesian statistics)

In recent years there has been a dramatic increase in the use of probability theory and Bayesian statistics (Malakov, 1999). Bayesian statistics can be used to calculate a probability distribution for any quantity of interest, such as a parameter of a model. This probability distribution summarises what is known about the parameter, given the data and any prior information. A probability distribution gives a simple visual description of what values of the parameter are most likely. Further, the probability distribution can be used to make statements about biologically relevant results (e.g. 'there is a probability of 0.73 that the population is declining at a rate greater than 10% per year').

For these reasons, the use of probability distributions has been advocated in ecology (Reckhow, 1990; Ellison, 1996; Hilborn & Mangel, 1997), fisheries biology (Hilborn & Walters, 1992; Hilborn, 1997; Punt & Hilborn, 1997), and conservation biology (Taylor *et al.*, 1996; Ludwig, 1998; Wade, 2000). Wade (2000) summarises the advantages of using probability distributions in this way:

1 Probability distributions are simple to understand and automatically include the uncertainty of the estimate.
2 Probability statements better represent the state of a population than *p* values generated from hypothesis tests.
3 The biological relevance of results is immediately apparent (in contrast to significance tests, where biological relevance is often ignored).
4 Decision theory can be applied to conservation and management to allow for consideration of the relative consequences of making incorrect decisions.
5 Uncertainty from important but poorly known parameters can be explicitly included in the results.
6 Uncertainty in model choice can be formally incorporated into analysis results by combining the results from different plausible models by weighting them by their probability.
7 Uncertainty can be reduced by incorporating additional information in a formal and transparent way, including combining various types of data, updating an analysis after the collection of additional data, or subjectively using information from similar populations or species.

The attractions of probability distributions can be seen in their increasing use in many fields of applied biology. Many fisheries assessments now use probability distributions and Bayesian statistics (e.g. Hilborn & Walters, 1992; Thompson, 1992; McAllister *et al.*, 1994; Walters & Ludwig, 1994; McAllister & Ianelli, 1997; Punt & Hilborn, 1997). Similarly, Bayesian methods are increasingly being used in the assessment of whale populations (e.g. Givens *et al.*, 1993, 1995; Raftery *et al.*, 1995; Punt &

Butterworth, 1997, 1999; Wade, 2001). There are many other examples of the use of Bayesian methods in ecology (Gazey & Staley, 1986; Reckhow, 1990; Shaughnessy et al., 1995; Ellison, 1996; Pascual & Kareiva, 1996; Omlin & Reichert, 1999). Within conservation biology, a few examples exist of Bayesian population viability analyses (Ludwig, 1996; Taylor et al., 1996, 2002; Wade, 2002). Hilborn & Liermann (1998) advocated the use of Bayesian methods and meta-analysis of historical datasets to improve estimation of parameters in fisheries biology. See Box 6.1 for a brief description of Bayesian statistics.

A simple example of the use of Bayesian methods can be seen in the most recent Comprehensive Assessment of the eastern stock of grey whale *Eschrichtius robustus* calculated by the International Whaling Commission (IWC, 1998). A Bayesian analysis was performed by fitting an age-structured population model to abundance estimates spanning 30 years (Wade, 2001). Previously, a harvest limit quantity was identified that would meet aboriginal subsistence harvest objectives agreed to by the IWC (Wade & Givens, 1997). This quantity, called Q_o, was derived from the model parameters. Therefore, the Bayesian analysis was used to calculate a probability distribution for Q_o (Wade, 2001). The Scientific Committee of the IWC recommended basing management advice on the lower fifth percentile of this distribution, which was 482 whales (IWC, 1998, pp. 241–244). This quantity has the interpretation that there is only a 0.05 probability that the harvest limit should actually be less than this amount in order to meet the management goals. Stated another way, this number provides a 0.95 probability that the management goals will be met. The requested number of takes was less than this number, so the Management Commission of the IWC approved the request.

Using a value based on a lower tail of the posterior distribution is similar to using a lower confidence limit from a traditional analysis. However, at least two points distinguish the Bayesian analysis from a traditional analysis using confidence limits. First, a traditional lower confidence limit cannot be used to make a statement about how likely it is that the management goals will be met (remember that a traditional confidence limit has the interpretation that if one collected one's data over and over, 95% of such calculated intervals will contain the true value, but it says nothing about the probability of the true value being in the one interval that was actually calculated). Secondly, the Bayesian analysis incorporated uncertainty from alternative sources in a way that could not be accomplished using traditional methods. For example, few data are available that describe the shape of the density-dependent response for any marine mammal population

Box 6.1 Bayesian statistics

The formula used to calculate a probability distribution for the value of a parameter was first solved by Bayes (1763). Statistical inference based on Bayes' theorem has come to be called Bayesian statistics, and credit is given to Jeffreys (1939) for founding the modern school of Bayesian statistical inference.

In Bayesian statistics, all inference is based on calculating a probability distribution for a parameter of interest. Specifically, Bayesian statistics provides the method for calculating the probability of a specific value of a parameter (θ) given the data (x), written as $p(\theta \mid x)$ (i.e. the probability of the parameter value θ given the data x). Bayes' theorem is a conditional probability statement that proves that $p(\theta \mid x)$ is proportional to the sampling distribution for the data, $p(x \mid \theta)$ (i.e., the probability of observing the data x given parameter value θ), multiplied by an independent probability distribution for the parameter, $p(\theta)$ (independent, in this case, of the specific data x). Therefore, Bayes' theorem can be written as

$$p(\theta \mid x) = p(x \mid \theta) \times p(\theta) \times c, \tag{6.1}$$

where c is a constant that normalises the distribution to a probability density. In this relationship, Bayesians have named $p(\theta)$ the *prior* probability for θ, and $p(\theta \mid x)$ the *posterior* probability for θ (in the sense that it summarises what is known about θ prior and posterior to the examination of the data x). In this context, the sampling distribution for the data, $p(x \mid \theta)$, is often referred to as the *likelihood function*. Therefore, Bayes' theorem can be represented verbally as

Posterior probability = likelihood function $\times$ prior probability
$\times$ normalising constant.

To calculate the normalising constant c, one needs to calculate the entire distribution of $p(x \mid \theta) \times p(\theta)$, so one automatically calculates the entire distribution for $p(\theta \mid x)$ as well. Therefore, one usually speaks in terms of the posterior and prior distributions. All statistical inference is then based on the posterior probability distribution. The mean of the posterior distribution can serve as a point estimate for the parameter. Uncertainty in the point estimate is directly expressed by the width of the posterior distribution, and can be summarised either as percentiles of the posterior distribution or as what is termed the highest posterior density interval (the Bayesian analogue to a confidence interval).

Additionally, probability statements can be made about the value of the parameter (e.g. 'the probability that the value of θ is greater than 0.0 is 0.879).

To calculate the posterior distribution, one has to integrate the product of the prior distribution and the likelihood function. In some simple cases, the integral can be calculated directly (in these cases it is said to have an analytical or 'closed-form' solution). If no analytical solution is available, the integration can be done using numerical methods.

As a simple example, suppose 30 (n) animals are randomly tagged and followed for one year. At the end of the year, 22 (y) remain alive. A binomial distribution can be used to estimate the annual survival rate of the population, using either traditional or Bayesian methods. For a Bayesian analysis, a prior distribution that is uniform from 0.0 to 1.0 can be chosen. This expresses the belief that (before data are collected) any value between 0.0 and 1.0 is equally as likely as any other. Most Bayesian textbooks (e.g. Press, 1989; Gelman et al., 1995) provide the analytical solution for a simple binomial analysis; with a uniform prior, the posterior is a beta distribution with parameters $y+1$ and $n-y+1$ (Figure 6.1). The mean of the posterior distribution is 0.719. In this example, the mode of the posterior is the same as the standard maximum likelihood estimate, 0.733 ($=y/n$). There is a 0.95 probability that the survival rate is between 0.562 and 0.864. Any other probability statement of interest can be made. For example, there is a probability of 0.151 that the survival rate is greater than 0.8.

(Ragen, 1995), but information from a variety of sources has been used to suggest a likely range for the response (Taylor & DeMaster, 1993). This range was incorporated into the analysis as a prior distribution for the parameter that determines the density-dependent response in the model (Wade, 2001). Because the available data for grey whales do not allow this parameter to be estimated, in a traditional analysis this parameter would have to be fixed at a single value, which would ignore the substantial uncertainty in the value of this parameter.

I will use a simple population trend analysis to provide a further illustration of the use of probability distributions and Bayesian methods in the conservation of exploited species. Beluga whales *Delphinapterus leucas* are harvested by native hunters throughout their range in the Arctic and Sub-Arctic (Reeves, 1990). An isolated population of beluga is found in

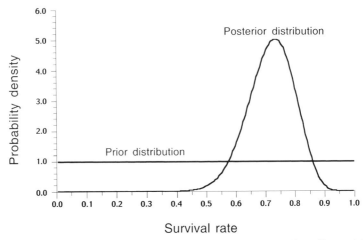

Figure 6.1. Example of the results of a Bayesian analysis (Box 6.1) of binomial survival data consisting of 30 tagged animals (trials) with 22 surviving one year (successes). A uniform prior probability distribution from 0.0 to 1.0 was selected, which expresses the belief that any survival rate is equally likely prior to examining the data. The posterior distribution represents the probability distribution for the survival rate after updating the prior distribution with the data.

Cook Inlet, Alaska (O'Corry-Crowe *et al.*, 1997), where they have been legally harvested by native Alaskans. The mean take from 1995 to 1997 was 87 whales per year (Hill & DeMaster, 1999). An immediate conservation issue is whether the harvest may have been large enough to cause a substantial decline in the population. Aerial surveys to estimate the abundance of this population have been conducted since 1994 using constant methods. These surveys produced counts of 281, 324, 307, 264, 193, 217 and 184 for the years 1994 to 2000, respectively (Rugh *et al*, 2001; Rugh, personal communication, National Marine Mammal Laboratory, National Marine Fisheries Service, 7600 Sand Point Way NE, Seattle, WA). As abundance estimates these counts are biased low for various reasons, primarily because not all animals are at the surface simultaneously, but the counts can serve as an index of abundance. Correction factors are used to scale these counts to absolute abundance estimates, with the most recent estimate for 1998 being 347, with a coefficient of variation of 0.29 (Hobbs *et al.*, 2001). Bayesian methods can be used to estimate a probability distribution for the abundance of the population in 1998 (Figure 6.2a). For simplicity here I have assumed normal sampling error, although often abundance estimates are assumed to have log-normal error structure (Buckland *et al.*, 1993).

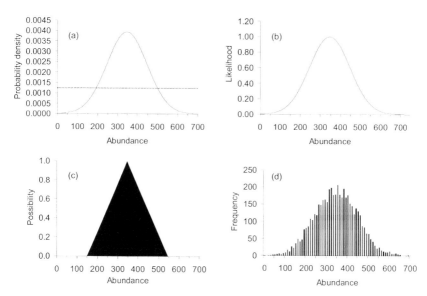

Figure 6.2. Examples of methods for expressing uncertainty in an abundance estimate as a distribution, or similar visual figure. (a) A Bayesian posterior probability distribution, which expresses the probability of each parameter value given the data and the prior distribution (straight line); (b) likelihood curve, which expresses the relative likelihood of each value of the parameter given the data; (c) a fuzzy number, which is a collection of nested sets expressing a possibility value for each set, where possibility is expressed as a number between 0.0 and 1.0, with a value of 1.0 used for the abundance number with the greatest possibility; (d) bootstrap frequency distribution, reinterpreted as a probability distribution for the parameter.

Trends in abundance can be estimated by the slope of a simple linear regression on the natural logarithm of abundance or an index of abundance (Eberhardt & Simmons, 1992). The standard hypothesis test in traditional statistics is a test of whether the slope is significantly different from a null hypothesis of zero (a stable population). Using this standard test with the index data, one could not conclude that the population was declining until the year 2000, as no significant difference was found until all seven years of data had been collected (Table 6.1).

When analysed using Bayesian methods, the same data led to different types of statement. By 1998 (after five years), there was an estimated probability of 0.926 that the population was declining, and a probability of 0.788 that the population was declining by 5% per year or more (Table 6.2). This latter probability went up to 0.831 and 0.928 with the addition of the 1999 and 2000 counts, respectively.

Table 6.1. Traditional population trend analysis of the Cook Inlet population of beluga whale, based on index count data from annual aerial surveys

Number of years	Years	Rate (r)	L95	U95	p value	Significance
4	1994–97	−0.024	−0.226	0.178	0.658	NS
5	1994–98	−0.096	−0.253	0.062	0.148	NS
6	1994–99	−0.086	−0.177	0.006	0.060	NS
7	1994–00	−0.091	−0.151	−0.030	0.012	*

Number of years is the sample size, Years identifies the range of years included in the analysis, Rate (r) is the estimated rate of change of the population per year as a fraction of the population size, L95 and U95 are the lower and upper confidence limits of r, respectively, the p value is for a test of significance from a rate of 0.0 (a stable population), NS represents a result that is not significant at the 0.05 level, and * represents a result that is significant at the 0.05 level.

Table 6.2. Bayesian population trend analysis of the Cook Inlet population of beluga whale, using the same data used in Table 6.1

Number of years	Years	$p(r < -0.05)$	$p(-0.05 < r < 0.0)$	$p(0.0 < r)$
4	1994–97	0.316	0.353	0.329
5	1994–98	0.788	0.138	0.074
6	1994–99	0.831	0.140	0.030
7	1994–00	0.928	0.066	0.006

The results are summarised as the probability of three separate hypotheses: (1) $p(r < -0.05)$, the probability the population is declining at a rate greater than 5% per year; (2) $p(-0.05 < r < 0.0)$, the probability the population is declining at a rate between 0 and 5% per year; (3) $p(0.0 < r)$, the probability the population is increasing.

The Bayes factor is used for Bayesian hypothesis comparison, in which one examines the probability of competing hypotheses. Briefly, if two hypotheses (H_1 and H_2) are considered to have equal prior probability, the Bayes factor is the ratio of the posterior probability of H_1 given the data to the posterior probability of H_2 given the data (Kass & Raftery, 1995). This quantity is also called the posterior odds ratio, and has this simple interpretation – a Bayes factor of 10 means that H_1 is 10 times more probable than H_2. Kass & Raftery (1995), adapting from Jeffreys (1961), have given recommended verbal interpretations of various values of the Bayes factor (Table 6.3).

Using this approach, I calculated Bayes factors (B) for three comparisons of hypotheses (Table 6.4). In 1998, after five years of counts, one could conclude that there was strong evidence that the Cook Inlet beluga popula-

Table 6.3. Interpretation of values of the Bayes factor, as recommended by Kass & Raftery (1995). $H1$ is hypothesis 1; $H2$ is hypothesis 2

Bayes factor	Interpretation
1 to 3	Not worth more than a bare mention
3 to 12	Positive evidence for $H1$ versus $H2$
12 to 150	Strong evidence for $H1$ versus $H2$
> 150	Decisive evidence for $H1$ versus $H2$

Table 6.4. Bayes' factor analysis of the population trend of Cook Inlet beluga whales

Number of years	Years	$r<0.0$ vs. $r>0.0$	$r<-0.05$ vs. $r>-0.05$	$r<-0.05$ vs. $r>0.0$	Conclusion
4	1994–97	2.0	2.2	1.0	Not worth more than a bare mention
5	1994–98	30.9	4.6	26.3	Strong evidence the population is declining, positive evidence the decline is >-0.05
6	1994–99	32.4	4.9	27.7	Strong evidence the population is declining, positive evidence the decline is >-0.05
7	1994–00	165.6	12.9	154.7	Decisive evidence the population is declining, strong evidence the decline is >-0.05

Bayes factors were calculated for three comparisons of hypotheses: (1) $r<0.0$ vs. $r>0.0$, $H1$ is the population is declining, $H2$ is the population is increasing; (2) $r<-0.05$ vs. $r>-0.05$, $H1$ is the population is declining at more than 5% per year, $H2$ is the population is increasing or declining at a rate less than 5%; (3) $r<-0.05$ vs. >0.0, $H1$ is the population is declining at more than 5% per year; $H2$ is the population is increasing.

tion was declining ($B=30.9$) and there was positive evidence that the decline was substantial (> 5% year) ($B=4.9$). Note that this means it was 30 times more probable that the population was declining than that it was stable or increasing. Furthermore, the data gave strong evidence that the population was substantially declining versus the possibility that the population was stable or increasing ($B=26.3$). After seven years of data, the evidence for a decline became decisive ($B=165.6$).

Whereas it took seven years of data to get a significant decline at the 0.05 level, the Bayesian analysis gave an indication the population was declining after only five years. The statement 'the data provided strong evidence that the population was declining and positive evidence the decline was substantial' is a more informative statement than 'no significant decline was found ($p = 0.148$)'. In particular, the Bayesian analysis was used to address the question of biological relevance, by being able to give a probability statement about the magnitude of the decline. While two years may not seem like a large difference, in percentage terms it means that the Bayesian analysis gave an indication the population was declining in 29% less time. Moreover, even a two-year delay in management action could substantially increase the risk to a small population. As a footnote, a temporary moratorium on the harvest was implemented in May 1999.

Likelihood inference

Likelihood inference is an alternative school of statistics that has recently developed. Although likelihood methods are a part of frequentist statistics, likelihood inference is something more than that – it is a new statistical philosophy based on Fisher's likelihood principle (Edwards, 1992; Royall, 1997), which states that statistical inference should be conditioned upon the observed data, and nothing else. Likelihood inference abandons the use of significance tests, which have been severely criticised by Edwards (1992) and Royall (1997), and instead uses the relative measure of the likelihood of the data, given values of the parameters. The likelihood curve provides a distribution that describes the relative likelihood of one parameter value versus others. For comparing hypotheses, one speaks of the 'support' the data give to one hypothesis versus another, where support is defined as the logarithm of the ratio of the likelihoods (Edwards, 1992).

Likelihood inference has many similarities with Bayesian inference, except one speaks in terms of relative likelihood rather than in terms of probability. On one hand, its advocates point out that likelihood inference has the advantage that prior distributions are not necessary (Royall, 1997), whereas the specification of prior distributions can sometimes be a difficulty in Bayesian statistics. On the other hand, likelihood inference does not have the advantage of being able to provide probability distributions, which in Bayesian methods leads to simple probability statements and the potential to use decision theory. Edwards (1992) acknowledged that critics have objected that the measure of support has 'no meaning' (no probability interpretation), but he does not consider this a difficulty. There are some additional technical problems in likelihood inference, such as the lack of a theoretical basis for the elimination of nuisance parameters (Royall, 1997). A discussion of likelihood inference, including these technical issues, can be found in Bernardo & Smith (1994).

Although an interesting theoretical development in statistics, there are few examples of pure likelihood inference being used in the literature. Schweder (1998) provided an example of a form of likelihood inference in an assessment of minke whales *Balaenoptera acutorostrata*. His focus was on incorporating indirect information into likelihood methods by treating 'prior' information as data. Schweder (1998) calculated point estimates and confidence limits, but did not continue on to use the 'method of support', as advocated by Edwards (1992). Wade (1999) used likelihood inference to examine the depletion level of spotted dolphins *Stenella attenuata* in the eastern tropical Pacific due to by-catch in the tuna fishery, and compared likelihood inference with traditional and Bayesian analyses of the same data. The data indicated that the hypothesis that the population was depleted had a likelihood twice as large as the hypothesis that the population was not depleted (Wade, 1999).

As a simple example of these methods, I have calculated the likelihood curve for the abundance of Cook Inlet beluga whales in 1998 (Figure 6.2), using a normal distribution (likelihood values only have relative meaning, so the curve has been arbitrarily scaled so that the largest value equals 1.0). The curve visually describes the relative likelihood of different abundance levels, given the data. As mentioned above, the 'support' of the data for a particular value is calculated by taking the logarithm of the ratio of the maximum likelihood value (the peak or mode of the likelihood curve) to the likelihood value at any other abundance level. In likelihood inference, one can calculate a 2-support interval by finding the locations in the tails of the distribution where the support equals 2. In this example, the maximum likelihood estimate is 347, and the 2-support interval is from 145 to 550. This interval has the interpretation that it defines a range of values for the abundance of the population that have the greatest relative likelihood given the data (i.e. the data 'support' that range of values). Note that this interval therefore has a different interpretation than the usual frequentist confidence interval, which expresses how often the interval will contain the true value if the data were resampled repeatedly.

Fuzzy numbers and logic

Another recent development has been the use of 'fuzzy' numbers and logic to express uncertainty. A fuzzy number is actually a series of nested sets that describe a range of values, along with a 'possibility' level for each value. For example, the abundance of a population can be expressed as a triangular fuzzy number where the x-axis is population size, the y-axis is the 'possibility' level, the peak of the triangle represents the point estimate of abundance, and the base of the triangle represents something analogous to a confidence limit (Figure 6.2c; Akçakaya *et al.*, 2000). Thus a fuzzy number is similar to a distribution and it expresses the degree of uncertainty about the quantity. It differs from a probability distribution in that the 'distribution' is really stacks of intervals that are nested such that an interval is always contained within the interval below it.

Fuzzy logic is just a set of mathematical rules for combining and performing logical operations on fuzzy numbers. Put most simply, fuzzy numbers can be viewed as a way of expressing uncertainty in the form of a distribution (although it is technically not a distribution). Similarly, fuzzy logic can be viewed as a way to combine fuzzy numbers and convert them into a 'distribution' for some quantity of interest, such as the certainty with which a population should be considered endangered.

Fuzzy logic evolved from set theory. It is not a statistical approach and it does not use probability theory (Laviolette *et al.*, 1995). Fuzzy set theory is an extension of regular ('crisp') set theory, the main difference being that objects can have partial membership in several sets at one time, rather than being unambiguously in a single set. These fuzzy sets can be used to describe uncertainty about the state of nature. Fuzzy logic is based on rules of the form 'if . . . then' that convert the inputs into new fuzzy sets that represent outputs. The rules define a system that relates a full range of inputs to a full range of outputs. These rules can be viewed as an approximation to a mathematical function (Kosko & Isaka, 1993; Zadeh, 1994).

Fuzzy logic has seen success in engineering applications such as the control of household appliances (Kosko & Isaka, 1993; Zadeh, 1994). It may be a useful approach for ecological management, where 'control' (management) of a system is desired. It appears to share some similarities with Bayesian methods in that distributions can be used to describe the uncertainty of parameters. In fact, Laviolette *et al.* (1995) argued that any situation where fuzzy logic is applied to a data analysis problem could also be handled through the use of Bayesian statistics. They suggested that lack of instruction in probability theory has led to engineers turning to the tool of fuzzy logic. Some statisticians have been harsh in their criticism of the use of fuzzy logic as a replacement for statistical inference, going so far as to term it 'embarrassingly naïve' (Efron, 1990, p. 450).

If Laviolette *et al.* (1995) are correct in their assertion that any fuzzy logic method could be equally implemented using probability theory, it is an interesting question as to what is gained by using fuzzy methods. The philosophical foundations of probability theory, along with the idea of remaining within the arena of statistical inference, are arguments for using probability theory rather than fuzzy methods. However, if fuzzy methods give one approximately the same answer as probability theory, there might be no particular reason to use it, but on the other hand there may be no particular reason not to use it, except on theoretical purist grounds. It is not clear whether there is any theoretical basis for demonstrating a convergence between fuzzy logic and probability theory, and there are few if any actual demonstrations that both techniques lead to the same results. From a pragmatic point of view, some people might find fuzzy methods easier to understand and implement. As someone who already has experience with Bayesian methods, my personal view is that the reverse is true, but it is unclear which method might be more approachable to someone without previous experience in either.

As a simple example, I used fuzzy methods to describe the abundance of Cook Inlet belugas, using a triangular fuzzy number (Figure 6.2c). Akçakaya *et al.* (2000, p. 1004) describe a triangular fuzzy number in this way: 'at each possibility level, there is an interval defined by the left and right sides of the fuzzy number. This level inversely measures the surety that the parameter is within the interval at that level: as the scale on the *y*-axis increases, the surety decreases that the parameter is within the corresponding interval.' Because fuzzy numbers are not actually distributions and are not based on statistical methods, there is no single accepted method for turning survey data into a fuzzy number for the abundance of a population. The base of the triangle can be determined from a statistical confidence interval, or it can be based on other information, such as the opinion of a group of experts (Akçakaya *et al.*, 2000). I used the 95% confidence interval to establish the base of the triangle. However, if fuzzy set membership is based on statistical estimates, it has been argued that it would be more sensible to use probabilities (Bayesian methods) throughout rather than converting to the architecture of fuzzy logic (Regan & Colyvan, 2000), but this point is disputed by Todd (2000).

Akçakaya *et al.* (2000) propose using fuzzy logic to incorporate uncertainty into IUCN (World Conservation Union) classifications. The IUCN system uses five criteria to evaluate the status of a population (population decline, restricted distribution and decline, small population size and decline, very small population size, and probability of extinction) (Mace & Lande, 1991). Each criterion has specific thresholds that identify a population as being in one of four risk categories: critically endangered, endangered, vulnerable, or low risk. In practice, a taxon has usually been assigned to the highest risk category that it qualifies for under any criterion. Akçakaya *et al.*'s (2000) proposed system uses fuzzy methods to accomplish two things. First, uncertainty is incorporated into the information by expressing numbers as fuzzy numbers (i.e. rather than a single number for abundance, a fuzzy number is used). Secondly, the information is combined across all five criteria to come up with a single evaluation of risk that integrates information from all five criteria. For example, once the information needed for the five criteria has been expressed as fuzzy numbers, one can then calculate the 'possibility' that a taxon is critically endangered under each criterion. Then these five calculations are combined into a single possibility value that the taxon is critically endangered. Similar calculations are done to give possibility values for being in the other risk categories. Finally, these possibility values are used to assign a taxon to a single risk category, in combination with specific rules that incorporate attitudes towards tolerance for risk and dispute.

Whether the procedure of Akçakaya et al. (2000) is the best approach to categorising exploited species as endangered or not remains to be seen. However, it is a step in the right direction compared with previous schemes that ignore uncertainty. Explicitly describing the uncertainty in information about a population, such as its abundance and trend, and incorporating that uncertainty into the decision-making process is the way forward, regardless of the specific technique used. As another example, Mackinson et al. (1999) have proposed using fuzzy methods to incorporate uncertainty into fisheries stock assessments and management.

Bootstrap distributions (reinterpreted)

The statistical procedure termed the bootstrap was originally developed as a non-parametric technique in frequentist statistics for estimating a sampling distribution, and thus standard errors and confidence limits (Efron & Gong, 1983; Efron & Tibshirani, 1993). It is based on resampling with replacement from one's data and recalculating a statistic of interest. This creates a distribution for the statistic, which is then used to estimate the standard error and confidence limits for the statistic.

The use of the bootstrap procedure has been extended by some users who have reinterpreted the bootstrap distribution as a probability distribution. This usage is most common in simulations where populations are repeatedly projected by randomly sampling parameter values from distributions for the parameter created by resampling the data in a bootstrap (e.g. Mohn, 1993; Annala et al., 1999). The results of the population projections are sometimes considered simultaneously to provide traditional confidence limits (a legitimate interpretation – see White, 2000) as well as probability (frequency) distributions (an illegitimate interpretation) that forecast the likely future state of the population. For example, Rosenberg &

Restrepo (1993) recommended using the bootstrap to create 'probability profiles' (their term) for model parameters, which are then used in a model projection to calculate the probability of various outcomes given a specified harvest level. This is a use of the bootstrap that goes beyond its original purpose as developed by Efron & Gong (1983).

Mohn (1993) provided a typical example. The bootstrap was used to calculate distributions for the standing stock, fishing mortality, and recruitment of a stock of cod in the Canadian Atlantic, using available data. These bootstrap distributions were then used as inputs into a risk analysis (see below), in combination with subjectively determined distributions for other parameters, including natural mortality and weight at age. Using these distributions as a starting point, the risk analysis projected the stock into the future under different harvest levels, and produced as output a comparison of the resulting total harvest of fish and standing biomass of fish. The outputs of the risk analysis were the frequency distributions for the parameters of interest that occur from the repeated simulation and projection. These frequency distributions are considered probability distributions for the future state of the stock (a Bayesian interpretation), and are also presented as approximate confidence regions (a traditional frequentist interpretation). Similar examples can be found in recent fisheries assessment work in New Zealand (Annala *et al.*, 1999), where bootstrap distributions are used to forecast the probability that the population achieves specified goals under various harvest levels.

This extension of the bootstrap for simulation and projection leads to difficult issues of statistical meaning and interpretation. First, it is well documented in the literature that standard frequentist distributions have no interpretation as a probability distribution for a parameter (DeGroot, 1973; Berger & Berry, 1988; Efron, 1993; Bernardo & Smith, 1994). Only Bayesian methods can provide a probability distribution for a parameter based on statistical inference. Therefore, the only way a bootstrap distribution (or other frequentist sampling distribution) can be reinterpreted as a probability distribution would be to consider it as an approximation to a Bayesian posterior distribution. DeGroot (1973) and Efron (1993) gave some simple examples of when this approximation may be good and when it may not. Unfortunately, bootstrap distributions used in this way are rarely, if ever, described as approximations to Bayesian methods, and therefore no consideration is given to how good the approximations might be.

Secondly, traditional frequentist methods do not provide a single method for combining the sampling uncertainty of data (as represented by the bootstrap) with the uncertainty of unknown parameters for which no data are available (note that this is handled through the use of prior distributions in Bayesian statistics). As this is a common circumstance in some applied problems, Restrepo *et al.* (1992) proposed a modification of the bootstrap that combines the resampling of data with random sampling of parameter values from subjectively determined probability distributions (analogous to the Bayesian prior distribution). They applied their method in a fisheries assessment problem to incorporate uncertainty in the natural mortality rate, a parameter that, when unknown, is often fixed at a single value (and uncertainty in its value is ignored). Restrepo *et al.* (1992) were clearly correct to be concerned about the traditional methods, which ignored uncertainty in certain parameters. However, it has been shown that this *ad hoc* frequentist approach generally performs no better than Bayesian methods, and sometimes much worse (Poole *et al.*, 1999). Mohn (1993) and Rosenberg & Restrepo (1993) also took this approach of mixing subjectively determined probability distributions for some parameters with frequency distributions for other parameters derived from bootstrapping the data. Although there is no theoretical justification for such an approach, it may be that incorporating uncertainty in this way is better than ignoring it entirely. These philosophical difficulties are real, but if the bootstrap is a method that will actually be used, these difficulties can perhaps be balanced against the desirable goal of explicitly addressing uncertainty.

As a simple example, I calculated a frequency distribution for the abundance of beluga whales in Cook Inlet, based on the estimate of 347. Again assuming a normal distribution, I performed a parametric bootstrap by randomly sampling 5000 values from a normal distribution with mean 347 and coefficient of variation of 0.29. These 5000 values were then tabulated as a frequency histogram (Figure 6.2d). In standard bootstrap methods, the variance of these 5000 values would be used to estimate the variance of the point estimate, and to calculate confidence intervals. Instead, here the distribution of bootstrap values is reinterpreted as a distribution that expresses the probability of different values of the parameter. This bootstrap distribution is sometimes used as the starting point for a population simulation to estimate the probability of extinction. For example, York *et al.* (1996) used what was essentially a parametric bootstrap distribution as the starting point for population projections to estimate the probability of extinction of Steller sea lions *Eumetopias jubata*.

INCORPORATING UNCERTAINTY INTO CONSERVATION DECISIONS

Along with the novel methods for incorporating uncertainty into analyses, there have also been several new developments on how to incorporate uncertainty into the decision-making process. Several of these methods build on the new analysis techniques discussed above. I first discuss formal decision-making procedures such as risk analysis and decision theory. I then describe procedures based on testing the performance of management systems using simulations. Most of these new methods share at least two qualities. First, uncertainty is explicitly incorporated into the decision-making process and a range of possible outcomes is considered. Secondly, the decision-making process is more formal, and often includes a set of rules or procedures for making decisions that can be agreed to before the data are analysed.

Formal procedures for making decisions

By a formal procedure, I mean there is a direct link between the analysis results and the management decision, and the decision is designed to accomplish a specific objective. Traditionally, procedures were often more informal in areas such as fisheries management. Scientists would use available data to perform a stock assessment to estimate quantities such as the current recruitment rate or the maximum sustainable yield of a population. Managers would consider the stock assessment results and then subjectively establish a quota. The managers may or may not have used the analysis results as the basis for setting the quota. Without agreed-upon rules, there would be no way of predicting what quota might be set for a given analysis result.

In contrast, in a formal procedure the decision would be more directly linked to the analysis results, and might even be predetermined for a given result. Moreover, the decision would be based on achieving a specified objective.

Risk assessment

In fisheries biology the term 'risk assessment' (or evaluation) has usually meant a prediction of future stock sizes under different fishing quotas or management schemes (e.g. Smith *et al.*, 1993; Reynolds & Mace, 1999). Sometimes this approach is formalised to a degree where scientists provide the prediction of future outcomes, and give this information to managers, who then choose a fishing quota from the different options presented (Hilborn *et al.*, 1993). The key difference between this and population assessment is the prediction of future performance under different options, whereas population assessment is simply a description of the current state of the population. An important point is that a range of expected outcomes is produced for each harvest level that is examined – this range of expected outcomes is the result of incorporating various types of uncertainty into the analysis. The risks and benefits of each possible harvest level are summarised. Hilborn *et al.* (1993) stressed that no attempt is made to produce a 'best' estimate of the stock condition, and the scientists make no recommendation about catch levels. The results are then considered by managers who can make a decision with a full understanding of the risks and benefits of the chosen harvest level.

Decision theory

Decision theory provides an established method for using scientific data to make decisions (Berger, 1985). A decision analysis can be viewed as an extension of risk assessment, as presented above. The management and conservation of populations involves making decisions, and therefore it is sensible to use decision theory. For example, categorising an endangered species is one form of decision, as is setting a quota on harvest.

Because decision analysis involves calculating the probability of events happening, it necessarily relies on Bayesian statistics (Bernardo & Smith, 1994). It starts by calculating the probability of the state of the world (or future states of the world) based on available data, as in risk assessment. Decision analysis adds an additional component, which is a loss function (or its reciprocal, a utility function). A loss function is a distribution that describes the consequence (the 'loss') for each possible outcome. A separate loss function is created for each possible decision, and the loss function gives a relative measure of the negative consequence of that decision for all possible true states of nature.

It is probably easiest to understand a loss function through an example. Suppose one performs a simple analysis of population trend in which two possible conclusions (decisions) can be reached: the population is declining or it is not. Now, if one concludes that the population is declining when it really is, then the correct decision has been made and one has suffered no loss. However, if the population is really not declining, then an incorrect decision has been made, and one has suffered a loss. A loss value of 1.0 could be assigned to this outcome. The scale of the loss function is not important – only the relative value of loss for one decision versus another is important. For example, if there are three possible outcomes, a loss func-

Table 6.5. Loss functions for three possible conclusions and three possible actual rates of population change

Decisions	Actual rate of population change		
	$r < -0.05$	$-0.05 < r < 0.00$	$r > 0.00$
Conclude population is declining rapidly	0	1	2
Conclude population is declining slowly	1	0	1
Conclude population is not declining	2	1	0

tion of 0, 1 and 2 for the three outcomes would be equivalent to loss functions of 1, 2 and 3 or 0, 5 and 10. All of these loss functions contain the same information – that the third outcome is twice as bad as the second outcome.

To perform the decision analysis, the probability distributions are combined with the loss functions to calculate the expected loss for each decision. A conclusion is then reached by choosing the decision that has the smallest expected loss. Consequently, this differs from risk assessment by having explicit functions that quantitatively describe the consequences of various outcomes. Once these loss functions are specified, the procedure will automatically recommend a decision based on the available data.

To illustrate a decision analysis, I return to the population trend analysis for Cook Inlet beluga whales. Wade (2000) describes a hypothetical decision analysis for population trend data, and identical methods are used here. Rather than simply deciding on whether a population is declining or not, suppose managers have decided that they want to consider three possible situations: (1) the population is declining rapidly $(r < -0.05)$; (2) the population is declining slowly $(-0.05 < r < 0.0)$; (3) the population is not declining $(r > 0.0)$. A different loss function is specified for each of the three possible conclusions and, within each loss function, a relative loss value is specified for each possible rate of population change. For example, for the decision to conclude that the population is declining rapidly, there is no loss if the population actually is declining rapidly, so a value of 0.0 is specified (Table 6.5). If the population is actually declining slowly, to conclude that it is declining rapidly is an error – a loss value of 1 is specified for that outcome. Finally, if the population is actually increasing, it is decided that this would be twice as bad an error as the previous one, and so a loss value of 2 is specified. Loss values are specified for the other two possible decisions in a similar way (Table 6.5).

Once the loss functions are specified, the decision analysis is performed

Table 6.6. Decision analysis for Cook Inlet beluga population

Years of data	Expected loss under different decisions			Conclusion
	Conclude population is declining rapidly	Conclude population is declining slowly	Conclude population is not declining	
4	1.011	0.645	0.985	Declining slowly
5	0.286	0.862	1.714	Declining rapidly
6	0.200	0.861	1.802	Declining rapidly
7	0.078	0.934	1.922	Declining rapidly

The expected loss for each decision is tabulated for different numbers of years of data, based on Tables 6.2 and 6.5 (see the text). The conclusion is reached by choosing the decision with the smallest expected loss in each row.

by combining the loss functions with the estimated probabilities from the Bayesian population trend analysis (Table 6.2). Specifically, the expected loss for each decision is calculated as the sum (or integral for a continuous loss function) of the product of the loss function and the probability of that rate of population change. Using the example with four years of data, the expected loss for the decision to conclude that the population is declining rapidly is calculated as the sum of the cross-products of the first row of Table 6.5 with the first row of Table 6.2: $(0 \times 0.316) + (1 \times 0.353) + (2 \times 0.329) = 1.011$ (Table 6.6). This calculation is repeated for each possible decision. For four years of data, the smallest expected loss occurs when one concludes that the population is declining slowly. For the Cook Inlet beluga example, this conclusion changes to 'declining rapidly' with five years of data, and remains there when additional years of data are analysed (Table 6.6).

Whereas the population trend analysis (using Bayes factors) indicated there was evidence of a decline after five years, the decision analysis concluded that there was a small decline after only four years (remember that a traditional significance test could only detect a decline after seven years). The decision analysis performs differently from the significance test because the error structure is different – stated in traditional terms, the decision analysis considers both Type I and Type II errors, whereas the traditional test is done by specifying only the Type I error rate. The traditional significance test sets the probability of rejecting a true null hypothesis (Type I error – concluding the population is declining when it is stable) to 0.05. The probability of not rejecting a false null hypothesis (Type II error – not rejecting the hypothesis that the population is stable when it is declining) is not explicitly set. In this case it will be a function of the Type

I error rate, the sample size, and the actual rate of decline of the population. The decision analysis has provided a mechanism for balancing the error rates – one can think of it as that the Type I error rate has been increased in order to decrease the Type II error rate. How the different error rates are balanced is determined by the loss functions, which describe the relative undesirability of making various errors. The point has been made that from a conservation point of view, Type II errors are worse than Type I errors (Taylor & Gerrodette, 1993). For example, not detecting the decline of a small population can be viewed as a graver error than incorrectly concluding that a population is declining when it is not.

Other examples of the use of decision analysis in the conservation and management of wild populations include: the establishment of listing criteria for spectacled eiders *Somateria fischeri* (Taylor *et al.*, 1996); and a hypothetical example using a Bayesian population viability analysis with decision theory in order to classify populations under IUCN criteria (Taylor *et al.*, 2001).

Testing the performance of management schemes with simulations

Another development has been the evaluation of management through the use of simulation models. In particular, simulations can be used to test whether a specified management scheme will achieve a specific quantitative goal, such as a target population level. An example is the Revised Management Procedure of the IWC, which can be used to set harvest quotas based on abundance estimates, the precision of the abundance estimates and previous harvest data (see descriptions in Kirkwood, 1992; Cooke, 1995). Specific performance goals of the procedure were to rehabilitate depleted stocks, prohibit whaling on stocks below 54% of their initial abundance, bring all exploited stocks to the target level of 72% of their initial abundance, and obtain the highest possible stable catch limits (Gambell, 1999). Extensive simulation modelling was used to select a numerical algorithm for calculating a quota from the available abundance and harvest data to meet these management goals (IWC, 1995). It should be noted that the selected procedure contains a Bayesian-like stock assessment algorithm that was 'tuned' to provide the desired performance (IWC, 1995), and incorporated uncertainty into the evaluation process. In particular, simulations were used to test the procedure under substantial levels of bias, process error and model error, while formally incorporating sampling error into the quota-setting routine. This procedure was turned into a computer program that takes inputs of abundance and previous harvest data, and outputs a harvest quota. In a system like this, once the procedure is agreed to, the

Table 6.7. Summary of attributes of different methods used to analyse data and summarise information about the conservation status of exploited species. 'Currency for inference' is the type of inferential statement that results from using that method

Method	Currency for inference	Uses distribution to visually describe uncertainty	Can incorporate uncertainty from alternative sources	Can incorporate model uncertainty	Statistically based procedure	Theoretical foundations
Traditional statistics	p value and confidence limits	No	No[a]	No	Yes	Frequentist sampling theory
Akaike's information criterion	AIC value	No	No	Yes	Yes	Information theory
Likelihood inference	Support, relative likelihood	Yes	No[b]	No	Yes	Fisher's likelihood principle
Probability distribution (Bayesian statistics)	Probability	Yes	Yes	Yes	Yes	Bayes' theorem, probability theory
Bootstrap distribution (reinterpreted)	Frequency distribution	Yes	Yes	Yes	No	?[c]
Fuzzy numbers and logic	Possibility value	Yes[d]	Yes	Yes	No	Set theory

[a] But see *ad hoc* method proposed by Restrepo *et al.* (1992), and critique by Poole *et al.* (1999).

[b] But see Schweder (1998) for proposed method for incorporating alternative information by treating it as data.

[c] Use of the bootstrap to estimate variances and confidence intervals has strong theoretical foundations (see Efron & Tibshirani, 1993), but reinterpretation of the bootstrap frequency distribution as a probability distribution for a parameter has no theoretical justification.

[d] Technically, fuzzy numbers are represented by a collection of nested sets, not by a distribution, but this gives the appearance of a distribution.

setting of harvest quotas becomes automatic rather than subjective.

A somewhat similar procedure was used to establish limits to fisheries' by-catch of marine mammals in the USA, as mandated by the US Marine Mammal Protection Act. The management goal was to prevent populations from becoming depleted. The specific performance criterion used was to establish a mortality limit such that populations had a 95% chance of recovering to or staying above 50% of their carrying capacity or initial (unexploited) population size (Barlow et al., 1995). A simulation model was used to select a procedure for calculating a mortality limit (termed the potential biological removal) that would achieve that specific performance goal (Wade, 1998). Again, simulations were used to test the procedure under a range of levels of sampling error and under conditions of substantial bias. Taylor et al. (2000) provide a description of the overall scheme, and a summary of the results of the scheme's application can be found in Read & Wade (2000).

CONCLUSIONS

The issue of uncertainty has clearly become an area of interest in the conservation and management of natural resources. The fact that several new methods have come into use in recent years indicates that this is a trend with widespread support. In comparing the various new methods with traditional techniques, some common themes emerge (Table 6.7). None of the novel methods retains the use of significance or hypothesis tests; in fact, many authors describing the new methods have specifically criticised the hypothesis-testing framework. Also, nearly all the new methods use distributions to describe uncertainty in parameters, rather than just confidence limits. Most of the new methods allow for uncertainty from alternative sources to be incorporated into the analysis, in contrast to traditional statistics. Finally, some of the new methods allow for model uncertainty to be explicitly incorporated. The use of several novel methods that specifically address the issue of incorporating uncertainty is a welcome change compared with traditional methods that often ignored uncertainty.

Now that these new analysis methods are available, it is natural that attention has also turned to new methods for incorporating uncertainty into conservation and management decisions. A common theme is that management procedures have become more structured and formal. In particular, new techniques have focused attention on the expected performance of the resource being exploited over the range of future possibilities, even if this range is large because available data are uncertain.

REFERENCES

Akçakaya, R. H., Ferson, S., Burgman, M. A., Keith, D. A., Mace, G.M. & Todd, C. R. (2000). Making consistent IUCN classifications under uncertainty. *Conservation Biology*, **14**, 1001–1013.

Allen, K. R. (1980). *Conservation and Management of Whales*. University of Washington Press, Seattle, WA.

Annala, J. H., Sullivan, K. J. & O'Brien, C. J. (Compilers) (1999). Report from the Fishery Assessment Plenary, April 1999: Stock Assessments and Yield Estimates. Unpublished report held in NIWA library, Wellington, New Zealand.

Barlow, J., Eagle, T., Swartz, S. & Wade, P. R. (1995). *U.S. Marine Mammal Stock Assessments: Guidelines for Preparation, Background, and a Summary of the 1995 Assessments*. NOAA Technical Memorandum NMFS-OPR-6.

Bayes, T. (1763). An essay towards solving a problem in the doctrine of chances. *Philosophical Transactions of the Royal Society of London*, **53**, 370–418.

Berger, J. O. (1985). *Statistical Decision Theory and Bayesian Analysis*. Springer-Verlag, New York.

Berger, J. O. & Berry, D. A. (1988). Statistical analysis and the illusion of objectivity. *American Scientist*, **76**, 159–165.

Bernardo, J. M. & Smith, A. F. M. (1994). *Bayesian Theory*. Wiley, Chichester.

Buckland, S. T., Anderson, D. R., Burnham, K. P. & Laake, J. L. (1993). *Distance Sampling: Estimating Abundance of Biological Populations*. Chapman & Hall, London.

Burnham, K. P. & Anderson, D. R. (1998). *Model Selection and Inference: A Practical Information-Theoretic Approach*. Springer-Verlag, New York.

Caswell, H., Fujiwara, M. & Brault, S. (1999). Declining survival probability threatens the North Atlantic right whale. *Proceedings of the National Academy of Sciences, USA*, **96**, 3308–3313.

Cooke, J. G. (1995). The International Whaling Commission's revised management procedure as an example of a new approach to fishery management. In *Whales, Seals, Fish and Man*, ed. A. S. Blix, L. Walloe & O. Woltang, pp. 647–657. Elsevier Science, Amsterdam.

Cox, D. R. (1977). The role of significance tests (with discussion). *Scandinavian Journal of Statistics*, **4**, 49–70.

Cox, D. R. (1982). Statistical significance tests. *British Journal of Clinical Pharmacology*, **14**, 325–331.

Cox, D. R. (1986). Some general aspects of the theory of statistics. *International Statistical Review*, **54**, 117–126.

DeGroot, M. H. (1973). Doing what comes naturally: interpreting a tail area as a posterior probability or as a likelihood ratio. *Journal of the American Statistical Association*, **68**, 966–969.

Eberhardt, L. L. & Simmons, M. A. (1992). Assessing rates of increase from trend data. *Journal of Wildlife Management*, **56**, 603–610.

Edwards, A. W. F. (1992). *Likelihood*. Johns Hopkins University Press, Baltimore and London.

Efron, B. (1990). Comment. *Statistical Science*, **5**, 450.

Efron, B. (1993). Bayes and likelihood calculations from confidence intervals. *Biometrika*, **80**, 3–26.

Efron, B. & Gong, G. (1983). A leisurely look at the bootstrap, the jackknife, and cross-validation. *American Statistician*, **37**, 36–48.

Efron, B. & Tibshirani, R. J. (1993). *An Introduction to the Bootstrap*. Chapman & Hall, London.

Ellison, A. M. (1996). An introduction to Bayesian inference for ecological research and environmental decision making. *Ecological Applications*, **6**, 1036–1046.

Flaaten, O., Salvanes, A.G.V., Schweder, T. & Ulltang, O. (1998). Fisheries management under uncertainty – an overview. *Fisheries Research*, **37**, 1–6.

Gambell, R. (1999). The International Whaling Commission and the contemporary whaling debate. In *Conservation and Management of Marine Mammals*, ed. J. R. Twiss & R. R. Reeves, pp. 179–198. Smithsonian Institution Press, Washington, DC.

Gazey, W. J. & Staley, M. J. (1986). Population estimation from mark-recapture experiments using a sequential Bayes algorithm. *Ecology*, **67**, 941–951.

Gelman, A, Carlin, J., Stern, H. & Rubin, D. (1995). *Bayesian Data Analysis*. Chapman & Hall, London.

Givens, G. H., Raftery, A. E. & Zeh, J. E. (1993). Benefits of a Bayesian approach for synthesizing multiple sources of evidence and uncertainty linked by a deterministic model. *Reports of the International Whaling Commission*, **43**, 495–503.

Givens, G. H., Zeh, J. E. & Raftery, A. E. (1995). Assessment of the Bering–Chukchi–Beaufort Seas stock of bowhead whales using the BALEEN II model in a Bayesian synthesis framework. *Reports of the International Whaling Commission*, **45**, 345–364.

Guttman, L. (1977). What is not what in statistics. *The Statistician*, **26**, 81–107.

Guttman, L. (1985). The illogic of statistical inference for cumulative science. *Applied Stochastic Models and Data Analysis*, **1**, 3–10.

Hilborn, R. (1997). Statistical hypothesis testing and decision theory in fisheries. *Fisheries*, **22**, 19–20.

Hilborn, R. & Liermann, M. (1998). Standing on the shoulders of giants: learning from experience in fisheries. *Reviews in Fish Biology and Fisheries*, **8**, 273–283.

Hilborn, R. & Mangel, M. (1997). *The Ecological Detective: Confronting Models with Data*. Princeton University Press, Princeton, NJ.

Hilborn, R. & Walters, C. J. (1992). *Quantitative Fisheries Stock Assessment: Choice, Dynamics and Uncertainty*. Chapman & Hall, New York and London.

Hilborn, R, Pikitch, E. K. & Francis, R. C. (1993). Current trends in including risk and uncertainty in stock assessment and harvest decisions. *Canadian Journal of Fisheries and Aquatic Sciences*, **50**, 874–880.

Hill, P. S. & DeMaster, D. P. (1999). *Alaska Marine Mammal Stock Assessments (1999)*. NOAA Technical Memorandum NMFS-AFSC-110.

Hobbs, R. C., Rugh, D. J. & DeMaster, D. P. (2001). Abundance of beluga whales in Cook Inlet, Alaska, 1994–1999. *Marine Fisheries Review*, in press.

Howson, C. & Urbach, P. (1991). Bayesian reasoning in science. *Nature*, **350**, 371–374.

IWC (International Whaling Commission) (1995). Chairman's report of the forty-sixth annual meeting. *Reports of the International Whaling Commission*, **45**, 15–52.

IWC (International Whaling Commission) (1998). Annex J. Report of the Sub-Committee on Aboriginal Subsistence Whaling. *Reports of the International Whaling Commission*, **48**, 241–244.

Jeffreys, H. (1939). *Theory of Probability*, 1st edn. Clarendon Press, Oxford.

Jeffreys, H. (1961). *Theory of Probability*, 3rd edn. Clarendon Press, Oxford.

Johnson, D. H. (1999). The insignificance of statistical significance testing. *Journal of Wildlife Management*, **63**, 763–772.

Jones, D. & Matloff, N. (1986). Statistical hypothesis testing in biology: a contradiction in terms. *Journal of Economic Entomology*, **79**, 1156–1160.

Kass, R. E. & Raftery, A. E. (1995). Bayes factors. *Journal of the American Statistical Association*, **90**, 773–795.

Kirkwood, G. P. (1992). Background to the development of revised management procedures. *Reports of the International Whaling Commission*, **42**, 236–243.

Knowlton, A. R. & Kraus, S. D. (2000). Mortality and serious injury in North Atlantic right whales. *Journal of Cetacean Research and Management*, in press.

Kosko, B. & Isaka, S. (1993). Fuzzy logic. *Scientific American*, **269**, 76–81.

Laviolette, M., Seaman, J. W., Barret, J.D. & Woodall, W. H. (1995). A probabilistic and statistical view of fuzzy methods. *Technometrics*, **37**, 249–261.

Ludwig, D. (1994). Bad ecology leads to bad public policy. *Trends in Ecology and Evolution*, **9**, 411.

Ludwig, D. (1996). Uncertainty and the assessment of extinction probabilities. *Ecological Applications*, **6**, 1067–1076.

Ludwig, D. (1998). Management of stocks that may collapse. *Oikos*, **83**, 397–402.

Ludwig, D., Hilborn, R. & Walters, C. (1993). Uncertainty, resource exploitation, and conservation: lessons from history. *Science*, **260**, 547–549.

Mace, G. & Lande, R. (1991). Assessing extinction threats: towards a re-evaluation of IUCN threatened species categories. *Conservation Biology*, **2**, 212–231.

Mackinson, S., Vasconcellos, M. & Newlands, N. (1999). A new approach to the analysis of stock-recruitment relationships: 'model-free estimation' using fuzzy logic. *Canadian Journal of Fisheries and Aquatic Sciences*, **56**, 686–699.

Malakov, D. (1999). News focus: Bayes offers a 'new' way to make sense of numbers. *Science*, **286**, 1460–1464.

Mangel, M., Talbot, L. M., Meffe, G. K., Agardy, M. T., Alverson, D. L., Barlow, J., Botkin, D. B., Budowski, G., Clark, T., Cooke, J., Crozier, R. H., Dayton, P. K., Elder, D. L., Fowler, C. W., Funtowicz, S., Giske, J., Hofman, R. J., Holt, S. J., Kellert, S. R., Kimball, L. A., Ludwig. D., Magnusson, K., Malayang III, B. S., Mann, C., Norse, E. A., Northridge, S. P., Perrin, W. F., Perrings, C., Peterman, R. M., Rabb, G. B., Regier, H. A., Reynolds III, J. E., Sherman, K., Sissenwine, M. P., Smith, T. D., Starfield, A., Taylor, R. J., Tillman, M. F., Toft, C., Twiss, J. R. Jr, Wilen, J. & Young, T. P. (1996). Principles for the conservation of wild living resources. *Ecological Applications*, **6**, 338–362.

Matloff, N. S. (1991). Statistical hypothesis testing: problems and alternatives. *Environmental Entomology*, **20**, 1246–1250.

McAllister, M. K. & Ianelli, J. N. (1997). Bayesian stock assessment using catch-age data and the sampling-importance-resampling algorithm. *Canadian Journal of Fisheries and Aquatic Sciences*, **54**, 284–300.

McAllister, M. K., Pikitch, E. K., Punt, A. E. & Hilborn, R. (1994). A Bayesian approach to stock asssessment and harvest decisions using the sampling/importance resampling algorithm. *Canadian Journal of Fisheries and Aquatic Sciences*, **51**, 2673–2687.

McBride, G. B., Loftis, J. C. & Adkins, N. C. (1993). What do significance tests really tell us about the environment? *Environmental Management*, **17**, 423–432.

McCloskey, D. N. (1995). The insignificance of statistical significance. *Scientific American*, **272**, 32–33.

Mohn, R. K. (1993). Bootstrap estimates of ADAPT parameters, their projection in risk analysis and their retrospective patterns. In *Risk Evaluation and Biological Reference Points for Fisheries Management*, ed. S. J. Smith, J. J. Hunt & D. Rivard, pp. 173–184. Canadian Special Publication of Fisheries and Aquatic Sciences, no. 120.

Myers, R. A., Hutchings, J. A. & Barrowman, N. J. (1997). Why do fish stocks collapse? The example of cod in Atlantic Canada. *Ecological Applications*, **7**, 91–106.

O'Corry-Crowe, G. M., Suydam, R. S., Rosenberg, A, Frost, K. J. & Dizon, A. E. (1997). Phylogeography, population structure, and dispersal patterns of the beluga whale *Delphinapterus leucas* in the western Nearctic revealed by mitochondrial DNA. *Molecular Ecology*, **6**, 955–970.

Omlin, M. & Reichert, P. (1999). A comparison of techniques for the estimation of model prediction uncertainty. *Ecological Modeling*, **115**, 45–59.

Pascual, M. A. & Kareiva, P. (1996). Predicting the outcome of competition using experimental data: maximum likelihood and Bayesian approaches. *Ecology*, **77**, 337–349.

Pearce, S. C. (1992). Data analysis in agricultural experimentation. II. Some standard contrasts. *Experimental Agriculture*, **28**, 375–383.

Poole, D., Givens, G.H. & Raftery, A. E. (1999). A proposed stock assessment method and its application to bowhead whales, *Balaena mysticetus*. *Fisheries Bulletin*, **97**, 144–152.

Press, S. J. (1989). *Bayesian Statistics: Principles, Models, and Applications*. Wiley, New York.

Punt, A. E. & Butterworth, D. S. (1997). Assessments of the Bering–Chukchi–Beaufort Seas stock of bowhead whales (*Balaena mysticetus*) using maximum likelihood and Bayesian methods. *Reports of the International Whaling Commission*, **47**, 603–618.

Punt, A. E. & Butterworth, D. S. (1999). An assessment of Bering–Chukchi–Beaufort Seas stock of bowhead whales (*Balaena mysticetus*) using a Bayesian approach. *Journal of Cetacean Research and Management*, **1**, 53–71.

Punt, A. & Hilborn, R. (1997). Fisheries stock assessment and decision analysis: the Bayesian approach. *Reviews in Fish Biology and Fisheries*, **7**, 35–63.

Quinn, J. F. & Dunham, A. E. (1983). On hypothesis testing in ecology and evolution. *American Naturalist*, **122**, 602–617.

Raftery, A. E., Givens, G. H. & Zeh, J. E. (1995). Inference from a determinsitic population dynamics model for bowhead whales. *Journal of the American Statistical Association*, **90**, 402–416.

Ragen, T. J. (1995). Maximum net productivity level estimation for the northern fur seal (*Callorhinus ursinus*) population of St. Paul Island, Alaska. *Marine Mammal Science*, **11**, 275–300.

Ralls, K. & Taylor, B. L. (2000). Better policy and management decisions through explicit analysis of uncertainty: new approaches from marine conservation. *Conservation Biology*, **14**, 1240–1242.

Read, A. & Wade, P. R. (2000). Status of marine mammals in the United States. *Conservation Biology*, **14**, 929–940.

Reckhow, K. H. (1990). Bayesian inference in non-replicated ecological studies. *Ecology*, **71**, 2053–2059.

Reeves, R. R. (1990). An overview of the distribution, exploitation and conservation status of belugas, worldwide. In *For the Future of the Beluga: Proceedings of the International Forum for the Future of the Beluga*, ed. J. Prescott & M. Gauquelin, pp. 47–58. University of Quebec Press, Sillery, Quebec.

Regan, H. M. & Colyvan, M. (2000). Fuzzy sets and threatened species classification. *Conservation Biology*, **14**, 1197–1199.

Restrepo, V. R., Hoenig, J. M., Powers, J. E., Baird, J. W. & Turner, S. C. (1992). A simple simulation approach to risk and cost analysis, with application to swordfish and cod fisheries. *Fisheries Bulletin*, **90**, 736–748.

Reynolds, J. D. & Mace, G. M. (1999). Risk assessments of threatened species. *Trends in Ecology and Evolution*, **14**, 215–217.

Rosenberg, A. A. & Restrepo, V. R. (1993). Uncertainty and risk evaluation in stock assessment advice for U.S. marine fisheries. *Canadian Journal of Fisheries and Aquatic Sciences*, **51**, 2715–2720.

Royall, R. (1997). *Statistical Evidence: A Likelihood Paradigm*. Chapman & Hall, London.

Rugh, D. J., Shelden, K. E. W. & Mahoney, B. (2001). Distribution of beluga whales in Cook Inlet, Alaska, during June and July, 1993–1998. *Marine Fisheries Review*, in press.

Schweder, T. (1998). Fisherian or Bayesian methods of integrating diverse statistical information? *Fisheries Research*, **37**, 61–75.

Shaughnessy, P. D., Testa, J. W, & Warneke, R. M. (1995). Abundance of Australian fur seal pups, *Arctocephalus pusillus doiferus*, at Seal Rocks, Victoria, in 1991–92 from Peterson and Bayesian estimators. *Wildlife Research*, **22**, 625–632.

Smith, S. J., Hunt, J. J. & Rivard, D. (eds.). (1993). *Risk Evaluation and Biological Reference Points for Fisheries Management*. Canadian Special Publication of Fisheries and Aquatic Sciences, **120**.

Taylor, B. L. & DeMaster, D. P. (1993). Implications of non-linear density dependence. *Marine Mammal Science*, **9**, 360–371.

Taylor, B. L. & Gerrodette, T. (1993). The uses of statistical power in conservation biology: the vaquita and northern spotted owl. *Conservation Biology*, **7**, 489–500.

Taylor, B. L. & Wade, P. R. (2000). 'Best' abundance estimates and best management: why they are not the same. In *Quantitative Methods for Conservation Biology*, ed. S. Ferson & M. Burgman, pp. 96–108. Springer-Verlag, New York.

Taylor, B., Wade, P. R., Stehn, R. & Cochrane, J. (1996). A Bayesian approach to classification criteria for spectacled eiders. *Ecological Applications*, **6**, 1077–1089.

Taylor, B. L., Wade, P. R., DeMaster, D. P. & Barlow, J. (2000). Incorporating uncertainty into management models for marine mammals. *Conservation Biology*, in press.

Taylor, B. L., Wade P. R., Ramakrishnan, U., Akçakaya R. & Gilpin, M. (2002). Incorporating uncertainty in PVAs for the purpose of classifying species by risk. In *Population Viability Analysis: Assessing models for Recovering Endangered Species*, ed. S. R. Beissinger & D. McCullough, University of Chicago Press, Chicago, in press.

Thompson, G. G. (1992). A Bayesian approach to management advice when stock-recruitment parameters are uncertain. *Fisheries Bulletin*, **90**, 561–573.

Todd, C. R. (2000). Perspectives on the definition of fuzzy sets: a reply to Regan and Colyvan. *Conservation Biology*, **14**, 1200–1201.

Wade, P. R. (1998). Calculating limits to the allowable human-caused mortality of cetaceans and pinnipeds. *Marine Mammal Science*, **14**, 1–37.

Wade, P. R. (1999). A comparison of statistical methods for fitting population models to data. In *Marine Mammal Survey and Assessment Methods*, ed. G. W. Garner, S. C. Amstrup, J. L. Laake, B. F. J. Manly, L. L. McDonald & D. G. Robertson, pp. 249–270. Balkema, Rotterdam.

Wade, P. R. (2000). Bayesian methods in conservation biology. *Conservation Biology*, **14**, 1308–1316.

Wade, P. R. (2001). A Bayesian stock assessment of the eastern Pacific gray whale using abundance and harvest data from 1967 to 1996. *Journal of Cetacean Research and Management, Special Volume*, in press.

Wade, P. R. (2002). Bayesian population viability analysis. In *Population Viability Analysis: Assessing Models for Recovering Endangered Species*, ed. S. R. Beissinger & D. McCullough. University of Chicago Press, Chicago, in press.

Wade, P. R. & Givens, G. (1997). Designing catch control laws that reflect the intent of aboriginal subsistence management principles. *Report of the International Whaling Commission*, **47**, 871–874.

Walters, C. & Ludwig, D. (1994). Calculation of Bayes posterior probability distributions for key population parameters. *Canadian Journal of Fisheries and Aquatic Sciences*, **51**, 713–722.

Wang, C. (1993). *Sense and Nonsense of Statistical Inference: Controversy, Misuse, and Subtlety*. Marcel Dekker, Inc., New York.

White, G. C. (2000). Population viability analysis: data requirements and essential analyses. In *Research Techniques in Animal Ecology: Controversies and Consequences*, ed. L. Boitani & T. K. Fuller, pp. 288–331. Columbia University Press, New York.

Yoccoz, N. G. (1991). Use, overuse, and misuse of significance tests in evolutionary biology and ecology. *Bulletin of the Ecological Society of America*, **72**, 106–111.

York, A. E., Merrick, R. L. & Loughlin, T. R. (1996). An analysis of the Steller sea lion metapopulation in Alaska. In *Metapopulations and Wildlife Conservation*, ed. D. R McCullough, pp. 259–291. Island Press, Washington, DC.

Zadeh, L. A. (1994). The role of fuzzy logic in modeling, identification, and control. *Modeling, Identification, and Control*, **15**, 191–203.

PART III

Taxonomic comparisons

7

Life histories of fishes and population responses to exploitation

JOHN D. REYNOLDS, SIMON JENNINGS & NICHOLAS K. DULVY

Most of the world's fisheries are either fully exploited or overexploited (Botsford *et al.*, 1997). While there is scope for further exploitation of some fish stocks, the global picture is not encouraging, with declining catches despite increasing fishing effort. We are running out of new stocks to exploit, as we fish in deeper waters (Merrett & Haedrich, 1997) and work our way down the food chain (Pauly *et al.*, 1998).

Are declines in exploited fish populations really conservation problems? Clearly, this depends on what we mean by 'conservation problem' (Mace & Reynolds, Chapter 1). If we are concerned about the continuing availability of a resource upon which people depend for their livelihoods and social traditions, the word 'problem' is obviously a considerable understatement. If we are concerned about possible effects on other parts of the ecosystem due to declines in specific species, this too may be an important problem, though generalisations are difficult (Kaiser & Jennings, Chapter 16; Hall, 1999; Gislason & Sinclair, 2000; Jennings *et al.*, 2001). If we are concerned with the possibility of extinction of fished species, the evidence is much less clear. In fact, there are still no documented cases of any marine fish species having yet become extinct due to exploitation (Roberts & Hawkins, 1999). However, local extirpations have definitely occurred (Brander, 1981; Casey & Myers, 1998; Dulvy *et al.*, 2000; Powles *et al.*, 2000; Stevens *et al.*, 2000), and some fish populations have declined by 99% in 20–30 years (Reynolds & Jennings, 2000).

We think it is useful to ask about fish conservation in relation to life histories for two reasons. First, on theoretical grounds exploited fish populations provide a good model system for establishing links between population dynamics under harvesting regimes and life histories. Fishes show a huge diversity of life histories, including fecundities that vary by five orders of magnitude, and fisheries create large-scale experiments that yield data on population dynamics over many generations. Secondly, and particularly relevant to the theme of this book, it is important to derive generalisations from species that we know a great deal about so that we can improve the conservation of species of which we know little. This is particularly true of tropical reef fisheries, where it will never be practical to collect the large amount of information that feeds the insatiable appetites of sophisticated models used in many temperate fisheries (Johannes, 1998). Yet some key tropical species such as groupers (Epinephelinae) are particularly susceptible to severe population declines and even extirpation under fishing pressure (Sadovy, 1994). Furthermore, even in temperate areas where research is well funded, the mandate of most scientists is geared strongly toward attaining sustainable exploitation of a small number of economically important species. This means that other species, which may be killed as a by-catch, can decline precipitously without anyone noticing. Thus the extirpation of the 'common' skate *Dipturus batis* from the Irish Sea and the decline of its western Atlantic counterpart, the barndoor skate *D. laevis* were not reported until at least 20 years after they occurred (Brander, 1981; Casey & Myers, 1998). We therefore need simple 'rules of thumb' for predicting population declines of poorly studied species, and life history characteristics such as body size, age at maturity, fecundity, and natural mortality rate seem fruitful avenues for exploration.

The aim of this chapter is to establish links between life histories, mortality rates and population trends. First, we provide a brief review of the theoretical links between life histories and population dynamics. Then we test predictions from this theory, based on comparative analyses of various species. Finally, we use the combination of theory and empirical observations to consider simple rules of thumb that might aid in making *a priori* predictions of responses to exploitation, and in prioritising species for conservation assessment.

THEORY

Links between life histories and sustainability

A number of theoretical analyses have indicated how life histories should determine responses to fishing (Adams, 1980; Stokes *et al.*, 1993; Kirkwood *et al.*, 1994; Pope *et al.*, 2000). These confirm the expectation that higher fishing mortality should be sustainable by species with faster life histories, i.e. earlier age at maturity and faster body growth. For example, Adams (1980) used classical yield-per-recruit analyses to show that species with faster life histories should both sustain higher mortality rates and produce higher yields per recruit. Kirkwood *et al.* (1994) used an age-structured population dynamics model that suggested that the potential

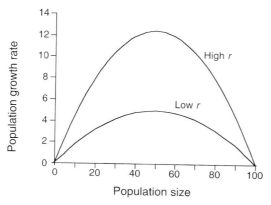

Figure 7.1. Population growth rate (individuals per unit time) as a function of population size for high ($r = 0.5$) and low ($r = 0.2$) intrinsic rates of natural increase. Species with higher intrinsic rates of increase provide greater yields to exploitation.

yield measured as a proportion of unexploited biomass should be proportional to natural mortality rates. For a range of potentially realistic levels of density dependence, they suggested that the percentage yield may be between about 10% and 15% of the natural mortality rate multiplied by the virgin biomass. This is a nice theoretical synthesis, but it is difficult to put these ideas into practice due to difficulties in measuring the key parameters in the sorts of data-poor situations where this sort of rule of thumb could be most useful.

The simplest way to incorporate life histories into predictions about sustainable exploitation is to consider the direct links between life history parameters and population dynamics. The intrinsic rate of population increase, denoted r, is a fundamental parameter in models that predict rates of population change per unit time. This is the rate of growth of a population at low densities (once it has reached a stable age distribution). Some authors also refer to this as r_{max}, to distinguish it from an observed rate of population increase at higher densities. If the population follows a logistic growth pattern, the rate of change in number of individuals per unit time, dN/dt, will depend on r and the carrying capacity, K (Ludwig, Chapter 2).

$$dN/dt = rN(1 - N/K).$$

$\qquad\qquad\qquad\qquad\qquad\qquad\qquad\qquad\qquad\qquad$ (7.1)

This provides the familiar parabolic relationship between population growth rate and population size shown in Figure 7.1. Two curves are shown, one for a species with a high intrinsic rate of population increase ($r = 0.5$), and the other for a lower one ($r = 0.2$). The maximum sustainable yield that can be taken occurs at intermediate population sizes. The species with the higher intrinsic rate of increase can provide a higher yield. Many species show strong density-dependent responses to the additional mortality imposed by fishing and can sustain fishing mortalities two to three times the natural mortality without declining to extinction (Shepherd & Cushing, 1990).

Obviously, the next step towards our goal of linking population productivity to life histories would be to measure *r* for different species. If only life were so simple! The problem is that empirical measurements of rates of increase rarely give useful values of *r* because they depend critically on density dependence, and density dependence is notoriously difficult to quantify in field studies of any species (Sutherland & Gill, Chapter 12). One might be tempted to measure surrogates for *r* by looking at fecundity and mortality rates in the laboratory under uncrowded conditions. But this value will be hopelessly artificial, depending on food, temperature, safety from predators and diseases. While we are on a pessimistic note, we should also mention that the so-called carrying capacity, *K*, is also a difficult parameter to measure with any confidence, especially in marine environments where fish population sizes often fluctuate wildly from year to year, according to biotic and abiotic conditions that affect recruitment.

Correlations among life history traits

If we cannot measure *r* directly, the next best thing might be to measure life history traits that are correlated with it. Classically, people have described *r*-selected species as those that live in environments that select for rapid production of many small offspring, and *K*-selected species as those living in stable environments that select for delayed reproduction of fewer, larger offspring. Today, these terms have gone out of fashion because additional forms of selection such as bet-hedging against unfavourable or variable conditions can produce similar or mixed suites of life history traits (Roff, 1992; Stearns, 1992). For example, a female Atlantic cod *Gadus morhua* may not reach maturity until it is seven years old, yet it may produce millions of tiny eggs. We see little point in trying to call this an *r*- or *K*-selected animal.

At first sight, the demise of the *r*–*K* continuum does not seem to bode well for our search for correlations among life history traits that can lead to predictions of sustainable levels of exploitation. However, it is still possible to find surrogate measures for those aspects of life histories that determine responses to exploitation because of fundamental trade-offs between life history parameters (Beverton & Holt, 1959; Beverton, 1963, 1987, 1992; Pauly, 1980; Charnov, 1993; Jensen, 1996; Stamps *et al.*, 1998). Some of

Table 7.1. Parameters used to describe fish life histories

Parameter	Meaning
T_{mat}	Age at maturity[a]
L_{mat}	Length at maturity[a]
T_{max}	Maximum recorded age[b]
k	Rate of growth from von Bertalanffy growth equation
L_∞	Theoretical maximum size from von Bertalanffy growth equation
M	Instantaneous rate of natural mortality

[a]For fish populations, T_{mat} and L_{mat} are usually taken as the age and length at which 50% of individuals in the population attain maturity. This is determined from a logistic curve fitted to the relationship between proportion of individuals that are mature and their age or size.
[b]Maximum recorded age in an unexploited or very lightly exploited population. Today, this usually has to be determined from historical data.

the main parameters used to describe fish life histories are given in Table 7.1. They include the rate of body growth, k towards a theoretical asymptotic size L_∞:

$$L_t = L_\infty(1 - e^{k(t - t_o)}) \qquad (7.2)$$

Where L_t is the length at age t, and t_o is the time at which length is zero on the modelled growth trajectory (Beverton & Holt, 1957). The equation provides a very good fit to size-at-age data for many species of fishes with indeterminate growth.

Beverton & Holt (1959) and Beverton (1963) were the first to study the interrelationships between life history parameters in fishes. They showed that: (1) body growth, k, is correlated with M, the rate of natural mortality (or $1/T_{max}$ as an index of M) (Figure 7.2); (2) body growth is inversely correlated with asymptotic size, L_∞; and (3) the length at maturity, L_{mat}, occurs at a similar proportion of asymptotic length. Such relationships have since been demonstrated for many other groups of vertebrates (Charnov, 1993), and have been particularly useful to fishery scientists because they allow parameters such as M to be estimated from the more easily measured von Bertalanffy growth parameters (Pauly, 1980). The ratios between parameters are dimensionless numbers and are relatively constant within taxonomic groups: the life history invariants. The existence of invariants suggests that the evolution of life histories is governed by some very general trade-offs (Charnov, 1993; see also Kokko et al., Chapter 14). For example, delayed reproduction might increase lifetime reproductive success through increases in age-specific fecundity, despite higher probabilities of mortality before the age of maturity (Roff, 1991, 1992). Maturation

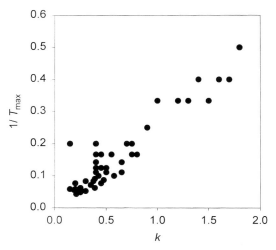

Figure 7.2. Cross-species relationship between $1/T_{max}$ (T_{max} = lifespan) and body growth rate, k, for clupeid and engraulid fishes. (Data from Beverton, 1963.)

has costs because energy has to be partitioned from growth to gonadal development. This implies that an early maturing female will be smaller at a given age. Smaller females produce fewer eggs and may compete less effectively for resources.

The net effect of these trade-offs is that fishes show life history strategies ranging from fast growth, high natural mortality, early maturity and small asymptotic size to slow growth, low natural mortality, late maturity and large asymptotic size. Reproductive output is closely linked to these characteristics (Beverton, 1987; Gunderson & Dygert, 1988; Jennings & Beverton, 1991; Gunderson, 1997). Gunderson & Dygert (1988), for example, showed that fish with higher gonad mass to body mass ratios had higher natural mortality, and Jennings & Beverton (1991) showed that herring populations with greater asymptotic size and higher age at maturity had lower annual reproductive output.

Thus, within and among species, generation time and reproductive output, which are key determinants of r, are themselves correlated with many easily measured life history parameters such as age and size at maturity, body growth rates, and body sizes. Body size data are available more often than the others. Asymptotic size, L_∞, is usefully approximated by the largest fish seen in a population, ideally an unexploited population. However, even if populations are already being fished intensively at the time of the assessment, we may still be able to use maximum size for predicting vulnerability in data-poor situations.

COMPARATIVE STUDIES

Phylogenies matter

We need to discuss phylogenetically based comparative methods because these are important for understanding the results of several recent studies. First, consider the traditional cross-species approach whereby one might regress changes in population sizes of various fish stocks against the life history variable of interest, such as age at maturity. One could then ask, for example, whether stocks with late maturity undergo a steeper decline in populations for a given level of fishing mortality. This approach is illustrated for four stocks in Figure 7.3. The table at the top of this figure shows data for two species from the Northeast Atlantic (Jennings *et al.*, 1998). When abundance data for the period 1975–94, controlled for differences in fishing mortality, are plotted against mean age at maturity for each stock, the trend supports the hypothesis that stocks with later maturity have declined more steeply. However, the two top data points are both for stocks of

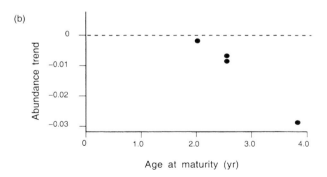

(a)

Stock	Age maturity (yr)	Abundance trend
North Sea Cod	3.8	−0.027
Irish Sea Cod	2.5	−0.009
North Sea Haddock	2.5	−0.008
W. Scotland Haddock	2.0	−0.003

(b)

Figure 7.3. Traditional cross-taxonomic comparisons of relationships between age at maturity and abundance trend of four stocks of Northeast Atlantic fishes, measured as the slope of the relationship between ln-transformed abundance and time (1975–94). (a) Data in tabular form. (b) Data plotted.

(a)

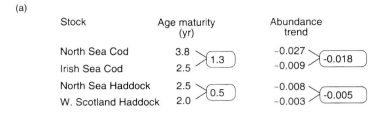

(b)

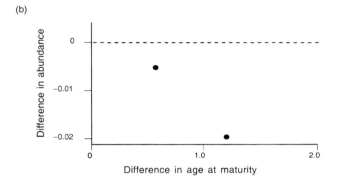

Figure 7.4. Derivation of phylogenetically based comparison of the same relationships as in Figure 7.3. Note that differences among pairs of stocks are (a) calculated and (b) plotted.

haddock *Melanogrammus aeglefinus* and the two bottom ones are for Atlantic cod. Therefore, we do not really have a sample of four independent data points that support the hypothesis: since the two stocks of haddock are obviously closely related to each other, as are the two cod stocks, one might argue that we have only two independent data points (Harvey & Pagel 1991; Harvey, 1996). The stocks will not have evolved their life history traits independently; they will have inherited many aspects of life histories, ecology and behaviour from common ancestors. Therefore, if we treat the stocks as statistically independent of one another we run a strong risk of pseudo-replication.

There are several ways to test for and avoid the problem of taxonomic non-independence in comparative studies, all of which incorporate the phylogenetic relationships of the taxa explicitly into the analyses (Harvey & Pagel, 1991; Pagel, 1999). In Figure 7.4 we present one of the simplest methods, which has been applied to several recent studies of life histories of exploited fishes. A phylogeny has been added beside the data to show the relationships between the pairs of stocks. Any differences between the two cod stocks must have evolved after the ancestor of this species split from the ancestor of the haddock. This means that *differences* between cod stocks in age at maturity will be independent of *differences* in age of maturity of haddock. Thus, subject to assumptions about the particular model of evolution underlying the divergence of the taxa, we can use 'paired independent contrasts' (Felsenstein, 1985) to calculate differences between close relatives in the variables of interest. This is shown in the circled numbers in Figure 7.4a. These differences, or 'contrasts', are now plotted against one another as in Figure 7.4b. One can also make an additional comparison between the species, based on the mean values for each stock within species (Harvey & Pagel, 1991). The data show that the pair of stocks with the greater difference in maturity also has the greater difference in abundance trend, as predicted by the hypothesis. Note that for presentational purposes the *x*-axis has been set to positive, i.e. by subtracting the smaller value of age at maturity from the larger one in each pair of taxa. Such data may be analysed statistically either by a binomial test or by a regression forced through the origin (Harvey & Pagel, 1991). Newer methods for testing for and correcting phylogenetic non-independence are given by Pagel (1999).

Tests for life history correlations with population changes

The first phylogenetically explicit test for relationships between life histories and population responses to fisheries involved a study of nine pairs of stocks or related species in the Northeast Atlantic (Jennings *et al.*, 1998). This study controlled for differences in fishing mortality. Differences among taxa in maximum length, age at maturity, and a crude surrogate for *r*, all proved to be related to changes in population size. Examples for age at maturity and maximum length are shown in the top panels of Figure 7.5. The key for interpreting such figures is that in all but two comparisons in each analysis, the stock or species with the latest age at maturity had declined more than its sister taxon. Interestingly, a traditional cross-taxonomic comparison that ignored phylogenetic relationships showed no patterns whatsoever, despite a doubling of apparent sample size (Figure 7.5, bottom panels). This shows a benefit of using phylogenetically based calculations; comparisons of differences between related taxa help to control for spurious differences among unrelated species in other variables that may obscure patterns. This increase in resolution is similar to the advantages of a paired design in experiments compared with an unpaired design.

As noted above, body size of fishes and other animals tends to be

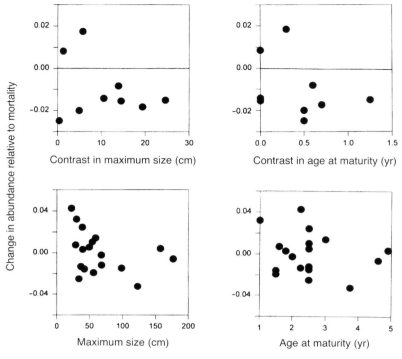

Figure 7.5. Relationships between trends in population size and life history characteristics of nine pairs of stocks or closely related species of Northeast Atlantic fishes. Top panels are phylogenetically based differences among pairs of stocks, and bottom panels are traditional cross-taxonomic comparisons. Abundance trends are the slopes of the relationships for each stock between ln-transformed abundance and time (mostly 1975–1994). (From Jennings *et al.*, 1998.)

strongly correlated with many other components of life histories, including growth rates, age at maturity, and fecundity (Roff, 1992). Thus it is not surprising that similar results were found in the Northeast Atlantic study for three of the four variables considered. It remains to be seen whether some are more relevant than others. However, from a pragmatic point of view, these correlations involving body size are helpful because size is often the only life history variable known for many fish species.

A similar approach has recently been used for reef fishes in Fiji (Jennings *et al.*, 1999a). This fishery exemplifies the kind of data-poor situation typical of tropical fisheries. Underwater visual censuses of fish species yielded data on abundance and a literature search was used to determine maximum body size of each of the 33 species of parrotfish (Scaridae), grouper (Epinephelinae) and snapper (Lutjanidae) species recorded. Fishing effort was estimated in 10 fishing grounds by dividing the length of productive reef fronts by the number of villagers, on the basis that all villagers have fishing rights. All of these estimates are imprecise, reflecting the realities of working with reef fisheries. The results showed that 11 of 17 parrotfishes, 5 of 6 groupers and 9 of 10 snappers decreased in abundance with increasing fishing intensity. Due to limited phylogenetic information only nine comparisons could be made between closely related species. These supported the hypothesis that larger species declined significantly more than smaller ones. As with the study of fishes in the Northeast Atlantic (Figure 7.5), a traditional cross-species analysis that ignored phylogenetic relationships missed this trend.

Two processes could account for the patterns documented in Fiji: differences in mortality (large species are more valuable), or differences in ability of populations to respond to mortality. Without data on species-specific mortality rates, we cannot distinguish between these alternatives. However, given that mortality data are almost never available for tropical reef fishes (Johannes, 1998), from a practical standpoint it is still helpful that predictions could be made about species-specific responses to fishing pressure based solely on body size.

Studies of the responses of tropical reef fishes to marine reserve protection also highlight the significance of life history in governing vulnerability. Russ & Alcala (1998) examined patterns of decline and recovery in families of fish as marine reserve protection first collapsed and was later reinstated. Large predatory species such as snappers, emperors (Lethrinidae), sea basses (Serranidae) and jacks (Carangidae) were fished intensively and had low rates of natural mortality and growth that should make them vulnerable to fishing (Bannerot et al., 1987; Sadovy, 1996). These species declined in abundance rapidly as fishing pressure increased, and recovered slowly when fishing ceased.

A recent meta-analysis of studies of the effectiveness of marine reserves for protecting fish populations has confirmed the expectation that the largest-bodied species of fishes would benefit most from protection (Mosquera et al., 2000). This result was not due simply to larger-bodied species being most heavily targeted by fishers, since the result held when the analyses were restricted to species that were not targeted directly but which were probably killed as by-catch.

Can we extrapolate from these studies to predict larger-scale community shifts over long time periods? This was attempted for the northern North Sea, based on a dataset extending from 1925 to 1996 (Jennings *et al.*, 1999b). Data were available for 23 species of fish, representing over 99% of all individuals caught during bottom-trawling surveys. All fish were pooled together, to examine gross trends in the community. The study showed that the mean growth rates of the community rose over this period. Furthermore, the mean age at maturity decreased from about 2.6 years at the start of the time series to about 2.3 years at the end. This was accompanied by a drop in mean maximum body length of about 10 cm, and mean length at maturity of about 5 cm. Phylogenetically based comparisons supported the hypothesis that these trends were due to differences among taxa in declines in abundance in relation to life histories. For example, in eight of nine pairs of taxa, the species that declined in abundance the most also had the largest body size. Interestingly, these trends were not revealed by traditional cross-taxonomic comparisons that ignored relatedness among taxa. There were no obvious environmental trends over this time period that could explain the combined species abundance trends (e.g. salinity, temperature, pollutants). Thus intensive commercial fishing over a 70-year period has shifted the average value of life history characteristics in the community.

Sharks and skates: particular causes for concern?

Sharks and skates (Elasmobranchii) have been well served by their 'slow' life histories for nearly all of the 400 million years since this superorder first arose. But of course evolution has no foresight, and ages of maturity of 10 years or more, combined with low fecundities and long gestation periods for live-bearers, have left elasmobranchs ill equipped to deal with modern fishing pressures. The cause of skates (Rajidae) has not been helped by a flat, square body shape which must be the worst possible design when encountering a fishing net! Indeed, the fact that some species are 10 cm or more from wingtip to wingtip when they emerge from their egg cases means that they may face fishing mortality from the moment they hatch.

Table 7.2 shows a sample of life history characteristics of selected skates and rays encountered by fisheries in the Northeast Atlantic. Note that even the smallest species, the starry ray, does not reach maturity until age five years, while common skates and thornback rays may take 10 or more years. These data, when cast in an age-specific context, can be used to calculate the maximum total mortality (fishing plus natural mortality) that the

Table 7.2. Life history characteristics of selected species of skates and rays (Rajidae) that are caught by commercial trawlers in the North Sea. Estimates are for females (Walker & Hislop, 1998; Walker, 1998, p. 121)

Species	Length maximum (cm)	Length mature (cm)	Age mature (yr)	Fecundity (eggs)	Growth rate (k)	Estimated mortality	Theoretical replacement mortality (r = 0)
Common skate *Dipturus batis*	237	180	11	40	0.06	0.70	0.38
Thornback ray *Raja clavata*	85	72	10	140	0.14	0.60	0.52
Spotted ray *R. montagui*	75	58	8	60	0.21	0.72	0.54
Cuckoo ray *Leucoraja naevus*	70	59	8	90	0.23	0.65	0.58
Starry ray *Raja radiata*	60	40	5	38	0.22	0.70	0.73

r, rate of population increase.

population could withstand, provided that each female replaces herself in the population (see e.g. Brander, 1981; Walker & Hislop, 1998). An age-structured Leslie matrix is used to estimate r, the intrinsic rate of population increase (see e.g. Kokko *et al.*, Chapter 14). This is based on the Euler–Lotka equation:

$$1 = \sum_{a}^{d} e^{-rx} l_x m_x. \tag{7.3}$$

Here a is the age at maturity, d is the maximum age attained, and l_x and m_x are, respectively, survival and number of offspring produced at each age, x. One can then calculate the replacement mortality, i.e. the total mortality where $r = 0$. This hypothetical mortality rate for a stable population is given in column 8 of Table 7.2, and can be compared with estimates of actual mortality in column 7. This comparison suggests that only the smallest species of ray is being killed sustainably. This result is particularly sensitive to age at maturity, rather than fecundity (Brander, 1981).

There are important caveats for these calculations. First, we have already seen that it is very difficult to make accurate measurements of r. Indeed, density dependence is rather lost in these calculations: the true sustainability of these populations depends on how the life history parameters that determine rates of population increase change with population size. Secondly, it was assumed that mortality is constant with age for individuals that were more than one year old. While predation risk will probably decrease with age, fishing mortality could either increase if older animals become more vulnerable because of their size, or it might decrease if older animals can actively avoid fishing gear. Nevertheless, the calculations provide a rough indication of the rank order of vulnerability of the various skates according to their life histories.

The links between life histories and vulnerability described for skates also apply to other elasmobranchs (Smith *et al.* 1998; Stevens *et al.* 2000; Frisk *et al.* 2001). For example, for Pacific sharks maximum age and to a lesser extent body size appear to be reasonable predictors of their rebound potential, r_{2M}, an estimate of the rate of potential population growth at a standard theoretical density (Smith *et al.* 1998). This was indicated by cross-species comparisons, and we have also verified these relationships by analysing the data with paired independent contrasts, based on the phylogeny by Dulvy and Reynolds (1997). As we indicated earlier, one needs to be cautious about inferences from surrogate measures of r because relationships with true r are not known. However, these studies provide compelling evidence that larger elasmobranchs are more vulnerable because they have reduced rates of population increase.

Studies of rays in the seas west of Britain have confirmed the predictions of life history theory regarding vulnerability, and highlighted potentially serious conservation concerns. The first warning came in 1981 when Keith Brander published a paper in the journal *Nature* warning that the 'common skate' had become extirpated from the Irish Sea during the 1960s. An age at maturity of approximately 11 years, combined with low fecundity, were blamed for the inability of this population to withstand mortality due to trawlers.

Recent analyses confirm that this species has still not recovered, with only six individuals having been caught during research surveys from 1988 to 1997 (Dulvy *et al.*, 2000). Unless trawling activity for targeted species such as cod and flatfish declines, there is no reason to expect recovery by common skates. Furthermore, two more species have disappeared from the Irish and Celtic Seas west of Britain – white skates *Rostroraja alba* and long-nose skates *Dipturus oxyrhinchus*. These species are reported as having been targeted by long-line fisheries during the late 1880s. Among five additional ray species for which there were sufficient data, the three largest species (blonde, thornback and painted rays *Raja microocellata*) have declined whereas the two smallest species (spotted and cuckoo rays) have increased in number. This increase may be due to competitive release as the larger species have declined. Thus the three largest species have been extirpated, the intermediate-sized species are declining, and the smallest species are increasing. Similar findings of size-related changes in populations of skates and rays have also been reported from the North Sea (Walker & Heessen, 1996).

From a conservation viewpoint these trends are particularly worrying because nearly all European countries have been pooling their fishery statistics among species. Therefore, while fisheries landings for all species of skates and rays combined look reasonably stable, this hides changes in species composition (Dulvy *et al.*, 2000). The extirpations and declines of European rays exemplify the differing goals of fisheries managers and conservationists (Mace & Reynolds, Chapter 1). Rays have not been of sufficient economic value in relation to other species to have been deemed worthy of any specific management to date. However, they are taken into account in new regulations implemented on the 1 January 1998 setting mesh size regulations for fixed nets, and scientists within the International Council for the Exploration of the Sea are aiming to improve data collection and develop assessment methods.

Nearly 20 years after the saga of the common skate was published, Casey & Myers (1998) discovered a similar extreme decline in another species on the other side of the Atlantic. The similarities are eerie. The barndoor skate also was extirpated over a large part of its range (formerly from the waters of the Maritime provinces in Canada to southern New England) during the 1960s, and again the collapse occurred without anyone noticing until decades later. As with the common skate, this species is vulnerable as a by-catch of other fishing operations. Finally, the barndoor skate is in the same genus as the common skate, and is also quite large. It undoubtedly shares the common skate's 'slow' life history, though little is known about its biology. Publication of Casey & Myer's paper led to a flurry of publicity that culminated in the barndoor skate being formally considered for listing under the United States Endangered Species Act. Further research by the National Marine Fisheries Service indicated that the skate's numbers have been on a slight upswing in recent years, and the decision was made not to include it in the Act.

INCORPORATING LIFE HISTORIES INTO CONSERVATION ASSESSMENTS

Towards rules of thumb

It is ironic that many of the species that cause the greatest conservation concern are those that we know least about. Species with slow life histories that are taken as by-catches are particularly vulnerable, as shown in the case of skates and rays. Yet, their low economic value renders them invisible to most fishery assessment biologists. Many fishes caught by developing nations are also beyond the reach of modern assessment techniques. Simple rules of thumb are needed for such species (Johannes, 1998).

We have reviewed a number of studies in both temperate and tropical regions which indicate that traits such as body size may provide some information about the likelihood of decline under fishing pressure. In the few studies that have compared body size with other traits including fecundity, body growth rate and age at maturity, body size has worked as well as or better than anything else. Can body size really be used for proactive conservation assessment? A recent attempt was made for the world's skates and rays (Dulvy & Reynolds, 2002). A database was assembled containing body sizes, latitudinal ranges and depth distributions for 230 species. All species were scrutinised to see whether there was evidence that larger species had undergone greater population declines than smaller ones. The body size of the barndoor skate was used as a specific benchmark, to see whether species larger than this were more apt to be of conservation concern. The analysis identified ten species larger than the barndoor skate and, among these, there was evidence to confirm that three have indeed undergone significant population declines. Three species inhabited deep, abyssal plains currently out of the range of fishing gears. No information could be found about the status of the remaining four species, and it was suggested that these should be prioritised for conservation assessment.

These results suggest that life history parameters might be used before formal population assessments have begun, to identify species that deserve a closer look. Thus, for the vast majority of the world's fish species whose population status is unknown, a manager might ask 'How big is it, and is it within reach of fisheries?' to help to decide whether to expend resources on population assessments of that species or a different one. Of course this is extremely crude, but for non-target species and many tropical reef species, it is often the best we can do, and, as the studies of skates and rays have shown, it might often work fairly well.

Classifying levels of threat

A more formal use of life histories in conservation assessment has been proposed to the American Fisheries Society (AFS) following their review of fish populations that are threatened or endangered (Coleman *et al.*, 1999; Musick *et al.*, 1999; Parker *et al.*, 2000). The idea is to incorporate life history information explicitly into the assignment of levels of threat faced by species (Musick, 1999). This is intended as an improvement over traditional categorisations of threat, as used in the *Red Lists* published by the World Conservation Union (IUCN). Under the IUCN rules, designations such as 'critically endangered', 'endangered', and 'vulnerable' are based solely on observed rates of population decline, small distributions, small population sizes, or quantitative predictions based on demographic parameters (IUCN, 1996). The suggestion to the AFS is to use a two-step process. First, one or more of the life history parameters listed in Table 7.1 (r, k, T_{mat}, T_{max}, or annual fecundity) would be used to assign species to a productivity index. If r is known, this is given precedence; otherwise the parameter corresponding to the lowest productivity category is used. For example, if r is estimated at > 0.5 or T_{mat} is < 1 year, the species is listed as having 'high' productivity. Conversely, 'very low' productivity would have $r < 0.05$ or $T_{mat} > 10$ years. These values are not meant as hard and fast criteria, but are intended as guidelines. The second step is to assign a threat category according to the combination of productivity as determined above, and observed population decline. For example, a 'high' productivity species would need to decline by 99% over 10 years or three generations in order to be considered as 'vulnerable'. In contrast, under existing IUCN guidelines productivity is ignored and the decline threshold is fixed at only 20%. The corresponding thresholds for a listing of 'vulnerable' for species whose productivity indices are 'medium', 'low', and 'very low' are suggested as 95%, 85% and 70%, respectively.

We appreciate the basic logic of this proposal, since the evidence available to date does support the expectation that life histories should be important for determining the ability of fishes to withstand exploitation. However, we have three concerns. First, the decline thresholds required to trigger a listing of 'vulnerable' strike us as too high. Even species with the slowest life histories would be allowed to decline by up to 69% in 10 years or three generations (whichever is longer) before raising the minimum level of concern. Secondly, as we have noted, there are severe practical problems in trying to measure r. It was suggested that if one cannot measure this, then it would be ideal if the alternative life history parameters come from unexploited populations (Musick, 1999). This is surprising, since the intrinsic rate of increase, r, is normally taken to refer to populations at the other end of the spectrum, i.e. very low density. In any case, while we agree that r ought to be important (see e.g. Figure 7.1), we are sceptical about the chances of measuring it accurately, and we share the concern of Sutherland & Gill (Chapter 12) about interpreting it with respect to density dependence. Thirdly, even if we wish to settle for the other life history characteristics, information on these, too, is available for only a small subset of fishes. One might counter that this does not mean that we should ignore the information when it is available.

We do not expect this debate to be settled anytime soon, but ultimately we consider this to be an empirical issue with two components. First, are stocks with high potential rates of population increase inherently resilient, as has been traditionally believed? Secondly, can fisheries managers control population sizes? If you believe that the answers to both of these questions are 'yes', you would be well justified in being dismayed by the IUCN's listing of species such as Atlantic cod as vulnerable to extinction. A recent analysis sheds some light on this. Hutchings (2000) showed that most of the 90 stocks of fish that he examined had shown little, if any, recovery 15 years after they had been reduced by 45–99% in population biomass. This suggests that we should be cautious in the assumption that most stocks can bounce back readily from low numbers. This analysis does not consider changes in fishing mortality over the time periods. It is therefore not clear whether the results represent a failure of the resiliency assumption, or a lack of effort to reduce fishing mortality. In other words, the explanation for the patterns may reside in either of the two questions we have posed above. Either way, it is an excellent first step towards an empirical resolution of how to reconcile differing views of conservationists and resource managers. Optimists argue that, although most populations have not been recovering, they still are not going extinct, and if there were clear signs that they were, managers would do something about it. Pessimists invoke the precautionary principle to argue that we should flag up declining species as vulnerable to extinction, and take them off the list after managers have proved that the populations have stabilised.

CONCLUSION

There is still much to be done to bring life history analyses more firmly into mainstream conservation assessments. Robust links to density dependence have been particularly elusive, and this is an area of theory development that would be well worth while. In addition, further comparative studies of population dynamics in relation to life histories should reveal the potential for the development of surrogates for more sophisticated modelling techniques. The relationship between life histories and population dynamics has featured prominently in debates concerning whether exploited fishes are threatened or safe. We feel that this is largely an empirical issue, which must be resolved before we can allow species to be declared safe on the basis of fast life histories. In the meantime, there is scope for using components of life histories to provide simple rules of thumb for prioritising conservation assessments of the many fish species about which little else is known.

REFERENCES

Adams, P. B. (1980). Life history patterns in marine fishes and their consequences for management. *Fishery Bulletin*, **78**, 1–12.

Bannerot, S. P., Fox, W. W. & Powers, J. E. (1987). Reproductive strategies and the management of tropical snappers and groupers. In *Tropical Snappers and Groupers: Biology and Fisheries Management*, ed. J. J. Polovina & S. Ralston, pp. 561–603. Westview Press, Boulder, CO.

Beverton, R. J. H. (1963). Maturation, growth and mortality of clupeid and engraulid stocks in relation to fishing. *Rapports et Procés-Verbaux des Réunions, Conseil International pour l'Exploration de la Mer*, **154**, 44–67.

Beverton, R. J. H. (1987). Longevity in fish: some ecological and evolutionary perspectives. In *Ageing Processes in Animals*, ed. A. D. Woodhead, M. Witten & K. Thompson, pp. 161–186. Plenum Press, New York.

Beverton, R. J. H. (1992). Patterns of reproductive strategy parameters in some marine teleost fishes. *Journal of Fish Biology*, **41** (Supplement B), 137–160.

Beverton, R. J. H. & Holt, S. J. (1957). *On the Dynamics of Exploited Fish Populations*. Ministry of Agriculture, Fisheries and Food, London.

Beverton, R. J. H. & Holt, S. J. (1959). A review of the lifespan and mortality rates of fish in nature and their relationship to growth and other physiological characteristics. *Ciba Foundation Colloquium on Ageing*, **5**, 142–180.

Botsford, L. W., Castilla, J. C. & Peterson, C. H. (1997). The management of fisheries and marine ecosystems. *Science*, **277**, 509–515.

Brander, K. (1981). Disappearance of common skate *Raia batis* from Irish Sea. *Nature*, **290**, 48–49.

Casey, J. M. & Myers, R. A. (1998). Near extinction of a large, widely distributed fish. *Science*, **281**, 690–692.

Charnov, E. L. (1993). *Life History Invariants: Some Explorations of Symmetry in Evolutionary Ecology*. Oxford University Press, Oxford.

Coleman, F. C., Koenig, C. C., Huntsman, G. R., Musick, J. A., Eklund, A. M., McGovern, J. C., Chapman, R. W., Sedberry, G. R. & Grimes, C. B. (1999). Long-lived reef fishes: the grouper–snapper complex. *Fisheries*, **25**, 14–21.

Dulvy, N. K. & Reynolds, J. D. (1997). Evolutionary transitions among egg-laying, live-bearing and maternal inputs in sharks and rays. *Proceedings of the Royal Society of London* B, **264**, 1309–1315.

Dulvy, N. K. & Reynolds, J. D. (2002). Predicting extinction vulnerability in skates. *Conservation Biology*, in press.

Dulvy, N. K., Metcalfe, J. D., Glanville, J., Pawson, M. K. & Reynolds, J. D. (2000). Local extinctions and shifts in community structure of skates masked by fishery stability. *Conservation Biology*, **14**, 283–293.

Felsenstein, J. (1985). Phylogenies and the comparative method. *American Naturalist*, **125**, 1–15.

Frisk, M. G., Miller, T. J. & Fogarty, M. J. (2001). Estimation and analysis of biological parameters in elasmobranch fishes: a comparative life history study. *Canadian Journal of Fisheries and Aquatic Sciences*, **58**, 969–981.

Gislason, H. & Sinclair, M. M. (eds.) (2000). Ecosystem effects of fishing. *ICES Journal of Marine Science*, **57**, 465–791.

Gunderson, D. R. (1997). Trade-off between reproductive effort and adult survival in oviparous and vivparous fishes. *Canadian Journal of Fisheries and Aquatic Sciences*, **54**, 990–998.

Gunderson, D. R. & Dygert, P. H. (1988). Reproductive effort as a predictor of natural mortality rate. *Journal du Conseil, Conseil International pour l'Exploration de la Mer*, **44**, 200–209.

Hall, S. J. (1999). *The Effects of Fishing on Marine Ecosystems and Communities*. Blackwell Science, Oxford.

Harvey, P. H. (1996). Phylogenies for ecologists. *Journal of Animal Ecology*, **65**, 255–263.

Harvey, P. H. & Pagel, M. (1991). *The Comparative Method in Evolutionary Biology*. Oxford University Press, Oxford.

Hutchings, J. A. (2000). Collapse and recovery of marine fishes. *Nature*, **406**, 882–885.

IUCN (World Conservation Union) (1996). *1996 IUCN Red List of Threatened Animals*. IUCN, Gland, Switzerland.

Jennings, S. & Beverton, R. J. H. (1991). Intraspecific variation in the life history tactics of Atlantic herring (*Clupea harengus* L.) stocks. *ICES Journal of Marine Science*, **48**, 117–125.

Jennings, S., Reynolds, J. D. & Mills, S. C. (1998). Life history correlates of responses to fisheries exploitation. *Proceedings of the Royal Society of London B*, **265**, 333–339.

Jennings, S., Reynolds, J. D. & Polunin, N. V. C. (1999a). Predicting the vulnerability of tropical reef fishes to exploitation: an approach based on phylogenies and life histories. *Conservation Biology*, **13**, 1466–1475.

Jennings, S., Greenstreet, S. P. R. & Reynolds, J. D. (1999b). Structural change in an exploited fish community: a consequence of differential fishing effects on species with contrasting life histories. *Journal of Animal Ecology*, **68**, 617–627.

Jennings, S., Kaiser, M. J. & Reynolds, J. D. (2001). *Marine Fisheries Ecology*. Blackwell, Oxford.

Jensen, A. L. (1996). Beverton and Holt invariants result from optimal trade-off of reproduction and survival. *Canadian Journal of Fisheries and Aquatic Science*, **53**, 820–822.

Johannes, R. E. (1998). The case for data-less marine resource management: examples from tropical nearshore finfishes. *Trends in Ecology and Evolution*, **13**, 243–246.

Kirkwood, G. P., Beddington, J. R. & Rossouw, J. A. (1994). Harvesting species of different lifespans. In *Large-Scale Ecology and Conservation Biology*, ed. P. J. Edwards, R. M. May & N. R. Webb, pp. 199–227. Blackwell Scientific, Oxford.

Merrett, N. R. & Haedrich, R. L. (1997). *Deep-Sea Demersal Fish and Fisheries*. Chapman & Hall, London.

Mosquera, I., Côté, I. M., Jennings, S. & Reynolds, J. D. (2000). Conservation benefits of marine reserves for fish populations. *Animal Conservation*, **4**, 321–332.

Musick, J. A. (1999). Criteria to define extinction risk in marine fishes. *Fisheries*, **24**, 6–14.

Musick, J. A., Berkeley, S. A., Cailliet, G. M., Camhi, M., Huntsman, G., Nammack, M. & Warren, M. L. (1999). Protection of marine fish stocks at risk of extinction. *Fisheries*, **25**, 6–8.

Pagel, M. (1999). Inferring the historical patterns of biological evolution. *Nature*, **401**, 877–884.

Parker, S. J., Berkeley, S. A., Golden, J. T., Gunderson, G. R., Heifetz, J., Hixon, M. A., Larson, R., Leaman, B. M., Love, M. S., Musick, J. A., O'Connell, V. M., Ralston, S., Weeks, H. J. & Yoklavich, M. M. (2000). Management of Pacific rockfish. *Fisheries*, **25**, 22–30.

Pauly, D. (1980). On the interrelationships between natural mortality, growth parameters and mean environmental temperature in 175 fish stocks. *Journal du Conseil, Conseil International pour l'Exploration de la Mer*, **39**, 175–192.

Pauly, D., Christensen, V., Dalsgaard, J., Froese, R. & Torres, F. (1998). Fishing down marine food webs. *Science*, **279**, 860–863.

Pope, J. G., MacDonald, D. S., Daan, N., Reynolds, J. D. & Jennings, S. (2000). Gauging the vulnerability of non-target species to fishing. *ICES Journal of Marine Science*, **57**, 689–696.

Powles, H., Bradford, M. J., Bradford, R. G., Doubleday, W. G., Innes, S. & Levings, C. D. (2000). Assessing and protecting endangered marine species.

ICES Journal of Marine Science, **57**, 669–676.

Reynolds, J. D. & Jennings, S. (2000). The role of animal behaviour in marine conservation. In *Behaviour and Conservation*, ed. L. M. Gosling & W. J. Sutherland, pp. 238–257. Cambridge University Press, Cambridge.

Roberts, C. M. & Hawkins, J. P. (1999). Extinction risk in the sea. *Trends in Ecology and Evolution*, **14**, 241–246.

Roff, D. A. (1991). The evolution of life-history parameters in fishes, with particular reference to flatfishes. *Netherlands Journal of Sea Research*, **27**, 197–207.

Roff, D. A. (1992). *The Evolution of Life Histories: Theory and Analysis*. Chapman & Hall, New York.

Russ, G. R. & Alcala, A. C. (1998). Natural fishing experiments in marine reserves 1983–1993: roles of life history and fishing intensity in family responses. *Coral Reefs*, **17**, 399–416.

Sadovy, Y. (1994). Grouper stocks of the western central Atlantic: the need for management and management needs. *Proceedings of the Gulf of Caribbean Fisheries Institute*, **43**, 43–64.

Sadovy, Y. J. (1996). Reproduction of reef fishery species. In *Reef Fisheries*, ed. N. V. C. Polunin & C. M. Roberts, pp. 15–59. Chapman & Hall, London.

Shepherd, J. G. & Cushing, D. H. (1990). Regulation in fish populations: myth or mirage. *Philosophical Transactions of the Royal Society B*, **330**, 151–164.

Smith, S. E., Au D. W. & Show, C. (1998). Intrinsic rebound potentials of 26 species of Pacific sharks. *Marine and Freshwater Research*, **49**, 663–678.

Stamps, J. A., Mangel, M. & Phillips, J. A. (1998). A new look at relationships between size at maturity and asymptotic size. *American Naturalist*, **152**, 470–479.

Stearns, S. C. (1992). *The Evolution of Life Histories*. Oxford University Press, Oxford.

Stevens, J. D., Bonfil, R., Dulvy, N. K. & Walker, P. A. (2000). The effects of fishing on sharks, rays and chimaeras (chrondrichthyans), and the implications for marine ecosystems. *ICES Journal of Marine Science*, **57**, 476–494.

Stokes, T. K., McGlade, J. M. & Law, R. (1993). *The Exploitation of Evolving Resources*. Springer-Verlag, Berlin.

Walker, P. A. (1998). Fleeting images: dynamics of North Sea ray populations. PhD thesis, University of Amsterdam.

Walker, P. A. & Heessen, H. J. L. (1996). Long-term changes in ray populations in the North Sea. *ICES Journal of Marine Science*, **53**, 1085–1093.

Walker, P. A. & Hislop, J. R. G. (1998). Sensitive skates or resilient rays? Spatial and temporal shifts in ray species' composition in the central and north-western North Sea between 1930 and the present day. *ICES Journal of Marine Science*, **55**, 392–402.

8

Mammalian life histories and responses of populations to exploitation

ANDY PURVIS

Overexploitation is the prime suspect in the global extinction of many mammalian species (Martin & Steadman, 1999) and is currently threatening extinction of hundreds more (Mace & Balmford, 2000). Harvesting theory predicts that reproductive rates will correlate positively with maximum sustainable yield, thereby linking life history to population vulnerability to exploitation. The theory underpinning that link has been well reviewed recently (Sutherland & Reynolds, 1998; Reynolds *et al.*, Chapter 7; Kokko *et al.*, Chapter 14), and I will not dwell on it here. My aims in this chapter are (1) to review briefly how reproductive rate is coupled with body size and mortality rate in mammals; (2) to explore what current theory predicts will happen to the life histories of sustainably exploited species; and (3) to test whether life history plays its predicted role in determining whether and how rapidly extant mammalian species decline in the face of exploitation.

PATTERNS IN MAMMALIAN LIFE HISTORY

Many key life history variables correlate with each other in placental mammals (for a review, see Harvey & Purvis, 1999). Some species live fast lives: they reach sexual maturity early, have large litters after short gestations and with short interbirth intervals, wean their offspring quickly and die young. Other species show the opposite suite of traits. This fast–slow continuum (Read & Harvey, 1989) covers an immense range in reproductive output. Table 8.1 compares some life history parameters for bank voles *Clethrionomys glareolus* and African elephants *Loxodonta africana*. The differences combine multiplicatively, such that a vole population could go through 17 generations in the time a newborn elephant is weaned, and over 50 by the time it first gives birth. If each vole were to live for 18 months, a single pregnant female could leave over 10^{26} descendants in this time. However,

Table 8.1. Selected life history parameters from a 'fast' species (bank vole *Clethrionomys glareolus*) and a 'slow' species (African elephant *Loxodonta africana*)

	Bank vole	African elephant
Wean age (days)	20	1890
Age 1st birth (days)	58	5460
Litter size	4.9	1.06
Litters/year	3.4	0.14
Instantaneous adult mortality rate/month	0.27	0.005
Adult size (g)	17	2766000

Data from Purvis & Harvey, 1995.

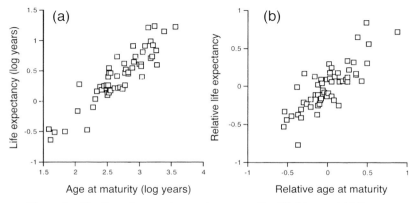

Figure 8.1. The fast–slow continuum in mammalian life history. (a) Life expectancy at maturity vs. age at maturity for 62 species of placental mammal. (b) The same relationship with body size effects removed by partial correlation. (Data from Purvis & Harvey, 1995.)

species that live fast also die young: Figure 8.1a shows the relationship between life expectancy at maturity (the reciprocal of the instantaneous mortality rate) and age at maturity for 62 species of placental mammal.

The most obvious difference between fast and slow species is that the former are physically smaller. This leads to a simple prediction that small mammals will tend to be more able than larger species to compensate for exploitation by increased recruitment. However, size and life history are not totally coupled: the fast–slow continuum persists even when body size effects are removed (Table 8.2; Figure 8.1b). For example, the greater horseshoe bat *Rhinolophus ferrumequinum* is only slightly larger than the bank vole (22 g vs. 17 g) but lives its life much more slowly: in the time taken for

Table 8.2. Significant interrelationships among some key mammalian life history variables when body size is held constant

Trait pair	Sign of correlation
Age at maturity & adult mortality rate	−
Age at maturity & juvenile mortality rate	−
Adult mortality rate & juvenile mortality rate	+
Age at maturity & annual fecundity	−
Annual fecundity & adult mortality	+
Annual fecundity & juvenile mortality	+
Gestation period & duration of lactation	+
Gestation period & age at maturity	+
Duration of lactation & age at maturity	+
Neonatal weight & litter size	−
Neonatal weight & gestation period	+

After Purvis & Harvey, 1996.

the vole population to reach 10^{26}, a pregnant female bat would leave fewer than 100 descendants. Body size differences therefore cannot be a sufficient explanation for why life history diversity has evolved – indeed, recent theoretical work by Kozlowski & Weiner (1997), reviewed below, has viewed mortality differences as a cause, rather than a result, of body size variation. Equally, they are unlikely to provide a complete explanation for the diversity of species' responses to exploitation.

This partial decoupling of body size and life history is important for conservation. It permits discrimination between competing hypotheses about why some species are more likely than others to decline in the face of human impact. Large-bodied mammals may be vulnerable because of a need for large home ranges (Woodroffe & Ginsburg, 1998), or because they face stronger hunting pressures (Cowlishaw & Dunbar, 2000) or because their low reproductive rates may make them less able to compensate for a given level of hunting (Kokko *et al.*, Chapter 14). Size, home range and reproductive rate are all intercorrelated, but the residual variation permits powerful statistical testing. I return to this topic in the last part of this chapter.

The link between body size and life history in mammals is also important for conservation. First, it focuses concern on large-bodied species as being potentially at risk of extinction through overexploitation, because their life histories are (on average) slower than those of smaller species. This approach has been used to identify fish species that may be particularly vulnerable to exploitation (Reynolds *et al.*, Chapter 7). Secondly, it can show how even sustainable exploitation is likely to affect mammalian diversity, by imposing a within-population selective force for smaller size. The next section develops this point within the framework of the most recent theoretical model to explain the evolution of mammalian life history differences.

EVOLUTIONARY RESPONSES TO EXPLOITATION

Kozlowski & Weiner's (1997) optimality model produces a very good fit to many observed life history patterns. In it, natural selection maximises life-time reproductive success by optimising the timing of sexual maturity. Briefly, each species' ecology is characterised by six parameters – the intercepts and slopes of the within-species allometric relationships of energy assimilation rate, respiration rate and mortality rate on body size. Individuals initially invest all their surplus energy (the difference between assimilation and respiration) into growth and none into reproduction. At a certain age and associated size, they make a once-and-forever switch from growth to reproduction – sexual maturity. What is the optimum age for this switch? There is a trade-off between potential reproductive rate and the chance of dying before reproducing – both are higher for organisms that delay maturity. The best decision turns out to be to mature as soon as the return from spending energy on reproduction now is as good as the expected future return from investing it in growth instead (Perrin & Sibley, 1993). The model can reproduce the observed interspecies allometries of life history traits on adult size, and also captures the fast–slow continuum: species with high mortality rates for their size also mature early for their size (Kozlowski & Weiner, 1997). Changing model parameters changes the optimal body size, making it possible to predict how body size should respond to particular hunting or harvesting regimes. Note that the model does not consider genetics at all: it is concerned with the stable evolutionary endpoint, assuming no constraints to optimality, and makes no predictions about the speed with which optimality will be achieved. But it provides a theoretical framework that can be used in conjunction with heritability estimates to predict evolutionary responses to exploitation (see Law, Chapter 15).

The full model is too complicated for mathematical analysis, but a computer program (*Allometries*: Gawelczyk, 1998) permits its exploration. Because an increase of mortality due to harvesting of 10–15% (as a percentage of natural mortality) is considered to be generally sustainable (Kirkwood et al., 1994), I examine the effect on life history of such an increase in mortality rate. The simplest mortality change to consider is an overall proportional increase in mortality rate at all sizes. A 10% proportional increase leads to a 21.3% decrease in adult weight and a 9% drop in age at maturity. Sustainable harvesting, even if it is not directly size selective, exerts a strong selection force for earlier maturity and smaller adult size. Size-selective harvesting, where larger individuals have higher harvesting mortality rates than do smaller animals, leads to even smaller adults and even faster life histories (results not shown). This supports the conclusion that, even if harvesting does not extirpate populations and species, it is likely to change them markedly (Law, Chapter 15).

The model also sheds light on changes seen in mammals subjected to a different form of exploitation – domestication. The early stages of domestication are usually indicated by a reduction in body size (Clutton-Brock, 1999) and often by the retention of juvenile characteristics (subcutaneous fat deposits, shorter jaws) into adulthood (paedomorphosis: McKinney & McNamara, 1991). Clutton-Brock (1999) attribute these changes to 'stress and hormonal changes as a result of the animal's emotional and physical dependence on humans'. However, they could also result from changes in mortality schedules plausibly associated with domestication (data from Mason, 1984; Clutton-Brock, 1999). Large species domesticated for food typically became smaller initially, consistent with higher mortality rates; if achieved through early sexual maturity, the small size would tend to be associated with paedomorphic features (progenesis). Species used mainly for power did not become smaller. Small food species, perhaps experiencing lower mortality than in the wild, became larger. Domestication is touted as one way of conserving species (e.g. farming species exploited for medicinal properties, see Parry-Jones & Vincent, 1998; making pets of threatened marsupials, Pain, 2000) but, as with exploitation, it can lead to marked change. The species may be conserved, but some of their characteristics may be lost.

LIFE HISTORY, EXPLOITATION AND POPULATION DECLINE

So far, this chapter has considered how populations might adapt to exploitation. Unfortunately, not all populations do adapt. If harvesting is too severe, it is not a microevolutionary selective force within populations and species, but a macroevolutionary selective force sorting lineages into those that have fast enough life histories to cope with the extra mortality and those that do not – the quick and the dead. This section starts with a brief review of characteristics that might be expected to increase species' vulnerability to overexploitation. Then I test the importance of life history traits in determining the sustainability of exploitation in mammals as a whole and, in more detail, carnivores and primates.

Theory predicts that populations with slower life histories will be more vulnerable to a given degree of exploitation (for a review, see Sutherland & Reynolds, 1998). However, it is important to remember that life history is only one factor determining whether exploitation is sustainable. The *level* of exploitation is obviously crucial too, and will depend on many things. Perhaps most importantly, human population density and land use patterns vary greatly over the globe, both regionally and locally (e.g. Alvard, 1995; World Resources Institute, 1996; Fa & Peres, Chapter 10). Moving to attributes of the species themselves, large-bodied species and those in large groups tend to be more obvious, to be more profitable to hunt, and perhaps to be perceived as more of a threat (e.g. Peres, 1990; Weaver *et al.*, 1996; Cowlishaw & Dunbar, 2000; Fa & Peres, Chapter 10). Animals active by day are more likely to be encountered by hunters (most hunting is done during the day: Cowlishaw & Dunbar, 2000), as are those with large home ranges (Woodroffe & Ginsberg, 1998). Species at high trophic level are more likely to be, or be viewed as, a threat to people or livestock, and so become targets for persecution (Weaver *et al.*, 1996). Lastly, animals of different species differ in their worth to exploiters. Some make better eating than others; some have finer fur than others; some allegedly have better medicinal properties than others. In all these cases, life history presumably plays little or no part in determining the intensity of exploitation.

Given that levels of exploitation vary greatly among species, is it none the less true that vulnerability to extinction through overexploitation is associated with large body size and slow life history? A simple analysis suggests that it is. The IUCN *Red List* (Baillie & Groombridge, 1996) contains assessments of extinction risk for virtually all mammalian species. For several orders, the relevant Action Plans go further and identify the nature of the process placing species at risk. Mace & Balmford (2000) collated these data, listing species as potentially threatened by habitat loss, overexploitation, introduced species, chains of extinction, natural rarity, or a combination of these. Table 8.3 ranks seven eutherian orders in terms of average size and speed of life history, and indicates the percentage of species in the order thought to be potentially threatened by overexploitation. Orders composed of large species with slow life histories (e.g. elephants and perissodactyls) have a high prevalence of threat due to overexploitation. At the other end of the scale, relatively few lagomorphs, primates and bats are at risk: these species are typically small and (except for primates) have faster life history. These patterns match findings with marine fishes (Jennings *et*

Table 8.3. Large body size and slow life history are associated with high prevalence of extinction risk from overexploitation, across seven eutherian orders

Order	Body size rank	Life history speed rank	% threatened by overexploitation
Proboscidea	1	7	100
Perissodactyla	2	6	88.2
Artiodactyla	3	4	61.8
Carnivora	4	3	40.1
Primates	5	5	18.8
Lagomorpha	6	1	17.0
Chiroptera	7	2	27.2

Data from Read & Harvey, 1989, and Mace & Balmford, 2000.

al., 1998; Dulvy *et al.*, 2000; Reynolds *et al.*, Chapter 7).

More sensitive and quantitative analysis of vulnerability is possible, using species-level information on extinction risk and life history. In what follows, I first describe and then build on (using the same procedures) an analysis of correlates of extinction risk in primates and carnivores by Purvis *et al.* (2000). We took IUCN (World Conservation Union) threat status as a quantitative measure of extinction risk for multiple regression analyses, predicting extinction risk from ecological, geographical and life history variables. Phylogenetic analysis was necessary because extinction risk and many of the predictor variables are often more similar among close relatives than would be expected if evolutionary history was not important. Statistical testing was therefore based on phylogenetically independent contrasts (Felsenstein, 1985), generated by the Comparative Analysis by Independent Contrasts (CAIC) program (Pagel, 1992; Purvis & Rambaut, 1995). This method is explained graphically by Reynolds *et al.* (Chapter 7, see Figures 7.3 and 7.4). Purvis *et al.* (2000) give details of the dataset and phylogenies used. In most analyses species were excluded from the analyses below if they were listed as threatened for reasons other than recent population decline (IUCN criterion A or A1: Mace & Lande, 1991; Baillie & Groombridge, 1996). This was to prevent the circularity that would arise if species were listed as threatened on the basis of, for instance, a very small geographical range.

Purvis *et al.* (2000) found that high extinction risk was associated independently with small geographical range, high trophic level, low population density, long gestation (in carnivores) and large body size (in primates). Do the same correlates hold when considering only those species potentially threatened by exploitation? Figure 8.2 provides informal

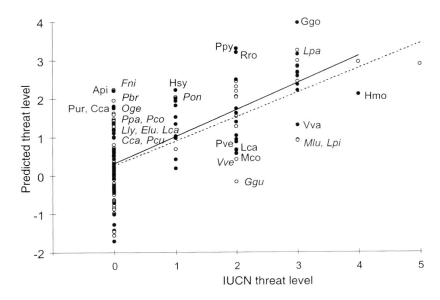

Figure 8.2. Predicted vs. observed threat in primates and carnivores. Threat levels: 0 = lower risk least concern, 1 = lower risk near-threatened, 2 = vulnerable or lower risk conservation-dependent, 3 = endangered, 4 = critically endangered, 5 = extinct or extinct in the wild. Species labels are as follows. Primates (solid circles, roman type, solid line): Api, *Alouatta pigra*; Cca, *Cebus capucinus*; Ggo, *Gorilla gorilla*; Hmo, *Hylobates moloch*; Hsy, *Hylobates syndactylus*; Lca, *Lemur catta*; Mco, *Mirza coquereli*; Ppy, *Pongo pygmaeus*; Pur, *Papio ursinus*; Pve, *Propithecus verreauxi*; Rro, *Rhinopithecus roxellana*; Vva, *Varecia variegata*. Carnivores (hollow circles, italics, dotted line): Cca, *Caracal caracal*; Elu, *Enhydra lutris*; Fni, *Felis nigripes*; Ggu, *Gulo gulo*; Lca, *Lynx canadensis*; Lly, *Lynx lynx*; Lpa, *Lynx pardinus*; Lpi, *Lycaon pictus*; Mlu, *Mustela lutreola*; Oge, *Oncifelis geoffroyi*; Pbr, *Parahyaena brunnea*; Pco, *Puma concolor*; Pcu, *Pseudalopex culpaeus*; Pon, *Panthera onca*; Ppa, *Panthera pardus*; Vve, *Vulpes velox*. (From Purvis *et al.* (2000), which also gives details of how the predicted threat levels were derived.)

evidence that they may. It compares the actual IUCN threat ratings for each species with the fitted values from the multiple regression model, i.e. the estimates of threat derived from each species' biological characteristics (for details of how Figure 8.2 was derived, see Purvis *et al.*, 2000). Labelled points are species poorly fitted by the model – the prediction is wrong by more than one threat level. Eleven of these species (*Enhydra lutris, Gorilla gorilla, Gulo gulo, Lemur catta, Lycaon pictus, Lynx pardinus, Mustela lutreola, Panthera onca, Pseudalopex culpaeus, Propithecus verreauxi* and *Varecia variegata*) are potentially at risk from overexploitation. If the characteristics predisposing overexploited species to high risk of extinction are markedly

Table 8.4. Multiple regression models predicting extinction risk in overexploited species of primate and carnivore. See text for explanation

Trait	Declining exploited species (35 species, 30 comparisons, $r^2 = 66.3\%$)			All exploited species (45 species, 37 comparisons, $r^2 = 64.3\%$)		
	Coefficient	t	p	Coefficient	t	p
Body mass	−0.38	−2.06	0.05	NS	NS	NS
Geographical range	−0.42	−6.40	<0.001	−0.42	−5.95	<0.001
Population density	−0.24	−2.92	0.007	−0.30	−3.97	<0.001
Gestation length	1.87	2.28	0.03	1.80	2.92	0.006
Trophic level	0.51	3.29	0.003	0.48	3.08	0.004

NS, not significant.

different from those operating in the sample as a whole, we might find these 11 to be predominantly on one side or other of the line. In fact, five are above the line and six below.

A more formal and rigorous analysis leads to similar conclusions. I extended the multiple regression modelling, using the same procedures, to predict extinction risk for exploited species only from the five variables in Purvis et al.'s (2000) model. Table 8.4 shows the results. All five predictors are significant, though body mass (the least significant) surprisingly has a negative coefficient. There was no significant difference between orders, i.e. there were no significant order × trait interactions. If, to achieve a larger sample, all exploited species are included (rather than only those listed for recent population decline), body mass is no longer a significant predictor ($p = 0.2$). Model simplification then leads to the regression results shown in the right-hand side of Table 8.4, in which the four remaining predictors are all highly significant (largest $p \leq 0.006$).

This model shows that, as expected, slow life history (as indicated by long gestation) predisposes overexploited species to decline more rapidly, when other important variables and phylogeny are taken into account. Interestingly, exploited species show almost the same set of correlates as all species, although they make up less than one-third of the species in Purvis et al.'s multiple regressions (35 of 120 species). This similarity may reflect the fact that overexploitation often goes hand-in-hand with habitat loss and degradation, the most prevalent threatening process. As habitats are disturbed, fragmented, and become accessible, so areas that were previously unprofitable for hunting become profitable (Milner-Gulland, Chapter 5).

In line with this argument, the outliers in Figure 8.2 are explained

Table 8.5. Life history predictors of extinction risk in overexploited carnivores and primates

Trait	N_S	N_C	A		B		C	
			t	p	t	p	t	p
Body mass	78	68	1.00	0.32	1.43	0.16	N/A	N/A
Interbirth interval	42	37	1.89	0.07	2.02	0.05	1.78[a]	0.08
Gestation length	60	52	2.24	0.03	2.53	0.01	2.07[a]	0.04
Litter size	70	61	−1.41	0.16	0.24	0.81	0.76	0.45
Age at sex. mat.	50	43	0.92	0.36	0.92	0.36	−0.63	0.54

A, as sole predictor. B, controlling for geographical range. C, controlling for geographical range and body size. N_S, number of species; N_C, number of contrasts (phylogenetically based comparisons). N/A, not applicable; sex. mat., sexual maturity.
[a]More significant than body mass in multiple regression.

better by the intensity of human impact than by the nature of the presumed threatening process. As discussed by Purvis *et al.* (2000), species for which the regression model most seriously underestimates threat tend to inhabit regions where recent human impacts have been particularly severe (e.g. Java and Madagascar). Conversely, species at lower risk than their biology would predict tend either to live in relatively undisturbed locations (such as northeast Amazonia) or to cope relatively well in disturbed habitats (e.g. *Gorilla gorilla*).

In the above analyses, gestation length was used as an indicator of a species' position on the slow–fast life history continuum. Do data on other aspects of life history yield similar patterns? Table 8.5 presents the results from a final set of phylogenetic analyses testing whether large body size, long interbirth interval, long gestation, small litter size and late sexual maturity are associated with high extinction risk among overexploited carnivores and primates. First, I tested each predictor in turn, without controlling for any other variables. I repeated this analysis controlling for geographical range size (easily the most important predictor of extinction risk in the regression models above). Then, I tested each life history variable in turn for significance while controlling for both geographical range size and body size. These results (Table 8.5) indicate a role for some but not all aspects of life history. Body mass is not a significant predictor of risk, whether or not geographical range is controlled for. Irrespective of whether geographical range and body size are taken into account, long gestation and (to a lesser degree) long interbirth interval are associated with high levels of risk. Both oust body mass from multiple regressions. Neither litter size, which shows little variance within some clades, nor age at sexual maturity is ever close to significance.

The new analyses reported in this section consistently show that the speed of life history plays a role in determining species' responses to exploitation. Mammalian orders made up of large, slow-living species show a high prevalence of overexploitation. Long gestation – one aspect of the fast–slow continuum – is correlated with high extinction risk among declining overexploited carnivores and primates, even when other important variables are taken into account. Long interbirth interval is also implicated as an important predictor of a species' fate. However, these analyses are preliminary, and care must be taken in interpreting the results. Ideally, data would be available indicating the intensity of exploitation faced by each species, or at least which species are exploited and which are not. Such data are not generally available, however, for global ensembles of species. Most species are probably exploited to a degree. Levels of exploitation are inevitably very difficult to quantify accurately (Bowen-Jones & Pendry, 1999; Fa & Peres, Chapter 10). The data here reflect instead opinions about whether or not the level of exploitation could threaten a species' survival. As such, there is the potential for circularity in the results.

CONCLUSIONS

Theory suggests that a given level of harvest is more likely to be sustainable for a species that has a 'fast' life history with early maturity and high reproductive rate. Empirical evidence from mammals backs up the theory: species placed at risk of extinction by exploitation tend to have slow life histories. Interestingly, the analyses suggest surprising similarity among the sorts of species put at risk by different threat processes. This similarity may reflect the tendency for different kinds of anthropogenic threat (habitat loss, overexploitation and introduced species) to go hand-in-hand.

Harvesting is a selective agent of extinction, preferentially pruning slow species from the phylogenetic tree of life and perhaps altering the body size distribution of mammals. However, even sustainable harvesting is a selective agent (unless care is taken to make it otherwise: Law, Chapter 15): large, slow species are expected to adapt to the new mortality regime by evolving smaller bodies and faster life histories. Either way, some of the character diversity – an important aspect of biodiversity (Williams & Humphries, 1996) – is lost.

ACKNOWLEDGEMENTS

I thank Georgina Mace, John Gittleman and Kate Jones for data and discussion, and the Natural Environment Research Council (GR3/11526) for support.

REFERENCES

Alvard, M. (1995). Shotguns and sustainable hunting in the Neotropics. *Oryx*, **29**, 58–65.

Baillie, J. E. M. & Groombridge, B. (1996). *IUCN Red List of Threatened Animals*. IUCN, Gland, Switzerland.

Bowen-Jones, E. & Pendry, S. (1999). The threat to primates and other mammals from the bushmeat trade in Africa, and how this threat could be diminished. *Oryx*, **33**, 233–246.

Clutton-Brock, J. (1999). *A Natural History of Domesticated Mammals*, 2nd edn. Cambridge University Press, Cambridge.

Cowlishaw, G. & Dunbar, R. I. M. (2000). *Primate Conservation Biology*. Chicago University Press, Chicago.

Dulvy, N. K., Metcalfe, J. D., Glanville, M. K., Pawson, M. K. & Reynolds, J. D. (2000). Fishery stability, local extinctions, and shifts in community structure in skates. *Conservation Biology*, **14**, 283–293.

Felsenstein, J. (1985). Phylogenies and the comparative method. *American Naturalist*, **125**, 1–15.

Gawelczyk, A. (1998). *Allometries*. Institute of Environmental Biology, Jagiellonian University, Krakow.

Harvey, P. H. & Purvis, A. (1999). Understanding the ecological and evolutionary reasons for life history variation: mammals as a case study. In *Advanced Ecological Theory,* ed. J. McGlade, pp. 232–248. Blackwells, Oxford.

Jennings, S., Reynolds, J. D. & Mills, S. C. (1998). Life history correlates of responses to fisheries exploitation. *Proceedings of the Royal Society of London B*, **265**, 333–339.

Kirkwood, G. P., Beddington, J. R. & Roussow, J. A. (1994). Harvesting species of different lifespans. In *Large-Scale Ecology and Conservation Biology,* ed. P. J. Edwards, R. M. May & N. R. Webb, pp. 199–227. Blackwell Science, Oxford.

Kozlowski, J. & Weiner, J. (1997). Interspecific allometries are byproducts of body size optimization. *American Naturalist*, **149**, 352–380.

Mace, G. M. & Balmford, A. (2000). Patterns and processes in contemporary mammalian extinction. In *Future Priorities for the Conservation of Mammalian Diversity,* ed. A. Entwhistle & N. Dunstone, pp. 27–52. Cambridge University Press, Cambridge.

Mace, G. M. & Lande, R. (1991). Assesing extinction threats: toward a reevaluation of IUCN threatened species categories. *Conservation Biology*, **5**, 148–157.

Martin, P. S. & Steadman, D. W. (1999). Prehistoric extinctions on islands and continents. In *Extinctions in Near Time: Causes, Contexts and Consequences,* ed. R. D. E. MacPhee, pp. 17–55. Kluwer/Plenum, New York.

Mason, I. L. (1984). *Evolution of Domesticated Animals*. Longman, London.

McKinney, M. L. & McNamara, K. J. (1991). *Heterochrony – The Evolution of*

Ontogeny. Plenum, New York.

Pagel, M. D. (1992). A method for the analysis of comparative data. *Journal of Theoretical Biology*, **156**, 431–442.

Pain, S. (2000). My pet possum. *New Scientist*, **166**(2236), 40.

Parry-Jones, R. & Vincent, A. (1998). Can we tame wild medicine? *New Scientist*, **157**(2115), 26.

Peres, C. A. (1990). Effects of hunting on western Amazonian primate communities. *Biological Conservation*, **54**, 47–59.

Perrin, N. & Sibley, R. M. (1993). Dynamic models of energy allocation and investment. *Annual Review of Ecology and Systematics*, **24**, 379–410.

Purvis, A. & Harvey, P. H. (1995). Mammal life history: a comparative test of Charnov's model. *Journal of Zoology (London)*, **237**, 259–283.

Purvis, A. & Harvey, P. H. (1996). Miniature mammals: life-history strategies and macroevolution. *Symposia of the Zoological Society of London*, **69**, 159–174.

Purvis, A. & Rambaut, A. (1995). Comparative analysis by independent contrasts (CAIC): an Apple Macintosh application for analysing comparative data. *Computer Applications in Bioscience*, **11**, 247–251.

Purvis, A., Gittleman, J. L., Cowlishaw, G. & Mace, G. M. (2000). Predicting extinction risk in declining species. *Proceedings of the Royal Society of London B*, **267**, 1947–1952.

Read, A. F. & Harvey, P. H. (1989). Life history differences among the eutherian radiations. *Journal of Zoology (London)*, **219**, 329–353.

Sutherland, W. J. & Reynolds, J. D. (1998). Sustainable and unsustainable exploitation. In *Conservation Science and Action*, ed. W. J. Sutherland, pp. 90–115. Blackwells, Oxford.

Weaver, J. L., Paquet, P. C. & Ruggiero, L. F. (1996). Resilience and conservation of large carnivores in the Rocky Mountains. *Conservation Biology*, **10**, 964–976.

Williams, P. H. & Humphries, C. J. (1996). Comparing character diversity across biotas. In *Biodiversity: A Biology of Numbers and Difference*, ed. K. J. Gaston, pp. 54–76. Blackwell Scientific, Oxford.

Woodroffe, R. & Ginsberg, J. R. (1998). Edge effects and the extinction of populations inside protected areas. *Science*, **280**, 2126–2128.

World Resources Institute (1996). *World Resources 1996–7*. Oxford University Press, Oxford.

9

Trade of live wild birds: potentials, principles and practices of sustainable use

STEVEN R. BEISSINGER

Each year millions of birds are captured alive and removed from the wild in developing countries in Latin America, Africa and Asia. If they survive, the birds either become pets in local homes, are transported to regional markets where they are sold for the same purpose, or are exported to developed countries where they are sold to pet owners or to aviculturists who breed birds as a hobby or as a business. Birds have made colourful and loved companion animals for centuries, and trade provides legal income for local peoples in a few nations.

The national and international trade in live birds has a somewhat different character than most other uses of wild populations discussed in this book. First, birds must be kept alive after harvest from the wild to have any value, but mortality in captivity is often high (Carter & Currey, 1987; Iñigo & Ramos, 1991). Secondly, some species can be bred in captivity by aviculturists, and this could decrease the economic value of and need for birds harvested from the wild. Thirdly, there is a 'collector mentality' and secrecy about breeding techniques in captivity that pervades aviculture and has hindered it from becoming a self-sufficient enterprise (Clubb, 1992; Derrickson & Snyder, 1992). This results in continued dependence by aviculturists on import of wild stock and creates a self-sustaining market.

There are many different actors involved in the trade of wild birds, each with vested interests. Multitudes of local extractors in developing countries remove birds from the wild and sell them to dozens of middle men, who, in turn, sell them to a handful of international importers that supply a large pet industry and aviculturists in developed countries with common or rare species. The Convention on International Trade in Endangered Species of Wild Fauna and Flora (CITES), which has been signed by 150 nations, regulates trade of species that are, or may soon become, endangered by listing them in one of the treaty's appendices (see below) and monitoring their legal trade. Each of these groups has vested interests that favour trade, including CITES, which was founded to track and regulate trade. In contrast, animal welfare groups and many conservation organisations in the countries of origin of the birds typically want an immediate stop to all bird trade. Finding themselves caught between these forces are governments, international conservation organisations and zoological parks. Only a few countries receive significant economic benefits from bird trade (Thomsen *et al.*, 1992). International conservation groups, such as the World Conservation Union (IUCN) and Worldwide Fund for Nature, have encouraged sustainable use of natural products as an approach to control trade, but have also supported decreased quotas and in some cases a moratorium on trade. Likewise, zoos have both supported trade in order to obtain birds for exhibit at reasonable prices and have discouraged it by participating in programmes to reduce the importation of wild birds. Thus the sociopolitical landscape of trade is complex, with many organisations each attempting to lobby for their own vested interests or conservation ethic.

In this chapter I review how the live trade in wild birds is implemented and examine whether it can become a sustainable enterprise. I begin by summarising the magnitude and effects of the bird trade. I then examine whether there is biological potential to sustainably harvest parrots, the group of birds most impacted on, given the current state of knowledge. Next I review what principles should guide the international trade of birds. Finally, I present evidence that suggests that trade, as currently practised, seems unlikely to conserve the species that it uses and the habitats on which they depend.

MAGNITUDE AND EFFECTS OF THE TRADE IN LIVE BIRDS

Captive breeding is the major source of individuals in trade for only a relatively few bird species: budgerigars *Melopsittacus undulatus*, cockatiels *Nymphicus hollandicus*, canaries *Serinus canaria*, zebra and Bengalese finches *Amandava subflava* and *Lonchura domestica*, most *Agapornis* lovebirds, several species of cockatoos *Cacatua*, and a number of Australian finches (e.g. *Chloebia gouldiae*, *Poephila cincta*, *Poephila acuticauda*). For most other birds, the majority of individuals in trade have come directly from wild sources, either trapped as free-flying adults or taken as nestlings.

Estimates of the annual numbers of birds extracted for international trade have ranged from 2 to 5 million individuals in the 1980s to 7.5 million birds during the peak of trade in the 1970s (Inskipp & Gamell, 1979; Thomsen *et al.*, 1992). Unfortunately, there is no monitoring system in place that can yield accurate numbers. Export and import permits for traded birds listed on CITES Appendices I (species threatened with extinction) and II (species that may become threatened if trade is not regulated) must be obtained from countries of both origin and destination, respectively. Export permits are also required for birds on Appendix III, which lists only species protected within the borders of a single nation. I analysed the numbers of birds recorded on CITES permits based on data from the World Conservation Monitoring Centre for the most recent period with complete records, 1991 to 1996.

The total number of birds reported to CITES that were traded among countries from 1991 to 1996 was 4 809 870 individuals (annual mean of 801 645 birds) of 519 species. Finches of the families Passeridae and Fringillidae comprised 70% of the trade (3 372 655 individuals of 70 species) and were exported primarily from Africa (mostly by Senegal and Tanzania, but also by Cameroon, Madagascar and Zaire), Asia (mostly by Vietnam and Malaysia) and Oceania (mostly by Indonesia and Singapore). Parrots (Psittacidae) accounted for 25% of the volume (1 215 020 individuals) and half the species (259). The greatest numbers of parrots came from Latin American countries (mostly Guyana, Surinam and Argentina, but also Nicaragua, Peru and Uruguay), and fewer were shipped from Africa. The remaining 5% of international trade was composed of 36 families and 190 species. Although finches comprise the greatest number of individuals in the trade, parrots account for the greatest monetary share of the commerce (Thomsen et al., 1992).

These figures greatly underestimate the numbers of birds extracted from the wild for the pet trade. They exclude mortality that takes place during capture, while confined by trappers, when transported within the country of origin, and while confined by the exporter before birds are granted CITES permits. Iñigo & Ramos (1991) estimated that 60% of the birds extracted from the wild may perish before export for international markets. Furthermore, the demand for pet birds within many Latin American and Asian countries may be as large or larger than the international market, although little is known about the size of internal markets. To the best of my knowledge, no systematic surveys have been published that estimate the number of pet birds in any exporting country, although even the casual traveller notices that many families have avian pets. In addition, China does not report avian export levels, which may be large (Thomsen et al., 1992: Yiming & Dianmo, 1999). Finally, export statistics track only the legal trade and therefore do not take into account the sizeable number of birds that are smuggled into international commerce. No firm estimates can be given for the size of illegal trade in birds, but it appears to be a profitable business because smuggled birds are thought to follow the same routes as illegal drugs.

Table 9.1. Comparison of levels of diversity, trade and threat in parrots
(Psittacidae) and finches (Passeridae and Fringillidae). Endangered and
threatened species are those listed by IUCN as critically endangered,
endangered or vulnerable

Comparison	Parrots	Finches
No. of species	358	1379
No. of endangered and threatened species	103	90
% endangered and threatened species	28.7	6.5
% endangered and threatened species affected by trade	47.5	13.3
No. of species traded 1991–96	259	70
% endangered and threatened species traded 1991–96	12.7	1.4

Thus, on the basis of pre-export mortality, sizeable internal markets in
many countries, missing data and a lucrative black market, it seems reasonable to conclude that the number of birds removed from the wild is probably two to four times the number reported to CITES. This would suggest
that 1 600 000 to 3 200 000 birds have been harvested annually from wild
populations for the live bird industry in the 1990s.

The impact of trade has not been equal for all traded species. Despite
the large numbers of finches traded, principal problems from the trade of
birds have been seen with parrots (Table 9.1). Nearly 29% of the world's
parrot species are listed by IUCN as threatened with extinction (Critical,
Endangered or Vulnerable categories), making this one the most
threatened families of birds (Collar et al., 1994). This is five times the rate of
threat to finches (Table 9.1). Nearly half of the threatened parrot species are
affected by trade compared with only 13% of threatened finches. Surprisingly, one of every eight threatened parrot species recently appeared in the
legal international trade, whereas trade of threatened species was negligible
for finches (Table 9.1). Examples of parrots now critically threatened by
trade include the Spix's macaw *Cyanopsitta spixii*, the hyacinth macaw
Anodorhynchus hyacinthinus, and the red-crowned Amazon *Amazona
viridigenalis*. Most parrots are threatened by a combination of trade and
habitat destruction (Beissinger & Bucher, 1992a; Collar & Juniper, 1992).
Nevertheless, trade may often be as threatening to most parrots as habitat
destruction because many parrots are habitat generalists. Flexible habitat
use by parrots is exemplified by the large number of species that have been
introduced, as a result of the pet trade, and have become established in
urban habitats around the world (Wiley et al., 1992).

Life history differences among species are often responsible for differential vulnerability to exploitation (Reynolds et al., Chapter 7; Purvis,

(a) Life cycle diagram and projection matrix

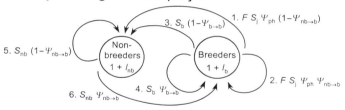

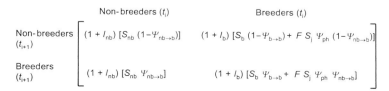

(b) Elasticity analysis

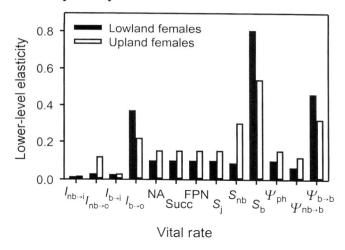

Figure 9.1. (a) Life cycle and (b) elasticity analyses of B. K. Sandercock & S. R. Beissinger (unpublished data, 2001) for the green-rumped parrotlet *Forpus passerinus* at Hato Masaguaral, Guarico, Venezuela. The life cycle diagram and the corresponding projection matrix were structured with breeder and non-breeder nodes to account for the high proportion of non-breeding males (50%) and females (20%) in the two populations (lowland and upland) that were studied (Sandercock *et al.*, 2000). Arcs 1 and 2 describe fecundity of breeders (*F*), weighted by the subsequent survival of fledglings produced (S_j), juvenile site fidelity (Ψ_{ph}) measured as the probability that a surviving juvenile remained in its natal population or dispersed to the other study population, and the probability that juveniles become breeders ($\Psi_{nb\rightarrow b}$) or non-breeders ($1 - \Psi_{nb\rightarrow b}$) by the next

Table 9.2. Comparison of the typical life history traits of parrots (Psittacidae) and finches (Passeridae and Fringillidae)

Life history trait	Parrots	Finches
Clutch size	Small	Large
No. of broods	Single	Multiple
Nest type	Cavity	Open cup or hanging
Age of first breeding	Delayed	Rapid
Adult survivorship rate	High	Intermediate
Primary habitat required	Forest	Grasslands

Chapter 8) and may explain why parrots are more susceptible to overharvesting than finches (Table 9.2). Annual fecundity of parrots is much less than finches by virtue of a smaller clutch size and fewer broods per year. Although parrots can use a variety of altered habitats for foraging, they typically nest in tree cavities, which are often in short supply. This may limit opportunities for nesting and result in large proportions of non-breeding males and females in parrot populations (Beissinger, 1996; Sandercock *et al.*, 2000). A large non-breeder population could create a surplus for harvesting, but may also result in a low rate of population growth. Finches usually make open cup or hanging nests, and do not require specialised structures for nesting. Furthermore, medium- and large-sized parrots may not reach an age of first breeding until two to five years of age, whereas finches usually mature within a year. Finally, most parrots are long-lived compared with finches.

Elasticity analyses of matrix population models (for a review, see Kokko *et al.*, Chapter 14) have shown that small changes in adult mortality rates have large effects on the rate of population change for long-lived species, such as most parrots, compared with small changes in reproductive success (Sæther & Bakke, 2000). B. K. Sandercock & S. R. Beissinger (unpublished data) present an example (Figure 9.1) for a small, highly fecund parrot

---

prebreeding census. Fecundity was calculated as the product of the percentage of nests that fledged at least one young (SUCC), the number of young fledged per successful nest (FPN), and the number of nesting attempts per year (NA). Arcs 3 and 4 parallel arcs 1 and 2, but are transition rates of adults, consisting of survival rates of breeders (S_b) and their likelihood of remaining a breeder ($\Psi_{b \to b}$) or becoming a non-breeder ($1 - \Psi_{b \to b}$). Finally, arcs 5 and 6 are life history pathways of non-breeders, and are composed of survival of adult non-breeders (S_{nb}) and their breeding status in the following year. Per capita immigration rates were incorporated into the breeder (I_b) and non-breeder (I_{nb}) nodes separately for juveniles moving from one population to another from within the study area (i) and for those entering from outside the study populations (o).

whose demography has been intensively studied (Beissinger & Waltman, 1991; Waltman & Beissinger, 1992; Stoleson & Beissinger, 1997a; Sandercock *et al.*, 2000). Despite the fact this species lays an average clutch size of seven eggs and can nest more than once a year, which are unusual traits compared with most parrots (Table 9.2), adult survivorship was by far the most elastic matrix parameter (i.e. small changes in this parameter had the greatest impact on population change). The probability of remaining a breeder was the next most important variable. Adult survival is likely to be even more important for larger parrots and macaws that lay fewer eggs and have higher survival rates than green-rumped Parrotlets *Forpus passerinus* (Sæther & Bakke, 2000).

POTENTIAL FOR SUSTAINABLE HARVESTING OF PARROTS

To harvest populations of wild animals sustainably, the rate of harvest (h) must not exceed the rate of productivity of the population at a particular size (N), which, in the simplest models of harvesting, is the difference between per capita birth (b) and death (d) rates (Caughley, 1977; Getz & Haight, 1989; Ludwig, Chapter 2) such that

$$(b - d)N - hN > 0. \tag{9.1}$$

The harvest rate should be set well below this level due to the effects of environmental stochasticity (Lande *et al.*, 1995; Engen *et al.*, 1997; Lande *et al.*, Chapter 4). If harvesting is mainly of adults or is equally implemented among age classes, the theory of maximum sustainable yield suggests that reducing population size to approximately one-half of carrying capacity (K) would maximise productivity (Figure 9.2a), depending on the shape of density dependence (Sutherland & Gill, Chapter 12). In the case of bird trade, sustainable yields would need to be set for each country, because that is how CITES sets export quotas.

To set harvest or export levels that are sustainable at large spatial scales for birds or other terrestrial wildlife, six areas of biological knowledge are needed (Beissinger & Bucher, 1992a):

1 *Population size and range*: Population trends must be detected, ideally by estimating population densities for different habitat types or land uses so that the effects of habitat change can be evaluated.
2 *Habitat requirements and movement*: Understanding habitat requirements, diet and ranging patterns is important for assessing the effects of landscape change on population viability. Different habitats

(a) Harvesting adults by increasing *K*

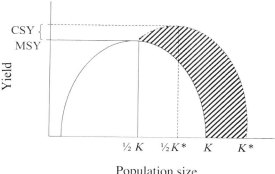

(b) Harvesting nestlings by adding nest sites

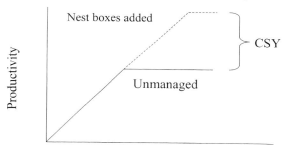

Figure 9.2. Two examples of the Conservative Sustainable Yield Model (Beissinger & Bucher, 1992a,b). (a) Comparison of harvesting of adults under the maximum sustainable yield model (MSY) and the conservative sustainable yield model (CSY), where the carrying capacity is increased to K^* by management actions. Yield is maximised at half carrying capacity for both MSY (K) and CSY (K^*). The harvest is large for MSY but only the increment between MSY and CSY is harvested under the Conservative Sustainable Harvest Model. (b) Effect of adding nest sites on the productivity and yield of nestlings from a parrot population under the Conservative Sustainable Yield Model. The unmanaged population has a large proportion of non-breeders due to nest site limitations. Productivity increases when nest boxes are added, as pairs that were unable to nest owing to lack of cavities begin to nest. The difference in productivity between the managed and unmanaged populations would be available to harvest as the CSY.

may be needed for breeding and feeding, for different stages of development and for the non-breeding season.

3 *Resilience to human disturbance and habitat changes*: Species differ in how

they respond to direct and indirect effects of human activities. Direct impacts of harvesting, such as abandonment of nests due to human visitation, may be easier to minimise than indirect effects that result from land use changes, such as regional shifts from grazing to agriculture.

4 *Estimates of demographic rates*: Harvesting potential is directly related to age- or stage-specific natality and mortality rates. For long-lived organisms, field studies may require 5–10 years to develop accurate estimates of these rates and longer to properly estimate their variances for use in population models (Beissinger & Westphal, 1998).

5 *Key factors that regulate populations*: Demographic factors that greatly affect population dynamics can be determined by correlation analyses using several annual life tables based on average estimates of vital rates (Varley & Gradwell, 1960) and by a variety of techniques for analysing sensitivity (Caswell, 1989).

6 *Effects of environmental variation*: Considering only averages for vital rates may lead to inaccurate estimates of harvest rates because annual variation in weather and natural catastrophes can strongly affect productivity and survivorship (e.g. Beissinger, 1986; Bayliss, 1989).

Efforts to set sustainable harvest rates for parrots and finches are greatly handicapped by a lack of good biological information for nearly all species. Although much information exists on the behaviour of parrots in captivity, they have typically proved to be difficult to study in the wild. Parrots may be noisy but they often inhabit the canopies of forests, making them hard to observe or census. Furthermore, nearly all species nest in cavities high in trees, which likewise are difficult to find and study. Most species are not plumage or size dimorphic, so the sexes cannot be readily distinguished. Because of their strong bills and hourglass-shaped legs, it has been difficult to develop adequate marking systems for banding parrots that do not result in injury to the birds (Meyers, 1995). Likewise only recently have neck-mounted radio transmitters been developed for parrots that allow detailed studies of movement to be made. This advance is important because many parrots fly long distances (> 25 km) across landscapes on a daily basis, making it difficult to determine movements and habitat requirements without telemetry. Thus few quantitative data are available on parrot demography (survival rates, longevity, recruitment, age of first breeding, annual productivity), annual population variation, diet and how it varies annually, habitat requirements, ranging behaviour, immigration and emigration, and social structure for parrots. Exceptions include the outstanding long-term studies of *Amazona vittata* on Puerto Rico (Snyder *et al.*, 1987; Meyers *et al.*, 1996), my on-going work with *Forpus passerinus* in the llanos of Venezuela (Beissinger & Waltman, 1991; Waltman & Beissinger, 1992; Stoleson & Beissinger, 1997a; Sandercock *et al.*, 2000), *Myiopsitta monachus* in Argentina (Bucher *et al.*, 1991; Navarro *et al.*, 1992, 1995; Martin & Bucher, 1993) and work done in Australia and New Zealand (Merton *et al.*, 1984; Rowley, 1990; Moorhouse *et al.*, 1999). The demography and population biology of traded finches appear to be equally poorly studied. Therefore it is not currently possible to set scientifically determined harvest quotas for any species of parrot or, for that matter, any species of bird currently traded.

Beissinger & Bucher (1992a,b) proposed a simple model for sustainable harvesting that could be used in the absence of detailed information discussed above, which is needed to set precise quotas. The Conservative Sustainable Harvest Model (Figure 9.2) suggested that if it can be demonstrated that a local population is stable or increasing ($(b - d)N \geq 0$), then any increase in the rate of population growth from increased productivity (b^*), decreased mortality (d^*) or increased carrying capacity (K^*) due to management programmes (mN) would lead to an increase in overall population size ($mN = (b^* - b)N$ and/or $mN = (d - d^*)N$), which could be harvested ($mN = hN$). Population trends and demography would need to be documented prior to the start of management programmes, and then compared with the increased rate of population growth or productivity produced from management activities. Once management begins, excess individuals produced by management could be harvested, and in theory should result in the maintenance of the population at preharvest levels. This is a cautious approach to resource use because it allows only extraction of excess produced by investments to improve the size of the population.

To apply the Conservative Sustainable Harvest Model, we must first determine which age classes should be harvested. Nestlings are the best age class for harvest in parrots (Beissinger & Bucher, 1992a,b). They adapt more easily to captivity, can be tamed and trained to talk, and their harvest has less of an impact on population dynamics than harvest of adults as discussed above. Harvesting nestlings also means that maximising sustainable harvests (hN) would not necessarily require reducing population size to one-half carrying capacity, the traditional approach to maximise sustainable yield (Ludwig, Chapter 2); instead, yields of nestlings are maximised by maximising productivity (bN) or the number of successfully nesting pairs, which would probably be accomplished by maintaining populations near carrying capacity (see also Lande *et al.*, Chapter 4). Density dependence seems unlikely to impact on the harvest of parrot nestlings in the manner in which it impacts on the harvest of adults because: (1) excess nestlings are removed before they have fledged, and (2) productivity can be increased without increasing population size by increasing the likelihood of becoming a breeder ($\Psi_{nb \to b}$ in Figure 9.1). Thus the juvenile survival rate of young that do fledge seems unlikely to be affected by an increase in population size or probability of becoming a breeder.

Productivity could be increased by management actions that increase the number of breeding pairs, percentage of nests fledging young or number of young fledged per nest. Methods to increase productivity include adding nest boxes to increase the number of nesting pairs, protecting nest sites from predators, supplementing food supplies, decreasing hatching asynchrony and deliberate multiple clutching (Beissinger & Bucher, 1992a,b). Adding nest sites is probably the easiest way to increase productivity for species that accept them, and determining the change in the number of breeding pairs should be straightforward (Figure 9.2b). Another easy and conservative way to harvest parrots and macaws would be to take advantage of the fact that most species exhibit hatching asynchrony, which leads to brood reduction of the last-hatched young (Stoleson & Beissinger, 1997b). Chicks that would normally die from brood reduction could be removed from the nest shortly after hatching, with little or no effect on population size.

Thus, if it is implemented properly and conservatively, sustainable harvesting may have potential advantages for conservationists, aviculturists, the pet industry, and local peoples. In theory, conservationists could gain by having healthy populations of wild parrots near carrying capacity, and by transmitting economic value to habitats to help to conserve them in their natural states. Aviculturists could obtain new genetic stock for their breeding programmes from birds harvested sustainably. The pet industry would have a steady but small inflow of legally imported birds already conditioned to captivity. Finally, if designed properly, the profits from these programmes could be directed to the local people in need of ways to support themselves and the economy of nations that are trying to develop.

On the basis of biological and sociological considerations of sustainable use of wildlife, Beissinger & Bucher (1992b) presented some criteria to judge the applicability of wildlife for sustainable use. It may be easier to implement the sustainable use of wildlife in systems with the following characteristics:

1 *Age classes with a low reproductive value (Fisher 1930) are harvested*: This would allow both productivity and population density to remain high (see Kokko *et al.*, Chapter 14).

2 *Products are marketed shortly after harvesting so that long periods (e.g. years) in captivity can be avoided*: This would act to minimise losses and expenses during captive husbandry.

3 *The potential to increase productivity through management is high*: Under such circumstances, sustainable harvests can be larger.

4 *Harvested species only require a small or moderate amount of land that is under the control of one owner*: Usually social species will require less land than territorial species because individuals group closer together and often occur in higher densities (Emmons, 1987). It will be easier to set and enforce harvest limits if one land owner controls the resource rather than many that must split the control.

5 Species that complete their life cycle within the management area will be easier to monitor and manage for sustainability.

6 Species that are fecund and adapted to earlier successional stages will be easier to sustain and be less susceptible to overharvesting than species with low rates of reproduction or requiring mature forests, which are disappearing rapidly.

Sustainable harvesting of parrots fits some of these criteria. Parrots can be harvested as nestlings, and do not have to be kept in captivity for years before being marketed. In the case of some species, parrots are capable of greatly increased productivity through intensive management, and may spend their complete life cycle within a management area. The potential for death in captivity may be the major disadvantage of harvesting parrots compared with other wildlife systems. Also many parrots have a relatively low reproductive potential and may be more susceptible to overharvesting than more fecund species (Bucher, 1992).

In conclusion, the above discussion suggests that there may be good potential to harvest some species of parrots from the wild for trade. In the next section, we move beyond potential to examine whether or not the harvest of wild birds for exportation is desirable.

PRINCIPLES TO GUIDE THE INTERNATIONAL TRADE IN LIVE BIRDS

The issues relating to the governance of the international trade in live birds are complex and transcend biology. Political, social and economic factors each affect the conditions under which trade has been or should be implemented. Little serious thought has been given to the implications of these factors in the international trade of live wildlife, including the role of biology.

In recognition of the pivotal role played by the USA as the largest importer of live birds in the world (Thomsen *et al.*, 1992) and the importance of legislation that was about to be introduced to the US Congress to decrease the importation of birds in 1990, the American Ornithologists' Union (AOU) formed a committee of ornithologists concerned with bird trade issues (Beissinger *et al.*, 1991). The charge of this subcommittee was to review the problems associated with the bird trade and to make recommendations for effective ways of dealing with the detrimental influences of trade on wild bird populations.

If there is to be a trade in live exotic birds for commercial purposes, it is important to state what conditions should be fulfilled. Focusing primarily on the implications for conserving wild bird populations in the country of origin as well as in North America, the committee developed seven principles to provide the basis for guiding an international trade in live birds (Beissinger *et al.*, 1991).

1   *The importation of live exotic birds should be sustainable, and should not pose risks for wild populations of species that are imported*: There is no justification for commercial endeavours that contribute to the extinction in the wild of a species, as discussed earlier for several parrots as the trade is currently practised. Export quotas for most countries need to be lowered drastically. Commercial harvesting of any of the 1183 bird species listed by IUCN as threatened with extinction is likely to increase their chances of extinction and should be prohibited.

2   *The importation of live exotic birds should not pose significant risks of disease transmission to native species, poultry or other birds held for legitimate purposes such as exhibition or scientific study*: Quarantine regulations around the world are, for the most part, unlikely to stop the importation of potentially threatening diseases. For example, all birds imported to the USA are held for 30 days of US Department of Agriculture regulated quarantine and tested only for exotic Newcastle disease (velogenic viscerotropic Newcastle disease, VVND). This period is too brief to allow the detection of other slow acting pathogens, many of which have recently been imported into collections of captive birds and could potentially be transferred to native species (Cooper, 1989; Nilsson, 1990). Difficulties with this one disease alone, which caused a massive loss to the poultry industry in 1972 and has continued to strike periodically since then (Nilsson, 1990), suggests that enormous economic losses may occur if worldwide shipments of birds continue and current quarantine procedures are not changed to require much

longer quarantine periods and testing for many more diseases. The massive extinctions of native Hawaiian birds, caused in part by diseases to which many species had no prior exposure, exemplify the potentials of exotic diseases to have tragic consequences (Warner, 1968; Van Riper et al., 1986).

3 *The importation of live exotic birds should not result in significant potentials for the establishment of feral populations*: Uncontrolled experiments in introductions of exotic bird species are already underway around the world as a result of continued international trade. Large numbers of exotic birds establishing themselves, so far mostly in urban environments but perhaps eventually spreading to natural ecosystems, may cause native populations to decline (Wiley et al., 1992).

4 *The importation of live exotic birds should be consistent with national policies concerning the use of native species*: To be ethically consistent, the trade in live exotic birds should be regulated by nations in the same manner that they regulate commercial uses of native wildlife. For example, the USA has prohibited most commercial uses of native wildlife species. Legal forms of utilisation of wild birds, for example sport hunting and falconry, are carefully regulated, require licenses, and require that wild populations of game birds or raptors be managed in a sustainable manner. Exotic birds were largely exempt from US regulations until the passage of the Wild Bird Conservation Act of 1992. So, although it is illegal to market or hold native bird species, except under permit, it is quite legal to practise these same activities with most non-native birds without a permit. This poses unfortunate ethical inconsistencies in the treatment of wildlife species.

5 *The trade of live exotic birds should be governed by regulations that are economically feasible, practically enforceable, simple, and effective. Regulations should not preclude scientific studies of birds in captivity, international recovery efforts, or public exhibitions for educational purposes*: Complicated regulations imply complicated bureaucracies and significant expense, and are susceptible to failure because of underfunding and difficulties in addressing complexities. Simplicity in regulations is an important goal.

6 *Captive breeding of exotic species for aviculture should be self-sustaining (i.e. without requiring the continued importation of wild-caught birds) and be conducted humanely*: The importation of wild birds for commercial aviculture is fuelled in part because it is often less expensive for aviculturists to import adult wild-caught birds and begin production immediately than to wait for years for captive-reared juvenile birds to

become mature (Clubb, 1992). Instead of supplementing captive birds with wild imports, private aviculturists must begin to adjust their practices towards the goal of self-sustaining captive populations, including better coordination of studbooks to maintain genetically viable captive gene pools.

7 *Captive breeding of exotic birds as a conservation strategy should be pursued only as a last resort, and only as part of internationally recognised and structured programmes*: The promotion of captive breeding as conservation is sometimes a rationalisation for keeping exotic birds in captivity. Captive breeding for conservation should be fully integrated with preservation and reintroduction efforts, conducted within the native range of the species, and internationally coordinated (Derrickson & Snyder, 1992). The many problems associated with captive breeding argue for using this technique with great discretion (Snyder *et al.*, 1996).

In conclusion, the seven principles discussed above provide a different perspective on trade that is not apparent when considering only the potential for sustainable harvest of birds in the preceding section. While harvest for the trade has the potential to offer certain benefits to exporting countries and aviculturists, there are a variety of reasons discussed above why trade in wild birds might not be desirable or advisable for importing countries. In the following section I examine how the trade actually functions in practice.

BIRD TRADE IN PRACTICE

Two factors work at different spatial scales to affect how the trade of birds is actually practised. First, market forces far from the source of the birds are so strong that it is attractive for local people to poach birds for the trade. In a unique meta-analysis, Wright *et al.* (2001) present data on poaching and mortality rates of 4024 wild nests for 21 species of parrots in 14 Neotropical countries. The average rate of poaching was 30%. Six studies reported no poaching and four studies found > 70% of the nests had had their young robbed. Mortality from poaching was higher than mortality due to natural causes in species that were poached. Poaching was significantly higher in unprotected sites than in protected sites. The rate of poaching was unrelated to the conservation status (i.e. IUCN rank). However, inexpensive species selling for less than $500 on the US retail market had lower poaching rates than those selling above that value. Because the demand far exceeds the capacity for breeders to produce exotic birds, there is great impetus to poach birds from the wild, where they may be sold as pets or falsely entered into the trade as captive-bred or sustainably harvested individuals.

Secondly, the practice of sustainable harvesting would require a degree of local control over harvests that is difficult and expensive to achieve. Presently no marking system, including closed-ring banding schemes, can reliably distinguish legal from illegally harvested birds, or identify illegally harvested birds that are 'laundered' through harvest programmes. Reliably distinguishing between legally and illegally harvested individuals requires a well-documented pedigree and tissue samples for DNA analyses. Without strong controls, attempts at sustainable harvesting could increase conservation problems rather than solve them. Most countries realise that they are incapable of controlling harvest of live birds and do not permit birds to be harvested from the wild for export or for national pet markets.

The USA recognised that, as the largest single importer of live wild birds (Thomsen *et al.*, 1992), it bore a responsibility for finding a solution to unsustainable use in many exporting countries and to the smuggling of wild birds out of countries that prohibited trade. The Wild Bird Conservation Act (WBCA) of 1992 was enacted to decrease the importation of wild birds for the pet trade. The act prohibits only importation of birds listed on CITES Appendices I and II, unless the birds come from licensed captive breeding facilities or sustainable harvesting programmes. These two appendices include most endangered and threatened species and all parrot species. The Act does not regulate other species and excludes importation of birds used for scientific study and zoological parks, as well as all game birds. The Act was acceptable under the General Agreement on Tariffs and Trade (GATT) that promotes free trade, because species that are prohibited from importation have already been identified by an international treaty (CITES).

Importation of live birds into the USA declined drastically after the WBCA took effect in October 1993 (Figure 9.3). The total numbers of live birds imported into the USA dropped from an average of 150 000– 200 000 per year in the 1980s and early 1990s to an average of 3500 birds per year from 1994 to 1997. Annual levels of legal import to the USA of psittacines, which mostly came from New World countries, declined from > 100 000 annually to hundreds of birds. A shift of Latin American parrots to markets in other parts of the world apparently has not occurred, and the total numbers of legally traded parrots has declined radically (Figure 9.3). Finches, on the other hand, were not greatly affected by the change in US laws. Although the number of finches imported into the USA declined

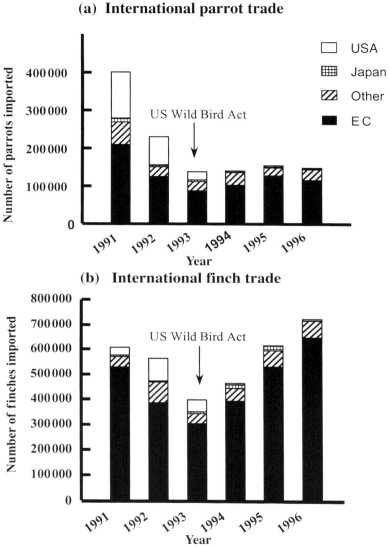

Figure 9.3. The annual numbers of (a) parrots and (b) finches in the international trade based on CITES permits issued from 1991 to 1996 for the USA, Japan, European Community countries, and other countries. The USA enacted the Wild Bird Conservation Act in 1992 and it came into effect in October 1993.

dramatically from around $> 50\,000$ per year to fewer than 3000 per year, the USA represented only a small market for finches compared with countries in the European Community (Figure 9.3). The source of most finches in the international trade is Africa and Asia. Finches appear to have found alternative markets in the European Union that are closer to exporting countries than is the USA. As a result, total trade in finches has remained as high or higher than it was before the WBCA came into effect (Figure 9.3).

There is not yet enough information to determine the effects of the WBCA on wild bird populations. It seems likely that the WBCA will decrease harvesting rates of parrots. Wright *et al.* (2001) found that poaching rates of Neotropical parrots were significantly lower after the enactment of the WBCA. However, no systematic surveys are available to indicate trends of wild populations of parrots or finches to determine whether populations have started to recover.

CONCLUSIONS

The international and national trade in live birds is a multimillion dollar industry that threatens rather than conserves birds. Although there is potential to harvest birds for the pet trade in a sustainable manner, harvest quotas are based on poor science. Furthermore, biological principles suggest that shipping birds around the world is unwise. Finally, poaching is pervasive as the trade is currently practised, and difficult to control. Only if sustainable harvesting can lead to robust bird populations and habitat preservation will giving a market value to birds by trading them achieve a conservation purpose. In the face of pressures from current unsustainable harvesting, most attempts at sustainable harvesting seem likely to fail.

Several changes in CITES are required to recreate a trade that conserves birds and ecosystems. First, to avoid the problem of introducing exotic species and diseases, CITES would have to switch its appendices from long 'dirty lists' of species that are too threatened to harvest to short 'clean lists' of species that are safe to import and whose quotas have been scientifically set at conservative levels. Secondly, international and national regulation of harvest of birds must shift from the use of national quotas to local harvest quotas. National quotas do not tie harvest levels into local conditions and provide no impetus for ecosystem conservation, because they mostly benefit economic interests that lie outside the region and that lack any commitment to sustaining the birds or their habitats. Quotas developed on a site-by-site basis, such as for a particular ranch or management area, would directly connect harvest levels to local population changes and habitat conditions.

REFERENCES

Bayliss, P. (1989). Population dynamics of magpie geese in relation to rainfall and density: implications for harvest models in a fluctuating environment. *Journal of Applied Ecology*, **26**, 913–924.

Beissinger, S. R. (1986). Demography, environmental uncertainty, and the evolution of mate desertion in the snail kite. *Ecology*, **67**, 1445–1459.

Beissinger, S. R. (1996). On the limited breeding opportunities hypothesis for avian clutch size. *American Naturalist*, **147**, 655–658.

Beissinger, S. R. & Bucher, E. H. (1992a). Can parrots be conserved through sustainable harvesting? *BioScience*, **42**, 164–173.

Beissinger, S. R. & Bucher, E. H. (1992b). Sustainable harvesting of parrots for conservation. In *New World Parrots in Crisis: Solutions from Conservation Biology*, ed. S. R. Beissinger & N. F. R. Snyder, pp. 73–115. Smithsonian Institution Press, Washington, DC.

Beissinger, S. R. & Waltman, J. W. (1991). Extraordinary clutch size and hatching asynchrony of a neotropical parrot. *Auk*, **108**, 863–871.

Beissinger, S. R. & Westphal, M. I. (1998). On the use of demographic models of population viability analysis in endangered species management. *Journal of Wildlife Management*, **62**, 821–841.

Beissinger, S. R., Snyder, N. F. R., Derrickson, S. R., James, F. C. & Lanyon, S. M. (1991). International trade in live exotic birds creates a vast movement that must be halted. *Auk*, **108**, 982–984.

Bucher, E. H. (1992). Neotropical parrots as pests. In *New World Parrots in Crisis: Solutions from Conservation Biology*, ed. S. R. Beissinger & N. F. R. Snyder, pp. 201–219. Smithsonian Institution Press, Washington, DC.

Bucher, E. H., Martin, L. F., Martella, M. B. & Navarro, J. L. (1991). Social behaviour and population dynamics of the monk parakeet. *Acta XX Congressus Internationalus Ornithologici*, pp. 681–689.

Carter, N. & Currey, D. (1987). *The Trade in Live Wildlife: Mortality and Transport Conditions*. Environmental Investigation Agency, London.

Caswell, H. (1989). *Matrix Population Models*. Sinauer, Sunderland, MA.

Caughley, G. (1977). *Analysis of Vertebrate Populations*. Wiley & Sons, New York.

Clubb, S. (1992). The role of private aviculture in the conservation of Neotropical psittacines. In *New World Parrots in Crisis: Solutions from Conservation Biology*, ed. S. R. Beissinger & N. F. R. Snyder, pp. 117–131. Smithsonian Institution Press, Washington, DC.

Collar, N. J. & Juniper, A. T. (1992). Dimensions and causes of the parrot crisis. In *New World Parrots in Crisis: Solutions from Conservation Biology*, ed. S. R. Beissinger & N. F. R. Snyder, pp. 1–24. Smithsonian Institution Press. Washington, DC.

Collar, N. J., Crosby, M. B. & Stattersfield, A. J. (1994). *Birds to Watch 2: The World List of Threatened Birds*. Birdlife, Cambridge.

Cooper, J. E. (1989). Birds and zoonoses. *Ibis*, **132**, 181–191.

Derrickson, S. R. & Snyder, N. F. R. (1992). Potentials and limits of captive breeding in conservation. In *New World Parrots in Crisis: Solutions from Conservation Biology*, ed. S. R. Beissinger & N. F. R. Snyder, pp. 133–163. Smithsonian Institution Press, Washington, DC.

Emmons, L. H. (1987). Ecological considerations on the farming of game animals: capybaras yes, pacas no. *Vida Silvestre Neotropical*, **1**(2), 54–55.

Engen, S., Lande, R. & Sæther, B.-E. (1997). Harvesting strategies for fluctuating populations based on uncertain population estimates. *Journal of Theoretical Biology*, **186**, 201–212.

Fisher, R. A. (1930). *The Genetical Theory of Natural Selection*. Dover, New York.

Getz, W. M. & Haight, R. G. (1989). *Population Harvesting*. Princeton University Press, Princeton, NJ.

Iñigo-Elias, E. E. & Ramos, M. A. (1991). The psittacine trade in Mexico. In *Neotropical Wildlife Use and Conservation*, ed. J. G. Robinson & K. H. Redford, pp. 380–392. University of Chicago Press, Chicago.

Inskipp, T. P. & Gamell, A. (1979). The extent of world trade in birds and the mortality involved. In *Thirteenth Bulletin of the International Council for Bird Preservation*, ed. P. Barclay-Smith & R. D. Chancellor, pp. 98–103. International Council for Bird Preservation, London.

Lande, R., Engan, S. & Sæther, B.-E. (1995). Optimal harvesting of fluctuating populations with a risk of extinction. *American Naturalist*, **145**, 728–745.

Martin, L. F. & Bucher, E. H. (1993). Natal dispersal and first breeding age in monk parakeets, *Auk*, **110**, 930–933.

Merton, D. V., Morris, R. B. & Atkinson, I. A. E. (1984). Lek behavior in a parrot: the Kakapo *Strigops habroptilus* of New Zealand. *Ibis*, **126**, 277–283.

Meyers, J.M. (1995). A colored leg banding technique for *Amazona* parrots. *Journal Field Ornithology*, **66**, 582–589.

Meyers, J. M., Arendt, W. J. & Lindsey, G. D. (1996). Survival of radio-collared nestling Puerto Rican parrots. *Wilson Bulletin*, **108**, 159–163.

Moorhouse, R. J., Sibley, M. J., Lloyd, B. D. & Greene, T. C. (1999). Sexual dimorphism in the North Island Kaka *Nestor meridionalis septentrionalis*: selection for enhanced male provisioning ability? *Ibis*, **141**, 644–651.

Navarro, J. L., Martella, M. B. & Bucher, E. H. (1992). Breeding season and productivity of monk parakeets in Cordoba, Argentina. *Wilson Bulletin*, **104**, 413–424.

Navarro, J. L., Martella, M. B. & Bucher, E. H. (1995). Effects of laying date, clutch size and communal nest size on the reproductive success of Monk Parakeets. *Wilson Bulletin*, **107**, 472–476.

Nilsson, G. (1990). *Importation of Birds into the United States in 1986–1988*. Animal Welfare Institute, Washington, DC.

Rowley, I. (1990). *The Galah*. Surrey Beatty, Chipping Norton, New South Wales.

Sæther, B.-E. & Bakke, Ø. (2000). Avian life history variation and contribution of demographic traits to population growth rate. *Ecology*, **81**, 642–653.

Sandercock, B. K., Beissinger, S. R., Stoleson, S. H., Melland, R. R. & Hughes, C. R. (2000). Survival rates of a Neotropical parrot: implications for latitudinal comparisons of avian demography. *Ecology*, **81**, 1351–1370.

Snyder, N. F. R., Wiley, J. W. & Kepler, C. B. (1987). *The Parrots of Luquillo: Natural History and Conservation of the Puerto Rican Parrot*. Western Foundation of Vertebrate Zoology, Los Angeles, CA.

Snyder, N. F. R., Derrickson, S. R., Beissinger, S. R., Wiley, J. W., Smith, T. B., Toone, W. D. & Miller, B. (1996). Limitations of captive breeding in endangered species recovery. *Conservation Biology*, **10**, 338–348.

Stoleson, S. H. & Beissinger, S. R. (1997a). Hatching asynchrony brood reduction and food limitation in a neotropical parrot. *Ecological Monographs*, **67**, 131–154.

Stoleson, S. H. & Beissinger, S. R. (1997b). Hatching asynchrony in parrots: boon or bane for conservation. In *Behavioral Approaches to Conservation in the Wild*, ed. J. R. Clemmons & R. Buchholtz, pp. 157–180. Cambridge University Press, Cambridge.

Thomsen, J. B., Edwards, S. R. & Mulliken, T. A. (eds.) (1992). *Perceptions, Conservation and Management of Wild Birds in Trade*. Traffic International, Cambridge.

Van Riper, C. III, Van Riper, S. G., Goff, M. L. & Laird M. (1986). The epizoology and ecological significance of malaria in Hawaiian land birds. *Ecological Monographs*, **56**, 327–344.

Varley, G. C. & Gradwell, G. R. (1960). Key factors in population studies. *Journal of Animal Ecology*, **29**, 399–401.

Waltman, J. R. & Beissinger, S. R. (1992). The breeding biology of the Green-rumped Parrotlet. *Wilson Bulletin*, **104**, 65–68.

Warner, R. E. (1968). The role of introduced diseases in the extinction of the endemic Hawaiian avifauna. *Condor*, **70**, 101–120.

Wiley, J. W., Snyder, N. F. R. & Gnam, R. S. (1992). Reintroduction as a conservation strategy for parrots. In *New World Parrots in Crisis: Solutions from Conservation Biology*, ed. S. R. Beissinger & N. F. R. Snyder, pp. 165–200. Smithsonian Institution Press, Washington, DC.

Wright, T. F., Toft, C. A., Enkerlin-Hoeflich, E., Gonzalez-Elizondo, J., Albornoz, M., Rodríguez-Ferraro, A., Rojas-Suárez, F., Sanz, V., Trujillo, A., Beissinger, S. R., Berovides A., V., Gálvez, A., X., Brice, A. T., Joyner, K., Eberhard, J. R., Gilardi, J., Koenig, S. E., Stoleson, S., Martuscelli, P., Meyers, J. M., Renton, K., Rodríguez, A. M., Sosa-Asanza, A. C., Vilella, F. J. & Wiley, J. W. (2001). Nest poaching in Neotropical parrots. *Conservation Biology*, **15**, in press.

Yiming, L. & Dianmo, L. (1999). The dynamics of trade in live wildlife across the Guangxi border between China and Vietnam during 1993–1996 and its control strategies. *Biodiversity and Conservation*, **7**, 895–914.

10

Game vertebrate extraction in African and Neotropical forests: an intercontinental comparison

JOHN E. FA & CARLOS A. PERES

There is mounting evidence that defaunation of the world's remaining tropical forests is a major cause of biodiversity loss, in some cases more important than deforestation (Redford, 1992; Robinson & Bennett, 2000). Forest vertebrates that are hunted for subsistence or commercial purposes are particularly affected. Such forest meat, game meat or bushmeat has long been a critical component of the diet of forest dwellers in tropical forest regions, often representing more than half of the animal protein intake (Chardonnet *et al.*, 1995). However, continuous offtake of game meat can only be sustained when hunting-induced mortality of target species does not exceed production. Yet, wild meat consumption has become more intensive in many moist tropical forest regions. This is largely because of rapidly increasing human populations, improved hunting technologies and a greater emphasis on commercialisation (Redford & Robinson, 1987; Wilkie & Carpenter, 1999). Increases in game extraction can aggravate pressures on local faunas, especially on large-bodied forest vertebrates, in some cases driving them to local extinction (Peres, 1990, 1996, 2000a; Redford, 1992; McRae, 1997).

Game hunting is the single most geographically widespread form of resource extraction in South America and Africa, and can affect the core of even the largest and least accessible nature reserves (Peres & Terborgh, 1995). Studies that have calculated sustainability of game harvests in these continents have almost invariably found that rates of extraction far exceed those of production (Robinson & Bodmer, 1999), even in the case of traditional aboriginal societies still using rudimentary hunting technology (Noss, 1995; Alvard *et al.*, 1997). Such uncontrolled exploitation will no doubt threaten to bring about marked population declines, and eventually the extinction of a number of game species. Coupled with threats from habitat loss, even from historical deforestation (Cowlishaw, 1999), global extinctions of the most sensitive species such as primates are likely to occur as an accumulation of local disappearances (Struhsaker, 1999). This may result in long-term changes in tropical forest dynamics through the loss of seed-dispersers, large granivores and frugivores, and 'habitat landscapers' such as large forest mammals (Dirzo & Miranda, 1991; Chapman & Onderdonk, 1998; Wright *et al.*, 2000).

Numerous international conservation organisations believe that tropical forest faunas are seriously endangered from current extraction levels of subsistence and commercial hunting (WSPA, 1995; Ape Alliance, 1998). However, few studies have quantified this at the scale of regions or continents. Such a broader picture would help us to understand the extent of the problem and serve to highlight differences and similarities among geographical areas. Moreover, intercontinental comparisons of consumption and extraction rates can shed light on the interactions between ecosystem productivity, harvestable game biomass and human consumers.

In this chapter we review the patterns of mammalian harvest in tropical moist forests in South America and Africa. We limit our comparison to these environments to maximise comparability in habitat structure. We discuss similarities and differences between primary consumer biomass in both continents and estimate the numbers and biomass of game animals harvested each year in the two continents. We focus on mammals because this class of vertebrates comprises a large proportion of hunting kills in both continents. To that end, we use data collected from different hunting studies within the major forest blocks in the two regions, the Amazon and Congo Basins.

TROPICAL FORESTS OF SOUTH AMERICA AND AFRICA: BACKGROUND

Rain forest is the primary biome between 8° N and 8° S of the equator in both Africa and South America. These forests are characterised by high rainfall, a high proportion of canopy cover (> 10%) and lack of a continuous grass layer (FAO, 1988, 1993). Attempts to review the forest typology in the two continents have been made by Sayer *et al.* (1992) for Africa and by Harcourt & Sayer (1996) for South America – based on the White (1983) and UNESCO classification systems, respectively. Mean annual rainfall was the primary variable used to distinguish between two broad forest types: wetland (mangrove and swamp forests) and dryland (lowland moist, submontane and montane forests) types (Harcourt & Sayer, 1996). These forests can be further classified into evergreen, semi-evergreen, semi-deciduous, humid, perhumid or variants of seasonal types.

Rain forests are structurally complex and are known for their remarkable richness of plants and animals. This diversity is not uniform, since plant richness in different forest regions can vary widely, decreasing with annual precipitation (for African and South American forests, respectively, see Hall & Swaine, 1981; Gentry, 1992). The flora is also related to soil type and geology of the area. In climatically similar areas, different soils can result in distinct forest types; leguminous tree species that can adapt to low nutrient conditions are often more abundant on poor acidic soils (Newbery et al., 1988; Maisels et al., 1994). Additionally, species diversity in the rain forest zones may have been affected by the oscillating climate during the late Pleistocene (Prance, 1987; Hamilton, 1988). Forest cover in much of Central Africa and South America may have been reduced prior to the end of the last glacial period (12 500 BP), remaining only in more mesic areas within the continents. As the last ice age gradually receded, rainfall increased, and the boundaries of the refuge forest expanded to fill the vast central Congo and Amazon Basins of Africa and South America.

Rain forests occupy 52% of the Neotropics (9.2 million km²), but only 7% (5.3 million km²) of the African continent (Sayer et al., 1992; Harcourt & Sayer, 1996). In Africa, rain forest is distributed from Senegal on the west coast of the continent to the eastern tip of Somalia, the vast proportion occurring within the lowlands of the Congo Basin (1.86 million km²). Most countries in West Africa were once covered in forests from the coastline to deep inland, but agricultural and urban expansion has led to large-scale deforestation and fragmentation. There are now only relict structurally complex and species-rich forest blocks remaining in West Africa, whereas a vast, more or less continuous expanse of relatively undisturbed rain forest still remains in Central Africa. Around 80% of the rain forest on the African continent is concentrated in this region, particularly in the Democratic Republic of Congo (Congo-Zaire). Rain forest outliers are found in suitable wet regions and along some rivers in other parts of tropical Africa. In the Neotropics, the vast proportion of remaining rain forest (8 million km²) is in South America, with 70% in Brazil. Rain forests are found from Mexico in the north, through the isthmus of Central America, to the Pacific countries of Colombia, Ecuador and Peru; across to Venezuela, Guyana, French Guyana and Surinam, through the vast Amazon forest in Brazil, and onto the landlocked countries of Bolivia and Paraguay. This area has a varied climate and relief that has resulted in a large variety of forest types.

Throughout the past 10 000 years, humans have had a major influence on the African scene. Hunter–gatherer communities were ubiquitous. However, the adverse climate in the humid forest regions, in comparison to savannah regions, limited penetration. At the time of European colonisation of sub-Saharan Africa in the sixteenth century, forests in high rainfall areas were mostly undisturbed and with sparse human populations (Aubréville, 1949). The introduction of South American maize, manioc, plantains and yams by the Portuguese provided the stimulus for colonisation and agricultural expansion in the forests. Subsequently, the development of trade with the outside world has had a profound impact on African forests. By the end of the twentieth century much of the East and West African forests had been fragmented, but those in Central Africa were still mostly intact. The aggregate figures from the Food and Agriculture Organization (FAO) suggest that less than 30% of the original forest cover remained in 1988. However, the whole of West Africa except Liberia has suffered severe deforestation, whereas in the Central African region, the most inaccessible areas remain relatively unbroken. Here, about 59% of the original forest cover of around 2 million km^2 still remain (Biodiversity Support Program, 1993; Wilkie & Carpenter, 1999). Forest loss in the different countries is correlated with the country's population density (Figure 10.1). Deforestation rates in central Africa pale in comparison with those in West Africa. Approximately only 0.2% of Central Africa's closed-canopy forests are cleared annually in contrast to a staggering rate of 4% in West Africa. However, some areas of Central Africa are experiencing extensive forest conversion as a result of agricultural clearing, mining and road building. The current human population in the six countries included in the Congo Basin (Cameroon, Central African Republic, Democratic Republic of Congo, Equatorial Guinea, Gabon and Congo) is around 24 million living in forest and another 9 million in urban centres (Bahuchet & de Maret, 1995).

Although South America was the last major continent to be invaded by humans, its contemporary vertebrates represent but a subset of a much larger fauna that existed prior to the Pleistocene megafaunal 'overkill'. This overkill may have been perpetrated by generations of Clovis hunters as they gradually advanced across the Panamanian isthmus all the way south to Patagonia (Martin, 1984; Ward, 1997). Mesoamerican, eastern and southern Brazilian forests have now been reduced to only shreds of their once majestic domain, but forest cover in much of Amazonia and the Guianan shields still remains relatively intact. Compared with Africa, relative deforestation rates have been modest (maximum 30%) in most countries (Figure 10.1), and demographic trends give some reason for optimism.

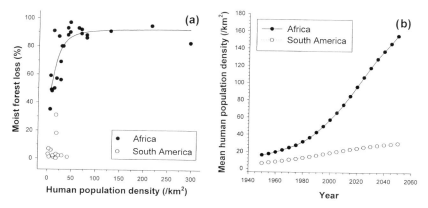

Figure 10.1. Inter-continental contrasts in (a) the relationship between human population density (inhabitants/km^2) and percentage moist forest loss in South American and African countries, and (b) projected human population density for countries in the Congo Basin (Africa) and the Amazon Basin (South America). Data from the World Resources Institute (1998).

Human populations in most of the continent show a greater than expected decline in growth rates, often as a consequence of rural exodus and urbanisation, which has relieved the pressure on forest frontiers. These trends are reflected in future projections of population growth, which are far more alarming in Africa than in South America. As we shall see, however, consumer pressure on terrestrial vertebrates is but one side of the equation in predicting the likelihood of local extinctions, which are also affected by morphoecological traits of the faunal assemblages and the structure and productivity of their forest habitats.

INTERCONTINENTAL DIFFERENCES IN MAMMAL ASSEMBLAGES

The numbers of families, genera and species inhabiting Africa and the Neotropics are similar, although bats are better represented in the latter (Keast, 1969). There is more than 90% endemism at the species level in both continents, and 29% and 54% of the families are exclusive to Africa and the Neotropics, respectively. Marsupials, edentates, pangolins, aardvarks, elephants and hyraxes have representatives in only one continent.

Although examples of convergent evolution have been documented across ecological vicariants from distinct orders or families (Keast, 1969; Bourlière, 1973), larger-bodied taxa are far more prominent in Africa than in the Neotropics (Fa & Purvis, 1997). African forests harbour a wider size range of diurnal primates, lorisids, squirrels, omnivorous Carnivora and hornbills (Bucerotidae) compared with their ecological analogues in the Neotropics, namely ceboid primates, didelphid possums, procyonids and toucans (Ramphastidae) (Cristoffer, 1987). The lowland tapir *Tapirus terrestris* is the only Neotropical forest mammal over 50 kg, whereas 13 frugivorous and browsing mammals can be assigned to this size class in African forests. This is partly a function of the more modest cervid radiation in the Neotropics, in contrast to that of African bovids, many of which occupy equatorial forest environments. Indeed, the most species-rich Neotropical forests typically contain only five sympatric ungulates (i.e. two peccaries *Tayassu* spp., two brocket deer *Mazama* spp. and tapir *Tapirus terrestris*), whereas as many as 10 ungulate species (*Cephalophus* spp., *Tragelaphus* spp., *Neotragus* spp., *Hyemoschus* sp., *Potamochoerus* sp., *Hylochoerus* sp., *Syncerus* sp.) can inhabit African forests. A similar phenomenon can be observed among the primates. In South America, prehensile-tailed (ateline) genera rarely exceed 10 kg, whereas several living or extinct Palaeotropical primate genera exceed 100 kg, including *Pongo* in Southeast Asia, *Gorilla* in mainland Africa, and *Archaeoindris* and other giant lemurs in Madagascar (Peres, 1994). This difference cannot be explained as an artefact of a less complete primate fossil record in the Neotropics (Fleagle *et al.*, 1997). The largest known platyrrhine species was a giant ateline from the Plio-Pleistocene boundary equivalent in size to only twice the weight of modern woolly spider monkeys *Brachyteles arachnoides* (Hartwig & Cartelle, 1996). In any case, environmental changes since then could have altered selection pressure on body size differentially.

The mean body mass of present-day non-volant forest mammals in Africa (37.45 ± 17.19 kg, $N = 284$; data from Kingdon, 1997) differs significantly from that in Amazonian forests (4.80 ± 1.44 kg, $N = 192$; data from Fonseca *et al.*, 1996). This is largely a function of the greater number of large-bodied species in Africa as compared to the Neotropics; in African forests, 60% of species are greater than 1 kg and 22% are greater than 10 kg whereas the equivalent figures are only 38% and 7% for the Neotropics (Figure 10.2). Moreover, the weights of the 66 species of mammalian primary consumers of a forest in northeast Gabon are uniformly distributed across five orders of magnitude (Emmons *et al.*, 1983), whereas those of a typical *terra firme* forest of central Amazonia are markedly skewed towards small- and mid-sized species (Peres, 1999a). These continental patterns are also reflected in the larger size of fruits consumed by Palaeotropical vertebrate frugivores compared with those in the Neotropics (Mack, 1993).

Various ecological hypotheses have been proposed to account for the narrower size range of Neotropical birds and mammals (Cristoffer, 1987;

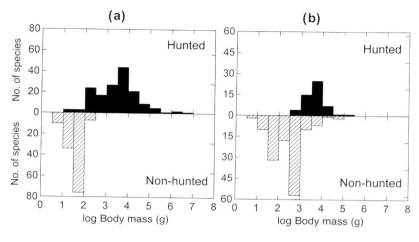

Figure 10.2. Distribution of body mass of hunted and non-hunted mammals in tropical rain forests of (a) Africa and (b) the Neotropics.

Fleming et al., 1987; Terborgh & van Schaik, 1987). However, many of the differences between African and South American species assemblages could also be attributed to the impact of humans on forest habitats and their faunas during the Pleistocene–Holocene. In particular, anthropogenic disturbance and forest fragmentation, more recent in the New World, could be implicated. The postulated overkill of most South American Pleistocene megafauna by the earliest human colonists (Martin, 1984) is highly unlikely in Africa, where human hunters and large vertebrates evolved side by side.

Intercontinental differences in forest structure may further reinforce differences in the size structure of the mammal fauna, although cause and effect here may often be confounded. A comparison of forest profiles from relatively undisturbed sites, the Urucú in the Amazon Basin (Peres, 1999a) and Lopé in Central Africa (White, 1994), show how forest structure often differs between the two continents (Figure 10.3). In Africa, forest elephants and other large mammals play a key role in the functioning and structure of rain forests (Prins & Reistma, 1989; Western, 1989). These mammals are attracted to areas with dense stands of herbaceous growth, common in the large gaps created by logging or natural disturbance (Chapman & Chapman, 1997). Unlike their Neotropical counterparts, African forests lack aggressive colonising tree species that can take advantage of large gaps. This appears to retard gap succession, allowing the herb and shrub layer to take hold, thus substantially increasing gap longevity in favour of large

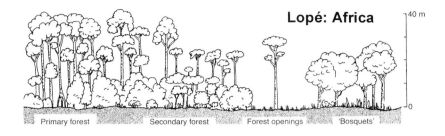

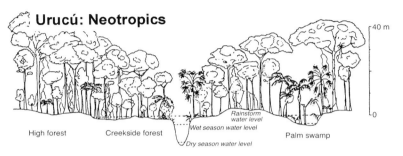

Figure 10.3. Vegetation profiles of rain forest in a Neotropical site (Urucú, Brazilian Amazonia; from Peres, 1999a, Copyright University of Chicago Press, 1999) and an African site (Lopé, Gabon; White, 1994).

terrestrial browsers feeding primarily on vegetative growth (Struhsaker *et al.*, 1996). Moreover, Neotropical forests appear to be generally more 'fragile' than those in Africa (Emmons & Gentry, 1983), where megaherbivores like forest elephants have a long history of structural influence on vegetation (Tutin *et al.*, 1997). Although tapirs can excavate salt-licks and selectively kill understorey saplings (C. Peres, personal observation), large forest 'landscapers' that can uproot small and medium-sized trees are conspicuously absent in the Neotropics.

HARVESTABLE FOREST MAMMAL BIOMASS: INTERCONTINENTAL DIFFERENCES

We compiled estimates of the total non-volant mammalian biomass for tropical forest sites in Africa and South America (Table 10.1). In Africa, non-volant mammal biomass has been estimated for a forest in southwestern Gabon (Prins & Reistma, 1989), and in more detail for five sites (Sites 1 to 5 in White, 1994) of differing logging history in the Lopé Reserve, also in Gabon (White, 1994). These estimates were based on censuses carried out concurrently for all species. We also calculated the mammal

Table 10.1. Estimates of crude mammalian biomass (kg/km^2) for forest sites in the Neotropics and Africa

Sites	Dominant vegetation type	Biomass (kg/km^2)	Sources
Neotropics			
Manaus, Brazilian Amazonia	Evergreen primary *terra firme* forest	206+	Malcolm, 1990; Emmons, 1984; Rylands & Keuroghlian, 1988
Urucú, Brazilian Amazonia	Evergreen primary *terra firme* forest	891	Peres, 1999a
Cosha Cashu, Peruvian Amazonia	Evergreen mature floodplain forest	1416	Janson & Emmons, 1990
Lago Teiú, Brazilian Amazonia	Evergreen annually flooded *várzea* forest	1987	Ayres, 1986
Guatopo, Venezuela	Secondary (30 years old) submontane forest	946	Eisenberg *et al.*, 1979
BCI, Panama	Evergreen late-secondary moist forest	2264	Eisenberg, 1980
Africa			
Ogooué-Maritime, southwest Gabon	Evergreen primary *terra firme* forest	1680	Prins & Reitsma, 1989
Makokou, northeast Gabon	Evergreen primary *terra firme* forest	2214	Barnes & Lahm, 1997
Parc Nacional des Volcans, Rwanda	Montane forest	3100	Plumptre, 1991
Lopé, Gabon	Evergreen primary *terra firme* forest	3101–6000	White, 1994
Ituri Forest, DRC	Evergreen primary *terra firme* forest	2743	Koster & Hart, 1988; Thomas, 1991; Wilkie, 1987

BCI, Barro Colorado Island; DRC, Democratic Republic of Congo.

biomass of forest sites in Makokou, northeast Gabon (Lahm, 1993; Barnes & Lahm, 1997), Ituri, northeast Democratic Republic of Congo (Koster & Hart, 1988; Wilkie & Finn, 1990; Thomas, 1991; Wilkie *et al.*, 1998; D. S. Wilkie, personal communication) and Virungas in Rwanda (Plumptre, 1991; A. J. Plumptre, personal communication). Density and body weight estimates (including corrections for the proportion of juveniles; see Coe *et al.*, 1976) for all censused mammals were used to calculate the crude primary consumer biomass. Data from five Neotropical closed-canopy forest sites (Urucú, Brazil, Peres, 1999a; Lago Teiú, Brazil, Ayres, 1986; Cocha Cashu, Peru, Janson & Emmons, 1990; Barro Colorado Island, Panama, Eisenberg, 1980) and two semi-open (Acurizal, Pantanal wetlands, Schaller, 1983; Masaguaral, Venezuelan llanos, Eisenberg *et al.*, 1979), and a semi-montane second-growth forest (Guatopo, Venezuela, Eisenberg *et al.*, 1979) were also available.

Average total crude primary consumer biomass of non-volant mammals in African forest sites (mean ± SD = 2 848.0 ± 1 129.3 kg/km², $N = 9$) far exceeded that in Neotropical sites (1108.7 ± 245.2 kg/km², $N = 5$). Biomass figures taken from these areas may not necessarily be representative of forests in the whole region, since there are considerable differences in soil type, elevation and climate. For example, total biomass among different sites within the Lopé Reserve (White, 1994), and the Virungas (Plumptre, 1991) in Africa, varied between 1000 and 6000 kg/km². This enormous range in productivity was attributed largely to differences in ungulate and proboscidean densities, namely elephants *Loxodonta africana* (Barnes *et al.*, 1993). However, in some areas duikers *Cephalophus* sp. can attain a bio-mass higher than that of elephants (Dubost, 1978, 1979) and in several other sites primates dominate the mammalian biomass (Oates *et al.*, 1990). The latter is probably typical of most tropical rain forest mammal communities, where a large proportion of the primary biomass is made up of folivorous primates (colobines (*Colobus* and *Procolobus* spp. in mainland Africa) and howler monkey (*Alouatta* spp. in South America)).

A further illustration of between-site variability can be seen in primates, the most intensively studied mammals in tropical forests. Primates are also the most important arboreal consumers in rain forests in Africa (Emmons *et al.*, 1983; Oates *et al.*, 1990) and South America (Peres, 1999a), often comprising a major part of the non-volant mammalian biomass. Although a broad link can be established between ecological variables (e.g. food supply) and primate abundance, the picture is complicated by the influence of human disturbance (logging and hunting), and historical and biogeographical factors (Oates, 1996). The considerable variation in primate den-

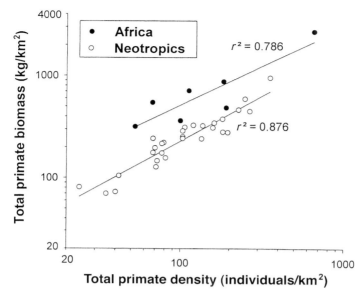

Figure 10.4. Variation of crude primate density and biomass at 29 Neotropical and 7 African forest sites, sourced from Peres (1999b, with permission from Cambridge University Press) and Chapman *et al.* (1999), respectively.

sity and biomass across a wide range of non-hunted and lightly hunted forest sites in Africa ($N=7$; Chapman *et al.*, 1999), and South America ($N=29$; Peres, 1999b) is therefore not surprising. However, overall primate community biomass in Africa is on average significantly larger than that in the Neotropics (Figure 10.4). African forests sustain a mean primate density of 194.8($\pm$210.5) individuals/km^2 (range 53 to 657 individuals/km^2), and a mean biomass of 857.8 $\pm$ 839.2 kg/km^2 (range 318 to 2710 kg/km^2), whereas South American sites exhibit much lower densities (123.6 $\pm$ 78.1 individuals/km^2, range 24 to 355 individuals/km^2) and biomass of 277.0 $\pm$ 177.7 kg/km^2 (range 70 to 953 kg/km^2). In general, most African forest sites are dominated by folivorous colobines, thus inflating figures of the number of animals present and their biomass. In Africa and Asia, colobines account for an average of 60% (range 28–91%, $N=10$) of the primate community biomass (Bourlière, 1985; Oates *et al.*, 1990; Oates, 1996). In Neotropical forests, the equivalent arboreal folivores often represent over half of the biomass of non-volant mammals (Eisenberg & Thorington, 1973; Peres, 1997).

Chapman *et al.* (1999) indicated that, in Africa, forest type correlates better with primate biomass than does forest productivity (as gauged from rainfall); biomass in the wettest locality (Douala-Edéa, Cameroon) with 4000 mm of rainfall is six times lower than that of Kibale (1662 mm). Peres (1999b) also showed that forest type, hydrology, and geochemistry were key determinants of primate biomass in Amazonia. Thus forests on nutrient-rich soils, and perhaps with a higher fruit production, sustain a greater primate biomass, even when differences in hunting pressure are taken into account (Peres, 1999b). Studies in Africa have suggested that soil chemistry is less important than growth stage, heterogeneity, taxonomic composition and history of the vegetation in determining the abundance of colobines (Oates *et al.*, 1990). In fact, Maisels *et al.* (1994) and Maisels & Gautier-Hion (1994) showed that the primate biomass can still be high in forests on nutrient-poor white-sand soils, where legume seeds and young leaves become prominent in their diets. The foraging plasticity of African monkeys may also explain why no clear relationship between frugivore primate biomass (guenons *Cercopithecus* and mangabeys *Lophocebus* and *Cercocebus*) and fruit availability has been found (Tutin *et al.*, 1997); frugivorous primates will increase their seed and leaf intake in forests where fleshy fruits are less diverse or absent (Maisels & Gautier-Hion, 1994).

The distribution of mammalian biomass, according to whether the species belong to arboreal or terrestrial guilds, differs significantly between continents. African forests are dominated by terrestrial species, whereas this trend is reversed towards arboreal taxa in Neotropical forests (Figure 10.5). Arboreal species account for more than 20% of the mammalian biomass in the few African forests surveyed to date, whereas this figure is typically 50–90% in the Neotropics. The structure and distribution of plant production in these forests may explain, to some extent, the spread of mammalian consumers. In general terms, continuous close-canopy forests, which are more typical of the Neotropics, will have more of their plant production in the tree canopy (Fittkau & Klinge, 1973), thus serving primarily the resource base of arboreal vertebrates. On the other hand, the terrestrial mammal biomass is expected to increase as large canopy gaps become increasingly common, allowing greater primary productivity for understorey shrubs and herbaceous layer. This trend is clearly uncovered when South American semi-open forest sites are compared with those under closed canopy (cf. Peres, 1999a). Indeed, these appear to converge with African forests in terms of their terrestrial mammal biomass. Canopy structure at these sites is far more heterogeneous, allowing a greater proportion of total solar radiation to filter through to the understorey and ground layers, favouring the primary production that sustains the large-bodied

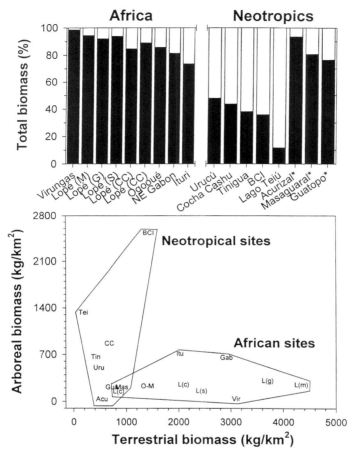

Figure 10.5. Between-site variation in mammalian biomass expressed as the proportion of biomass accounted for by terrestrial (black bars) and arboreal species (open bars), and the relationship between the crude biomass of arboreal and terrestrial species (below). M, Marantaceae forest: s, *Sacoglottis* forest; G, galleries and bosquets; CC, closed canopy forest; BCI, Barro Colorado Island, Panama; Tei, Teiú, Brazil; Tin, Tinigua, Brazil; Uru, Urucú, Brazil; CC, Cocha Cashu, Peru; Gua, Guatopo, Venezuela; Mas, Masaguaral, Venezuela; Acu, Acurizal, Brazil; Itu, Ituri, Democratic Republic of Congo; Gab, Makokou, northeast Gabon; O-M., Ogooué-Maritime, Gabon; Vir, Virungas, Rwanda; L(g), Lopé Reserve, galleries & bosquets, Gabon; L(m), Lopé Reserve, Marantaceae forest, Gabon; L(c), Lopé Reserve, closed canopy forest, Gabon; L(s), Lopé Reserve, *Sacoglottis* forest, Gabon.

terrestrial fauna. Although large frugivores and browsers occur at relatively low densities in both Neotropical (Robinson & Redford, 1986; Peres, 1999a) and African (Fa & Purvis, 1997) forests, these taxa can adjust to a relatively low quality diet, and hence harvest a greater fraction of the forest primary production. As we shall see, African forests should be able to sustain a relatively higher harvest rate per unit area, particularly at the higher end of the prey size spectrum, because they can support a far greater number of large-bodied herbivores.

GAME SPECIES AND EFFECTS OF HUNTING

Game harvest profiles obtained from the two continents (see below) clearly demonstrate that a wider range of species is hunted in Africa than in the Neotropics (Figure 10.6). From the body size distribution compiled here (Figure 10.2), 55% of 284 African forest mammals have been considered as game species in the literature, compared with only 28% of 192 species in Amazonian forests. This can be attributed partly to the greater number of larger-bodied and substantially higher mean body mass of African game mammal species (mean $\pm$ SE $= 37\,450 \pm 17\,186$ g, $N = 284$; range $= 8$ to 4.0×10^6 g), compared with those in Amazonia (4803 ± 1440 g, $N = 192$; range $= 10$ to 2.4×10^5 g). There are 110 mid-sized to large-bodied mammal species equal to or exceeding 1 kg in body mass in African forests ($96\,504 \pm 43\,905$ g), representing 70% of the 157 species recorded in African game harvest profiles. In contrast, only 73 of the Neotropical forest mammal species are 1 kg in body mass ($12\,154 \pm 3640$ g), including 50 game species that represent 94% of all species known to be hunted. Moreover, a total of 39 very large game species (> 10 kg) can be found in African forests (mean body mass $= 264\,107 \pm 120\,208$ g) as opposed to only 13 species in Neotropical forests ($50\,869 \pm 17\,093$ g). The prominent role of large-bodied mammals in African game harvests can also explain their greater vulnerability to indirect hunting techniques (e.g. traps, nets, snares), which opens the possibility for hunters to pursue more efficiently a greater range of game species (Bahuchet & de Garine, 1990; Wilkie & Curran, 1991; Noss, 1998). The use of snares, especially cable snares, is currently widespread in African forests, and accounts for the extraction of more game species (and biomass) than do firearms. Because cable snares are more affordable and accessible to local hunters than are firearms, extensive areas can be operated. Snare densities reported for Bayanga, Central African Republic, were 3.6 and 4.2 snares/km^2 in two separate hunting ranges (Noss, 1995), but in some areas, snare density could be as high as 13 snares/km^2

Figure 10.6. Mammal species used as bushmeat in Africa: (a) gorilla *Gorilla gorilla*, (b) moustached guenon *Cercopithecus cephus*, (c) rodents and duikers. Photo: J. E. Fa.

(southeast Bioko Island; Colell *et al.*, 1994). Cable snares are known to capture virtually all species in African rain forests, except elephant and hippopotamus, as well as several species of birds and reptiles. In contrast, snare hunting is virtually absent in the Neotropics. To some degree, snares are replaced in the Neotropics by shotgun traps, which tend to be restricted to species that remain faithful to particular paths in the forest. Furthermore, the lower population densities recorded for Neotropical forest mammals (Fa & Purvis, 1997; Peres, 2000b) could also explain why game traps were never developed in the hunting technology of native Amazonians. A widespread and near-random deployment of snares in a Neotropical forest would bring limited rewards, since only tapirs, armadillos and pacas *Agouti paca* exhibit a predictable ranging ecology in terms of habitual use of forest paths.

There is no doubt that tropical forest vertebrates have been subjected to human hunting pressure for millennia. In Africa, they have coexisted with humans for many millennia longer than in the Neotropics (see de Maret *et al.*, 1987), and several species have evolved antipredator responses to cope with this. Tutin & White (1999) suggested, for example, that intimidation displays exhibited by terrestrial African primates could be explained partly by the long history of exposure to human hunting. However, greater vulnerability to game traps as well as the higher baseline densities of African rain forest vertebrates would have clearly influenced the extent to which these are hunted relative to Neotropical species. Hunting of the more prominently arboreal (and often smaller) taxa in the Neotropics, would have been more difficult prior to firearms, and specific strategies have been developed for different vertebrate taxa (Stahl, 1995). This can be illustrated by the elaborate use of blowguns and neurotoxic arrowheads when targeting prehensile-tailed primates, which often remain secured to the upper canopy even after *rigor mortis* when killed with unpoisoned projectiles. In contrast, the rather simple use of net hunting by Mbuti hunters and other indigenous peoples in African forests is probably a good indicator of the relative ease at which high returns can be obtained from terrestrial mammals (Noss, 1995).

The exact impact of past hunting on large vertebrate assemblages is difficult to assess. It is likely that prior to the arrival of firearms and dogs, hunters would have had more limited consequences on prey populations. Decisions on prey choice would have been guided primarily by relative abundance, ease of capture and hunter preference (Stahl, 1995). In contrast, current practices, vested with more sophisticated hunting tools (including automatic rifles; see de Merode, 1998) and motivated by financial aims, can have devastating effects on the fauna. The issue is not merely one of changes in technology but one embracing complex linkages between socioeconomics and behavioural ecology of hunting decisions (FitzGibbon, 1998). An example of this is when the individual hunter's rationale is to maximise their returns from hunting, since restraint would give advantages to others showing no or little restraint (Smith, 1983; Milner-Gulland & Leader-Williams, 1992). The same 'tragedy of the commons' argument explains the failure of many other open-access extraction systems (see Ludwig, Chapter 2). None the less, at a broader geographical level, total harvests are less likely to be correlated with technology (although the use of wire snares and firearms has increased efficiency), but will be a function of consumer numbers. Indeed, factors that limit consumer population size and market participation may be more important than technological limitations (Alvard, 1995).

Hunters in tropical forest regions target primarily large-bodied species (Peres, 1990; Bodmer, 1995; FitzGibbon, 1998), as would be expected from classic foraging models. Larger-bodied species are more susceptible to over-harvesting because these tend to have lower reproductive rates and lower densities (Purvis, Chapter 8). These species provide hunters with a greater return on investment in weapons and ammunition. However, the level of risk to the hunter and the technology available will influence which species are targeted first. In African forests, two of the most sought-after prey are the large-bodied red colobus *Piliocolobus* spp. and black-and-white colobus *Colobus* spp. monkeys (Oates, 1996). This is because these monkeys are more vocal (especially the red colobus), live in large groups, are found in the upper canopy, are generally slower-moving than other primates, and pose no danger to the hunter (Struhsaker, 1999). Larger prey (e.g. elephants, buffalo, great apes), on the other hand, involve more risk to the hunter and therefore are usually hunted once the easier, more abundant prey have been depleted. Because hunters target large game in forests near long-established communities, populations of these animals are often much reduced near human habitation, as shown for apes (Tutin & Fernandez, 1983) and elephants (Barnes *et al.*, 1991) in Gabon.

The enormous impact of hunting on mammal communities in tropical forests has only recently been documented (Redford & Robinson, 1985; Robinson & Bennett, 2000; Peres, 2000a). Some studies suggest the impact of hunting on game mammals such as primates is greater than moderate habitat disturbance such as logging (Oates, 1996; Peres, 1999b; Wilkie *et al.*, 2001). The available information indicates that if hunting pressure is not too heavy, and large neighbouring tracts of undisturbed forest can

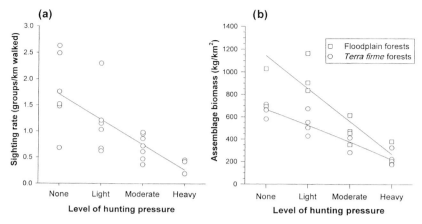

Figure 10.7. Relationship between the level of hunting pressure and game abundance of (a) African forest anthropoid primates ($N = 22$ sites) in terms of sighting rates (data from Oates, 1996); and (b) biomass of game species ($N = 25$ sites) in Amazonian floodplain and *terra firme* forests (data from Peres, 1999b, with permission from Cambridge University Press).

buffer and replenish hunted areas, game populations can readily bounce back after exploitation. Density and biomass estimates of vertebrate assemblages at 25 Amazonian forest sites declined significantly with increased levels of hunting pressure (Peres, 2000a). For these sites, the resulting depletion curves (Figure 10.7) illustrate that mammal biomass can decline dramatically from as much as 1200 kg/km² in non-hunted floodplain forest sites, to around 200 kg/km² in heavily hunted areas (Peres, 2000b). These data are mirrored in similar trends from 22 African forest sites that clearly demonstrate a decrease in anthropoid primate numbers as hunting pressure becomes increasingly heavier (Oates, 1996).

Although a reduction in game vertebrate densities is expected in over-harvested areas, Peres (2000a) has shown that overall game densities in hunted and non-hunted Amazonian forest sites do not differ significantly. Because game harvest is highly selective towards larger-bodied species, the biomass of small and mid-sized species greatly increases as a proportion of the overall community, whereas that of the largest size classes was significantly depressed at moderately to heavily hunted sites (Peres, 1999a; Figure 10.8a). For Amazonian primates, for instance, Peres & Dolman (2000) found reasonably good evidence of density compensation (or under-compensation) of the residual assemblage of non-hunted mid-sized species, where their large-bodied (ateline) counterparts had been severely reduced in numbers. The available data for Africa, although limited in com-

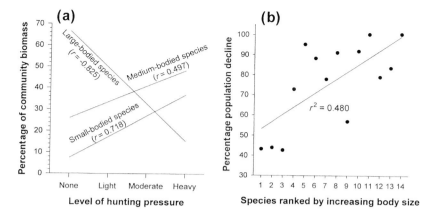

Figure 10.8. Relationships between level of hunting pressure and impact on different sized game species in terms of (a) changes in percentage contribution of different primate size classes to the total biomass of diurnal primates at 56 Amazonian sites (from Peres, 1999b), and (b) percentage impact on game species in Makokou, Gabon (Lahm, 1993).

parison to those from the Neotropics, point to a similar depletion pattern. From estimates of mammal abundance in non-hunted and hunted sites in Makokou, Gabon, Lahm (1993) showed that body mass and population density were negatively correlated with impact on the species (Figure 10.8b). Whether or not density compensation occurs in African hunted sites, as observed in the Neotropics, remains to be demonstrated. Shifts to smaller prey are the expected scenario in overhunted areas. Peres (1999b) and A. Jerozolimski & C. Peres (unpublished results) have demonstrated that the mean body mass of all target species was significantly reduced in response to hunting pressure. Counts of the number of animal carcasses arriving at Malabo market, Bioko Island, Equatorial Guinea, were made during two eight-month study periods in 1991 and 1996. Between-year comparisons of these harvests showed that the number of species and carcasses in 1996 was greater than in 1991. In biomass terms, the increase was significantly less, only 12.5%, when compared with almost 60% more carcasses entering the market in 1996. A larger number of carcasses of the smaller-bodied species, such as rodents and the blue duiker *Cephalophus monticola*, were recorded in the latter study period. Concurrently, there was a dramatic reduction in the larger-bodied species, the Ogilby's duiker *Cephalophus ogilbyi* and the seven diurnal primates (Fa *et al.*, 2000).

Studies of how hunting might affect the population dynamics of game species are sorely lacking for both Africa and the Neotropics. Some data are, however, available on the impact of hunting on animals of different age classes. For example, Dubost (1978, 1980) and Feer (1988) concluded that hunting and trapping by Gabonese villagers most severely affect young adult water chevrotain *Hyemoschus aquaticus* and duikers, the age class with the greatest reproductive potential. However, population age structures and demographics of hunted versus non-hunted sites are rarely available (but see Bodmer *et al.*, 1997; Hart, 2000). The fact remains that all investigations into the sustainability of game hunting in South America and Africa have shown that most species have been overexploited (Bodmer, 1995; Noss, 1995; Ráez-Luna, 1995; FitzGibbon *et al.*, 1996; Muchaal & Ngandjui, 1999; Mena *et al.*, 1999; Townsend, 1999; Fa, 2000; Peres, 2000b).

ESTIMATES OF GAME HARVESTS IN AFRICA AND THE NEOTROPICS

Estimates of game offtakes in tropical forests range from global appraisals of what proportion wild animal protein contributes to people's diets (Prescott-Allen & Prescott-Allen, 1982), to extrapolations of numbers and biomass consumed within particular regions. For Neotropical forests, Redford & Robinson (1987) reviewed wildlife use patterns of Indian and colonist communities from subsistence hunting studies ($N = 23$) and developed an index that measured number of individuals of each taxon killed per consumer-year (per capita per annum, or p.c.p.a.). Using this index, Redford (1993) estimated a total of 19 million vertebrates harvested annually in rural Brazilian Amazonia, for the 1980 Brazilian national census. Using eight additional samples ($N = 31$), Peres (2000a) recalculated average extraction rates of game species by the entire no-income rural population of Brazilian Amazonia, and concluded that between 67 and 164 thousand tonnes of terrestrial vertebrates are harvested annually, including over 50 different taxa, particularly mammals (primates, ungulates, caviomorph rodents), birds (cracids, tinamous, trumpeters), and reptiles (tortoises). For mammals alone, between 6.4 and 15.8 million individuals, comprising 60–148 tonnes, are harvested every year (Peres, 2000a). From these average estimates, basin-wide extraction rates per species can be calculated for hunted species (Table 10.2a). Extraction figures varied from 0.0001 kg/km^2 per year for forest cottontail rabbits *Sylvilagus brasiliensis* to 7.6 kg/km^2 per year for collared peccaries *Tayassu pecari*. Extraction rates for taxa larger than 10 kg are 2.7 ± 2.9 kg/km^2 per year ($N = 8$) whereas for those smaller than 10 kg, the mean value is 0.4 ± 0.7 kg/km^2 per year ($N = 23$).

To generate equivalent bushmeat extraction data for Africa, we compiled a total of 14 hunting profiles from forest sites in Cameroon, Congo-Zaire, Gabon and Equatorial Guinea (Wilkie, 1987; Infield, 1988; Lahm, 1993; Colell *et al.*, 1994; Noss, 1995; DelVingt, 1997; Fotso & Ngnegueu, 1997; Muchaal & Ngandjui, 1999). From these studies spanning 12 months in duration on average, we estimated p.c.p.a. values for consumers. Once corrected for area of occupancy of each species, extraction rates could be calculated for 57 reported mammalian taxa (Table 10.2b). This corresponds to the consumption of a rural human population of 24 million within a forest area of 1.8 million km² (taken from Wilkie & Carpenter, 1999). By species, figures ranged from a minimum extraction of 0.01 kg/km² per year for squirrels *Funisciurus* spp. to a maximum of 1348.9 kg/km² per year for the bay duiker *Cephalophus dorsalis*. Taxa > 10 kg provided 177.7 ± 358.4 kg/km² per year ($N = 24$) whereas smaller-bodied species (< 10 kg) contributed significantly less (35.4 ± 72.2 kg/km² per year, $N = 33$). In total, an estimated 579 million animals are consumed in the Congo Basin annually; around 5 million tonnes of dressed bushmeat (Fa *et al.*, 2001). This figure contrasts somewhat with Wilkie & Carpenter's (1999) estimate of only 1 million tonnes based on extrapolations of actual meat consumed. Although it could be argued that extrapolations of this kind are too crude, given that data on bushmeat consumption patterns and animal densities are only available for a few areas, our total estimate of bushmeat consumed does not seem unrealistic.

The above figures are still underestimates, since they do not account for a large fraction of rural and even urban households (especially in Africa) that also consume large amounts of bushmeat. Despite this caveat, the amount of bushmeat extracted and consumed per unit area in the Congo Basin is still orders of magnitude higher than in the Amazon. In terms of actual yields of edible meat (given that muscle mass and edible viscera account on average for 55% of body mass), 62 808 tonnes is consumed in the Amazon (Peres, 2000a), but around 2 million tonnes in Africa. For both continents, regressions of extraction rates against body mass show that rates rise steeply with increasing body size, reflecting hunters' preferences for large-bodied species (Figure 10.9). Slopes are statistically indistinguishable ($p = 0.27$), while intercepts differ significantly ($p < 0.0005$). Whether such removal rates are sustainable within each forest region, on a basin-wide level, most species are exploited unsustainably in the Congo, while all hunted Amazonian taxa fall below the minimum sustainable quotas (Fa *et al.*, 2001). This is largely a result of larger human population sizes within a smaller forest area in the Congo, and the fact that a large proportion of the hunter's bag is sold in towns and villages for profit.

Table 10.2. Estimates of mammal numbers and biomass harvested per year in the Amazon and Congo Basins. Species names for the Congo Basin follow Kingdon (1997)

Species	Body mass (kg)	Consumption rate (p.c.p.a.)	No. of animals consumed	Biomass harvested (tonnes)	Extraction (kg/km² per year)
(a) Amazon Basin					
Artiodactyla					
Tayassu pecari	35.00	0.67	1 499 318	38 382.5	10.23
Tayassu tajacu	25.00	0.61	1 353 248	27 065.0	7.22
Mazama spp.	22.25	0.31	683 317	13 119.7	3.50
Perissodactyla					
Tapirus terrestris	160.00	0.05	116 269	14 882.4	3.97
Rodentia					
Cuniculus paca	8.00	0.81	1 791 959	13 977.3	3.73
Dasyprocta spp.	3.50	0.66	1 479 177	5325.0	1.42
Myoprocta spp.	1.50	0.04	97 270	58.4	0.02
H. hydrochaeris	45.00	0.09	206 179	3298.9	0.88
Sciurus spp.	0.60	0.14	316 256	151.8	0.04
Coendou spp.	4.50	0.03	66 768	113.5	0.03
Lagomorpha					
Sylvilagus brasiliensis	1.00	0.0004	781	0.6	0.0001
Primates					
Alouatta spp.	6.40	0.34	762 850	3966.8	1.06

Ateles spp.	8.11	0.25	557 704	4026.6	1.07
Lagothrix lagotricha	7.04	0.56	1 250 539	8716.3	2.32
Cebus spp.	2.72	1.07	2 384 846	5556.7	1.48
Pithecia spp.	2.35	0.05	103 554	182.3	0.05
Cacajao spp.	3.17	0.01	20 663	52.2	0.01
Chiropotes spp.	2.77	0.03	77 308	167.0	0.05
Callicebus spp.	0.93	0.04	89 833	75.5	0.02
Aotus spp.	0.94	0.04	99 260	95.3	0.03
Saimiri spp.	0.76	0.01	16 454	12.3	0.003
Saguinus spp.	0.39	0.01	20 697	9.7	0.003

Xenathra

Bradypus spp.	4.28	0.06	139 401	292.7	0.08
Myrmecophaga tridactyla	30.50	0.01	29 056	174.3	0.05
Tamandua tetradactyla	5.00	0.09	193 746	581.2	0.16
Dasypus spp.	7.33	0.67	1 498 045	5243.2	1.40
Priodontes maximus	30.00	0.004	8273	206.8	0.06

Carnivora

Nasua nasua	4.50	0.37	829 470	2057.1	0.55
Potos flavus	2.20	0.01	31 064	46.6	0.01
Eira barbara	4.85	0.01	18 682	71.7	0.02
Felis spp.	6.75	0.02	48 042	240.2	0.06

(b) Congo Basin

Artiodactyla

Potamochoerus porcus	61.90	0.3701	9 013 047	557 908	300.56
Hylochoerus meinertzhageni	178.75	0.0106	258 177	46 149	24.86
Hymoshcus aquaticus	10.40	0.4974	12 114 173	125 987	67.87
Neotragus batesi	3.75	0.1025	2 495 711	9359	5.04

Table 10.2. (cont.)

Species	Body mass (kg)	Consumption rate (p.c.p.a.)	No. of animals consumed	Biomass harvested (tonnes)	Extraction (kg/km² per year)
Cephalophus monticola	3.90	5.3320	129 859 710	506 453	272.84
Cephalophus nigrifrons	13.90	0.0624	1 519 067	21 115	11.38
Cephalophus sylvicultor	56.70	0.1851	4 508 441	255 629	137.72
Cephalophus callipygus	14.80	1.1749	28 614 612	423 496	228.15
Cephalophus dorsalis	17.90	5.7434	139 878 605	2 503 827	1348.89
Cephalophus ogilbyi	17.00	1.2386	3 016 516	51 281	276.27
Cephalophus leucogaster	13.90	0.0739	1 798 941	25 005	16.84
Tragelaphus spekei	83.80	0.0121	293 986	24 636	13.27
Syncerus caffer	237.50	0.0130	317 670	75 447	40.65
Okapia johnsoni	230.00	0.0106	258 177	59 381	79.98
Proboscidea					
Loxodonta africana cyclotis	1741.70	0.0495	1 204 826	2 098 446	1130.50
Rodentia					
Heliosciurus rufobrachium	0.33	0.0107	260 218	85	0.05
Protoxerus stangeri	0.77	0.0438	1 066 308	821	0.44
Paraxerus poensis	0.12	0.0333	811 823	97	0.05
Anomalurus spp.	0.79	0.0133	324 729	257	0.14
Funisciurus spp.	0.16	0.0065	158 835	25	0.01
Epixerus ebii	0.58	0.0026	62 448	36	0.02
Atherurus africanus	2.88	2.7122	66 055 471	190 240	102.49
Cricetomys emini	1.95	2.5333	61 698 934	120 313	64.82
Thryonomys swinderianus	5.05	0.0272	663 349	3350	1.80

Primates

Cercopithecus neglectus	4.44	0.0026	62 448	277	0.15
Cercopithecus ascanius	3.70	0.0071	172 118	637	0.34
Cercopithecus cephus	2.00	0.2794	6 805 711	13 611	7.33
Cercopithecus nictitans	5.30	1.1642	28 354 724	150 280	80.96
Cercopithecus preussi	5.25	0.0267	649 459	3410	183.69
Cercopithecus mona	5.00	1.0065	24 513 278	122 566	66.03
Cercopithecus erythrotis	3.44	0.3994	97 283	335	18.03
Cercopithecus pogonias	2.20	0.0866	2 110 323	4643	2.50
Lophocebus albigena	4.10	0.0417	1 014 601	4160	2.24
Cercocebus torquatus	8.13	0.1502	3 656 931	29 731	16.02
Mandrillus sphinx	10.20	0.0077	14 988	153	1.03
Mandrillus leucophaeus	15.00	2.3160	564 043	8461	455.80
Colobus angolensis	13.13	0.0123	299 076	3928	2.12
Colobus guereza	16.50	0.0048	117 283	1935	1.04
Colobus satanas	8.40	0.0200	487 094	4092	2.20
Colobus badius	7.75	2.5779	37 670 229	291 944	262.13
Papio anubis	28.25	0.0035	3442	97	1.31
Pan troglodytes	38.70	0.0031	75 848	2935	1.58
Gorilla gorilla	78.10	0.0013	31 224	2439	1.31

Carnivora

Aonyx congica	20.00	0.0027	65 236	1305	0.70
Nandinia binotata	2.60	0.0221	539 218	1402	0.76
Viverra civetta	13.50	0.0289	703 678	9500	5.12
Genetta servalina	1.65	0.0096	233 805	386	0.21
Bdeogale nigripes	2.75	0.0526	1 281 013	3523	1.90
Herpestinae spp.	3.60	0.0228	555 923	2001	1.08
Xenogale naso	3.60	0.0504	1 227 042	4417	2.38

Table 10.2. (*cont.*)

Species	Body mass (kg)	Consumption rate (p.c.p.a.)	No. of animals consumed	Biomass harvested (tonnes)	Extraction (kg/km² per year)
Atilax paludinosus	3.60	0.0281	684 976	2466	1.33
Crossarchus obscurus	1.25	0.0180	437 897	547	0.29
Felis aurata	11.75	0.0085	206 578	2427	1.31
Panthera pardus	55.00	0.0071	172 118	9466	5.10
Pholidota					
Phataginus tricuspis	2.30	0.0175	425 612	979	0.53
Smutsia gigantea	32.50	0.0048	116 903	3799	2.05
Hyracoidea					
Dendrohyrax dorsalis	3.00	0.0027	65 236	196	0.11

p.c.p.a., per capita per annum.
Data for Amazonia based on the sources reported by Peres (2000a). Data for Africa based on: Infield, 1988; Muchaal & Ngandjui, 1999; DelVingt, 1997; Fotso & Ngnegueu, 1997; Colell *et al.*, 1994; Noss, 1995; Lahm, 1993; Wilkie, 1987; Adeola & Decker, 1987.

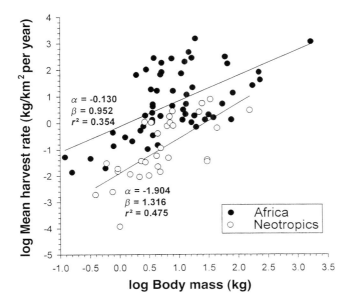

Figure 10.9. Relationship between the estimated game extraction rate and log body mass of forest mammals in Africa and the Neotropics.

Therefore, per capita harvest rates (kg/person per year) in relation to number of consumers show a lower variation for South American settlements, whereas for Africa they decline significantly from an average of about 500 kg/person per year in smaller settlements to 1 kg/person per year in the largest settlements (Figure 10.10). This does not necessarily reflect differential consumption rates of bushmeat per person but differences in commercialisation of wild meat. Hunting does not just provide meat for household consumption but is an important source of income for many hunters, and the distinction between subsistence and commercial hunting is often blurred. This is because many subsistence hunters will sell a portion of their bag under certain circumstances. Whether meat is consumed locally or sold, this further goes to show that African forests can sustain far greater biomass harvests than can Neotropical forests, particularly in areas supplying smaller numbers of consumers. Per capita harvest rates in both continents, however, decline substantially and converge at very low levels in intensively harvested areas.

In terms of marketing of game, most authors agree that there are significant differences between Africa and South America, both in emphasis and volume of wild meat sold. Despite reports of around 100 tonnes of

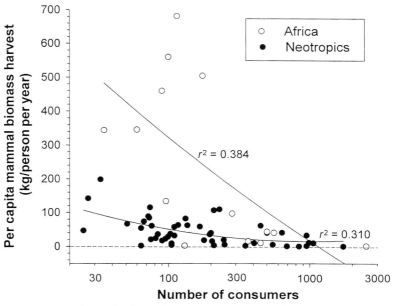

Figure 10.10. Relationship between consumer numbers and mammal meat extracted in villages studied in African and Neotropical forests.

game meat marketed in a year in Iquitos, Peru (Castro *et al.*, 1976), this is extremely atypical throughout South and Central America (Redford, 1992). In comparison, most towns and cities in African rain forest regions operate markets that regularly extract well in excess of 100 tonnes monthly (Colyn *et al.*, 1987; Steel, 1994; Juste *et al.*, 1995). Such produce also constitutes an important, though often underestimated, part of the economy of many African countries (Butynski & von Richter, 1974; Feer, 1993). Structural adjustment programmes and a general decline in the export of agricultural products in the 1980s has forced small communities in Africa to rely on local natural resources for generating revenue. Infield (1988) showed that, on average, around 80% of all bushmeat hunted was sold in villages around Korup National Park, Cameroon. Similar figures for the proportion of meat sold appear in Lahm (1993) and Steel (1994) for Gabon, and Colell *et al.* (1994) for Bioko Island.

CONCLUSIONS

Extraction of game vertebrates in tropical forests is a diffuse and rather inconspicuous activity conducted by millions of African and South American hunters. However, the impact of hunting can be a more critical concern for biodiversity conservation than is deforestation. We conclude that hunted species in both continents are, by and large, being exploited unsustainably, particularly in the case of large-bodied taxa. At present, this appears to be especially alarming in Central and West African forests, given the much higher consumer pressure and expansion of the commercial hunting catchment areas mediated by the logging industry. Against a background scenario of rapidly increasing human populations and an accelerating demand for animal protein, the survival prospects for game species in African forests is even less certain than those in the Neotropics.

Although our intercontinental comparison provides some reason for guarded optimism for South America, there is no doubt that exploitation of forest wildlife is increasing in both continents and will result in local extinctions of several bird and mammal species. This can be attributed primarily to human population growth and the greater access to previously roadless frontier forests through logging and roads. The paved road network in the Brazilian Amazon alone (excluding the states of Mato Grosso and Maranhão) will increase in the next few years from 6300 km to 11 000 km (IPAM and ISA, 2000). This will generate access to an additional 470 000 km^2 of forest considering only a 50 km band on each side of the road, a conservative estimate in terms of game harvest given the migratory fluxes, secondary roads, and regional development that these new roads will stimulate. Additionally, the emergence of new agricultural settlements, larger urban markets, introduction of new hunting technologies, and lack of (or non-compliance with) effective legislation on game hunting exacerbates the situation. Even in Brazil, which has arguably developed the most elaborate conservation legislation of all African and South American forest countries, there are virtually no enforced restrictions on game extraction in terms of protection of sensitive species, age–sex classes, breeding seasons and bag limits. Spatial harvest gradients made possible by the establishment of wildlife sanctuaries and internal zonation of indigenous and extractive reserves have often been considered in reserve management plans but in practice remain either unfeasible or unenforceable. Although significant progress has been made in recent years in advancing sustainable management of wildlife, few workable models have been demonstrated. Various authors have suggested plans that span reduction of local supply, quota systems, local and government enforcement and limitation of commercial supply (Bowen-Jones & Pendry, 1999; Inamdar et al., 1999). However, most solutions have been unsuccessful in linking community participation, land tenure reforms and traditional control systems and thus have led to even more indiscriminate hunting (but see Bodmer & Puertas, 2000). The complex political contexts within which wildlife harvest occurs often precludes effective solutions (see Sanderson, Chapter 21).

The prospects for attaining a sustainable harvest are even worse in equatorial Africa. Here, wildlife extraction and participation in what is known as 'the bushmeat trade' are presently the most insidious threat to wildlife in this continent. The trade is highly decentralised and primary markets are dispersed throughout the forest areas. Secondary markets in towns and cities are equally important. The problem in Africa has complex socioeconomic and gender dimensions (generally men are the hunters while women dominate the commerce) that make it difficult to manage. Essentially, because bushmeat offers quick benefits to forest-dwelling populations, it has few rivals in terms of trade value in poverty-stricken environments (Inamdar *et al.*, 1999). Because bushmeat is highly transportable, has a high value/weight ratio, is preserved at low cost, and has good storage qualities when smoked, bushmeat extraction is lucrative to a wide range of individuals from local communities to professional hunters (often sponsored by urban entrepreneurs with access to modern weapons). Moreover, penetration of untapped areas is provided by the timber industry (Ape Alliance, 1998).

There is no doubt that consumer pressure per se is far greater in Africa than in South America. The data compiled here show that game harvests can have a marked effect on absolute numbers of animals in hunted areas and can also change the structure of vertebrate communities. From the South American data, we have shown that mammal assemblages exposed to increasingly heavier hunting pressure not only decline in absolute numbers but shift to predictably smaller-bodied species in the residual faunas. The contrasts revealed between harvestable amounts of meat and differing extraction levels in each continent also point to the fact that the two forest regions are in markedly different developmental stages in relation to human disturbance. African tropical forests have vastly greater human densities, and the emphasis on commercial exploitation of bushmeat further exacerbates the problem. Despite this, African forests may have actually been intrinsically more resilient to disturbance because of their history, structure and productivity. However, current extraction most definitely supersedes production. Resolving the role of the hunted species' ecological attributes (such as comparisons of r values) on their recovery rates has now become purely academic. Our data show that the trends do not bode well for the future of wildlife for either continent if hunting pressure continues unchecked. Defaunation thus emerges as one of the most significant concerns for biodiversity conservation in Afrotropical and Neotropical forests.

ACKNOWLEDGEMENTS

We thank R. F. W. Barnes, A. Plumptre, J. Oates, D. Wilkie and V. Reynolds, for providing us with biomass and density data on different forest sites in Africa. A. Jerozolimski helped to compile the Neotropical game harvest data on which one figure in this paper is based. The Josephine Bay and Michael Paul Foundations, Conservation International Center for Applied Biodiversity Sciences and Wildlife Conservation Society funded the fieldwork conducted by C.A.P. C. Cristoffer, R. F. W. Barnes, J. Oates, A. Plumptre and D. Wilkie made useful comments on the manuscript.

REFERENCES

Adeola, M. O. & Decker, E. (1987). Utilisation de la faune sauvage en milieu rural au Nigeria. *Nature et Faune*, **3**, 15–21.

Alvard, M. (1995). Shotguns and sustainable hunting in the Neotropics. *Oryx*, **29**, 58–66.

Alvard, M., Robinson, J., Redford, K. & Kaplan, H. (1997). The sustainability of subsistence hunting in the Neotropics. *Conservation Biology*, **11**, 977–982.

Ape Alliance (1998). *The African Bushmeat Trade: A Recipe for Extinction*. Fauna and Flora International, Cambridge.

Aubréville, A. (1949). *Climats, forêts et désertification de l'Afrique tropicale*. Société d'Éditions Géographiques, Maritimes et Coloniale, Paris.

Ayres, J. M. (1986). Uakaris and Amazonian flooded forest. Unpublished PhD thesis, University of Cambridge.

Bahuchet, S. & de Garine, I. (1990). The art of trapping in the rain forest. In *Food and Nutrition in the African Rain Forest*, eds. C. M. Hladik, S. Bahuchet & I. de Garine, pp. 24–35. UNESCO/MAB, Paris.

Bahuchet, S. & de Maret, P. (1995). *State of Indigenous Populations Living in Rainforest Areas*. European Commission DGXI Environment, Brussels.

Barnes, R. F. W. & Lahm, S. A. (1997). An ecological perspective on human densities in the central African forests. *Journal of Applied Ecology*, **34**, 245–260.

Barnes, R. F. W., Barnes, K. L., Alers, M. P. T. & Blom, A. (1991). Man determines the distribution of elephants in the rain forests of northeastern Gabon. *African Journal of Ecology*, **29**, 54–63.

Barnes, R. F. W., Agnagna, M., Alers, M. P. T., Blom, A., Doungoube, G., Fay, M., Masunda, T., Ndo Nkoumou, J. C., Sikubwabo Kiyengo, C. & Tchamba, M. (1993). Elephants and ivory poaching in the forests of equatorial Africa. *Oryx*, **27**, 27–34.

Biodiversity Support Program (1993). *Central Africa: Global Climate Change and Development – Overview*. World Wildlife Fund, Washington, DC.

Bodmer, R.E. (1995). Managing Amazonian wildlife: biological correlates of game choice by detribalized hunters. *Ecological Applications*, **5**, 872–877.

Bodmer, R.E. & Puertas, P.E. (2000). Community-based comanagement of wildlife in the Peruvian Amazon. In *Sustainability of Hunting in Tropical Forests*, eds. J. G. Robinson & E. L. Bennett, pp. 395–412. Columbia University Press, New York.

Bodmer, R.E., Eisenberg, J. & Redford, K. (1997). Hunting and likelihood of extinction of Amazonian mammals. *Conservation Biology*, **11**, 460–466.

Bourlière, F. (1973). The comparative ecology of rain forest mammals in Africa and Tropical America: some introductory remarks. In *Tropical Forest Ecosystems in Africa and South America: A Comparative Review*, eds. B. J. Meggers, E. S. Ayensu & W. D. Duckworth, pp. 279–292. Smithsonian Institution Press, Washington, DC.

Bourlière, F. (1985). Primate communities: their structure and role in tropical ecosystems. *International Journal of Primatology*, **6**, 1–26.

Bowen-Jones, E. & Pendry, S. (1999). The threat to primates and other mammals from the bushmeat trade in Africa, and how this threat could be diminished. *Oryx*, **33**, 233–246.

Butynski, T. M. & von Richter, W. (1974). In Botswana most of the meat is wild. *Unasylva*, **26**, 24–29.

Castro, N., Revilla, J. & Neville, M. (1976). Carne de monte como una fuente de proteínas en Iquitos, con referencia especial a monos. *Revista Forestal del Peru*, **6**, 19–32.

Chapman, C. A. & Chapman, L. J. (1997). Forest regeneration in logged and unlogged forests of Kibale National Park, Uganda. *Biotropica*, **29**, 396–412.

Chapman, C. A. & Onderdonk, D. A. (1998). Forests without primates: primate/plant codependency. *American Journal of Primatology*, **45**, 127–141.

Chapman, C. A, Gautier-Hion, A., Oates, J. F. & Onderdonk, D. A. (1999). African primate communities: determinants of structure and threats to survival. In *Primate Communities*, eds. J. G. Fleagle, C. Janson & K. E. Reed, pp. 1–37. Cambridge University Press, Cambridge.

Chardonnet, P., Fritz, H., Zorzi, N. & Feron, E. (1995). Current importance of traditional hunting and major contrasts in wild meat consumption in sub-saharan Africa. In *Integrating People and Wildlife for a Sustainable Future*, eds. J. A. Bissonette & P. R. Krausman, pp. 304–307. The Wildlife Society, Bethesda, MD.

Coe, M. J., Cumming, D. M. & Phillipson, J. (1976). Biomass and production of large African herbivores in relation to rainfall and primary production. *Oecologia*, **22**, 341–354.

Colell, M., Maté, C. & Fa, J. E. (1994). Hunting among Moka Bubis in Bioko: dynamics of faunal exploitation at the village level. *Biodiversity and Conservation*, **3**, 939–950.

Colyn, M. M., Dudu, A. & Mbaelele, M. M. (1987). Data on small and medium scale game utilization in the rain forest of Zaire. In *Wildlife Management in Sub-Saharan Africa: Sustainable Economic Benefits and Contribution Towards Rural Development*, pp. 109–145. World Wide Fund for Nature, Harare.

Cowlishaw, G. (1999). Predicting the pattern of decline of African primate diversity: an extinction debt from historical deforestation. *Conservation Biology*, **13**, 1183–1193.

Cristoffer, C. (1987). Body size differences between New World and Old World arboreal tropical vertebrates: cause and consequences. *Journal of Biogeography*, **14**, 165–172.

de Maret, P., Clist, B. & van Neer, W. (1987). Résultats des premières fouilles dans un abri de Shum Lae et d'Abeke au nord-ouest Cameroun. *L'Anthropologie*, **91**, 559–584.

de Merode, E. (1998). Protected areas and local livelihoods: contrasting systems of wildlife management in the Democratic Republic of Congo. PhD thesis, University of London, UK.

DelVingt, W. (1997). La chasse villageoise: Synthèse régionale des études réalisées durant la première phase du Programme ECOFAC au Cameroun, au Congo et en Republique Centrafricaine. Unpublished report, AGRECO-CTFT, ECOFAC, Brussels.

Dirzo, R. & Miranda, A. (1991). Altered patterns of herbivory and diversity in the forest understorey: a case study of the possible consequences of contemporary defaunation. In *Plant–Animal Interactions: Evolutionary Ecology in Tropical and Temperate Regions*, eds. P. W. Price, P. W. Lewinsohn, G. W. Fernandes & W. W. Benson, pp. 273–287. Wiley, New York.

Dubost, G. (1978). Un aperçu sur l'ecologie du chevrotain africain *Hyemoshus aquaticus* Ogilby. *Mammalia*, **42**, 1–62.

Dubost, G. (1979). The size of African forest artiodactyls as determined by vegetation structure. *African Journal of Ecology*, **17**, 1–17.

Dubost, G. (1980). L'écologie et la vie sociale du cephalophe bleu (*Cephalophus monticola* Thunberg) petit ruminant forestier africain. *Zeitschrift für Tierpsychologie*, **54**, 205–266.

Eisenberg, J. F. (1980). The density and biomass of tropical mammals. In *Conservation Biology: An Evolutionary–Ecological Perspective*, ed. M. E. Soulé & B. A. Wilcox, pp. 35–55. Sinauer, Sunderland, MA.

Eisenberg, J. F. & Thorington, R. W. Jr (1973). A preliminary analysis of a neotropical mammal fauna. *Biotropica*, **5**, 150–161.

Eisenberg, J. F., O'Connell, M. A. & August, P. V. (1979). Density, productivity, and distribution of mammals in two Venezuelan habitats. In *Vertebrate Ecology in the Northern Neotropics*, ed. J. F. Eisenberg, pp. 187–207. Smithsonian Institution Press, Washington, DC.

Emmons, L. (1984). Geographic variation in densities and diversities of non-flying mammals in Amazonia. *Biotropica*, **16**, 210–222.

Emmons, L. H. & Gentry, A. H. (1983). Tropical forest structure and the distribution of gliding and prehensile-tailed vertebrates. *American Naturalist*, **121**, 513–524.

Emmons, L. H., Gautier-Hion, A. & Dubost, G. (1983). Community structure of the frugivorous–folivorous forest mammals of Gabon. *Journal of Zoology, London*, **199**, 209–222.

Fa, J. E. (2000). Hunted animals in Bioko Island, West Africa: sustainability and future. In *Sustainability of Hunting in Tropical Forests*, eds. J. G. Robinson & E. L. Bennett, pp. 165–195. Columbia University Press, New York.

Fa, J. E. & Purvis, A. (1997). Body size, diet and population density in Afrotropical forest mammals: a comparison with Neotropical sites. *Journal of Animal Ecology*, **66**, 98–112.

Fa, J. E., Juste, J., Perez del Val, J. & Castroviejo, J. (1995). Impact of market hunting on mammal species in Equatorial Guinea. *Conservation Biology*, **9**, 1107–1115.

Fa, J. E., Garcia Yuste, J. E. & Castelo, R. (2000). Bushmeat markets in Bioko Island as a measure of hunting pressure. *Conservation Biology*, **14**, 1602–1613.

Fa, J. E., Peres, C. A. & Meeuwig, J. (2001). Bushmeat exploitation in tropical forests: an intercontinental comparison. *Conservation Biology*, in press.

FAO (Food and Agriculture Organization) (1988). *An Interim Report on the State of Forest Resources in the Developing Countries*. FAO, Rome.

FAO (Food and Agriculture Organization) (1993) *Forest Resources Assessment 1990: Tropical Countries*. FAO Forestry Paper no. 112. FAO, Rome.

Feer, F. (1988). Strategies écologiques de deux éspèces de bovides sympatriques de la forêt sempervirante Africaine (*Cephalophus callipygus* et *C. dorsalis*): influence du rhythme d'activité. PhD thesis, Université Pierre et Marie Curie, Paris.

Feer, F. (1993). The potential for sustainable hunting and rearing of game in tropical forests. In *Tropical Forests, People and Food: Biocultural Interactions and Applications to Development*, Eds. C. M. Hladik, A. Hladik, O. F. Linares, H. Pagezy, A. Semple & M. Hadley, pp. 691–708. Parthenon, Carnforth.

Fittkau, E. J. & Klinge, H. (1973). On biomass and trophic structure of the central Amazonian rain forest ecosystem. *Biotropica*, **5**, 2–14.

FitzGibbon, C. (1998). The management of subsistence harvesting: behavioral ecology of hunters and their mammalian prey. In *Behavioral Ecology and Conservation Biology*, ed. T. Caro, pp. 449–473. Oxford University Press, New York.

FitzGibbon, C., Mogaka, H. & Fanshawe, J. H. (1996). Subsistence hunting and mammal conservation in a Kenyan coastal forest: resolving a conflict. In *The Exploitation of Mammal Populations*, ed. V. J. Taylor & N. Dunstone, pp. 147–159. Chapman & Hall, London.

Fleagle, J. G., Kay, R. F. & Anthony, M. R. L. (1997). Fossil New World monkeys. In *Vertebrate Paleontology in the Neotropics: the Miocene Fauna of La Venta, Colombia*, ed. R. F. Kay, R. H. Madden, R. L. Cifelli & J. J. Flynn, pp. 473–495. Smithsonian Institution Press, Washington, DC.

Fleming, T. H., Breitwisch, R. & Whitesides, G. H. (1987). Patterns of tropical vertebrate frugivore diversity. *Annual Review of Ecology and Systematics*, **18**, 91–109.

Fonseca, G. A. B., Herrmann, G., Leite, Y. L. R., Mittermeier, R. A., Rylands, A. B. & Patton, J. L. (1996). *Lista anotada dos mamíferos do Brasil*. Occasional Papers in Conservation Biology no. 4. Conservation International, Washington, DC.

Fotso, R. C. & Ngnegueu, P. R. (1997). Commercial hunting and its consequences on the dynamic of duiker population. Unpublished report, ECOFAC, Cameroon.

Gentry, A. (1992). Tropical forest biodiversity: distributional patterns and their conservational significance. *Oikos*, **63**, 19–28.

Hall, J. B. & Swaine, M. D. (1981). *Distribution and Ecology of Vascular Plants in a Tropical Rain Forest*. Dr W. Junk Publishers, Hague.

Hamilton, A. C. (1988). Guenon evolution and forest history. In *A Primate Radiation: Evolutionary Biology of the African Guenons*, ed. A. Gautier-Hion,

F. Bourlière, J. P. Gautier & J. Kingdon, pp. 13–34. Cambridge University Press, Cambridge.

Harcourt, C. S. & Sayer, J. A. (1996). *The Conservation Atlas of Tropical Forests: The Americas*. Simon & Schuster, New York.

Hart, J. A. (2000). Impact and sustainability of indigenous hunting in the Ituri forest, Congo-Zaire. In *Sustainability of Hunting in Tropical Forests*, ed. J. G. Robinson, & E. L. Bennett, pp. 106–153. Columbia University Press, New York.

Hartwig, W. & Cartelle, C. (1996). A complete skeleton of the giant South American primate *Protopithecus*. *Nature*, **381**, 307–311.

Inamdar, A., Brown, D. & Cobb, S. (1999). *What's Special about Wildlife Management in Forests? Concepts and Models of Rights-Based Management, with Recent Evidence from West-Central Africa*. Natural Resources Perspectives no. 44. Overseas Development Institute, London.

Infield, M. (1988). *Hunting, Trapping and Fishing in Villages Within and on the Periphery of the Korup National Park*. World Wide Fund for Nature, Godalming.

IPAM and ISA (2000). Avança Brasil: os custos ambientais para a Amazônia. Instituto de Pesquisa Ambiental da Amazônia and Instituto Socioambiental. Belém, Brazil.

Janson, C. H. & Emmons, L. H. (1990). Ecological structure of the non-flying mammal community at the Cocha Cashu biological station, Manu National Park, Peru. In *Four Neotropical Rainforests*, ed. A. Gentry, pp. 314–338. Yale University Press, New Haven, CT.

Juste, J., Fa, J. E., Perez del Val, J. & Castroviejo, J. (1995). Market dynamics of bushmeat species in Equatorial Guinea. *Journal of Applied Ecology*, **32**, 454–467.

Keast, A. (1969). The evolution of mammals on southern continents: comparisons of the contemporary mammalian faunas of the southern continents. *Quarterly Review of Biology*, **44**, 121–167.

Kingdon, J. (1997). *The Kingdon Field Guide to African Mammals*. Academic Press, London.

Koster, S. H. & Hart, J. A. (1988). Methods of estimating ungulate populations in tropical forests. *African Journal of Ecology*, **26**, 117–127.

Lahm, S. A. (1993). Ecology and economics of human/wildlife interaction in northeastern Gabon. PhD thesis, University of New York.

Mack, A. L. (1993). The sizes of vertebrate-dispersed fruits: a neotropical–paleotropical comparison. *American Naturalist*, **142**, 840–856.

Maisels, F. & Gautier-Hion, A. (1994). Why are Caesalpinoideae so important for monkeys in hydromorphic rainforests of the Zaire Basin? In *Advances in Legume Systematics 5: The Nitrogen Factor*, pp. 189–204. Royal Botanic Gardens, Kew.

Maisels, F., Gautier-Hion, A. & Gautier, J.-P. (1994). Diets of two sympatric colobines in Zaire: more evidence on seed-eating in forests on poor soils. *International Journal of Primatology*, **15**, 681–701.

Malcolm, J. R. (1990). Estimation of mammalian densities in continuous forest north of Manaus. In *Four Neotropical Rainforests*, ed. A. Gentry, pp. 339–357. Yale University Press, New Haven, CT.

Martin, P. S. (1984). Prehistoric overkill: the global model. In *Quaternary Extinctions: A Prehistoric Revolution*, ed. P. S. Martin & R. G. Klein, pp. 354–403. University of Arizona Press, Tucson, AZ.

McRae, M. (1997). Road kill in Cameroon. *Natural History*, **106**, 36–47.

Mena, P., Stallings, J. R., Regalado, J. & Cueva, R. (1999). The sustainability of current hunting practices by the Huaorani. In *Hunting for Sustainability in Tropical Forests*, ed. J. G. Robinson & E. L. Bennett, pp. 57–78. Columbia University Press, New York.

Milner-Gulland, E. J. & Leader-Williams, N. (1992). A model of incentives for the illegal exploitation of black rhinos and elephants: poaching pays in Luangwa Valley. *Journal of Applied Ecology*, **29**, 388–401.

Muchaal, P. K. & Ngandjui, G. (1999). Impact of village hunting on wildlife populations in the western Dja Reserve, Cameroon. *Conservation Biology*, **13**, 385–396.

Newbery, D. McC, Alexander, I. J., Thomas, D. W. & Gartlan, J. S. (1988). Ectomycorrhizal rain forest legumes and soil phosphorus in Korup National Park, Cameroon. *New Phytologist*, **109**, 433–450.

Noss, A. J. (1995). Duikers, cables and nets: a cultural ecology of hunting in a Central African forest. PhD thesis, University of Florida.

Noss, A. J. (1998). The impacts of cable snare hunting on wildlife populations in the forests of the Central African Republic. *Conservation Biology*, **12**, 390–398.

Oates, J. F. (1996). Habitat alteration, hunting and the conservation of folivorous primates in African forests. *Australian Journal of Ecology*, **21**, 1–9.

Oates, J. F., Whitesides, G. H., Davies, A. G., Waterman, P. G., Green, S. M., Dasilva, G. L. & Mole, S. (1990). Determinants of variation in tropical forest primate biomass: new evidence from West Africa. *Ecology*, **71**, 328–343.

Peres, C. A. (1990). Effects of hunting on western Amazonian primate communities. *Biological Conservation*, **54**, 47–59.

Peres, C. A. (1994). Which are the largest New World monkeys? *Journal of Human Evolution*, **26**, 245–249.

Peres, C. A. (1996). Population status of white-lipped and collared peccaries in hunted and unhunted Amazonian forests. *Biological Conservation*, **77**, 115–123.

Peres, C. A. (1997). Effects of habitat quality and hunting pressure on arboreal folivore densities in Neotropical forests: a case study of howler monkeys (*Alouatta* spp.). *Folia Primatologia*, **68**, 199–222.

Peres, C. A. (1999a). The structure of nonvolant mammal communities in different Amazonian forest types. In *Mammals of the Neotropics: The Central Neotropics*, vol. 3, ed. J. F. Eisenberg & K. H. Redford, pp. 564–581. University of Chicago Press, Chicago.

Peres, C. A. (1999b). Effects of subsistence hunting and forest types on Amazonian primate communities. In *Primate Communities*, ed. J. G. Fleagle, C. Janson & K. E. Reed, pp. 268–283. Cambridge University Press, Cambridge.

Peres, C. A. (2000a). Effects of subsistence hunting on vertebrate community structure in Amazonian forests. *Conservation Biology*, **14**, 240–253.

Peres, C. A. (2000b). Evaluating the sustainability of subsistence hunting at multiple Amazonian forest sites. In *Hunting for Sustainability in Tropical*

Forests, ed. J. G. Robinson & E. L. Bennett, pp. 31–56. Columbia University Press, New York.

Peres, C. A. & Dolman, P. M. (2000). Density compensation in neotropical primate communities: evidence from 56 hunted and unhunted Amazonian forests of varying productivity. *Oecologia*, **122**, 175–189.

Peres, C. A. & Terborgh, J. (1995). Amazonian nature reserves: an analysis of the defensibility status of existing conservation units and design criteria for the future. *Conservation Biology*, **9**, 34–46.

Plumptre, A. J. (1991). Plant–herbivore dynamics in the Birungas. PhD thesis, University of Bristol.

Prance, G. T. (1987). Biogeography of neotropical plants. In *Biogeography and Quaternary History in Tropical America*, ed. T. C. Whitmore & G. T. Prance, pp. 46–65. Clarendon Press, Oxford.

Prescott-Allen, R. & Prescott-Allen, C. (1982). *What's Wildlife Worth?* International Institute for Environment and Development, Washington, DC.

Prins, H. H. T. & Reistma, J. M. (1989). Mammalian biomass in an African equatorial rain forest. *Journal of Animal Ecology*, **58**, 851–861.

Ráez-Luna, E. F. (1995). Hunting large primates and conservation of the Neotropical rain forests. *Oryx*, **29**, 43–48.

Redford, K. (1992). The empty forest. *BioScience*, **42**, 412–422.

Redford, K. (1993). Hunting in Neotropical forests: a subsidy from nature. In *Tropical Forests, People and Food: Biocultural Interactions and Applications to Development*, ed. C. M. Hladik, A. Hladik, O. F. Linares, D. Pagezy, A. Semple & M. Hadley, pp. 227–246. Parthenon Publishing, Carnforth.

Redford, K. H. & Robinson, J. G. (1985). Hunting by indigenous peoples and conservation of game species. *Cultural Survey Quarterly*, **9**, 41–43.

Redford, K. H. & Robinson, J. G. (1987). The game of choice. Patterns of Indian and colonist hunting in the Neotropics. *American Anthropologist*, **89**, 650–667.

Robinson, J. G. & Bennett, E. L. (eds.) (2000). *Hunting for Sustainability in Tropical Forests*. Columbia University Press, New York.

Robinson, J. G. & Bodmer, R. E. (1999). Towards wildlife management in tropical forests. *Journal of Wildlife Management*, **63**, 1–13.

Robinson, J. G. & Redford, K. H. (1986). Body size, diet and population density of neotropical forest mammals. *American Naturalist*, **128**, 665–680.

Rylands, A. B. & Keuroghlian, A. (1988). Primate populations in continuous forest and forest fragments in central Amazonia. *Acta Amazonica*, **18**, 291–307.

Sayer, J. A., Harcourt, C. S. & Collins, N. M. (1992). *The Conservation Atlas of Tropical Forests: Africa*. Macmillan, Basingstoke.

Schaller, G. B. (1983). Mammals and their biomass on a Brazilian ranch. *Arquivos de Zoologia, Universidade de São Paulo*, **31**, 1–36.

Smith, E. A. (1983). Anthropological applications of optimal foraging theory: a critical review. *Current Anthropology*, **24**, 625–651.

Stahl, P. W. (1995). *Archaeology in the Lowland American tropics*. Cambridge University Press, Cambridge.

Steel, E. A. (1994). *Study of the Value and Volume of Bushmeat Commerce in Gabon*. World Wide Fund for Nature, Libreville.

Struhsaker, T. T (1999). Primate communities in Africa: the consequence of long-term evolution or the artifact of recent hunting? In *Primate Communities*, ed. J. G. Fleagle, C. Janson & K. E. Reed, pp. 289–294. Cambridge University Press, Cambridge.

Struhsaker, T. T., Lwanga, J. S. & Kasanene, J. M. (1996). Elephants, selective logging and forest regeneration in the Kibale forest. *Journal of Tropical Ecology*, **12**, 45–64.

Terborgh, J. & van Schaik, C. P. (1987). Convergence vs. nonconvergence in primate communities. In *Organization of Communities: Past and Present*, ed. J. H. R. Gee & P. S. Giller, pp. 205–226. Blackwell Scientific, Oxford.

Thomas, S. C. (1991). Population densities and patterns of habitat use among anthropoid primates in the Ituri Forest, Zaire. *Biotropica*, **23**, 68–83.

Townsend, W. (1999). The sustainability of subsistence hunting by the Sirionó Indians of Bolivia. In *Hunting for Sustainability in Tropical Forests*, ed. J. G. Robinson & E. L. Bennett, pp. 267–281. Columbia University Press, New York.

Tutin, C. E. G. & Fernandez, M. (1983). Nationwide census of gorilla (*Gorilla g. gorilla*) and chimpanzee (*Pan t. troglodytes*) populations in Gabon. *American Journal of Primatology*, **6**, 313–336.

Tutin, C. E. G. & White, L. J. T. (1999). The recent evolutionary past of primate communities: likely environmental impacts during the past three millennia. In *Primate Communities*, ed. J. G. Fleagle, C. Janson & K. E. Reed, pp. 220–236. Cambridge University Press, Cambridge.

Tutin, C. E. G., White, L. J. T. & Mackanga Missandzou, A. (1997). The use by rain forest mammals of natural forest fragments in an equatorial African savanna. *Conservation Biology*, **11**, 1190–1203.

UNESCO (1981). *Vegetation Map of South America: Explanatory Notes*. UNESCO, Paris.

Ward, P. D. (1997). *The Call of Distant Mammoths*. Copernicus Press, Springer-Verlag, New York.

Western, D. (1989). The ecological value of elephants: a keystone role in African ecosystems. In *The Ivory Trade and the Future of the African Elephant*, Chapter 5.2, ed. S. Cobb, pp. 25–36, IUCN, Gland, Switzerland.

White, F. (1983). *The Vegetation of Africa: A Descriptive Memoir to Accompany the UNESCO/AETFAT/UNSO Vegetation Map of Africa*. UNESCO, Paris.

White, L. J. T. (1994). Biomass of rain forest mammals in the Lopé Reserve, Gabon. *Journal of Animal Ecology*, **63**, 499–512.

Wilkie, D. S. (1987). Impact of swidden agriculture and subsistence hunting on diversity and abundance of exploited fauna in the Ituri forest of Northeastern Zaire. PhD thesis, University of Massachusetts.

Wilkie, D. S. & Carpenter, J. F. (1999). Bushmeat hunting in the Congo Basin: an assessment of impacts and options for mitigation. *Biodiversity Conservation*, **8**, 927–955.

Wilkie, D. S. & Curran, B. (1991). Why do Mbuti hunters use nets? Ungulate hunting efficiency of bows and nets in the Ituri rain forest. *American Anthropologist*, **93**, 680–689.

Wilkie, D. S. & Finn, J. T. (1990). Slash–burn cultivation and mammal abundance in the Ituri Forest, Zaire. *Biotropica*, **22**, 90–99.

Wilkie, D. S., Curran, B., Tshombe, R. & Morelli, G. A. (1998). Managing
bushmeat hunting in Okapi Wildlife Reserve, Democratic Republic of Congo.
Oryx, **32**, 131–144.

Wilkie, D. S., Sidle, J. G., Boundzanga, G. C., Blake, S. & Auzel, P. (2001).
Deforestation or defaunation: commercial logging and market hunting in
Northern Congo. In *Wildlife Logging Interactions in Tropical Forests*, ed. R.
Fimbel, A. Grajal & J. G. Robinson. Columbia University Press, New York,
in press.

WRI (World Resources Institute) (1998). *World Resources 1998–1999*. Oxford
University Press, Oxford.

Wright, S. J., Zeballos, H., Dominguez, I., Gallardo, M. M., Moreno, M. C. &
Ibáñez, R. (2000). Poachers alter mammal abundance, seed dispersal and
seed predation in a Neotropical forest. *Conservation Biology*, **14**, 227–239.

WSPA (World Society for the Protection of Animals) (1995). *Slaughter of the Apes*.
WSPA, London.

11

Lessons from the plant kingdom for conservation of exploited species

CHARLES M. PETERS

Plants are some of the most intensively exploited of all biological resources. The current annual harvest of wood products is approximately 3.3 million m^3; over half of this total is burned for fuel (FAO, 1999). International trade in sawtimber, plywood and paper is valued at more than $(US)142 billion a year (FAO, 1997). In terms of non-wood resources, the world market for rattan involves more than 150 000 tonnes/year (Caldecott, 1988), 6.7 million tonnes of natural rubber are tapped annually, and more than 45 tonnes of Brazil nuts are collected from Amazonian forests each year (FAO, 1999). In 1998 alone, over 14.2 million tonnes of fresh tropical fruit were harvested (FAO, 1999).

Given that plants are stationary and less cryptic than animals, the ecological impacts of their exploitation are frequently easier to observe. A series of stumps and a bulldozed skid trail or the herringbone pattern of a rubber tapper's incisions are lasting imprints of forest exploitation. The selective removal of a primate does not leave such an obvious, quantifiable trace. For plants, it is usually a much simpler proposition to determine whether a population is being conserved or overexploited.

Plants are also the base of the food chain on which all other organisms depend. If certain plant species are eliminated from the forest through excessive harvest or habitat disruption, this loss will undoubtedly be reflected in the feeding habits of local herbivores. The links between plants and animals are the threads from which forest communities are woven, and the conservation and use of these communities must, by necessity, include both sets of players (Redford & Feinsinger, Chapter 17).

For all of these reasons, an analysis of plant populations would seem to have much to offer to a discussion of the conservation of exploited species. The objective of this chapter, therefore, is to summarise what can be learned about species conservation from the exploitation and management of plant populations. The chapter opens with a brief discussion of the ecological characteristics that differentiate the exploitation of plant and animal

Table 11.1. Frequency of different breeding systems among tree species in temperate and tropical forests. Monoecious species have unisexual male and female flowers within a single crown; dioecious species have separate male and female trees

Forest type	Perfect flowers (%)	Monoecious (%)	Dioecious (%)	Source
Temperate forest				
Northeastern USA	13	81	6	Braun, 1950
Tropical forest				
Costa Rica	68	10	22	Bawa, 1974
Sarawak	60	14	26	Ashton, 1969

resources. The overall impact of harvesting plant products is then examined and the various factors that control the intensity and permanence of these impacts are outlined. Finally, several basic lessons from the plant kingdom about the conservation of exploited species are presented together with recommendations for closing the gap between research and application. Based on my experience and interests, the focus of this chapter is on tropical forests and the various timber and non-wood plant resources that grow in these habitats.

DIFFERENCES BETWEEN PLANTS AND ANIMALS

There are several differences between plants and animals that play a key role in determining the response of each group to exploitation. Perhaps the first and most important of these is that plants are autotrophs and, as such, they have the ability to make complex sugar molecules from carbon dioxide, water and light energy from the sun. They make their own food and they release oxygen in the process. From a practical standpoint, this means that plants do not have the same food procurement priorities as animals. A reduction in the abundance of prey species or a decrease in the amount of quality browse are not issues to plants.

There are also notable differences in the reproductive characteristics of plants and animals. As is shown in Table 11.1, most of the plants in both temperate and tropical forests are hermaphrodites, i.e. they possess both male and female floral structures on the same plant. Interestingly, there are differences in the way that this hermaphroditism is expressed in the temperate zone and the tropics. Most of the tree species in temperate forests are monoecious, meaning that they have separate male and female flowers, while the majority of the trees in the wet tropics have perfect flowers with both male (staminate) and female (pistillate) floral structures. The percentage of species that exhibit dioecy, with separate male and female trees, is somewhat higher in tropical forests than in temperate forests, but in neither environment does it represent more than about one-quarter of all plant taxa. An obvious benefit of being a hermaphrodite is that sexual reproduction does not require the services of a mate.

In contrast to most terrestrial animals, the reproductive output of plants is prodigious and widely dispersed. A single, large tropical tree may produce in excess of 25 000 seeds in a season (see e.g. Peters, 1991), and these seeds may be carried by wind or animals for several hundred metres. Species with smaller seeds produce them in even greater quantities and the tiny propagules may be dispersed for several kilometres. Assuming a lifespan of several hundred years for long-lived canopy species, the total reproductive output of these trees may surpass several million progeny. Litter size for most plant species is measured in the hundreds, thousands or tens of thousands.

The seeds of many plant species can remain dormant in the soil for years in response to adverse environmental conditions. The exact stimulus required for germination varies from species to species, but usually involves some combination of increased light, increased soil temperature or an increased concentration of solutes in the soil solution (Vazquez-Yanes & Orozco-Segovia, 1993). All of these changes are indications that the canopy has been opened and that the shady, physiologically stressful conditions of the forest understorey have been removed. Rather than germinating, and ultimately dying, in a limiting environment, the seed opts to wait until conditions become better. A similar avoidance strategy is exhibited by trees in the temperate zone during the onset of winter, when they drop their leaves and enter a state of low metabolic activity.

In addition to seed production by sexual means, many plant species have the ability to reproduce vegetatively. Adventitious buds are released on the parent plant, frequently in response to disturbance, and new clonal individuals are produced from sprouts along the stem, roots or branches. This strategy is apparently quite successful. Vegetatively produced groves of quaking aspen *Populus tremuloides* cover hundreds of hectares in the western USA, and dense clones of the bamboo *Guadua weberbaueri* extend over 92 000 km^2 in the Brazilian Amazon (Nelson, 1994). Vegetative reproduction can be used to regenerate body parts, to expand a population rapidly in response to favourable environmental conditions, to invade new habitats or to maintain a desirable genotype over time. With a few notable exceptions (e.g. corals and bryozoans), animal populations do not have these clonal options.

A final characteristic of plants that can play a major role in shaping the pattern and intensity of resource exploitation is that many species, especially tropical species, are very well protected. Although they cannot move to escape predation or harvest, many tropical plants are armed with thick bark, sharp thorns, stinging hairs, and a host of insidious secondary metabolites that can cause contact dermatitis, disrupt cell functioning, inhibit key physiological processes or produce deadly cyanide gas. Many of these individuals are also extremely big and very hard to harvest. Felling a buttressed, 60 m tall canopy tree by hand can take longer and involve more work than trapping a rodent or shooting a monkey.

THE BAD NEWS

On the basis of the preceding discussion, it would seem that plant populations are better able to withstand the impacts of repeated commercial harvesting than animal populations. However, there are unfortunate correlates to the generalisations presented above that drastically alter this picture. For example, the majority of plants are indeed hermaphrodites, but many of them possess mechanisms that force outcrossing or the exchange of genetic material with other individuals through cross-pollination (Bawa, 1983). In some species, the emergence of female and male floral structures are timed so that stigma receptivity and pollen release in a single flower are out of synchronisation. Other species have spatially separated the male and female flowers within the crown so that the probability of self-pollination is greatly reduced. A final group of species has evolved genetic incompatibility mechanisms that effectively eliminate any possibility of self-fertilisation (de Nettancourt, 1977; Williams *et al.*, 1994). Through a series of ingenious biochemical processes, the genetic make-up of the pollen arriving at the stigmatic surface is evaluated, and germination is restricted only to those grains that have been produced by individuals with a different genotype.

Given the strict requirements for cross-pollination exhibited by many tropical trees, some mechanism is needed to carry the pollen from one tree to another. Wind is the preferred pollen carrier in temperate forests, and this vector works quite well in low diversity forests where the constituent plant species occur in relatively high density populations. Wind pollination, however, is not effective in tropical forests. The first problem is that there is very little wind in the interior of a multi-storeyed forest. The second problem is that the plant populations in species-rich forest occur at very low densities; many species may be represented by only one or two adult trees per hectare (Whitmore, 1998). What vector can carry pollen over long distances and be selective about the taxonomic identity of the donor and the recipient? The answer is animals. A great majority of tropical plants rely on animals to pollinate their flowers and disperse their fruit (Bawa, 1983). Without these animals, there is no pollination, no seed set, no population recruitment and no sustainable harvesting (see also Redford & Feinsinger, Chapter 17).

A second piece of bad news concerns the reproductive output of tropical plants. Tropical forest plants do produce a very large number of seeds and these seeds are frequently dispersed over a great distance. Unfortunately, most of these seeds, as well as the seedlings that grow from them, die within one year following seedfall. For some species, the mortality at the seedling stage is so severe that only 1–2% of the initial cohort will survive (see e.g. Sarukhan, 1981). Seeds are eaten by animals and preyed upon by insects. Young seedlings are defoliated by herbivores, smashed by falling branches, ripped out of the soil by rolling rocks, and desiccated by wildly fluctuating levels of soil moisture. Given the high rates of mortality that characterise many tropical plant populations, it is somewhat surprising that they maintain themselves even in the absence of repeated exploitation.

Finally, tropical plants are undeniably well protected and they possess a diverse arsenal of chemical and physical defences. The current search for new medicines in tropical forests gives some indication of the complicated chemistry found in the leaves, seeds and wood of these plants. However, just as there are animals that can eat the most toxic leaves and insects that can oviposit on the most deadly seeds, human beings have repeatedly demonstrated that they are very clever at circumventing plant defences. The hydrogen cyanide in the tubers of *Manihot esculenta* is routinely removed by native Amazonians, and all it takes to fell a 60 m tall rain forest tree is a big chainsaw and some fuel.

THE IMPACT OF EXPLOITATION

In reality, the exploitation of tropical plant resources can have a notable impact on the species and populations involved. Although there is much variation between species, sites and harvest methods, the overall magnitude of this impact is controlled by the type of resource or plant tissue that is harvested, the intensity of harvest and the ecological characteristics of the species under exploitation. Sporadic tapping of latex for subsistence use may have little impact on the long-term stability of a tree population, while intensive, annual collection of a valuable fruit or oil seed can gradually eliminate a species from the forest. The felling of large adult trees can produce a similar ecological result in a much shorter time period.

Type of plant tissue

For the purpose of this chapter, the enormous variety of plant resources produced by tropical forests can be grouped into three categories based on the type of plant tissue or compound exploited: vegetative tissues, reproductive propagules and plant exudates. Vegetative tissues are a diverse assemblage of plant tissues used for fibres, building material, medicines and food. The plant part exploited may be the root, stem, leaf, bark or apical bud. Although the origin and use of these plant products are very different, their harvest produces a similar ecological impact. The individual will either be killed during the collection process or, in a limited number of cases, it will survive and later regenerate the tissues removed. Timber and rattan are probably the best-known examples of vegetative tissues whose harvest results in the death of the plant. Uncontrolled harvesting has caused notable shortages of the most desirable rattan species in Southeast Asia, e.g. *Calamus caesius* and *Calamus manan* (Dransfield & Manokaran, 1994) and several valuable woods have become locally extinct in many parts of Amazonia, e.g. *Ceiba pentandra*, *Aniba duckei* and *Caesalpinia echinata* (Gentry & Vasquez, 1988; Grieser Johns, 1997). In many respects, the exploitation of vegetative tissues is like hunting. Harvesting involves the death of large adult individuals with high fecundity, and the resultant decline in recruitment rate can ultimately drive the population to extinction. The ecological impacts of logging are immediate and high profile, and they have been documented in numerous studies (e.g. Johns, 1988; Uhl & Guimaraes, 1989; Pinard *et al.*, 1996).

Reproductive propagules are fruits, nuts, oil seeds and arils that are produced by the plant as a result of sexual reproduction. The collection of these resources does not kill or wound the plant, and it is tempting to assume that the harvest of reproductive propagules has only a minimal impact on the population. It should be remembered, however, that fruits contain the seeds that produce the seedlings that are necessary to maintain the population in the forest. Removing large quantities of fruits and seeds can have a significant, albeit gradual and very subtle, effect on the structure and dynamics of the population under exploitation.

The gradual disintegration of a plant population subjected to intensive seed collection is depicted in Figure 11.1 using demographic data for *Grias peruviana*, an edible forest fruit from the Peruvian Amazon, and the

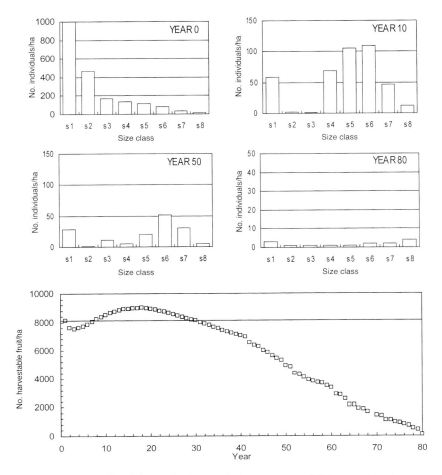

Figure 11.1. Simulated change in the population structure of *Grias peruviana* in response to excessive fruit collection. Results are based on stepwise analyses using a transition matrix model and demographic data reported by Peters (1990a). Harvest intensity is set at 85% of the total annual fruit production. Note the change in scale in the last three time periods to account for a progressive decrease in population size.

stepwise results from computer simulations of a transition matrix model (Peters, 1990a). Size classes s1 to s3 are based on height measurements of seedlings, saplings, and juveniles, while classes s4 to s8 reflect a 5.0 cm diameter interval for adults. For the purpose of the simulation, the harvest intensity was set at 85% of the total annual fruit production. Note the change of scale at years 10, 50 and 80 to compensate for the gradual decrease in population size. The scatterplot in the lower half of Figure 11.1 shows the total number of fruits harvested from the *Grias* population during each year of the simulation.

As is shown at year 0, the *G. peruviana* population initially displays the inverse J-shaped, or negative exponential, size class distribution of a shade-tolerant canopy tree with abundant regeneration. After 10 years of fruit collection, however, the structure of the population has been notably changed. The infrequency of seedling establishment has caused a reduction in the smaller size classes; the greater number of stems in the intermediate size classes reflects the growth of saplings that were established prior to exploitation. By year 50, the population has been even further degraded by the chronic lack of regeneration. Some of the intermediate size classes contain fewer than 10 individuals, and the existing level of seedlings and saplings appears to be insufficient to restock the adult classes. The size class histogram at year 80 represents the culmination of a long process of overexploitation. The population consists only of large, old adult trees, none of which is regenerating. In the absence of remedial action, it is only a matter of time before *G. peruviana* becomes locally extinct.

The important message to be gained from this simulation is that at no point during the process of overexploitation is there any dramatic visual evidence, for example dead or dying trees, that something is wrong. Fruit production and harvest levels do not begin to drop below baseline until year 30, and commercial quantities of fruit continue to be available for several decades after this (see scatterplot in Figure 11.1). Even during the later stages, the forest still contains a considerable number of adult *G. peruviana* trees that are producing fruit. Harvesting undoubtedly would continue until these trees begin to die, at which point collectors would be forced to move into a new area of forest in search of *Grias* fruits.

The example shown in Figure 11.1 represents an extreme case of overexploitation, and does not imply that every level of harvesting reproductive propagules leads directly to species extinction. The simulation is useful, however, because it shows that even though the ecological impacts of this type of resource use are very gradual and essentially invisible, in the long run they can be as devastating as logging in causing the disruption of local populations.

In addition to the impact on seedling establishment and population structure, the collection of reproductive propagules can also affect the genetic composition of the population being exploited (Peters, 1990b). A population of forest trees, for example, will usually contain several individuals that produce large, succulent fruits, a great number of individuals that produce fruits of intermediate size and quality, and a few individuals that produce fruits that, from a commercial standpoint, are inferior because of small size, bitter taste, or poor appearance. If this population is subjected to intensive fruit collection, the 'inferior' trees invariably will be the ones whose fruits and seeds are left in the forest to regenerate. Over time, the selective removal of only the best fruit types will result in a population dominated by trees of marginal economic value. This process is identical to the 'high-grading' or 'creaming' of the best tropical timbers that occurs in many logging operations.

When properly conducted, the tapping of plant exudates, i.e. latex, resins and gums, does not disturb the forest canopy, kill the exploited tree, or remove its seeds from the site. In theory, this activity probably comes the closest to conforming to the ideal of sustainable exploitation. It should be noted, however, that maintaining a continual supply of latex or resin is contingent upon the harvest species being able to replace itself in the forest. There is currently a large number of rubber trees growing in the lowland forests of Amazonia. These trees will eventually die. Are any provisions being made to recruit a second and third generation of *Hevea* trees? This is an important question given that the demands of continually producing large amounts of latex are frequently at odds with the ecological imperative of producing seeds. Polhamus (1962), for example, reported fruit sets of only 2–4% in high yielding plantations of *Hevea* clones, even after controlled hand pollinations.

Harvest intensity

The intensity of harvest can either exacerbate or alleviate the ecological impacts of exploitation. Low level selective logging, for example, may leave sufficient seed trees in the population to maintain natural rates of seedling establishment, and the periodic collection of a few fruits for subsistence use actually may function as a type of compensatory mortality by removing fruits and seeds that would have died or been eaten anyway. Unfortunately, 'How much is too much?' is a key question without an easy answer. The basic issue here relates to the interaction between resource abundance or stock, resource yield, and harvest level (see e.g. Ludwig, Chapter 2). Highly productive resources growing in high density populations will have a higher sustainable off-take than sparse populations with low productivity.

A hypothetical example of overexploitation is shown in Figure 11.2 to illustrate the relationships between stock and harvestable yield. The shaded bars in the histogram represent the current stock of rattan cane at the start of the year; the open bars shown at the top of each shaded bar represent the

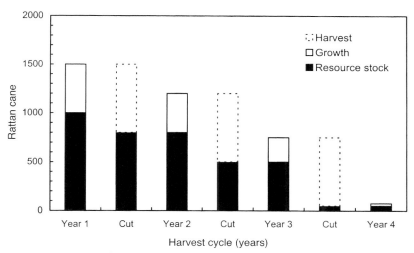

Figure 11.2. Hypothetical example of overexploitation of rattan illustrating the relationship between resource stock and annual productivity. See the text for explanation of stock, growth and harvest parameters.

total growth by the end of the year. The dotted bars show the amount of rattan cane that is harvested each year.

The current stock of rattan in the forest at the start of year 1 is 1000 canes. This stock produces 500 new canes during the year. A larger stock would have produced more canes, a smaller one would have produced fewer canes. At the end of the first year, 700 rattan canes are harvested – 200 more than were produced during the year – leaving a stock of 800 canes in the forest. These plants are left to grow for a year and they produce 400 new canes. The next year, 700 canes – 300 more than were produced – are harvested again. The remaining rattan plants produce 250 new canes, yielding a total stock of 750 canes. A final harvest of 700 canes at the end of year 3 reduces the total stock to only 50. At this point, commercial rattan harvesting is no longer possible, and the annual growth of the resource has been reduced to only 25 canes/year. If nothing is done to remedy the situation, rattan will probably disappear from the forest as it has in many parts of Southeast Asia.

On the basis of what is presented in Figure 11.2 about the density and yield of rattan, a more sustainable level of harvest can be estimated. The initial stock of rattan produces 500 new canes each year. By harvesting only this amount and leaving the basic stock untouched, rattan cane could be exploited on the site for a long time. The key is to cut only as much rattan as the basic stock produces in one year. This simple prescription of 'cut only the growth' is (theoretically) the basic premise of sustainable forestry.

Ecological characteristics of harvest species

Some species, because of their reproductive biology, regeneration and growth strategies, or population structure, are inherently better able to withstand the continual perturbations of exploitation than other species. A listing of the key ecological factors that determine the adaptability or resilience of different plant species to harvesting is shown in Table 11.2. The values of each parameter are classified as low, medium and high, based on the potential for sustainable exploitation.

As is shown in Table 11.2, the life cycle characteristics of a species can either facilitate or severely complicate exploitation. Species that fruit at unpredictable intervals and require a specific animal for pollination and seed dispersal probably represent the worst case scenario. An annually fruiting species serviced by more common, generalist pollinators such as small insects or bees is much easier to work with. In terms of regeneration guilds, primary forest species adapted for growth and regeneration under a closed canopy will, in most cases, be preferable to fast-growing pioneer species that require the occurrence of large gaps for seedling establishment.

The density and distribution of the species can also play an important role here. Abundant species that are clearly regenerating in the forest are much more tolerant of harvesting than low density, scattered populations. The forest types within which a species occurs must also be taken into consideration. If the desired habitat occupies only a very small area, or is inaccessible during certain times of the year, for example seasonally flooded forests, resource supply can quickly become a problem as collectors harvest too much too soon.

Even more important than the overall abundance of the plant species, however, is the size class distribution of the individuals within its populations. A species may be the most abundant in the forest in terms of total number of stems, but if all of these stems are of similar size or if the population is characterised by a preponderance of large adult trees and exhibits no regeneration, the species is obviously having trouble establishing seedlings. If the establishment of seedlings is a problem in the absence of harvesting, imagine the difficulty the species will experience when commercial collectors start picking up large quantities of fruit, or loggers start felling the largest adult trees.

Table 11.2. *Potential for sustainable exploitation of different plant species based on their botanical characteristics, reproductive biology, and population structure*

	Potential for sustainable exploitation		
	Low	Medium	High
Botanical characteristics			
Flowers	Few, large	Intermediate	Small, many
Fruits	Few, large	Intermediate	Small, many
Seed germination	Low viability	Intermediate	High viability
Sprouting ability	None	Low	High
Population structure			
Size-class distribution	Little regeneration	Sporadic regeneration	Abundant regeneration
Tree density/ha	0–5 adults	5–10 adults	10 + adults
Spatial distribution	Scattered	Clumped	Homogeneous
Regeneration guild	Early pioneer	Late secondary	Primary
Flower/fruit phenology	Unpredictable	Supra-annual	Annual
Reproductive biology			
Pollination	Biotic; with specialised vector	Biotic; with generalist vector	Abiotic
Pollinator abundance	Rare; bats, hummingbirds	Intermediate; beetles, moths	Common; small insects, abiotic
Seed dispersal	Biotic; with specialised vector	Biotic; with generalist vector	Abiotic
Disperser abundance	Rare; large birds, primates	Intermediate; small mammals	Common; bats, small birds

Adapted from Peters, 1994.

LESSONS FROM THE PLANT KINGDOM

Current patterns of harvesting in wild plant populations suggest several trends of relevance to the conservation of exploited populations. The first of these is that plants are surprisingly resilient to disturbance, and subsistence-level exploitation of many botanical resources has only minimal impact on forest populations. If the harvests of vegetative tissues are kept small and do not surpass the annual yield of the species, and if reproductive propagules and exudates are collected at a level that does not impact on the regeneration and growth of the species, resource extraction can be viewed as a relatively benign intervention that mimics natural events such as tree falls, seed predation and occasional wounding.

The second trend is that the commercial exploitation of timber and non-timber resources is plagued by destructive harvesting, overexploitation and a basic disregard for the functional ecology of tropical plant populations. Timber trees are logged without replacement, rattan canes are cut and dragged out of the forest without there being a clue as to the initial density and productivity of the target species, and Brazil nuts have been collected commercially for so long in Amazonia that residual populations consist entirely of large adult trees (see Figure 11.1). I would contend that a similar pattern is characteristic of the exploitation of animal populations.

The third trend is that the few documented examples of sustainable resource use in the tropics invariably involve a deliberate and informed management effort. In each case, the species under exploitation continues to produce, and reproduce, because someone has invested the time and the energy to ensure that this happens. The unavoidable conclusion from all of this is that the conservation of plant species under exploitation requires management. The same, no doubt, will be true for animals.

It is a curious feature of the historical relationship between people and plants that management efforts are usually undertaken only when desirable species are severely in peril. The development of silviculture in Germany during the mid 1700s, for example, was largely in response to the devastation of local forests by an increasing population. Only recently have any attempts been made to develop a silviculture for non-timber tropical forest resources (see e.g. Stockdale, 1994; Peters, 1996). Perhaps now is the time to move forward with the development of innovative systems for the management of the animal populations found in tropical forests.

The management of any biological resource has an ecological side, an economic side, and a social side, i.e. the prescription, the compensation and the actors involved. A viable management strategy must integrate these three variables in such a way that the prescription is implemented, the relevant actors are compensated, and the exploited species are conserved. There are several steps that could be taken to enhance the possibility that this happens. First, great care needs to be exercised in selecting the taxa, the community groups and the environment within which management operations are to be implemented. Select the most robust species, the most organised and responsible community, and the most well-known habitat. Secondly, the highest priority should be given to applied research. We need to move beyond the description of population declines caused by overharvesting and start addressing the hard questions about what can be done to restore certain species. This will invariably involve more sociology and community extension than biology. Thirdly, start small, start inexpensive, but start some participatory management projects and carefully monitor what happens over time. Provide a firm scientific basis to the project and do everything possible to ensure that the science is done by local people. Finally, perhaps the most useful lesson to be learned from the plant kingdom about the conservation of exploited species is also the simplest. In spite of everything we might do from afar to protect an organism, ultimately we must touch the thing we wish to save.

REFERENCES

Ashton, P. S. (1969). Speciation among tropical forest trees: some deductions in the light of recent evidence. *Biological Journal of the Linnean Society*, **1**, 155–196.

Bawa, K. S. (1974). Breeding systems of tree species of a lowland tropical community. *Evolution*, **29**, 167–179.

Bawa, K. S. (1983). Patterns of flowering in tropical plants. In *Handbook of Experimental Pollination Biology*, ed. C. E. Jones & R. J. Little, pp. 394–410. Van Nostrand Reinhold, New York.

Braun, E. L. (1950). *Deciduous Forests of Eastern North America*. Blakiston Publishers, Philadelphia.

Caldecott, J. (1988). Climbing towards extinction. *New Scientist*, **9**, 62–66.

de Nettancourt, D. (1977). *Incompatibility in Angiosperms*. Springer-Verlag, Berlin and New York.

Dransfield, J. & Manokaran, N. (1994). *Rattan: Plant Resources of Southeast Asia*, no. 6. PROSEA, Bogor.

FAO (Food and Agriculture Organization) (1997). *State of the World's Forests 1997*. FAO, Rome.

FAO (Food and Agriculture Organization) (1999). FAOSTAT Statistics Database http://apps.fao.org. FAO, Rome.

Gentry, A. & Vazquez, R. (1988). Where have all the ceibas gone? A case history of mismanagement of a tropical forest resource. *Forest Ecology and Management*, **23**, 73–76.

Grieser Johns, A. (1997). *Timber Production and Biodiversity Conservation in Tropical Rain Forests*. Cambridge University Press, Cambridge.

Johns, A. (1988). Effects of 'selective' timber extraction on rain forest structure and composition and some consequences for frugivores and folivores. *Biotropica*, **20**, 31–37.

Nelson, B. W. (1994). Natural forest disturbance and change in the Brazilian Amazon. *Remote Sensing Reviews*, **10**, 105–125.

Peters, C. M. (1990a). Population ecology and management of forest fruit trees in Peruvian Amazonia. In *Alternatives to Deforestation: Steps Toward Sustainable Use of the Amazon Rain Forest*, ed. A. B. Anderson, pp. 86–98. Columbia University Press, New York.

Peters, C. M. (1990b). Plenty of fruit but no free lunch. *Garden*, **14**, 8–13.

Peters, C. M. (1991). Plant demography and the management of tropical forest resources: a case study of *Brosimum alicastrum* in Mexico. In *Rain Forest Regeneration and Management*, ed. A. Gomez-Pompa, T. C. Whitmore & M. Hadley, pp. 265–272. UNESCO, Paris; Parthenon Publishing Group, Carnforth.

Peters, C. M. (1994). *Sustainable Harvest of Non-Timber Plant Resources in Tropical Moist Forest: An Ecological Primer*. Biodiversity Support Program, Washington, DC.

Peters, C. M. (1996). *The Ecology and Management of Non-Timber Forest Resources*. Technical paper no. 322. World Bank, Washington, DC.

Pinard, M., Howlett, B. & Davidson, D. (1996). Site conditions limit tree recruitment after logging of dipterocarp forests in Sabah, Malaysia. *Biotropica*, **28**, 2–12.

Polhamus, L. G. (1962). *Rubber: Botany, Production, and Utilization*. Leonard Hill Ltd, London.

Sarukhan, J. (1981). Demographic problems in tropical systems. In *Demography and Evolution of Plant Populations*, ed. O. Solbrig, pp. 161–188. Blackwell Scientific, Oxford.

Stockdale, M. C. (1994). Inventory methods and ecological studies relevant to the management of wild populations of rattan. PhD thesis, Oxford Forestry Institute, Oxford University.

Uhl, C. & Guimaraes, I. (1989). Ecological impacts of selective logging in the Brazilian Amazon: a case study from the Paragominas region of the state of Para. *Biotropica*, **21**, 98–106.

Vazquez-Yanes, C. & Orozco-Segovia, A. (1993). Patterns of seed longevity and germination in the tropical rain forest. *Annual Review of Ecology and Systematics*, **24**, 669–687.

Whitmore, T. C. (1998). *An Introduction to Tropical Rain Forests*, 2nd edn. Oxford University Press, Oxford.

Williams, E. G., Clarke, A. E. & Know, R. B. (1994). *Genetic Control of Self-Incompatibility in Flowering Plants*. Kluwer Academic, Dordrecht and Boston, MA.

PART IV

From individuals to communities

12

The role of behaviour in studying sustainable exploitation

WILLIAM J. SUTHERLAND & JENNIFER A. GILL

Behavioural ecology has flourished over the last few decades and there is currently considerable interest in combining the fields of behaviour and conservation (Ulfstrand, 1996; Clemmons & Bucholz, 1997; Sutherland, 1998a; Caro, 1999; Gosling & Sutherland, 2000). In this chapter we consider the role that behavioural investigations can play in the study of exploitation. Behaviour may influence the susceptibility to exploitation of different species when coexisting, may cause species to decline further when the population has been reduced by exploitation and may determine the response to the human disturbance resulting, for example, from hunting. Furthermore, behavioural studies often take an evolutionary approach to attempt to understand why animals behave as they do, which provides the opportunity of understanding population-level responses from fundamental behavioural decisions. It should then be possible to use these models to predict the consequences of exploitation for conservation.

A range of aspects of behaviour will affect susceptibility to exploitation. Thus, whether a species is social or solitary, sedentary or active, living in the open or hidden in cover will all considerably influence its likelihood of capture (Reynolds & Jennings, 2000). Age differences in behaviour may produce age differences in the risk of being captured. Young individuals are usually less successful foragers and take greater risks, which makes them more susceptible to predation and exploitation (Cresswell, 1994). The mating system will usually result in sex differences in activity and thus sex differences in vulnerability to exploitation. For example, the sex (often the male) that is more active in seeking mates may be more visible or more likely to enter a trap (Kohlmann *et al.*, 1999). In addition, sex differences in levels of parental care may influence exploitation rates through, for example, the risks to parents of protecting slow-moving, vulnerable young. There is clearly a wide range of behavioural factors that will influence susceptibility to exploitation. Here, we concentrate on aspects of behaviour that apply generally but for which the consequences for exploited populations are less intuitively obvious.

In this chapter we consider seven issues relating to exploitation in which we believe behavioural studies can play an important role: (1) understanding levels of sustainable exploitation, (2) determining the susceptibility of different species to accidental mortality, (3) the buffer effect, (4) the Allee effect, (5) the response to hunting disturbance, (6) the behaviour of exploiters, and (7) economic discounting.

CALCULATION OF MAXIMUM SUSTAINABLE YIELD

The classic theoretical approach for estimating sustainable yields is based on the density-dependent relationship between population growth rate and population size (Figure 12.1; see Ludwig, Chapter 2). The fraction of the population that can be exploited can be considered as equal to the population growth rate that is surplus to that required for maintaining the population. Thus, in theory, if the population growth rate is 1.09 then the surplus of 9% per year can be removed and the population will be maintained at the same level. There is, of course, a range of good reasons, such as uncertainty or environmental stochasticity, to be conservative and exploit below this level (Beddington & May, 1977; see Punt & Smith, Chapter 3). The classic approach for calculating maximum sustainable yield is to multiply the population growth rate at each population size by the population size to give the yield available, while maintaining the population at a constant level (Figure 12.1).

As shown in Figure 12.1, a simple consequence of the linear density-dependent relationship is that maximum sustainable exploitation is expected to occur at 50% of the unexploited population size. This figure also shows, however, that this result depends upon the shape of the density-dependent relationship. If the relationship between growth rate and density is convex then the maximum sustainable level of exploitation will occur at above 50% of the initial population size. If the relationship is concave then the maximum sustainable level of exploitation will occur at below 50% of the initial population size.

The actual shape of the relationship between population growth rate and population density will depend upon a number of aspects of behaviour such as resource depletion rates, interference competition, dominance rank and territoriality, and in each case we expect the impact on population growth rate to increase with density (Sutherland, 1996). Depletion acts through a reduction in the available food supplies, resulting in a lower rate

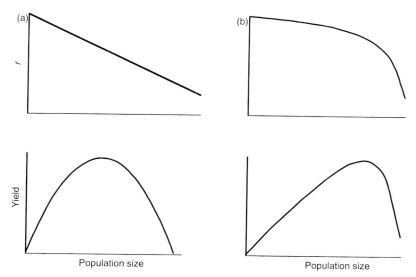

Figure 12.1. Importance of the nature of density dependence for linking per capita growth rates *r* (above) with yields (below). (a) A linear relationship between population growth rate and population size results in a symmetrical curve with the highest yield at a population at half of the unexploited level. (b) A convex curve results in an asymmetrical curve with the highest yields above 50% of the unexploited level.

of intake. The reduced intake may affect population growth by either reducing survival or lowering the probability of having sufficient reserves to breed successfully. As the number of competing individuals increases, the effects of depletion thus increase disproportionately (Sutherland & Anderson, 1993). Interference is the short-term and reversible decline in intake rate resulting from the presence of others owing, for example, to fighting or disturbance of the prey, and it usually increases disproportionately with population density (Hassall & Varley, 1969). As an example, Stillman *et al.* (1997) showed that interference amongst Eurasian oystercatchers *Haematopus ostralegus* increased markedly with local population density. The occurrence of dominance behaviour means that as population size increases, a higher proportion of individuals will be of low rank and will thus experience reduced survival or reproductive output. Finally, the exclusion of individuals from the better-quality territories or even from obtaining a territory at all is likely to act more strongly at higher population sizes (Kokko & Sutherland, 1998).

As a result of three of these four processes – interference, depletion and dominance – we expect population growth rate to be increasingly reduced by population density (see Figure 12.1b). For territoriality there may be a more complex relationship but population growth rate will still be increasingly reduced by population density. This pattern is also likely to be true for many other density-dependent processes, such as disease and parasite infection levels, which will become increasingly important at high densities. An important consequence of the patterns shown in Figure 12.1b is that the maximum yield will occur above 50% of the unexploited population size.

There is also the possibility of more complex relationships, for example, for a population with a fixed number of equal-quality territories. At population sizes below this threshold set by the number of territories, all individuals will breed and the population growth rate will be high. Once the population exceeds this threshold, all territories will be occupied and any remaining individuals will fail to breed. This is also likely to result in a maximum sustainable yield above 50% of initial population size.

Thus knowledge of behaviour provides insights into the nature of density dependence, which in turn determines the response to exploitation. We believe there is considerable potential to derive density-dependent responses from behavioural processes and to use these to answer a wide range of questions, including population responses to exploitation.

NON-TARGET SPECIES

Many conservation issues relate to non-target species caught intentionally or inadvertently (Kaiser & Jennings, Chapter 16). Most target species have some measure of protection from negative feedback: as they become scarce they are usually less profitable to target. Non-target species have no such protection, as their exploitation is largely unaffected by their abundance (Milner-Gulland, Chapter 5). Thus blue whales *Balaenoptera musculus* continued to be exploited even when extremely rare because it was profitable to hunt fin whales *Balaenoptera physalus* (Clark, 1990), and black rhinoceros *Diceros bicornis* hunting only persisted in some areas because it was profitable to hunt African elephants *Loxodonta africana* in the same area (Milner-Gulland & Leader-Williams, 1992). This is likely to be a very common mechanism for driving rare species towards extinction.

The potential impact of hunting on these non-target species can depend to a large extent on differences in behaviour. For example, the dilution effect (Hamilton, 1971) is the phenomenon whereby individuals in large groups are less likely to be preyed upon than those in small groups, if hunting rates do not scale up perfectly with group size. In species that show conspecific aggregation, scarcer species are likely to occur in smaller groups and hence each attack on such groups results in a proportionately greater loss to the population. Predation and hunting are also usually likely to be greater for individuals on the periphery of groups and if scarcer species tend to occur on group edges, they will be more likely to be killed. Any differences in ecology or behaviour among species are likely to result in the scarcer species occurring in smaller groups, or on the periphery of larger groups.

The dilution effect considers the relationship between group size and per capita mortality resulting from a given predation (or hunting) event. Thus the number killed per group may be independent of group size but the proportion killed decreases with group size. This can help to explain the frequent conservation problem that occurs when rare and supposedly protected species coexist with commoner, exploited species. Lesser white-fronted geese *Anser erythropus* are declining in Europe, probably as a result of severe exploitation (Madsen, 1996). It is likely that the tendency of lesser white-fronted geese to occur in the same area but fly separately from large flocks of white-fronted geese *Anser albifrons* may increase their vulnerability to hunting. The decline of slender-billed curlew *Numenius tenuirostris* could potentially have a similar explanation. Although this species is protected, it is extremely similar to the Eurasian curlew *Numenius arquata*, which is heavily hunted during migration and in the wintering areas. These examples are somewhat speculative but it is likely to be generally true that differences in behaviour and ecology between species (e.g. a different migration schedule, a different habitat preference or different roost arrival time) will often result in higher mortalities for the rarer species simply because of the dilution effect.

BUFFER EFFECT

The buffer effect (Brown, 1969) refers to the pattern of habitat selection of a species changing in response to population size. Thus, at low population density, species would occur in the optimal habitat type and as the population expands an increasing proportion will occur in poorer-quality habitats. This pattern of altering habitat selection in response to population size can have important consequences for harvested populations. If a population is being harvested in a poor-quality location then numbers are likely to decline and not to be replaced at that site. However, if a population is being harvested in a good-quality site, then reductions in number through hunting will be offset by movement of individuals from the poorer habitats into the good habitat. This will result in harvesting apparently having little impact on a population until the point at which the supply of immigrants from poorer sites has been exhausted. At this point the population may decline rapidly.

A good example of this is the Atlantic cod *Gadus morhua*. Cod populations in the Northwest Atlantic apparently underwent a dramatic crash during the 1980s. However, the population decline had in fact been continuing for some time prior to this but had gone unnoticed by fishermen (Hutchings, 1996). This was because at high population density the cod had a wide spatial distribution, within which they occurred at a range of densities. Fishing activity was concentrated in the most profitable, high density aggregations. As the cod population started to decline, recruitment from the low and medium density aggregations to the high density aggregations occurred, possibly as a result of the benefits to individuals of being members of a large group, through enhanced abilities to locate prey or avoid predation. The result was that the catches experienced by offshore fisherman did not change until there were virtually no fish occurring outside of the high density, heavily fished areas, at which point continued fishing caused the population to collapse rapidly. This resulted in a great deal of debate as to whether or not overfishing was the cause of the collapse (Walters & Maguire, 1996). Examination of cod survey data collected from stratified random locations clearly showed this decline in medium and low density aggregations and demonstrated that overfishing was the cause of the decline (Hutchings, 1996). Had there been consideration of the habitat selection behaviour of cod prior to this time it may have been possible to predict the collapse of this fishery well before it happened.

ALLEE EFFECT

The Allee effect (Allee, 1931, 1938; Allee *et al.*, 1949) (also known as depensation in the fisheries literature; Alvarez, 1998) is the decline in per capita survival or breeding output at low population size (see Petersen & Levitan, Chapter 13). There are numerous behavioural mechanisms for the Allee effect (for reviews, see Courchamp *et al.*, 1999; Stephens & Sutherland, 1999, 2000) such as an inability to find mates at low densities, increased predation in small groups (see e.g. Berg *et al.*, 1992), improved vigilance in larger groups (Kenward, 1978; Jennings & Evans, 1980), reduced parasitism (Côté & Poulin, 1995) and improved foraging success with co-operative hunting or enhanced fertilisation success (Levitan *et al.*, 1992).

The Allee effect may have considerable implications for exploitation.

Incorporating the Allee effect into the classic density-dependent relationship between population growth rate and population size (Figure 12.1) results in three equilibria: an upper stable point, a lower unstable one and extinction (Petersen & Levitan, Chapter 13). If the population size falls below the lower unstable point it is likely to become extinct. It is as yet far from clear how important the Allee effect is in exploited populations, but it has the potential to be extremely important, especially for population recovery.

Population modellers and those studying behaviour often have different definitions of the Allee effect, which is important for interpreting its consequences. Stephens *et al.* (1999) suggested that it is useful to distinguish between a component Allee effect and a demographic Allee effect. Most empirical studies of behaviour or ecology examine a component of the population growth rate, such as predation risk or the inability to find a mate. However, these need to be combined with all other density-dependent processes in order to determine how overall growth rate changes with density (the demographic Allee effect). Thus there may be a component Allee effect but other processes may override its effects. It is the demographic Allee effect, a decline in population growth rate at low population sizes, that most population modellers consider and it is this that determines the consequences of the Allee effect for exploitation.

Although there is considerable evidence for behavioural and ecological processes generating Allee effects, the confusion over its meaning has resulted in its importance being uncertain. The Allee effect clearly has the potential to increase the probability of local extinction for exploited populations, and an understanding of the behavioural processes resulting in Allee effects is therefore important.

HUMAN DISTURBANCE

Human disturbance of animal populations is often considered an important conservation problem (Hockin *et al.*, 1992). The concern is that the presence of humans in areas of high conservation value may cause animals to move away from these areas, fail to settle or have a lower survival or breeding output. Thus, in addition to the direct increase in mortality from intentional killing, the simple presence of hunters in an area may have indirect effects on populations, for both target and non-target species.

The problem of disturbance needs therefore to be addressed in a two-stage process (Gill & Sutherland, 2000). The first stage is to consider whether or not there is a localised effect of human presence, such as animals avoiding the area. The second stage is to determine the consequences of this localised effect for population size.

The localised effect of human disturbance

The localised effect is the reduction in numbers of individuals using a site in the presence of disturbance compared with those that would use it in the absence of disturbance. There are three ways of determining the local effect (Table 12.1). A common method is to compare numbers in disturbed and undisturbed sites. This is a perfectly acceptable method if all other factors that are important to the species in question do not differ between the disturbed and undisturbed sites and if the comparisons take place over the whole period of use of the sites. Studies that are carried out over very short periods may simply be recording short-term redistributions, which may be reversed at a later date. Thus, if hunting causes animals to avoid particular parts of the habitat but they return to those sites on days without hunting, then the overall use of the site may not be reduced.

A second method of predicting the effect of disturbance on local population size is through experimental manipulations. For example, Madsen (1998) examined the impact of hunting disturbance on the distribution of wildfowl by creating an experimental set of hunting-free refuges in Denmark. This resulted in considerable local increases in wildfowl numbers within the refuges, indicating that the pattern of distribution was greatly affected by hunting.

The third means of examining the local effect of disturbance is to consider disturbance as analogous to predation risk. Animals show clear trade-offs between predation risk and resource use (Ydenberg & Dill, 1986). For example, Milinski (1985) showed that depletion of food patches by three-spined sticklebacks *Gasterosteus aculeatus* was reduced in those patches with high predation risk. Exactly the same process determines the response to disturbance; if animals avoid disturbed areas consistently, then the levels of resource use in these sites will be lower than in undisturbed sites. This method was used to examine the effect of disturbance on the manner in which pink-footed geese *Anser brachyrhynchus* use fields of sugar beet *Beta vulgaris* (Gill *et al.*, 1996). The amount of sugar beet consumed in different fields was strongly, negatively related to the distance of the fields from roads, indicating that the geese were trading off use of the food supply against the avoidance of disturbance. The strength of this response is likely to be the result of this species being heavily hunted in the UK. Pink-footed geese are both an important UK conservation issue – over 90% of the world population winter there – and an important agricultural problem, as recent increases in population size have resulted in increased grazing of arable crops by the geese. Understanding the behavioural trade-off against disturbance can potentially allow manipulations of the system to minimise the impact of the birds on these crops.

A second study examined the effect of human presence on the distribution of black-tailed godwits *Limosa limosa* feeding on bivalves in estuaries. Estuaries are habitats that have both extremely high conservation value and high levels of human recreational use. This has resulted in concerns that human presence may be constraining numbers of birds using these sites. The study was carried out on estuaries with a wide range of levels of recreational use, but found no evidence that human presence resulted in any change in distribution at a range of spatial scales (Gill *et al.*, 2001b). This behavioural study therefore indicated that disturbance was not an important conservation problem in this instance. The lack of a behavioural response to disturbance in the godwits may also be linked to the fact that they are not hunted in the UK.

The consequences of localised effects for global population size

Many animal species do show localised avoidance of disturbed areas. However, the concern of biologists is usually whether such avoidance behaviour has any consequences for the population. This brings us to the second phase of the analysis, in which the consequences of density dependence must be considered. Most studies concentrate on localised avoidance but the impact of disturbance on populations is determined by the combination of localised avoidance and the density-dependent consequences of altering densities between sites. An important complication is that the two factors may be interrelated. Gill & Sutherland (2000) show that species with weak density dependence (e.g. because there is abundant food for the existing population) can move more readily in response to disturbance than can species with strong density dependence, the latter experiencing considerable competition for resources. For example, a species such as wigeon *Anas penelope*, which move readily in response to disturbance (Mayhew, 1988; Madsen, 1998), may be able to do so because its required habitat (short grass near to water) is reasonably abundant. This has important implications for conservation strategies because, although initially it seems intuitively obvious that species that move readily when disturbed are those that are in need of most protection, in fact these may be the species for which the costs of moving are least and hence they are not in need of protection (Gill *et al.*, 2001a).

The process of determining the change in total population size

Table 12.1. Representative studies of disturbance in a range of species and using a variety of methods. Note that such studies are almost entirely restricted to birds and mammals. The relative merits of the different methods are discussed in the text

Species	Type of disturbance	Method	Effect	Reference
Elk *Cervus elaphus*	Roads	Radio-tracking of individuals	Avoidance of surrounding area	Czech, 1991
Moose *Alces alces*	Military	Radio-tracking of individuals	Slight increase in home range size during disturbance	Andersen *et al.*, 1996
Alpine chamois *Rupicapra r. rupicappa*	Recreation	Comparison of numbers before and after disturbance	Reduction in numbers after disturbance	Gander & Ingold, 1997
Bighorn sheep *Ovis canadensis*	Helicopters	Comparison of behaviour in the presence and absence of helicopters	Reduction in time spent foraging during winter	Stockwell *et al.*, 1991
American flamingos *Phoenicopterus ruber*	Tour boats	Comparison of behaviour in disturbed and undisturbed flocks	Reduction in time spent foraging during disturbance	Galicia & Baldassarre, 1997
Bald eagles *Haliaeetus leucocephalus*	Development and recreation	Analysis of effect of disturbance on distribution	Lower densities in areas of high human activity	Stalmaster & Newman, 1978
Greater snow geese *Chen caerulescens atlantica*	Recreation and hunting	Comparison of numbers before and after disturbance	Reduction in numbers following disturbance	Bélanger & Bédard, 1989
Pink-footed geese *Anser brachyrhynchus*	Roads	Trade-off between disturbance and use of food supplies	Reduction in use of the food supplies	Gill *et al.*, 1996

Wigeon *Anas penelope*	Hunting	Experimental manipulation	Increase in numbers on sites without hunting	Madsen, 1998
Waterfowl spp.	Recreation	Analysis of effect of human activity on distribution	Lower densities close to sites with high human activity	Klein *et al.*, 1995
Purple sandpiper *Calidris maritima* and turnstone *Arenaria interpres*	Construction	Comparison of numbers before and after disturbance	No reduction in numbers	Burton *et al.*, 1996
Bar-tailed godwit *Limosa lapponica* and Redshank *tringa totanus*	Bait-digging	Comparison of numbers in presence and absence of bait-digging	Increase in numbers in years when bait-digging restricted	Townshend & O'Connor, 1993
Passerine spp.	Road traffic	Comparison of breeding densities in relation to distance from roads	Reduced densities in 17 of 23 species studied	Reijnen *et al.*, 1995

resulting from human disturbance involves considering the consequences of increasing population density on the undisturbed areas, as a result of density dependence. Thus individuals disturbed from one site will accumulate elsewhere and may therefore experience higher mortality or reduced fecundity due to the competition within those areas. The density dependence is critical; if there is no density dependence then the displacement caused by disturbance has no impact. The reduction in total population size ΔN, resulting from disturbance, can be calculated from

$$\Delta N = \gamma N d' / (b' + d'), \tag{12.1}$$

where γ is the local decline in numbers as a result of disturbance as described above, N is the population size at the site prior to disturbance, d' is the slope of the density dependence in winter mortality, and b' is the slope of the density dependence in breeding output (Sutherland, 1998b).

This method can thus be used to determine the change in the total population across all sites, even outside the area in which the disturbance takes place, given measures of the local displacement effect and density-dependent survival and fecundity.

Human disturbance, such as that caused by hunting, may well be a serious local problem but the fact that most studies do not consider whether behavioural changes result in a change in mortality or breeding output means that the conclusions drawn by many of these studies on the importance of disturbance cannot be justified.

BEHAVIOUR OF EXPLOITERS

Exploiters also behave. They make decisions as to where to hunt or set their nets, which prey to target and which prey should be captured or ignored. Foraging behaviour theory has been used to explain not only the behaviours of the exploited prey, but also the behaviour of exploiters (Alvard, 1993). There are four main concepts from foraging behaviour that can be applied to interpreting the behaviour of exploiters. These are the optimal diet model, the marginal value theorem, central place foraging and the ideal free distribution.

The optimal diet model (Charnov, 1976a) can be used to describe which items to take and which to ignore. Prey types can be ranked according to their profitability (i.e. energy or economic value divided by handling time). The most profitable prey types are always taken but the decision of whether to take the less profitable prey types depends upon the rate at which more profitable prey are encountered (Charnov, 1976a). As an example of this,

Winterhalder (1981) showed that, after acquiring snowmobiles, Cree Indians became more selective and ignored less profitable prey (with a lower energy gain per unit handling time) as a consequence of their increased encounter rates with profitable prey.

The marginal value theorem (Charnov, 1976b) predicts the point at which it pays exploiters to leave a patch and move to a new one. The prediction is that the marginal gain at leaving should be the same in all patches visited. This can be used to explain harvesting patterns in patchy environments. Central place foraging (Orians & Pearson, 1979) considers the response of foragers to prey at different distances from a location to which their prey is transported. Behavioural ecologists usually consider this location to be a breeding or resting site but the same concept applies to exploitation away from a fishing port or hunting camp. There are two classes of central place foraging models depending upon whether the hunting individual returns after catching a single prey (as might happen when it is not possible to continue hunting and carry the captured prey) or whether they can return with many prey items (as would be the case with a fishing boat). The models of single-prey loaders predict that the minimum acceptable prey value increases with travel time (Lessells & Stephens, 1983). The pattern of depletion around central places, such as villages or hunting camps (Hill et al., 1997; Peres, 2000), should then differ according to the value of the prey, with more valuable prey being depleted over a greater distance. The prediction from central place models that incorporate multiple-prey loading (Orians & Pearson, 1979), in which hunting efficiency declines with the number of prey already caught (e.g. because it slows down the hunter or fishing boat), is that the extent of loading should increase with the average travel distance. Thus, as prey become scarcer and exploiters have to travel further, they are likely to stay for longer within each patch and return with higher loads than they would if travelling short distances. This could clearly confound the interpretation of fisheries and hunting statistics and mask population declines.

The ideal free distribution (Fretwell & Lucas, 1970) describes the game theoretical solution to the problem of the expected distribution of competing individuals. The ideal free distribution has been applied to describe the spatial pattern of whaling boats (Whitehead & Hope, 1991) and fishing boats (Abrahams & Healy, 1990). The basic theoretical concept is that patches will differ in quality (e.g. prey density) but that there is negative feedback amongst the competing individuals as a result of interference (e.g. prey becoming harder to catch or interference between capture techniques) or depletion of prey. The theoretical expectation is that the distribution will be such that a higher number of individuals in the better sites will result in the same mean success rate as a smaller number exploiting poorer sites but with less competition. This is the game theoretical solution: if an individual can gain from moving it should do so and as a result all individuals have the same expected reward rate.

The prediction of equal rewards for each individual applies only if all individuals are equal (Parker & Sutherland, 1986). However, variation between individuals will result in differences in capture rate but does not necessarily result in differences in distribution (Sutherland & Parker, 1992). Thus, if individuals differ in their efficiency, for example because some individuals are better shots or some boats have more efficient nets, then the optimal distribution for each is likely to be the same, although the efficient hunters will obtain higher rewards. It is only if they differ in their response to competition (e.g. those that try to stalk undisturbed prey may experience more interference than those that chase prey into nets) that they might be expected to differ in distribution, with those most susceptible to competition occupying the poorer patches (Sutherland & Parker, 1992). This then leads to the possibility of predicting the distribution of exploiters and hence the spatial distribution of exploitation.

DISCOUNTING

Discounting is the preference for possessing money now rather than in the future, even when the amount is corrected for inflation (Schmid, 1989; see Ludwig, Chapter 2). It is considered important for understanding exploitation patterns, as it favours overexploitation. Some slow-growing species, such as whales and tropical forest trees, may grow at a lower rate than the discounting rate. In theory, it is not financially worth while retaining such populations as it would be more profitable to exploit the population and place the money in the bank and live off the interest (Lande *et al.*, 1994, 1995).

Discounting is a behavioural process as it is entirely based upon preferences of individuals. If individuals did not have a preference for short-term rewards there would be no discounting. We will describe a curious conflict between the concepts of economists and behaviourists that has yet to be resolved, but has important consequences for exploitation.

It is possible to consider the current value of future rewards, allowing for discounting. This can be thought of as asking how much you would pay now to be given an amount of money in a certain number of years (see Figure 12.2). As the discounting rate d is usually expressed over a set time

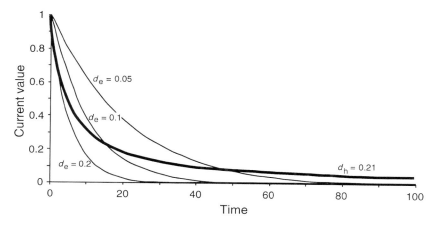

Figure 12.2. The current value of future benefits or costs after incorporating hyperbolic and exponential discounting. The current value can be considered as the amount that individuals would be prepared to pay now for a benefit in the future. The thin lines show a range of exponential relationships with different discount rates d_e. The thick line shows a hyperbolic relationship fitted to data on human preferences for saving current lives or lives in the future $d_h = 0.21$ (Henderson & Sutherland, 1996). Over short periods (less than 10 years) the exponential and hyperbolic relationships are similar but over long periods (50–100 years) the differences are marked, with hyperbolic relationships giving a considerably higher current value.

(e.g. 5% a year) then economists quite rightly argue that the current value declines exponentially over time giving an annual discount rate of d_e. Thus the present value V_p of a future value V_f received after a time delay of t is:

$$V_p = V_f / (1 + d_e)^t. \qquad (12.2)$$

Over long periods the current value therefore becomes a small fraction of the actual sum. The consequence is that a gain in the future (e.g. the benefit from leaving individuals to breed or allowing small individuals to grow before exploitation) has negligible value now when discounted exponentially. However, studies of rats, pigeons and humans who are given the choice between a food item now or a larger reward in the future show that they do not show the expected exponential discounting but instead show hyperbolic discounting (Rachlin, 1991) whereby:

$$V_p = V_f / (1 + d_h t), \qquad (12.3)$$

where d_h is the hyperbolic discount rate. Compared with exponential discounting, hyperbolic discounting gives much greater value to the long term. Calculations incorporating hyperbolic discounting will thus be more favourable to maintaining populations for long-term sustainable exploitation.

Although economists argue for exponential rather than hyperbolic discounting there is some evidence that in practice even economists use hyperbolic discounting. For example, there is evidence that the US government applies reduced discount rates to water development projects and the UK government does the same when considering forestry projects. This suggests they are adjusting their exponential framework to apply to the hyperbolic curve (Henderson & Sutherland, 1996).

Discounting is widely used by governmental economists and is often critical in determining whether projects are considered financially viable. If it is true that we should be using hyperbolic discounting rather than exponential discounting then this makes the long term of greater importance for schemes that rely on benefits accruing over long time periods. Thus, for exploitation schemes involving slow-growing species, the nature of discounting may be critical in determining whether they are considered financially viable.

DISCUSSION

It is widely accepted that behavioural differences between species will affect their susceptibility to exploitation. Similarly, age and sex differences in behaviour will affect individual susceptibility. Although important, the role of such behaviours is conceptually obvious. In this chapter, we have concentrated on components of behaviour that are less obvious yet may be critically important in exploited populations. Thus the buffer effect was probably critical in misleading the fishing industry to believe there were abundant cod stocks on the Grand Banks, when in fact they were about to collapse due to overfishing. Behaviours that lead to an Allee effect (also known as depensation) may well be critical in enhancing the rate of population decline in overexploited populations and so increase the probability of extinction. The dilution effect may mean that behavioural or ecological differences between coexisting species will result in the scarcer species experiencing disproportionate mortality.

There are a number of fields in which behavioural ecologists and those studying exploitation have been studying the same subject, but by working in isolation they have produced different results. In the study of discounting, economists have always assumed exponential discounting while behaviourists have evidence for hyperbolic discounting, yet these two fields have not confronted the discrepancy. The foraging behaviour of animals has usually been considered separately from the foraging behaviour of humans (with a few notable exceptions). Yet the predictive framework of optimal foraging theory has clear implications for understanding patterns of exploitation by humans.

Why then does it seem that the role of behaviour has been so under-represented in studies of exploitation? A major reason may be that those interested in behaviour and those interested in exploitation tend to have different philosophies, use different study animals, read different journals and attend different meetings. Behavioural ecologists usually pick common species and often avoid those that are heavily exploited.

Behavioural models can be used to provide an understanding of density dependence, which is essential for understanding the direct and indirect consequences of exploitation. Empirical assessments of the strength of density dependence suffer from a range of problems (Schenk *et al.*, 1998). However, as we have described in this chapter, density dependence can be estimated using behavioural processes such as depletion rates, interference, dominance and territoriality. We believe that there is considerable potential here for future work.

CONCLUSIONS

Behavioural ecology can provide insights into underlying mechanisms, which can have considerable implications for the processes and consequences of exploitation. We give seven examples.

1 An understanding of behavioural decisions made by individuals can lead to a greater understanding of the nature of density dependence, which is fundamental to understanding sustainable levels of exploitation.
2 Some species may be caught accidentally or may not be the main target of exploitation yet may sometimes experience higher mortality than the target species. The extent to which they are caught may often be influenced by their behaviour.
3 Changing patterns of habitat selection in response to changing population size (the buffer effect) can result in populations apparently being robust to exploitation until a threshold density is reached, after which they may collapse rapidly.
4 The Allee effect (the decline in survival or breeding output at low

population sizes) greatly increases the risk of extinction in exploited populations and often has a behavioural component.

5 Exploitation may also result in disturbance, both to the exploited species and to others sharing the habitat. The change in distribution of populations in response to disturbance is best considered from a behavioural perspective as being analogous to predation risk. Extending this to predicting the population consequences requires knowledge of density dependence.

6 Foraging theory has occasionally been applied to humans but has wider utility.

7 Economic discounting is a behavioural phenomenon in which the conclusions differ between economists and behaviourists, with considerable consequences.

Understanding the behavioural processes of both exploited species and exploiters will reduce the risks of unexpected phenomena, such as sudden population collapses, and so improves the ability to exploit populations sustainably. We therefore suggest a need for those studying behavioural ecology and those studying exploitation to find ways of increasing collaboration.

ACKNOWLEDGEMENTS

We thank the Natural Environment Research Council and the Royal Society for the Protection of Birds for funding some of the work described here. We thank the editors for inviting us to participate in this meeting and for providing useful comments on an earlier draft.

REFERENCES

Abrahams, M. V. & Healy, M. C. (1990). Variation in the competitive abilities of fishermen and its influence on the spatial distribution of the British Columbian salmon troll fleet. *Canadian Journal of Fisheries and Aquatic Sciences*, **6**, 1116–1121.

Allee, W. C. (1931). *Animal Aggregations, A Study in General Sociology*. University of Chicago Press, Chicago.

Allee, W. C. (1938). *The Social Life of Animals*. William Heinemann, London.

Allee, W. C., Emerson, A. E., Park, O., Park, T. & Schmidt, K. P. (1949). *Principles of Animal Ecology*. W. B. Saunders, Philadelphia.

Alvard, M. S. (1993). Testing the ecological noble savage hypothesis – interspecific prey choice by Piro hunters of Amazonian Peru. *Human Ecology*, **21**, 355–387.

Alvarez, L. H. R. (1998). Optimal harvesting under stochastic fluctuations and critical depensation. *Mathematical Biosciences*, **152**, 63–85.

Andersen, R., Linnell, J. D. C. & Langvatn, R. (1996). Short term behavioural and physiological response of moose *Alces alces* to military disturbance in Norway. *Biological Conservation*, **77**, 169–176.

Beddington, J. R. & May, R. M. (1977). Fluctuating natural populations in a naturally fluctuating environment. *Science*, **197**, 463–465.

Bélanger, L. & Bédard, J. (1989). Responses of staging greater snow geese to human disturbance. *Journal of Wildlife Management*, **53**, 713–719.

Berg, A., Lindberg, T. & Källebrink, K. G. (1992). Hatching success of lapwings on farmland: differences between habitats and colonies of different sizes. *Journal of Animal Ecology*, **61**, 469–476.

Brown, J. L. (1969). The buffer effect and productivity in tit populations. *American Naturalist*, **103**, 347–354.

Burton, N. H. K., Evans, P. R. & Robinson, M. A. (1996). Effects on shorebird numbers of disturbance, the loss of an artificial roost site and its replacement by an artificial island at Hartlepool, Cleveland. *Biological Conservation*, **77**, 193–201.

Caro, T. (ed.) (1999). *Behavioural Ecology and Conservation Biology*. Oxford University Press, Oxford.

Charnov, E. L. (1976a). Optimal foraging: attack strategy of a mantid. *American Naturalist*, **110**, 141–151.

Charnov, E. L. (1976b). Optimal foraging: the marginal value theorem. *Theoretical Population Biology*, **9**, 129–136.

Clark, C. W. (1990). *Mathematical Bioeconomics: The Optimal Management of Renewable Resources*. Wiley Interscience, New York.

Clemmons, J. R. & Bucholz, R. (eds.) (1997). *Behavioural Approaches to Conservation in the Wild*. Cambridge University Press, Cambridge.

Côté, I. M. & Poulin, R. (1995). Parasitism and group-size in social animals – a metaanalysis. *Behavioral Ecology*, **6**, 159–165.

Courchamp, F., Clutton-Brock, T. H. & Grenfell, B. (1999). Inverse density dependence and the Allee effect. *Trends in Ecology and Evolution*, **14**, 405–410.

Cresswell, W. (1994). Age-dependent choice of redshank (*Tringa totanus*) feeding location – profitability or risk. *Journal of Animal Ecology*, **63**, 589–600.

Czech, B. (1991). Elk behavior in response to human disturbance at Mount St. Helens National Volcanic Monument. *Applied Animal Behaviour Science*, **29**, 269–277.

Fretwell, S. D. & Lucas, H. L. (1970). On territorial behaviour and other factors influencing habitat distribution in birds. *Acta Biotheoretica*, **19**, 16–36.

Galicia, E. & Baldassarre, G. (1997). Effects of motorized tourboats on the behavior of nonbreeding American Flamingos in Yucatan, Mexico. *Conservation Biology*, **11**, 1159–1165.

Gander, H. & Ingold, P. (1997). Reactions of male alpine chamois *Rupicapra r. rupicappa* to hikers, joggers and mountainbikers. *Biological Conservation*, **79**, 107–109.

Gill, J. A. & Sutherland, W. J. (2000) Predicting the consequences of human disturbance from behavioural decisions. In *Behaviour and Conservation*, eds. M. Gosling & W. J. Sutherland, pp. 51–64. Cambridge University Press, Cambridge.

Gill, J. A., Sutherland, W. J. & Watkinson, A. R. (1996). A method to quantify the effects of human disturbance on animal populations. *Journal of Applied Ecology*, **33**, 786–792.

Gill, J. A., Norris, K. & Sutherland, W. J. (2001a). Why behavioural responses may not reflect the population consequences of human disturbance. *Biological Conservation*, **97**, 265–268.

Gill, J. A., Norris, K. & Sutherland, W. J. (2001b). The effects of disturbance on habitat use by black-tailed godwits, *Limosa Limosa*. *Journal of Applied Ecology*, in press.

Gosling, M. & Sutherland, W. J. (eds.) (2000). *Behaviour and Conservation*. Cambridge University Press, Cambridge.

Hamilton, W. D. (1971). Geometry of the selfish herd. *Journal of Theoretical Biology*, **31**, 295–311.

Hassall, M. P. & Varley, G. C. (1969). New inductive population model for insect parasites and its bearing on biological control. *Nature*, **223**, 1133–1136.

Henderson, N. & Sutherland, W. J. (1996). Two truths about discounting and their environmental consequences. *Trends in Ecology and Evolution*, **11**, 527–528.

Hill, K., Padwe, J., Bejyvagi, C., Bepurangi, A., Jakugi, F., Tykuarangi, R. & Tykuarangi, T. (1997). Impact of hunting on large vertebrates in the Mbaracayu reserve, Paraguay. *Conservation Biology*, **11**, 1339–1353.

Hockin, D., Ounsted, M., Gorman, M., Hill, D., Keller, V. & Barker, M. A. (1992). Examination of the effects of disturbance on birds with reference to its importance in ecological assessments. *Journal of Environmental Management*, **36**, 253–286.

Hutchings, J. A. (1996). Spatial and temporal variation in the density of northern cod and a review of hypotheses for the stock's collapse. *Canadian Journal of Fisheries and Aquatic Sciences*, **53**, 943–962.

Jennings, T. & Evans, S. M. (1980). Influence of position in the flock and flock size on vigilance in the starling, *Sturnus vulgaris*. *Animal Behaviour*, **28**, 634–635.

Kenward, R. E. (1978). Hawks and doves: factors affecting success and selection in goshawk attacks on woodpigeons. *Journal of Animal Ecology*, **47**, 449–460.

Klein, M. L., Humphrey, S. R. & Percival, H. F. (1995). Effects of ecotourism on distribution of waterbirds in a wildlife refuge. *Conservation Biology*, **9**, 1454–1465.

Kohlmann, S. G., Green, R. L. & Trainer, C. E. (1999). Effects of collection method on sex and age composition of black bear (*Ursus americanus*) harvest in Oregon. *Northwest Science*, **73**, 34–38.

Kokko, H. & Sutherland, W. J. (1998). Optimal floating strategies: consequences for density dependence and habitat loss. *American Naturalist*, **152**, 354–366.

Lande, R., Engen, S. & Sæther, B. (1994). Optimal harvesting, economic discounting and extinction risk in fluctuating environments. *Nature*, **372**, 88–90.

Lande, R., Engen, S. & Sæther, B. (1995). Optimal harvesting of fluctuating populations with a risk of extinction. *American Naturalist*, **145**, 728–745.

Lessells, C. M. & Stephens, D. W. (1983). Central place foraging: single prey loaders again. *Animal Behaviour*, **31**, 238–243.

Levitan, D. R., Sewell, M. A. & Chia, F.-S. (1992). How distribution and abundance influence fertilisation success in the sea urchin *Strongylocentrotus franciscanus*. *Ecology*, **73**, 248–254.

Madsen, J. (1996). Lesser white-fronted goose. In *Globally Threatened Birds in Europe: Action Plans*, ed. B. Heredin, L. Rose & M. Painter, pp. 67–78. Council of Europe Publishing, Strasburg.

Madsen, J. (1998). Experimental refuges for migratory waterfowl in Danish wetlands. II. Tests of hunting disturbance effects. *Journal of Applied Ecology*, **35**, 398–417.

Mayhew, P. W. (1988). The daily energy intake of European wigeon in winter. *Ornis Scandinavica*, **19**, 217–223.

Milinski, M. (1985). Risk of predation taken by parasitised fish under competition for food. *Behaviour*, **93**, 203–216.

Milner-Gulland, E. J. & Leader-Williams, N. (1992). A model of incentives for the illegal exploitation of black rhinos and elephants: poaching pays in Luangwa Valley, Zambia. *Journal of Applied Ecology*, **29**, 388–401.

Orians, G. H. & Pearson, N. E. (1979). On the theory of central place foraging. In *Analysis of Ecological Systems*, ed. D. J. Horn, R. D. Mitchell & G. R. Stairs, pp. 154–177. Ohio State University Press, Columbus, OH.

Parker, G. A. & Sutherland, W. J. (1986). Ideal free distribution when individuals differ in competitive ability: phenotype-limited ideal free models. *Animal Behaviour*, **34**, 1222–1242.

Peres, C. A. (2000). Effects of subsistence hunting on vertebrate structure in Amazonian forests. *Conservation Biology*, **14**, 240–255.

Rachlin, H. (1991). *Introduction to Modern Behaviourism*. Freeman, New York.

Reijnen, R., Foppen, R, Terbraak, C. & Thissen, J. (1995). The effects of car traffic on breeding bird population in woodland. 3. Reduction in density in relation to the proximity of main roads. *Journal of Applied Ecology*, **32**, 187–202.

Reynolds, J. D. & Jennings, S. (2000). The role of behaviour in marine conservation. In *Behaviour and Conservation*, ed. M. Gosling & W. J. Sutherland, pp. 238–259. Cambridge University Press, Cambridge.

Schenk, T. M., White, G. C. & Burnham, K. P. (1998). Sampling-variance effects on detecting density dependence from temporal trends in natural populations. *Ecological Monographs*, **68**, 445–463.

Schmid, A. (1989). *Benefit–Cost Analysis*. Westview, Boulder, CO.

Stalmaster, M. V. & Newman, J. R. (1978). Behavioral responses of wintering bald eagles to human activity. *Journal of Wildlife Management*, **42**, 506–513.

Stephens, P. A. & Sutherland, W. J. (1999). Consequences of the Allee effect for ecology and conservation. *Trends in Ecology and Evolution*, **14**, 401–405.

Stephens, P. A. & Sutherland, W. J. (2000). Vertebrate mating systems, rarity and conservation. In *Vertebrate Mating Systems*, ed. M. Apollonio, M. Festa-Bianchet & D. Mainardi, pp. 186–213. World Scientific Publishing Co., Singapore.

Stephens, P. A., Sutherland, W. J. & Freckleton, R. P. (1999). What is the Allee effect? *Oikos*, **87**, 185–190.

Stillman, R. A., Goss-Custard, J. D. & Caldow, R. W. G. (1997). Modelling interference from basic foraging behaviour. *Journal of Animal Ecology*, **66**, 692–703.

Stockwell, C. A., Bateman, G. C. & Berger, J. (1991). Conflicts in national parks: a case study of helicopters and bighorn sheep time budgets at the Grand Canyon. *Biological Conservation*, **56**, 317–328.

Sutherland, W. J. (1996). *From Individual Behaviour to Population Ecology*. Oxford University Press, Oxford.

Sutherland, W. J. (1998a). The role of behaviour in conservation biology. *Animal Behaviour*, **56**, 801–809.

Sutherland, W. J. (1998b). The effect of change in habitat quality on populations of migratory species. *Journal of Applied Ecology*, **35**, 418–421.

Sutherland, W. J. & Anderson, C. A. (1993). Predicting the distribution of individuals and the consequences of habitat loss: the role of prey depletion. *Journal of Theoretical Biology*, **160**, 223–230.

Sutherland, W. J. & Parker, G. A. (1992). The relationship between continuous input and interference models of ideal free distributions with unequal competitors. *Animal Behaviour*, **44**, 345–355.

Townshend, D. J. & O'Connor, D. A. (1993). Some effects of disturbance to waterfowl from bait-digging and wildfowling at Lindisfarne National Nature Reserve, north-east England. *Wader Study Group Bulletin*, **68**, 47–52.

Ulfstrand, S. (1996). Behavioural ecology as a tool in conservation biology: an introduction. *Oikos*, **77**, 183.

Walters, C. & Maguire, J.-J. (1996). Lessons for stock assessment from the northern cod collapse. *Reviews in Fish Biology and Fisheries*, **6**, 125–137.

Whitehead, H. & Hope, P. L. (1991). Sperm whalers off the Galápagos Islands and in the Western North Pacific, 1830–1850. Ideal free whalers? *Ethology and Sociobiology*, **12**, 147–161.

Winterhalder, B. (1981). Foraging strategies in the boreal forest: an analysis of Cree hunting and gathering. In *Hunter-Gatherer Foraging Strategies*, ed. B. Winterhalder & E. A. Smith, pp. 66–98. University of Chicago Press, Chicago.

Ydenberg, R. C. & Dill, L. M. (1986). The economics of fleeing from predators. *Advances in the Study of Behaviour*, **16**, 229–249.

13

The Allee effect: a barrier to recovery by exploited species

CHRISTOPHER W. PETERSEN & DON R. LEVITAN

Small populations are at an increased risk of extinction, and to the extent that exploitation reduces those populations it will contribute towards this problem. Although habitat loss or degradation and non-sustainable exploitation of species have been strongly implicated in the decline of many populations, once small, these populations often face additional threats that raise their probability of extinction. In this chapter we focus on one of these threats, the Allee effect (often called 'depensation' in the fisheries literature). This is a syndrome in which populations at low density or size exhibit a positive relationship between per capita population growth rate and population size (Courchamp *et al.*, 1999a; Stephens & Sutherland, 1999). The processes that can decrease per capita growth rates at low population size are quite broad, and can include genetic effects such as increased inbreeding, facilitation of conspecifics through modification of the environment, and facilitation through social behaviours (Allee, 1931; Allee *et al.*, 1949; Courchamp *et al.*, 1999a; Stephens & Sutherland, 1999). Allee effects can occur in all environments for any type of organism, although many of the examples used in this chapter come from the marine realm, owing to the authors' background as marine biologists and the extreme exploitation that has come to characterise human interactions with marine populations.

After first discussing the history and definition of the term Allee effect, we then examine three specific cases, often cited as classic examples of the Allee effect. We then explore how Allee effects can affect population growth through specific aspects of reproductive biology, focusing on the fertilisation dynamics of external fertilisers. Finally, we address the question of why Allee effects are rarely documented in natural populations, which types of species may be more vulnerable to Allee effects, and how conservation biology can affect the recovery of exploited populations suffering from Allee effects.

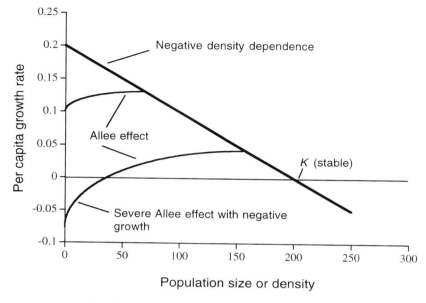

Figure 13.1. The Allee effect demonstrated as the negative deviation of the per capita growth rate of a population at low population size compared with the predicted linearly increasing growth rate at lower population numbers. The linearly decreasing population growth rate derives from the logistic growth equation. At extreme levels the Allee effect can lead to negative population growth (illustrated on graph).

WHAT IS AN ALLEE EFFECT?

Warder Clyde Allee devoted a large portion of his research effort to understanding how changing density or population size affects the fitness of individuals (Allee, 1931, 1932, 1938). His later work reflects a much stronger interest in cases where individual fitness was positively correlated with density or population size, and how this was related to the evolution of social behaviour. Even before his death in 1955, the term Allee principle appeared in the literature as the concept that 'undercrowding (or lack of aggregation) may be limiting' (Odum, 1953). Odum (1963) later referred to a growth curve as the 'Allee growth type' when the per capita growth rate showed an intermediate maximum with population density, as opposed to density-dependent relationships that reflect intraspecific competition, such as the logistic growth curve, which show decreases in growth rate versus density over all possible densities (Figure 13.1). This early work appears to define the Allee effect as a positive relationship between individual fitness and either numbers or density of conspecifics.

As recently pointed out by Stephens *et al.* (1999), there has been considerable confusion about the exact meaning of the Allee effect. A more limited definition of the Allee effect restricts this term to cases where there is negative growth rate at low density or population size (see e.g. Courchamp *et al.*, 1999b). Given Allee's work and previous descriptions of this effect, this definition seems too narrow; indeed, Courchamp *et al.* (1999a) provide the broader definition.

Confusion also exists over the use of the term 'inverse density dependence'. Inverse density dependence has been used to refer to curves of the type $y = x^1$ (cf. Odum, 1963), while others use it to refer to a relationship where x is monotopically increasing with y (Allee, 1941, as cited by Fowler & Baker, 1991; Courchamp *et al.*, 1999a). In this chapter we use positive density-dependent growth rates to refer to cases where the per capita growth rate increases with density.

In an attempt to provide clarity to the definition of the Allee effect, Stephens *et al.* (1999) distinguished two types of Allee effect, which they call the component Allee effect and the demographic Allee effect. The component Allee effect focuses on positive effects of density or population size on individual components of fitness, and does not require positive density dependence at the population level. The demographic Allee effect refers to the per capita growth rates of a population as a function of population size, and requires that the net effect of increasing group or population size is an increase in population growth rate. Because several factors may result in negative density dependence, most prominently intraspecific competition, we expect component Allee effects to be much more common than demographic Allee effects. In this chapter we have decided to follow the 'component Allee effect' definition of Stephens *et al.* (1999), and also discuss demographic effects of the Allee effect. The 'component' definition closely follows several earlier definitions of the term (Dennis, 1989).

Allee effects are commonly considered in both the botanical and fisheries literature, but are known under different names. Individual plants may enhance the environment for conspecifics by modifying physical aspects of the environment. This Allee effect via environmental modification has been most frequently discussed in plants under the title of positive switches (for a review, see Wilson & Agnew, 1992). In plants, environmental modification has been shown to occur through a wide variety of resources or physical conditions, including water, pH, soil elements, light, temperature, wind and fire (Wilson & Agnew, 1992). In the fisheries literature, the term depensation is used synonymously with a demographic Allee effect. A variety of processes might lead to Allee effects in fisheries species, including increased per capita predation rates and decreased individual reproductive success. Generally, facilitation may occur through social behaviours or aggregation that increase feeding rates, survival rates or reproductive rates of individuals (Courchamp et al., 1999a; Stephens & Sutherland, 1999). The common element of all of these examples is that, when population density or size decreases, individuals do not fare as well.

The detrimental genetic effects of small population size, including increased inbreeding depression and increased fixation of alleles due to genetic drift, have been cited as examples of the Allee effect. Although Allee (1949) explicitly discussed some of these issues, genetic effects of population size in conservation biology have also been discussed at length elsewhere (e.g. Allendorf & Leary, 1986; Gilpin & Soulé, 1986; Lande, 1988, 1995) and we focus our discussion here on the non-genetic mechanisms.

ALLEE EFFECTS: THREE CLASSIC EXAMPLES

The passenger pigeon and the Allee effect

Perhaps the most famous case of exploitation and extinction that has implicated the Allee effect is the extermination of the passenger pigeon *Ectopistes migratorius* in North America. This species at one time made up an estimated 25–40% of the birds in the USA (Schorger, 1955). Their numbers during the mid 1800s have been estimated at 3–5 billion, with several independent estimates of single flock sizes of over 1 billion. Yet, the last known individual of this species died in 1914 at the Cincinnati Zoo. The demise of the passenger pigeon has been linked with the idea of an Allee effect in the general literature (Owen, 1980; Cockburn, 1991; Hunter, 1996), and the fate of this phenomenally abundant bird has served as a warning for conservation biologists that no exploited species is safe. But how strong is the evidence that Allee effects were important in the extinction of the passenger pigeon?

In the largest summary of the biology of the passenger pigeon, Schorger (1955) hypothesised that continued hunting and poaching, even after restrictions on hunting and netting were enacted in various US states over the second half of the nineteenth century, led to the demise of this species. He did not invoke the Allee effect. However, Halliday (1980) argued that, as colonies dwindled in size, the impact of hawk predation intensified, leading to declining per capita rates of reproduction and survival. Halliday used this hypothesis as a cautionary note for conservation biologists, arguing that maintaining large breeding colonies might be more important than a large overall population size and that a species may be doomed to extinction even when it is still abundant. He also clearly labelled the Allee effect as an untested and probably untestable hypothesis for this species given the lack of appropriate data. Blockstein & Tordoff (1985) reiterated the idea that, at low numbers, passenger pigeons suffered higher mortality and nest predation from natural predators.

Bucher's (1992) analysis of passenger pigeon extinction attempted to reconcile these various hypotheses, and he concluded that food availability was the predominant factor causing the extinction of the passenger pigeon. He emphasised the temporal and spatial unpredictability of the main food source of passenger pigeons, masting species of trees, especially beech *Fagus grandifolia* and oak *Quercus* spp., in the eastern forest of the USA at a time when forests were severely reduced relative to historical levels. He hypothesised that this species had a relatively high minimal viable population (MVP), owing to the necessity of social facilitation in finding an unpredictable food source, and that shrinking populations were due more to deforestation than to hunting. Both Bucher and Halliday thus invoked an Allee effect in the extinction of the passenger pigeon. Unfortunately, virtually no data exist with which to test the role of the Allee effect in declining passenger pigeon populations, and its extinction precludes any direct tests.

Thus, with the passenger pigeon, we are left with several viable hypotheses and no data to distinguish among them. Of course, these hypotheses are not mutually exclusive, so it is possible that the passenger pigeon went extinct from a combination of loss of food trees, disease or storms, Allee effects on reproduction or predation by raptors, and exploitation (Owen, 1980). The lack of any clear evidence for a demographic Allee effect in this species leads to a more general question: are there any good, documented examples of demographic Allee effects in exploited species?

Fisheries

The decline or collapse of many fisheries around the world over the last few decades and their slow recovery has led several authors to consider the possibility of a population or community-wide effect in preventing the populations from successfully recovering. The continued exploitation of the population or general degradation of the habitat has been implicated as restricting population recovery in some cases (Myers *et al.*, 1995). In other cases neither of these circumstances seems to apply and yet the population still is not recovering. Two general types of explanation have been suggested for the absence of strong recovery after exploitation has been reduced.

The first is that the overexploitation of one species has led to a dramatic change in the community, with a change in the dynamics of population growth for the exploited species. Other than the case of herbivorous fishes and sea urchins in tropical reefs, the evidence for this type of effect is fairly weak (Kaiser & Jennings, Chapter 16).

A second explanation for the slow recovery of populations of exploited fishes is decreased population growth at low densities, a demographic Allee effect. This effect is typically seen as a positive slope over early parts of the recruit/spawner versus stock relationship. These graphs are similar to those in Figure 13.1, with some measure of adult abundance (stock) on the x-axis substituting for population size and recruits/spawner taking the place of per capita growth rate on the y-axis. This Allee effect can be caused by a variety of mechanisms including impaired aggregation, reduced reproductive success, or increased per capita predation at low population size (Hilborn & Walters, 1992; Liermann & Hilborn, 1997).

One of the premises of the Allee effect is that animals can be selected to aggregate when there are benefits from conspecific facilitation. Although direct evidence for demographic Allee effects is lacking in fishery species, clumped distributions are common, and may help to lead to their overexploitation. Clumping has the unfortunate side effect of concentrating the remaining individuals in an exploited population and allowing for their continued capture at economically acceptable rates, even when the population has experienced high levels of exploitation. This overexploitation is not an Allee effect, but has the result of lowering populations to levels where Allee effects might become important impediments to stock recovery. Such a pattern appears to have occurred in Atlantic cod *Gadus morhua* in the Northwest Atlantic (Hutchings, 1996). The high variance in local population density made it difficult for fisheries biologists to detect the severe declines in abundance and allowed offshore fishermen the false sense of security that the population was still at exploitable densities. Density-dependent spatial distributions, with densities remaining high but the geographical range of an exploited species shrinking as population size decreases, may be common in exploited schooling species (Hilborn & Walters, 1992). This increased aggregation with decreasing local abundance can make fisheries much more likely to undergo a population crash due to exploitation than was previously thought possible. At the time of writing, most of these stocks are still not recovering, and there is speculation that Allee effects could be partly to blame.

Exploitation in fishery populations may reduce densities of a population to a level where they are unable to successfully obtain certain types of resource. For example, a major function of schooling in coral reef fishes is to be able to overwhelm territorial fishes and obtain access to their resources (Robertson *et al.*, 1976; Foster, 1985). On some reefs, solitary individuals are virtually excluded from defended resources, where schools of individuals can regularly gain access to these same defended resources (Foster, 1985). The high level of artisanal nearshore fishing in many coral reefs has the potential to decrease the resource availability to species of surgeonfish (Acanthuridae) and parrotfish (Scaridae) that regularly gain access to algae defended by damselfishes (Pomacentridae). However, despite documented component Allee effects, we know of no instances where demographic Allee effects related to food acquisition in an exploited species have been documented.

A positive relationship between population growth and population size, indicative of an Allee effect, can also be caused by the covariance of environmental quality and population size. If, for example, the environment has been degrading over time due to anthropogenic effects, and during this same time a population is being overexploited, then a lower per capita recruit success at low population size would be due to the coincidence of low population size and poor environmental quality for recruitment. Strong environmental change, anthropogenic or otherwise, has the potential to cloud attempts to understand how population size affects per capita recruitment into populations.

Myers *et al.* (1995) attempted to test for Allee effects (depensation) in marine fisheries with long data histories (15 years or more), but found evidence for Allee effects in only 3 of 128 stock datasets analysed. In those three, there was some evidence for either environmental change or habitat loss as a potential alternative explanation. A reanalysis of these data by Liermann & Hilborn (1997) using a Bayesian technique called hierarchical modelling (Wade, Chapter 6) confirmed that the most likely correct interpretation of the data was that there was no depensation. However, they also noted that the range of possible interpretations of the data was quite broad (i.e. the results had low power to distinguish among hypothetical population growth curves), and cautioned that fishery data analysis should include the possibility of depensation. In neither the original analysis by Myers *et al.* (1995) nor the reanalysis by Liermann & Hilborn (1997) is there strong evidence for an Allee effect in exploited fishery stocks.

Reproductive success of colonial or socially nesting species

Seabirds have been exploited for meat, eggs, feathers and down by diverse groups of people from sailors to coastal inhabitants. In colonially nesting birds there are some clear potential benefits of joining a colony, including swamping of predators, increased predator vigilance, predator mobbing, and the colony acting as an information centre for food availability (Wittenberger & Hunt, 1985; Brown *et al.*, 1990). Andrewartha & Birch (1954) stated that small colonies of gulls 'are unable to establish themselves in situations where large ones would have no difficulty', but do not give references or data. According to Wittenberger & Hunt (1985), there is little clear evidence of an Allee effect in terms of increased reproductive success due to increased colony size. In some species smaller colonies have been shown to be more likely to be abandoned, but this has been attributed to less reliable food supplies associated with the small colonies (Wittenberger & Hunt, 1985).

In one experimental study, Götmark & Andersson (1984) showed that solitary nesters were less successful than colonial nesters and that egg predation rates in experimental nests were lower near a colony, implying a potential benefit from the colony in mobbing potential egg predators. In separate studies, Hatchwell (1991) and Birkhead (1977) found a positive effect of colony synchrony and neighbour synchrony on the probability of successful fledging in common murres *Uria aalge*.

For populations of colonial birds that have been exploited, there appears to be no evidence that reductions in colony size have affected per capita reproductive success and thus have hindered recovery from exploitation. For colonial nesting seabirds, such as the species of terns and gulls on the eastern seaboard of the USA that were exploited for the making of ornate hats for women (millinery trade) during the late 1800s, once the exploitation ceased, birds appeared to return from locations more isolated from human disturbance and quickly increased in numbers from small to large colonies. Terns declined in the 1950s and 1960s, but these declines were associated with increased population sizes of gulls along the eastern coast of the USA and their predation on tern chicks and adults (J. G. T. Anderson, personal communication). There is no evidence that these colonies had to reach a critical size before they could become successful, and no evidence that even large tern colonies were able to reduce predation from gulls.

In fishes, some species also form locally synchronised nesting colonies for short periods (e.g. *Abudefduf troschelii*). There is evidence that survivorship of young in nests is positively associated with colony size in the freshwater bluegill sunfish *Lepomis macrochirus*, both through mobbing of predators and possibly through predator dilution, with nests at the periphery of the colony under more intense predation risk than more central nests

(Gross & MacMillan, 1981). Côté & Gross (1993) additionally showed that fungal infection rates were lower in colonial nests of *L. macrochirus*, owing to colonial males having decreased time allocated to vigilance against potential predators and more time to clean infected eggs from the nest.

ALLEE EFFECTS: CONTEMPORARY EXAMPLES

Recent examples of populations experiencing an Allee effect involve the detrimental effects of reduced population size on per capita reproductive success. The Allee effect can be manifested in the reproductive biology of an organism at several levels. Positive density-dependent effects have been attributed to fertilisation success of free-spawned gametes (Hughes, 1994), mate-finding ability (Allee *et al.*, 1949), induction of reproduction (Darling, 1938) and reproductive success of colonial or socially nesting species (Andrewartha & Birch, 1954). Although the logic for a potential Allee effect exists in many cases, there is not always strong empirical support for the Allee effect. We start this section with a discussion of fertilisation and Allee effects, and then discuss other examples of reproductive biology that might lead to an Allee effect.

A possible Allee effect: external fertilisation

Fertilisation rate can clearly be a positive density-dependent phenomenon; as the number of local males increases we would expect an equal or higher proportion of eggs to be fertilised. This effect might apply to a wide range of taxa (algae, marine invertebrates, wind-pollinated plants, animal-pollinated plants) with a diversity of reproductive modes, but we focus here on aquatic species that release both sperm and eggs into the water column (broadcast spawners), since it is here that fertilisation success, exploitation and the Allee effect have been discussed recently. We use the examples of sea urchin fertilisation and abalone population dynamics, since they are both examples of exploited species where limitation of fertilisation success has been implicated as a major conservation concern.

Sperm limitation in broadcast spawners

Sea urchins are harvested for their gonads, which serve as energy storage organs and are rich in fat before and during the early portion of the reproductive season. Gametes dilute quickly in the water column, and Pennington (1985) was the first to show that fertilisation could be quite low if females spawned several metres from spawning males. Highly synchronised spawning in many marine broadcast spawners has been considered as an adaptation both to increase fertilisation success (marine invertebrates, Oliver & Babcock, 1992; Sewell & Levitan, 1992; marine algae, Pearson & Brawley, 1996; Serrao et al., 1996) and to reduce egg and zygote mortality through predator dilution (Oliver & Babcock, 1992); however, the evidence for tight spawning synchrony, while occasionally observed, is not ubiquitous (Levitan, 1998).

Fertilisation experiments in sea urchins are conducted by putting either individuals or recently collected gametes in arrays where sperm or both sperm and eggs are released into the water column. After either sperm (with eggs exposed to ambient sperm concentration) or both sperm and eggs are allowed to dilute under natural flow conditions, eggs are collected, and fertilisation rate measured (Pennington, 1985; Levitan, 1995; Wahle & Peckham, 1999). Under these experimental conditions, fertilisation is greatly reduced at densities that are typical of postexploitation levels (Wahle & Peckham, 1999). In a study of the green sea urchin *Strongylocentrotus droebachiensis* in Maine, Wahle & Peckham (1999) concluded that fertilisation rate decreased at a faster rate than either individual growth or gonadal size increased for individuals at lower postexploitation densities, leading to reduced fitness of individuals in exploited populations despite their lower densities and more available food per individual.

There is some evidence in unexploited populations of sea urchins that dramatically reduced densities have resulted in no or slow recovery of decimated populations. *Diadema antillarum* experienced a catastrophic die-off throughout the Caribbean basin during the winter of 1983–84 owing to an unknown pathogen. The species showed no recovery in density in the next 10 years, and some authors have suggested that fertilisation failure of this previously high density species may have retarded the recovery (Levitan, 1991; Hughes, 1994). Evidence supporting this suggestion is the low spawning synchrony following the die-off, with many individuals spawning in isolation (Levitan, 1988), experimental evidence that, at the densities noted post die-off, fertilisation success is predicted to be very low (Levitan, 1991) and the poor larval recruitment following the die-off (Lessios, 1988). However, because of the 99% reduction in the number of adults in the Caribbean following the die-off, it is difficult to untangle any per capita reduction in offspring production from the expected reduction in larval production caused by the overall reduction in population size. There is no conclusive evidence to implicate Allee effects in this slow recovery. Similarly, in the green sea urchin study discussed above, although the experimental arrays are suggestive of severe fertilisation reductions at postexploitation densities, there are no data from natural fertilisation events to corroborate this experimental result.

However, there is some evidence from natural spawning events which strongly suggests that sperm numbers and spawning synchronisation of large numbers of individuals is important for successful reproduction. Where predictable spawning events occur, such as in the corals of the Great Barrier Reef (Harrison *et al.*, 1984), measures of fertilisation success show a clear peak in fertilisation during the peak spawning time, with reduced fertilisation success for eggs collected either before or after the peak of spawning for a species (Oliver & Babcock, 1992).

These results have led some authors to suggest that establishing high density refuges in marine protected areas might be important to maintain high levels of zygote production (Quinn *et al.*, 1993). Levitan *et al.* (1992) suggested that, given the wide range of densities where sperm limitation existed in experimental arrays, Allee effects might operate over a much wider range of densities in free-spawning populations than previously considered.

The importance of the Allee effect in free-spawning populations at extremely low density is almost certain, and the case of the white abalone *Haliotis sorenseni* is a striking example. Abalone are large, herbivorous gastropods found in the temperate Pacific. Most species have been heavily exploited for food, both by commercial and sport divers, with the fisheries for all five California species of *Haliotis* exhibiting a dramatic increase in landings followed by a complete or near complete collapse of the fishery (Murray *et al.*, 1999; see Figure 16.1, p. 344). The white abalone population in particular has been decimated off California, and the species appears to be on the brink of extinction. All abalone are broadcast spawners, and at their current density (one individual per hectare in one census; Davis *et al.*, 1996) there is little doubt that fertilisation limitation is a real problem in white abalone populations. Recruitment appears minimal and sporadic in this species, and it is a likely example of an Allee effect through limitation of fertilisation. Although disease and poaching might also have played a role in this species' decline and lack of recovery in protected areas, at its current numbers the population does not appear to be self-sustaining in the wild (Tegner *et al.*, 1996). Abalone have an unfortunate juxtaposition of characteristics; they are harvested individually by divers, they are worth substantial amounts of money ($(US)450 per dozen in February 1996 for the one harvested species in southern California; Tegner *et al.*, 1996), and they do not appear to have habitats that provide an escape from exploitation.

This species may represent the first imminent extinction of a marine invertebrate due to overexploitation (Tegner *et al.*, 1996). At the time of writing, white abalone have been proposed for listing as an endangered species under the Endangered Species Act in the USA (Federal Register, 2000).

In addition to sea urchin and abalone fertilisation, Allee effects have been implicated in the local extinction of giant clams in parts of the Indo-Pacific, and are thought to be important considerations in the population dynamics of other externally fertilising species that are currently being exploited such as scallops and sea cucumbers (for references, see Murray *et al.*, 1999).

POLLEN LIMITATION IN EXPLOITED PLANT SPECIES

Just as broadcast spawning marine organisms are susceptible to Allee effects from decreases in fertilisation success with population density, so both wind- and animal-pollinated plants are susceptible to pollen limitation at low density. Some degree of pollen limitation appears to be common in natural populations (Burd, 1994). In tropical forest trees, human disturbance and exploitation can lead to decreased seed or fruit set in more isolated trees. This may exacerbate the better-known direct effects of harvesting (see Peters, Chapter 11). In *Shorea siamensis*, a tropical forest tree in Thailand, Ghazoul *et al.* (1998) studied fruit set at three population densities, which represented a relatively unexploited population within a wildlife reserve, an intermediately disturbed forest near the border of the reserve, and a relatively more exploited forest outside of the reserve. Tree density varied by approximately an order of magnitude between sites, and the low density, exploited site had the lowest fruit set for each of two years (0.7–1.5%) compared with the densest population in the reserve (2.5–5.5%). Although a demonstration of reduced fruit set at low density is real in natural populations, Allee effects in reproduction will be limited to those exploited forests where recruitment is accomplished by natural regeneration of forest trees after harvest, as opposed to planting of the next generation by foresters.

Pollination success in plants in response to changes in density brought about by exploitation will be complex, depending on the foraging behaviour of pollinators, the physical environment in the case of wind-pollinated plants, and the degree of selfing in the population. Although most extractive plant industries are heavily farmed and managed through agriculture, exploitation of species in forests where recruitment is not supplemented by plantings could threaten the persistence of local populations.

SPAWNING AGGREGATIONS, PREFERENTIAL MALE CAPTURE AND THE ALLEE EFFECT

Allee effects certainly can occur when populations reach such small numbers that one sex is rare or absent (e.g. dusky seaside sparrow *Ammodramus maritimus nigrescens*; Hedrick *et al.*, 1996). However, Allee effects may also be important in cases where low density and skewed sex ratios combine to substantially reduce average individual reproductive success in a population. Exploitation skews sex ratios in many taxa (Kokko *et al.*, Chapter 14). Skewed sex ratios, combined with low populations densities, can be a particularly potent combination for Allee effects.

Several species of large groupers and snappers migrate tens to hundreds of kilometres to spawn in large aggregations for limited times at traditional sites during the year. These aggregations have been the focus of intense fishing activity, with a predictable, economically rewarding resource that can be easily captured. In Nassau grouper *Epinephelus striatus* aggregation sites have been fished heavily and many of these have ceased to exist (Sadovy, 1993), while in gag grouper *Mycteroperca microlepis* there has been a reduction in the geographical range of concentrations of spawning individuals along a preferred depth (Koenig *et al.*, 1996).

Not only have absolute numbers been reduced, but the sex ratio in the remaining populations has been altered, further limiting the potential for recovery. Biased sex ratios in these species to some extent stem from their unique reproductive biology. The grouper species are sequential protogynous hermaphrodites; they start out life as females and later become males. For the change to be evolutionarily stable, sex-changed males must have higher average reproductive success than the smaller females, and because the total male and female reproductive success of the population must be equal, the sex ratios are expected to be female biased in the absence of any exploitation (Charnov, 1982). Two factors appear to have led to strong female biases in adult sex ratios: differential male mortality and lack of sex change of females in response to changes in the sex ratio. Fishing is most intense at spawning aggregations, and males tend to arrive at aggregations first and stay longer than females. The larger size of males also makes them differentially sought by spear fishermen. Males lost to fishing are not replaced via sex change in proportion to their removal, which has led to a decrease of from 17% to 2% of mature males in one population of gag grouper and to a suggestion of the possibility of reduced fertilisation rate due to a shortage of males in the population (Koenig *et al.*, 1996).

It is difficult to predict the long-term life history responses of these fishes to exploitation because we do not know what cues are used to induce sex change in these species. Sex change has been studied in many species of reef fish, but always in species with localised social groups, while in groupers it appears that interactions among individuals at spawning aggregations are not related to their social behaviour during the rest of the year (see e.g. Shapiro *et al.*, 1994). Extreme changes in the sex ratio make it possible that sperm limitation is occurring or could potentially occur in the near future for this and other species of aggregating groupers.

Similarly biased sex ratios are occurring in African elephants *Loxodonta africana* in locations where males, which are larger and have larger tusks, have been preferentially killed for their tusks. The paucity of males that this exploitation creates led Dobson & Poole (1998) to model female reproductive rates with different sex ratios and densities, and successfully predicted the nearly 50% decrease in pregnant or lactating females in a population where the adult sex ratio was 74:1 as compared with a less exploited population where the sex ratio was 26:1 (Dobson & Poole, 1998).

WHY ARE POPULATION-LEVEL ALLEE EFFECTS SO SELDOM OBSERVED?

Despite large numbers of examples of component Allee effects, there is little evidence in the literature for widespread population-level Allee effects. Recent papers on Allee effects include long and diverse lists of species where per individual success increased with density for one aspect of survival, reproduction, or growth (Courchamp *et al.*, 1999a,b; Stephens & Sutherland, 1999, 2000). However, examples of Allee effects that are currently acting at the population level are rare not just for exploited species but also for any natural populations of organisms.

There are several possible reasons for this discrepancy. The first, and perhaps most straightforward, explanation is that the lack of observations reflects reality: population-level Allee effects really are rare in nature. Perhaps the magnitude of intraspecific competition is too large relative to countering demographic Allee effects to produce positive density dependence at the population level.

Demographic Allee effects might also be difficult to observe in nature because, once these effects occur, the populations quickly become extinct. Allee effects may be so severe as to cause negative growth rates below an unstable population equilibrium point (Figure 13.1), or perhaps populations kept at small size due to Allee effects become more vulnerable to both demographic and environmental stochasticity, which increases the probability of extinction by causing population fluctuations. At small population size, demographic stochasticity appears to create unstable equilibrium population sizes, below which populations show negative growth (Lande, 1998).

A third and final possibility is that population-level Allee effects may be more common than they appear, but they typically occur in populations where exploitation and habitat degradation covary with Allee effects, making it difficult to partition Allee effects from the other insults to population growth.

CONSERVATION AND THE ALLEE EFFECT

Allee effects may be particularly important in species that have typically occurred at relatively high densities and only recently had their densities dramatically reduced by exploitation. It is just these types of species that may be unsuited for success at low densities. Passenger pigeons probably fall into this category. Some marine species might lack the behaviour and life histories necessary to survive at low densities (Levitan & McGovern, 2001).

Allee effects are expected to be more common in species that actively aggregate, which may be a characteristic that also makes the species more likely to be exploited. Because species that experience Allee effects gain benefits from increased local density or aggregations or social grouping, we would expect them to form groups under natural conditions. Species where individuals are either aggregated in space or synchronised in time (e.g. for reproduction) are more likely to suffer disproportionately as their numbers are reduced.

Creating regions with locally high density may be an effective management strategy for exploited species at low overall population density. For organisms such as sea urchins with a highly dispersive larval stage, marine protected areas which allow for population densities that permit effective fertilisation could be an effective means to minimise Allee effects in fertilisation. For managers of populations, it may be more valuable to keep a local population at high density compared with a similar number of individuals over a broader geographical range. This might also make management and protection of the remaining individuals easier. However, having individuals spatially concentrated will increase the effects of environmental stochasticity, reducing the long-term probability of successful recovery in the absence of an Allee effect. In the case of white abalone, the possibility of an Allee effect has led the National Marine Fisheries Service to propose collecting and aggregating individuals in the wild as one of its conservation measures (Federal Register, 2000).

CONCLUSIONS

Perhaps one of the most serious concerns about a potential Allee effect is not that it causes extinction directly by itself, but that it decreases the rate of recovery of small populations, leaving them vulnerable for a longer period than would occur in the absence of the effect. The longer the population remains at a small size, the more likely that environmental or demographic stochasticity will lead to catastrophic reproduction or recruitment failures. The effect would operate in the extreme case where average per capita growth was negative, but also would have an impact over a broad range of population sizes where population growth was reduced.

Despite the increased attention to genetic problems with small populations, including inbreeding and loss of genetic diversity, environmental or demographic stochasticity and loss of habitat appear to be the greatest threats to species on the brink of extinction (Caughley, 1994; Lande, 1998). Other than severe cases where it leads to complete reproductive failure (such as a lack of induction of reproduction or fertilisation failure due to low density of males), Allee effects are most likely to be one of many causes hindering the recovery of small, exploited populations.

REFERENCES

Allee, W. C. (1931). *Animal Aggregations, A Study in General Sociology*. University of Chicago Press, Chicago.

Allee, W. C. (1932). *Animal Life and Social Growth*. Williams & Wilkins, Baltimore, MD.

Allee, W. C. (1938). *The Social Life of Animals*. William Heinemann, London.

Allee, W. C., Emerson, A. E., Park, O., Park, T. & Schmidt, K. P. (1949). *Principles of Animal Ecology*. W. B. Saunders, Philadelphia.

Allendorf, F. W. & Leary, R. F. (1986). Heterozygosity and fitness in natural populations of animals. In *Conservation Biology: The Science of Scarcity and Diversity*, ed. M. E. Soulé, pp. 57–76. Sinauer Associates, Sunderland, MA.

Andrewartha, H. G. & Birch, L. C. (1954). *The Distribution and Abundance of Animals*. University of Chicago Press, Chicago.

Birkhead, T. R. (1977). The effect of habitat and density on breeding success in the common guillemot (*Uria aalge*). *Journal of Animal Ecology*, 46, 751–764.

Blockstein, D. E. & Tordoff, H. B. (1985). Gone forever: a contemporary look at the extinction of the passenger pigeon. *American Birds*, 39, 845–851.

Brown, C. R., Stutchbury, B. J. & Walsh, P. D. (1990). Choice of colony size in birds. *Trends in Ecology and Evolution*, 5, 398–403.

Bucher, E. H. (1992). The causes of extinction of the passenger pigeon. *Current Ornithology*, **9**, 1–36.

Burd, M. (1994). Bateman's principle and plant reproduction: the role of pollen limitation in fruit and seed set. *Botanical Review*, **60**, 83–139.

Caughley, G. (1994). Directions in conservation biology. *Journal of Animal Ecology*, **63**, 215–244.

Charnov, E. L. (1982). *The Theory of Sex Allocation*. Princeton University Press, Princeton, NJ.

Cockburn, A. (1991). *An Introduction to Evolutionary Ecology*. Blackwell, Oxford.

Côté, I. M. & Gross, M. R. (1993). Reduced disease in offspring: a benefit of coloniality in sunfish. *Behavioral Ecology and Sociobiology*, **33**, 269–274.

Courchamp, F., Clutton-Brock, T. & Grenfell, B. (1999a). Inverse density dependence and the Allee effect. *Trends in Ecology and Evolution*, **14**, 405–410.

Courchamp, F., Grenfell, B. & Clutton-Brock, T. (1999b). Population dynamics of obligate cooperators. *Proceedings of the Royal Society of London B*, **266**, 557–563.

Darling, F. F. (1938). *Bird Flocks and the Breeding Cycle: A Contribution to the Study of Avian Sociality*. Cambridge University Press, Cambridge.

Davis, G. D., Haaker, P. L. & Richards, D. V. (1996). Status and trends of white abalone at the California Channel Islands. *Transaction of the American Fisheries Society*, **125**, 42–48.

Dennis, B. (1989). Allee effects: population growth, critical density and the chance of extinction. *Natural Resources Modelling*, **3**, 481–538.

Dobson, A. & Poole, J. (1998). Conspecific aggregation and conservation biology. In *Behavioral Ecology and Conservation Biology*, ed. T. Caro, pp. 193–208. Oxford University Press, Oxford.

Federal Register (2000). Endangered and threatened species; proposed endangered status for white abalone. *Federal Register (USA)*, **65**, 26167–26176.

Foster, S. A. (1985). Group foraging by a coral reef fish: a mechanism for gaining access to defended resources. *Animimal Behaviour*, **33**, 782–792.

Fowler, C. W. & Baker, J. D. (1991). A review of animal population dynamics at extremely reduced population levels. *Report of the International Whaling Commission*, **41**, 545–554.

Ghazoul, J., Liston, K. A. & Boyle, T. J. B. (1998). Disturbance-induced density dependent seed set in *Shorea siamensis* (Dipterocarpaceae), a tropical forest tree. *Journal of Ecology*, **86**, 462–473.

Gilpin, M. E. & Soulé, M. E. (1986). Minimum viable populations: processes of species extinction. In *Conservation Biology: The Science of Scarcity and Diversity*, ed. M. E. Soulé, pp. 19–34. Sinauer Associates, Sunderland, MA.

Götmark, F. & Andersson, M. (1984). Colonial breeding reduces nest predation in the common gull (*Larus canus*). *Animal Behaviour*, **32**, 485–492.

Gross, M. R. & MacMillan, A. M. (1981). Predation and the evolution of colonial nesting in bluegill sunfish (*Lepomis macrochirus*). *Behavioral Ecology and Sociobiology*, **8**, 163–174.

Halliday, T. R. (1980). The extinction of the passenger pigeon *Ectopises migratorius* and its relevance to contemporary conservation. *Biological Conservation*, **17**, 157–162.

Harrison, P. L., Babcock, R. C., Bull, G. D., Oliver, J. K., Wallace, C. C. & Willis, B. L. (1984). Mass spawning in tropical reef corals. *Science*, **223**, 1186–1189.

Hatchwell, B. J. (1991). An experimental study of the effects of timing of breeding on the reproductive success of common guillemots (*Uria aalge*). *Journal of Animal Ecology*, **60**, 721–736.

Hedrick, P. W., Lacy, R. C., Allendorf, F. W. & Soulé, M. E. (1996). Directions in conservation biology: comments on Caughley. *Conservation Biology*, **10**, 1312–1320.

Hilborn, R. & Walters, C. J. (1992). *Quantitative Fisheries Stock Assessment: Choice, Dynamics and Uncertainty*. Chapman & Hall, New York.

Hughes, T. P. (1994). Catastrophes, phase shifts, and large-scale degradation of a Caribbean coral reef. *Science*, **265**, 1547–1551.

Hunter, M. L. Jr (1996). *Fundamentals of Conservation Biology*. Blackwell Scientific, Cambridge, MA.

Hutchings, J. A. (1996). Spatial and temporal variation in the density of northern cod and a review of hypotheses for the stock's collapse. *Canadian Journal of Fisheries and Aquatic Sciences*, **53**, 943–962.

Koenig, C. C., Coleman, F. C., Collins, L. A., Sadovy, Y. & Colin, P. L. (1996). Reproduction in gag, *Myctroperca microlepis* (Pisces: Serranidae) in the eastern Gulf of Mexico and the consequences of fishing spawning aggregations. In *Biology, Fisheries, and Culture of Tropical Groupers and Snappers*, ed. F. Arreguín-Sanchez, J. L. Munro, M. C. Balgos & D. Pauly, pp. 307–323. ICLARM Conference Proceedings no. 48, Manila.

Lande, R. (1988). Genetics and demography in biological conservation. *Science*, **241**, 1455–1460.

Lande, R. (1995). Mutation and conservation. *Conservation Biology*, **9**, 782–791.

Lande, R. (1998). Demographic stochasticity and Allee effect on a scale with isotropic noise. *Oikos*, **83**, 353–358.

Lessios, H. A. (1988). Mass mortality of *Diadema antillarum* in the Caribbean: what have we learned? *Annual Review of Ecology and Systematics*, **19**, 371–393.

Levitan, D. R. (1988). Asynchronous spawning and aggregative behavior in the sea urchin *Diadema antillarum* Philippi. In *Echinoderm Biology*, Proceedings of the 6th International Echinoderm Conference, ed. R. Burke, pp. 181–186. Balkema, Rotterdam.

Levitan, D. R. (1991). Influence of body size and population density on fertilization success and reproductive output in a free-spawning invertebrate. *Biological Bulletin*, **181**, 261–268.

Levitan, D. R. (1995). The ecology of fertilization in free-spawning invertebrates. In *Ecology of Marine Invertebrate Larvae*, ed. L. McEdward, pp. 123–156. CRC Press, Boca Raton, FL.

Levitan, D. R. (1998). Sperm competition, gamete competition, and sexual selection in external fertilizers. In *Sperm Competition and Sexual Selection*, ed. T. Birkhead and A. P. Møller, pp. 175–217. Academic Press, San Diego.

Levitan, D. R. & McGovern, T. M. (2001). The Allee effect in the sea. In *Marine Conservation Biology: The Science of Maintaining the Sea's Biodiversity*, ed. E. A. Norse & L. B. Crowder. Island Press, Washington, DC, in press.

Levitan, D. R., Sewell, M. A. & Chia, F. S. (1992). How distribution and abundance influences fertilization success in the sea urchin *Strongylocentrotus franciscanus. Ecology*, **73**, 248–254.

Liermann, M. & Hilborn, R. (1997). Depensation in fish stocks: a hierarchic Bayesian meta-analysis. *Canadian Journal of Fisheries and Aquatic Sciences*, **54**, 1976–1984.

Murray, S. N and 18 co-authors (1999). No-take reserve networks: sustaining fishery populations and marine ecosystems. *Fisheries*, **24**, 11–25.

Myers, R. A., Barrowman, N. J., Hutchings, J. A. & Rosenberg, A. A. (1995). Population dynamics of exploited fish stocks at low population levels. *Science*, **269**, 1106–1108.

Odum, E. P. (1953). *Fundamentals of Ecology*. W. B. Saunders, Philadelphia.

Odum, E. P. (1963). *Ecology*. Holt, Reinhart, and Winston, New York.

Oliver, J. & Babcock, R. (1992). Aspects of the fertilization ecology of broadcast spawning corals: sperm dilution effects and in situ measurements of fertilization. *Biological Bulletin*, **183**, 409–417.

Owen, O. S. (1980). *Natural Resource Conservation: An Ecological Approach*. Macmillan, New York.

Pearson, G. A. & Brawley, S. H. (1996). Reproductive ecology of *Fucus distichus* (Phaeophyceae): an intertidal alga with successful external fertilization. *Marine Ecological Program Series*, **143**, 211–223.

Pennington, J. T. (1985). The ecology of fertilization of echinoid eggs – the consequences of sperm dilution, adult aggregation and synchronous spawning. *Biological Bulletin*, **169**, 417–430.

Quinn, J. F., Wing, S. R. & Botsford, L. W. (1993). Harvest refugia in marine invertebrate fisheries: models and applications to the red sea urchin, *Strongylocentrotus fransciscanus. American Zoologist*, **33**, 537–550.

Robertson, D. R., Sweatman, H. P. A., Fletcher, E. A. & Cleland, M. G. (1976). Schooling as a mechanism for circumventing the territoriality of competitors. *Ecology*, **57**, 1208–1220.

Sadovy, Y. (1993). The Nassau grouper, endangered or just unlucky? *Reef Encounters*, **13**, 10–12.

Schorger, A. W. (1955). *The Passenger Pigeon, its Natural History and Extinction*. University of Wisconsin Press, Madison, WI.

Serrao, E. A., Pearson, G., Kautsky, L. & Brawley, S. H. (1996). Successful external fertilization in turbulent environments. *Proceedings of the National Academy of Sciences, USA*, **93**, 5286–5290.

Sewell, M. A. & Levitan, D.R. (1992). Fertilization success during a natural spawning of the dendrochirote sea cucumber *Cucumaria miniata. Bulletin of Marine Science*, **51**, 161–166.

Shapiro, D. Y., Garcia-Moliner, G. & Sadovy, Y. (1994). Social system of an inshore stock of the red hind grouper, *Epinephelus guttatus* (Pisces: Serranidae). *Environmental Biology of Fishes*, **41**, 415–422.

Stephens, P. A. & Sutherland, W. J. (1999). Consequences of the Allee effect for behaviour, ecology and conservation. *Trends in Ecology and Evolution*, **14**, 401–405.

Stephens, P. A. & Sutherland, W. J. (2000). Vertebrate mating systems, rarity and conservation. In *Vertebrate Mating Systems*, ed. M. Apollonino,

M. Festa-Bianchet & D. Mainardi, pp. 186–213. World Scientific Publishing Co., Singapore.

Stephens, P. A., Sutherland, W. J. & Freckleton, R. P. (1999). What is the Allee effect? *Oikos*, **87**, 185–190.

Tegner, M. J., Basch, L. V. & Dayton, P. K. (1996). Near extinction of an exploited marine invertebrate. *Trends in Ecology and Evolution*, **11**, 278–280.

Wahle, R. A. & Peckham, S. H. (1999). Density-related reproductive trade-offs in the green sea urchin, *Strongylocentrotus droebachiensis*. *Marine Biology*, **134**, 127–137.

Wilson, W. G. & Agnew, A. D. Q. (1992). Positive-feedback switches in plant communities. *Advances in Ecological Research*, **23**, 263–336.

Wittenberger, J. F. & Hunt, G. L. Jr (1985). The adaptive significance of coloniality in birds. *Current Ornithology*, **8**, 1–78.

14

Life histories and sustainable harvesting

HANNA KOKKO, JAN LINDSTRÖM & ESA RANTA

Life histories encapsulate the patterns of individual growth, survival and reproduction. These individual-based traits all influence the rate at which the target population renews itself. Since the sustainable use of any resource is clearly dependent on the rate of its renewal, life history characteristics are obviously of interest in considerations of sustainable exploitation. Were there no trade-offs between life history traits such as reproduction and survival, natural selection would be expected to mould every species into 'Darwinian demons' (Law, 1979) that mature immediately after birth, have zero natural mortality and produce offspring at an infinite rate. Sustainable harvesting in such a world would not require much intelligent thought. Existing life histories, however, abound in compromises that limit the rate at which new individuals are being produced (Roff, 1992; Stearns, 1992; Reynolds *et al.*, Chapter 7). As a result, species and populations differ widely in their most basic traits, including their intrinsic growth rate. It is easy to see that a population that has twice the growth rate of another target population can be harvested at twice the rate, when similar requirements of sustainability are expected (Figure 14.1).

A dilemma is that the largest individuals are nearly always the most profitable ones, but life history trade-offs often tend to assign them the lowest growth rates (e.g. Caughley & Sinclair, 1994; Calder, 1996). This is true within a species, and even more so among harvestable species differing greatly in size. Severe declines in populations of various whale species worldwide serve as a good example: very low growth rates (4–7% annual increase in non-exploited populations; Allen & Kirkwood, 1988) make overexploitation by humans easy and recovery by whales slow (May, 1976; Gulland, 1990). Similar arguments of course apply to the harvest of large, slowly growing plants such as tropical trees (e.g. Olmsted & Alvarez-Buylla, 1995). In the case of whales, the problem is aggravated by very high profits from catching large individuals, difficulties in estimating population sizes reliably enough, and high mobility of individuals that render it

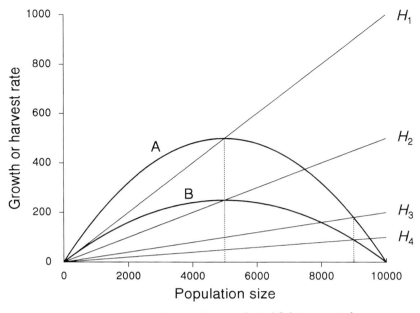

Figure 14.1. Population growth rate is the most basic life history trait that influences prospects of sustainable harvesting. All other factors being equal, a population with twice the growth rate of another can be harvested twice as much. This principle is here illustrated with deterministic logistic growth, with an intrinsic 20% annual growth in population A, and 10% in population B. In both cases, the maximum sustainable yield (MSY; Ricker, 1975) occurs when populations have been reduced to 50% of their carrying capacity, and the yield from A, obtained, for example, by following the constant effort harvest rate H_1, is double that from B with harvest rate H_2. A twofold difference in yield also arises at more prudent harvesting rates, H_3 versus H_4, that lead to smaller (10%) reductions in population size, and do not suffer from the instability problems associated with the MSY concept (see Ludwig, Chapter 2).

difficult to reach an agreement among countries that participate in exploitation of the natural resources (Gulland, 1990). Although modern harvesting techniques such as trawling have brought species with much higher reproductive capacities into the realm of overexploitation (e.g. Atlantic cod *Gadus morhua*; Cook *et al.*, 1997; Myers *et al.*, 1997), large-bodied species seem to be generally more vulnerable to exploitation (Gaston & Blackburn, 1995; Jennings *et al.*, 1998). As this is also apparent in the fate of Pleistocene megafauna (Lessa & Farina, 1996; McKinney, 1997), it seems that any mismatch between exploitation and sustainability has the most detrimental effects in large-bodied and thus typically highly profitable species.

How, then, to sustainably exploit species when life history trade-offs so often translate into trade-offs in the choice of species as targets of harvest as well? Clearly, harvest limits must be tailored to the rates of increase and patterns of density dependence of each particular species and population. The among-species variation in life histories is treated elsewhere in this book (Reynolds *et al.*, Chapter 7; Purvis, Chapter 8). Our focus is on the management consequences of schedules of growth and reproduction, as well as sex differences in the reproductive roles, within a species. Knowledge of the life history of a particular species has the potential to improve management practices considerably, because individuals may differ drastically in their expected contribution to population growth, depending on their age. We do not dwell on effects of the opposite direction: harvesting may act as a selection agent in life history evolution itself, leading to the evolution of smaller body size or earlier maturation (see e.g. Heino, 1998). Law (Chapter 15) considers such processes in more detail.

REPRODUCTIVE VALUES

Derivations of sustainable offtake, such as that presented in Figure 14.1, suffer from several unrealistic assumptions. Apart from ignoring processes such as stochasticity and economic considerations (but see Lande *et al.*, Chapter 4), such models implicitly assume that all individuals have an equal impact on the growth of a population. Especially in long-lived species, this is a most unlikely assumption: as an extreme example, postreproductive animals can be removed from a population without adversely affecting population growth (Law, Chapter 15). This is indicated in their reproductive value – their expected contribution to future generations (Fisher, 1930; Caswell, 1989) – being zero.

In a population that grows at rate r, reproductive value v at age i is defined as

$$v_i = \frac{e^{ri}}{l_i} \sum_{j=i}^{k} e^{-rj} l_j m_j, \tag{14.1}$$

where l_i equals the probability that a newborn individual survives up to age i, and m_j gives its fecundity at age j (e.g. Stearns, 1992). MacArthur (1960) conjectured that harvesting should generally take individuals with the smallest reproductive values, since this will minimise the impact that harvesting has on population growth. Again, however, trade-offs may enter the equation if individuals also differ in their profitability, i.e. the value of an individual to humans when caught, which is often measurable in monetary units. Obvious examples are provided by slowly growing species: the profitability of felling a tall tree is not equal to that of removing a seedling, and big fish yield more value than their larvae. This may cause a conflict if individuals most profitable to exploit are also those with the highest reproductive values, which is often expected, especially if fecundity is linked to body size.

Reproductive value changes over season and over age groups

Reproductive value of an individual changes with age, but in seasonally breeding species it also varies over shorter time scales, peaking just before reproduction, and being at the lowest after the breeding season when there is a higher chance that an individual will die before it produces offspring again the next season. This forms a theoretical background to the intuitively clear result that it is wiser to harvest after rather than before the breeding season (Doubleday, 1975; Kokko & Lindström, 1998; Kokko *et al.*, 1998; Kokko, 2001). Nevertheless, hunting before or during the breeding season is relatively common, for example in ungulate (for a review, see Ginsberg & Milner-Gulland, 1994) and waterfowl (Kokko *et al.*, 1998) populations, and in fisheries where harvesting often occurs throughout the year. In an example from fisheries, Matsuda *et al.* (1994) calculated seasonal reproductive values to evaluate the impact of two different types of fishery, dip netting and purse seine netting, on chub mackerel *Scomber japonicus* populations. The dip net fishery exploits mackerels in winter and spring, which is before and during the spawning season, whereas the purse seine net fishery occurs in summer and autumn, after the spawning season. On the basis of estimates of age-specific fishing mortalities, natural mortalities and reproduction rates, they concluded that each fish caught in the dip net fishery causes a 46% larger reduction in the growth rate of the population than each fish caught in the purse seine fishery. Yet, because of a much lower total catch (1.5% of the total), the impact of dip netting as a whole falls clearly below that of purse seine netting. Despite a higher impact per fish caught, banning dip netting is unlikely to happen, since the fisheries operate at different localities and the price of dip netted chub mackerels is almost 13 times that of those caught in the purse seine fishery (Matsuda *et al.*, 1994).

Whenever a part of a cohort dies before reproducing, any single young individual may die before it has a chance to reproduce, and its expected contribution to population growth is therefore low. A reproducing adult, on the other hand, has already surpassed the dangers of youth, and will therefore have a higher impact on population growth. Reproductive values are thus typically low for young animals, peak at the onset of maturity, and – especially in long-lived animals – may decline slowly thereafter as reproduction and/or survival deteriorates. Examples of age-specific reproductive values are shown in Figure 14.2 for various animal taxa.

If age-specific kills are based on reproductive values, the initial increase in the reproductive value is often more important to consider than the final decline. First, young animals are more numerous than very old ones. This is why data that pool adult age groups typically show a continuous increase of reproductive value with age, as for the sage grouse *Centrocercus urophasianus* (Figure 14.2). A second, practical, reason is that in many species the appearance of animals changes relatively little in the adult age classes, and juveniles are therefore more easily distinguished as a separate age class than are very old animals. This suggests that young animals should often become a preferred target of the harvest (assuming their profitability is not much lower than that of older animals). This statement may certainly sound counterintuitive, since the future of any population relies on its young, and below we discuss cases where it indeed does not apply.

Several case studies show that harvesting adults has a greater impact on a population than harvesting immature individuals. If harvesting is biased towards adults with high reproductive value, the assumption that underlies derivations such as Figure 14.1 – that a 10% annual growth in a population means that 10% of the individuals may be safely removed – is not valid. For example, in a Chilean population of vicuñas *Vicugna vicugna*, the annual growth rate was estimated as 16.4%, yet a simulated harvest rate of 15% led to a 3% annual decline of the population when harvesting concentrated on three 'adult' age classes (Cattan & Glade, 1989). In plants, reproductive value differences among age groups may be huge (Figure 14.2d), leading to accordingly large discrepancies between simplistic models and stage-structured analyses: with a 5% annual growth rate and a density of 760 individuals/ha in the tropical palm *Coccothrinax readii*, one might estimate the upper limit for an annual sustainable harvest to be $0.05 \times 760 = 38$ individuals/ha, yet a stage-specific analysis shows that not even one adult individual/ha may be harvested sustainably every year (Olmsted & Alvarez-Buylla, 1995). Similarly, population growth in the forest herb *Allium tricoccum* is heavily dependent on reproductive individuals that have large, edible bulbs, and relatively low harvest rates prove sufficient to cause a population decline (Nault & Gagnon, 1993). Further examples come from seal populations: Hårding & Härkönen (1999) and Kokko *et al.* (1999) showed that the drastic decline in seal populations in the Baltic Sea during the twentieth century has been much steeper in scenarios where the catch consists

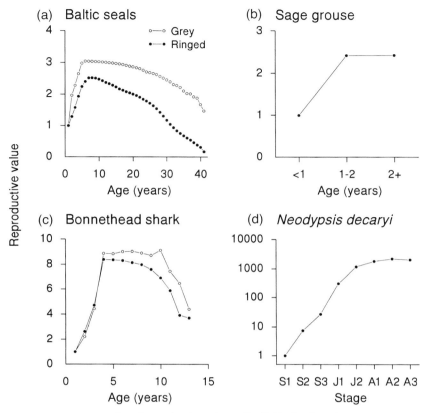

Figure 14.2. Examples of reproductive values of individuals of varying age or stage, calculated according to Caswell (1989). (a), Grey seal *Halichoerus grypus* and ringed seal *Phoca hispida* (data from Kokko *et al.*, 1997; reprinted by permission of Blackwell Science, Inc.); (b) sage grouse *Centrocercus urophasianus*, stages classified as juveniles (age ≤ 1 year), yearlings (1–2 years) and adults (age ≥ 2 years), data from Johnson & Braun (1999); (c) bonnethead shark *Sphyrna tiburo*, two alternatives based on different methods of estimating adult survival (open dots, Pauly, 1980; filled dots, Hoenig, 1983) (data from Cortés & Parsons, 1996); (d) Tropical palm *Neodypsis decaryi*, classified in stages S1 to S3, seedlings with leaf length < 15 cm, 15–60 cm and > 60 cm, respectively; J1 and J2, immature juveniles with visible stem and height < 80 cm and > 80 cm, respectively; A1 to A3, mature adults with stem height < 200 cm, 200–350 cm and > 350 cm, respectively. (Data (pooled matrix from all plots) from Ratsirarson *et al.*, 1996.)

mainly of adult seals rather than of pups and immature individuals. Finally, a switch from an adult-biased to juvenile-biased hunting policy has been suggested as the likely cause for a drastic increase, accompanied by an increase in the total yield, in Finnish moose *Alces alces* populations during the 1970s (Nygrén & Pesonen, 1993; Lehtonen, 1998).

Elasticity and sensitivity

If age-specific survival and fecundity values are known, reproductive values can be calculated from transition matrices that summarise the survival, fecundity and state change probabilities of individuals (Caswell, 1989). However, the most common way to estimate the effects of human intervention, either positive or negative, that focuses on a specific age class is to analyse the elasticity of the transition matrix directly (de Kroon *et al.*, 1986; Charron & Gagnon, 1991; Nault & Gagnon, 1993; Benton & Grant, 1999). This procedure (for details, see e.g. Caswell, 1989; Benton & Grant, 1999) first quantifies the sensitivity of the population growth rate λ to changes in one of the transitions a_{ij} (stage-specific fecundity or survival) that form the elements of the transition matrix **A** (see Box 14.1). Sensitivities $\partial\lambda/\partial a_{ij}$ will then be scaled to represent proportional changes in survival or fecundity values, which yields elasticities $e_{ij} = (a_{ij}/\lambda)(\partial\lambda/\partial a_{ij})$. If, say, survival from age two to age three years has a low elasticity value, this means that two-year olds may be removed without causing too much harm to the population. Unsurprisingly, elasticities and sensitivities bear a direct relationship to the reproductive value: Caswell (1989, p. 138) shows that transitions to stages of high reproductive value will have highest sensitivities.

However, sensitivities and elasticities have to be used with care. That a population responds strongly to a change in a specific life history trait does not imply that the dynamics are driven mainly by variations in that trait. How much variation actually occurs in that trait is of equal importance to the observed outcome (Silvertown *et al.*, 1996; Ehrlén & van Groenendael, 1998; de Kroon *et al.*, 2000; Gaillard *et al.*, 2000). In the context of harvesting, elasticities specify only the population-wide response to a small change in survival, but they do not indicate how large the survival change will be when one is following a given harvesting strategy.

That this may be highly relevant can be illustrated by a hypothetical example. Consider a slowly growing species, where natural mortality depends on body size, and only individuals of age three years or older are economically worth harvesting (Figure 14.3). Maturation occurs at age four years, and the expected annual fecundity of mature individuals equals five female offspring. Natural mortality is lowest in third-year immature

Box 14.1 Matrix notation of life cycles

Transition matrices (Caswell, 1989) are tables that list the expected number of individuals 'produced' by an individual of a specific stage during one time unit (e.g. one year). Here, 'production' may refer to fecundity, but also to the survival of the individual itself. For example, the life cycle in Figure 14.3 specifies that an adult individual (age class $4+$) will produce, on average, five juveniles (age class 1). In matrix notation, this is listed as $a_{14} = 5$ (first row, fourth column). The adult may also survive and continue being an adult. When adult survivorship equals 90%, this means that each adult that is alive in a specific year 'produces' 0.9 adults to the following year ($a_{44} = 0.9$). Likewise, each one-year-old individual produces 0.2 two-year-olds ($a_{21} = 0.2$). Combining all transitions of the life cycle graph yields the matrix

$$\mathbf{A} = \begin{pmatrix} 0 & 0 & 0 & 5 \\ 0.2 & 0 & 0 & 0 \\ 0 & 0.3 & 0 & 0 \\ 0 & 0 & 0.95 & 0.9 \end{pmatrix}. \tag{14.2}$$

$\mathbf{A}$ can be used to predict the numbers of individuals after one time unit has elapsed, when the initial number of individuals is known and written in vector format. For example, if a population had 200 juveniles and 100 individuals in every other age class, the population size after one time unit would equal

$$\begin{pmatrix} 0 & 0 & 0 & 5 \\ 0.2 & 0 & 0 & 0 \\ 0 & 0.3 & 0 & 0 \\ 0 & 0 & 0.95 & 0.9 \end{pmatrix} \cdot \begin{pmatrix} 200 \\ 100 \\ 100 \\ 100 \end{pmatrix} = \begin{pmatrix} 500 \\ 40 \\ 30 \\ 185 \end{pmatrix} \tag{14.3}$$

individuals, i.e. 500 juveniles, 40 two-year-olds, 30 three-year-olds, and 185 adults. This calculation follows the rules of matrix multiplication. Numbers in age class i are obtained by summing the products of numbers in the ith row of the transition matrix, and in the population vector. For example, the number of individuals in the fourth age class is obtained by multiplying the elements of the fourth row with those in the vector, $0 \times 200 + 0 \times 100 + 0.95 \times 100 + 0.9 \times 100 = 185$.

Caswell (1989) described how matrix algebra can be used to derive important characteristics of the demography of the population. Most importantly, the equation $\lambda\mathbf{w} = \mathbf{Aw}$ (for details see Caswell, 1989) specifies both the growth rate λ and the stable age structure **w** of the population (**w** is called the right eigenvector of the matrix). A similar equation, $\mathbf{v}\lambda = \mathbf{v}\mathbf{A}$, yields the stage-specific reproductive values **v**. Procedures for computing these values, as well as sensitivities and elasticities of population growth rates to changes in the elements of the matrix, are available in many mathematical software packages.

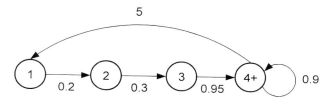

Figure 14.3. A hypothetical life cycle of an animal with three immature age classes (1, 2, 3), and an age class of mature adults (4 +). Arrows indicate the expected contribution of an animal to a future age class. A contribution can arise either through reproduction (arrow from class 4 + to 1; value can exceed 1) or survival (all other arrows; value cannot exceed 1).

individuals (survival $p_3 = 0.95$), which have attained the adult body size but do not yet engage in costly breeding activities. Survival of mature individuals is also high ($p_4 = 0.90$), whereas it is low in the first two age classes ($p_1 = 0.2$, $p_2 = 0.3$). From this information, we may build a transition matrix **A** (Box 14.1) that describes population growth.

The population growth rate can be computed from the eigenvalue equation $\lambda \mathbf{w} = \mathbf{A}\mathbf{w}$ (Box 14.1; Caswell, 1989). For our example, the solution is $\lambda = 1.11$, meaning that the population increases annually by 11%. The right eigenvector $\mathbf{w} = [0.689, 0.124, 0.034, 0.153]^T$ gives the stable age structure of the population, indicating that 15.3% of all individuals are mature at any given time. The corresponding left eigenvector $\mathbf{v} = [1.0, 5.5, 20.5, 23.9]^T$ reveals that the expected contribution of a mature individual is almost 24 times that of the youngest age class, and 17% larger than that of a three-year-old. The elasticity values are 0.1204 for fecundity and for the survival of the first three age classes, and 0.5185 for the survival of mature individuals.

Clearly, the difference in reproductive values and especially elasticities strongly suggests concentrating the harvest on immature three-year-olds rather than on mature individuals of age four years or older. However, if we

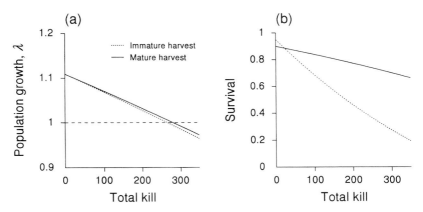

Figure 14.4. (a) Relationship between population growth rate λ and the total quota K that consists either purely of three-year-old immatures (dotted line) or mature individuals (solid line). Population growth follows the transition matrix **A** as given in the text, hunting mortality occurs after the breeding season and before natural mortality, and there is no compensatory mortality. Total population size is 10 000, and growth λ and the age structure **w** are iterated from a modified matrix $\mathbf{B} = \{b_{ij}\}$ that takes into account hunting mortality: $\lambda\mathbf{w} = \mathbf{Bw}$, $\Sigma_i w_i = 10\,000$, and either $b_{43} = (w_3 - K)p_3/w_3$ (immature hunting) or $b_{44} = (w_4 - K)p_4/w_4$ (mature hunting). Note that an annual harvest of 3% of the population (300 individuals out of 10 000) is sufficient to cause a population decline, despite the intrinsic growth rate exceeding 10%. The decline occurs sooner if immatures are harvested. This is surprising, given that reproductive values v_i and elasticities e_i are smaller for immature three-year-olds than for adults both in the unharvested ($v_3 = 20.5$, $v_4 = 23.9$; $e_3 = 0.12$, $e_4 = 0.52$) and harvested populations (e.g. at $K = 250$ in the immature harvest: $v_3 = 16.9$, $v_4 = 46.7$; $e_3 = 0.08$, $e_4 = 0.68$). (b) The actual survival of three-year-old immatures (b_{43}) declines faster with the total quota K than that of matures (b_{44}), in settings where either immatures (dotted line) or matures (solid line) are harvested. This results from the adult age class (4 +) being larger than the immature age class, and it accounts for the severe consequences of harvesting immature individuals, despite the low elasticity value of their survival. The discrepancy shows that elasticities or reproductive values should not be used without assessing the actual change caused to survival probabilities in the different life history stages. Also note that the relationship between total kill and survival is non-linear, which results from changes in the age structure when hunting focuses on a specific life history stage.

assume a total population size of 10 000 individuals and compute the actual values of λ with a hunting quota from 0 to 350 individuals, the population response to the harvest hardly depends on whether immatures or matures are taken (Figure 14.4a). Indeed, in the scenario of hunting immatures only, a *lower* hunting quota is sufficient to cause a population decline (Figure 14.4a). What went wrong with our elasticities?

One possible caveat is that elasticity analysis by definition considers only small changes in survival. When hunting mortality is considerable, the transition matrix itself changes, thus weighting age classes differently from those in the initial, natural setting (Mills *et al.*, 1999; de Kroon *et al.*, 2000). While this certainly applies to our case, it is not the cause of the discrepancy. Instead, tracking the declining survival of immatures in the transition matrix as they are increasingly hunted only increases the difference between immature and mature elasticities or reproductive values (see caption to Figure 14.4). This would suggest that, as hunting pressure on immatures increases, it becomes ever more important to spare the adults. The key to this problem lies in recognising that mature individuals, a class that consists of all ages above four years (15% of the population), are much more numerous than three-year-olds (3.4% of the population). Because of this, a given quota causes a much higher relative increase in the mortality of immatures than matures, especially when very few surviving immatures remain. Furthermore, in a scenario where hunting affects both immatures and matures, harvest of immatures not only will decrease their survival but also will decrease the total number of mature individuals – and therefore will also increase the impact caused by killing a single *mature* individual.

The example of Figure 14.4a also indicates that the relationship between reproductive value and the reduction of population growth is not straightforward: immatures have lower reproductive values yet harvesting them is more harmful. This discrepancy turns out to indicate a rather delicate timing problem when one is modelling population growth with transition matrices. The matrix **A** describes the values of individuals, including current reproduction. Hence, removing a mature individual in the autumn, as assumed in the derivation of Figure 14.3, does not in fact remove its whole reproductive value v_4 from the population. It has already reproduced and killing it in the autumn will not affect this contribution. Instead, the true value of the removal equals 0.9×23.9 (v_4 weighted by the probability of again reaching this reproductive stage) $= 21.5$. Likewise, killing a three-year-old in the autumn removes a potential four-year-old, with the value $0.95 \times 23.9 = 22.7$. This is indeed a slightly higher value than that of already matured individuals, and it explains the higher impact of killing immature individuals in the example given in Figure 14.4.

Conclusions: reproductive values

Apart from emphasising the importance of careful modelling of life history stages, our results highlight the difference between the elasticity of a stage transition and the actual variation that the transition probability will exhibit. This difference is often underlined in studies of natural variation in life history traits (de Kroon *et al.*, 2000) or management practices that aim to improve population growth of endangered species (e.g. Ehrlén & van Groenendael, 1998), but it is of equal importance in the context of harvesting where it is less often mentioned (although see Benton & Grant, 1999). Humans are interested in catching animals or plants, not survival percentages. This means that, while taking young individuals with low reproductive value can be the least damaging option when hunting quotas are small as compared with the population size, this is not a safe option if quotas may take a considerable fraction of a young age class. It is not sustainable to collect all eggs year after year from a goose colony, even if each egg has a very low reproductive value compared with that of its parents!

Indeed, when 'optimal harvesting' is given a mathematical definition that maximises the sustainable yield (in absolute numbers), optimal policies may involve a total harvest of certain age classes. It is then logically clear that these must be the oldest ones, and the optimal strategy is then to remove an old age class completely, combined with a partial harvest in a younger age class (Beddington & Taylor, 1973; Doubleday, 1975; Rorres & Fair, 1975; Grey & Law, 1987; Arditi & Dacorogna, 1992). The same result applies in models that include density-dependence (Getz, 1980; Reed, 1980; Grey, 1988; Law & Grey, 1988; Murphy & Smith, 1991; Dacorogna *et al.*, 1994). Thus, even though taking individuals with lowest reproductive values minimises the loss of population growth, the yield per recruit is not necessarily maximised with this strategy (Grey & Law, 1987; Law & Grey, 1988). Considering somewhat more realistic situations where no age class is completely killed, Goodyear (1996) derived MSY values (in units of weight, which takes account of varying biomass in different age classes) for the red snapper *Lutjanus campechanus*. Of 10 hypothetical selectivity regimes, the maximum sustainable yield was found to peak when oldest individuals were taken.

If hunting mortality can potentially reach very high levels in any single age class, the safest option is to ensure that individuals have had a chance to leave enough progeny to replace themselves before they are taken, since even severe overexploitation of oldest age classes cannot then threaten sustainability (Myers & Mertz, 1998). Clearly, this strategy is not very easy to implement in species with determinate growth, as it would be difficult to recognise individuals that have crossed the safety threshold. In species with indeterminate growth, however, recommendations such as enforced minimum sizes of individuals taken can be the simplest way to achieve this condition, despite the fact that fecundity generally increases with size in such species. Such limits have the additional advantages of being easy to control and allowing capture of the largest and thus the most profitable individuals. Such limits are indeed a common practice in recreational fishing and in exploitation of shellfishes (Jennings *et al.*, 2001). They may also be technically vastly easier to implement than more detailed policies: in fisheries, gill net mesh size sets a physical threshold for the size of fish that are caught, and this naturally restricts other possible harvest strategies to adjusting this size threshold (Reed, 1980).

Overall, it must be recommended to calculate total yields – and mortalities resulting from taking that quota as a whole – rather than merely comparing stage-specific elasticities or reproductive values. As always (see Lande *et al.*, Chapter 4), it should also be kept in mind that blind predictions of deterministic models may overlook safety issues, which in a life history context mean ensuring high enough survival of the immature age classes, to avoid destroying the regeneration potential of the whole population. Finally, even in species where harvesting at old age or large size is preferable either because of safety criteria or due to the high profitability of large individuals, the generally increasing relationship between reproductive value and age means that reducing the *overall* harvest mortality will lead to a higher proportion of individuals entering the most productive age classes, thus boosting the productivity of the whole population (e.g. in brook trout *Salvelinus fontinalis*; Robinson & Bolen, 1989, pp. 53–54). The increase of reproductive values with age can therefore significantly influence total productivity and yield even in cases where harvesting cannot be made age specific.

SEX RATIOS

Apart from age, individuals differ from each other in other aspects affecting their reproduction, of which sex is the most obvious and probably the most important example. The different reproductive roles of males and females have profound consequences for their impact on population growth. Killing a female will certainly lead to the loss of her subsequent offspring, but killing a male does not necessarily alter the population growth rate at all, if the females he would have fertilised instead become inseminated by other males.

Clearly, whether or not this happens depends on the mating system of the species. In polygynous pheasants, hens do not suffer from decreased fertility when the male:female sex ratio drops to 1:10 in a harvested population, or to 1:50 in captive animals (Hill & Robertson, 1988). In strict monogamy, killing either sex would be equally harmful for the population. But strict sexual monogamy is a very rare mating system (Andersson, 1994), and we may therefore expect population growth to depend generally less on males than on females. Since males often have higher catch value as well, heavily male-biased harvesting strategies seem a wise rule of thumb. A favourable combination of high profitability and low reproductive value would be especially easy to attain in species where some males defend large harems, and the rest form a group of non-reproductives (e.g. as in pheasants; Hill & Robertson, 1988). Killing males will be even better if the presence of males harms productivity of the population, either because females and males may compete for the same resources (e.g. Alexander & Taylor, 1983; Kokko *et al.*, 1998) or because of direct harassment arising from a conflict between the sexes (Reale *et al.*, 1996).

But how far can one go with this 'kill happily all the males' conclusion? Clearly, there is a biological limit to it: shooting every male in a sexually reproducing population will certainly have a drastic impact on population growth. Theoretical studies that seek to quantify optimal sex-specific harvesting policies need to assume a relationship between the availability of males as mates and the females' fertility – leading to the so-called birth function that relates the number of males and females to the number of births in the population (Caswell & Weeks, 1986; Hill & Robertson, 1988; Vlad, 1988; Lindström, 1998). When the proportion of males decreases, an increasing fraction of individuals will produce young (since there are, by definition, more females), but this is ultimately limited by declining fertility (Figure 14.5). The optimal sex ratio will reflect a trade-off between these two factors, and it will depend crucially on the efficiency of fertilisation when females greatly outnumber males. Actual measurements of the birth function are extremely scarce (Caswell & Weeks, 1986). However, some declines in female fertility have been documented in polygynous species: caribou *Rangifer tarandus* females appear to suffer a decline in fecundity at sex ratios greater than 1 : 12 (Bergerud, 1974), and moose *Alces alces* females have been observed to show the same pattern already at a 1 : 2 sex ratio (Bannikov, 1970) – although another study reports a sex ratio of 1 : 10 in this species with no reduction in fecundity (Markgren, 1974). Conflicting results have also been reported in Dall sheep *Ovis dalli* (Heimer, 1980; Murphy *et al.*, 1990).

In less polygynous species, the role of males is likely to be greater, and sex ratio distortions will reduce fecundity more easily. Common eider ducks *Somateria mollissima* form pair bonds yet females take care of offspring by themselves. Still, shooting the males during springtime was

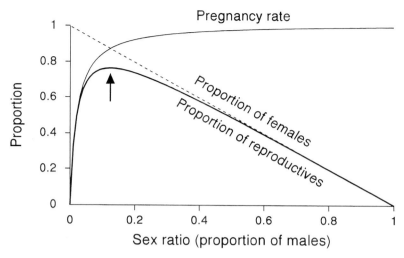

Figure 14.5. A hypothetical example of population growth under sex-specific harvesting. The proportion of reproductives in a population is the product of the number of females and the probability that a female reproduces (the pregnancy rate). If harvesting biases sex ratios towards fewer males, the proportion of reproductive individuals in the population grows, as long as reproduction is limited by the number of females rather than males. This means higher offspring production – and a larger yield – for a given population size if most individuals are female. However, the probability that a given female becomes inseminated must ultimately drop to zero if no males are available for matings. This decline may be very steep in polygynous systems that tolerate heavily biased sex ratios without a significant drop in female fertility, and it means that the sex ratio that yields maximum reproduction (arrow) occurs not far from a drastic decline in productivity.

found to reduce female fertility by about 50% (Hario et al., 1995). This is probably a typical outcome. Killing a female is certain to remove all of her future offspring, whereas killing her mate harms her fecundity by a factor that depends on the extent to which she relies on a single mate to provide sperm and paternal care. For example, in a study of captive mallards *Anas platyrhynchos*, widowed females were usually able to find a new mate, but they laid fewer viable eggs (Lercel et al., 1999). Therefore, killing males is expected to reduce population growth but not as strongly as killing females. The exact impact of sex-specific harvesting will depend on the role that the male plays in reproduction, on the availability of mates to each sex (sex ratios), and on the relative strength of density dependence within and between the sexes (Kokko et al., 1998).

As an example, biasing the sex ratio to 1:7.3 males:females, compared with an original 1:1 sex ratio, leads to a 57% increase in productivity in the hypothetical population given in Figure 14.5. Even populations that naturally have female-biased sex ratios could significantly benefit from further biasing. A study of an impala *Aepyceros melampus* population predicts a 30% increase in productivity by achieving a 1:10 ratio instead of the extant 1:3 (Fairall, 1985) – though this assumes no decline in female fertility. Sex-specific harvesting may thus strongly improve yields or the sustainability of a given quota, but since there is limited knowledge concerning population responses when sex ratios deviate much from their natural values, generating strong biases should be followed by careful monitoring. Strongly polygynous species should allow for the largest biases in sex ratios without adversely affecting fertility, but this also means that the function relating fertility to sex ratio (Figure 14.5) will be steep, making it difficult to estimate a sufficient male:female ratio without accidental and drastic overexploitation of males.

Furthermore, surprising responses may lie hidden in the biology and the social system of a species (for a more detailed treatment of behavioural topics see Sutherland & Gill, Chapter 12). Swenson *et al.* (1997) reported that, in brown bears *Ursus arctos*, killing one male has a population effect equivalent to killing 0.5 to 1 adult female. This is a result of a disrupted social structure, where immigrant males arrive to replace the male, and kill the cubs of the female. Such behaviour is likely to be adaptive from the male's viewpoint as it shortens the time to the female's next conception. Ginsberg & Milner-Gulland (1994) listed more potentially deleterious effects of killing males: artificial selection for inferior males, disruption of territorial structure, and increased mortality of offspring born out of season (if females are unable to locate males at an optimal time). The last effect, as well as the danger that some females are unable to mate at all, is most likely to threaten synchronously breeding populations (Ginsberg & Miller-Gulland, 1994). As a general conclusion, it appears that there are strong arguments for male-biased harvesting, but to avoid unexpected consequences of 'unnatural' sex ratios, extreme biases should be avoided, and less extreme biasing should always be accompanied by monitoring the reproductive output of the population.

CONCLUSIONS

Animals or plants are not all alike. They differ in their age, size, prospects of survival and reproduction, and these are often linked to sex. To some extent these differences can be summarised by the concept of reproductive value. Where it can be derived, it quantifies the contribution of an individual belonging to a given stage to future population growth. Clearly, harvesting should, as a rule of thumb, spare individuals with highest reproductive values. Yet, this strategy does not maximise the yield per recruit, and we have also outlined cases where issues of precaution and simplicity favour alternative approaches (e.g. size limits for harvesting). Management plans cannot always be based on detailed life history data, and even where this is possible, our examples demonstrate that reproductive values or elasticities must be evaluated with great care. Furthermore, trade-offs often exist between reproductive value and profitability of the catch, and optimising a harvesting strategy must take these into account.

Our examples have concentrated on age- and sex-specific harvesting. However, the conclusion that individuals that 'do not matter' for population growth should be favoured as quarry, can be extended to cases where the social system or population-wide density dependence affects some individuals more adversely than others. In the context of density dependence and the question of overall compensatory responses to hunting mortality, Errington (1934) coined the term 'doomed surplus', meaning individuals that can be killed without harming the population as they would otherwise die of natural causes. It is clear that whenever density dependence occurs mainly within a specific age, size or social stage, harvesting can be preferentially directed towards individuals of that stage even if no single individual is 'doomed'. Again, this naturally assumes that the stage fulfils some requirements of profitability. The analysis of density-dependent situations is not too different from the simplistic examples that we have used (e.g. Alvarez-Buylla, 1994), and can be extended to include effects of seasonally operating density dependence (e.g. Kokko & Lindström, 1998; Boyce *et al.*, 1999; Jonzén & Lundberg, 1999).

Subtle differences in life histories can manifest themselves in strong effects on the outcome of harvesting. Unfortunately, this often means that sustainable harvesting practices must be more prudent than simplistic calculations of population growth would suggest. Yet the recognition that all individuals are not alike also allows for fine-tuning the harvest in a way that can improve the yield of the harvest, without compromising the requirements of sustainability.

ACKNOWLEDGEMENTS

We thank Per Lundberg, Jörgen Ripa and Bill Sutherland for extremely helpful discussions, and Mikko Heino, Richard Law and Bill Sutherland for comments on the manuscript. Funding was provided by the TMR programme of the European Commission (H.K., J.L.) and by the Academy of Finland (E.R.); our joint research on population management is funded by the Ministry of Agriculture and Forestry in Finland.

REFERENCES

Alexander, W. C. & Taylor, R. J. (1983). Sex ratio and optimal harvest of canvasback ducks, a model. *Ecological Modelling*, **19**, 285–298.

Allen, K. R. & Kirkwood, G. P. (1988). Marine mammals. In *Fish Population Dynamics*, ed. J. A. Gulland, 2nd edn, pp. 251–269. Wiley, Chichester.

Alvarez-Buylla, E. R. (1994). Density dependence and patch dynamics in tropical rain forests: matrix models and application to a tree species. *American Naturalist*, **143**, 155–191.

Andersson, M. (1994). *Sexual Selection*. Princeton University Press, Princeton, NJ.

Arditi, R. & Dacorogna, B. (1992). Maximum sustainable yield of populations with continuous age-structure. *Mathematical Biosciences*, **110**, 253–270.

Bannikov, A. G. (1970). Moose in the USSR and its exploitation. *Finnish Game Research*, **30**, 273–276.

Beddington, J. R. & Taylor, D. B. (1973). Optimum age-specific harvesting of a population. *Biometrics*, **29**, 801–809.

Benton, T. G. & Grant, A. (1999). Elasticity analysis as an important tool in evolutionary and population ecology. *Trends in Ecology and Evolution*, **14**, 467–471.

Bergerud, A. T. (1974). Rutting behaviour in the Newfoundland caribou. *The Behaviour of Ungulates and its Relation to Management*, ed. V. Geist & F. Walther, pp. 395–435. International Union for Conservation of Nature, Morges, Switzerland.

Boyce, M. S., Sinclair, A. R. E. & White, G. C. (1999). Seasonal compensation of predation and harvesting. *Oikos*, **87**, 419–426.

Calder, W. A. III (1996). *Size, Function and Life History*. Dover, Mineola, TX.

Caswell, H. (1989). *Matrix Population Models*. Sinauer, Sunderland, MA.

Caswell, H. & Weeks, D. E. (1986). Two-sex models: chaos, extinction, and other dynamic consequences of sex. *American Naturalist*, **128**, 707–735.

Cattan, P. E. & Glade, A. A. (1989). Management of the vicuna *Vicugna vicugna* in Chile: use of a matrix model to assess harvest rates. *Biological Conservation*, **49**, 131–140.

Caughley, G. & Sinclair, A. R. E. (1994). *Wildlife Ecology and Management*. Blackwell, Boston, MA.

Charron, D. & Gagnon, D. (1991). The demography of northern populations of *Panax quinquefolium* (American Ginseng). *Journal of Ecology*, **79**, 431–445.

Cook, R. M., Sinclair, A. & Stefánsson, G. (1997). Potential collapse of North Sea cod stocks. *Nature*, **385**, 521–522.

Cortés, E. & Parsons, G. R. (1996). Comparative demography of two populations of the bonnethead shark (*Sphyrna tiburo*). *Canadian Journal of Fisheries and Aquatic Sciences*, **53**, 709–718.

Dacorogna, B., Weissbaum, F. & Arditi, R. (1994). Maximum sustainable yield with continuous age structure and density-dependent recruitment. *Mathematical Biosciences*, **120**, 99–126.

de Kroon, H., Plaisier, A., van Groenendael, J. & Caswell, H. (1986). Elasticity: the relative contribution of demographic parameters to population growth rate. *Ecology*, **67**, 1427–1431.

de Kroon, H., van Groenendael, J. & Ehrlén, J. (2000). Elasticities: a review of methods and model limitations. *Ecology*, **81**, 607–618.

Doubleday, W. G. (1975). Harvesting in matrix population models. *Biometrics*, **31**, 189–200.

Ehrlén, J. & van Groenendael, J. (1998). Direct perturbation analysis for better conservation. *Conservation Biology*, **12**, 470–474.

Errington, P. L. (1934). Vulnerability of bobwhite populations to predation. *Ecology*, **15**, 110–127.

Fairall, N. (1985). Manipulation of age and sex ratios to optimize production from impala (*Aepyceros melampus*) populations. *South African Journal of Wildlife Research*, **15**, 85–88.

Fisher, R. A. (1930). *The Genetical Theory of Natural Selection*, 1st edn. Clarendon Press, Oxford.

Gaillard, J.-M., Festa-Bianchet, M., Yoccoz, N. G., Loison, A. & Toïgo, C. (2000). Temporal variation in fitness components and population dynamics of large herbivores. *Annual Review of Ecology and Systematics*, **31**, 367–393.

Gaston, K. J. & Blackburn, T. M. (1995). Birds, body size and the threat of extinction. *Philosophical Transactions of the Royal Society B*, **347**, 205–212.

Getz, W. M. (1980). The ultimate-sustainable-yield problem in nonlinear age-structured populations. *Mathematical Biosciences*, **45**, 279–292.

Ginsberg, J. R. & Milner-Gulland, E. J. (1994). Sex-biased harvesting and population dynamics in ungulates: implication for conservation and sustainable use. *Conservation Biology*, **8**, 157–166.

Goodyear, C. P. (1996). Variability of fishing mortality by age: consequences for maximum sustainable yield. *North American Journal of Fisheries Management*, **16**, 8–13.

Grey, D. R. (1988). Harvesting under density-dependent mortality and fecundity. *Journal of Mathematical Biology*, **26**, 193–197.

Grey, D. R. & Law, R. (1987). Reproductive values and maximum yields. *Functional Ecology*, **1**, 327–330.

Gulland, J. A. (1990). Commercial whaling – the past, and has it a future? *Mammalian Review*, **20**, 3–12.

Hårding, K. C. & Härkönen, T. (1999). Development in the Baltic grey seal (*Halichoerus grypus*) and ringed seal (*Phoca hispida*) populations during the 20th century. *Ambio*, **28**, 619–627.

Hario, M., Hollmén, T. & Selin, K. (1995). Kevätmetsästyksen vaikutus haahkan pesintään. [In Finnish, with English summary.] *Suomen Riista*, **41**, 13–20.

Heimer, W. E. (1980). A summary of Dall sheep management in Alaska during 1979 (or how to cope with a monumental disaster). *Symposium of Northern Wild Sheep and Goat Council*, **2**, 355–380.

Heino, M. (1998). Management of evolving fish stocks. *Canadian Journal of Fisheries and Aquatic Sciences*, **55**, 1971–1982.

Hill, D. A. & Robertson, P. (1988). *The Pheasant*. BSP, Oxford.

Hoenig, J. M. (1983). Empirical use of longevity data to estimate mortality rates. *Fishery Bulletin*, **82**, 898–903.

Jennings, S., Reynolds, J. D. & Mills, S. C. (1998). Life history correlates of responses to fisheries exploitation. *Proceedings of the Royal Society of London B*, **265**, 333–339.

Jennings, S., Kaiser, M. K. & Reynolds, J. D. (2001). *Marine Fisheries Ecology*. Blackwell, Oxford.

Johnson, K. H. & Braun, C. E. (1999). Viability and conservation of an exploited sage grouse population. *Conservation Biology*, **13**, 77–84.

Jonzén, N. & Lundberg, P. (1999). Temporally structured density-dependence and population management. *Annales Zoologici Fennicae*, **36**, 39–44.

Kokko, H. (2001). Optimal and suboptimal use of compensatory responses to harvesting: timing of hunting as an example. *Wildlife Biology*, in press.

Kokko, H. & Lindström, J. (1998). Seasonal density dependence, timing of mortality, and sustainable harvesting. *Ecological Modelling*, **110**, 293–304.

Kokko, H., Lindström, J. & Ranta, E. (1997). Risk analysis of hunting of seal populations in the Baltic. *Conservation Biology*, **11**, 917–927.

Kokko, H., Pöysä, H., Lindström, J. & Ranta, E. (1998). Assessing the impact of spring hunting on waterfowl populations. *Annales Zoologici Fennici*, **35**, 195–204.

Kokko, H., Helle, E., Lindström, J., Ranta, E., Sipilä, T. & Courchamp, F. (1999). Backcasting population sizes of ringed and grey seals in the Baltic and Lake Saimaa during the 20th century. *Annales Zoologici Fennici*, **36**, 65–73.

Law, R. (1979). Ecological determinants in the evolution of life histories. In *Population Dynamics*, ed. R. M. Anderson, B. D. Turner & L. R. Taylor, pp. 81–103. Blackwell, Oxford.

Law, R. & Grey, D. R. (1988). Maximum sustainable yields and the self-renewal of exploited populations with age-dependent vital rates. In *Size-Structured Populations*, ed. B. Ebenman & L. Persson, pp. 140–154. Springer-Verlag, Berlin.

Lehtonen, A. (1998). Managing moose, *Alces alces*, populations in Finland: hunting virtual animals. *Annales Zoologici Fennici*, **35**, 173–179.

Lercel, B. A., Kaminski, R. B. & Cox, R. R. (1999). Mate loss in winter affects reproduction of mallards. *Journal of Wildlife Management*, **63**, 621–629.

Lessa, E. P. & Farina, R. A. (1996). Reassessment of extinction patterns among the Late Pleistocene mammals of South America. *Paleontology*, **39**, 651–662.

Lindström, J. (1998). Harvesting and sex differences in demography. *Wildlife Biology*, **4**, 213–221.

MacArthur, R. H. (1960). On the relation between reproductive value and optimal predation. *Proceedings of the National Academy of Sciences, USA*, **46**, 143–145.

Markgren, G. (1974). The question of polygamy at an unbalanced sex ratio in the moose. In *The Behaviour of Ungulates and its Relation to Management*, ed. V. Geist & F. Walther, pp. 888–892. International Union for Conservation of Nature, Morges, Switzerland.

Matsuda, H., Mitani, I. & Asano, K. (1994). Impact factors of purse seine net and dip net fisheries on a chub mackerel population. *Research on Population Ecology*, **36**, 201–207.

May, R. (1976). *Theoretical Ecology. Principles and Applications*. Blackwell Press, London.

McKinney, M. L. (1997). Extinction vulnerability and selectivity: combining ecological and paleontological views. *Annual Review of Ecology and Systematics*, **28**, 495–516.

Mills, L. S., Doak, D. F. & Wisdom, M. J. (1999). Reliability of conservation actions based on elasticity analysis of matrix models. *Conservation Biology*, **13**, 815–829.

Murphy, L. F. & Smith, S. J. (1991). Maximum sustainable yield of a nonlinear population model with continuous age structure. *Mathematical Biosciences*, **104**, 259–270.

Murphy, E. C., Singer, F. J. & Nichols, L. (1990). Effects of hunting on survival and productivity of Dall sheep. *Journal of Wildlife Management*, **54**, 284–290.

Myers, R. A. & Mertz, G. (1998). The limits of exploitation: a precautionary approach. *Ecological Applications*, **8**, S165–S169.

Myers, R. A., Hutchings, J. A. & Barrowman, N. J. (1997). Why do fish stocks collapse? The example of cod in Atlantic Canada. *Ecological Applications*, **7**, 91–106.

Nault, A. & Gagnon, D. (1993). Ramet demography of *Allium tricoccum*, a spring ephemeral, perennial forest herb. *Journal of Ecology*, **81**, 101–119.

Nygrén, T. & Pesonen, M. (1993). The moose population (*Alces alces* L.) and methods of moose management in Finland, 1975–89. *Finnish Game Research*, **48**, 46–53.

Olmsted, I. & Alvarez-Buylla, E. R. (1995). Sustainable harvesting of tropical trees: demography and matrix models of two palm species in Mexico. *Ecological Applications*, **5**, 484–500.

Pauly, D. (1980). On the interrelationships between natural mortality, growth parameters and mean environmental temperature in 175 fish stocks. *Journal du Conseil, Conseil International pour l'Exploration de la Mer*, **39**, 175–192.

Ratsirarson, J., Silander, J. A. & Richard, A. F. (1996). Conservation and management of a threatened Madagascar palm species, *Neodypsis decaryi*, Jumelle. *Conservation Biology*, **10**, 40–52.

Reale, D., Bousses, P. & Chapuis, J. L. (1996). Female-biased mortality induced by male sexual harassment in a feral sheep population. *Canadian Journal of Zoology*, **74**, 1812–1818.

Reed, W. J. (1980). Optimal age-specific harvesting in a nonlinear population model. *Biometrics*, **36**, 579–593.

Ricker, W. E. (1975). Computation and interpretation of biological statistics of fish populations. *Fisheries Research Board of Canada Bulletin*, **191**.

Robinson, W. L. & Bolen, E. G. (1989). *Wildlife Ecology and Management*, 2nd edn. Macmillan, New York.

Roff, D. A. (1992). *The Evolution of Life Histories*. Chapman & Hall, London.

Rorres, C. & Fair, W. (1975). Optimal harvesting for an age-specific population. *Mathematical Biosciences*, **24**, 31–47.

Silvertown, J., Franco, M. & Menges, E. (1996). Interpretation of elasticity matrices as an aid to the management of plant populations for conservation. *Conservation Biology*, **10**, 591–597.

Stearns, S. C. (1992). *The Evolution of Life Histories.* Oxford University Press, Oxford.

Swenson, J. E., Sandegren, F., Söderberg, A., Bjärvall, A., Franzén, R. & Wabakken, P. (1997). Infanticide caused by hunting of male bears. *Nature*, **386**, 450–451.

Vlad, M. O. (1988). The optimal sex ratio for age-structured populations. *Mathematical Biosciences*, **93**, 181–190.

15

Phenotypic and genetic changes due to selective exploitation

RICHARD LAW

Exploitation of species in the wild has several effects. Most obviously and immediately, it reduces the abundance of the target species. Resource managers and conservationists have a common interest in maintaining exploited species at a level that does not place the species' survival in jeopardy. There is also concern about trickle-down effects to other components of the ecosystem (see Kaiser & Jennings, Chapter 16; Redford & Feinsinger, Chapter 17), and there may be a strong motivation to hold the abundance of exploited species below a level that damages these other components (Grigg & Pople, Chapter 18).

Less obvious effects of exploitation are changes in the genetic structure of species. These changes are of two sorts: directional and random. Directional genetic change is a consequence of selective exploitation – the tendency for some kinds of individual to be removed in preference to others. Bearing in mind the intense, relentless and often highly selective methods by which species are exploited in the wild, such genetic change is potentially important. The effects of selective exploitation on evolution of the harvested species are important both for the conservationist and for the resource manager. Is it sensible to change the genetic structure of exploited species, either deliberately or inadvertently? What kind of organism will be appropriate for exploitation in the future, once evolution caused by exploitation has taken place? Extinction is not the main conservation issue here – it is a concern about the genetic structure of the populations that survive exploitation (Ledig, 1992).

Effects of exploitation on random genetic change (genetic drift) are less clear cut. Genetic drift caused by random sampling of small gene pools leads to fluctuations in gene frequency and eventually to complete loss of genes. The consequences of loss of genetic variability are potentially serious in small populations, and erosion of genetic variability has become a major theme in conservation biology (Frankham, 1995). Small population size can also result in inbreeding, with the consequence that deleterious genes are expressed. However, most commercially exploited species, even when seriously depleted by exploitation, have effective population sizes above the level at which serious erosion of genetic variability takes place, and genetic drift and inbreeding are likely to be second-order processes in such cases. Exceptions to this are certain taxa such as the barndoor skate *Dipturus laevis* that have been driven to the verge of extinction (Casey & Myers, 1998), and taxa such as bighorn sheep *Ovis canadensis* that are still exploited despite small population sizes (Fitzsimmons *et al.*, 1995); in such cases genetic drift and inbreeding under exploitation are potentially important. Genetic drift would be of particular concern if exploitation were to lead to an effective population size (N_e) that is a small fraction of the actual population size (*N*) (Ryman *et al.*, 1981).

This chapter focuses on directional genetic change generated by exploitation. Specifically, this chapter addresses the following questions. How large are the selection differentials caused by exploitation? How much genetic variation is there for selection to operate on? What information can be gleaned from changes over time in trait values of exploited species? Do the changes matter from the points of view of resource managers and conservationists? If they do matter, what should the interested parties be doing about it?

SELECTION DIFFERENTIALS

Exploitation is inherently selective. Loggers remove trees of highest quality (Ledig, 1992). Trophy hunters prefer large moose with the best antler conformation (Teer, 1997; Solberg *et al.*, 2000), deer with high-quality antlers (Scribner *et al.*, 1984), and rams with large horns (Jorgensen *et al.*, 1993). Hunters of ivory stand to gain only from killing elephants with tusks (Jachmann *et al.*, 1995). Marine fisheries are most often exploited using size-selective fishing gear (Myers & Hoenig, 1997).

In spite of the apparent selectivity of exploitation, there has been little attempt to estimate the selection differentials that exploitation generates on harvested populations. This is surprising for two reasons. First, quantitative estimates of selection differentials are a prerequisite to any informed discussion of selection caused by exploitation. Secondly, the estimates ought to be relatively straightforward to obtain because the number and properties of individuals removed are often known quite precisely (though an estimate of population size is also needed). The little information that is available comes from commercially exploited fish stocks, as described below.

Selection on body size

Much effort in fisheries management goes into control of fishing gear to ensure that small (young) fish grow without being caught. This is because it is usually more profitable to leave the fish to grow larger and also because the chance that some individuals will survive to reproduction is increased. Such selectivity of fishing gear generates a selection differential on body size as cohorts (year classes) of fish grow.

Law & Rowell (1993) investigated the selection differentials on length-at-age of Atlantic cod *Gadus morhua* in the North Sea in the 1980s. The selection differential can be thought of as the difference between the mean length observed and the mean length the cohort would have had in the absence of fishing, all other things being equal. Estimation requires information on the length-at-age distribution of the stock, the length-at-age distribution of the catch, and the length-dependent fishing mortality rate. Detailed information on length-at-age was available only for the landed catch, and information about the stock had to be inferred from this (the calculations are given in Law & Rowell, 1993).

Law & Rowell (1993) estimated that one-year-old cod surviving fishing in the period July to September were about 0.25 cm smaller than they would have been in the absence of fishing. Although this selection differential may seem small, it refers to just three months of a longer period during which the cohort enters the fishery. In addition, there are strong phenotypic correlations between size at different ages (fish that are large for their age in one year also tend to be large the next year), so selection continues even when the trait is not expressed. Overall, the mean length of a cohort after entering the fishery is probably about 1 cm smaller than it would have been in the absence of fishing. Morover, this refers to only one cohort, yet directional selection continues cohort after cohort, as long as similar patterns of fishing are kept in place. (This is not to suggest that each cohort is 1 cm smaller than the cohort that came before, because the selection response depends on the generation time and also on the heritability of the trait as described below; but it does mean that the population is under continuing directional selection.)

Information is also available on the selection differential on length-at-age of cod in the Gulf of St Lawrence (Sinclair *et al.*, 1999). This geographical region is particularly interesting because exploitation became so intense that stocks collapsed, leading to closure of the fishery in 1992. The study by Sinclair and his colleagues was cohort based, and entailed sampling individuals in each cohort as the cohort grew older (ages four, five, six, . . . years), measuring the length each individual had at an earlier fixed age (three years). (Size at age 3 could be back-calculated from growth rings in the otolith.) In the absence of selection, the mean length at age 3 would not change as the cohort gets older. If larger individuals were more likely to die, the survivors would be those that had smaller length at age 3. They plotted length at age 3 as a function of the age of the individual at the time of sampling, estimated the regression equation, and used the gradient of the equation as a measure of selection.

Sinclair and his colleagues found that cohorts born between 1974 and 1984 had selection differentials of about −0.5 cm/year, a figure of the same order as that of the North Sea cod, above. Before 1974, there seems to have been a period in which the selection differentials were zero or positive. Whether the selection differentials were a response to fishing can be resolved by noting any change following closure of the fishery. The 1985 to 1987 cohorts, for which an estimate of the selection before and after closure is possible, show much reduced selection after closure of the fishery, implying that a substantial part of the selection was due to fishing. Subsequent cohorts also show little sign of selection, although the variability associated with these estimates is large.

Selection on life history traits

Life history traits – age- and size-dependent rates of reproduction and mortality (Kokko *et al.*, Chapter 14) – may also be under selection due to exploitation. Such selection might easily be overlooked, because the traits are not themselves the direct target of selection (whether an individual becomes sexually mature at age 3 or at age 4 is not of immediate interest to a fisher). However, the pattern of mortality imposed by exploitation changes the benefit to an individual (in terms of the contribution it makes to future generations) of reproduction and survival at different ages (Law, 1979) and generates selection, as described below.

Consider a life history defined by the schedule of age-specific rates of reproduction b_i and survival l_i, the population being censused each year immediately after reproduction. Here b_i is the mean number of daughters per female aged i, l_i is the proportion of females surviving natural mortality from a reference point soon after birth to age i. (The reason for not measuring mortality from birth itself is to permit 'nursery' competition among newborn individuals before reaching this point; it is assumed that such density dependence leads to a stable equilibrium population size.) Write the proportion of females that escape being caught between age i and $i+1$ as θ_i. The expected lifetime's production of daughters, R_o, is then

Table 15.1. Expected lifetime's production of daughters per female (R_0) for two simple life histories, A and B, calculated under contrasting patterns of exploitation

	Age i			
	1	2	3	4
Life history A				
l_i	0.667	0.167	0.083	0.042
b_i	0	4	8	16
Life history B				
l_i	0.667	0.167	0.083	0.042
b_i	0	0	16	16

	Survival under exploitation					
	θ_0	θ_1	θ_2	θ_3	$R_0(A)$	$R_0(B)$
No exploitation	1	1	1	1	2	2
Exploitation at age 3	1	1	1	0.8	1.87	1.87
Exploitation at ages 2 and 3	1	1	0.8	0.8	1.63	1.49
Exploitation at ages 1, 2 and 3	1	0.8	0.8	0.8	1.30	1.20

l, survival rate; b, reproductive rate.

$$R_0 = \sum_{i=1}^{k} \left(\prod_{j=0}^{i-1} \theta_j \right) l_i b_i, \tag{15.1}$$

where k is the maximum age. In words, the expected lifetime's production of daughters is the sum over all ages of the production of offspring at each age, after allowing for natural mortality and mortality caused by exploitation. Under such density dependence, R_0 gives a direct measure of fitness, and a mutant life history $\{l_i', b_i'\}$ will invade the resident life history only if the corresponding $R_0' > R_0$ (Law & Grey, 1989). Table 15.1 gives a numerical example of two life histories chosen such that they would have exactly the same $R_0 = 2$ in the absence of exploitation, but having different distributions of reproduction over age. When exploitation at ages 1 or 2 is introduced, the delayed maturation in B becomes disadvantageous, i.e., $R_0(B) < R_0(A)$, because such a delay makes it more likely that an individual is culled before it reproduces.

The life history of the North Sea cod illustrates the strong selection on age at maturation that exploitation can introduce (Rowell, 1993). Rowell constructed a model for age-specific reproduction of cod maturing at different ages using (1) the von Bertalanffy growth equation with a well-established relationship between body weight and egg production, and (2) a

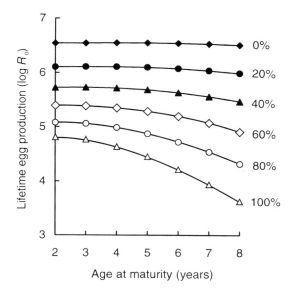

Figure 15.1. Expected lifetime's production of eggs of North Sea cod for individuals maturing at different ages. The lines refer to contrasting levels of fishing mortality from 0% to 100% of the values that applied in the 1980s. (From Law, 2000; recalculated and redrawn from Rowell, 1992, with permission from the *ICES Journal of Marine Science*.)

trade-off arising from transfer of resources from growth to reproduction. Combining reproduction with age-specific natural and fishing mortalities (both assumed to be independent of age at maturation), the expected lifetime's production of eggs R_0 of a female maturing at each age could be determined.

Figure 15.1 shows the effect of fishing mortality on the lifetime's reproductive success of cod maturing at different ages. To demonstrate the effect of fishing mortality, the age-specific fishing mortality rates that applied in the 1980s have been weighted by the factors 0, 20%, . . . , 100%. The top line gives R_0 in the absence of any fishing mortality. In the absence of fishing there is rather little advantage of one age of maturation over another because the gain in reproduction due to early maturation is countered by the smaller body size subsequently, and the resulting loss in later reproduction. But, as fishing mortality is increased to the level that applied in the 1980s (lines lower down the figure), it can be seen that late maturation becomes highly disadvantageous. Note the logarithmic scale of R_0: R_0 for a cod maturing at age 8 is an order of magnitude less than that of a cod maturing at age 2 under the level of fishing mortality that prevailed in the

1980s. In other words, such a delay in maturation is strongly disadvantageous when there is a high probability of being caught.

These examples illustrate a much more general phenomenon. When an exploiter removes individuals with one trait value in preference to another, a selection differential is generated. This applies just as much to trophy hunters choosing deer with large antlers, ivory hunters choosing elephants with tusks, and harvesters choosing fruits from high yielding plants as it does to size-selective fisheries. At present, however, the strength of selection is generally unknown.

GENETIC VARIATION

For exploitation to bring about directional genetic change there must be genetic variation in the traits under selection, and this genetic variation must be of a kind that can lead to a change in the mean value of the traits when exploitation takes place.

The morphological and life history traits under selection are most often continuous traits affected by genes at many loci. In other words, the traits are quantitative, and can be analysed within the framework of quantitative genetics (Falconer & Mackay, 1996). The selection response R (how much the mean trait value changes from one generation to the next) is proportional to the selection differential S:

$$R = h^2 S, \tag{15.2}$$

where the constant of proportionality h^2 is the heritability. The heritability depends on the genetic architecture of the trait, the contribution to the trait value made by the additive effects of genes, the non-additive effects of genes and the environment. In short, the heritability is the ratio of the additive genetic variance to the total phenotypic variance in a population of individuals. Equation 15.2 shows that the heritability is an important indicator of the tendency to change under directional selection due to exploitation: a trait with a heritability close to zero changes very slowly even if the selection differential is large, whereas a trait with a heritability close to unity can change rapidly.

In a review of more than 1000 estimates of heritability in wild, outbred species, Mousseau & Roff (1987) found a mean heritability of morphological traits of 0.46 and of life-history traits of 0.26. The lower heritability of life history traits is expected from the fact that genetic variation is eroded faster from traits the more closely associated they are with fitness. But a heritability of 0.26 is large enough to bring about observable genetic change on a decadal time scale, given the levels of selection that apply at least in fisheries.

For fish, much is known about heritabilities of production-related traits, as a consequence of domestication of species, particularly salmonids, for the aquaculture industry. The picture that emerges from these studies is in keeping with that of Mousseau & Roff (1987), with mean heritabilities 0.24 for body weight (28 studies), 0.30 for body length (17 studies), and 0.31 for age at maturity (8 studies) (Law, 2000). Reproductive output is typically proportional to body size in fish, and body size is therefore closely related to fitness.

Under the more variable conditions in wild populations, heritabilities might be expected to be smaller than in controlled experiments. Surprisingly, where it has been possible to obtain estimates of heritability both in the wild and under laboratory conditions, the heritabilities have turned out to be quite similar (Weigensberg & Roff, 1996). For instance, Jónasson *et al.* (1997) estimated heritability of the body weight of Atlantic salmon *Salmo salar* after one winter at sea by tagging parr of known parents, releasing the parr and recapturing the survivors on their return; the heritability obtained, 0.36 (standard error 0.11), is similar to that estimated in a farming environment.

With the exception of fish, information on heritabilities of traits selected by exploitation is scarce. However, it is likely that antler conformation in deer has a heritable component, and probably other traits of deer such as growth rate and maturation as well. For instance, Andrew de Nahlik (personal communication) observed the antlers in a herd of red deer *Cervus elaphus* in an English deer park, after the introduction of a stag and three hinds of an unrelated strain from another park. The structure and colour of the antlers of the introduced stag were different from those of the residents. Antlers of some stags born in the following years were recognisably different in shape, size and colour from those of typical residents, and showed some similarity to the antlers of the introduced stag.

It is sometimes argued that the great increase in antler size of deer that can be achieved from generation to generation by improved nutrition (Geist, 1986) indicates that any genetic component of variation in antler conformation would be swamped by environmental variation. However, in estimating the heritability, the additive genetic variance needs to be set against the environmental variance that applies to the population in its natural setting, not against the much greater environmental variance that could be achieved by placing the deer in a wide range of different nutritional environments. In fact, exaggerated sexual traits often have greater additive genetic variation than comparable non-sexually selected ones, not-withstanding the history of directional sexual selection that gives rise to them (Pomiankowski & Møller, 1995). In view of the increasing interest in deer breeding, information on the genetics of antlers is likely to become available in the near future.

Wood volume in certain tree species has demonstrably a substantial additive genetic component. This is known from the rapid response to selection for wood volume sometimes observed during domestication (Ledig, 1992). For example, Eldridge (1982) obtained increases in wood volume of 5%, 25% and 29% in three trials after a single generation of selection on *Pinus radiata*. Such observations imply the existence of substan-tial additive genetic variation for wood volume in the unselected population. If, therefore, individuals with high wood volume at a given age were re-moved, a change to the reverse direction in the population would be expected.

The genetic architecture of quantitative traits affects the response to selection. Antler size in white-tailed deer *Odocoileus virginianus* is greater in individuals that are heterozygous at more protein loci (Scribner *et al.*, 1989), and a similar result has been found for horn size in bighorn sheep (Fitzsimmons *et al.*, 1995). If the marker loci reflect the genetic architecture of these ornaments, the non-additive components of genetic variance of the ornaments are large, and the heritability is correspondingly small. Prefer-ential removal of individuals with larger ornaments would then have rela-tively little effect on the mean trait values.

The message from quantitative genetics is that the morphological and life history traits under selection from exploitation are likely to have non-negligible additive genetic variance. This general message must be quali-fied by an awareness that each trait in each exploited population has its own particular genetic architecture that will affect the response to selection.

PHENOTYPIC CHANGE UNDER EXPLOITATION

The information above points to strong selection caused by exploitation acting on traits of individuals, and to an additive genetic component of variation in the traits. Given these ingredients for evolutionary change, it is of interest to examine exploited species to see what, if any, evidence there is of phenotypic change associated with exploitation.

Elephants
In the African elephant *Loxodonta africana* females as well as males often (but not always) have tusks. Observations by Jachmann *et al.* (1995) on

groups of elephants in the wild suggest that crosses between tusked males and tuskless females give rise to tusked sons and tuskless daughters; there is evidently a genetic basis for the presence and absence of tusks in females that is in part sex linked. One might expect a gene for tusklessness to be advantageous under conditions in which tusks are exploited for ivory. Jachmann *et al.* (1995) showed an increase in the frequency of tuskless females in the central Luangwa Valley in Zambia from about 10% in 1969 to as high as 38% towards the end of the 1980s. Over this period, aerial surveys recorded substantial numbers of dead elephants on the ground. Interestingly, following the introduction of more effective law enforcement in 1988, the number of dead elephants was greatly reduced, and there has been a corresponding decline in the frequency of tusklessness since then. The immediate change in frequency of tusklessness was presumably at least in part a demographic consequence of the greater proportion of tusked females surviving within cohorts; it takes some time for the frequency of genes causing tusks to build up in new cohorts.

There is also substantial variation in tusklessness in the Asian elephant *Elephas maximus* (Kurt *et al.*, 1995). In this species females are always tuskless, and males are usually tusked. In some remoter areas, such as northeastern India, an increase in the frequency of tuskless males is associated with poaching for ivory and meat, as in the African elephant above. Elsewhere hunting and capturing (for work in forest camps, and for ceremonial purposes) has a long history of careful management. Yet, in Sri Lanka, the frequency of tuskless males is high relative to other areas. Kurt *et al.* (1995) argued that this is a consequence of continual restocking of a large captive population of tusked males from the relatively small wild population that exists in Sri Lanka.

Cervids

Exceptionally large antlers of red deer have been preserved for many centuries, and it is evident that the largest antlers of contemporary red deer in the wild or in deer parks are small relative to those in the records (Geist, 1986). As noted above, such changes are thought to be due to nutrition. But these changes are also consistent with an evolutionary response to selection. In the absence of information on nutrition at earlier times, we cannot distinguish between these alternatives, or indeed the likely possibility that both environmental and genetic change have played a part.

More informative are observations by Andrew de Nahlik (personal communication) of a significant improvement in antler quality (length and thickness) in roe deer *Capreolus capreolus* that colonised part of central

Hampshire in England in the late 1940s and early 1950s. Roe deer were unknown there previously, and they colonised an area of several thousand hectares without human intervention. The population grew to an estimated size in the region of 150 to 200 individuals, and had to be reduced. Heavy selective culling was introduced in the late 1960s, and the population settled at a maximum of about 100 individuals. The environment for feeding was good and changed little, though there was less food available when the herd was large. The initial colonists had rather poor antlers, and, in the course of culling, strong directional selection was applied, favouring bucks with the best antlers (unlike most deer culling, no high quality bucks were removed at all). Andrew de Nahlik interpreted the improvement as an outcome of selective culling, although pointing out the possibility of later colonisation by higher quality animals.

Solberg & Sæther (1994) observed a trend towards declining body mass in moose *Alces alces* over a 23 year period, correlated with increasing population density and a decreasing proportion of males (there is selective hunting for males in some populations). More recently, Solberg *et al.* (2000) showed that culling mortality in males increased with age; females were culled mostly when young or old. The authors note that such hunting generates a selective advantage for smaller individuals, although at present it is not possible to disentangle the effect genetic change has on the time series of body mass from direct effects of population density and sex ratio.

Fish

Commercial fish stocks, as globally important sources of protein, are often carefully monitored for changes in production-related traits, such as body growth and sexual maturation. Striking phenotypic changes have been observed, as reviewed by Trippel (1995) and Law (2000). For example, most of the gadoid stocks in the northwest Atlantic have been undergoing reductions in length and age at maturation through the 1980s and 1990s (Trippel *et al.*, 1997). Age at maturation in northeast Arctic cod has been decreasing since the 1940s (Jørgensen, 1990). Age and length at maturation are decreasing in Baltic Sea cod (Cardinale & Modin, 1999). Age and length at maturation in North Sea plaice *Pleuronectes platessa* have decreased substantially since the beginning of the twentieth century (Rijnsdorp, 1993). Weight of Pacific salmon species on return from the marine environment has been declining (Ricker, 1981; McAllister *et al.*, 1992); Figure 15.2 shows the change that has occurred in one area of British Columbia, Canada. Weight of Atlantic salmon caught after two sea years declined over a 120 year period in a Canadian river in Quebec (Bielak &

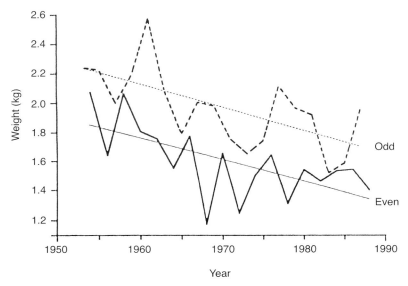

Figure 15.2. Time series of mean adult body weight of pink salmon *Oncorhynchus gorbuscha*. This species has a two-year life cycle, so there are two separate populations, one spawning in even years (solid lines) and the other in odd years (dashed lines). (From McAllister *et al.*, 1992, reprinted with permission of NRC Press.)

Power, 1986). Weight at age of North Sea sole *Solea solea* increased when heavy beam trawlers were brought into use in the 1960s (de Veen, 1976).

Although there is no doubt about the existence of large directional phenotypic changes in exploited fish stocks, there is some debate as to the part played by genetic and non-genetic factors. First, exploitation, because it reduces abundance, increases the availability of food for surviving fish; this itself can have a direct effect on individual growth and maturation. Such density dependence has been suggested as the cause of decreased age at maturation in Northeast Arctic and Baltic Sea cod (Jørgensen, 1990; Cardinale & Modin, 1999). Secondly, exploitation can have a direct effect on the environment. For example, the introduction of heavy beam trawlers in the North Sea led to greater disturbance of the sea bed; de Veen (1976) suggested that this made more food available for sole, and led to an increase in growth. Thirdly, gradual changes in the physical environment, quite apart from those caused by exploitation, could bring about phenotypic change. For example, the temperature of the North Sea increased by a small amount during the twentieth century, and this could account for some of the change in age and size of maturation of the North Sea plaice (Rijnsdorp, 1993).

These possible determinants of phenotypic change notwithstanding, a reduction in length and age at maturation is also consistent with genetic change caused by selective exploitation. The problem we face is how to establish the relative contribution of genetic and non-genetic causes of change. The only attempt to do this has been by Rijnsdorp (1993). He found that a substantial part of the change in maturation of the North Sea plaice still remained unexplained after allowing for density-dependent effects and changes in water temperature; this remaining component was consistent with genetic change caused by selective fishing.

CONSEQUENCES FOR MANAGEMENT AND CONSERVATION

The consequences of directional genetic change driven by exploitation are profound for both resource managers and conservationists for at least three reasons. First, phenotypic evolution can mean that the resource becomes more or less valuable as time progresses. Consider, for example, the major decline in body weight of pink salmon *Oncorhynchus gorbuscha* returning to rivers on the west coast of Canada illustrated in Figure 15.2 (McAllister *et al.*, 1992), a change which has been interpreted as a genetic response to selective fishing (Ricker, 1981). Such a reduction in body weight is of concern to fishery managers, because, all other things being equal, it leads to a major loss in value of the resource.

Secondly, genetic change is not readily reversed. Exploited species will not necessarily bounce back to some earlier phenotypic state simply by altering the environmental conditions. This needs emphasis given the increasing adoption of a precautionary approach to management with the intention of avoiding irreversible change in exploited species (FAO, 1995). Still more problematic, selection pressures generated by exploitation may not themselves be easily reversed. This problem can be seen in Figure 15.1; the current pattern of harvesting of North Sea cod generates a strong selective advantage for fish with early maturation, but complete cessation of fishing simply makes selection on age at maturation rather weak. Directional genetic change caused by exploitation is not easily undone.

Thirdly, how does genetic change impact on ecosystems in which exploited species live? Although there are serious problems in understanding the linking of species in complex food webs and the effects these links have on dynamics, predator and prey body size are critical determinants of food web links (Cohen *et al.*, 1993; Kaiser & Jennings, Chapter 16). As the body sizes of exploited species change, what impacts does this change have elsewhere on the ecosystem? For instance, cod, a major component of the

North Sea ecosystem, are now maturing at lengths as small as 15 cm, in contrast to smallest lengths of 58 cm at the end of the nineteenth century (Rowell, 1993). Quite apart from the demographic change in size structure caused by fishing, cod may complete their lives at much smaller sizes than in earlier times. The consequences of such changes are not known, but might be significant in conservation of the North Sea ecosystem.

MANAGEMENT OF SELECTIVE EXPLOITATION

What patterns of exploitation would it be sensible for resource managers and conservationists to employ, given the tendency of exploitation to be selective? Evolutionary goals are less straightforward to specify than ecological goals of maintaining yields while keeping the risk of extinction small. Below, two possible goals are suggested: to make selection as small as possible, and to use selection to enhance qualities desirable for management and conservation.

Minimising directional selection

Theory gives the following three results. First, for a trait expressed at some point in life and neutral with respect to reproduction and survival, there is no selection if individuals are culled at random with respect to trait value. Secondly, for an age-dependent life history trait in a population increasing exponentially, there is no selection if individuals at all ages are culled to the same degree (Law, 1979). The reason for this is that the reduction in the contribution of older individuals to production of offspring when culled in this way is exactly balanced by the reduction in growth of the population. Thirdly, for an age-dependent life history trait in a population with density-dependent competition among newborn individuals (leading to a stable equilibrium point), there is no selection if individuals are culled when younger than the earliest age at which can reproduction occur.

The selectively neutral harvest on life history traits in a density-regulated population is illustrated in Figure 15.3a and b using the model of North Sea cod introduced above (see Selection differentials) (Rowell, 1993). Exploitation confined to one-year-olds has no effect on the relative advantage of females maturing at age two to eight years: comparing the continuous lines in Figure 15.3a and b, it can be seen that the harvest reduces all the R_0 values by the same proportion. On the other hand, exploitation at subsequent ages gives an advantage to females maturing at ages up to the harvested age over females maturing after the harvested age.

A variation on this theme is to cull individuals with the lowest reproduc-

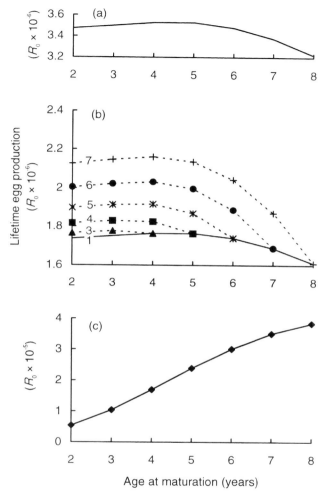

Figure 15.3. Contrasting patterns of harvesting applied to the North Sea cod, showing how the expected lifetime's production of eggs R_o by females maturing at different ages is affected by harvesting. (a) No harvesting. (b) Exploitation of one age class only. (Numbers refer to age of exploited age-class in years.) (c) Exploitation of females only after reaching sexual maturity.

tive value (see Kokko et al., Chapter 14). For instance, if it were possible to harvest individuals after the end of reproductive life, this ought to have no effect on the trait in future generations. Exploitation of individuals with low reproductive value has special interest because these individuals also have little effect on self-renewal of populations. Harvesting to minimise the loss in self-renewal is closely related to harvesting to maximise the yield (MacArthur, 1960; Law & Grey, 1988).

Minimising directional selection is easier said than done. Exploitation typically leads to selection on several traits simultaneously, and the traits themselves are unlikely to be independent; this makes non-selective exploitation regimes hard to specify. There is also a practical problem of how to put in place a pattern of exploitation that is non-selective, and at the same time compatible with other goals, such as minimising the risk of extinction. For instance, the reproductive value of young individuals well before sexual maturation might be relatively low, making such individuals appropriate for harvesting; on the other hand, if harvesting is too intense, the existence of the whole population would be put in jeopardy. One may have to accept that exploitation is going to be selective, and consider the kinds of selection appropriate for the goals of management and conservation.

Selection to enhance quality

A common goal of management is to keep populations at a level that habitats can sustain, and to maintain healthy populations. For instance, in Europe there is a strong culture of selective culling in deer management to maintain high-quality males (A. de Nahlik, personal communication), although the effectiveness of selection is debated in some quarters. de Nahlik (1992) made specific recommendations for selective culling of deer to improve quality of populations, including removal of sick individuals, individuals below the local 'quality' standard, males with malformed heads, excess females and females that are regularly barren. In recognition of the needs of trophy hunting of deer, which is of significant economic importance, he also suggested removing trophy males once they reach old age and have low reproductive potential. He also noted that such culling should be done in a way that maintains an appropriate age structure and approximate parity of sex ratio (Kokko et al., Chapter 14). Scribner et al. (1984) also considered the role that selective culling could have in reducing the frequency of inferior spike bucks in white-tailed deer.

Sometimes the goal of quality enhancement is not so obvious. A case in point is the Northeast Arctic cod (Law & Grey, 1989). This stock supports two fisheries, one on the spawning grounds along the Norwegian coast that has operated for at least 1000 years, and the other on the feeding grounds in the Barents Sea that began in the first half of the twentieth century. The spatial separation of the spawning and feeding grounds has the effect that fishing generates quite different selection pressures in the two areas. Fishing on the spawning grounds gives a small selective advantage for delayed maturation, because late-maturing females are larger and have greater egg production when they eventually visit the spawning grounds and have to run the gauntlet of the fishery there. Fishing on the feeding grounds causes a large selective advantage for early maturation, because late maturing individuals are likely to be caught before they reproduce at all. It is interesting that age at maturation has been decreasing since the fishery in the Barents Sea was opened (Jørgensen, 1990), although the cause of this change is debated.

In principle, fishing mortality on the Northeast Arctic cod in the Barents Sea and along the Norwegian coast could be controlled to select for early or late maturation. Because somatic growth and reproduction are in competition for the same resource, this translates to selection for small or large size-at-age. One could therefore select either for smaller earlier-reproducing fish or for larger late reproducers. Which is better, or does it matter at all? Calculations of the yield after evolution under different regimes of fishing suggest that the yield would be much larger if fishing were confined to the spawning grounds (Law & Grey, 1989; Heino, 1998). Thus, from the perspective of resource management, it appears that the productivity of the stock could be improved by fishing just on the spawning grounds. On the other hand, there would clearly be social and political considerations to take into account due to the seasonality of the spawner fishery and its geographical location (Heino, 1998).

It is notable that the conventional wisdom as to how species should be exploited in the wild does not apply when evolution is taken into account. Consider, for example, the North Sea cod: as noted above, even the selectively neutral harvest requires targeting the youngest individuals. If one wished to reverse selection for early maturation in the North Sea cod, exploitation of spawning aggregations appears to be required, as in the case of the Northeast Arctic cod (Figure 15.3c). In a sense it is not surprising that such a fundamental change is needed to undo the effects of current selective exploitation. But there is clearly a tension between what is desirable over a short (ecological) and a longer (evolutionary) time period, and great care would be needed not to place the short-term survival of the population in jeopardy when one is implementing exploitation to reverse current patterns of selection.

CONCLUSIONS

The purpose of this chapter has been to raise awareness of the inherent selectivity of exploitation, and the consequences of this selection. While some theory is in place, the information available is fragmentary, and a firmer empirical foundation is badly needed. None the less, where it has been possible to estimate selection caused by exploitation, the selection differentials have proved to be substantial. In addition, the limited information available on genetic variation indicates that heritabilities of traits likely to be under selection, while not large, are not negligible. It is therefore not surprising that phenotypic change is being observed in exploited species, although a genetic basis for such change has yet to be unequivocally demonstrated.

Resource managers and conservationists need to be conscious of phenotypic evolution caused by exploitation, in addition to more obvious matters of maintaining yields and minimising extinction risks. The nature of exploited organisms may be changing simply as a result of the exploitation. At the moment we are usually blind to directional genetic change that results from exploitation.

ACKNOWLEDGEMENTS

I thank the editors of the volume for an introduction to the literature on selective culling of terrestrial mammals, A. J. de Nahlik for information on selective culling of deer, and E. J. Solberg and B.-E. Sæther for information on culling moose.

REFERENCES

Bielak, A. T. & Power, G. (1986). Changes in mean weight, sea-age composition, and catch-per-unit-effort of Atlantic salmon (*Salmo salar*) angled in the Godbout River, Quebec, 1859–1983. *Canadian Journal of Fisheries and Aquatic Sciences*, **43**, 281–287.

Cardinale, M. & Modin, J. (1999). Changes in size-at-maturity of Baltic cod (*Gadus morhua*) during a period of large variations in stock size and environmental conditions. *Fisheries Research*, **41**, 285–295.

Casey, J. M. & Myers, R. A. (1998). Near extinction of a large, widely distributed fish. *Science*, **281**, 690–692.

Cohen, J. E., Pimm, S. L., Yodzis, P. & Saldaña, J. (1993). Body sizes of animal predators and animal prey in food webs. *Journal of Animal Ecology*, **62**, 67–78.

de Nahlik, A. J. (1992). *Management of Deer and Their Habitat: Principles and Methods*. Wilson Hunt, Gillingham.

de Veen, J. F. (1976). On changes in some biological parameters in the North Sea sole (*Solea solea* L.). *Journal du Conseil, Conseil International pour l'Exploration de la Mer*, **37**, 60–90.

Eldridge, K. G. (1982). Genetic improvements from a radiata pine seed orchard. *New Zealand Journal of Forestry Science*, **12**, 404–411.

Falconer, D. S. & Mackay, T. F. C. (1996). *Introduction to Quantitative Genetics*, 4th edn. Longman, Harlow.

FAO (Food and Agriculture Organization) (1995). Guidelines on the precautionary approach to capture fisheries and species introductions. FAO Fisheries Technical Paper no. 350, Part 1.

Fitzsimmons, N. N., Buskirk, S. W. & Smith, M. H. (1995). Population history, genetic variability, and horn growth in bighorn sheep. *Conservation Biology*, **9**, 314–323.

Frankham, R. (1995). Conservation genetics. *Annual Review of Genetics*, **29**, 305–327.

Geist, V. (1986). Super antlers and pre-World War II European research. *Wildlife Society Bulletin*, **14**, 91–94.

Heino, M. (1998). Management of evolving fish stocks. *Canadian Journal of Fisheries and Aquatic Sciences*, **55**, 1971–1982.

Jachmann, H., Berry, P. S. M. & Imae, H. (1995). Tusklessness in African elephants: a future trend. *African Journal of Ecology*, **33**, 230–235.

Jónasson, J., Gjerde, B. & Gjedrem, T. (1997). Genetic parameters for return rate and body weight of sea-ranched Atlantic salmon. *Aquaculture*, **154**, 219–231.

Jorgensen, J. T. Festa-Bianchet, M. & Wishart, W. D. (1993). Harvesting bighorn ewes: consequences for population size and trophy ram production. *Journal of Wildlife Management*, **57**, 429–435.

Jørgensen, T. (1990). Long-term changes in age at sexual maturity of Northeast Arctic cod (*Gadus morhua* L.). *Journal du Conseil, Conseil International pour l'Exploration de la Mer*, **46**, 235–248.

Kurt, F., Hartl, G. B. & Tiedemann, R. (1995). Tuskless bulls in Asian elephant *Elephas maximus*. History and population genetics of a man-made phenomenon. *Acta Theriologica Supplement*, **3**, 125–143.

Law, R. (1979). Optimal life histories under age-specific predation. *American Naturalist*, **114**, 399–417.

Law, R. (2000). Fishing, selection and phenotypic evolution. *ICES Journal of Marine Science*, **57**, 659–668.

Law, R. & Grey, D. R. (1988). Maximum sustainable yields and the self-renewal of exploited populations with age-dependent vital rates. In *Size-Structured Populations*, ed. B. Ebenman & L. Persson, pp. 140–154. Springer-Verlag, Berlin.

Law, R. & Grey, D. R. (1989). Evolution of yields from populations with age-specific cropping. *Evolutionary Ecology*, **3**, 343–359.

Law, R. & Rowell, C. A. (1993). Cohort-structured populations, selection responses, and exploitation of the North Sea cod. In *The Exploitation of Evolving Resources*, ed. T. K. Stokes, J. M. McGlade & R. Law, pp. 155–173. Lecture Notes in Biomathematics no. 99. Springer-Verlag, Berlin.

Ledig, F. T. (1992). Human impacts on genetic diversity in forest ecosystems. *Oikos*, **63**, 87–108.

MacArthur, R. H. (1960). On the relation between reproductive value and optimal predation. *Proceedings of the National Academy of Sciences, USA*, **46**, 143–145.

McAllister, M. K., Peterman, R. M. & Gillis, D. M. (1992). Statistical evaluation of a large-scale fishing experiment designed to test for a genetic effect of size-selective fishing on British Columbia pink salmon (*Oncorhynchus gorbuscha*). *Canadian Journal of Fisheries and Aquatic Sciences*, **49**, 1294–1304.

Mousseau, T. A. & Roff, D. A. (1987). Natural selection and the heritability of fitness components. *Heredity*, **59**, 181–197.

Myers, R. A. & Hoenig, J. M. (1997). Direct estimates of gear selectivity from multiple tagging experiments. *Canadian Journal of Fisheries and Aquatic Sciences*, **54**, 1–9.

Pomiankowski, A. & Møller, A. P. (1995). A resolution of the lek paradox. *Proceedings of the Royal Society of London B*, **260**, 21–29.

Ricker, W. E. (1981). Changes in the average size and average age of Pacific salmon. *Canadian Journal of Fisheries and Aquatic Sciences*, **38**, 1636–1656.

Rijnsdorp, A. D. (1993). Fisheries as a large-scale experiment on life-history evolution: disentangling phenotypic and genetic effects in changes in maturation and reproduction of North Sea plaice, *Pleuronectes platessa* L. *Oecologia*, **96**, 391–401.

Rowell, C. A. (1992). Selection differentials imposed by fishing activity on the North Sea cod (*Gadus morhua* L.). D Phil thesis, University of York.

Rowell, C. A. (1993). The effects of fishing on the timing of maturity in North Sea cod (*Gadus morhua* L.). In *The Exploitation of Evolving Resources*, ed. T. K. Stokes, J. M. McGlade & R. Law, pp. 44–61. Lecture Notes in Biomathematics no. 99. Springer-Verlag, Berlin.

Ryman, N., Baccus, R., Reuterwall, C. & Smith, M. H. (1981). Effective population size, generation interval, and potential loss of genetic variability in game species under different hunting regimes. *Oikos*, **36**, 257–266.

Scribner, K. T., Smith, M. H. & Johns, P. E. (1984). Age, condition, and genetic effects on incidence of spike bucks. *Proceedings of the Annual Conference of the Southeastern Association of Fish and Wildlife Agencies*, **38**, 23–32.

Scribner, K. T., Smith, M. H. & Johns, P. E. (1989). Environmental and genetic components of antler growth in white-tailed deer. *Journal of Mammalogy*, **70**, 284–291.

Sinclair, A. F., Hanson, J. M., Swain, D. P. & Currie, L. (1999). Size selective mortality of cod in the southern Gulf of St Lawrence. *Canadian Stock Assessment Proceedings*, series 99/05, pp. 43–48. Fisheries and Oceans, Ottawa.

Solberg, E. J. & Sæther, B.-E. (1994). Male traits as life-history variables: annual variation in body mass and antler size in moose (*Alces alces*). *Journal of Mammalogy*, **75**, 1069–1079.

Solberg, E. J., Loison, A., Sæther, B.-E. & Strand, O. (2000). Age-specific harvest mortality in a Norwegian moose *Alces alces* population. *Wildlife Biology*, **6**, 41–52.

Teer, J. G. (1997). Management of ungulates and the conservation of biodiversity. In *Harvesting Wild Species: Implications for Biodiversity Conservation*, ed. C. H. Freese, pp. 424–464. Johns Hopkins University Press, Baltimore, MD.

Trippel, E. A. (1995). Age at maturity as a stress indicator in fisheries. *BioScience*, **45**, 759–771.

Trippel, E. A., Morgan, M. J., Fréchet, A., Rollet, C., Sinclair, A., Annand, C., Beanlands, D. & Brown, L. (1997). Changes in age and length at sexual maturity of Northwest Atlantic cod, haddock and pollock stocks, 1972–1995. *Canadian Technical Report of Fisheries and Aquatic Sciences* no. 2157.

Weigensberg, I. & Roff, D. A. (1996). Natural heritabilities: can they be reliably estimated in the laboratory? *Evolution*, **50**, 2149–2157.

16

An ecosystem perspective on conserving targeted and non-targeted species

MICHEL J. KAISER & SIMON JENNINGS

Human harvesting activities might be considered as the largest on-going manipulative ecological experiment ever conducted. Left uncontrolled, human harvesting has often led to drastic changes in landscape, species composition and population structure. This is not a recent phenomenon as paleoecological studies provide strong evidence that extinctions of large animals on land were closely associated with human migrations into new areas (Alroy, 1999).

Humans are capable of being highly selective in their choice of species to harvest and often are not constrained by the usual energetic restrictions that apply to the individual foraging of most other animals. Most predatory animals evaluate their prey in terms of the potential energetic reward offset against the risks involved in acquiring that energy (Hughes, 1993). This principal is still applicable to those humans who are subsistence foragers (Winterhalder, 1981; Hill & Hawkes, 1983). Humans have evolved different currencies for attributing value to prey species other than their intrinsic energetic value. As hunting capabilities have exceeded mere subsistence needs, prey species have become a tradable commodity. For example, subsistence hunting is crucial to the livelihoods of the native peoples who live in the forests of Amazonia (Redford & Robinson, 1987). However, the growing human population and improvements in hunting technology (i.e. the introduction of shotguns, cf. bows and arrows) and the market demands for bush meat have increased the value of these species beyond their mere energetic content. The introduction of shotguns has improved success rate during hunting despite dwindling populations of target species. Thus improved technology has maintained success rate despite a reduction in the number of encounters per hour hunting. As a result many Neotropical prey species are being hunted to extinction (see e.g. Bodmer *et al.*, 1997). While habitat destruction is currently the greatest overall threat to rain forest wildlife, hunting is the greatest threat to terrestrial tropical biodiversity in those areas in which the forests remain intact (Redford, 1992).

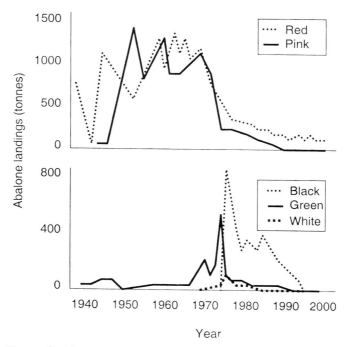

Figure 16.1. The expansion and contraction of the Californian abalone fishery portrayed in terms of annual landings, showing the successional exploitation of each of the abalone species (see also Petersen & Levitan, Chapter 13). The species were sequentially removed such that the largest and most abundant species were exploited first. (Adapted from Murray *et al.*, 1999.)

For some prey, the inverse relationship between financial value and prey availability means that it is profitable for humans to invest enough effort to harvest certain species to close to extinction. A marine example is that of the white abalone *Haliotis sorenseni* that was harvested by divers in the shallow inshore waters of California. The demand for, and high cash value of, the abalone promoted more and more fishing effort to eke out dwindling stocks until they inevitably crashed in the early 1970s (Davis *et al.*, 1996; Figure 16.1). Prey species would be depleted rarely to the same extent if they were harvested only on the basis of their energetic content.

The gradual decline in populations of target species is the most obvious response to human harvesting activity. However, harvesting activities affect far more than just the target species (Pace *et al.*, 1999). All species fulfil a functional role within the ecosystem of which they are a component (they may be predators, prey, scavengers, competitors, form habitat structures and maintain patchiness and habitat heterogeneity). The consequences of harvesting a particular species will depend on its role and dominance within that ecosystem. Hence, harvesting a top predator might relieve predation on its prey species while harvesting prey species will increase predation pressure on alternative prey types. However, the relation between trophic position and harvest potential is never so deterministic. Yodzis (1998) described the arguments usually put forward for marine mammal culling in the Benguela ecosystem off the coast of southern Africa: 'We harvest the target species; marine mammals eat the target species; if marine mammal populations are reduced by some amount X, then we can increase our harvest by the amount those X marine mammals would have eaten, without any net decrease in target species stock.' Yodzis' (1998) study highlights the pitfalls in these oversimplistic predictions of the outcome of predator removal in marine ecosystems. Even in this well-quantified ecosystem the outcome of culling top predators is highly variable. Variation might arise either from random variation in the outcome of predictive models that reflects current ignorance of the system due to limitations in the measurements of parameters taken (Figure 16.2), or from random influences that are experienced in the system that cannot be eliminated (e.g. climatic variation).

In addition to the effects of harvesting the target species, the actual harvesting techniques employed can have direct and indirect consequences for non-target species and habitats. Harvesting species that are integral structural components of a particular habitat will have negative effects on those species directly associated with them and release space for opportunistic species to colonise the harvested area. Obvious examples of this include the harvesting of forests in which the trees are the fundamental component of the habitat that is inhabited by a multitude of associated species (Pimm *et al.*, 1995).

In this chapter we explore the various ecosystem responses to human harvesting activities in aquatic and terrestrial environments. We suggest that more traditional single-species approaches to management are no longer adequate to maintain ecosystem integrity, given the evidence of the wider ecosystem effects of human harvesting activity. Finally, we explore those management techniques that are most likely to mitigate the negative effects of human harvesting activities.

HARVESTING PREDATORS AND GRAZERS

Repeated intensive hunting has led to substantial reductions in the abundance of some target species in both terrestrial and aquatic ecosystems (see

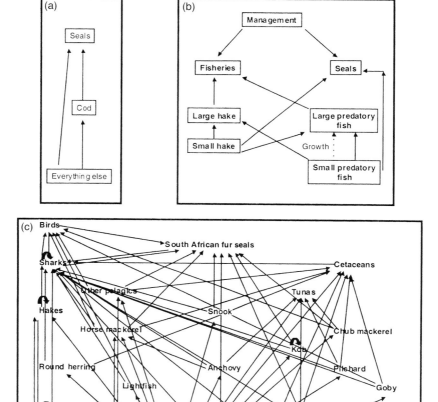

Figure 16.2. A variety of food webs as conceived for the Benguela system: (a) the most simplistic point of view, (b) a slightly more realistic view and (c) a much simplified version of the full food web (the full version is too complex to see clearly each of the interactions). (Adapted from Yodzis, 1998.)

e.g. Redford, 1992; Myers *et al.*, 1996; Bodmer *et al.*, 1997) and has caused changes in the structure of species composition within animal communities (see e.g. Greenstreet & Hall, 1996). Those species from higher trophic levels (Pauly *et al.*, 1998) and large-bodied or slow-growing species with late maturity (Kirkwood *et al.*, 1994) tend to decline in abundance more rapidly than those that have small body size and are faster growing (Reynolds *et al.*, Chapter 7). These life history correlates that are linked to susceptibility to decline are common to both terrestrial and aquatic systems. Bodmer *et al.* (1997) calculated differences in the relative abundance of large-bodied mammals in the northeastern Peruvian Amazon in different areas with either persistent or infrequent hunting pressure. For Amazonian mammals that weighed more than 1 kg the degree of population decline was correlated with the species' intrinsic rate of natural increase, longevity and generation time. Those species most vulnerable to extinction had relatively low rates of natural increase, greater longevity and longer generation times. Jennings *et al.* (1998) found similar results when they examined in detail the long-term trends in the abundance of exploited stocks of bottom-dwelling fishes in the North Sea. They used a comparative approach based on phylogenetic comparisons to examine the differential effects of fishing on individual species with contrasting life histories. As in Bodmer *et al.*'s (1997) study, they found that those species that decreased in abundance relative to their nearest phylogenetic relative matured later, achieved a greater maximum size, and had lower rates of potential population increase.

The responses of predator populations in aquatic and terrestrial systems to human harvesting seem to follow similar patterns, with removal of the largest-sized fauna from the system ultimately leading to dominance by smaller-bodied fauna. Sustained and uncontrolled harvesting will lead to a gradual decline in the body size spectrum of the animal population (Figure 16.3; Rice & Gislason, 1996). The consequences of these shifts in body size spectra are likely to have the greatest ramifications in those ecosystems in which trophic cascades have been reported (Table 16.1; Pace *et al.*, 1999). In the main, these ecosystems tend to be relatively simple with few, but strongly linked, interactions between different trophic levels.

Interactions that result from exploitation of species in terrestrial ecosystems

Ecosystem changes will be most obvious when the linkages between different trophic levels or individual species are very strong. Pace *et al.* (1999) cite Leopold's (1949) observations of the results of extirpating wolves *Canis lupus* that led to an increase in deer populations with the consequence that 'I have seen every edible tree defoliated to the height of a saddlehorn'. In this case, wolves might be thought of as keystone species. Keystone species are defined as those species for which a change in their population size will have knock-on effects for other components of the ecosystem (e.g. their

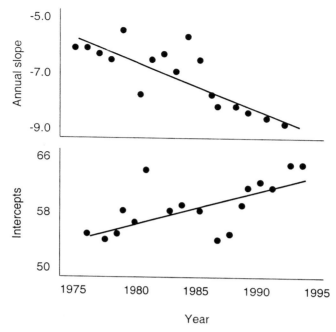

Figure 16.3. Regression of the slope of annual number spectra of fish sampled in annual trawl surveys between 1977 and 1993 in the North Sea. Number spectra are the mean number of individual fish in each size class category occurring in all samples. The less negative the slope, the greater the proportion of individuals in high size class categories. The regression of the intercepts of the number spectra from these surveys suggests an increase in the actual numbers of small size class fishes, although this may be a result of autocorrelation between slopes and intercepts. (Adapted from Rice & Gislason, 1996.)

prey). Population fluctuations in wolf density have also been shown to indirectly affect tree growth through their regulatory effect on moose *Alces alces* populations (McLaren & Peterson, 1994). The idea of keystone species and their influence on systems has most of its origins in the marine and freshwater literature (Paine, 1980; Flecker & Townsend, 1994), but they are equally apparent in terrestrial systems. For example, North American bison *Bison bison athabascae* as they move across the land alter plant community structure through their grazing activities and increase habitat heterogeneity in the tallgrass prairies (Knapp *et al.*, 1999). The bison can be considered to be keystone species through the impact of their grazing and migratory activities on plant species and habitat diversity. As bison migrate across the prairies, they open up space for opportunistic species as they graze vegetation and trample migration routes through the foliage. Similarly, the Serengeti wildebeest *Connochaetes taurinus* is a keystone species that determines the rest of the Serengeti ecosystem (Sinclair & Arcese, 1995). Population fluctuations in this wildebeest population are determined by environmental parameters such as rainfall that influence the quality of grazing at critical times of the year. In contrast to many other systems, predation has relatively little impact on the wildebeest populations (Mduma *et al.*, 1999).

Evidence for cascades has been found also in highly speciated tropical food webs. Removal experiments of lizards (mainly *Anolis* spp.) led to greater leaf damage by the herbivorous insects on which they normally prey (Dial & Roughgarden, 1995). In meadow communities, lizards that prey upon insects have been shown to influence grasshopper density such that plant biomass is greatly reduced in the absence of lizards (Chase, 1998).

Interactions that result from exploitation of target species on tropical reefs

The overexploitation of fishes on tropical reefs can affect community structure and a range of ecosystem processes. Many reefs provide the main sources of protein and income for coastal people. Reef fishers target species from all trophic groups, and on many fished reefs the abundance of herbivorous and invertebrate feeding fishes has been reduced by an order of magnitude or more (Russ, 1991).

The main algal consumers on reefs are herbivorous fishes and sea urchins. The abundance of sea urchins (Echinoidea) is regulated by recruitment success, food supply and natural mortality due to predation and disease. The main sea urchin predators are fishes such as emperors (Lethrinidae) and triggerfishes (Balistidae) that are also targeted by human fishers (McClanahan, 1995b). On some reefs in the Caribbean and off East Africa, fish predation appears to play a key role in controlling the abundance of sea urchin populations and the latter have proliferated following the overfishing of their predators (McClanahan & Muthiga, 1988; McClanahan, 1992, 1995a).

Once sea urchins have become abundant, they graze the majority of algal production. Urchins can tolerate low algal biomass because they have low consumption and respiration rates. This allows them to outcompete herbivorous fishes that have higher consumption and respiration rates and reach maximum biomass levels an order of magnitude higher (McClanahan, 1992). Since the herbivorous fishes are poor competitors under these conditions, they may not recover to former levels of abundance when fishing is stopped (McClanahan, 1995a).

Table 16.1. Examples of studies that have identified trophic cascades in the recent literature. These examples are illustrative and are not meant to be an exhaustive list

Ecosystem	Cascade	Evidence	Effects	References
Marine				
Oceanic	Salmon–zooplankton–phytoplankton	Ten-year time series	Increased phytoplankton when salmon abundant	Shiomoto et al., 1997
Coastal	Whales–otter–urchins–kelp	Long-term data and behavioural studies	Predation by whales on otters led to urchin population expansion and increased grazing of kelp	Estes et al., 1998
Intertidal	Birds–urchins–macroalgae	Manipulation of bird predation on urchins	Algal cover greatly increased when urchins reduced	Wooton, 1995
Fresh water				
Streams	Fish–invertebrates–periphyton	First- and second-degree production affected by predation of invertebrate populations	Annual first-degree production affected by sixfold difference	Huryn, 1998
Shallow lake	Fish–zooplankton–phytoplankton	Observations of lakes under clear and turbid conditions	Reductions in fish abundance led to shift in zooplankton size–structure with consequent effects on phytoplankton	Jeppesen et al., 1998
Terrestrial				
Meadow	Lizards–grasshopper–plants	Observations and experimental studies	Grasshopper density mediated by lizards; plant biomass decline with decreasing lizard predation	Chase, 1998

Tropical forest	Beetles–ants–insects–piper plants	Observations and manipulation of beetle density in enclosures	Beetles prey upon ants that remove herbivorous insects that consume plants. More foliage consumed in presence of beetles	Letourneau & Dyer, 1998
Boreal forest	Wolves–moose–balsam fir	Study of moose grazing over 30 years	Population cycles of wolves, moose and balsam fir	McLaren & Peterson, 1994

Adapted from Pace *et al.* (1999).

As they graze, sea urchins erode the reef matrix and prevent the settlement and growth of coral recruits. Unless recruitment failure or disease leads to a collapse of urchin populations, other intervention is needed to promote recovery of the reef ecosystem. McClanahan and co-workers (1996) attempted such intervention on a small scale by deliberate removal of sea urchins. When they removed the urchins from unfished experimental plots on Kenyan reefs, there were significant increases in algal cover and fish abundance within one year. However, on fished reefs, herbivorous fishes were less abundant, and the algae rapidly overgrew corals as they proliferated. The ecosystem shifts that McClanahan *et al.* (1996) induced in fished areas by urchin removal were remarkably similar to those observed in the heavily fished Caribbean when there was mass urchin mortality following disease. Here, the loss of urchins led to heavy growth of algae that soon dominated the reef community (Carpenter, 1985; Lessios, 1988).

The effects of predator removal on urchin populations contrast with the effects of piscivore removal on reef fish populations. Several studies have documented significant decreases in the abundance of piscivorous target species following fishing and yet there was no evidence for a corresponding increase in the abundance of their prey (Bohnsack, 1982; Russ, 1985; Jennings & Polunin, 1997). The reasons for this are likely to be linked to the structure of reef fish communities, where phylogenetic groupings contain many species, with a wide range of life history traits, behavioural differences and feeding strategies (Hiatt & Strasburg, 1960; Parrish *et al.*, 1985, 1986; Hixon, 1991). Moreover, most fish species undergo marked ontogenetic changes in diet, and act as the prey and predators of other species in the course of their life history. As a result, while the collective impacts of predators are large, the impacts of individual predator species on the dynamics of their prey are minor. This effect was termed diffuse predation by Hixon (1991).

It is worth noting that on much smaller scales (square metres rather than square kilometres) there is some evidence for the role of predation as a structuring force, particularly when habitat or refuge space is directly limited. Thus Caley (1993), Hixon & Beets (1993) and Carr & Hixon (1995) have conducted elegant studies demonstrating that experimental reductions in piscivore abundance lead to detectable increases in the abundance and diversity of their prey. However, even at these scales, it is widely accepted that recruitment variation has a more significant impact on population structure (Sale, 1980; Doherty, 1991; Doherty & Fowler, 1994).

Interactions following removal of predatory fish in temperate marine fisheries

Fishing has a marked impact on the dynamics of exploited fish populations. Many species, both target (caught intentionally) and non-target (caught as bycatch), can sustain fishing mortality rates two to three times their natural mortality rates, but are ultimately depleted as fishing mortality rises (Jennings & Kaiser, 1998). Even in the most intensively fished marine ecosystems such as the Benguela upwelling, Georges Bank, Bering Sea and North Sea, piscivorous fish are more important consumers of fish biomass than humans, marine mammals or birds (see e.g. Bax, 1991; Yodzis, 1998). Long-term studies of fish populations have suggested that the intensive fishing of such piscivorous fish has allowed other species to proliferate. For example, Sherman et al. (1981) showed that population explosions of sand-eels *Ammodytes* spp. in the northeast and west Atlantic coincided with the depletion of their predators such as Atlantic herring *Clupea harengus* and mackerel *Scomber scombrus*. However, it is very difficult to establish causality given the range of environmental factors that could also account for these links.

In a recent review of the effects of predator depletion on non-target species in temperate marine ecosystems, Jennings & Kaiser (1998) concluded that there were relatively few circumstances in which changes in the abundance of piscivorous fishes in marine ecosystems have cascading impacts on other parts of the system. High fish consumption rates by marine predators did not consistently imply that predation was a structuring force when most species can act as predators and prey in the course of their life history and when adult predators are still capable of switching diet and feeding strategy in response to prey availability. Indeed, in temperate systems, the strongest evidence for the predator-based control of prey species came from the impact of humans on their target species. The strength of this relationship is likely to result from the conservative fishing strategies employed by humans, who, in the majority of commercial fisheries, are unwilling to be flexible in their aims and target a relatively small proportion of the total fish fauna. Most predatory fish, conversely, are very generalist feeders, often switching to invertebrate prey or cannibalism and eating many species of fish at different stages in their life history.

Interactions after removal of predatory fish from fresh waters

Some of the best evidence for cascading trophic effects following the exploitation of target fishes comes from freshwater lakes (Marten, 1979; Carpenter et al., 1985). In many cases, the removal of predatory fish has impacts throughout the ecosystem, and the conservation of these target species can influence the structure and functioning of the entire system.

Two recent examples of trophic cascades were reported by Pace *et al.* (1999). Flecker & Townsend (1994) and McIntosh & Townsend (1996) have shown that the presence of a brown trout *Salmo trutta* predator in a New Zealand stream led to increased predation on herbivorous mayfly larvae *Delatidium* spp. As a result, the mayfly larvae spent more time sheltering under rocks and less time foraging on their upper surfaces. This allowed epilithic algae to proliferate. Conservation or fisheries management action that affects the trout would therefore have knock-on effects on other aspects of ecosystem function.

Carpenter *et al.* (1987) manipulated the fish populations of three entire North American lakes to test whether species at higher trophic levels could regulate the abundance, productivity and community structure of phytoplankton and zooplankton. In their control lake, productivity varied from year to year, predominantly in response to climatic factors. However, in a lake where piscivorous largemouth bass *Micropterus salmoides* were added and potentially planktivorous fish removed, there was an increase in zooplankton biomass and a shift from a copepod and rotifer zooplankton assemblage to one dominated by cladocerans. Algal biomass and primary productivity also fell. Moreover, in a lake where most largemouth bass were removed and potentially planktivorous fish added, the planktivores remained in refuges to avoid predation. As a result, zooplankton biomass and the dominance of large cladocerans increased. Carpenter *et al.* (1987) had provided convincing evidence that fish populations could be important regulators of primary productivity. Their study was also important because it showed that the presence of a few predators, and the predator avoidance reactions that they stimulated, had a fundamental impact on the structure of the food web. The results of this study and others that have shown similar cascading effects (Neill, 1994) suggest that the effective conservation of piscivores has the potential to reduce primary production in lakes.

Why systems respond differently to predator removal

In marine ecosystems, the loss of fish predators can have limited consequences for prey species. While there are well-known exceptions, such as those we have cited, the more general conclusion is that scientists have looked very hard for interactions in terrestrial and aquatic ecosystems and failed to find them. For example, Milchunas *et al.* (1998) synthesised the literature on experimental manipulations and comparative studies of the effects of livestock grazing on shortgrass steppes and its relationship to ecosystem function. They found that some groups, particularly birds, were strongly affected by even light grazing pressure, but at the community level, trophic structure composition did not vary greatly across grazing treatments. Even when there were relatively large effects of grazing on consumer groups, this did not alter ecosystem processes such as primary production or soil nutrient pool and cycling rates. Since an effect is perceived as a positive result, while no effect may go unreported, the existing literature is strongly biased towards significant interactions.

In general, there are much closer links between predator and prey dynamics in freshwater ecosystems. We suggest that the indirect effects of fish predator removal are greater and more predictable in freshwater lakes. Within lake ecosystems the majority of biomass is aggregated into a few relatively distinct size classes that correspond loosely to phylogenetic groupings (Sprules *et al.*, 1983; Sprules & Goyke, 1994; Sprules & Stockwell, 1995). Phylogenetic diversity is considerably lower in most freshwater lakes than in marine ecosystems, and the lake organisms within size groups tend to have a relatively limited range of life history traits and morphologies. Size has a key role in determining the potential predators or prey of the organisms within food webs (Peters, 1983) and thus the organisation of limnetic communities places strong constraints on community structure that do not occur in many marine environments (Neill, 1994). In many of the more species-rich marine ecosystems the biomass spectrum is extended and there is more variance in size within the main phylogenetic groupings with a wider range of life history traits, behavioural differences and feeding strategies (Jennings & Kaiser, 1998). As a result, predation is diffuse (Hixon, 1991) and the overall effect of all piscivores on their prey can be substantial, although the impact of any individual species, or small group of species, is minor.

From a management perspective, it is desirable to be able to predict the potential for the occurrence of a trophic cascade as a result of harvesting activities. During the course of our consideration of the literature on aquatic and terrestrial ecosystems, several rules of thumb have emerged that should be considered in a management context.

1 None of the examples of cascades given in Table 16.1 involves more than three interactions between different species, i.e. they are simple systems regardless of the fact that they may be embedded within highly complex systems of high biodiversity (e.g. the beetle–ant–insect–piper plant example from tropical forests). These minisystems within larger more complex systems are perhaps to be expected in high diversity

ecosystems in which there is a greater tendency towards specialist feeding interactions.

2 The interactions within the cascade are between organisms that are assigned to major trophic levels within a system, e.g. predator–herbivore–primary producer; very few involve intermediate trophic levels. This contrasts sharply with the food web of the Benguela system in which there are at least seven interactions between the bottom and the top of the system. These more complex systems are expected to be more resistant to cascading effects.

3 The key predators or herbivores in the examples of cascades are most usually the dominant organisms at their trophic level. Hence, in the case of significant decrease in the population of predator or herbivore, there are few others to take their place in the short term. This contrasts sharply with many of the more 'open' marine ecosystems where there may be three or more predators that exert similar levels of predation on one or more species (e.g. sharks, cetaceans and marine mammals all eat pilchard in the Benguela system).

4 Cannibalism is rare within species involved in systems prone to trophic cascades, in sharp contrast to many marine ecosystems in which canni- balism is common (Figure 16.2). Even in the absence of major pred- ators, cannibalism can limit species density, as indicated in Figure 16.2.

OVEREXPLOITATION DECREASES ENERGY SUBSIDIES TO ECOSYSTEMS

Energy subsidies are inputs of nutrients or organic material that supple- ment the regular supply of these resources within an ecosystem. Energy subsidies occur naturally or their occurrence can increase or decrease as a result of human activities. It is difficult to envisage terrestrial subsidies that arise from hunting practices, apart from carcasses left by poachers who remove only certain body parts (e.g. hunting of elephants for ivory, fur seals for their pelts, or North American bison for their skins) or carrion which arises from forest areas that have been burnt for agricultural development. Despite our best efforts to find examples, there appear to be few records of the ecological significance of carrion in terrestrial systems other than for those species that specifically feed on this material (Polis et al., 1997). En- ergy subsidies are only likely to have ecological significance if the inputs are concentrated and frequent enough and of sufficient magnitude to contrib- ute significantly to a particular ecosystem (Polis & Strong, 1996). A good example of an important contribution of nutrients and energy to aquatic and terrestrial ecosystems involves carcasses of Pacific salmon *Oncorhynchus* spp. (Cederholm *et al.*, 1999). Pacific salmon migrate to sea where they grow to maturity before migrating back to their native rivers to spawn and die. Thus Pacific salmon are important vectors of marine-derived nutrients that are moved upstream. These mass spawning aggregations of salmon are important sources of food for many terrestrial animals and bird species that inhabit the watershed. Studies that have examined $^{15}N/^{14}N$ ratios in food webs of systems with anadromous salmon and those without indicate that the decomposing carcasses of salmon are remineralised by primary producers that are consumed by fish, including young salmon (Kline *et al.*, 1993; Cederholm *et al.*, 1999).

Salmon carcasses can supply a critical source of energy for some terrestrial vertebrates and provide nutrients for riparian vegetation along some spawning streams. Salmon are now viewed by some as keystone species in terrestrial vertebrate communities (Willson & Halupka, 1995). Indeed, the reproduction cycle and seasonal distribution of some animals is tied directly to a spawning run of salmon. For example, the number of bald eagles *Haliaeetus leucocephalus* wintering along salmon rivers and their reproductive success is directly correlated with the availability of spawning salmon (McClelland *et al.*, 1982; Hansen, 1987). It is clear that salmon provide an important source of nutrient input into terrestrial and limnetic systems, but salmon stocks are, in general, overexploited (Nehlsen *et al.*, 1991). Hence the present-day inputs of marine nutrients from salmon carcasses are probably much lower than they were prior to overexploitation. While it is not possible to attribute differences in past and present-day community structure to decreases in the amount of energy and nutrient subsidies passing into watershed systems, the importance of the role of salmon carcasses has prompted management action to ensure their continued presence (Cederholm *et al.*, 1999).

Energy subsidies from killing non-target species

Terrestrial hunting and artisanal fishing activities tend to be relatively 'clean' in that hunters tend to stalk or target individual prey or set traps that catch only the desired range of species. Subsistence hunters retain all prey and none goes to waste (Winterhalder, 1981). In contrast, large-scale commercial fisheries use relatively indiscriminate techniques such as drift nets, towed fishing gear and long lines set with thousands of hooks (Jennings & Kaiser, 1998). These fishing techniques yield by-catches of species that are not utilised by the fishers. By-catches are discarded dead or dying either for legal reasons or because there is insufficient money to be gained by sorting or landing them. This material is dumped back into the ocean. Thus fishing activities redirect energy in marine ecosystems by the production of carrion that becomes available to both scavengers on the seabed and those that feed at the surface of the sea.

Anyone who has witnessed a fishing boat returning to port will have observed the flock of seabirds that compete for the offal and discarded fish thrown overboard. In the North Sea alone, approximately 235 000 tonnes of discarded fish are consumed by seabirds each year and this has led in part to increases in bird populations and distribution (Furness *et al.*, 1988, 1992; Camphuysen *et al.*, 1993; Furness, 1996; Garthe *et al.*, 1996). These patterns of increase in seabird populations are also seen elsewhere around the world (Jennings & Kaiser, 1998).

We know from deep-sea studies that food-falls of carrion have a profound effect on local diversity and production processes (Dayton & Hessler, 1972). However, the majority of the world's fishing activities are confined to more shallow coastal waters. Experimental studies have demonstrated that the responses of animals to carrion in continental shelf areas may be equally rapid (Jennings & Kaiser, 1998). It is common practice in the North Sea for trawlers to fish one after the other along the same navigational plot. As the first bottom fishing trawls pass across the seabed, benthic fauna are dug up, damaged or killed by the gear, which in turn attracts scavenging fish into the area of disturbance. Examination of the gut contents of these scavenging fish reveals that they eat a wider variety and larger rations of prey in areas of trawl disturbance (Kaiser & Ramsay, 1997).

While the responses of populations of scavenging seabirds have been strongly correlated with subsidies from discarding practices, the responses of fish and invertebrate scavenger populations to fisheries subsidies are not clear. Several studies indicate that populations of flatfish species that are known to be facultative scavengers have increased in abundance or increased their growth rate in response to increased fishing effort. For example, the growth rates of plaice *Pleuronectes platessa* and sole *Solea solea* have increased in relation to the increase in bottom fishing effort and hence disturbance of the seabed (Millner & Whiting, 1996; Rijnsdorp & van Leeuwen, 1996). However, there are many factors that might contribute to the increased growth of plaice and sole. In general, flatfish are small sized, grow rapidly and mature early and may have replaced slower-growing species such as cod *Gadus morhua* as their populations have been fished down (Jennings *et al.*, 1998). Furthermore, eutrophication has increased populations of polychaetes and brittlestars *Ophiothrix fragilis* in coastal waters, thereby increasing the food supply for juvenile flatfishes and probably also increasing their growth rate.

So far, there is little evidence that populations of benthic invertebrate scavengers have increased in response to fisheries-generated carrion (Ramsay et al., 2000). Why should there be such large differences in the responses of scavenging seabirds and invertebrates to energy subsidies? Seabirds are able actively to search for fishing vessels over large areas and hence discards from trawlers are a relatively reliable and constant source of high-quality food (Camphuysen et al., 1993). In contrast, benthic invertebrates are unable to actively seek out fisheries-generated carrion and rely on its chance occurrence on the seabed. Thus this source of carrion is probably too unpredictable to give significant benefit to most invertebrate populations.

IMPLICATIONS OF HABITAT DAMAGE AND CHANGE

It is now well established that losses in forest habitat greatly reduce the loss of species diversity and greatly increase the risk of endemic species' extinctions (Pimm & Askins, 1995; Pimm et al., 1995). For example Estrada et al. (1994) compared the non-flying mammal diversity found in a range of Neotropical rain forests that were subject to different levels of human disturbance with the diversity in cleared areas that had become pastures. They found that disturbed forests had the lowest mammal diversity of habitats that incorporated trees and that pastures had the lowest mammal diversity of all habitats. Diversity increased with increasing habitat complexity measured in terms of vertical foliage diversity. In contrast to deforestation, hunting practices in terrestrial systems lead to minor modifications of habitat through the creation of paths to gain access to remote areas of forest or heathland. Occasionally, habitats are burnt to flush out wildlife into the path of waiting hunters. Humans also manage landscapes or freshwater habitats for the purpose of promoting populations of species that are hunted for recreation. With the exception of the removal of selected trees from forests, it is unusual for existing habitat structures to be intentionally destroyed with the aim of capturing or harvesting targeted species, as the association of one with the other is often very close.

Fishing in the marine environment is perhaps the best example of a method of hunting that causes habitat change either intentionally or unintentionally. In a recent article, Watling & Norse (1998) compared the effects of fishing with towed bottom-fishing gears with clear-cutting of forests in terrestrial systems. Their assertion was that the incidental or even deliberate removal of topographically complex seabed habitats would have similar detrimental effects on the associated species assemblage as in terrestrial systems. This is perhaps not surprising and there is good evidence to demonstrate these effects. For example, Sainsbury and co-workers (Sainsbury, 1987; Sainsbury et al., 1998) reported that, as sponges and soft-coral communities were removed as by-catch in trawls off the northwestern shelf of Australia, the associated fish species were greatly reduced in abundance. Only after these areas were protected from bottom fishing did they observe slow regeneration of the habitat as sponges and corals began to recolonise and grow. Once this process had begun, then the populations of associated fish species began to increase once again.

In temperate estuarine systems, oysters (Ostreiidae) are important reef-forming organisms that add structural complexity to the seabed and increase species and habitat diversity. Oysters also improve water quality through their filtration activities as they bind particulate organic matter and remove pollutants and nutrients from the water column. The functional role of oysters in coastal ecosystems is now deemed to be of such importance that in many areas large sums of money are spent attempting to re-establish degraded oyster reefs (Lenihan, 1999).

MANAGEMENT MEASURES

Conservation of species to conserve ecosystems

In cases where the loss of a species has adverse impacts on ecosystem processes, their effective conservation will also benefit the ecosystem. Let us look at an example from terrestrial systems. A conservation focus on a single species – the wildebeest – is justified in the Serengeti because wildebeest have an important role in the maintenance of plant diversity and seed dispersal, and they provide a food source for all the carnivores and scavengers in the system. In aquatic systems there are examples where the conservation of emperor and triggerfish species on some reefs will keep sea urchin abundance low and maintain the system in a state where corals can grow effectively. Similarly, the effective conservation of sea otters *Enhydra lutris* helps to keep sea urchin populations under control and to promote the growth of kelp beds. Maintenance of these habitats has important implications for the other species that use them and for coastal protection.

On the west coast of North America, the effective conservation of the sea otter may have helped to conserve kelp beds that provide important habitats for many fish and invertebrates. Historically, the hunting of sea otters so depleted their populations that they no longer exerted any predatory control over sea urchin populations and the urchins began to destroy kelp beds. Ultimately, the kelp beds became barren grounds, where the rock was colonised by small epilithic algal species and sea urchins. In the late twentieth century, otter populations have grown following hunting bans and improved conservation, so they have exerted in turn more predation pressure on the sea urchins. This has allowed new kelp beds to grow on areas of barren ground. Clearly, these effects are confounded by many other factors such as oceanographic effects on sea urchin recruitment and interactions between sea urchin and abalone fisheries. Nevertheless, in general terms, the effective conservation of otters has helped to conserve the kelp beds that provide important habitats for many species of fish and invertebrates (Estes & Van Blaricom, 1985; Estes & Duggins, 1995).

On those reefs where the relationships between fishes and sea urchins can be predicted reliably by models, effective conservation of fish species that consume sea urchins may help to ensure continued growth of the reef. This provides collateral benefits for coral communities, helps coastal protection and aids those species of fish and invertebrates that rely on a structured and complex coral community. After removing sea urchins from unfished experimental plots, McClanahan et al., (1996) showed that there were significant increases in fish density, fish species richness and algal cover within one year. On fished reefs, where herbivorous fishes were scarce, algal cover increased as corals were overgrown by algae. However, on unfished reefs, where herbivorous fishes were abundant, the algae were grazed and coral cover increased. The authors cautioned that sea urchin removal would not be a good strategy on reefs where no attempt was made to prevent fishing. While McClanahan et al., (1996) achieved rehabilitation of these reefs by using humans to control sea urchin populations, the urchins could equally be controlled by effective conservation of their fish predators.

Maintaining energy subsidies as a way to conserve ecosystems

Cederholm et al. (1999) outlined some of the measures taken to ensure that energy subsidies are maintained in those systems in which such subsidies have a significant role. Clearly, overexploitation of salmon stocks at sea will limit the number of fish that eventually migrate back to their home stream or river. In an attempt to counteract the effect of the occurrence of fewer salmon carcasses in river systems, carcasses of hatchery-reared salmon are substituted into the system. In addition, carcass retention devices are introduced into the stream flow that will reduce the effects of washout before the carcass material can be incorporated into the system. These devices are simple, involving the introduction of felled tree branches into the path of the stream on which the salmon carcasses become entrapped.

While the previous example deals with management to alleviate the problems of reductions in energy subsidies, the population increases in seabirds observed globally are directly linked to artificially elevated levels of energy subsidies. Since the large quantities of fish discarded in the North-east Atlantic support populations of scavenging seabirds (Furness, 1996; Garthe *et al.*, 1996), some people have cautioned that plans to reduce discarding could have profound effects on bird populations (Furness *et al.*, 1992). Moreover, Camphuysen *et al.* (1993) advocated that any changes in mesh-size regulations that reduce the proportion of catch discarded should be introduced gradually to avoid adverse effects for competitively inferior seabird species.

Habitat management as a way to conserve ecosystems

We have seen earlier that the alteration of habitats either as a direct result of harvesting (e.g. logging activities) or indirectly as a result of incidental disturbances (e.g. fishing in complex and structured habitats) has detrimental effects on either the target or associated non-target species (Sainsbury, 1987; Pimm *et al.*, 1995; Watling & Norse, 1998). In these circumstances, the habitat is regarded as the main focus of conservation efforts in addition to the target species. Severe alteration of habitat structure can make a habitat entirely unsuitable for the associated species such that there is little opportunity for population recovery. Undoubtedly, the best method of preserving a habitat is the use of reserves, although relatively few exist in marine systems. There are two main reasons for using reserves as a management tool: the conservation of habitat and species of conservation interest and/or the promotion of populations of target species. While the former goal is eminently achievable using reserves as a management tool, there is much debate about the size and number of reserves required to achieve the latter (Murray *et al.*, 1999).

Brooks *et al.* (1999) presented convincing evidence that only large reserves will prevent species extinctions for threatened species in terrestrial habitats. While fairly localised reserves are appropriate for populations of species that show high site fidelity throughout their life history (e.g. tropical reef fishes) (Mangel, 1998; Roberts, 1998), species that range uninhibited over much greater areas will require far larger reserves in order for the measures to have any significant effect on their populations. For example, there is some debate regarding the closure of areas even as large as one-quarter of the North Sea; some have suggested that this might do little or nothing to protect widely dispersed and mobile fish such as cod (Horwood, 2000). Furthermore, the goals of reserves can be confounded by non-marine influences such as inundation of pollutants or sediment as a result of agricultural activities hundreds of kilometres distant. Thus effective use of reserves requires an integrated approach that incorporates a consideration of both aquatic and terrestrial influences.

CONCLUSIONS

We have selected several examples where humans understand the links between species in ecosystems and some management of ecosystem function is possible through the effective conservation of target species. However, in most ecosystems, such management is impossible and investigators still have little or no power to predict the effects of species removal on ecosystem function. Shifts in exploited communities, particularly in the marine environment, may often have more to do with differential vulnerability of target species to fishing than with changes in the community due to the removal of certain species. There have been massive reductions in the abundance of top predators in many marine systems, but despite numerous attempts to find changes in their prey, these are rarely strong or consistent and can be confounded by environmental factors. This supports the view of many ecologists that the majority of links in food webs are weak and that multichannel omnivory is very common (Polis & Strong, 1996). However, in circumstances where managers can demonstrate that the depletion of certain species has indirect effects on the ecosystem, and that the effects can be reversed by effective conservation of that species, then they have an opportunity to act.

REFERENCES

Alroy, J. (1999). Putting North America's end-Pleistocene megafaunal extinction in context. In *Extinctions in Near Time*, ed. R. D. E. MacPhee, pp. 105–143. Kluwer, Dordrecht.

Bax, N. J. (1991). A comparison of the biomass flow to fish, fisheries and mammals in six marine ecosystems. *ICES Marine Science Symposia*, **193**, 217–224.

Bodmer, R. E., Eisenberg, J. F. & Redford, K. H. (1997). Hunting and the likelihood of extinction of Amazonian mammals. *Conservation Biology*, **11**, 460–466.

Bohnsack, J. A. (1982). Effects of piscivorous predator removal on coral reef fish community structure. In *Gutshop '81: Fish Food Habits and Studies*, ed. G. M. Caillet & C. A. Simenstad, pp. 258–267. University of Washington, Seattle.

Brooks, T. M., Pimm, S. L., Kapos, V. & Ravilious, C. (1999). Threat from deforestation to montane and lowland birds and mammals in insular South-east Asia. *Journal of Animal Ecology*, **68**, 1061–1078.

Caley, M. J. (1993). Predation, recruitment and the dynamics of communities of coral-reef fishes. *Marine Biology*, **117**, 33–43.

Camphuysen, C. J., Ensor, K., Furness, R. W., Garthe, S., Huppop, O., Leaper, G., Offringa, H. & Tasker, M. L. (1993). *Seabirds Feeding on Discards in Winter in the North Sea*. Netherlands Institute for Sea Research, Den Burg, Texel.

Carpenter, R. C. (1985). Sea urchin mass-mortality: effects on reef algal abundance, species composition and metabolism and other coral reef herbivores. *Proceedings of the Fifth International Coral Reef Symposium*, **4**, 53–60.

Carpenter, S. R., Kitchell, J. F. & Hodgson, J. R. (1985). Cascading trophic interactions and lake productivity. *Bioscience*, **35**, 634–639.

Carpenter, S. R., Kitchell, J. F., Hodgson, J. R., Cochran, P. A., Elser, J. J., Elser, M. M., Lodge, D. M., Kretchmer, D., He, X. & von Ende, C. N. (1987). Regulation of lake primary productivity by food web structure. *Ecology*, **68**, 1863–1876.

Carr, M. H. & Hixon, M. A. (1995). Predation effects on early post-settlement survivorship of coral-reef fishes. *Marine Ecology Progress Series*, **124**, 31–42.

Cederholm, C. J., Kunze, M. D., Murota, T. & Sibatani, A. (1999). Pacific salmon carcasses: essential contributions of nutrients and energy for aquatic and terrestrial ecosystems. *Fisheries*, **24**, 6–15.

Chase, J. M. (1998). Central-place forager effects on food web dynamics and spatial patterns in Northern California meadows. *Ecology*, **79**, 1236–1245.

Davis, G., Haaker, P. & Richards, D. (1996). Status and trends of white abalone at the California Channel Islands. *Transactions of the American Fisheries Society*, **125**, 42–48.

Dayton, P. K. & Hessler, R. R. (1972). Role of biological disturbance in maintaining diversity in the deep sea. *Deep-Sea Research*, **19**, 199–208.

Dial, R. J. & Roughgarden, J. (1995). Experimental removal of insectivores from rain forest canopy: direct and indirect effects. *Ecology*, **76**, 1821–1834.

Doherty, P. J. (1991). Spatial and temporal patterns in recruitment. In *The Ecology of Fishes on Coral Reefs*, ed. P. F. Sale, pp. 261–293. Academic Press, San Diego, CA.

Doherty, P. J. & Fowler, T. (1994). An empirical test of recruitment limitation in a coral reef fish. *Science*, **263**, 935–939.

Estes, J. A. & Duggins, D. O. (1995). Sea otters and kelp forests in Alaska: generality and variation in a community ecological paradigm. *Ecological Monographs*, **65**, 75–100.

Estes, J. A. & Van Blaricom, G. R. (1985). Sea-otters and shellfisheries. In *Marine Mammals and Fisheries*, ed. J. R. Beddington, R. J. H. Beverton & D. M. Lavigne, pp. 187–235. George Allen & Unwin, London.

Estes, J. A., Tinker, M. T., Williams, T. M. & Doak, D. F. (1998). Killer whale predation on sea otters linking oceanic and nearshore ecosystems. *Science*, **282**, 473–476.

Estrada, A., Coates-Estrada, R. & Meritt, D. Jr (1994). Non-flying mammals and landscape changes in the tropical rain forest region of Los Tuxtlas, Mexico. *Ecography*, **17**, 229–241.

Flecker, A. S. & Townsend, C. R. (1994). Community wide consequences of trout introduction in New Zeland streams. *Ecological Applications*, **4**, 798–807.

Furness, R. W. (1996). A review of seabird responses to natural or fisheries-induced changes in food supply. In *Aquatic Predators and their Prey*, ed. S. P. R. Greenstreet & M. L. Tasker, pp. 168–173. Blackwell Scientific Publications, Oxford.

Furness, R. W., Hudson, A. V. & Ensor, K. (1988). Interactions between scavenging seabirds and commercial fisheries around the British Isles. In *Seabirds and Other Marine Vertebrates: Competition, Predation and Other Interactions*, ed. J. Burger, pp. 240–268. Columbia University Press, New York.

Furness, R. W., Ensor, K. & Hudson, A. V. (1992). The use of fishery waste by gull populations around the British Isles. *Ardea*, **80**, 105–113.

Garthe, S., Camphuysen, C. J. & Furness, R. W. (1996). Amounts of discards by commercial fisheries and their significance as food for seabirds in the North Sea. *Marine Ecology Progress Series*, **136**, 1–11.

Greenstreet, S. P. R. & Hall, S. J. (1996). Fishing and ground-fish assemblage structure in the north-western North Sea: an analysis of long-term and spatial trends. *Journal of Animal Ecology*, **65**, 577–598.

Hansen, A. J. (1987). Regulation of bald eagle reproductive rates in southeast Alaska. *Ecology*, **68**, 1387–1392.

Hiatt, R. W. & Strasburg, D. W. (1960). Ecological relationships of the fish fauna on coral reefs of the Marshall Islands. *Ecological Monographs*, **30**, 65–127.

Hill, K. & Hawkes, K. (1983). Neotropical hunting among the Ache of eastern Paraguay. In *Adaptive Responses of Native Amazonians*, ed. R. Hames & W. Vickers, pp. 139–188. Academic Press, New York.

Hixon, M. A. (1991). Predation as a process structuring coral reef fish communities. In *The Ecology of Fishes on Coral Reefs*, ed. P. F. Sale, pp. 475–508. Academic Press, San Diego, CA.

Hixon, M. A. & Beets, J. P. (1993). Predation, prey refuges and the structure of coral reef fish assembleges. *Ecological Monographs*, **63**, 77–101.

Horwood, J. W. (2000). No-take zones: a management context. In *Effects of Fishing on Non-target Species and Habitats: Biological, Conservation and Socioeconomic Issues*, ed. M. J. Kaiser & S. J. de Groot, pp. 302–312. Blackwell Science, Oxford.

Hughes, R. N. (1993). Introduction. In *Diet Selection: An Interdisciplinary Approach to Foraging Behaviour*, ed. R. N. Hughes, pp. 1–9. Blackwell Science, Oxford.

Huryn, A. D. (1998). Ecosystem-level evidence for top-down and bottom-up control of production in a grassland stream system. *Oecologia*, **115**, 173–183.

Jennings, S. & Kaiser, M. J. (1998). The effects of fishing on marine ecosystems. *Advances in Marine Biology*, **34**, 201–352.

Jennings, S. & Polunin, N. V. C. (1997). Impacts of predator depletion by fishing on the biomass and diversity of non-target reef fish communities. *Coral Reefs*, **16**, 71–82.

Jennings, S., Reynolds, J. D. & Mills, S. D. (1998). Life history correlates of responses to fisheries exploitation. *Proceedings of the Royal Society of London B*, **265**, 333–339.

Jeppesen, E., Sondergaard, M., Jensen, J. P., Mortensen, E., Hansen, A. M., Jorgensen, T. *et al.* (1998). Cascading trophic interactions from fish to bacteria and nutrients after reduced sewage loading: an 18-year study of a shallow hypertrophic lake. *Ecosystems*, **1**, 250–267.

Kaiser, M. J. & Ramsay, K. (1997). Opportunistic feeding by dabs within areas of trawl disturbance: possible implications for increased survival. *Marine Ecology Progress Series*, **152**, 307–310.

Kirkwood, G. P., Beddington, J. R. & Rossouw, J. A. (1994). Harvesting species of different lifespans. In *Large-scale Ecology and Conservation Biology*, ed. P. J. Edwards, R. M. May & N. R. Webb, pp. 199–227. Blackwell Science, Oxford.

Kline, T. C. Jr, Goering, J. J., Mathisen, O. A., Poe, P. H., Parker, P. L. & Scalan, R. S. (1993). Recycling of elements transported upstream by runs of Pacific salmon: II. ^{15}N and ^{13}C evidence in the Kvichak River watershed, Bristol Bay, south-western Alaska. *Canadian Journal of Fisheries and Aquatic Sciences*, **50**, 2350–2365.

Knapp, A. K., Blair, J. M., Briggs, J. M., Collins, S. L., Hartnett, D. C., Johnson, L. C. & Towne, E. G. (1999). The keystone role of bison in north American tallgrass prairie – bison increase habitat heterogeneity and alter a broad array of plant, community and ecosystem processes. *Bioscience*, **49**, 39–50.

Lenihan, H. S. (1999). Physical–biological coupling on oyster reefs: how habitat structure influences individual performance. *Ecological Monographs*, **69**, 251–275.

Leopold, A. (1949). *A Sand County Almanac and Sketches from Here and There.* Oxford University Press, Oxford.

Lessios, H. A. (1988). Mass mortality of *Diadema antillarum* in the Caribbean: what have we learned? *Annual Reviews of Ecology and Systematics*, **19**, 371–393.

Letourneau, D. K. & Dyer, L. A. (1998). Experimental test in a lowland tropical forest shows top-down effects through four trophic levels. *Ecology*, **79**, 1678–1687.

Mangel, M. (1998). No-take areas for sustainability of harvested species and a conservation invariant for marine reserves. *Ecology Letters*, **1**, 87–90.

Marten, G. G. (1979). Predator removal: effects on fisheries yields in Lake Victoria (East Africa). *Science*, **203**, 646–648.

McClanahan, T. R. (1992). Resource utilization, competition and predation: a model and example from coral reef grazers. *Ecological Modelling*, **61**, 195–215.

McClanahan, T. R. (1995a). A coral-reef ecosystem–fisheries model – impacts of fishing intensity and catch selection on reef structure and processes. *Ecological Modelling*, **80**, 1–19.

McClanahan, T. R. (1995b). Fish predators and scavengers of the sea urchin *Echinometra mathaei* in Kenyan coral-reef marine parks. *Environmental Biology of Fishes*, **43**, 187–193.

McClanahan, T. R. & Muthiga, N. A. (1988). Changes in Kenyan coral reef community structure and function due to exploitation. *Hydrobiologia*, **166**, 269–276.

McClanahan, T. R., Kakamura, A. T., Muthiga, N. A., Gilagabher Yebio, M. & Obura, D. (1996). Effects of sea-urchin reductions on algae, coral and fish populations. *Conservation Biology*, **10**, 136–154.

McClelland, B. R., Young, L. S., Shea, D. S., McClelland, P. T., Allen, H. L. & Spettigue, E. B. (1982). The bald eagle concentration in Glacier National Park, Montana: origin, growth and variation in numbers. *The Living Bird*, **19**, 133–155.

McIntosh, A. R. & Townsend, C. R. (1996). Interactions between fish, grazing invertebrates and algae in a New Zealand stream: a trophic cascade mediated by fish induced changes in behaviour. *Oecologia*, **108**, 174–181.

McLaren, B. E. & Peterson, R. O. (1994). Wolves, moose, and tree rings on Isle Royale. *Science*, **266**, 1555–1558.

Mduma, S. A. R., Sinclair, A. R. E. & Hilborn, R. (1999). Food regulates the Serengeti wildebeest: a 40-year record. *Journal of Animal Ecology*, **68**, 1101–1123.

Milchunas, D. G., Lauenroth, W. K. & Burke, I. C. (1998). Livestock grazing: animals and plant biodiversity of shortgrass steppe and the relationship to ecosystem function. *Oikos*, **83**, 65–74.

Millner, R. S. & Whiting, C. L. (1996). Long-term changes in growth and population abundance of sole in the North Sea from 1940 to the present. *ICES Journal of Marine Science*, **53**, 1185–1195.

Murray, S. N. and 18 co-authors (1999). No-take reserves networks: sustaining fishery populations and marine ecosystems. *Fisheries*, **24**, 11–25.

Myers, R. A., Hutchings, J. A. & Barrowman, N. J. (1996). Hypothesis for the decline of cod in the North Atlantic. *Marine Ecology Progress Series*, **138**, 293–308.

Nehlsen, W., Williams, J. E. & Lichatowich, J. A. (1991). Pacific salmon at the crossroads: stocks at risk from California, Oregon, Idaho, and Washington. *Fisheries*, **16**, 4–21.

Neill, W. M. (1994). Spatial and temporal scaling and the organisation of limnetic communities. In *Aquatic Ecology: Scale, Pattern and Process*, ed. P. S. Giller, A. G. Hildrew & D. G. Rafaelli, pp. 189–231. Blackwell Scientific, Oxford.

Pace, M. L., Cole, J. J., Carpenter, S. R. & Kitchell, J. F. (1999). Trophic cascades revealed in diverse ecosystems. *Trends in Ecology and Evolution*, **14**, 483–488.

Paine, R. T. (1980). Food web linkage, interaction strength and community structure. *Journal of Animal Ecology*, **49**, 667–685.

Parrish, J. D., Callahan, M. W. & Norris, J. E. (1985). Fish trophic relationships that structure reef communities. *Proceedings of the Fifth International Coral Reef Symposium*, **4**, 73–78.

Parrish, J. D., Norris, J. E., Callahan, M. W., Magarifugi, E. J. & Schroeder, R. E. (1986). Piscivory in a coral reef community. In *Gutshop '81: Fish Food Habits and Studies*, ed. G. M. Caillet & C. A. Simenstad, pp. 73–78. University of Washington, Seattle.

Pauly, D., Christensen, V., Dalsgaard, J., Froese, R. & Torres, F. (1998). Fishing down marine food webs. *Science*, **279**, 860–863.

Peters, R. H. (1983). *The Ecological Implications of Body Size*. Cambridge University Press, Cambridge.

Pimm, S. L. & Askins, R. A. (1995). Forest losses predict bird extinctions in eastern North America. *Proceedings of the National Academy of Sciences*, **92**, 9343–9347.

Pimm, S. L., Russell, G. J., Gittleman, J. L. & Brooks, T. M. (1995). The future of biodiversity. *Science*, **269**, 347–350.

Polis, G. A. & Strong, G. R. (1996). Food web complexity and community dynamics. *American Naturalist*, **147**, 813–846.

Polis, G. A., Anderson, W. B. & Holt, R. D. (1997). Toward an integration of landscape and food web ecology: the dynamics of spatially subsidized food-webs. *Annual Review of Ecology and Systematics*, **28**, 289–316.

Ramsay, K., Kaiser, M. J., Rijnsdorp, A. D., Craeymeersch, J. & Ellis, J. (2000). The impact of beam trawling on populations of the benthic scavenger *Asterias rubens* L. In *The Effects of Trawling on Non-target Species and Habitats: Biological, Conservation and Socio-economic Issues*, ed. M. J. Kaiser & S. J. de Groot, pp. 151–162. Blackwell Science, Oxford.

Redford, K. H. (1992). The empty forest. *BioScience*, **42**, 412–422.

Redford, K. H. & Robinson, J. G. (1987). The game of choice: patterns of Indian and colonist hunting in the neotropics. *American Anthropologist*, **89**, 650–667.

Rice, J. & Gislason, H. (1996). Patterns of change in the size spectra of numbers and diversity of the North Sea fish assemblage, as reflected in surveys and models. *ICES Journal of Marine Science*, **53**, 1214–1225.

Rijnsdorp, A. D. & van Leeuwen, P. I. (1996). Changes in growth of North Sea plaice since 1950 in relation to density, eutrophication, beam-trawl effort and temperature. *ICES Journal of Marine Science*, **53**, 1199–1213.

Roberts, C. M. (1998). Sources, sinks and the design of marine reserve networks. *Fisheries*, **23**, 16–19.

Russ, G. R. (1985). Effects of protective management on coral reef fishes in the central Philippines. *Proceedings of the Fifth International Coral Reef Symposium*, **4**, 219–224.

Russ, G. R. (1991). Coral reef fisheries: effects and yields. In *The Ecology of Fishes on Coral Reefs*, ed. P. F. Sale, pp. 601–635. Academic Press, San Diego, CA.

Sainsbury, K. J. (1987). Assessment and management of the demersal fishery on the continental shelf of northwestern Australia. In *Tropical Snappers and Groupers – Biology and Fisheries Management*, ed. J. J. Polovina & S. Ralston, pp. 465–503. Westview Press, Boulder, CO.

Sainsbury, K. J., Campbell, R. A., Lindholm, R. & Whitlaw, A. W. (1998). Experimental management of an Australian multispecies fishery: examining the possibility of trawl-induced habitat modification. In *Global Trends: Fisheries Management*, ed. E. K. Pikitch, D. D. Huppert & M. P. Sissenwine, pp. 107–112. American Fisheries Society Symposium no. 20, Bethesda, MD.

Sale, P. F. (1980). The ecology of fishes on coral reefs. *Oceanography and Marine Biology: An Annual Review*, **18**, 367–421.

Sherman, K., Jones, C., Sullivan, L., Smith, W., Berrien, P. & Ejsymont, L. (1981). Congruent shifts in sandeel abundance in western and eastern North Atlantic ecosystems. *Nature*, **291**, 486–489.

Shiomoto, A., Tadokoro, K., Nagasawa, K. *et al.* (1997). Trophic relations in the subarctic North Pacific ecosystem: possible feeding effects from pink salmon. *Marine Ecology Progress Series*, **150**, 75–85.

Sinclair, A. R. E. & Arcese, P. (eds.) (1995). *Serengeti II: Research, Management and Conservation of an Ecosystem.* University of Chicago Press, Chicago.

Sprules, W. G. & Goyke, A. P. (1994). Size-based structure and production in the pelagia of Lakes Ontario and Michigan. *Canadian Journal of Fisheries and Aquatic Sciences*, **51**, 2603–2611.

Sprules, W. G. & Stockwell, J. D. (1995). Size based biomass and production models in the St Lawrence Great Lakes. *ICES Journal of Marine Science*, **52**, 705–710.

Sprules, W. G., Casselman, J. M. & Shuter, B. J. (1983). Size distributions of pelagic particles in lakes. *Canadian Journal of Fisheries and Aquatic Sciences*, **40**, 1761–1765.

Watling, L. & Norse E. A. (1998). Disturbance of the seabed by mobile fishing gear: a comparison to forest clearcutting. *Conservation Biology*, **12**, 1180–1197.

Willson, M. F. & Halupka, K. C. (1995). Anadromous fish as keystone species in vertebrate communities. *Conservation Biology*, **9**, 489–497.

Winterhalder, B. (1981). Foraging strategies in the boreal environment: an analysis of Cree hunting and gathering. In *Hunter-Gatherer Foraging Strategies*, ed. E. A. Smith & B. Winterhalder, pp. 13–35. Chicago University Press, Chicago.

Wooton, J. T. (1995). Effects of birds on sea urchins and algae: a lower-intertidal trophic cascade. *Ecoscience*, **2**, 321–328.

Yodzis, P. (1998). Local trophodynamics and the interaction of marine mammals and fisheries in the Benguela ecosystem. *Journal of Animal Ecology*, **67**, 635–658.

The half-empty forest: sustainable use and the ecology of interactions

KENT H. REDFORD & PETER FEINSINGER

Exploitation by humans has been the cause of much of the Earth's biotic impoverishment. Ecosystems have been extensively altered or eliminated, biological communities have been modified through extinction and alien species' introduction, and species have been driven extinct. A voracious appetite for natural resources, combined with a virtual disregard for the consequences of this appetite for the Earth's biota, has typified humans through much of the last millennium.

It is therefore somewhat of a paradox that relatively recently exploitation has emerged as a proposed solution to biotic impoverishment and extinction. Advocates of this position point to two factors, a pattern of human-engendered extinction of those elements of biodiversity that are perceived to have no value, and the successes that humans have had in managing some species of animals and plants for sustainable harvesting. This 'use it or lose it' philosophy has come to dominate thinking and action in some ecological and political settings (e.g. Hutton & Dickson, Chapter 20).

In this approach, advocates postulate that sustainable exploitation of a target species will create the social, economic and ecological conditions for continued existence not only of that species but also of the ecosystem that supports it. In other words, sustainable exploitation can be used as a tool not only for economic benefits but also for biodiversity conservation. In this approach, exploited populations, while undergoing harvesting, are assumed to continue to play functional roles in their species assemblages and ecosystems and not to cause the collapse of the ecological system of which they are a part.

But can biodiversity be conserved while species are being sustainably exploited? The answer to this question is usually assumed to be 'yes, if we get the target species harvesting right'. In the enthusiasm for exploitation as a conservation tool, science has been largely neglected. Many questions poised by the 'sustainable use approach' remain unanswered and the political and social climate is often not supportive of criticism of this approach.

It is assumed that science has little to bring to the debate and is being used as a subterfuge by critics of the approach.

In this chapter we examine one of the assumptions underlying the sustainable use approach, i.e. that substantially decreasing the density of a species by harvesting will not negatively influence conservation of the biodiversity of which that species is a part. We bring to bear scattered, and sometimes contradictory, evidence from a variety of disciplines. In an effort to unite disparate data, we provide three hypothetical examples that illustrate our argument. Unfortunately, the available evidence does not provide an unequivocal answer to the question of the impact of sustainable harvesting on biodiversity conservation. In fact, attempting to answer this question reveals a fundamental uncertainty in our understanding of ecological systems: to what extent are communities of plants and animals tightly ecologically organised and to what extent is their organisation loose? In other words, to what extent can the population level of a target species, reduced by harvesting, continue to function in the same ecological manner in the community it inhabits?

While acknowledging this uncertainty we conclude that the evidence is not conclusive that sustainably exploiting a target species can result in conservation of biodiversity. We acknowledge that there is undoubtedly enormous variation between species and ecosystems. We further acknowledge that very few of these systems or species have not been affected by human activities. However, the strategy of sustainable exploitation for conservation has been offered as a blanket solution, ignoring this very same variation. In the absence of certainty we conclude that the precautionary principle strongly suggests that we exercise great caution in proceeding with an approach that may do more harm than good.

THE HALF-EMPTY FOREST

Our argument is based on tropical forests though we are convinced that it could be extended to marine systems, freshwater systems and other terrestrial biomes as well. Some years ago one of us (K.R.) coined the term 'the empty forest' to define a landscape in the tropics (or elsewhere) whose verdant appearance today masks a serious wasting disease that tomorrow might greatly modify the assemblage of plant and animal species present (Redford, 1992). The disease begins when some animal populations become entirely extinct or nearly so, progresses through drastic changes in the species interactions in which those animals had participated directly when the forest was 'full', and leads to cascading effects throughout the remainder of the biota. Redford (1992) drew special attention to tropical forests that human hunters had emptied of those mammals and large birds whose absence would strongly affect the plant–animal and predator–prey interactions in which they had formerly participated. His concern followed Janzen's (1974) warning based on plants and the insects that pollinate them: to sustain a tropical landscape and its biota, conserve species interactions, not just species.

Redford's (1992) argument explored the two extreme states – the empty forest with animal populations locally extinct and the full forest with populations at 'traditional densities' or at carrying capacity. Clearly, though, intermediate conditions exist. In fact, contemporary approaches to animal harvesting rely on a reduction of animal populations below 'traditional' densities, to maximise productivity, without extinguishing them. We thus define the 'half-empty forest' (*sensu lato*) as an area where population densities of some animals or plants, key participants in species interactions, are substantially below traditional levels but still comfortably above minimum viable population (MVP) size from the demographer's, the geneticist's and the resource manager's point of view.

In this chapter, we integrate a variety of themes from animal behaviour, ecology, conservation and management to show that in the half-empty forest species interactions and community dynamics might be disrupted in the long term in a similar way to what might happen in the empty forest, although in different and much less obvious ways. We use this argument to suggest the need to evaluate the utility of sustainable harvest as a tool for biodiversity conservation.

Before exploring the chain of events initiated by partial reductions in animal population densities (the half-empty forest), though, we must review the more extreme cases of reductions – all the way to extinction – and the 'cascading effects' that these initiate.

RESULTS OF EXTINCTIONS: CASCADING EFFECTS

Whether an animal species goes extinct globally or a specific population goes extinct locally, the effects may cascade through the remainder of the biota and lead to dramatic shifts in community composition, structure, and function (see Kaiser & Jennings, Chapter 16). One compelling recent demonstration of cascading effects and the role that conservation measures can take in preventing these involves a forest, a marine kelp forest. Off the shore of southern California, Estes *et al.* (1989) showed that kelp forests flourish in the presence of sea otters (*Enhydra lutris*), whereas local extinc-

Table 17.1. *Examples of putative or demonstrated cascading effects*

Extinction of taxon	Location	References
Anadromous fish	Northwest North America	Francis, 1997; Willson *et al.*, 1998
Grizzly bears and wolves	Greater Yellowstone, USA	Berger, 1999; Berger *et al.*, 2001
Top predators and resultant meso-predator release	USA and worldwide	Leigh *et al.*, 1993; Palomares *et al.*, 1995; Ostfeld *et al.*, 1996; Crooks & Soulé, 1999; Terborgh *et al.*, 1999
Ecosystem engineers: beaver, bison, detritivorous fish	North America and Venezuela	Jones *et al.*, 1994; Pollock *et al.*, 1995; Flecker, 1996; Naiman *et al.*, 1988; Knapp *et al.*, 1999
Large mammals and birds	Neotropical forests	Dirzo & Miranda, 1991; Redford, 1992; Terborgh & Wright, 1994; Chapman & Onderdonk, 1998; Andersen, 1999; Ganzhorn *et al.*, 1999; Hamann & Curio, 1999; Wright *et al.*, 2000

tion of otters permits sea urchins to multiply, overgraze, and virtually extinguish kelp. That is, sea otter predation appears to hold sea urchin populations in check, while sea urchin grazing limits populations of fleshy algae. Since kelp forests shelter a horde of marine species (Dayton *et al.*, 1998), sea otter conservation is urgent not only for its own sake but also for the sake of preventing, or reversing, cascading effects that change the nature of that entire marine landscape.

Other cascading effects that have resulted, appear to result, or are predicted to result from extinctions are listed in Table 17.1. In short, cascading effects of local and global extinctions certainly have occurred in the past, are occurring at present, and will undoubtedly occur with increasing frequency as the rate of extinctions accelerates (Pace *et al.*, 1999).

ECOLOGICAL EXTINCTION AND ITS COMPLICATIONS

Our argument is that exploitation might result in extinction, not extinction of a global or local nature but an ecological one. Estes *et al.* (1989) have defined three types of extinction: global extinction, the universal disappearance of a species; local extinction, the disappearance of the species from a particular part of its historical range, such as a forest; while ecological extinction is 'the reduction of a species to such low abundance that, although it is still present in the community, it no longer interacts significantly with other species'.

The first two types of extinction are easy to understand and measure – when all individuals are gone, the population or species is extinct. However, ecological extinction is much more difficult to understand and even more difficult to measure. Perhaps the major challenge facing those interested in studying ecological extinction is defining what the term 'significant' means in terms of a species no longer interacting 'significantly' with other species. As discussed below, the meaning of this 'significance' raises issues of underlying models of ecological organisation and change. These difficulties in definition, however, do not mean that ecological extinction does not exist. Recent work by marine scientists has been critical in documenting ecological extinction (Dayton *et al.*, 1998) and the concept has been applied to terrestrial settings as well (Novaro *et al.*, 2000).

Even if interactive species such as those mentioned in Table 17.1 are extinct neither globally nor locally, and their local population densities are maintained above the MVP size as calculated on the basis of genetic and demographic parameters, cascading effects will not necessarily be averted. Conner (1988) discussed cases where wildlife populations are reduced but not extinguished, and defined the concept of 'ecologically functional populations' as 'populations at levels above that of minimum viability . . . in sufficient abundance to be ecologically functional in their community'. That is, vertebrate populations which meet demographic and genetic criteria for viability could still be so sparse that their historically intense participation in species interactions is now inconsequential. According to Estes *et al.* (1989), for all intents and purposes these species are ecologically extinct. For example, if populations of seed-dispersing birds were maintained only at MVP levels, total numbers of seeds dispersed might decline abruptly and vegetation dynamics would be affected. Small-mammal populations maintained only at MVP levels might be insufficient to disperse spores of mycorrhizal fungi throughout the forest, again with drastic effects on species composition and ecosystem function (Conner, 1988; see also Novaro *et al.*, 2000). In the cases listed in Table 17.1, local or global extinction is sufficient but not necessary to initiate the cascading effects. If the token population of species A can no longer maintain interactions with species B to Z in the style to which they had been accustomed, the cascading effects that result will be indistinguishable from those where species A has gone completely extinct. That is, the 'nearly empty' forest with demographically viable but ecologically extinct animal populations may be simply another 'empty forest' from the perspective of species interactions.

To examine the impacts of population reduction of a target species due to harvesting we present two models of species interaction in the half-empty forest: the uniform model and the differential model. These models are drastic simplifications of the real world and we use them more to raise questions concerning assumptions underlying current practices than to resolve fundamental ecological issues. We suggest that the first, or uniform, model underlies the philosophy, if not the practice, of many advocates of sustainable use. This position is held despite the ecological evidence that suggests the inappropriateness of the model. After a refutation of this model we offer a second model, the 'differential' model, that seems to better describe current ecological understanding.

THE UNIFORM MODEL AND ITS REJECTION

The half-empty forest may still retain its entire species list of eye-catching vertebrates at reduced but not inconsequential population densities. Furthermore, a non-critical appraisal of the forest's key species interactions might suggest that harvesting wildlife populations or reducing them by other means has not substantially threatened either the half-empty forest's network of interactions or the sustainability of its present composition.

To examine species interactions more closely, consider a single animal population at traditional population levels (a population in the 'full forest'), the individuals of which collectively use six discrete classes of resources that differ somewhat in availability (Figure 17.1a). The classes could be distinct species of prey animals or plants, or individuals with distinct properties within a single species of prey animal or plant. As a whole, the consumer population under consideration uses some classes relatively more intensively than others; in other words, the population displays selectivity among the resources available (Figure 17.1a).

In the case of the uniform model, let us assume that harvesting or another phenomenon reduces the consumer population by 50%. All else being equal, this should simply lead to a 50% reduction in use, on average, across the six classes of resources, i.e. the response is 'uniform' (Figure 17.1a). The population displays the same pattern of relative selectivity as before, and even the least preferred class of resource still has its share of users. The goodness-of-fit between relative availability and relative use of resources has not changed. In this scenario, half-emptying the forest has quantitative but not qualitative effects. No reason exists to expect

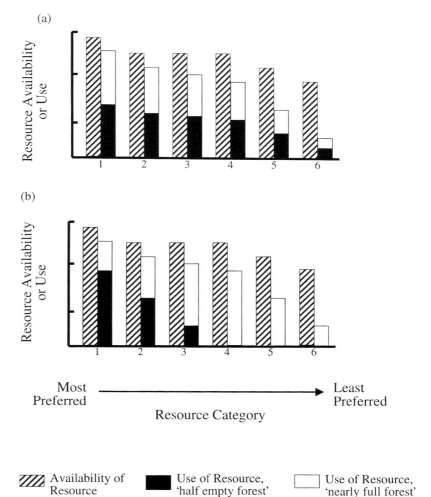

Figure 17.1. Six classes of resources and their relative availability to, or collective use by, an animal population. (a) The uniform model for resource use. Even in the nearly full forest the animal population displays selectivity among resources, but it uses even the least preferred class to some extent. When the population is halved and the amount of resources it collectively uses is reduced, the collective diet maintains the same relative pattern as before. (b) The differential model. When the population and its total resource use are halved, the pattern of collective resource use 'migrates' to the most preferred classes, the least preferred resources are used little if at all, and the goodness-of-fit between availability and use is much lower than before.

disruptions in community function or cascading effects anywhere near the magnitude of those in the empty forest.

Though not appreciated by many ecologists, this uniform model appears to underlie, often only implicitly, the actions of many advocates and practitioners of sustainable harvesting when they argue that such actions will conserve biodiversity. However, the available ecological data do not support this assumption. In particular, the assumption that individuals within a population will respond in a homogeneous fashion irrespective of that population's density is not supported. In order to refute the 'uniform' model we present a brief summary of the ecological evidence against it.

The evidence suggests that changes in animal population density appear to have qualitative as well as quantitative effects through either one or both of two mechanisms:

1 The individuals that make up the consumer population are not identical. One animal's choices may differ consistently from those of its neighbour.
2 An individual may change its choices as a direct or indirect result of the density of competitors of the same species.

In fact, the collective diet, or other pattern of resource use, displayed by an animal population is simply the sum of the choices made by the different individuals that happen to make up that population (Feinsinger, 1976).

For over 30 years, population biologists and behavioural ecologists have devoted a great deal of attention to each of these means, but almost exclusively in the context of basic biology rather than wildlife management and conservation (but see Sutherland, 1996; Goss-Custard & Sutherland, 1997). Analyses of field data on such themes as interspecific competition, predation and wildlife food habits have tended to lump individuals together and treat the population's use of resources as a whole. To our knowledge, though, nearly all of the investigations into diets of conspecific individuals have found that differences do exist and that the uniform model is not supported. These differences may result from four different factors: (1) individual differences with a morphological basis; (2) individual differences without an evident morphological basis; (3) individual differences with a cultural basis; and (4) individual differences among opportunistic foragers in different microhabitats (see Table 17.2 for examples and citations).

These four factors have found considerable support in the literature of basic ecology and animal behaviour. Reviews of 'optimal foraging theory' (Pyke et al., 1977; Pyke, 1984; Stephens & Krebs, 1986) and many empirical studies these cite, buttressed by more recent studies, show that

Table 17.2. Mechanisms responsible for individual differences in foraging

Mechanisms	Sample taxa	References
Individual differences with a morphological basis	Sunfish	Ehlinger & Wilson, 1988
	Galapagos finches	Boag & Grant, 1984; Grant, 1986
	Centrarchid fishes	Keast, 1977
	Deermice	Smartt & Lemen, 1980
	Kites	Smith & Temple, 1982
	Garter snakes	Arnold, 1981a,b
	Hummingbirds	Feinsinger & Colwell, 1978; Feinsinger et al., 1988
	Leopards	Bailey, 1992
Consistent individual differences without an evident morphological basis	Cocos Island finch	Werner & Sherry, 1987
	Marine snails	West, 1986; Burrows & Hughes, 1991
	Harvester ants	Rissing, 1981
	Piscivorous African cichlids	Kohda, 1994
	Trout	Bryan & Larkin, 1972
	Largemouth bass	Schindler et al., 1997
	Crows	Powell, 1974
	Ducks	Hohman, 1985
	American redstarts	Holmes et al., 1978
	Hyaenas	Kruuk, 1972
Individual differences with a cultural basis	Herbivorous insects	Fox & Morrow, 1981
	Bees	Linsley, 1978; Eickwort & Ginsberg, 1980
	Gulls	Annett & Pierotti, 1999
	Wild dogs	Schaller, 1972
	Hyaenas	Kruuk, 1972
	Sloths	Montgomery & Sunquist, 1978
Individual differences among opportunistic foragers in different microhabitats	Bees	Heinrich, 1976, 1979
	Blackbirds	Orians, 1980
	Neotropical flycatchers	Sherry, 1984
	North American warblers	Morse, 1971, 1973
	Lions	Schaller, 1972

neighbouring, conspecific foragers modify the food choices made by each other, while isolated foragers consistently select those resources that are intrinsically the most rewarding. A general model, the 'ideal free distribution' (Fretwell & Lucas, 1970), predicted similar outcomes but as a result of individual choice, not coercion.

The conclusion from review of these data is inexorable: the uniform model does not adequately describe the interactions between animals in the half-empty forest. Rather there seem to be complicated rules governing the extent and nature of these interactions that are strongly affected by population density.

THE DIFFERENTIAL MODEL

The second model for examining the impacts of population reduction of a target species due to harvesting is the 'differential model'. Substantial reductions in animal population density (i.e. half-emptying the forest) will rarely if ever result in the uniform model across the various classes of foods. Instead, depending on which particular individuals vanish and take their unique diets with them, some kinds of food may be consumed nearly as frequently as in the full forest, while others will scarcely be consumed at all. Goodness-of-fit between relative availability and use of the different resources will almost certainly be poorer than in the full forest. Figure 17.1b introduces the second model, the differential model. This has also been called the 'buffer effect' (Brown, 1969), and is now generally known as density-dependent habitat selection (for a review, see Rosenzweig, 1991).

The differential model suggests that the change in goodness-of-fit will follow a pattern: not just any resources but instead those less preferred will be passed over by the surviving foragers. Whether mechanism 1, mechanism 2, or both operate (see above), effects of the reduction in animal density will be heterogeneous across the classes of resources. In the half-empty forest, according to the preceding argument some kinds of food may not be consumed at all. Not being eaten may be a bad thing from the perspective of food items such as fruits on plants that wait in vain for their seeds to be dispersed. If the different classes of resources are different species, as in the other examples below, population dynamics of the species less preferred by consumers might change dramatically, with effects that cascade through the entire landscape. To paraphrase Janzen (1986), the half-empty forest may contain many species interactions that appear healthy on the surface but are really 'living dead' relicts in which animals no longer participate. The living dead interactions may occur in the same forest as, and even side by side with, the perfectly viable interactions that still involve the very same animal populations (cf. Figure 17.1b).

THREE HYPOTHETICAL CASES

In order to illustrate how the differential model might work in specific settings, we provide three hypothetical examples below. As mentioned

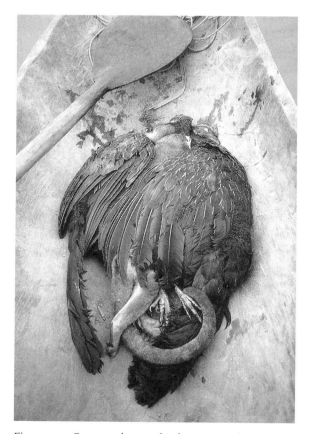

Figure 17.2. Guans and potos shot by Yuqui Indians, Bolivia.

previously, the species involved are not ones that would normally be expected to be prime targets for commercial exploitation but the examples are based on the best information that we could collect and on settings closest to our experience.

Case 1. Frugivores and fleshy fruits

Let us say that a cloud forest in Central America initially supports a robust population of black guans (Aves: Cracidae: *Chamaepetes unicolor*; Figure 17.2). During the wet season a tree species of the family Lauraceae ripens its fruit. Fruiting among the trees making up the population is not uniform: on average, smaller, younger, or more stressed individuals produce much sparser fruit crops than do large, robust trees, while genetic variation among trees occasions differences in the pulp biomass and/or the pulp: seed ratio per fruit. Most guans move among only the most reward-ing trees, those having the largest fruit crops and/or the greatest reward per fruit. Nevertheless, solitary individuals and some guan groups – as well as the first-mentioned guans, once they deplete the fruit crops in the most popular trees – are stuck with the less rewarding trees. As a result, the guan population as a whole consumes at least some fruits from virtually every tree of the population in question regardless of the nature of fruit crop and fruit characteristics. Over decades or centuries, by chance nearly every tree produces at least one seed that ends up in a 'safe site' on the forest floor and grows to maturity.

Now, hunting pressure depletes the guan population but does not extin-guish it. The half-empty forest that results still supports guan numbers well above MVP size, so conservation biologists see no reason to worry about the fate of the guan population per se. Nor do they worry about guans' role in seed dispersal, for guans still flock to the conspicuously fruiting trees as before. What the guan-focused biologists do not notice, though, is that now the birds scarcely deplete even the fruit crops on the preferred trees before the fruiting season ends. That is, those trees provided enough fruits for all the surviving guans. In consequence, there has been no incentive for guans to visit the less preferred trees, and all the fruits on these less-preferred trees have fallen, much to the joy of insects, fungi and seed-eating rodents on the forest floor. The marginal trees retain an 'ecological memory' of when times were good and guans were visiting, but now they are far less likely than their larger-fruited neighbours to contribute to the next tree generation. The result is possible loss of genetic variation.

To our knowledge this scenario, which emphasises mechanism 2, has not yet been demonstrated in full. All the elements, however, are in place. Conspecific trees produce different numbers of fruits, and those with larger fruit crops tend to attract more frugivores. Fruit traits such as pulp biomass or pulp: seed ratio vary among conspecific trees of the family Lauraceae and others, are heritable and relate to selection by birds (Wheelwright, 1993). Local populations of guans and other Cracidae are frequently depleted, if not extinguished, by human hunters (Silva & Strahl, 1991). In a somewhat similar case, depletion of the spider monkey *Atelus paniscus* appears to lead to demographic and genetic changes in *Inga ingoides* (Mimosaceae), a tree population for which it is the principal disperser (Pacheco & Simonetti, 1998; L. F. Pacheco, personal communication).

Among other frugivores mechanism 1 may be more important than mechanism 2, although both may operate simultaneously. In the cloud forests of Monteverde, Costa Rica, the demography of three species of understorey plants depends primarily on consumption of their small watery fruits, and subsequent seed dispersal, by one highly frugivorous bird population and secondarily on two others. Yet, only 35% of faecal samples from these birds contained seeds from at least one of the three plant species (Murray, 1988). In Costa Rican dry forest, frugivorous bats (*Carollia perspecillata*) from the same roost have different foraging routes. These often remain quite consistent over time and appear to result in individual differences in diets (Fleming, 1988). Although he did not document individual differences per se, Fleming showed that diets varied with sex, age and social status. Furthermore, seeds of even the most popular and bat-dependent fruiting plants showed up in only a small fraction of bat faecal samples at any one time (Fleming, 1988). In short, differential but cryptic effects of half-emptying the forest on plant–frugivore interactions may initiate an impressive cascade of effects through processes that resemble those given in Figures 17.1a,b (see Bond, 1995).

Case 2. Bumblebees in a half-empty field

In a north temperate field filled with wildflowers and bumblebees, virtually every plant whose floral traits match bumblebees' capabilities are visited by queen or worker bees (Apidae: *Bombus*) that seek nectar or pollen and unintentionally pollinate the plants they visit (Heinrich, 1976, 1979). On a given day in mid to late summer, even the few dozen workers of a small bumblebee colony might collectively exploit flowers of nearly all such plant species in flower. Nevertheless, the individual worker has a much narrower diet, 'majoring' on only one plant species at a time while 'minoring' on one or two others. Heinrich (1976, 1979) and other authors (e.g. Laverty, 1980) showed that a young bee just entering the workforce settles on its major plant species through trial and error, based on the food reward it encounters per unit effort it expends. Often bees with seniority are already heavily exploiting the best nectar producers. The neophyte bee will encounter only the dregs left behind in those flowers, will perceive the species as being unrewarding, and most likely will select as its major another species that is less exploited by senior bees. The net result is that bumblebee foragers spread out over the full range of flowers available.

Heinrich (1976, 1979) experimentally limited bee numbers relative to flowers and found that all neophytes chose the one plant species whose flowers provided the greatest intrinsic nectar rewards – perhaps the clearest demonstration ever of mechanism 2. Likewise, an open field half-emptied of bumblebees, perhaps by insecticides used nearby or through a decline in cats and the explosion of mouse populations (Darwin, 1896), might produce more nectar and pollen than the surviving bees with seniority can possibly exploit (cf. Kearns *et al.*, 1998). It follows that neophyte and senior bees alike may now perceive the same small subset of plant species, those with the greatest intrinsic production of nectar or pollen per unit bee effort, as being the most rewarding. Thus, during a given day or week, most or all bees from the colony will major on the same plant species, ignoring the intrinsically less rewarding plants flowering nearby. Pollination, fertilisation, seed production and contributions to the soil seed bank will become skewed in favour of those few, popular majors that replace one another over the growing season. This simple behavioural phenomenon – flower choice by flexibly foraging bumblebees – could have profound effects on vegetation dynamics and lead to an increasingly simplified plant assemblage in the half-empty field. As for the guan story above, we are unaware of studies that document this entire scenario from start to finish, but the plethora of studies on bumblebee foraging indicate that the scenario is realistic.

Case 3. Hummingbirds in a half-empty cloud forest

Hummingbirds in Neotropical cloud forests visit the flowers of many plant species and pollinate most of these, including epiphytes (especially Bromeliaceae and shrubby Ericaceae), climbers and understorey shrubs and herbs. At Monteverde, Costa Rica, two hummingbird populations are responsible for most such pollination. Long-billed *Phaethornis guy* exploits and pollinates many plants with long flowers, while shorter-billed *Lampornis castaneoventris* exploits and pollinates nearly all plants with short flowers but still adapted for bird pollination (Feinsinger *et al.*, 1986). The flower species exploited by either hummingbird vary widely in nectar production and in popularity with hummingbird visitors (Feinsinger *et al.*, 1987). On some days many flowers of the least preferred species go unpollinated. Over time, though, even the least preferred plants achieve some pollination and set abundant seeds (Figure 17.1a).

Most individual *Lampornis* and *Phaethornis* visit flowers of several different species daily or even during a single foraging bout. At any one moment an individual may carry pollen grains of as many as 15 (*Lampornis*) or 16 (*Phaethornis*) plant species on its bill and head (Feinsinger *et al.*, 1987). Nevertheless, the pollen loads carried by different individuals are rarely identical, and direct observations of foraging hummingbirds confirm that different individuals of both species make different choices. For example, male *Lampornis* often defend densely flowering shrubs in the understorey, or flower-rich ericaceous shrubs in the forest canopy, but not both at the same time. Females scrounge among plants with sparser flower crops or those belonging to less preferred species (Feinsinger *et al.*, 1988). A *Phaethornis* that imbibes the nectar in its favourite flowers lowers their value to the next *Phaethornis* to come along, forcing the second to seek out alternative plant individuals or species (see Gill, 1988).

During a long-term study at Monteverde, one of us (P.F.) and colleagues collected the pollen load from each mist-netted hummingbird, then counted the pollen grains per plant species (Feinsinger *et al.*, 1987). Using the methodology of Ebenman & Nilsson (1982) for calculating the inter- and intraindividual components of 'niche width', we now estimated the contribution of the average hummingbird individual to the total diversity of pollen carried by its population in that month, over 12 months. Collectively, the 2–14 *Phaethornis* mist-netted in a given month carried pollen grains from 8–21 (average 16) plant species. Considering not only species richness but also grains per pollen species, on average each individual contributed 57.5% towards the *Phaethornis* population's 'pollen breadth', while differences among individuals contributed 42.5%. Collectively, the 3–20 *Lampornis* mist-netted in a given month carried 7–26 pollen species (average 16). On average, each *Lampornis* contributed 44.9% towards its population's 'pollen breadth' while differences among individuals contributed 55.1%. Thus, on average, about half of a population's pollen breadth consisted of differences among individuals.

If the forest were suddenly half-emptied of hummingbirds, as has happened with other pollinator species, how might plants be affected? Even if there were no change in the flower choices made by each hummingbird survivor, clearly mechanism 1 would come into play as fewer birds contributed to the between-individual component of pollen breadth. That is, the collective diversity of pollen carried by a hummingbird population would decline as fewer individuals, and consequently fewer interindividual differences, were involved. In such a circumstance, it follows that some plant species might experience decreased pollination success and decreased seed output. Furthermore, flower choices made by hummingbird survivors would almost certainly change (mechanism 2). With less jostling for nectar esources the hummingbirds of one species, like guans or bumblebees, might all concentrate at their preferred plant species and the most abundantly flowering individuals, ignoring the scattered or intrinsically less rewarding flowers that some bird or another had formerly visited in the full forest. In the extreme case the low-ranked plant species, as well as sparsely flowering plants of preferred species, might achieve virtually no pollination whatsoever, resulting not only in genetic impoverishment within the preferred species themselves but also in decreased diversity in the seed bank and eventual cascading effects throughout the forest.

Fortunately, this scenario remains hypothetical, for hummingbirds as a group often seem quite oblivious to moderate disturbance (Feinsinger *et al.*, 1988) and clearly are not high on the hit lists of human hunters. Other animal pollinators, however, are more sensitive to various forms of human interference and may already have initiated cascading effects similar to the ones just described (Rathcke & Jules, 1993; Aizen & Feinsinger, 1994a,b, 2001; Buchmann & Nabhan, 1996; Murcia, 1996; Allen-Wardell *et al.*, 1998; Kearns *et al.*, 1998; Renner, 1998). Particular attention has focused on the fragmentation of habitats, which may 'half-empty' the remnants of their pollinators and generate cascading effects at the fragment or land-scape.

Conclusion

Clearly hummingbirds and bumblebees are not targets of sustainable harvesting programs; guans themselves are also unlikely to be targeted. However, all three taxa have been shown, in some places, to be negatively impacted on by human actions. The taxa that have been most studied by population biologists, community ecologists, and behavioural ecologists are those that currently provide the data most germane to our argument. Unfortunately, it is not these taxa that are usually targeted for sustainable harvesting. These target taxa, the focus of resource managers, have not often been the subject of relevant ecological work.

We are left hoping that scientists with a conservation interest will begin to examine the scenario laid out in this chapter, study taxa that are subject to sustainable use schemes, and collect the data necessary to evaluate our argument in their own systems.

IMPLICATIONS OF THE DIFFERENTIAL MODEL TO SUSTAINABLE HARVESTING OF WILDLIFE

The examples above deal with only a few of the multitude of species interactions that might be derailed in the half-empty forest. Of course, even without any human intervention there is no such thing as a full forest. Densities of all consumer populations involved in species interactions never remain in perfect equilibrium at all times with their food species such that the mutualistic interactions function and exploitation interactions constantly control prey populations (see Levey & Benkman, 1999). All landscapes have always experienced, and will always experience, spatial and temporal changes not only in the species identity of interactors but also in the goodness-of-fit between one side and the other.

Our argument is not based on the existence of a 'pristine' state of tropical forests, in which all species are in ecological harmony, with this pristine state disturbed by human actions. Rather, our argument concerns the relative difference between the extent and magnitude of ecological interactions in tropical forests relatively little affected by human actions and those that more recently have been heavily impacted on by human hunting. We suggest that there are two factors which contribute to the appropriateness of this comparison. First, the intensity and rate of recent human-induced change are unparalleled in the ecological history of most taxa. Secondly, human-induced change is often unidirectional – ecological systems rarely have the opportunity to rebound – as they might have in their less-human-dominated pasts.

Recent work has strongly supported the incredible impact that contemporary human hunting is having on tropical forest faunas (see cases in Robinson & Bennett, 2000; Fa & Peres, Chapter 10). As an example, based on an exhaustive study of the impacts of human hunting at 24 Amazonian sites, Peres (2000b) concludes: 'Subsistence hunting in Amazonia . . . can result in profound changes in the structure of tropical forest vertebrate communities through (a) shifts in the relative abundance of different size classes, (b) significant reductions in the overall community biomass, and (c) changes in guild structure' (see also Fa & Peres, Chapter 10). The impacts of commercial hunting in tropical forests are even more severe, with extraction rates many times higher than those reported for subsistence hunting (Robinson *et al.*, 1999).

Human-driven decreases in population densities of tropical forest faunas have been shown to have knock-on ecological effects. A variety of studies have shown that the demographic structure of some plant populations that have long depended on strong interactions with large tropical forest vertebrates may be disrupted in the absence of those animals and their ecological actions (for reviews see Redford, 1992; Peres, 2000a). In a case study of the impact of human poaching on Panamian tropical forests Wright *et al.* (2000) conclude that 'The net effect of removal of game species . . . varies among plant species, and altered plant species composition is likely to be a widespread consequence of poaching'. In this case, as in many others, the species of mammals have not been completely removed, but have been greatly reduced in density.

Less preferred species or individuals, whether flowering plants, fruiting plants, or potential prey, will often suffer, or profit, from the decrease in consumer densities, resulting in short-term shifts in their reproductive success or population dynamics relative to those of the more popular individuals or species. The arguments and examples presented above suggest that a forest that is abruptly half emptied through human intervention may display departures from interactors' 'goodness-of-fit' that are orders of magnitude more intense and prolonged than those occurring when the forest was nearly full. In other words, removal of significant numbers of individuals will probably move the ecological system outside of its historical range of variability (Morgan *et al.*, 1994).

Wright *et al.* (2000) also point out that studies of the impact of decrease in faunas in tropical forests have produced inconsistent outcomes. In a comparison of studies in Mexico, Uganda and Panama, investigators found that the net effect of anthropogenic disturbance on plant density and diversity is unpredictable. In all cases there were results, but in differing directions. There clearly remains a tremendous amount to learn concerning the ecological impacts of tropical forest vertebrates in the half-empty forest.

Sustainable harvesting and ecological extinction

Not all decreases in population density are unplanned by-products of human exploitation. One increasingly popular form of exploitation whose effect is to half-empty the forest, while conscientiously avoiding emptying it entirely, is the management of wildlife populations for sustainable harvest. The concept of sustainable harvesting presupposes that populations can be managed so as to remain viable demographically and genetically while being continuously culled at rates sufficient to provide significant quantities of food or revenue (Grigg *et al.*, 1995; Grigg & Pople, Chapter 18). This concept sometimes includes the assumption – implicit or explicit – that a harvested population, viable in itself, will maintain the network of its species interactions and thereby conserve the biodiversity. In most cases where this reasoning is used, the biodiversity in question is implied as being biodiversity in all of its components and attributes (*sensu* Redford & Richter, 1999).

Frequently, though, the sole concern of a harvesting protocol appears to be the viability of the target population, without conscious thought towards sustaining its biological interactions and therefore conserving the biodiversity in which it is imbedded. If there is an underlying model in the mind of most implementers, it is the uniform model. To the resource manager, the subtle behavioural differences expressed by individuals seem to be of no relevance to the success of the sustainable harvest. However, as we have shown, consideration of these differences may be vital to success.

Focusing on the population as the level of concern has allowed a perceived alliance between harvesters and conservationists. In fact, harvesting sustainably is regarded as equivalent to conservation in this perspective as expressed by Shea *et al.* (1998): 'In conservation, we aim to minimize the chance that a population declines to extinction. In harvesting, we seek to maintain exploited populations at productive levels'.

Ostfeld *et al.* (1996), among others, have pointed out that sustainable harvesting protocols that take such myopic viewpoints could result in unintended consequences such as cascading effects throughout the landscape. As Freese (1998) emphasised, 'sustainable off-take and ecological sustainability are two separate, and often divergent, goals'. Our argument throughout this chapter suggests that harvesting animal populations with the sole goal of managing for a sustained off-take while ignoring possible knock-on effects may result in ecological extinction that might seriously alter the fate of the entire landscape, even if those populations maintain themselves at quite respectable levels and appear superficially to maintain key interactions with other species.

We do not mean to disparage the goals of sustainable harvesting. In particular, harvesting may provide substantial calorific or economic benefits to local people (Figure 17.3). Often sustainable harvesting is the only practical means of preserving some original habitat, staving off complete conversion of the landscape, and preserving some, if not all, species interactions (Grigg *et al.*, 1995; Hutton & Dickson, Chapter 20). We do, however, urge wildlife ecologists and wildlife managers to consider that harvesting may create a half-empty forest, probably leads to differential effects on species interactions, and most likely initiates cascading effects. Ecological complexity being what it is, those cascading effects could well double back to haunt the sustainable harvest itself.

As a coda: rather than half-emptying the forest of harvested species, game management in the North Temperate zone, at least, has sometimes turned the full forest into a 'supersaturated' forest. The most compelling example may be white-tailed deer *Odocoileus virginianus* in the eastern USA, which have reached pest proportions. In this case, the forest, now supersaturated with white-tails, is experiencing quite dramatic cascading effects (Stromayer & Warren, 1997; Waller & Alverson, 1997). While it concentrates on the scenario of the half-empty forest, our argument could easily be modified for the scenario of the supersaturated forest as well.

The half-empty ocean?

Though our argument has focused on tropical forests, it is possible that a similar situation might be occurring in the world's oceans. Exploitation of fish in the ocean does not appear to be sustainable even when only the

Figure 17.3. A Kayapo hunter in eastern Amazonia, Brazil.

exploited populations themselves are considered (Roberts, 1997; Dayton *et al.*, 1998). As one fish stock plummets to commercially unprofitable levels, exploitation turns to other stocks, which are often of smaller species and/or of species at lower trophic levels (Roberts, 1997; Pauly *et al.*, 1998; Jennings *et al.*, 1999; National Academy Press, 1999). Most seriously, in some cases fisheries practices have already initiated dramatic cascading effects throughout marine ecosystems (Parsons, 1993; Dayton *et al.*, 1995).

Some of these cascading effects may result from a very simple action: selective harvesting of the larger individuals within an exploited population. Mechanism 1 clearly operates among fishes and other marine food species such as lobsters *Homarus americanus*: individual diets change with increasing size. Thus selective harvesting of large individuals may affect one entire segment of the span of resources used by the predator population. This freedom from predation now enjoyed by large prey items may reverberate throughout the local seascape (Steneck, 1996; Dayton *et al.*, 1998 cf. Kaiser & Jennings, Chapter 16).

'Subtle effects' and the precautionary principle

In an important book, McDonnell & Pickett (1993) pointed out the urgency of ecologists beginning to study the 'subtle' effects of human influence. They defined subtlety as covering a variety of often inconspicuous or un-expected interactions of humans with ecosystems including indirect effects and lagged effects. The effects we are highlighting in this chapter fall squarely into this category. Their subtlety does not negate their signifi-cance.

Subtle interactions were not a part of early ecological thinking which suggested that species were tightly bound to one another by a web of eco-logical interactions. More recent thinking, such as that exemplified in Pimm's 1991 book *The Balance of Nature?* questioned this approach, sug-gesting instead that community composition was fluid and interactions were more opportunistic than tightly deterministic. Most ecologists have rejected the equilibrium models and turned enthusiastically to non-equilibrium models (McDonnell & Pickett, 1993).

The current ecological literature is replete with arguments about the effect of species' loss on the stability and productivity of ecosystems. The message of these studies seems to be that some species matter more than others in terms of various measures of ecosystem processes and that differ-ent ecological systems function in different ways (Kaiser & Jennings, Chap-ter 16). In general, though, it appears that there is more redundancy and resilience than had been assumed under the 'balance of nature' view of ecological systems. As F. Micheli (unpublished n.d.) wrote: 'Theory and data indicate that there is considerable indeterminacy about the type, mag-nitude and direction of community changes following food-web alterations . . . Because of the inherent variability of ecological processes and the frag-mentary data available, we will never be able to fully explain and predict species dynamics and community change.'

Most work has dealt with the presence/absence of species and has not examined the impacts of decreased density. It does seem clear though that species vary in their susceptibility to the impacts of changing density with perhaps many showing only limited response. As Winemiller & Polis (1993) wrote, 'changes in the abundance of focal species are often accom-panied by changes in the abundance of species linked both directly via consumer–resource interactions, and indirectly via competition and trophic cascades.' Those species most likely to be targeted by humans for sustainable exploitation schemes may be those most affected. As an example, there are very few large or very large organisms that have not been in the past, or are not now, targets for use. Those species most often targeted by humans may also be disproportionately strong interactors, whose decreased density may disproportionately affect their ecosystem. The science of ecology has been devoted to discovering universal organising principles, many of which have been found. But it appears that human intervention can reshuffle the ecological pack, resulting in ecological outcomes that are different over time, ecological setting, and type and extent of human interaction. Human activity appears to be capable of decoupling basic ecological drivers from species' 'natural' responses, creating a novel ecology (Foster et al., 1998). Winemiller & Polis (1993) in their review of food webs emphasise this point: 'It is uncertain how the structure of natural systems and those altered by humans correspond to one another: we are unsure to what extent knowledge gained in one system applies to the other.' Food web theory and understanding is not at a state to allow managers to feel any confidence in predicting the outcome of changes of density of target species (cf. Abrams et al., 1993).

In these conditions of uncertainty it seems prudent to evoke the precautionary principle. As human pressures grow on what remains of wild nature, we must be very careful in claiming an understanding that we do not have of ecological interactions. We must be explicit about the limits of our science and not endorse approaches that may do more harm than good. We should work to shift the burden of proof 'from requiring regulators to demonstrate that ecosystem alterations have consequences to require users to demonstrate that alterations have no consequences' (Angermeier, 2000). We should seriously consider Sanderson's suggestion (Chapter 21) that 'there should be a kind of Hippocratic oath for conservation'. Taking such an oath should be an integral part of assessing the efficacy of sustainable use as a tool for conservation.

On a broader scale, perhaps the species-centred and global extinction-centred approach to conservation has prevented us from seeing the (half-empty) forest for the trees. The powerful public conservation movement is based primarily on conserving species, particularly endangered ones, not on conserving ecological processes or species interactions (cf. Buchmann & Nabhan, 1996). Once a species has declined to the point where it is on the CITES (Convention for International Trade in Endangered Species of Flora and Fauna) list and featured in a full-colour brochures, it is long past the point of ecological extinction. Little attention is paid to species, especially less charismatic ones, responsible for the half-empty forest but still in good shape from their own particular point of view. While the species- and extinction-centred approach to conservation appears to appeal best to the general public, perhaps it should not dictate the ways in which conservation professionals perceive potential dangers to the ecological integrity of the landscapes that they investigate or manage.

CONCLUSION

If we are to gain the critical conservation benefits that sustainable harvesting programmes can provide then we must explicitly recognise, and incorporate into our calculations, the costs as well as the benefits that such exploitation may bring. The link between species conservation and biodiversity conservation is a confused one. Whereas species are clearly one of the components of biodiversity, conservation of species is not equivalent to conservation of biodiversity with all its components (genes, populations/species; communities/ecosystems) and attributes (structure, function and composition; Redford & Richter, 1999). It is probable that all significant use, especially at the species level, has its biodiversity costs. We are increasingly coming to the realisation that 'more traditional single-species approaches to management are no longer adequate to maintain ecosystem integrity, given the evidence of the wider ecosystem effects of human harvesting activity' (Kaiser & Jennings, Chapter 16).

Concerns about the efficacy of exploitation as a conservation tool should not always deter us from contemplating such use, but should propel us into thinking at a broader scale and ensuring that those components of biodiversity negatively affected by sustainable harvesting are conserved in other parts of the ecosystem. It should also strengthen the growing realisation that if conservation of biodiversity is the objective then in many cases it must be the direct objective of policy, rather than a desired by-product (Guillison *et al.*, 2000).

REFERENCES

Abrams, P. A., Menge, B. A., Mittelbach, G. G., Spiller, D. A. & Yodzis. P. (1993). The role of indirect effects in food webs. In *Food Webs. Integration of Patterns and Dynamics*, ed. G. A. Polis & K. O. Winemiller, pp. 371–395. Chapman & Hall, New York.

Aizen, M. A. & Feinsinger, P. (1994a). Forest fragmentation, pollination, and plant reproduction in a Chaco dry forest, Argentina. *Ecology*, **75**, 330–351.

Aizen, M. A. & Feinsinger, P. (1994b). Habitat fragmentation, native insect pollinators, and feral honey bees in Argentine 'Chaco Serrano'. *Ecological Applications*, **4**, 378–392.

Aizen, M. A. & Feinsinger, P. (2001). Bees not to be? Responses of insect pollinator faunas and flower pollination to habitat fragmentation. In *How Landscapes Change: Human Disturbance and Ecosystem Disruptions in the Americas*, ed. G. A. Bradshaw, P. A. Marquet & H. A. Mooney. Springer-Verlag, New York, in press.

Allen-Wardell, G., Bernhardt, P., Bitner, R., Burgess, A., Buchmann, S., Cane, J. *et al.* (1998). The potential consequences of pollinator declines on the conservation of biodiversity and stability of crop yields. *Conservation Biology*, 12, 8–17.

Andersen, E. (1999). Seed dispersal by monkeys and the fate of dispersed seeds in a Peruvian rainforest. *Biotropica*, 31, 145–158.

Angermeier, P. L. (2000). The natural imperative for biological conservation. *Conservation Biology*, 14, 373–381.

Annett, C. A. & Pierotti, R. (1999). Long-term reproductive output in western gulls: consequences of alternative tactics in diet choice. *Ecology*, 80, 288–297.

Arnold, S. J. (1981a). Behavioral variation in natural populations. I. Phenotypic, genetic and environmental correlations between chemoreceptive responses to prey in the garter snake, *Thamnophis elegans*. *Evolution*, 35, 489–509.

Arnold, S. J. (1981b). Behavioral variation in natural populations. II. The inheritance of a feeding response in crosses between geographic races of the garter snake, *Thamnophis elegans*. *Evolution*, 35, 510–515.

Bailey, T. N. (1992). *The African Leopard*. Columbia University Press, New York.

Berger, J. (1999). Anthropogenic extinction of top carnivores and interspecific animal behaviour: implications of the rapid decoupling of a web involving wolves, bears, moose and ravens. *Proceedings of the Royal Society of London B*, 266, 2261–2267.

Berger, J., Stacey, P. B., Bellis, L. & Johnson, M. P. (2001). A mammalian predator–prey disequilibrium: how the extinction of grizzly bears and wolves affects the biodiversity of avian neotropical migrants. *Ecological Applications*, in press.

Boag, P. T. & Grant, P. R. (1984). Darwin's finches (*Geospiza*) on Isla Daphne Major, Galápagos: breeding and feeding ecology in a climatically variable environment. *Ecological Monographs*, 54, 463–489.

Bond, W. J. (1995). Assessing the risk of plant extinction due to pollinator and disperser failure. In *Extinction Rates*, ed. J. H. Lawton & R. M. May, pp. 130–146. Oxford University Press, New York.

Brown, J. L. (1969). The buffer effect and productivity in tit populations. *American Naturalist*, 103, 347–354.

Bryan, J. E. & Larkin, P. A. (1972). Food specialization by individual trout. *Journal of the Fisheries Research Board of Canada*, 29, 1615–1624.

Buchmann, S. L. & Nabhan, G. P. (1996). *The Forgotten Pollinators*. Island Press, Covelo, CA.

Burrows, M. T. & Hughes, R. N. (1991). Variation in foraging behaviour among individuals and populations of dogwhelks, *Nucella lapillus*: natural constraints on energy intake. *Journal of Animal Ecology*, 60, 497–514.

Chapman, C. A. & Onderdonk, D. A. (1998). Forests without primates: primate/plant codependency. *American Journal of Primatology*, 45, 127–241.

Conner, R. N. (1988). Wildlife populations: minimally viable or ecologically functional? *Wildlife Society Bulletin*, 16, 80–84.

Crooks, K. R. & Soulé, M. E. (1999). Mesopredator release and avifaunal extinctions in a fragmented system. *Nature*, **400**, 563–566.

Darwin, C. H. (1896). *The Origin of Species by Means of Natural Selection; Or, The Preservation of Favored Races in the Struggle for Life*. Reprinted from the 6th London edn. A. L. Burt, New York.

Dayton, P. K., Thrush, S. F., Agardi, M. T. & Hofman, R. J. (1995). Environmental effects of marine fishing. *Aquatic Conservation: Marine and Freshwater Ecosystems*, **5**, 205–232.

Dayton, P.K., Tegner, M. J., Edwards, P. B. & Riser, K. L. (1998). Sliding baselines, ghosts, and reduced expectations in kelp forest communities. *Ecological Applications*, **8**, 309–322.

Dirzo, R. & Miranda, A. (1991). Altered patterns of herbivory and diversity in the forest understory: a case study of the possible consequences of contemporary defaunation. In *Plant–Animal Interactions: Evolutionary Ecology in Tropical and Temperate Regions*, ed. P. W. Price, P. W. Lewinshon, G. W. Fernandes & W. W. Benson, pp. 273–287. Wiley, New York.

Ebenman, B. & Nilsson, S. G. (1982). Components of niche width in a territorial bird species: habitat utilization in males and females of the chaffinch (*Fringilla coelebs*) on islands and mainland. *American Naturalist*, **119**, 331–344.

Ehlinger, T. J. & Wilson, D. S. (1988). Complex foraging polymorphism in bluegill sunfish. *Proceedings of National Academy of Sciences, USA*, **85**, 1878–1882.

Eickwort, G. C. & Ginsberg, H. S. (1980). Foraging and mating behavior in Apoidea. *Annual Review of Entomology*, **25**, 421–446.

Estes, J. A., Duggins, D. O. & Rathbun, G. B. (1989). The ecology of extinctions in kelp forest communities. *Conservation Biology*, **3**, 251–264.

Feinsinger, P. (1976). Organization of a tropical guild of nectarivorous birds. *Ecological Monographs*, **46**, 257–291.

Feinsinger, P. & Colwell, R. K. (1978). Community organization among neotropical nectar-feeding birds. *American Zoologist*, **18**, 779–795.

Feinsinger, P., Murray, K. G., Kinsman, S. & Busby, W. H. (1986). Floral neighborhood and pollination success in four hummingbird-pollinated cloud forest plant species. *Ecology*, **67**, 449–464.

Feinsinger, P., Beach, J. H., Linhart, Y. B., Busby, W. H. & Murray, K. G. (1987). Disturbance, pollinator predictability, and pollination success among Costa Rican cloud forest plants. *Ecology*, **68**, 1294–1305.

Feinsinger, P., Busby, W. H., Murray, K. G., Beach, J. H., Pounds, W. Z. & Linhart, Y. B. (1988). Mixed support for spatial heterogeneity in species interactions: hummingbirds in a tropical disturbance mosaic. *American Naturalist*, **131**, 33–57.

Flecker, A. S. (1996). Ecosystem engineering by a dominant detritivore in a diverse tropical stream. *Ecology*, **77**, 1845–1854.

Fleming, T. H. (1988). *The Short-Tailed Fruit Bat: A Study in Plant–Animal Interactions*. University of Chicago Press, Chicago.

Foster, D.R., Motzkin, G. & Slater, B. (1998). Land-use history as long-term broad-scale disturbance: regional forest dynamics in central New England. *Ecosystems*, **1**, 96–119.

Fox, L. R. & Morrow, P. A. (1981). Specialization: species property or local phenomenon? *Science*, **211**, 887–893.

Francis, R. C. (1997). Sustainable use of salmon: its effect on biodiversity and ecosystem function. In *Harvesting Wild Species: Implications for Biodiversity Conservation*, ed. C. H. Freese, pp. 626–670. Johns Hopkins University Press, Baltimore, MD.

Freese, C. H. (1998). *Wild Species as Commodities*. Island Press, Washington, DC.

Fretwell, S. D. & Lucas, H. L. Jr (1970). On territorial behavior and other factors influencing habitat distribution in birds. I. Theoretical development. *Acta Biotheoretica*, XIX(1), 16–36.

Ganzhorn, J. U., Fietz, J., Rakotovao, E., Schwab, D. & Zinner, D. (1999). Lemurs and the regeneration of dry deciduous forest in Madagascar. *Conservation Biology*, **13**, 794–804.

Gill, F. B. (1988). Trapline foraging by hermit hummingbirds: competition for an undefended, renewable resource. *Ecology*, **69**, 113–117.

Goss-Custard, J. D. & Sutherland, W. J. (1997). Individual behaviour, populations and conservation. In *Behavioural Ecology*, 4th edn, ed. J. R. Krebs & N. B. Davies, pp. 373–395. Blackwell, Oxford.

Grant, P. R. (1986). *Ecology and Evolution of Darwin's Finches*. Princeton University Press, Princeton, NJ.

Grigg, G., Hale, P. & Lunney, D. (eds.) (1995). *Conservation through Sustainable Use of Wildlife*. Centre for Conservation Biology, University of Queensland, Brisbane.

Guillison, R. E., Rice, R. E. & Blundell, A. G. (2000). 'Marketing' species conservation. *Nature*, **404**, 923–924.

Hamann, A. & Curio, E. (1999). Interactions among frugivores and fleshy fruit trees in a Philippine submontane rainforest. *Conservation Biology*, **13**, 766–773.

Heinrich, B. (1976). Foraging specializations of individual bumblebees. *Ecological Monographs*, **46**, 105–128.

Heinrich, B. (1979). Majoring and minoring by foraging bumblebees, *Bombus vagans*: an experimental analysis. *Ecology*, **60**, 245–255.

Hohman, W. L. (1985). Feeding ecology of ringnecked ducks in northwestern Minnesota. *Journal of Wildlife Management*, **49**, 546–557.

Holmes, R. T., Sherry, T. W. & Bennett, S. E. (1978). Diurnal and individual variability in the foraging behavior of American redstarts (*Setophaga ruticilla*). *Oecologia*, **36**, 141–149.

Janzen, D. H. (1974). The deflowering of Central America. *Natural History*, **83**, 49–53.

Janzen, D. H. (1986). Blurry catastrophes. *Oikos*, **47**, 1–2.

Jennings, S., Greenstreet, S. P. R. & Reynolds, J. D. (1999). Structural changes in an exploited fish community: a consequence of differential fishing effects on species with contrasting life histories. *Journal of Animal Ecology*, **68**, 617–627.

Jones, C. G., Lawton, J. H. & Shachak, M. (1994). Organisms as ecosystem engineers. *Oikos*, **69**, 373–386.

Kearns, C. A., Inouye, D. W. & Waser, N. M. (1998). Endangered mutualisms: the conservation of plant–pollinator interactions. *Annual Review of Ecology and Systematics*, **29**, 83–112.

Keast, A. (1977). Mechanisms expanding niche width and minimizing competition in two centrarchid fishes. *Evolutionary Biology*, **10**, 333–395.

Knapp, A. K., Blair, J. M., Briggs, J. M., Collins, S. L., Hartnett, D. C., Johnson, L. C. & Towne, E. G. (1999). The keystone role of bison in North American tallgrass prairie. *BioScience*, **49**, 39–50.

Kohda, M. (1994). Individual specialized foraging repertoires in the piscivorous cichlid fish *Lepidiolamprologus profundicola*. *Animal Behaviour*, **48**, 1123–1131.

Kruuk, H. (1972). *The Spotted Hyaena*. University of Chicago Press, Chicago.

Laverty, T. M. (1980). The flower-visiting behavior of bumblebees: floral complexity and learning. *Canadian Journal of Zoology*, **58**, 1324–1335.

Leigh, E. G., Wright, S. J., Putz, F. E. & Herre, E. A. (1993). The decline of tree diversity on newly isolated islands: a test of a null hypothesis and some implications. *Evolutionary Ecology*, **7**, 76–102.

Levey, D.J. & Benkman, C. W. (1999). Fruit-seed disperser interactions and timely insights from a long term perspective. *Trends in Ecology and Evolution*, **14**, 41–43.

Linsley, E. G. (1978). Temporal patterns of flower visitation by solitary bees, with particular reference to the southwestern United States. *Journal of the Kansas Entomological Society*, **51**, 531–546.

McDonnell, M. J. & Pickett, S. T. A. (1993). Introduction: scope and need for an ecology of subtle human effects and populated areas. In *Humans as Components of Ecosystems*, ed. M. J. McDonnell & S. T. A. Pickett, pp. 1–5. Springer-Verlag, New York.

Micheli, F. (n.d.). Consumer resource interactions in aquatic ecosystems: research priorities for conservation and management. Unpublished report for the Society for Conservation Biology.

Montgomery, G. G. & Sunquist, M. E. (1978). Habitat selection and use by two-toed sloths and three-toed sloths. In *The Ecology of Arboreal Foliovores*, ed. G. G. Montgomery, pp. 329–360. Smithsonian Institution Press, Washington, DC.

Morgan, P., Aplet, G. H., Haufler, J. B., Humphries, H. C., Moore, M. M. & Wilson, W. D. (1994). Historical range of variability: a useful tool for evaluating ecosystem change. *Journal of Sustainable Forestry*, **2**, 87–111.

Morse, D. H. (1971). The foraging of warblers isolated on small islands. *Ecology*, **52**, 216–228.

Morse, D. H. (1973). The foraging of small populations of yellow warblers and American redstarts. *Ecology*, **54**, 346–355.

Murcia, C. A. (1996). Forest fragmentation and the pollination of neotropical plants. In *Forest Patches in Tropical Landscapes*, ed. J. Schelhas & R. Greenberg, pp. 19–36. Island Press, Covelo, CA.

Murray, K. G. (1988). Avian seed dispersal of three neotropical gap-dependent plants. *Ecological Monographs*, **58**, 271–298.

Naiman, R. J., Johnson, C. A. & Kelley, J. C. (1988). Alteration of North American streams by beaver. *BioScience*, **38**, 753–762.

National Academy Press (1999). *Sustaining Marine Fisheries*. National Academy Press, Washington, DC.

Novaro, A. J., Funes. M. C. & Walker, R. S. (2000). Ecological extinction of native prey of a carnivore assemblage in Argentine Patagonia. *Biological Conservation*, **92**, 25–34.

Orians, G. H. (1980). *Some Adaptations of Marsh-Nesting Blackbirds.* Princeton University Press, Princeton, NJ.

Ostfeld, R. S., Jones, C. G. & Wolff, J. O. (1996). Of mice and mast. *BioScience,* **46**, 323–330.

Pace, M.L., Cole, J. J., Carpenter, S. R & Kitchell, J. F. (1999). Trophic cascades revealed in diverse ecosystems. *Trends in Ecology and Evolution,* **14**, 483–488.

Pacheco, L. F. & Simonetti, J. A. (1998). Consecuencias demográficas para *Inga ingoides* (Mimosoideae) por la pérdida de *Ateles paniscus* (Cebidae), uno de sus dispersores de semillas. *Ecología en Bolivia,* **31**, 67–90.

Palomares, F., Gaona, P., Ferreras, P. & Delibes, M. (1995). Positive effects on game species of top predators by controlling smaller predator populations: an example with lynx, mongooses, and rabbits. *Conservation Biology,* **9**, 295–305.

Parsons, T. R. (1993). The impact of industrial fisheries on the trophic structure of marine ecosystems. In *Food Webs. Integration of Patterns and Dynamics,* ed. G. A. Polis & K. O. Winemiller, pp. 352–357. Chapman & Hall, New York.

Pauly, D., Christensen, V., Dalsgaard, J., Froese, R. & Torres, F. Jr (1998). Fishing down marine food webs. *Science,* **279**, 860–863.

Peres, C. A. (2000a). Effects of subsistence hunting on vertebrate community structure in Amazonian forests. *Conservation Biology,* **14**, 240–253.

Peres, C. A. (2000b). Evaluating the impact and sustainability of subsistence hunting at multiple Amazonian forest sites. In *Hunting for Sustainability in Tropical Forests,* ed. J. G. Robinson & E. L. Bennett, pp. 31–56. Columbia University Press, New York.

Pimm, S. (1991). *The Balance of Nature?* University of Chicago Press, Chicago.

Pollock, M. M., Naiman, R. J., Erickson, H. E., Johnston, C. A. & Pinay, G. (1995). Beaver as engineers: influences on biotic and abiotic characteristics of drainage basins. In *Linking Species and Ecosystems,* ed. C. G. Jones & J. H. Lawton, pp. 117–126. Chapman & Hall, New York.

Powell, R. W. (1974). Some measures of feeding behavior in captive common crows. *Auk,* **91**, 571–574.

Pyke, G. H. (1984). Optimal foraging theory: a critical review. *Annual Review of Ecology and Systematics,* **15**, 523–576.

Pyke, G. H., Pulliam, H. R. & Charnov, E. L. (1977). Optimal foraging: a selective review of theory and tests. *Quarterly Review of Biology,* **52**, 137–154.

Rathcke, B. J. & Jules, E. S. (1993). Habitat fragmentation and plant–pollinator interactions. *Current Science (India),* **65**, 273–277.

Redford, K. H. (1992). The empty forest. *BioScience,* **42**, 412–422.

Redford, K. H. & Richter, B. D. (1999). Conservation of biodiversity in a world of use. *Conservation Biology,* **13**, 1246–1256.

Renner, S. S. (1998). Effects of habitat fragmentation on plant pollinator interactions in the tropics. In *Dynamics of Tropical Communities,* ed. D. M. Newbery, H. H. T. Prins & N. D. Browne, 37th Symposium of the British Ecological Society, pp. 339–359. Blackwell, London.

Rissing, S. (1981). Foraging specialization of individual seed-harvester ants. *Behavioral Ecology and Sociobiology,* **9**, 97–111.

Roberts, C. M. (1997). Ecological advice for the global fisheries crisis. *Trends in Ecology and Evolution,* **12**, 35–38.

Robinson, J. G. & Bennett, E.L. (eds.) (2000). *Hunting for Sustainability in Tropical Forests.* Columbia University Press, New York.

Robinson, J. R., Redford, K. H. & Bennett, E. L. (1999). Wildlife harvest in logged tropical forest. *Science,* **284,** 595–596.

Rosenzweig, M. L. (1991). Habitat selection and population interactions: the search for mechanism. *American Naturalist,* **137,** S5–S28.

Schaller, G. B. (1972). *The Serengeti Lion.* University of Chicago Press, Chicago.

Schindler, D. E., Hodgson, J. R. & Kitchell, J. F. (1997). Density-dependent changes in individual foraging specialization of largemouth bass. *Oecologia,* **110,** 592–600.

Shea, K. & NCEAS Working Group on Population Management (1998). Management of populations in conservation, harvesting, and control. *Trends in Ecology and Evolution,* **13,** 371–375.

Sherry, T. W. (1984). Comparative dietary ecology of sympatric, insectivorous neotropical flycatchers (Tyrannidae). *Ecological Monographs,* **54,** 313–338.

Silva, J. L. & Strahl, S. D. (1991). Human impacts on populations of chachalacas, guans, and currasows (Galliformes: Cracidae) in Venezuela. In *Neotropical Wildlife Use and Conservation,* ed. J. G. Robinson & K. H. Redford, pp. 37–52. University of Chicago Press, Chicago.

Smartt, R. A. & Lemen, C. (1980). Intrapopulational morphological variation as a predictor of feeding behavior in deermice. *American Naturalist,* **116,** 891–894.

Smith, T. B. & Temple, S. A. (1982). Feeding habits and bill polymorphism in hook-billed kites. *Auk,* **99,** 197–207.

Steneck, R. S. (1996). The Gulf of Maine. In *Fundamentals of Conservation Biology,* ed. M. L. Hunter, pp. 209–212. Blackwell Science, Cambridge, MA.

Stephens, D. W. & Krebs, J. R. (1986). *Foraging Theory.* Princeton University Press, Princeton, NJ.

Stromayer, K. A. K. & Warren, F. J. (1997). Are overabundant deer herds in the eastern United States creating alternate stable states in forest plant communities? *Wildlife Society Bulletin,* **25,** 227–234.

Sutherland, W. J. (1996). *From Individual Behaviour to Population Ecology.* Oxford University Press, Oxford.

Terborgh, J. & Wright, S. J. (1994). Effects of mammalian herbivores on plant recruitment in two neotropical forests. *Ecology,* **75,** 1829–1833.

Terborgh, J., Estes, J. A., Paquet, P., Ralls, K., Boyd, D., Miller, B. & Noss, R. (1999). Role of top carnivores in regulating terrestrial ecosystems. In *Continental Conservation,* ed. M. E. Soulé & J. Terborgh, pp. 39–64. Island Press, Washington, DC.

Waller, D. M. & Alverson, W. S. (1997). The white-tailed deer: a keystone herbivore. *Wildlife Society Bulletin,* **25,** 217–226.

Werner, T. K. & Sherry, T. W. (1987). Behavioral feeding specialization in *Pinaroloxias inornata,* the 'Darwin's Finch' of Cocos Island, Costa Rica. *Proceedings of the National Academy of Sciences, USA,* **84,** 5506–5510.

West, L. (1986). Interindividual variation in prey selection by the snail *Nucella* (= *Thais) emarginata. Ecology,* **67,** 798–809.

Wheelwright, N. T. (1993). Fruit size in a tropical tree species: variation, preference by birds, and heritability. *Vegetatio,* **107/108,** 163–174.

Willson, M. F., Gende, S. M. & Marston, B. H. (1998). Fishes and the forest. *BioScience*, **48**, 455–462.

Winemiller, K. O. & Polis, G. A. (1993). Food webs: what can they tell us about the world? In *Food Webs. Integration of Patterns and Dynamics*, ed. G. A. Polis & K. O. Winemiller, pp. 1–16. Chapman & Hall, New York.

Wright, S. J., Zeballos, H., Dominguez, I., Gallardo, M. M., Moreno, M. C. & Ibanez, R. (2000). Poachers, mammals, seed dispersal and seed predation in a neotropical forest. *Conservation Biology*, **14**, 227–239.

PART V

Conservation meets sustainable use

18

Sustainable use and pest control in conservation: kangaroos as a case study

GORDON C. GRIGG & ANTHONY R. POPLE

Sustainable use of wildlife throws into conflict the opposing paradigms of conservation, in which resources are saved *for* use, and preservation, in which resources are saved *from* use (Passmore, 1974). Sugg & Kreuter (1994) have written eloquently about this in the context of African elephants *Loxodonta africana* and the ban on trade in ivory, and they have also suggested how the African elephant epitomises the debate over the sustainable use of wildlife.

Kangaroos also epitomise that debate, and African and Australian wildlife biologists have had to wrestle with these conflicts and find ways to conserve wildlife species, and their habitats, in the face of great alienation of wildlife habitat for domestic stocking. Putting an economic value on wildlife, in their habitats, appears to offer a constructive way forward. Kangaroos are an excellent case study of sustainable wildlife use. They take the debate beyond simply valuing wildlife to ensure that it is conserved. The added dimension is that kangaroos are considered to be pests, so that harvests provide both an income and a reduction in damage. Kangaroos are also numerous and relatively well studied, providing a solid scientific basis to their management.

Over the last 20 years, 1.3 million to 3.2 million kangaroos have been harvested annually for their skins and meat from about 40% of mainland Australia and from populations that have ranged from about 16 million to 34 million. The populations of the three main harvested species are thought to be much higher now than they were before the arrival of Europeans, because of dingo *Canis lupus dingo* control, tree clearing to promote grasslands and the introduction of millions of watering points for introduced stock. Harvesting is thought to maintain a 30–40% reduction in numbers, compared with what unharvested populations would be, but most landholders still regard kangaroos as pests, competing with sheep or damaging crops. The harvest is managed by extensive population monitoring and by the setting of annual harvest quotas, state by state. In practice, the full national quota has never been taken, because economics dictate harvests lower than the maximum permissible.

The three large species are very widespread and abundant, and over most of their ranges they coexist with sheep, often at similar densities, on land which is very heavily degraded through overstocking.

Kangaroos are strongly identified with Australia, as a national symbol, and have a very high conservation status. Policies that regulate and dictate kangaroo management are a compromise between demands for greater pest control on the one hand and for complete protection on the other. Interestingly, their high conservation status and their value as a resource are not in conflict, because both favour kangaroos remaining widespread and abundant. Arguments can be easily made, in fact, that the harvesting of kangaroos is beneficial for kangaroos because it encourages their conservation and, further, that it has the potential to encourage conservation of their habitat.

Not surprisingly the harvesting of kangaroos attracts criticism. This chapter explores the issues surrounding the commercial harvesting of kangaroos in Australia, including the science and some of the politics. A fuller review of the biology of kangaroos and their commercial exploitation can be found in Pople & Grigg (1998). Before we proceed, we should explore a dichotomy in the reasons for harvesting kangaroos.

We, and many other conservationists, agree with wool growers that kangaroo harvesting is desirable from a conservation point of view. But our reasons for holding this position would probably be completely different. Wool growers typically see kangaroos as competitors for sheep, as direct agents of land degradation and, therefore, see commercial kangaroo harvesting as self-funding pest control. However, we see difficulties with this approach. First, it is not clear that reducing kangaroo numbers leads automatically to improved pasture and/or increased wool productivity (see later). Secondly, a significant further reduction in the numbers of these iconic species would probably be unacceptable to the Australian and world communities. Thirdly, if kangaroo numbers are reduced significantly, the kangaroo industry may fold and its present control role cease.

Therefore, as conservation biologists, we see instead the possibility of a radical new approach, a sustainable harvest of kangaroos, at higher prices, as an alternative to sheep, presenting wool growers with the opportunity to diversify, and redefining the status of kangaroos from pest to resource. This could improve the economic equation in the rangelands, at a lower herbivore density, setting the scene for long-term rehabilitation of the landscape. This is still in the future, but trends are in the right direction and the mechanism to drive it would be better market recognition of the products, particularly meat. So both conservation biologists and graziers may advocate kangaroo harvesting, but for totally different reasons. Most of this chapter focuses on the present situation, rather than the future, to which we will return at the very end.

KANGAROO POPULATIONS

The harvested species

Of the 50 or so species of the Macropodoidea, about half have declined significantly in range or numbers since the European invasion, 10 to extinction on the Australian mainland (four species survive on islands) and about half remain common, in some cases, very common (Calaby & Grigg, 1989). Habitat changes and foxes are thought to account for most of the declines, with the extinction of one species of wallaby thought to have been accelerated by hunting. The four species of large kangaroos that are harvested on the mainland are likely to be at much higher numbers now than at the time of European arrival, because of the addition of watering points for stock, clearing of vegetation to promote grasslands, and the control of their main pre-European predator, the dingo. Where dingoes are present, kangaroo numbers are generally greatly reduced, with some evidence of their regulation by dingoes (Pople *et al.*, 2000).

The four large kangaroos harvested are the red kangaroo *Macropus rufus*, eastern grey kangaroo *M. giganteus*, western grey kangaroo *M. fuliginosus*, and the common wallaroo or euro *M. robustus*. Three other species are harvested, a small number of whiptail wallabies *M. parryi* and, in Tasmania, where they occur in very large numbers and are regarded as pests, red-necked wallabies *M. rufogriseus* and Tasmanian pademelons *Thylogale billardierii*. The first four species are the most abundant. The first three make up over 95% of the commercial harvest, and only these are discussed in this chapter.

Distribution and abundance

The large kangaroos are among the most numerous of all of the large terrestrial mammals. They are monitored only in that part of their ranges where they are harvested (Figures 18.1 and 18.2). However, an Australia-wide estimate was made over 1980–82 (Caughley *et al.*, 1983), describing the density and distribution of the species (Figure 18.1) and indicating that > 85% of the combined total numbers of the three main commercial species occur within the harvest zone.

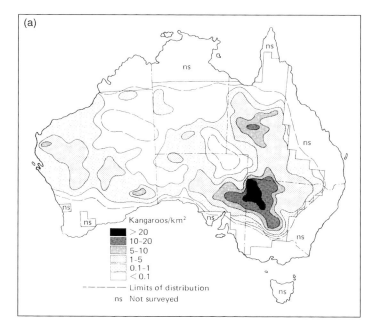

Figure 18.1. Density and distribution of (a) red kangaroos, (b) eastern grey kangaroos and (c) western grey kangaroos, determined from aerial surveys over 1980–82 (after Caughley, 1987b). Estimates for both species of grey kangaroos are conservative; recent work suggests they are about half of the true density. Ground surveys of much of the eastern part of the eastern grey kangaroo range over 1987–92 estimated a density of 10 kangaroos/km². (From Southwell *et al.*, 1997. Reproduced with the permission of Cambridge University Press.)

There are very good records of numbers of kangaroos from annual aerial surveys in the commercial areas, incorporating the sheep rangelands in Queensland, New South Wales, South Australia and Western Australia (Figure 18.2), as well as good harvest statistics. These population estimates are shown in Figure 18.3 and indicate that the total Australian kangaroo population has ranged between about 16 million and 38 million over the past 24 years. For the eastern states, there has been a general increase through the late 1970s, in years of above-average rainfall, a big decline following the 1982–83 drought, and recovery to pre-drought levels by 1990.

The population estimates in Figure 18.3 have been determined largely from aerial surveys that have been conducted in New South Wales annually since 1975, in South Australia annually since 1978, in Queensland in 1980 then annually since 1984, and in Western Australia triennially since 1981

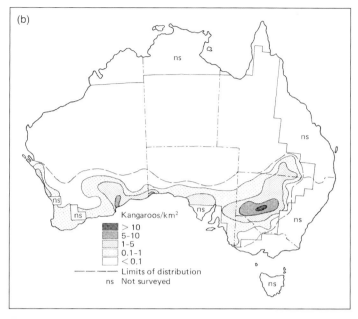

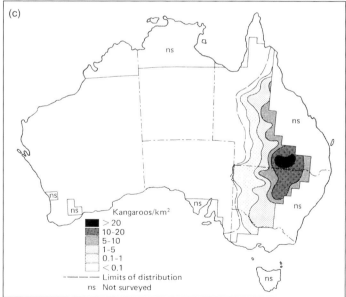

Figure 18.1 (*cont.*)

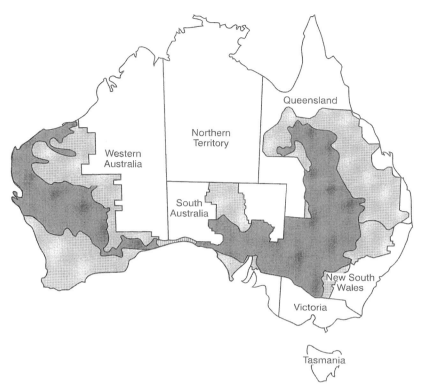

Figure 18.2. Main area in Australia where kangaroos are commercially harvested (dark and light shading). Relatively small numbers are harvested outside this zone, in the Northern Territory, far western Queensland and occasionally Victoria. Also shown are the sheep rangelands (dark shading) in which the predominant land use is low intensity sheep grazing (approximately 0.2 sheep/ha). *Vertical-line shading* indicates sheep rangelands where there is no commercial harvesting of kangaroos. (Figures 18.2 to 18.5 are also accessible on the World Wide Web, see Pople & Grigg, 1998.)

and partial surveys conducted annually since 1995. Estimates have been extrapolated in line with rainfall for Western Australia and in line with New South Wales for the other states. Increases in the size of the commercial area over time have resulted in relatively slight increases in population size.

Population processes

Most kangaroos live in the drier parts of the continent and are very responsive to rainfall, which may be very variable from year to year. Droughts, which are rarely continent wide, bring about big reductions in numbers

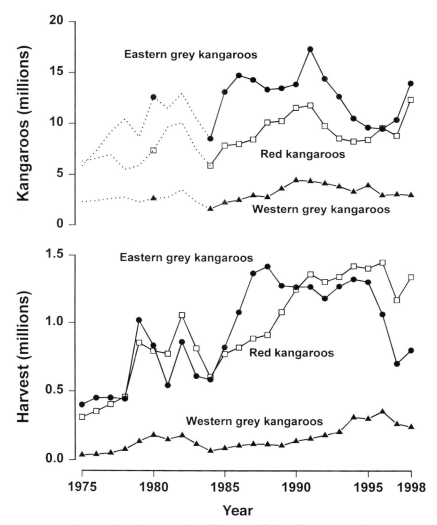

Figure 18.3. Combined state totals and harvest off-take of eastern grey kangaroos, red kangaroos and western grey kangaroos in the commercial area (Figure 18.2). Extrapolations and interpolations are shown as dotted lines.

(Caughley et al., 1985). The effect of rainfall will depend on its timing and there will be differences between regions and kangaroo species (Bayliss, 1987; Cairns & Grigg, 1993; Cairns et al., 2000). The effect of kangaroo density itself on these dynamics, at least in the semi-arid rangelands, is considered weak and results from kangaroos reducing their food supply rather than from spacing behaviour (Caughley, 1987a). Obviously, this regulation keeps the population within limits and allows collection of a sustainable harvest. However, the fact that density dependence is weak means the limits are broad and the fluctuations in numbers can be marked. In the absence of dingoes, therefore, food supply (governed largely by rainfall) and predation by the commercial kangaroo industry are the main factors limiting kangaroo numbers within the sheep rangelands.

Harvesting can have a number of sometimes opposing influences on a kangaroo population's dynamics. Because regulation is weak and largely extrinsic, harvest mortality is likely to be additive to the overall mortality when pasture conditions are good. During drought, mortality is more likely to be compensatory, with many harvested animals either likely to die anyway or using scarce food that could ensure survival for others. Overall, this will result in a dampening of a population's fluctuations.

This dampening effect will be partly countered by alterations to the population's age structure. Kangaroos display marked sexual size dimorphism and, because value is attached to the size of skins and weight of carcasses, this results in selective harvesting of males. Harvested populations therefore have a strong female bias and high potential rates of increase (r_p) (Pople & Cairns, 1995; Kokko et al., Chapter 14). The potential rate of increase is the rate a population would achieve if harvesting stopped. However, the disparity in the potential rate of increase of harvested and unharvested populations may only be obvious when pasture conditions are good, because unstable age distributions are also a feature of unharvested kangaroo populations in a fluctuating environment. In drought, marked male-biased mortality and minimal recruitment results in populations with potential rates of increase ($r_p = 0.3$ to 0.6) much higher than the maximum suggested for a population with a stable age distribution and sex ratio at parity (i.e. intrinsic rate of increase r_{max}, which for red kangaroos is 0.25) (Bayliss, 1985; Pople, 1996).

Monitoring the populations

Direct monitoring is undertaken by foot survey, vehicle survey and aerial survey, the latter being the most extensively employed. Methods have been reviewed extensively by Southwell (1989) and Pople (1999). Although estimates of relative density are generally adequate for monitoring population trends, estimates of absolute density are required to set a quota as a proportion of population size (Caughley & Sinclair, 1994). Hence, considerable effort has gone into finding ways to correct for the bias intrinsic to aerial surveys. Luckily, the large commercial species occur in more open, relatively flat rangeland habitat and are still active during daylight hours near sunrise and sunset (crepuscular). This makes them amenable to ground and aerial surveys, the latter allowing counts to be made relatively cheaply over very large areas.

HOW QUOTAS ARE SET

Species-specific quotas for harvests in each state are proposed each year by state conservation agencies to be approved by the Federal Minister for the Environment on the recommendation of a national committee of scientists, the Scientific Committee for Wildlife Use. Typically quotas have been set at 10–20% of population estimates, a rate developed empirically, but with an eye to theory.

Caughley (1987a) developed an interactive model incorporating the dynamics of a red kangaroo population driven by pasture whose biomass, while grazed by kangaroos, was determined largely by rainfall. Caughley & Gunn (1993) described the model and argued that, in deserts, plant–herbivore systems are best described by the functional and numerical responses of herbivores to their food supply. An exception is where spacing behaviour regulates the herbivore population (i.e. intrinsic regulation). Caughley's model suggested that an instantaneous harvest rate of 10–15% per year would represent the maximum sustainable yield (MSY) for red kangaroo populations subjected to an unselective harvest (see Figure 18.4). A slightly lower value was likely for grey kangaroos and wallaroos, and selective harvesting would result in a MSY at higher rates. An unselective harvest of 10–15% would reduce the long-term mean population density by 30–40%. Caughley & Sinclair (1994) suggested that, for populations limited by a consumable resource, an estimate of the MSY by the logistic model would be conservative. Figure 18.4 indicates that this is true for a deterministic interactive model, but the MSY is overestimated (in terms of either proportional or absolute off-take) for a stochastic model. This highlights the relative safety of a proportional harvesting strategy in a fluctuating environment (see Lande *et al.*, Chapter 4).

The population estimates on which the quotas are based are obtained primarily from aerial surveys and have been since the late 1970s. Consideration is given also to factors such as overall population trends, climatic conditions (mainly rainfall) and trends in various harvest statistics (e.g. carcass weight, sex ratio, skin size). If conditions change once the quota is set (e.g. onset of a drought) managers may place restrictions on the harvest by closing certain areas or stipulating size limits.

The present system of management has been in place for more than 20

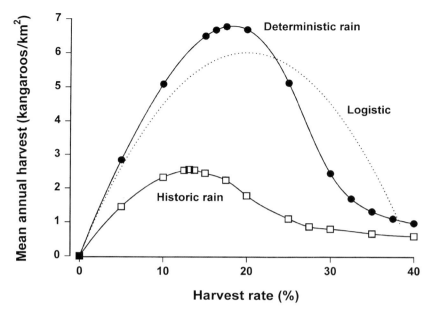

Figure 18.4. Yield curves for red kangaroo harvests based on three models of population growth. Historic rain (□) is used to provide stochasticity in driving a simplified version of Caughley's (1987a) model describing the interaction between kangaroos and pasture biomass. Every three months, a constant percentage of the population at the start of the quarter was removed. These isolated rates were equivalent to the annual instantaneous harvest rates shown here (Caughley, 1976). The yields are determined from 100-year runs of the same rainfall series. A deterministic version of this model (●) was run using unvarying long-term average rainfall. The yield curve for logistic population growth, using essentially the same parameters (r_{max} = 0.4, carrying capacity K = 60 kangaroos/km^2), is shown as a dotted line.

years now, through some wide fluctuations of kangaroo populations correlating with years of above and below average rainfall. There is thus experience to build on, even though the harvests usually fall below the quotas.

COMMERCIAL HARVESTING

Temporal trends

Aboriginal rock art shows that kangaroos have been used by humans in Australia for more than 20 000 years (Chaloupka, 1984). A single animal would feed several people, and provide material for rugs and clothes (Tunbridge, 1991). The history of European use of kangaroos following European settlement is described by several authors (see Pople & Grigg,

1998). Early on, kangaroos were killed for food, sport and as pests. It was not until the middle part of the nineteenth century that kangaroos were killed in any great numbers, when they were regarded as vermin and bounties for their destruction were introduced. A hide harvest was under way by the end of the nineteenth century. By the 1950s, the trade extended to pet meat, which soon became a significant component of the industry. An export trade in game meat for human consumption developed from 1955 (McFarlane, 1971; Corrigan, 1988). However, in the 1970s there was a ban on the export of kangaroo products and a US import ban. By the mid 1980s, after development of the Australian Wildlife Protection (Regulation of Exports and Imports) Act 1982, which required management plans to have Commonwealth approval, the export ban was lifted and the export trade gradually resumed. Important elements in the management plans are population monitoring and the identification of maximum harvest quotas in each state.

Over the past 25 years the national harvest of each species has been increasing (Figure 18.3), with the recent drop resulting from a fall in demand for skins. Annual harvest rates have generally been higher for red kangaroos (8–17%) than for eastern greys (4–13%) and western greys (3–12%) (Figure 18.5). This is at least partly because of the preference for open country by red kangaroos, to which shooters have greater access. Harvest rates have been increasing recently, but then so has the quota as a proportion of the population (Figure 18.5) as managers in some states seek greater damage mitigation. Thus the proportion of the national quota taken each year has fluctuated around 75%. However, quotas have been reached and harvest seasons closed at both a state level and for regions within states.

Harvest rates tend to be higher during drought, when kangaroos are more accessible because they aggregate around remaining water and food, vehicles are less likely to be bogged, and graziers press for protection of dwindling pastures. Inadvertently, this pattern of harvesting kangaroos more heavily during drought approaches Stocker & Walters' (1984) optimal strategy for an ungulate population, which was based upon Caughley's (1976) interactive model. Using stochastic dynamic programming (SDP), Stocker & Walters were able to increase harvest off-take over a number of alternative strategies, including fixed-rate harvesting. The optimal strategy called for a fixed escapement of animals, which increased with increasing pasture biomass, and a high harvest rate at low pasture biomass. Using SDP, McLeod & Pople (1998) conducted similar modelling for kangaroos, reporting only slight improvements in off-take using a variable harvest rate. They considered it unlikely that the kangaroo industry would adopt the

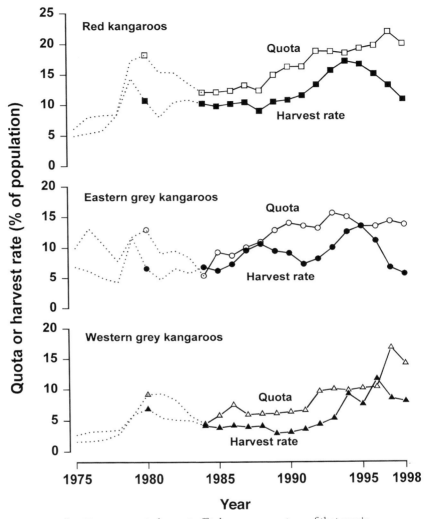

Figure 18.5. Harvest rate (= harvest off-take as a percentage of that year's population size) and quotas (as a percentage of the previous year's population size) of eastern grey kangaroos, red kangaroos and western grey kangaroos in the commercial area (Figure 18.2). Extrapolations and interpolations are shown as dotted lines.

optimal strategy, which involved increased variation in harvest off-take, including periods of zero yield.

Current annual quotas are set at about 15–20% (Figure 18.5). Actual harvest rates, however, are limited by access and economic factors, and are usually lower than this, < 12% in recent years (Figure 18.5). Where 15–20%

harvests have been achieved, for example the take of red kangaroos in Queensland, such rates appear to be sustainable. However, these rates are probably overestimates as the population estimates are conservative. While harvests do not exceed the quota, the harvest rate may exceed the quota as a proportion of population size, because the latter is based on the previous year's population estimate.

Current economic value of kangaroos

Kangaroos are an important drawcard for tourists, which puts an additional economic incentive on kangaroo conservation, but the focus of this chapter is on their direct harvest. They are valuable for their meat and hides. Ramsay (1994) reviewed the export trade, which showed comparative stability through the 1980s, with annual values of exported products of $(Aus)10 million to 15 million, rising to $30 million by 1992. The total value of the kangaroo industry to Australia is hard to estimate but is now likely to be in the vicinity of $(Aus)100 million annually, mostly from the hides.

The leather is fine and pliable, with a particularly high strength:weight ratio. It is used for sports shoes and other footwear, belts, gloves, leather clothing and footballs. Twenty-one countries imported kangaroo leather in 1991–92 (Ramsay, 1994). The trend in prices has been upwards, but skin prices rise and fall according to demand and, at higher prices, manufacturers often switch to goat and calf leather. Because of this, the capacity for sustained higher prices is limited. The meat, however, is a largely unrecognised product, which has still not found its logical place in the world market for game meat. This is understandable because until 1993 most Australian states allowed it to be sold only for pet food, because of prejudice, and because of pressure by beef and lamb producers who feared competition from another red meat. However, it can now be sold for human consumption throughout the country, and kangaroo is found in restaurants, including many of the very best. Grigg (1988, 1997a) has argued that the qualities of kangaroo meat, coupled with its comparatively short supply (limited ultimately by harvest quotas), give it a potential to achieve high prices on the world market as a speciality game meat. Despite the qualities of the meat, more than half of the kangaroos shot in Australia each year are used for their hides only, so meat production could be increased greatly without more kangaroos being killed and without quotas being raised.

The harvesting process

Free-range kangaroos are harvested by shooting, at night, on private leasehold or freehold land, and only with the permission of the landholder. Most pastoralists allow the shooters, who are almost always self-employed, on to their properties free of charge (this may not always remain the case, see later). Because properties in the sheep rangelands may be very large, shooters often fulfil a useful watchdog role over domestic stock, water supplies, fences and gates.

Shooters are increasingly being called 'wildlife harvesters' and, with the move towards increasing use of the carcasses as meat for human consumption as well as for hides and pet food, are gradually gaining increased status, with qualifications in meat handling now being required to ensure the hygienic handling of field-shot game.

Shooters usually work alone, from a four-wheel-drive vehicle, with a high powered spotlight and a high powered rifle, and work commonly throughout much of the night. This takes advantage of the behaviour of kangaroos, which is to stand, transfixed, if caught in the beam of a high powered light. The shooting is required to be conducted according to a code of practice designed in consultation with the Australian Royal Society for the Prevention of Cruelty to Animals. This requires that the animal is shot through the head so that death is instantaneous, so great skill as a marksman is required. The cost of ammunition gives an economic incentive to kill with a single shot, quite apart from any humane considerations. Another aspect of the code of practice requires pouch young to be dispatched swiftly with a blow to the head. Interestingly, with greater awareness of animal welfare issues, many people see kangaroo harvesting, with swift slaughter of free-range animals, unaware of danger, as an analogue of free-range chickens and free-range pigs, and preferable to the way in which traditional livestock is handled.

With kangaroo meat now legal for human consumption in all states, stricter regulations have been brought in to ensure hygienic handling of the meat. The load of carcasses is required to be delivered to a refrigerated field 'chiller' in the early morning, before temperatures begin to rise. Subsequently, the carcasses are collected and transported to the processing works in refrigerated transport. At the processing works the skins are removed for tanning and the carcasses are butchered in the same way as meat from domestic stock. The meat is usually packed in cryovac containers and the remainder goes to make fertiliser.

ARE KANGAROOS REALLY PESTS?

Kangaroos cause damage to fences, compete with stock for drinking water in droughts and frequently cause damage (sometimes human injury) when vehicles collide with them. They also cause damage to crops, through foraging and camping there, but the largest numbers of kangaroos are in areas where cropping is infrequent.

The main concern is that they consume pasture and, when this is scarce, the concern is heightened. A survey of 906 pastoralists by Gibson & Young (1988) showed that, of annual losses of $(Aus)113 million attributed to kangaroos (3% of production), the largest loss (51%) was attributed to the consumption of pasture that would otherwise have been available for sheep. This was followed by lost crop production (27%), fence repairs (14%) and the cost of water consumed (8%). This assessment was based solely on the perceptions of farmers and graziers, and its relation to reality is quite unknown. However, it does provide a quantitative assessment of those perceptions, and a measure of the extent to which kangaroos are seen as pests.

Accordingly, pastoralists look towards the kangaroo industry to reduce numbers, and this is often supplemented by shooting (legal under a pest destruction permit) and poisoning and clearance of sheltering vegetation (illegal). In the past, animals were shot *en masse* after being herded in organised drives or battues (Kirkpatrick & Amos, 1985; Barker & Caughley, 1992).

This concern about competition and damage from kangaroos is heightened because the rangelands have become degraded by overgrazing by domestic stock. Estimates vary, but Newman & Condon (1969) estimated 1.85 million km² of the rangelands are degraded (out of an area of 7.61 million km² in mainland Australia). Woods (1984) estimated 2.18 million km², and concluded that much of the substantially degraded land will become desertified if land use and management do not change. There is now a strong recognition that land management practices must change, and graziers and government agencies have identified the management of 'total grazing pressure' as a very high priority, particularly in the sheep rangelands.

Typically, options identified for the rehabilitation of the sheep rangelands include destocking or lowered stocking, altering the season of use, resting or 'spelling' certain areas, and culturing and seeding treatments. Kangaroos are seen as being inimical to all of these, because a destocked or spelled paddock, or a seeded paddock, is likely to attract kangaroos to the resultant green pick, because of their mobility through stock fences. Norbury & Norbury (1993) described preferential grazing of kangaroos in spelled paddocks, and discussed the potential benefits of closing waters to discourage this, either through turning the water off or the use of Finlayson troughs or similar devices (see later).

Thus kangaroos constrain opportunities for graziers to modify grazing pressure by moving sheep about. Certainly, small exclosures show that completely removing kangaroos and sheep can allow vegetation regeneration. However, the densities to which kangaroos need to be reduced to achieve effective regeneration of vegetation is unknown, particularly when it is still grazed by sheep, cattle, feral goats and rabbits (Pople & McLeod, 2000).

There is also the bigger question of whether competition between sheep and kangaroos is of serious economic significance. The hard evidence is limited and somewhat equivocal (for reviews, see Pople & Grigg, 1998; Pople & McLeod, 2000). Clearly a resolution of this question is very important because of the present belief that there is a productivity benefit to be gained from lowering kangaroo numbers. At very high densities this is likely to be the case, but the gains expected from lowering typical densities may be illusory.

More experimental, manipulative research is needed to determine land management practices that will best rehabilitate the sheep rangelands. If continued overgrazing turns these rangelands into deserts, they will be economically unproductive, even for the kangaroo industry if there is a greatly diminished kangaroo population.

The kangaroo industry and pest control

If pest control has been and continues to be the main reason for the harvest, has the industry been, and can it be, effective? The answer has to be 'no', if the perceptions of pastoralists are any guide, because kangaroo harvesting has been in full swing since long before the study by Gibson & Young (1988) quantified their considerable dissatisfaction. Because actual harvest rates in recent years have been close to 10–15%, it can be assumed that harvesting has lowered the populations by about the 30–40% estimated by Caughley (1987a). However, there are frequent calls from graziers' organisations for higher quotas or for the implementation of additional control measures.

What other methods are on offer? Additional (legal) control measures include the issue of 'shoot-and-let-lie' permits, electrification of water troughs to stop kangaroos drinking (Norbury, 1992; Hacker & Freudenberger, 1997) and, most recently, proposals to use immunocontraceptive techniques.

The idea of controlling kangaroos by immunocontraception has received some attention recently, particularly from animal rights groups who see it as more humane than shooting. On this promise, The Cooperative Research Centre for Marsupial Conservation and Management, based at

Sydney's Macquarie University, was funded to develop techniques by which, using immunogenic antigens, kangaroos could be made sterile for long periods, probably up to about a year. This may be useful for controlling kangaroos in contained or suburban situations such as golf courses, wildlife parks and public reserves. Doubts about the practicality of its use in the rangelands, however, have been raised by McCallum (1996) and Grigg (1997a,b) on a number of grounds, including difficulties with species specificity and gauging the dose rate to reduce populations without compromising conservation objectives. To quote McCallum, 'the notion that one can "control" species with highly variable populations, both temporally and spatially, given that a response will not be apparent immediately, is one which would surprise most population ecologists'. A more comprehensive review of the difficulties was presented by Pople & Grigg (1998).

In the absence of natural predators, therefore, there seems to be no better way to control kangaroo numbers than by harvesting and without the industry it could be expected that kangaroo numbers would become very large indeed. But if really serious pest control became the aim, its effectiveness would be limited because it can survive only if kangaroos remain numerous. We think that an alternative approach is necessary, which recognises kangaroos as a resource, rather than a pest, and we now turn again to thoughts about the future.

From pest to resource

Changing the pest status of kangaroos is about changing their economic status. If more money could be made from kangaroos than sheep, the change in status will surely follow. Can this happen? Perhaps, because kangaroo meat is a good product looking for a bigger market. If the present trend towards better recognition continues, and landholders begin to see the potential and put some money into marketing, it is easy to forecast a time when kangaroos will be regarded as a legitimate and valued component of the economic as well as the faunal fabric of Australia's rangelands. Such a development could give landholders an incentive to reduce sheep numbers, opening the way for a reduction in overgrazing, a vision for the future which has been referred to as 'sheep replacement therapy for rangelands' (Grigg, 1997b).

This possible scenario has been explored and advocated in a series of publications (Grigg, 1987, 1995, 1997a; Lunney & Grigg, 1988). A crucial element, apart from active marketing to promote the meat on the world game meat market, would be to find a way that would enable landholders to gain advantage directly from the kangaroos on their property. To do this, the issue of ownership is important, but ownership of kangaroos is vested in the state. Already, when kangaroos are shot, they are identified with numbered tags so that their legality under the quota system can be established, species by species. The solution may be for the wildlife management agency in each state to issue tags to individual properties, proportional to estimates of kangaroo numbers there, by species. Tags could then be sold by landholders to the kangaroo industry, at prices determined by market forces. Ownership of the kangaroo would be transferred to the owner of the tag at the time it is attached to the freshly shot carcass. The total number of tags issued would dictate the size of the harvest, quotas being set for individual properties or regions, as required to ensure adequate conservation or population control.

This is not an outcome that would automatically be favoured by the present kangaroo industry, which now gains access to its product free of charge. The envisaged future price rise, however, would have to cover the purchase of harvesting rights from landholders who do, after all, raise the animals. A small number of landholders, perhaps seeing a changed future, have already taken out kangaroo processors' licenses themselves. It is an outcome, too, which would not please animal preservationists and animal rights activists who, of course, can be counted on to oppose a kangaroo industry as a matter of principle, no matter how much ecosystem-wide conservation benefit accrues.

CONCLUSION

In Africa, the CAMPFIRE programme is well known (website: http://www.campfire-zimbabwe.org), and aims to reclaim land previously alienated to cattle, by making wildlife viewing and wildlife harvesting more rewarding economically (Hutton & Dickson, Chapter 20). In Australia, debate about kangaroos has been the driving force behind much discussion; current thinking is reviewed in a conference on the topic organised by the University of Queensland's Centre for Conservation Biology (Grigg *et al.*, 1995). The Australasian Wildlife Management Society, too, has been active in promoting discussion and has developed a general Position Statement on wildlife harvesting, which serves as a background for a statement about kangaroos specifically (both accessible at website: www.awms.org).

The most salient points are that every case of wildlife harvesting (including fish and trees) should be examined on its merits and that the main criteria should be that the harvesting can be done humanely, that the populations can sustain a harvest at economically viable levels, and that biodiversity conservation is not compromised. Whenever there can be a conservation gain, for the species or their habitats, this needs to be identified and encouraged.

Australia's harvesting of kangaroos is often said by its opponents to be one of the world's largest harvests of wildlife. We believe it to be one of the best managed, too. It is still the subject of much vigorous debate and continuing research and, if developed in concert with control of feral animals, the industry has a great potential to set in motion a reclamation and restoration of habitat across much of inland Australia.

REFERENCES

Barker, R. D. & Caughley, G. (1992). Distribution and abundance of kangaroos (Marsupalia: Macropodidae) at the time of European contact: Victoria. *Australian Mammalogy*, **15**, 81–88.

Bayliss, P. (1985). The population dynamics of red and western grey kangaroos in arid New South Wales, Australia. II. The numerical response function. *Journal of Animal Ecology*, **54**, 127–135.

Bayliss, P. (1987). Kangaroo dynamics. In *Kangaroos: Their Ecology and Management in the Sheep Rangelands of Australia*, ed. G. Caughley, N. Shepherd & J. Short, pp. 119–134. Cambridge University Press, Cambridge.

Cairns, S. C. & Grigg, G. C. (1993). Population dynamics of red kangaroos (*Macropus rufus*) in relation to rainfall in the South Australian pastoral zone. *Journal of Applied Ecology*, **30**, 444–458.

Cairns, S. C., Grigg, G. C., Beard, L. A., Pople, A. R. & Alexander, P. (2000). Western grey kangaroos (*Macropus fuliginosus*) in the South Australian pastoral zone: the dynamics of populations at the edge of their range. *Wildlife Research*, **27**, 309–318.

Calaby, J. H. & Grigg, G. C. (1989). Changes in macropodoid communities and populations in the past 200 years, and the future. In *Kangaroos, Wallabies and Rat-kangaroos*, vol. 2, ed. G. Grigg, P. Jarman & I. Hume, pp. 813–820. Surrey Beatty, Sydney.

Caughley, G. (1976). Wildlife management and the dynamics of ungulate populations. In *Applied Biology*, vol. 1, ed. T. H. Coaker, pp. 183–246. Academic Press, London.

Caughley, G. (1987a). Ecological relationships. In *Kangaroos: Their Ecology and Management in the Sheep Rangelands of Australia*, ed. G. Caughley, N. Shepherd & J. Short, pp. 159–187. Cambridge University Press, Cambridge.

Caughley, G. (1987b). Introduction to the sheep rangelands. In *Kangaroos: Their Ecology and Management in the Sheep Rangelands of Australia*, ed. G. Caughley, N. Shepherd & J. Short, pp. 1–13. Cambridge University Press, Cambridge.

Caughley, G. & Gunn, A. (1993). Dynamics of large herbivores in deserts: kangaroos and caribou. *Oikos*, **67**, 47–55.

Caughley, G. & Sinclair, A. R. E. (1994). *Wildlife Ecology and Management*. Blackwell Scientific, London.

Caughley, G., Grigg, G. C. & Short, J. (1983). How many kangaroos? *Search*, **14**, 151–152.

Caughley, G., Grigg, G. C. & Smith, L. (1985). The effect of drought on kangaroo populations. *Journal of Wildlife Management*, **49**, 679–685.

Chaloupka, G. (1984). From paleoart to casual paintings. *Northern Territory Museum of Arts and Sciences Monograph*, **1**, 1–60.

Corrigan, P. (1988). Export of kangaroo meat. *Australian Zoologist*, **24**, 179–180.

Gibson, L. M. & Young, M. D. (1988). *Kangaroos: Counting the Cost. The Economic Effects of Kangaroo Culling on Agricultural Production*. CSIRO, Melbourne.

Grigg, G. C. (1987). Kangaroos – a better economic base for our marginal grazing lands? *Australian Zoologist*, **24**, 73–80.

Grigg, G. (1988). Kangaroo harvesting and the conservation of the sheep rangelands. *Australian Zoologist*, **24**, 124–128.

Grigg, G. C. (1995). Kangaroo harvesting for conservation of rangelands, kangaroos, .and graziers. In *Conservation through Sustainable Use of Wildlife*, ed. G. C. Grigg, P. T. Hale & D. Lunney, pp. 161–165. Centre for Conservation Biology, University of Queensland, Brisbane.

Grigg, G. C. (1997a). A crossroads in kangaroo politics. *Australian Biologist*, **10**, 12–22.

Grigg, G. (1997b). Making a living from roos, not sheep. *Australian Geographic*, **45**, 33.

Grigg, G. C., Hale, P. T. & Lunney, D. (eds.) (1995). *Conservation through Sustainable Use of Wildlife*. Centre for Conservation Biology, University of Queensland, Brisbane.

Hacker, R. B. & Freudenberger, D. (1997). The effect of short-term exclosure of watering points on the behaviour and harvesting efficiency of grey and red kangaroos. *Rangeland Journal*, **19**, 145–156.

Kirkpatrick, T. H. & Amos, P. J. (1985). The kangaroo industry. In *The Kangaroo Keepers*, ed. H. J. Lavery, pp. 75–102. University of Queensland Press, St Lucia.

Lunney, D. & Grigg, G. (1988). Kangaroo harvesting and the conservation of arid and semi-arid lands. *Australian Zoologist*, **24**, 121–193.

McCallum, H. (1996). Immunocontraception for wildlife population control. *Trends in Ecology and Evolution*, **11**, 491–493.

McFarlane, J. D. (1971). Exports of kangaroo meat. *Australian Zoologist*, **16**, 62–64.

McLeod, S. & Pople, T. (1998). Optimal exploitation strategies for kangaroo populations in variable environments. In *Proceedings of the 11th Australian Veterbrate Pest Conference*, Bunbury, Western Australia, pp. 375–380.

Newman, J. C. & Condon, R. W. (1969). Land use and present condition. In *Arid Lands of Australia*, ed. R. O. Slatyer & R. A. Perry, pp. 105–129. Australian National University Press, Canberra.

Norbury, G. L. (1992). An electrified watering trough that selectively excludes kangaroos. *Rangeland Journal*, **14**, 3–8.

Norbury, G. L. & Norbury, D. C. (1993). The distribution of red kangaroos in relation to range regeneration. *Rangeland Journal*, **15**, 3–11.

Passmore, J. (1974). *Man's Responsibility for Nature*. Scribner, New York.

Pople, A. R. (1996). Effects of harvesting upon the demography of red kangaroos in western Queensland. PhD thesis, University of Queensland.

Pople, A. R. (1999). Aerial surveys for kangaroo management. *Australian Zoologist*, **31**, 266–320.

Pople, A. & Cairns, S. (1995). Impact of harvesting on kangaroos. In *Conservation through Sustainable Use of Wildlife*, ed. G. Grigg, P. Hale & D. Lunney, pp. 224–229. Centre for Conservation Biology, University of Queensland, Brisbane.

Pople, A. R. & Grigg, G. C. (1998). Commercial harvesting of kangaroos in Australia. Unpublished document prepared for Environment Australia, Canberra. (Website: http://www.anca.gov.au/plants/wildlife/roo/roobg.htm)

Pople, A. R. & McLeod, S. R. (2000). Kangaroo management and the sustainable use of rangelands. In *Management for Sustainable Ecosystems*, ed. P. T. Hale, A. Petrie, D. Moloney & P. Sattler, pp. 78–86. Centre for Conservation Biology, University of Queensland, Brisbane.

Pople, A. R., Grigg, G. C., Cairns, S. C., Beard, L. A. & Alexander, P. (2000). Trends in the numbers of red kangaroos and emus on either side of the South Australian dingo fence: evidence for predator regulation? *Wildlife Research*, **27**, 269–276.

Ramsay, B. J. (1994). *Commercial Use of Wild Animals in Australia*. Australian Government Publishing Service, Canberra.

Southwell, C. (1989). Techniques for monitoring the abundance of kangaroo and wallaby populations. In *Kangaroos, Wallabies and Rat-kangaroos*, vol. 2, ed. G. Grigg, P. Jarman & I. Hume, pp. 659–693. Surrey Beatty, Sydney.

Southwell, C. J., Cairns, S. C., Palmer, R., Delaney, R. & Broers, R. (1997). Abundance of large macropods in the eastern highlands of Australia. *Wildlife Society Bulletin*, **25**, 125–132.

Stocker, M. & Walters, C. J. (1984). Dynamics of a vegetation–ungulate system and its optimal exploitation. *Ecological Modelling*, **25**, 151–165.

Sugg, I. & Kreuter, U. (1994). *Elephants and Ivory: Lessons from the Trade Ban*. Institute of Economic Affairs, London.

Tunbridge, D. (1991). *The Story of the Flinders Ranges Mammals*. Kangaroo Press, Kenthurst, New South Wales.

Woods, L. E. (1984). *Land Degradation in Australia*. Australian Government Publishing Service, Canberra.

19

Conservation and resource use in Arctic ecosystems

ANNE GUNN

Arctic ecosystems are still functionally intact and robust. Most threats typical for elsewhere in the world – habitat loss through agriculture, industry and urbanisation are either non-existent or localised, and introduced species are scarce. Within Arctic ecosystems, resource use (hunting) is the most conspicuous influence that people have on wildlife.

Hunting has a high profile in Arctic wildlife management not least because it is so important in the mixed subsistence economy that is still characteristic in many northern countries. And among the factors that can influence Arctic wildlife, hunting is the most manageable and it can be relatively easily quantified. Across the two Canadian territories of the Northwest Territories (NWT) and Nunavut (NT), hunting is not currently a threat to most wildlife, because numbers are adequate to support the level of hunting. However, on the Arctic islands of Banks (Nagy *et al.*, 1996) and northwest Victoria (Gunn *et al.*, 2000), where caribou are classified as endangered, hunting has accelerated the declines.

From a technical wildlife conservation point of view, whether or not hunting is a threat depends on whether it causes undesired declines, thus reducing sustainability. However, hunting is more than a technical issue as wildlife conservation also has to take into account people's attitudes and perceptions (see Sanderson, Chapter 21). Urban and rural cultures often diverge about how hunting can be a threat or benefit and, for example, they will probably differ as to whether hunting endangered wildlife is anything but a threat. The Canadian Arctic is largely populated by aboriginal people and hunting is inextricably part of the long relationship between them and their environment; they see themselves as part of the Arctic ecosystem (e.g. Berkes & Folke, 1998). Urban and rural cultures often diverge about whether hunting can threaten or benefit wildlife, and this divergence can include views on endangered species.

The chapter starts with a brief description of Arctic ecology and trends in wildlife numbers. A brief description of historic hunting and its regulation leads to an explanation of the current wildlife management regimes. Having established the background, I discuss hunting and other threats to the Arctic ecosystems before closing the chapter by describing how hunting can be a benefit. Although the Arctic is normally defined as being as north of the treeline, I include examples from caribou *Rangifer tarandus*, many of which migrate seasonally between the treeless tundra and the treed taiga. I also draw examples from muskox *Ovibos moschatus*, polar bear *Ursus maritimus* and whale management in the NWT and NT.

ARCTIC ECOSYSTEMS

The Arctic has a severe and unpredictably variable climate that limits vegetation to low shrub and grass–sedge communities with extensive polar deserts on the high Arctic islands (Edlund & Alt, 1989). Climate severity is conspicuous in, for example, annually limiting plant growth and nutrient recycling to only three months or less (Maxwell, 1981). Annual variability is high – for example, on Banks Island, the coefficient of variation for snowfall at the end of winter (May) is 87% and for the length of the plant growing season is 47% (Caughley & Gunn, 1993). Imposed on annual variations are interannual trends that persist over decades and are driven by large-scale circulation anomalies (Barnston & Livezey, 1987; Hurrell, 1995). The signature of large-scale circulation anomalies (Pacific North American and North Atlantic Oscillations) is discernible in the timing of plant growth, herbivore body weights and population trends, although effects vary between regions and species (Sinclair *et al.*, 1993; Post & Stenseth, 1999).

The link between climate and herbivore population ecology is through the effect of weather on forage availability. Immediately after spring snowmelt, caribou and muskox feed selectively, switching between plant species to track the flowering and leafing sequence as early plant growth has the highest nutritional value (Kuropat & Bryant, 1983; Figure 19.1). Forage intake largely determines body condition and both caribou and muskox have to reach a threshold of body condition to successfully breed and raise a calf (Parker *et al.*, 1990; Adamczewski, 1995). Winter conditions add further variability in the supply of forage to mammalian herbivores beyond that imposed by limits on plant growth. Winter conditions vary annually and determine relative forage availability when snow and ice affect the energetics of foraging for mammalian herbivores.

The annually variable and regionalised climate (Maxwell, 1981) and its effects on forage availability suggest that generalisations about trends in abundance of wildlife across the Arctic have to be cautious. Those

Figure 19.1. Adult and young Peary caribou *Rangifer tarandus pearyi*, in the Canadian High Arctic. (Copyright Greenpeace/Morgan.)

variations also suggest that the relationship between rate of increase and food availability is complex, unpredictable and drives fluctuations in herbivore numbers (see e.g. Caughley & Gunn, 1993).

The Canadian Arctic is populated by Inuit and Inuvialuit who have settled land claims with the federal government. The Inuvialuit Final Agreement, signed in 1984, covers 168 350 km² and has 2500 beneficiaries in the Northwest Territories. The Nunavut Land Claim Agreement followed in 1993. Nunavut was established as a separate territory in 1999, with an area of just over 1.9 million km² and 17 500 beneficiaries.

POPULATION TRENDS

Fluctuations in caribou numbers over decades is a frequently reiterated observation in aboriginal knowledge (see e.g. Ferguson & Messier, 1997). The increased hunting that followed European colonisation (introduction of rifles, commercial hunting) accentuated or overrode natural fluctuations in caribou numbers and contributed to the so-called caribou crisis of low numbers between 1949 and 1955 (Kelsall, 1968). The reality of further declines in the early 1980s was controversial and, by the 1990s, it became obvious that the herds of barren-ground caribou *R. t. groenlandicus* had increased in size up to fivefold. Currently, on the mainland tundra, the four largest herds of barren-ground caribou (Bathurst, Beverly, Qamanirjuaq, Queen Maud Gulf) totalled 1.4 million caribou in the mid 1990s and are probably stable or increasing (Figure 19.2).

Peary caribou *R. t. pearyi* are found only on Canada's High Arctic islands. Trends in population size are available only from the western High Arctic islands, where numbers have fluctuated (Figure 19.3) within a long-term decline from 26 000 in 1961 to 1100 by 1997 (Gunn *et al.*, 2000). In 1991, the Committee on the Status of Endangered Wildlife in Canada classified caribou on the High Arctic and Banks Island as 'endangered' (Miller, 1990) based on the steep population declines during the 1970s and 1980s (Figure 19.3).

Historically, muskox were numerous enough to be important in the aboriginal cultures on the mid-Arctic islands and mainland. Sharp declines in muskox numbers on the NWT mainland followed unregulated commercial harvest in the late 1800s and early 1900s (Barr, 1991). The trade in muskox hides peaked and collapsed within 30 years and only a handful of scattered herds remained on the mainland Arctic (Barr, 1991). Subsequently muskox hunting was banned between 1917 and 1967, when populations had started to recover and restrictive hunting quotas were implemented. Currently, muskox numbers in the NWT and Nunavut are about 103 000 on the Arctic islands and about 26 000 on the mainland (Gunn & Fournier, 1998).

Hunting was not the cause of all historic wildlife declines everywhere – muskox virtually disappeared from Banks and Victoria Islands, probably in the late 1800s, before European influences. Inuvialuit elders remember that an ice storm encased vegetation in ice and many muskox died (Gunn *et al.*, 1991). Muskox numbers rebounded on Banks Island from a few hundred to 3000 by 1972 and 64 000 by 1994 before declining to 46 000 (Nagy *et al.*, 1996; J. Nagy, personal communication).

The number of polar bears hunted increased with European exploration and trading in the Arctic. Hunting for hides was not significant until the 1950s, when prices climbed in response to markets. Snowmobiles were becoming available in the 1960s and hunting increased, adding to international concerns for polar bears. In 1968, regulations imposed quotas to reduce hunting. Currently, Canada has about 14 800 polar bears of a global population estimated to number between 25 000 and 30 000 bears (IUCN Polar Bear Specialists Group, 1998).

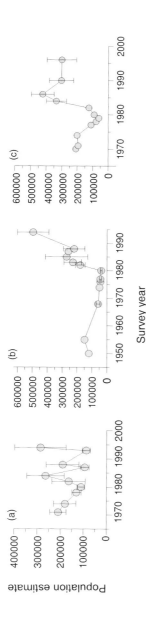

Figure 19.2. Population estimates for three barren-ground caribou herds in the Northwest Territories and Nunavut: (a) Beverly herd, (b) Qamanirjua herd and (c) Bathurst herd. Bars indicate standard errors.

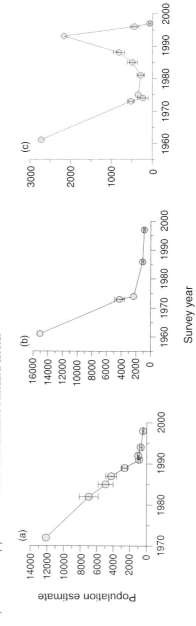

Figure 19.3. Population estimates for Peary caribou and Arctic Island caribou on three western High Arctic Islands: (a) Banks Island, (b) Melville and Prince Patrick Islands and (c) Bathurst Island. Bars indicate standard errors.

WILDLIFE MANAGEMENT STRUCTURES AND CO-MANAGEMENT

Governments responded to the wildlife declines in the NWT during the early 1900s with well-meaning but often poorly explained regulations to restrict hunting. Those regulations largely ignored local knowledge and emphasised hunting as a threat, thereby alienating aboriginal hunters, leaving them with bitter feelings. Those feelings still influence discussions about hunting, although changes to the management structures may be reducing mistrust (see e.g. Richard & Pyke, 1993; Usher, 1995). Those changes began in 1975 when the settlement of land claims established a new regime that gave hunters a more direct say in wildlife management.

The post-land claims regime is now termed co-management, to signify that government has shifted some power and responsibility to co-management boards. Both the federal and territorial governments nominate appointees to represent the public interest on the boards, while the hunters are represented by regional appointees. The boards have authority for wildlife management subject only to conservation, public safety and public health interests. Although final authority is invested in the appropriate government minister, the boards make day-to-day management decisions on wildlife. The boards have authority for harvest allocation issues and provide advice on wildlife management to the government agencies, who almost invariably adopt the advice.

Co-management helps to ensure that aboriginal ecological knowledge is included in wildlife management, although there is debate about how effectively (see e.g. Usher, 1995). Under land claim legislation, the territorial government determines a total allowable harvest using species-specific methods and recommends the total allowable harvest to the boards. The boards estimate basic needs levels from personal interviews with hunters to record harvest levels. If the total allowable harvest exceeds the basic needs levels, then the surplus will be allocated to non-beneficiaries or for commercial wildlife use (meat sales and guided hunts for trophy bulls).

The territorial governments (NWT and NT) determine total allowable harvest, but the extent and method of carrying this out varies between species. The differences are a complex of practicality, life history and management history. For caribou and muskox harvest management, pragmatic flexibility takes precedence over application of theory as outlined by, for example, Caughley (1977), Milner-Gulland & Mace (1998) and many chapters in this book. Aerial surveys are used to track caribou and muskox population trends, although the use of the resulting information differs. For caribou, the survey findings for barren-ground caribou are not currently used to limit subsistence hunting, but they have been used to cap commercial use. In the few current instances where caribou are declining (on some Arctic islands), communities voluntarily reduced harvesting when they began to have difficulty finding caribou.

In contrast to caribou, muskox are hunted under an annual quota based on a rule of thumb – 3–5% of the most recently estimated number of muskox in the management unit. The annual quota is a fixed number of muskox (either sex) and effort is limited by season and assignment to geographical management units. The nearby community decides whether the quota is for subsistence or commercial use, as in 1979 commercial use either for sport hunting or meat sales was written into regulations. The quotas have increased since they began in 1967 to 13 000 tags available in 2000.

Managing polar bears has taken a different direction from caribou and muskox harvest management because tracking abundance is logistically difficult and prohibitively expensive. The total allowable harvest is based on modelling the maximum number of female bears that can be taken without causing a population decline (Taylor *et al.*, 1987). The total allowable harvest is applied as sex-selective hunting through a 'flexible quota system'. The flexible quota system assumes that the sustainable annual harvest of adult females (of more than two years of age) is 1.6% of the estimated population, and that males can be harvested at double that rate (for the theory behind sex-biased harvesting, see Kokko *et al.*, Chapter 14). Within the annual total quota, each community is annually allocated a maximum number of males, and a maximum number of females. Conservatism is built in by ensuring that if the number of females killed exceeds the allocated maximum in a given year, there is a decrease in the total quota for the following year. Between 1994 and 1999, in the NWT and NT, the average annual sustainable harvest was 624 and the kill averaged 598 (IUCN Polar Bear Specialists Group, 1998).

In the mid 1990s, to involve hunters more in the decisions about quotas and to manage polar bears on a population basis, communities and territorial government signed Local Management Agreements. The Agreements describe the background, use of both scientific and traditional knowledge and the rationale for the population estimate upon which the total allowable harvest is based.

Progress has also been made in developing co-management for other marine mammals, notably small whales in the eastern and western Arctic. The conservation and management of beluga *Delphinapterous leucas* in Alaska and the NWT is through the Alaskan and Inuvialuit Beluga Whale

Committee, which includes representatives from communities and governments as well as technical advisors (Adams *et al.*, 1993). However, only the representatives from the beluga hunting communities vote on hunting issues. In the eastern Arctic progress toward co-management for narwhal *Monodon monocerus* was less smooth partly because of a failure to openly and completely include the Inuit hunters (Richard & Pyke, 1993).

The advisory and co-management boards and agreements are not necessarily a guarantee of widespread hunter support (Usher, 1995). This was apparent in Klein *et al.*'s (1999) appraisal of the effectiveness of the Beverly–Qamanirjuaq Caribou Management Board. The authors (Klein *et al.*, 1999) identified that information was not flowing from the user representatives back to the communities and thus the users did not feel involved.

HUNTING AS A THREAT TO WILDLIFE CONSERVATION

The circumstances under which hunting is more likely to be a threat causing unintentional declines in wildlife can be divided into ecological and institutional. Ecological circumstances include the severity and variability of the Arctic environments that buffet populations. I have lumped as institutional those circumstances dealing with the detection and diagnosis of population declines as well as socioeconomic factors that affect hunting.

Hunting can become a threat if population size changes unpredictably in response to environmental perturbations and/or density-dependent changes (unless the population size is closely monitored and hunting quickly adjusted). Caribou, muskox and polar bears are relatively long lived and thus resilient to environmental variability. Muskox are large-bodied grazers with a predominantly conservative lifestyle adapted to buffering much of the variable weather and forage supplies (Adamczewski, 1995). Caribou are probably less strongly coupled by feedback loops to their forage (Jefferies *et al.*, 1992) which suggests that caribou will show less density dependence and be more buffeted by environmental variability.

On the northern-most Arctic islands, environmental variability becomes more significant as many processes are near limits, for example plant growth which plays a large role in determining herbivore reproduction and survival. Consequently, annual variation in population attributes such as pregnancy rates and calf survival is high. Thomas (1982) documented annual pregnancy rates varying between 0 and 80% for Peary caribou and the range of calf production and survival between 1982 and 1998 was 23 to 76 calves per 100 cows for caribou on Banks Island (Larter

& Nagy, 1999). The amount of environmental buffeting may exceed the capability of large mammals to buffer changes and lead to unexpected surges in recruitment or mortality. Population rate of change and size will be more unpredictable and thus hunting at more of a risk of being out of phase with the population trend.

Changes in caribou numbers on Banks Island provide an example of hunting accelerating a decline that is probably already underway in response to an environmental change (severe winters). Caribou declined from 11 000 in 1972 to about 450 by 1998 (Nagy *et al.*, 1996; J. Nagy, personal communication). At least two winters in the 1970s were severe enough to cause caribou to starve to death and one winter in the 1990s reduced productivity and calf survival. In the 1970s and 1980s, hunting (annually 300–450 caribou) did not decrease and accelerated the decline in caribou numbers before hunters agreed to reduce the hunting to an annual take of 30 caribou (Nagy *et al.*, 1996).

Institutional circumstances that increase wildlife vulnerability to hunting start with detecting population declines. The ability to detect declines in caribou or muskox numbers depends partly on estimating trends in population size (Heard, 1985; Graf & Case, 1989). The aim is to conduct surveys at five year intervals but high costs and large survey areas have increased survey intervals to the extent that population declines have been missed. For example, the inter-island caribou population of Prince of Wales and Somerset Islands was considered to be relatively stable between 1974 and 1980 (estimated 5000 caribou in 1980). Inuit hunters reported seeing fewer caribou on those two islands in the early 1990s, which triggered a survey but not until 1995. The survey revealed that caribou had declined to fewer than 100 (Gunn *et al.*, 2000).

Problems with detecting declines are not just technical but include the fact that hunters frequently distrust survey techniques and disbelieve the results (Klein *et al.*, 1999). This disbelief is not confined to management of caribou and muskox but also includes whales (Richard & Pyke, 1993). Disbelief stems from historical relationships, poor communication and cultural differences between aboriginal and non-aboriginal peoples in a willingness to rely on abstract concepts and numbers as opposed to personal observations. Further differences arise over interpretation of factors causing declines – for example, whether caribou have moved away from the survey area or numbers declined because deaths exceeded births (Freeman, 1975; Miller and Gunn, 1978).

Socioeconomic factors are another institutional circumstance that can affect the vulnerability of wildlife to hunting. The two territories (NWT and

NT) have a 'Fourth World' economy (Weissling, 1989), with indigenous minorities forming an enclave within the larger and economically dominant North American society. The young and growing human population still depends on hunting and fishing. Over 90% of aboriginal households in the NWT used wild meat or fish in 1991 (Bureau of Statistics, 1996). Wage earning provides cash for equipment and supplies necessary for hunting and fishing (see e.g. Wenzel, 1991), which creates a need for at least part-time work. However, wage-earning opportunities are relatively limited, shifting the emphasis to commercial use of wildlife and fisheries, but the distinction between subsistence and commercial use is by no means simple. Not all commercial use is necessarily about maximising profits, which, as Clark (1976) spelled out, leads to an economic rationale for overharvesting, especially for long-lived species with low rates of reproduction (see Ludwig, Chapter 2). In western Greenland, for example, small-scale sales of minke whale *Balaenoptera acutorstrata* and fin whale *B. physalua* were necessary to maintain cashflow to purchase supplies for subsistence hunting (Caulfield, 1993).

Finally, in the background to discussions on hunting is a mixture of concern and defensiveness in response to 'outside' (i.e. southern Canada and elsewhere) opinions. For example, in a workshop on future action over the endangered Peary caribou, this was recognised as a serious issue (Gunn *et al.*, 1998), especially in the context of allowing caribou hunting while considering reducing wolf predation (through translocations or subsistence hunting). Partly the response to 'outside' opinions is from previous experience with some non-governmental organisations. Those organisations cover a spectrum that includes animal rights activists, some of whom see hunting as a threat to conservation, and, conversely, aboriginal hunters who perceive the organisations as a threat to their way of life. For example, the movement against seal hunting led to the European Community's ban on sealskins, which resulted in a substantial loss of income from selling sealskins in some Inuit communities (Wenzel, 1991).

ADDITIONAL THREATS

The greater risk that hunting could become unsustainable and cause or contribute to population declines may lie in the unexpected (Holling, 1986). 'The unexpected' ranges from shortcomings in data collection or predictive models to environmental changes accumulating in unanticipated ways. I include in this context threats to wildlife from outside the territories, such as atmospheric transfer of contaminants and climate change, even if we are uncertain as to how those threats may act in practice.

Global climate change and the atmospheric transport of contaminants are factors that will affect or already are affecting populations. Global climate change is predicted to warm the western Arctic and increase precipitation (Maxwell, 1997). Global warming is predicted to trigger a cascade of effects (see e.g. Oechel *et al.*, 1997). Evidence consistent with predictions for global climate change in the western Arctic include Inuvialuit reports of ecological changes following trends of warmer weather (IISD, 1999).

Effects on population ecology that could affect sustainability of hunting are possible. For example, an increase in difficulty of finding winter forage is likely for caribou on the western Arctic islands if warmer temperatures bring a greater frequency of freezing rain and deeper snow. Annual snowfall for the western High Arctic increased during the 1990s and the three heaviest snowfall winters coincided with Peary caribou numbers on Bathurst Island dropping from 3000 to an estimated 75 between 1994 and 1997; muskox declined by 80% during the same three winters (Gunn *et al.*, 2000).

Atmospheric and aquatic transport of contaminants has resulted in contaminants reaching detectable levels in Arctic wildlife (Elkin & Bethke, 1995; AMAP, 1997), although effects on population ecology are unknown. Persistent organochlorine contaminants are carried in the atmosphere, but cadmium is almost entirely from natural sources and mercury is from ocean degassing, natural breakdown and atmospheric and anthropogenic sources (AMAP, 1997).

If global warming imposes greater environmental stress on wildlife, then it may interact with contamination. Polar bears, at the top of the food chain, accumulate contaminants from eating ringed seals and other marine mammals. Relatively high levels of organochlorines and metals are found in polar bears and exhibit relatively strong regional patterns (AMAP, 1997). In female polar bears, although the existing body levels of organochlorines may be sequestered effectively when fat reserves are high, the sequestration may be inadequate during a poor feeding season (Polischuk *et al.*, 1994; AMAP, 1997). On western Hudson Bay, there is a trend for female bears having less fat reserves as progressively earlier sea ice break-up forces them ashore and they have to fast for longer (Stirling *et al.*, 1999).

HUNTING AS BENEFICIAL TO WILDLIFE CONSERVATION

Viewed scientifically, hunting can benefit conventional North American wildlife conservation in two ways. First, hunting can either stimulate a population's rate of increase as the initial phase of sustained yield management (Caughley, 1977; Milner-Gulland & Mace, 1998) or reduce a population considered to be too large. Secondly, from the point of view of wildlife conservation, a tangible benefit is that hunters are directly 'sampling' wildlife and habitat while they are hunting and this knowledge accumulates over time and wide areas. Gradually, the hunters' knowledge is being used in management (see e.g. Kofinas *et al.*, 1997).

Some of the first formalised involvement of hunter's local ecological knowledge in wildlife management was through the advisory boards for caribou management. The Beverly–Qamanirjuaq Caribou Co-Management Board was established in 1982 partly as a result of controversy over whether surveys suggested a decline in the Qamanirjuaq herd and partly after an unexpected excursion of the Beverly herd into northern Saskatchewan triggered a massive caribou harvest. The Board includes jurisdictional representatives and an equal number of aboriginal users, and advises the governments of each jurisdiction. In 1985, an international co-management board was created for the Porcupine Caribou herd. Those advisory boards broke new ground in bringing together the users and managers (Peter & Urquhart, 1991; Thomas & Schaefer, 1991).

The next step in attempting to ensure that hunters' knowledge is incorporated into wildlife conservation came with the establishment of co-management boards starting in the NWT with the Inuvialuit Final Agreement in 1985. However, as Usher (1995) has written, the incorporation of traditional knowledge into co-management is less than satisfactory given the very different cultural concepts of wildlife. Despite all the changes and uncertainties brought about by European contact, hunting is still an integral part of aboriginal life. Hunting is bound up in cultural and individual identity and relationships with wildlife and the land rather than a simple statement about hunting being the removal of *x* individuals from a wildlife population.

Given its cultural significance, hunting has an intangible benefit to wildlife conservation because acceptance of hunting has the connotation of, at least, recognition of a hunting culture, its values and knowledge. In turn, that recognition and its inclusion in decisions about wildlife conservation build support for conservation. For example, the draft National Recovery Strategy for Peary caribou and Arctic island caribou includes hunting as a recovery action. Under draft federal legislation, wildlife nationally recognised to be endangered requires a National Recovery Strategy that sets out actions for recovery. If recovery strategies are not automatically against hunting, this may build hunters' support for the other recovery actions.

CONCLUSIONS

The potential for hunting as a threat depends not only on the technical ability to track trends in population size to ensure that the hunting is sustainable but also on the credibility of those efforts with aboriginal hunters. Hunting is, and has been, an essential part of aboriginal culture in circumpolar arctic regions, and wildlife conservation cannot happen without their support and involvement. A recent and still-developing mechanism to give hunters an effective voice in wildlife conservation is through shared responsibilities with government (co-management). Co-management is less than 30 years old and coincidentally, during that time, most wildlife abundance has increased or is stable. Wildlife fluctuates in abundance and sooner or later populations will decline, especially if global climate change increases demand for wildlife or other outside influences change the sustainability of hunting. Decreases in sustainability will raise special issues of access to wildlife that will test co-management. Even so, co-management is a step forward in sharing knowledge and developing trust to conserve wildlife in the Northwest Territories and Nunavut.

ACKNOWLEDGEMENTS

Siu-Ling Han and Mitch Taylor (Department of Sustainable Development, Government of Nunavut) gave freely of their time to provide information. Lynda Yonge and Judy Dragon (Department of Resources, Wildlife and Economic Development, Government of the Northwest Territories) helped with manuscript production.

REFERENCES

Adamczewski, J. (1995). Digestion and body composition in the muskox. PhD thesis, University of Saskatchewan.

Adams, M., Frost, K. J., Harwood, L. A. (1993). Alaska and Inuvialuit Beluga Whale Committee (AIBWC) – an initiative in 'at home management'. Community-based whaling in the North. *Arctic*, **46**, 134–137.

AMAP (Arctic Monitoring and Assessment Programme) (1997). *Arctic Pollution Issues: A State of the Arctic Environment Report*. AMAP, Oslo.

Barnston, A. G. & Livezey, R. F. (1987). Classification, seasonality and persistence of low-frequency atmospheric circulation patterns. *Monthly Weather Review*, **115**, 1083–1126.

Barr, W. (1991). *Back from the Brink: the Road to Muskox Conservation in the Northwest Territories*. The Arctic Institute of North America, University of Calgary, Calgary, AB. Komatik Series 3.

Berkes, F. & Folke, C. (1998). *Linking Social and Ecological Systems*. Cambridge University Press, Cambridge.

Bureau of Statistics (1996). *Statistics Quarterly*, vol. 18. Department of Public Works and Services, Government of the Northwest Territories, Yellowknife, NT.

Caughley, G. (1977). *Analysis of Vertebrate Populations*. Wiley, Chichester.

Caughley, G. & Gunn, A. (1993). Dynamics of large herbivores in deserts: kangaroos and caribou. *Oikos*, **67**, 47–55.

Caulfield, R. A. (1993). Aboriginal subsistence whaling in Greenland: the case of Qeqertarsuaq municipality in west Greenland. Community-based whaling in the north. *Arctic*, **46**, 144–155.

Clark, C. W. (1976). *Mathematical Bioeconomics: The Optimum Management of Renewable Resources*. Wiley Interscience, New York.

Edlund, S. & Alt, B. (1989). Regional congruence of vegetation and summer climate patterns in the Queen Elizabeth Islands, Northwest Territories, Canada. *Arctic*, **42**, 3–23.

Elkin, B. T. & Bethke, R. W. (1995). Environmental contaminants in the Northwest Territories, Canada. *Science of the Total Environment*, **160/161**, 307–321.

Ferguson, M. A. D. & Messier, F. (1997). Collection and analysis of traditional ecological knowledge about a population of Arctic tundra caribou. *Arctic*, **50**, 17–28.

Freeman, M. M. R. (1975). Assessing movement in an Arctic caribou population. *Journal of Environmental Management*, **3**, 251–257.

Graf, R. & Case, R. (1989). Counting muskoxen in the Northwest Territories. *Canadian Journal of Zoology*, **67**, 1112–1115.

Gunn A. & Fournier, B. (1998). *Muskox Numbers and Distribution in the Northwest Territories, 1997*. Northwest Territories Department of Resouces, Wildlife and Economic Development. File Report no. 121.

Gunn, A., Shank, C. C. & McLean, B. (1991). The status and management of muskoxen on Banks Island. *Arctic*, **44**, 188–195.

Gunn, A., Seal, U. S. & Miller, P. S. (eds.) (1998). *Population and Habitat Viability Assessment Workshop for Peary Caribou and Arctic-Island Caribou* (Rangifer tarandus). CBSG, Apple Valley, MN.

Gunn, A., Miller, F. L. & Nishi, J. (2000). Status of endangered and threatened caribou on Canada's Arctic islands. *Rangifer Special Issue*, no. 12, pp. 39–50.

Heard, D. C. (1985). Caribou census methods used in the Northwest Territories. *McGill Subarctic Research Papers* no. 40, pp. 229–238.

Holling, C. S. (1986). The resilience of terrestial ecosystems: local surprise and global change. In *Sustainable Development of the Biosphere*, ed. W. C. Clark & R. E. Munn, pp. 292–317. Cambridge University Press, Cambridge.

Hurrell, J. W. (1995). Decadal trends in the North Atlantic Oscillation: regional temperatures and precipitation. *Science*, **269**, 676–679.

IISD (International Institute for Sustainable Development) (1999). *Inuit Observations on Climate Change*. Trip report no. 1. IISD, Winnipeg, Canada.

IUCN Polar Bear Specialists Group (1998). Worldwide status of the polar bear. In *Proceedings of the 12th Working Meeting of the IUCN Polar Bear Specialists*, January 1997. Oslo, Norway, pp. 23–44.

Jefferies, R. L., Svoboda, J., Henry, G., Raillard, M. & Ruess, R. (1992). Tundra grazing systems and climatic change. In *Arctic Ecosystems in a Changing Climate: An Ecophysiological Perspective*, ed. F. S. Chapin, R. L. Jefferies, J. F. Reynolds, G. R. Shaver, J. Svoboda & E. W. Chu, pp. 391–412. Academic Press Inc., New York.

Kelsall, J. (1968). *The Migratory Barren-Ground Caribou of Canada*. Canadian Wildlife Service Monograph, Ottawa.

Klein, D.R., Moorhead, L., Kruse, J. & Braund, S. R. (1999). Contrasts in use and perceptions of biological data for caribou management. *Wildlife Society Bulletin*, **27**, 488–498.

Kofinas, G. P., Tetlichi, J., Arey, C., Peterson, D. & Neryshoo, M. (1997). *Community-Based Ecological Monitoring: A summary of 1996–97 Observations & Pilot Project Evaluation*. North Yukon Ecological Knowledge Co-Operative, Whitehorse, Yukon Territory, Canada.

Kuropat, P. & Bryant, J. P. (1983). Digestibility of caribou summer forage in arctic Alaska in relation to nutrient, fiber, and phenolic constituents. *Acta Zoologica Fennica*, **175**, 51–52.

Larter, N. & Nagy, J. (1999). *Sex and Age Classification Surveys of Peary Caribou on Banks Island, 1982–1998: A Review*. Northwest Territories Department of Resouces, Wildlife and Economic Development. Manuscript Report no. 114.

Maxwell, B. (1981). Climatic regions of the Canadian Arctic Islands. *Arctic*, **34**, 225–240.

Maxwell, B. (1997). *Responding to Global Climate Change in Canada's Arctic*. Environment Canada, Downsview, Ontario.

Miller, F. L. (1990). *Peary Caribou Status Report*. Environment Canada, Canadian Wildlife Services West & North Region. Alta, Edmonton.

Miller, F. L. & Gunn, A. (1978). Inter-island movements of Peary caribou south of Viscount Melville Sound, Northwest Territories. *Canadian Field Naturalist*, **92**, 331–333.

Milner-Gulland, E. J. & Mace, R. (eds.) (1998). *Conservation of Biological Resources*. Blackwell Science, Cambridge, MA.

Nagy, J. A., Larter, N. C. & Fraser, V. P. (1996). Population demography of Peary caribou and muskox on Banks Island, N.W.T., 1982–1992. *Rangifer Special Issue* no. 9, pp. 213–222.

Oechel, W. C., Callaghan, T., Holten, J. I., Maxwell, B., Molau, U. & Sveinbjornsson, B. (eds.) (1997). *Global Change and Arctic Terrestial Ecosystems*. Springer-Verlag, New York.

Parker, K., White, R. G., Gillingham, M. P. & Holleman, D. F. (1990). Comparison of energy metabolism in relation to daily activity and milk consumption by caribou and muskox neonates. *Canadian Journal of Zoology*, **68**, 104–114.

Peter, A. & Urquhart, D. (1991). One caribou herd, two native cultures, five political systems: consensus management of the Porcupine Caribou range. *Transactions of North American Wildlife and Natural Resources Conference*, **56**, 321–325.

Polischuk, S. C., Letcher, R. J., Norstrom, R. J., Atkinson, S. A. & Ramsay, M. A. (1994). Relationship between PCB concentration, body burden and percent body fat in female polar bears while fasting. Dioxin '94, Department of

Environmental Sanitary Engineering, Kyoto University, Japan. *Organohalogen Compounds*, **20**, 535–539.

Post, E. L. & Stenseth, N. C. (1999). Climatic variability, plant phenology, and northern ungulates. *Ecology*, **80**, 1322–1339.

Richard, P. R. & Pike, D. G. (1993). Small whale co-management in the eastern Canadian Arctic: a case history and analysis. *Arctic*, **46**, 138–155.

Sinclair, A. R. E., Gosline, J. M., Holdsworth, G., Krebs, C. R., Boutin, S., Smith, J. N. M., Boonstra, R. & Dale, M. (1993). Can the solar cycle and climate synchronize the snowshoe hare cycle in Canada? Evidence from tree rings and ice cores. *American Naturalist*, **141**, 173–198.

Stirling, I., Lunn, N.J. & Iacozza, J. (1999). Long-term trends in the population ecology of polar bears in western Hudson Bay in relation to climatic change. *Arctic*, **52**, 294–306.

Taylor, M., DeMaster, D., Bunnell, F. L. & Schweinsburg, R. E. (1987). Modeling the sustainable harvest of female polar bears. *Journal of Wildlife Management*, **51**, 811–820.

Thomas, D. C. (1982). The relationship between fertility and fat reserves of Peary caribou. *Canadian Journal of Zoology*, **60**, 597–602.

Thomas, D. C. & Schaefer, J. (1991). Wildlife co-management defined: the Beverly and Kaminuriak Caribou Management Board. *Rangifer Special Issue* no. 7, pp. 73–89.

Usher, P. (1995). Comanagement of natural resources: some aspects of the Canadian experience. In *Human ecology and climate change*, ed. D. L. Peterson & D. R. Johnson, pp. 197–206. Taylor & Francis, Washington, DC.

Weissling, L. E. (1989). Arctic Canada and Zambia: a comparison of the development processes in the Fourth and Third Worlds. *Arctic*, **42**, 206–216.

Wenzel, G. W. (1991). *Animal Rights, Human Rights. Ecology, Economy and Ideology in the Canadian Arctic*. University of Toronto Press, Toronto.

20

Conservation out of exploitation: a silk purse from a sow's ear?

JON HUTTON & BARNEY DICKSON

This chapter contends that the well-managed utilisation of wildlife resources can be an effective conservation strategy. It also acknowledges that the economic exploitation of wild species and ecosystems may sometimes lead to misuse. But while the conventional wisdom is that consumptive use must be either stopped or heavily regulated, we argue that even the commercial use of wildlife is not, in itself, incompatible with conservation. Indeed, there is increasing evidence that, particularly where habitat loss is a critical threat to species, sustainable use may be the chief mechanism through which conservation is achieved. Conservation biologists have been slow to recognise this, in part because they overemphasise the biological aspects of conservation at the expense of a proper acknowledgement of the social and economic factors that shape conservation outcomes. We use the example of the bushmeat trade in Central Africa to illustrate the importance and complexity of the latter set of factors. Nevertheless, there is some evidence from the Convention on International Trade in Endangered Species of Wild Fauna and Flora (CITES) that conservationists are beginning to understand the importance of the socioeconomic dimensions of sustainability. In the second half of the chapter we consider the socioeconomic context of conservation in southern Africa. There the inexorable spread of agriculture results in pressures on wildlife and wildlife habitats. We examine well-established programmes of sustainable use in Zimbabwe that encourage the commercial consumptive use of the very species that are to be conserved. We conclude that conservation can indeed be achieved from the unlikely starting point provided by exploitation.

EXPLOITATION AND SURVIVAL, MARKETS AND SUSTAINABILTY

The use of wild species is still commonly the foundation for human survival in the developing world. In Tanzania, for example, a recent study of six typical rural villages has demonstrated that 58% of household income is derived from the harvesting and sale of wild honey, wild fruits, charcoal and fuel wood (Monela *et al.*, 1999). Under these conditions, where people are so dependent on biodiversity resources, the exploitation of wild species and ecosystems is not going to stop – even if it is biologically unsustainable. Indeed, exploitation is likely to increase for the foreseeable future as people in developing countries seek to meet their needs from 'free' wild resources under a range of adverse economic conditions, or in other situations of stress, such as drought, which may be increasing in frequency as a result of global climate change (Scoones *et al.*, 1992). In Africa a combination of factors, including economic structural readjustment programmes, in which developing countries are encouraged to cut state employment and social services to win financial support from the International Monetary Fund and World Bank (Stepanek, 1999), have resulted in severe under-employment, with millions of people forced into greater reliance on meeting their basic needs of food, shelter and medicine from the wild.

Some conservationists from the developed world imply that hunting for subsistence is acceptable, while hunting for commercial purposes is not. However, in practice it is impossible to make a sharp distinction. Even among indigenous peoples with traditional economies, wild products are traded and the income used to buy the 'essentials' of modern living (Wenzel, 1991; Department of Environment, Transport and the Regions, 1999). Nevertheless, it must be acknowledged that markets and commerce have been a major factor in the increased rate at which animals and plants with relatively slow rates of reproduction have been overharvested, locally extirpated and even driven to extinction in the last two centuries (Clark, 1990). One fairly simple explanation for this would cite the greater return to be expected from liquidating the stock and investing the proceeds else-where, in comparison to harvesting the stock in a sustainable way (Clark, 1990; Barbier *et al.*, 1994; Ludwig, Chapter 2). Another, not necessarily inconsistent explanation would emphasise the role that inappropriate systems of proprietorship can play in leading to the unsustainable exploitation of species. For example, if a wild species becomes a *de facto* open access resource it may be threatened by overuse. Both these explanations cite the socio-economic circumstances in which the human exploitation of wildlife takes place in order to explain why such exploitation can pose a threat. But they both imply that there is no necessary link between the exploitation of a species for the market and a decline in that species. In the right circumstances exploitation can be sustainable (Barbier *et al.*, 1994; Swanson, 1997). However, for some mainstream conservationists markets are invariably associated with conservation failure (Caughley & Gunn, 1996; Milner-

Gulland & Mace, 1998). This fear is so deeply entrenched that it might be described as part of the 'world view' of many conservationists (Clarke, 1992), particularly those whose formative experiences were divorced from the problems of the developing world. According to this group, species must be strictly protected and markets in wildlife and wildlife products outlawed (Dickson, 1994). In arriving at this conclusion they often pay scant attention to the social and economic factors that shape the impact of exploitation. Instead they focus on the biology of exploited populations.

SOLUTIONS FROM BIOLOGY?

In most of the analyses of exploitation that we have heard in recent years the discussion among conservationists has revolved around biological factors such as population numbers or density, reproductive potential and life history parameters, sometimes to the exclusion of all other considerations. In many cases any suggestion that this may not be an entirely adequate framework for problem solving has been met with consternation. Happily the situation is changing, but it is just as necessary to challenge the notion that the cure for overexploitation is to be found in the biological sciences as it is to question the belief that commercial exploitation is incompatible with conservation.

The sustainability of use – whether subsistence or commercial use – hinges as much on the human institutions that shape the relations between the resource and the users as on the biological productivity of the species concerned. The issues of tenure and rights of access and the array of incentives and disincentives facing potential users are of central importance (Oglethorpe, 1999).

This observation is particularly well supported by the study of bushmeat exploitation in the forests of Central Africa (for a review, see Fa & Peres, Chapter 10). While there is some debate as to the biological sustainability of current harvest levels for some of the commoner species (Inamdar et al., 1999), there is little argument that the exploitation of the great apes is uncontrolled and growing in such a way that it cannot hope to be sustainable, even over relatively short time scales. The problem is driven largely by the flow of meat from the forest to urban areas in a system of commercial harvest and trade that has grown from traditional subsistence roots and which has profound social impacts at both the rural point of production and the urban point of consumption (Ape Alliance, 1998; Department of Environment, Transport and the Regions, 1999). In rural areas the exploitation of wild species not only provides up to a third of village income, but is sometimes the only reliable source of highly nutritious animal protein (CITES Secretariat, 2000a). In addition the harvest offers benefits to both men (as hunters) and women (as traders and 'chop bar' owners) and provides a safety net for many sectors of the population in times of stress (CITES Secretariat, 2000a). Smoked bushmeat enjoys high value in urban areas, where it is often preferred for cultural reasons and, when this is coupled with its good storage qualities and relative ease of transport, a lively trade is ensured (Cowlishaw, 1999; Inamdar *et al.*, 1999).

With a harvest and trade so wedded to human survival, only a profoundly human-hostile conservationist would disagree that 'biodiversity conservation needs to be seen in the context of the vulnerability of the rural and urban poor' (CITES Secretariat, 2000a). We would go further, however, by suggesting that the bushmeat case illustrates the more general point that biodiversity conservation *depends* on the rural and urban poor and that the importance of this harvest for human livelihoods and social welfare must be a pivotal consideration in any policy that aims to achieve biological sustainability. While helping to quantify the problems, neither biological research to fill the many gaps in our knowledge of the species concerned (IUCN, 1996) nor a better understanding of the biological processes involved (Cowlishaw, 1999) will be of much value in the search for conservation solutions. Even where we know enough about the status and biology of the species involved to determine their response to harvesting, simple policy responses that hinge on codified protection, exclusion and punitive sanctions (which are the tools of choice of many conservationists) are unlikely to work. Moreover, the costs will fall on those who can least afford them. Solutions, if they exist, are likely to revolve around locally administered rights-based systems (of which tenure is one form), which experience has demonstrated are much harder to achieve where authority is consolidated at the national or international level (Murphree, 2000). In the bushmeat case, the situation is so complex and the options so limited that there is a question about whether *any* policy will be able to secure sustainable off-takes within the available biological time frames (Inamdar *et al.*, 1999). Even in economically powerful countries the historical experience suggests that the prerequisites for sustainability are rarely introduced until the 'eleventh hour', when, at the very least, exploitation has led to the local extirpation of species (Mann & Plummer, 1995).

The notion that sustainability may not be primarily a biological issue has not always been well understood or accepted by those who view conservation from a biological perspective. At their most naive and extreme, conservation organisations have suggested that the sustainability of a consumptive use programme can only be demonstrated with a 'vast amount of information' including:

> population, age to maturity, breeding cycle, recruitment and mortality rates, age structure, size and sex distribution, density, growth rates, behaviour, ecosystem conditions, relationships with associated species, abiotic factors, seasons, levels of use, catch per unit, markets, economics . . .
>
> *(Environmental Investigation Agency, 1992)*

It is symptomatic of this view that while the biological factors are specified in some detail, the socioeconomic factors are simply referred to under the catch-all terms 'markets' and 'economics'. Of course, some are opposed to the exploitation of wildlife even when it is sustainable. David Favre of the Animal Legal Defence Fund clearly expresses this view in relation to elephants:

> That a particular use of wildlife may be biologically and ecologically sustainable does not mean that it is ethically acceptable. Elephants are not turnips . . . To kill elephants for the sole purpose of selling their body parts like ivory is unacceptable.
>
> *(Favre 1993)*

Those who share this position have no interest in the social and economic factors that might make use sustainable, because they are opposed to all use. Nevertheless, they still need to address the socioeconomic circumstances in which the protectionist policies they favour are implemented, if they are to show that such policies can be both effective and equitable.

Among those who do not rule out sustainable use altogether, there are signs of a recognition that conservation biology on its own has little to offer by way of solutions. Many key social and economic concepts are quickly entering the scientist's lexicon, and in many cases it is 'retooled' biologists who are advancing new concepts of sustainability. This is illustrated by a recent development in CITES. The Convention is a conservation tool that aims to ensure that wild species are not driven towards extinction by international commercial trade. Experience has demonstrated that a major shortcoming in the operation of the convention has been the failure of many parties to fully implement the requirements of Article IV. This article is, in many ways, at the heart of the Convention (Jenkins, 2000). It requires that exports of species included in Appendix II of the Convention only be allowed if the export is deemed, by a registered Scientific Authority, to be 'non-detrimental' to the long-term survival of that species. Failure to make the non-detriment finding has seen a stream of species declining to such low levels that they have become endangered and are transferred from

Appendix II to Appendix I. Once on Appendix I they are effectively re-moved from international commercial trade.

There are a number of reasons why non-detriment findings are not properly made. They include shortages of expertise and capacity, but, even where these exist, the judgement about whether the export of a species (or the original harvest from the wild) is detrimental is not an easy one. There are several different models of harvesting (Caughley, 1977), but although these can, in theory, identify when overuse is occurring (Caughley, 1992), the sort of information needed (on off-take rates, population size and life history) to apply the models in practice is rarely available. Even where the information is available, biological science alone is an inadequate predictor of the sustainability of a harvesting regime and, because of the number of variables, certainly cannot be achieved (Holling, 1993; Ludwig et al., 1993). Recently, a workshop was convened by the World Conservation Union (IUCN) Species Survival Commission in co-operation with the CITES Sec-retariat and a number of Scientific Authorities from parties to the Conven-tion. It was designed to provide some guidance to those making a non-detriment finding in CITES. At the workshop an expert group, comprising almost exclusively biological scientists, drew up a list of the factors that would be relevant in assessing the management of harvesting regimes for animal species (Table 20.1). Of the 26 issues that were identified, fewer than half were related to population and life history parameters, which are so fundamental to conventional harvesting theory. The majority of issues were included in recognition that, while the biology of the species can indi-cate the degree of risk inherent in harvesting, sustainability will depend on management issues (such as resource tenure and access) with a strong role for resource monitoring and adaptive management (CITES Secretariat, 2000b).

The list drawn up by the workshop will, no doubt, be modified with time, but the participants included a number of factors affecting sustaina-bility that would, at best, be irrelevant had they constrained their deliber-ations strictly within the articles of the convention. CITES deals exclusively with the threat posed to individual taxa (usually species) by international trade. It contains no scope for weighing up the costs and benefits of various conservation approaches and it does not discriminate between the destruc-tive and constructive use of the wildlife trade, presumably because those drafting it more than 20 years ago did not recognise the possibility of bene-ficial trade (Hutton & Dickson, 2000). The participants in the workshop, however, acknowledged that harvesting for international trade is usually just one element of a programme of exploitation and that controlling the

Table 20.1. Factors affecting management of the harvesting regimes for animal species (CITES Secretariat, 2000b)

Factor	Questions
Life history	
1. Life history	What is the species' life history?
2. Ecological adaptability	Is the species adaptable (habit, diet, environmental tolerance etc)?
3. Dispersal efficiency	How efficient is the species dispersal mechanism?
4. Interaction with humans	Is the species tolerant to human activity other than harvest?
National status	
5. National distribution	How is the species distributed nationally?
6. National abundance	What is the abundance nationally?
7. National population trend	What is the recent national population trend?
8. Quality of information	What type of information is available to describe abundance and trend in the national population?
9. Major threats	What major threat is the species facing (overuse/habitat loss and alteration/invasive species/other) and how severe is it?
Harvest management	
10. Illegal off-take or trade	How significant is the national problem of illegal and unmanaged off-take or trade?
11. Management history	What is the history of harvest?
12. Management plan or equivalent	Is there a management plan related to the harvest of the species?
13. Aim of harvest regimen in management planning	What is harvest aiming to achieve?
14. Quotas	Is the harvest based on a system of quotas?
Control of harvest	
15. Harvesting in protected areas	What percentage of the legal national harvest occurs in state-controlled Protected Areas?
16. Harvesting in areas with strong resource tenure or ownership	What percentage of the legal national harvest occurs outside Protected Areas, in areas with strong local control over resource use?
17. Harvesting in areas with open access	What percentage of the legal national harvest occurs in areas where there is no strong local control, giving *de facto* or actual open access?
18. Confidence in harvest management	Do budgetary and other factors allow effective implementation of management plan(s) and harvest controls?
Monitoring of harvest	
19. Methods used to monitor the harvest	What is the principal method used to monitor the effects of the harvest?

Table 20.1. (*cont.*)

Factor	Questions
20. Confidence in harvest monitoring	Do budgetary and other factors allow effective harvest monitoring?
21. Utilisation compared to other threats	What is the effect of the harvest when taken together with the major threat that has been identified for this species?
22. Incentives for species conservation	At the national level, how much conservation benefit accrues from harvesting?
23. Incentives for habitat conservation	At the national level, how much habitat conservation benefit is derived from harvesting?
Protection from harvest	
24. Proportion strictly protected	What percentage of the species' natural range or population is legally excluded from harvest?
25. Effectiveness of strict protection methods	Do budgetary and other factors give confidence in the effectiveness of measures taken to afford strict protection?
26. Regulation of harvest effort	Are there restrictions on harvesting (such as season or equipment) for preventing overuse?

trade across borders alone is commonly inadequate to prevent overexploitation. They also acknowledged the possibility that, notwithstanding the fact that overexploitation is all too common, a preoccupation with the exploitation of individual species may act as a blinker to more serious problems that arise out of the exploitation and modification of whole ecosystems for agriculture (Swanson, 1997).

Given that in the vast majority of cases it is the relentless loss of wild habitat that constitutes the most serious threat to the long-term survival of wild species (Groombridge, 1992; but see Fa & Peres, Chapter 10), there is an often overlooked paradox in the fact that, at the same time as they champion the 'protection' of wild species within the framework of CITES, economically powerful countries not only destroy their own natural ecosystems to produce agricultural crops but commonly encourage (and often subsidise) similar processes in developing countries (Rosenblum & Williamson, 1987). In the next section we examine the system of incentives and disincentives that has driven the depletion of species and habitats over large parts of southern Africa, starting with a historical perspective and ending with a description of a broad ecosystem approach to conservation that revolves around the sustainable use of a range of species.

HISTORICAL MISTAKES

Colonial governments will be remembered for their two-pronged approach to conservation in Africa: they created large protected areas, often evicting those who were living on the land, and they made laws prohibiting the use of many wild species by rural African people. There is currently considerable debate about the intent, outcome and continued appropriateness of 'preservationist' wildlife policies that have often been maintained subsequent to independence (Child, 1995b; Spinage, 1996, 1998; Martin, 1999). Although it is unlikely to be the last word, Martin (1999) leaves little doubt that, in southern Africa at least, reliance on these twin strategies severed the link between African communities and wildlife, setting the scene for contemporary conservation problems. These are problems that have been exacerbated by the region's history of severe racial inequity.

In the absence of meaningful industrialisation in most of southern Africa, the hunger for land has grown and rural poverty remains widespread (UNEP, 1999). Even in South Africa, which has a significant degree of industrial development, rural poverty and land hunger are pivotal development issues. Protected areas are under pressure because they are seen by rural people as under used and serving the needs only of social elites. They are also unpopular because they harbour dangerous wild animals that do not respect boundaries between different land types, however distinct those boundaries are on a map (Adams & McShane, 1992). As a result, these areas are increasingly being fenced, ostensibly to keep animals in, but also to keep people and their cattle out (BBC Assignment, 1992). Use of the land outside urban areas is being polarised: elephants *Loxodonta africana* and lions *Panthera leo* have right of way in protected areas, but have to give way *absolutely* to humans outside. In effect this means that much wildlife outside protected areas is being eradicated.

This ecological apartheid relies on strict policing. Africa's rural people, who once lived off wildlife, for which they often had traditional rules of access and management, are forbidden from using wildlife for food and those who continue to do so are outlawed as 'poachers' and accordingly harassed and hounded as criminals (Matowanyika, 1989). This type of protection, which operates against the interests of most local people, is doomed to failure in many, if not most, circumstances. Africa's rural poor rely on natural resources for their survival and cannot easily be separated from the wildlife. The levels of poverty experienced by many communities make bushmeat the only affordable source of protein (Chardonnet *et al.*, 1995). The alternative to using wildlife is commonly severe malnutrition (Makombe, 1993). Despite the law, rural people continue to use wildlife on a daily basis. The real effect of laws has not been to stop use, but to drive it underground. Because of the difficulties of stopping illegal use there is a strong tendency for wildlife to become a *de facto* open-access resource (Swanson & Barbier, 1992; Swanson, 1997). Traditional, *sustainable use* has been replaced by institutionalised *abuse*.

As a result of preservationist approaches, applied without regard to the prevailing socioeconomic circumstances, parks and other areas protected for wildlife are often under severe pressure in southern Africa. Other parts of the continent are littered with protected areas that exist only on maps and in the memories of old game rangers. When they have the opportunity, rural people have wasted no time in helping themselves to park resources, and that often includes the land itself (Turton, 1987). Even where there are thriving tourism industries, African governments are failing to invest in parks and wildlife. Throughout the continent, budgets for protected area management have fallen steadily in real terms over the last decade, and, with many structural readjustment programmes in place, this rate of fall appears to have increased (Munthali, 1996). It is naive to think that this trend will be easily reversed – the rural African voter simply has little or no sympathy for wildlife and the areas set aside for it to live in (Matowanyika, 1989).

But this is far from the end of the story. Prevented from using wildlife legally, rural Africans have no alternative but to turn to domestic livestock and crops for their survival, even on the poorest land. This leads to the tragedy of the cow and the plough (Swanson, 1997). Much of southern Africa is arid or semi-arid and far from suitable for agriculture, but more and more marginal land is being cleared, settled and cultivated (Moyo *et al.*, 1991). Wild land is disappearing, partly because its wildlife products cannot compete economically with subsistence agriculture (Swanson & Barbier, 1992). Where cash crops are concerned, the imbalance between the revenue potential of those crops and the wildlife is even greater. Huge tracts of land have been irreversibly degraded by inappropriate use (Iliffe, 1995). It is no exaggeration to describe this destruction of land and loss of productivity as southern Africa's *greatest* environmental problem.

As far as wildlife is concerned, settlement and agriculture turn the ratchet of extinction another notch. Once cultivation is undertaken, wildlife does not simply have a zero value – more often than not it represents a major cost to rural people. Animals commonly destroy growing crops and foodstores and loss of human life is all too common (Bell & McShane-Caluzi, 1984). The solution is then seen by farmers as inevitable. The wildlife has to go.

There is one final irony. While land is being degraded outside national parks, land inside often fares little better. We tend to assume that parks constitute an ecological nirvana, but sadly this is increasingly far from the truth. In particular, elephants do not magically maintain static numbers. Unless held back by the 'hand of man' they increase and ultimately are responsible, in confined conditions, for destroying their own environment (Hanks, 1979). In the 1992–93 drought in Zimbabwe it was difficult to distinguish the wasteland in parks caused by elephants from the wasteland outside caused by people and cattle forced to live on inhospitable land.

In short, preservationist strategies have:

- Been unenforceable.
- Removed traditional controls and incentives.
- Turned wildlife into a *de facto* open-access resource and rural Africans who use wildlife into criminals.
- Made protected areas economic 'black holes' in the rural landscape.
- Created conflict between humans and wildlife around protected areas.
- Severely reduced the value of wild habitats and wild species to rural people.
- Promoted agriculture on ecologically fragile land.

This dysfunctional catalogue may not have been foreseen when the strategies were introduced. Now that the shortcomings are obvious, the persistence of these strategies and, indeed, their vigorous defence in some quarters, is perplexing (Spinage, 1996).

THE VALUE OF WILDLIFE

The problems we have outlined have been recognised in southern Africa for some years, together with an appreciation that progress under these conditions depends not on fine-tuning the system but on changing the overall strategy. The lesson of the southern African experience is that conservationists must not focus on taking value away from wildlife, but on finding ways to increase it. Of course, some wildlife still needs to be protected. Protected areas have played an important part in conservation in Africa and will continue to do so. Nevertheless, even protected areas need to be managed in a way that does more to meet the needs of local people, since their continued integrity ultimately depends on the support of these people. Overall there needs to be more emphasis on conservation *outside* protected areas.

Several studies have demonstrated that on the arid and semi-arid savannahs of East and southern Africa, wildlife assemblages, which include species such as elephant, buffalo *Syncerus caffer*, leopard *Panthera pardus* and lion, can out-compete domestic livestock in terms of both net revenue and return on investment (Bond, 1993; Elliot & Mwangi, 1997). In so doing, wildlife moves from being a pest to an asset (see also Grigg & Pople, Chapter 18). On a large ranch in a semi-arid part of southern Zimbabwe in 1992 the net revenue from wildlife was $(US)1.11 per hectare, compared to $0.6 per hectare from cattle. The return on investment was more than three times higher for wildlife (8.6%) than for cattle (2.5%) (Jansen *et al.*, 1992). In this case, the revenue from wildlife was generated by sport hunting and cropping. In Kenya a more recent study has shown that, where there is no sport hunting, the revenue from wildlife cropping ($0.2–0.4 per hectare) is comparable with that from livestock ($0.2–1.4 per hectare) (Elliot & Mwangi, 1997). But where wildlife tourism (without sport hunting) is introduced, the revenues climb to $4.4–4.7 per hectare. Another study has shown that, where landholders have been able to combine photo-tourism, sport hunting and cropping, net revenues have been between 10 and 20 times larger than from livestock (Child, 1995a). Nevertheless, in conditions where arable crops can be grown, revenues from both wildlife and livestock are uncompetitive. The Kenya study demonstrates that arable revenues can be over 100 times greater ($132–166 per hectare) than those from livestock and more than 20 times greater than from wildlife photo-tourism.

However, to generate value from wildlife is one thing, to ensure that this contributes to conservation is another. But in southern Africa it has been clearly demonstrated that where it has been possible for private landowners and rural communities to receive economic benefits from the wildlife on their land they have responded by investing in the wildlife 'resource' with demonstrable conservation advantages (Kiss, 1990; Cumming, 1994).

The earliest attempts to create conservation incentives for landholders in southern Africa were based around private property, partly because of the racial history of land tenure and governance in large parts of the region, but also because it has proved much harder to construct similar mechanisms for common property systems (IIED, 1994). In neither instance is a positive conservation outcome inevitable. Even where value is generated it is essential to have the right institutional framework. This involves such factors as policy, legislation and market access (IUCN, 1997). This is the point at which CITES is brought into sharp focus. Whether on private or community property, the common features of successful programmes of sustainable use are access to the resource and access to markets. Access to resources is, by and large, a matter for national policy. But access to markets, where the markets are international ones, is most definitely not. Some of the most profitable uses of wildlife are based on the export of durable wildlife products. CITES determines what can be traded, with whom, under what conditions and, in consequence, at what price. It sets the terms of trade for wildlife products from the devolved systems of tenure in southern Africa. It therefore has an enormous impact on the struggle to allow wild ecosystems to be financially competitive and hence on the success of conservation-based community development (Murphree, 2000). Small wonder then that CITES is taken very seriously by southern African countries (Mofson, 2000). They have been at the forefront of calls for the Convention to be interpreted in a way that encourages systems of exploitation that result in beneficial trade.

CONSERVATION-BASED COMMUNITY DEVELOPMENT

Programmes in which wild resources directly contribute to conservation in the communal areas of southern Africa are known as Conservation-based Community Development (CBCD) or Community-based Natural Resource Management (CBNRM). These programmes, such as CAMPFIRE in Zimbabwe, ADMADE in Zambia and LIFE in Namibia are most prominent in highly traditional and poor subsistence farming communities around protected areas. These are the villagers whose livelihoods are threatened by wild animals and who therefore directly pay the costs of Africa's national parks.

CAMPFIRE has been examined and described in some detail (Metcalfe, 1994; Olthof, 1995; Child et al., 1997; Murombedzi, 1999). In brief, it returns the right of rural communities to manage and use wildlife to their own benefit. And, by and large, they are doing it well. In many areas they are making money from wild animals and they recognise that only through conservation can these benefits be continued (Child et al., 1997). After only a few years, some of the trends resulting from the old practices have been reversed. The depredations of wild animals continue, but are more stoically borne (Taylor, 1995). There are clear examples, even in crowded communal lands, of reductions in unregulated hunting (Kalen & Tragardh, 1998) and of new land being set aside for wildlife (Matzke, 1993). However, though important, the new conservation areas are relatively small scale and the overall pattern both inside and outside CAMPFIRE areas remains one of ongoing clearance for cultivation and settlement (WWF, 1997). Nevertheless, the rate of loss in CAMPFIRE areas has been shown to be slower than in non-CAMPFIRE areas (Conybeare, 1998). In some cases wild areas are viewed more favourably, as a reservoir of economic resources rather than a harbour for dangerous threats (Kalen & Tragardh, 1998). Among the most obvious benefits of community wildlife management programmes is the supply of meat in protein-deficient rural areas, but arguably the biggest boon to communities has been the cash brought in by tourists. In Namibia this is largely photo-tourism (Ashley, 1995). By contrast, in Zimbabwe more than 90% of these earnings come from tourists who wish to hunt animals. Elephant hunting alone has contributed a massive 64% of annual income, making this species the mainstay of CAMPFIRE (Bond, 1994). This provides good reason for communities to carefully husband their elephant resources. Overall elephant numbers in Zimbabwe climbed from 49 000 in 1983 to more than 63 000 in 1995 (Price Waterhouse, 1996). The introduction of CAMPFIRE over this period has played a role in this trend. For example, it is notable that following the introduction of functional CAMPFIRE programmes the number of elephants killed as problem animals decreased steadily from 200 in 1986 to just 54 in 1992 (Hutton & Dawe, 1994).

At this point it is valuable to provide a case study that illustrates the way that the profits of exploitation have provided conspicuous economic incentives for conservation to villagers involved in CAMPFIRE. From 1990 until 1994 the total revenue from CAMPFIRE that was returned to the people of Masoka Ward in northern Zimbabwe increased from $(US)31 268 to $77 692 (Murphree, 1996). All of this was derived from the sport hunting of wild animals and most of it from elephant hunting. In 1994, every household earned $366 from wildlife revenues. Each allocated approximately 50% of the money to community development projects, invested about 20% in further resource management and kept roughly $122 in cash. In a community in which the average annual household cash income was below $40, wildlife was suddenly a significant asset (M. W. Murphree, personal communication). Here it is important to stress that the people of Masoka were not passive recipients of this income. Examination of the way that the community managed its wildlife revenue year by year demonstrated that peasant farmers make rational choices about resource management and about the way that the income from wild resources is best deployed to community benefit. In 1991, following severe drought and almost total crop failure, the allocation of funds to household dividends and drought relief jumped to almost 80%. By contrast, in 1992, 1993 and 1994, revenues were used primarily for community projects and resource management (Table 20.2). The community was shrewdly using their wildlife

Table 20.2. Masoka wildlife revenues and budget allocations 1990–94

Year	Revenues (after deduction of council levies) $(US)	Budget allocations						
		Resource management		Household dividends/ drought relief		Community projects	
	$(US)	$(US)	%	$(US)	%	$(US)	%
1990	31 268	4104	13	10 080	32	17 084	55
1991	24 804	2166	8	19 355	78	3283	13
1992	54 264	8682	16	2086	4	43 495	80
1993	70 752	10 092	14	19 538	28	41 122	59
1994	77 962	16 865	22	20 122	26	40 976	52

From Murphree, 1996. NB: Murphree's original figures have been converted into $(US).

Table 20.3. Mahenye tourism revenue by category, 1991–1997

Year	Hunting safari revenue	Tourism lodge revenue	Total
1991	19 111	—	19 111
1992	35 294	—	35 294
1993	24 308	—	24 308
1994	19 968	—	19 968
1995	6787	291	7078
1996	6074	6162	12 236
1997	6814	15 516	22 330

Adapted from Murphree, 2000. NB: Murphree's original figures have been converted into $(US).

revenues flexibly, in good years for community development and in bad years as food security (Murphree, 1996).

An additional case study, that of the community of Mahenye in the southeast of Zimbabwe, serves to demonstrate the importance of hunting revenue to CAMPFIRE. It also shows how communities have expanded the scope of their income-generating activities so that photo-tourism has been added to consumptive exploitation in a way that has increased the total revenue extracted from a fairly constant resource base (Murphree, 2000). After almost a decade of institutional difficulties in which the government was reluctant to devolve responsibility and revenues to the community, CAMPFIRE suddenly took off in Mahenye in 1991 when the community received a cheque for $(US)19 111 from the hunting concession that made use of 'their' wildlife. Within one year, however, hunting safari revenues had reached a peak and thereafter declined. In order to break through the income ceiling, which was determined by the level of harvest that would be sustainable, the community entered into a commercial venture to open a lodge for photo-tourists. Lodge revenues quickly overtook hunting revenues and within only three years far exceeded them (Table 20.3). As far as local benefits are concerned in 1997 the $14 923 wages of the local employees can be added to the $15 516 earned by the community from the lodge. Marshall Murphree's summation of the situation is telling:

> Mahenye is no longer a community of subsistence farmers, where wildlife is a liability rather than an asset. It now has a collective natural resource enterprise which forms an important component of the livelihood and investment strategy of its members. (*Murphree* 2000)

It would be nice at this point to claim that all is rosy in these community programmes in Africa, but of course this is not the case. There is nothing simple about the involvement of communities in the sustainable use of wild resources (Inamdar & Cobb, 1998), especially when this involves the reversal of many years of colonial rule. Even if they are successful, schemes in which the value of 'wild' species is used as a conservation tool will bring their own (often predictable) problems (Freese, 1997). These include political resistance to the devolution of proprietorship over wildlife to the level of the community. In the case of CAMPFIRE proprietorship has remained at the level of district councils. Other problems are caused by population movements that are themselves the result of rapid social and economic change. A population influx into a CAMPFIRE area can make the sustainable management of wildlife a more difficult task. Some of the difficulties associated with CAMPFIRE have been described in various donor-driven analyses of the programme (The Mitchell Group & South-East Consortium for International Development, 1998; Royal Netherlands Embassy Harare, 1998). A bogus though widely distributed review (Patel, 1998) has served to obfuscate the issues, making serious discussion of the problems more difficult (A. Inamdar, personal communication). This incident appears to have arisen from the concerns of a sector of the animal rights constituency. Having declared themselves philosophically opposed to the sustainable use of wildlife (Hoyt, 1994), they fear the consequences of communities successfully demonstrating the conservation value of CAMPFIRE. At the moment one can say that the results are promising, mirroring the undoubted success of sustainable use on private land, but there will be many hurdles to overcome in the future. In our opinion, therefore, the fairest thing to say about conservation-based community development in general, and CAMPFIRE in particular, is that it is an honest attempt to do the right thing under conditions where the alternatives have performed poorly for a century and still show little promise.

CONCLUSIONS

It is not possible to analyse wildlife conservation problems or to develop effective solutions by drawing only on the biological sciences. The fate of many wild species is now dependent on human action and addressing these issues requires an understanding of the dynamics of human societies and their interactions with wildlife. Perhaps the point is an obvious one but conservationists have been surprisingly slow to take it on board. The result has been that for too long conservationists have been prepared to advocate strategies based on the creation of protected areas and legal restrictions on use. While such strategies may have some immediate appeal, they do not take sufficient account of the social and economic factors affecting wildlife and wildlife habitat and were often imposed in highly inequitable ways. It is not surprising that the record of this protectionist approach has been a mixed one.

The experience of southern Africa and elsewhere has shown that the greatest threat to wildlife is the conversion of their habitat to agriculture. A protectionist approach has actually promoted this conversion because it reduces the incentive to retain wildlife habitat. Of course, wild species continue to be used by millions of rural people and this use plays a big part in meeting their basic needs. Indeed, such use would be almost impossible to stop. But as long as local people do not have security of tenure over all their wildlife resources they do not have a strong incentive to manage those resources sustainably. But if they do gain tenure rights, and the other appropriate conditions are in place, then the use of wildlife can become a successful conservation strategy. Rural people would then have good reason to conserve wildlife habitat rather than convert it to agriculture – a use for which it may, in any case, be ill suited. Thus, while there is no *necessary* connection between the exploitation of wild species and their conservation, exploitation can be harnessed to produce effective conservation. A silk purse can indeed be made out of a sow's ear.

ACKNOWLEDGEMENTS

This paper would not have been possible without the enduring support of our many friends and colleagues in southern Africa. We are grateful to Marshall Murphree for permission to use his data, to the IUCN/SSC Wildlife Trade Programme and the CITES Secretariat for information on the non-detriment finding process, and to the Department of Geography at the University of Cambridge for access to its research facilities. This document was prepared as a contribution to the Africa Resources Trust that seeks to highlight the important relationship between international trade and the rights and aspirations of rural communities seeking to improve the quality of their lives through the sustainable use of natural resources.

REFERENCES
Adams, N. S. & McShane, T. O. (1992). *The Myth of Wild Africa: Conservation without Illusion*. W. W. Norton, New York.
Ape Alliance (1998). *The African Bushmeat Trade – A Recipe for Extinction*. Flora and Fauna International, Cambridge.
Ashley, C. (1995). Community based tourism as a strategy for CBNRM. Paper

presented at the 1995 Annual Conference of the Regional Natural Resource Management Programme ('The Commons without the Tragedy'), Kasane, Botswana, 3–6 April 1995.

Barbier, E. B., Burgess, J. C. & Folke, C. (1994). *Paradise Lost? The Ecological Economics of Biodiversity.* Earthscan, London.

BBC Assignment (1992). *War of the Wild.* First broadcast February 1992.

Bell, R. & McShane-Caluzi, E. (1984). The man–animal interface: an assessment of crop damage and wildlife control. In *Conservation and Wildlife Management in Africa,* ed. R. Bell & E. McShane-Caluzi, pp. 48–60. US Peace Corps Seminar, Washington, DC.

Bond, I. (1993). The economics of wildlife and land-use in Zimbabwe: an examination of current knowledge and issues, WWF Project Paper no. 36, Harare, Zimbabwe.

Bond, I. (1994). The importance of sport-hunted African elephants to Campfire in Zimbabwe. *Traffic Bulletin,* **14**, 117–119.

Caughley, G. (1977). *Analysis of Vertebrate Populations.* Wiley, Chichester.

Caughley, G. (1992). Utilisation and overutilisation. In *Applying New Criteria for Listing Species on the CITES Appendices,* pp. 12–18. IUCN/SSC, Gland, Switzerland.

Caughley, G. & Gunn, A. (1996). *Conservation Biology in Theory and Practice.* Blackwell, Oxford.

Chardonnet, P., Fritz, H., Zorzi, N. & Feron, E. (1995). Current importance of traditional hunting and major contrasts in wild meat consumption in sub-Saharan Africa. In *Integrating People and Wildlife for a Sustainable Future,* ed. J. Bisonnette & P. Kraussman, pp. 304–307. The Wildlife Society, Bethesda, MD.

Child, B., Ward, S. & Tavengwa, T. (1997). *Zimbabwe's CAMPFIRE Programme: Natural Resource Management by the People.* IUCN-ROSA Environmental Issues Series no. 2. IUCN-ROSA, Harare.

Child, G. (1995a). *Wildlife and People: The Zimbabwe Success.* Wisdom Foundation, Harare and New York.

Child, G. (1995b). Managing wildlife successfully in Zimbabwe. *Oryx,* **29**, 171–177.

CITES Secretariat (2000a). A discussion paper on 'Bushmeat as a trade and wildlife management issue'. Doc. 11.44.

CITES Secretariat (2000b). Draft Manual to make Non-Detriment Findings. Document Inf. 11.3. In *Proceedings of the 11th Conference of the Parties II,* Gigiri, Kenya, 10–20 April 2000. CITES-UNEP, Geneva.

Clark, C. W. (1990). *Mathematical Bioeconomics.* Wiley, Chichester.

Clarke, M. E. (1992). Worldviews, science, and the politics of social change. Paper presented at the Third Annual Conference of the International Association for the Study of Common Property, Washington, DC, 17–20 September 1992.

Conybeare, A. (1998). Assessment of habitat maintenance, diversity and productivity under communal management. Report to WWF Resource Management Support to Campfire Project.

Cowlishaw, G. (1999). Predicting the pattern of decline of African primate diversity: an extinction debt from historical deforestation. *Conservation Biology,* **13**, 1183–1193.

Cumming, D. H. M. (1994). Are multi-species systems a viable land use option for southern African savannas? MAPS Project Paper no. 46. WWF, Harare.

Department of Environment, Transport and the Regions (1999). Bushmeat as a Trade and Wildlife Management Issue. A discussion paper submitted to the CITES Secretariat by Department of Environment, Transport and the Regions, UK.

Dickson, B. (1994). *What's Wrong with Consumptive Use?* Africa Resources Trust, Harare.

Elliot, J. & Mwangi, M. (1997). Making wildlife 'pay' in Laikipia, Kenya. Laikipia Wildlife Economics Study Discussion Paper no. CEC-DP-1. African Wildlife Foundation, Nairobi and Washington, DC.

Environmental Investigation Agency (1992). Comments on IUCN Second Draft Criteria and Requirements for Sustainable Use of Wild Species. Unpublished report available from EIA, 69–85 Old Street, London EC1V 9HX.

Favre, D. (1993). Debate within the CITES community: What direction for the future? *Natural Resources Journal*, **33**, 875–918.

Freese, C. H. (ed.) (1997). *Harvesting Wild Species: Implications for Biodiversity Conservation*. Johns Hopkins University Press, Baltimore, MD.

Groombridge, B. (ed.) (1992). *Global Biodiversity: Status of the Earth's Living Resources*. Chapman & Hall, London.

Hanks, J. (1979). *The Struggle for Survival*. Mayflower Books, New York.

Holling, C. S. (1993). Investing in research for sustainability. *Ecological Applications*, **3**, 552–555.

Hoyt, J. (1994). *Animals in Peril: How Sustainable Use is Wiping Out the World's Wildlife*. Avery Publishing Group, New York.

Hutton, J. & Dawe M. (1994). An analysis of the production and economic significance of elephant hide in Zimbabwe. Report to the Director, Department of National Parks and Wildlife Management. Africa Resources Trust, Harare.

Hutton, J. & Dickson, B. (2000). Introduction. In *Endangered Species, Threatened Convention*, ed. J. Hutton & B. Dickson, pp. xv–xx. Earthscan, London.

IIED (International Institute for Environment and Development) (1994). *Whose Eden? An Overview of Community Approaches to Wildlife Management*. IIED/Overseas Development Agency, London.

Iliffe, J. (1995). *Africans: The History of a Continent*. Cambridge University Press, Cambridge.

Inamdar, A. & Cobb, S. (1998). Wildlife as wealth: can wildlife contribute to poverty elimination? Wildlife Issues Paper, Linking Policy and Practice in Biodiversity. DFID, London.

Inamdar, A., Brown, D. & Cobb, S. (1999). *What's Special about Wildlife Management in Forests? Concepts and Models of Rights-based Management, with Recent Evidence from West-Central Africa*. ODI Natural Resource Perspectives no. 44.

IUCN (1996). *1996 IUCN Red List of Threatened Animals*. IUCN, Gland, Switzerland.

IUCN (1997). *Sustainable Use Issues and Principles*. IUCN/SSC Southern African Sustainable Use Specialist Group, Harare.

Jansen, D., Bond, I. & Child, B. (1992). Cattle, wildlife, both or neither.

A summary of survey results for the commercial ranches in Zimbabwe. WWF Project Paper no. 30. Harare.

Jenkins, R. W. G. (2000). The significant trade process: making Appendix II work. In *Endangered Species, Threatened Convention*, ed. J. Hutton & B. Dickson, pp. 47–56. Earthscan, London.

Kalen, C. & Tragardh, N. (1998). *Sustainable Use of Wildlife: A Case Study of the Campfire Programme in Zimbabwe*. Lund University, Lund.

Kiss, A. (1990). Living with wildlife: wildlife resource management with local participation in Africa. World Bank Technical Paper no. 130, Washington, DC.

Ludwig, D., Hilborn, R. & Walters, C. (1993). Uncertainty, resource exploitation and conservation: lessons from history. *Science*, **260**, 17, 36.

Makombe, K. (ed.) (1993). *Sharing the Land: Wildlife, People and Development in Africa*. IUCN, Harare.

Mann, C. C. & Plummer, M. L. (1995). *Noah's Choice: The Future of Endangered Species*. Knopf, New York.

Martin, R. B. (1999). The rule of law and African game, and social change and conservation misrepresentation – a reply to Spinage. *Oryx*, **33**, 89–97.

Matowanyika, J. Z. Z. (1989). Cast out of Eden: peasants versus wildlife policy in savanna Africa. *Alternatives*, **16**, 30–39.

Matzke, G. (1993). *Chawarura Community use of Mavuradonha Wilderness*. CASS Occasional Papers in Natural Resource Management. CASS, Harare.

Metcalfe, S. (1994). The Zimbabwe Communal Areas Management Programme for Indigenous Resources (CAMPFIRE). In *Natural Connections*, ed. D. Western & R. Wright, pp. 161–192. Island Press, Washington, DC.

Milner-Gulland, E. J. & Mace, R. (1998). *Conservation of Biological Resources*. Blackwell, Oxford.

Mitchell Group & South-East Consortium for International Development (1998). Mid-Term Evaluation of Zimbabwe Natural Resources Management Project, Phase II: Communal Areas Management Programme for Indigenous Resources. Report produced for USAID, available from the Mitchell Group, 18161 11th Street NW, Washington, DC, USA.

Mofson, P. (2000). Zimbabwe and CITES: influencing the international regime. In *Endangered Species, Threatened Convention*, ed. J. Hutton & B. Dickson, pp. 107–122. Earthscan, London.

Monela, G. C., Kajembe, G. C., Kaoneka, A. R. S. & Kowero, G. (1999). *Household Livelihood Strategies in the Miombo Woodlands: Emerging Trends*. Sokoine University of Agriculture, Tanzania.

Moyo, S., Robinson, P., Katerere, Y., Stevenson, S. & Gumbo, D. (1991). *Zimbabwe's Environmental Dilemma*. ZERO, Harare.

Munthali, S. (1996). Policy, financial, legislative and institutional arrangements. In *African Wildlife Policy Consultation*, pp. 205–217. ODA, London.

Murombedzi, J. (1999). Devolution and Stewardship in Zimbabwe's CAMPFIRE Programme. *Journal of International Development*, **11**, 287–293.

Murphree, M. (1996). The cost/benefit approach to wildlife management and the 'producer community' in the CAMPFIRE programme. Presentation to Members of Parliament, Zimbabwe.

Murphree, M. (2000). The lesson from Mahenye. In *Endangered Species, Threatened Convention*, ed. J. Hutton & B. Dickson, pp. 181–196. Earthscan, London.

Oglethorpe, J. (ed.) (1999). *Tenure and Sustainable Use*. IUCN, Gland, Switzerland.

Olthof, W. (1995). Wildlife resources and local development: experiences from Zimbabwe's CAMPFIRE Programme. In *Local Resource Management in Africa*, ed. J. Breemer, C. van den Drijver & L. Venema, pp. 111–128. Wiley, Chichester.

Patel, H. (1998). *Sustainable Utilization and African Wildlife Policy*. Indigenous Environmental Policy Centre, Washington, DC.

Price Waterhouse (1996). *Elephant Census in Zimbabwe 1980–1995: An Analysis and Review*. Ministry of Environment and Tourism, Harare.

Rosenblum, M. & Williamson, D. (1987). *Squandering Eden: Africa at the Edge*. Bodley Head, London.

Royal Netherlands Embassy Harare, Zimbabwe (1998). Combined Review of Strategic Support Through ZimTrust to CAMPFIRE and Institutional Support to the CAMPFIRE Association. Unpublished report available from the Netherlands Embassy, Harare.

Scoones, I., Melnyk, M. & Pretty, J. N. (1992). *The Hidden Harvest: Wild Foods and Agricultural Systems. A Literature Review and Annotated Bibliography*. IIED, London.

Spinage, C. (1996). The rule of law and African game – a review of some trends and concerns. *Oryx*, **30**, 178–186.

Spinage, C. (1998). Social change and conservation misrepresentation in Africa. *Oryx*, **32**, 265–276.

Stepanek, J. F. (1999). *Wringing Success from Failure in Late-Developing Countries*. Praeger, Westport, CT.

Swanson, T. (1997). *Global Action for Biodiversity*. Earthscan, London.

Swanson, T. & Barbier, E. (eds.) (1992). *Economics for the Wilds*. Earthscan, London.

Taylor, R. (1995). *From Liability to Asset: Wildlife in the Omay Communal Land of Zimbabwe*. IIED, London.

Turton, D. (1987). The Mursi and the National Park development in the Lower Omo Valley. In *Conservation in Africa*, ed. D. Anderson & R. Grove, pp. 169–186. Cambridge University Press, Cambridge.

UNEP (United Nations Environment Programme) (1999). *Global Environmental Outlook 2000*. Earthscan, London.

Wenzel, G. (1991). *Animal Rights, Human Rights: Ecology, Economy and Ideology in the Canadian Arctic*. Belhaven Press, London.

WWF (World Wide Fund for Nature) (1997). *Landuse Changes, Wildlife Conservation and Utilisation and the Sustainability of Agro-ecosystems in the Zambezi Valley*. WWF Final Report B7-5040/93/06.

21

Getting the biology right in a political sort of way

STEVEN SANDERSON

Over the course of the past two decades, conservationists have appealed to anthropologists, economists, public policy analysts and political scientists to figure out strategies that align social policy with wild species, biodiversity and ecosystem conservation. In that same period, due to the demands of conservation in the field, some of the best work in the politics of conservation has come from conservationists themselves, as evidenced in the literature. Recent landmark volumes that consider wild species as commodities (e.g. Freese, 1999), and the conservation of biological resources (Milner-Gulland & Mace, 1998), build importantly on earlier work by McNeely (1988) on the economics of conservation; Robinson & Redford (1991) on wildlife in the Neotropics; and Redford & Padoch (1992) on neotropical forests. Recent examples have struggled to assess the relationship between conservation and development, with indifferent success (Neumann, 1998; Oates, 1999; Terborgh, 1999). Suffice it to say that the world of conservation politics has been amply served by its leading scientists and practitioners.

The continuing struggle to find political solutions to ongoing biodiversity loss speaks volumes about the complexity of politics, its poor connection to scientific inference, and persistent weaknesses of public policy. Policy advocates and critics have not been silent. Policy reductionists the world around have made wildlife conservation easy, at least in rhetoric, by reducing the daunting dilemmas of conservation to easy slogans or one-dimensional solutions. For the 20 years in which biodiversity conservation has held some part of the environmental centre stage, one observer or another has asserted that keystone species, habitat preservation, the presence (or absence) of local peoples, extractive reserves, 'hard-edged' or 'soft-edged' parks, or some similar nostrum holds the key to conservation in a given place. International accords have blossomed, as have new non-governmental organisations (NGOs), who have charged themselves with a global conservation mandate. High profile interventions in natural and human systems of production have proliferated, with variable effects.

At the same time, many policy analysts have submitted problems of conservation to conceptual slimming, even as the scope of the idea of conservation has grown. Conservation is now almost universally associated with 'sustainable use', whereas conservation that does not include human use has been relegated to 'preservation', which strangely has taken on a very negative connotation, based on imperial models of preservation in Africa and Asia. It is only a small exaggeration to say that in the course of this simplification, advocates of conservation *sensu late* have been pitted against each other in the most stylised ways: 'preservationists' are forced to be 'anti-people', which fits only a small subset of those lumped in this category. Conservationists who acknowledge the inevitability (but not necessarily the desirability) of increasing human use are seen as traitors to the Earth, running with the enemies of real conservation, i.e. those who are interested in exploiting the Earth for its consumptive use. Those who have signed on to the sustainability bandwagon have tagged all kinds of development practices with the sustainable label, while those who are steadfastly anti-development, or anti-multinational corporation, refuse to see the gradations in sustainability that appear in local practices.

The result of this disappointing tussle in the conservation community has been the political and polemical insistence of one group or another that certain axioms of conservation are true and all action should derive therefrom. This chapter questions some of those postulates, but cannot take on what may be the more telling critique: that the very idea of axiomatic conservation flies in the face of the uniquely variable environments in which conservation problems take place. It may well be that a much less deterministic and more contingent notion of conservation must be developed in order to ensure the conservation of wild exploited species.

Contemporaneously, just as ecologists have recognized the system complexity of natural resource management efforts (Mangel *et al.*, 1996), policy solutions have simplified, and the putative problems of conservation have become unidimensional: the lack of sustainability, we have learned, is due to failures of politics, markets, institutions or public policies, which, in turn, derive from human greed, ignorance, the tragedy of the commons, or other failings, depending on the experience and disposition of the observer (Ludwig, Chapter 2).

The result is distressing: the potential dialogue over conservation has become a polemic, in which elements of the conservation community are travelling in divergent directions for several reasons. On one hand, the political 'solutions' to conservation 'problems' often begin with proposals whose scale is impossible: 'Society' at the global level must consume less.

Population growth must stop. Migration must stop or slow. Global capitalism triumphant must appreciate the diverse cultures it is bent on homogenising under market strategies for human development. Biodiversity must be appreciated for its own sake. In other words, the world needs to be different from what it is.

On the other hand, others dismiss the possibility of virtue altogether. The irreducible and conscious 'undifferentiation' of the human subjects of conservation in today's world appears to validate game theorists' and rational choice proponents' emphasis on action based on individual self-interest, in which short-term gains trump all long-term solutions (Roe, 1998). In a world of undifferentiated rational individuals each seeking gain, what kind of intergenerational conservation could one expect? If conservation must be self-seeking, no wonder the proofs of its necessity turn to contingent valuation, discount rates, and ideas of natural capital formation, in which conservation is the sum of the residuals of individual greed.

Conservation-oriented scientific research has not been immune to these allures, partly because they show such apparent similarity to ecological models. Following the lead of students of *Homo economicus*, scientists have staked out two strategies that both end up in a reductionist approach, too. Modellers of wildlife populations or natural ecosystems have concentrated on a deductive, rule-derived approach to understanding their subjects, with the result that scale tends to be fixed, change is endogenous to the model, empirical data become secondary to theory, and variables tend towards the discrete, generally for reasons of model-building. On the other hand, field ecologists have been relentlessly empirical and inductive, with similar scale rigidities (produced by exigencies of research rather than models), a tendency towards single-species orientation, and less time devoted to enriching theory.

Careful readers of the literature can see these stereotypes as oversimple, even though the latter thrive on the seemingly endless supply of less careful pundits, practitioners, and PhD students. For every careful assessment of environmental futures, there is a Robert Kaplan (1997), whose observations of Africa are as popular as they are cartoonish and pontifical (Englund, 1996). For every field conservationist with deep appreciation of local peoples and their rights (Oldfield & Alcorn, 1991; Karlsson, 1999), someone rises to propose evacuating parks or building fences (Oates, 1999; Terborgh, 1999). For every advocate of getting prices right, there is an advocate of non-market cultural approaches (Freehling & Marks, 1998). And the North–South divide between rich and poor countries inexorably deepens, as conservation remedies to property, population and politics are applied with fervour in developing countries and not in developed countries.

STERILE DEBATE, DEEPENING PROBLEMS

In the end, the debate often has the sterility of old family arguments, in which stylised positions are taken at the beginning, and little of the heat generated in argument results in improvement. Most often, one or another stunningly general culprit (e.g. global capitalism or poor people) is blamed for the current predicament, in the tautological way prices are blamed for inflation.

Whether or not the simplest ideas are complex enough to describe the many difficulties of conservation and its policy failures, the fact is that things do not appear anywhere to be improving at a fast enough rate, if at all. Human populations and consumption are growing in alarming ways. Agricultural transformation leads the way. According to one recent estimate, by 2020, world rice, wheat and maize demand will be up by 20% over current levels, livestock by 60%. Demand for wood will double over the next half-century, a time frame in which virtually all fresh water will be used for human consumption (Ayensu *et al.*, 1999). Deforestation seems inexorable. According to a recent estimate, something like 5% of tropical forests and 10% of temperate and boreal forests are being sustainably managed (Freese, 1999), and this is probably an overestimate. With the rapid urbanisation of developing countries, the political and social coalitions that connect with life in the countryside become more stylised and remote. Energy demands go up, dependence on agriculture increases on a reduced land base. Meanwhile, growing rural populations are consuming wild species in ways harmful to the species' long-term survival. Small wonder, then, that sustainability demands less consumption on a global scale.

We all know what this means for wild species. Previously uncultivated land is being converted to agriculture at stunning rates, and the biosphere is already human dominated (Vitousek *et al.*, 1992). Agricultural transformation predicts biodiversity loss beautifully, not just in terrestrial ecosystems, either, since more than one-quarter of world marine fisheries products go to animal feed or other uses not directly related to human food consumption (National Research Council, 1999). Fresh water resources are diverted to human use or contaminated by agricultural nutrients and pesticides, transnational atmospheric deposition, and local-to-regional storm water run-off. Marine and coastal fisheries are grossly overfished, tropical forests overlogged and human-inhabited lands degraded season by season.

The fact that these generalisations are challenged by field anthropologists and sociologists is interesting; the dominance of the crisis narrative is often questionable. The crisis mentality gripping the environmental community gives 'the cause' special urgency; it also allows a certain kind of thinking that may not serve the cause in the longer term. A crisis mentality allows complex problems to be addressed 'at the point of attack', as if they were linear. It may be that such an approach biases policy towards future adaptive failures rather than to successes.

Frustration with the prescriptive give-and-take occasioned by these phenomena may be beside the point, but some of the political ramifications for conservation science are not. The crisis proportions of world environmental management do not absolve either management or the treatment of history from criticism. In fact, some would argue that the entire construction of environmental management is set up in such a way as to guarantee a continuation of the bureaucratic rigidities, policy hegemony and intellectual vacuousness that has characterised much of the so-called debate over sustainability (Roe, 1998).The debate over sustainability has never engaged what really is sustainable in terms of what values in relation to what ecosystem dynamics over what time scales. It is a phony debate in the sense of actually moving towards definitional consensus or rigour. In that respect, it follows in the footsteps of the postwar development debate, which likewise has sidestepped its goals in favour of agreeing on simple ideas, such as 'development is good'.

In conservation politics, as in any bureaucratic competition for resources, agencies large and small tend to defend themselves in terms of war against one enemy or another, and propose their alternatives (and their funding proposals) in terms of a single goal, such as park protection, local peoples' rights, animal welfare and the like. Increasingly, advocacy positions such as these seem to distance themselves from advances in the literature, which are becoming more place based, integrative and critical. At times, it seems that the subtleties generated by field research are set aside by global actors in favour of a more general political position designed to 'advance the cause'.

Conservation itself has muddied the waters with its own internal tensions between preservation and use. Mainly, conservationists have distanced themselves from preservation, for some good political reasons and bad. The name of preservation in Africa has an undeniable imperial past, whose centrepiece was the alienation of land and biota from aboriginal peoples (Marks, 1983; Neumann, 1998; Hutton & Dickson, Chapter 20). Analogous processes of local exclusion have taken place in the Neotropics, under very different political regimes. Faced with hostility toward preservation, increasing pressure on protected areas, and the impossibility of accomplishing conservation goals within a protected area regime, conservationists adopted sustainable use as their principal policy mantra a decade ago. Since then, most conservationists and their programmatic documents have stopped contesting the transformation of biota into 'biological resources', socially constructed for the purpose of use (commodities), elimination (pests), or, rarely, non-use. The rigour and subtlety of conservation science has proceeded, while its political advocates have allowed the exigencies of economic production to adumbrate its scope.

In a stunning show of optimism or obduracy, conservation managers and science advocates alike propose more management as the answer to badly managed systems (Ludwig, 1993; Ludwig et al., 1993). Leaving aside the more systemic cultural premises that underpin Roe's critique of the power politics of management, the practical line of argument of pro-management conservationists seems to be as follows: preservation cannot prevail in the face of human exploitation; conservation (meaning use) without policy is no conservation, given the much-abused 'tragedy of the commons'; and, even though policy has not slowed the pace of destruction satisfactorily or shown durable evidence of success (i.e. restoration or recovery or improvement, as opposed to slowed rates of degradation or loss), more policy is called for.

Accordingly, given the weaknesses of protected areas in terrestrial ecosystems, multiple use strategies, or complex zoning is proposed instead of protection. Acknowledging the limits of the public conservation estate (Lugo, 1995; Soulé & Sanjayan, 1998), even privatisation of preservation is proposed (Inamdar et al., 1999). In view of the budgetary cost of maintaining a conservation presence, or in order to have influences in the corridors of power, NGOs have adopted the discourses of powerful monied organisations (e.g. the World Bank), the United Nations system or national governments. In marine systems, proposals show striking similarity: marine reserves, sea tenure, licensing based on stock assessments, and so on. These policies have not been submitted to rigorous evaluation within the sponsoring agencies themselves, though they have been criticised widely in the conservation literature. In the absence of serious evaluation (serious being defined by the real prospect that a large-scale conservation and development programme might actually be closed for non-performance), one policy failure leads to another, without serious examination of what might be wrong with the concepts or the politics behind the failures (or proposed next steps).

The reasons for this lack of serious assessment are not difficult to divine: large organisations (World Bank, World Wide Fund for Nature (WWF), other large agencies, whether governmental or not) have huge organisational and financial stakes in their chosen strategies. The multilateral development assistance community must justify itself in terms of funded projects, and the countries that can absorb those efforts are typically the large countries with large NGOs amply represented (Brazil, Indonesia). In small countries with anaemic NGOs or local organisations (namely Vietnam), international organisations do not hesitate to steamroll local interests with globally planned conservation plans. Conservation projects have to happen, and the competition for funds and concepts is as desperate as the multilateral need to be invested in conservation.

In this increasingly desperate policy environment, wild species are losing, inexorably, it seems, and conservation scientists and field adepts are suffering great discouragement, even as they withstand the many discomforts and difficulties of their jobs. In many cases, these field ecologists and conservationists become extreme in their views, even advocating armed expulsion of humans from protected areas.

THE POLITICAL DIMENSIONS OF CONSERVATION SCIENCE

The point of this chapter, then, is to address some important political dimensions of conservation from a pragmatic perspective. It is, perhaps, less important at this point to attempt to assess systematically the many approaches to conservation. Maybe the more important priority is to question the science insofar as it is contested publicly – i.e. is politicised. Underlying this analysis is one general stipulation, and a few political propositions, which are not offered as if they are commonly accepted, but as initial ideas that guide the analysis and allow it to move beyond first steps. The point, after all, is not so much to be absolutely right, but to point to some new political directions that might be right.

The stipulation is that conservation science, in the common sense of the term, is a political affair as much as a scientific enterprise (Ludwig *et al.*, 1993; Sanderson & Redford, 1996; Shafer, 1999). That is so by definition, because scientific evidence is brought to bear on a constructed problem in order to affect the discourse about the distribution of biological resources. Perhaps the clearest evidence in the world of the interrelationship between conservation science and politics can be found in perennial debates over park policy in Kenya (McRae, 1998), or the highly contested Florida Everglades restoration project, or in fisheries management (Gray, 1998; National Research Council, 1999).

The political propositions, to which we will return, are as follows:

1 It is not necessary to prove that a field-based strategy for conservation is, in fact, sustainable. One only needs to assert credibly that it is the best option available. No one has proved that alternatives to field-based attempts at conservation are superior, especially those who would advocate globalist and centralising management ideas that have no foundation in real places or real societies.

2 The practice of getting the biology right in a political way must be empirically based, contingent, adaptive and only modestly sold on the promise of success. Too often, conservation scientists are required to prove the long-term virtue of their hypotheses, either to themselves and their own communities, or to the communities of sceptics who oppose conservation or a given approach to conservation. Sceptics have derailed science-based proposals from fisheries to global change by questioning the 'proof' of their foundations. Likewise, failures in conservation efforts are trotted out to discredit conservation itself, rather than as an acknowledgment of the inevitably high rate of failure in conservation, as in development. To use a somewhat frivolous parallel, if the same standards of success were applied to small business projects in the USA, no small businesses would ever be supported, as their failure rate is about 70%. The point here is twofold: first, that conservation cannot tie itself to a guarantee of success in order to experiment; and, secondly, that an experimental, empirical, and adaptive approach to conservation is more likely to be robust than a formulaic design that does not admit surprise or stochasticity in natural systems.

3 Conservation of wild species requires strange bedfellows, sometimes the stranger the better. Coalition-building must be as contingent as the management goals. Rigidities in politics are as dangerous as linear thinking in complex situations.

THE GAINS OF THE LAST DECADE AND THEIR SOBERING CONCLUSION

Longstanding partisans and early analysts of biodiversity conservation can remember when the discussion had lost its way (Redford & Sanderson, 1992), with biodiversity becoming an unsatisfying kind of shorthand for species richness, or emphasised charismatic megafauna. Despite the dismal description above, to read the current literature is to recognise what profound and positive changes characterise the politics of conservation science and practice. A much deeper appreciation for local peoples is evident, at the same time the romanticisation of local practices is much diminished. The empirical literature is substantially stronger, especially in critical areas such as primate hunting, inshore fisheries losses, and the role of keystone species in ecological communities.

As mentioned early in this chapter, conservationists have handled most of the political load of conservation by themselves. In that process, though, science itself has been humbled, as it struggles to find a way of communicating effectively for policy outcomes – i.e. speaking truth to power. When categorical arguments are made (Dobson *et. al.*, 1997), effective counterarguments appear, which scale down the inferences and question the political implications of even simple statements (Czech & Krausman, 1997). This is both a vice, in the sense that it undermines the power of generalisations, and a virtue, in the sense that it keeps science parsimonious and avoids categorical solutions of the kind that have failed so uniformly in the recent past.

What is sobering to the social scientist is the conclusion that the gains of the last decade have come without much help from mainstream economics or political science, much less the world ostensibly charged with development, those involved with multilateral development assistance. In the world of academic research and in large organisations alike, leaders have mainly appended sustainability to what they were doing in the service of other goals. The similarity in World Bank sustainable development to prior periods is striking, despite the great (and recent) effort to understand environmental impacts. Trade-offs between capital accumulation or enhanced infrastructure versus the preservation of natural systems is a virtual shutout in favour of economic growth. The policy literature is involuted, too, with some notable exceptions (Leach & Mearns, 1996; Roe, 1998). Too often, the critique of our currently unsustainable world is made in categorical terms that are unhelpful to prospective change. This criticism is important to understand, as it should affect the kinds of strategies undertaken by conservationists in politics and it must indicate some traps to avoid.

GETTING THE BIOLOGY RIGHT IN A POLITICAL WAY MEANS GETTING SOMEONE ELSE TO UNDERSTAND IT TOO

As I argued in an earlier paper (Sanderson, 1997), science-based conservation politics suffers enormously from a lack of a common language. Extending that argument, one could remark on the familiar tendency of professionals to develop their own specialised languages, not to communicate with the general public, but to assert their own technical knowledge against common knowledge. Lindblom (1990) contended that professionals select and structure social questions in ways that impair enquiry, often to partisan advantage. As Coles (1989) pointed out in a different connection, professional jargon becomes a way of asserting power and falling into a position of moral thoughtlessness.

From a political standpoint this is disastrous, as can be seen most obviously – but by no means exclusively – in fisheries management, where scientific knowledge, management knowledge, and users' knowledge are commonly opposed to each other in stylised ways, destined to undermine, rather than to reinforce, coalitions, and to guarantee blame-seeking and disdain by one group towards another.

The kind of discussion common to scientists and academics does not work well in conservation. First, politics is not an open scientific debate, in the sense that science should be without preferences, or without any disposition towards plausible explanations. Conservation science does not fit the ideal of scientific investigation, posing as it does questions that are intended to produce evidence in favour of a given outcome. In that regard, though, conservation science has much in common with other 'applied' sciences, in that the questions posed are socially constructed around 'problems', and not just questions of knowledge. This distinction is not merely a question of semantics. Practically speaking, when one scientist argues with another over evidence related to a conservation goal (e.g. that preservation of the snail kite *Rostrhamus sociabilis* supersedes ecosystem values such as water depth or hydroperiod in the Florida Everglades, or that ecosystem structure and function are relatively independent of diversity), often conservation loses in the mix. The internal squabble generates the so-called Type II error, in which scientists avoid a proper conclusion for lack of conclusive evidence (Freese, 1999). While that prudence is acceptable in the laboratory, it is paralysing in the practice of conservation policy.

More important, still, is the political appropriation by stakeholders of terms in common conservation use, such as maximum sustainable yield (MSY), minimum viable populations or minimum critical size. The political impotence of MSY can be seen in its results in fisheries, where it has been downgraded from a target to a reference point (Punt & Smith, Chapter 3). Minimum viable population has been used more constructively, in some cases, but Grumbine (1992) showed its power to govern an approach to the conservation of grizzly bears in the greater Yellowstone Park ecosystem, to variable effect. Moreover, MSY, along with minimum viable population and minimum critical size, practically invites political compromise around the least demanding constraint. So, minimum viable population becomes the maximum population worried about, or minimum critical size becomes the most acreage policy-makers must leave intact. MSY, despite loud voices calling for below-maximum harvest to allow for the imprecision in MSY or stock or recruitment estimates (e.g. Ludwig, Chapter 2), becomes sustainable yield or, worse, some fraction of total allowable catch. This tendency to misuse MSY or its analogues is seen vividly in the case of Atlantic cod *Gadus morhua* (National Research Council, 1999). In general, the precautionary principle is a hope expressed, rather than a policy implemented, and a system goal tends to be fixed by social organisations, rather than allowed to reflect the intertemporal and spatial variability that natural systems require (Holling & Sanderson, 1996). This does not even address the additional complexity of creating a management design that actually tries to mimic or replicate natural variability. How a highly managed system can reflect natural system stochasticity, or the pulses of large system-changing events such as storms, is not evident.

A similar danger exists in the way conservationists contest the social construction of pests, wildlife or even preservation as concepts. It is commonly known that elephants are favourite conservation targets, but their parallel local characterisation as pests makes conservation efforts difficult 'in really existing communities' (Roe, 1998). Similar arguments could be made about game species of wildlife, especially when they are both trophy animal and pest (the mountain lion *Felis concolor*), or traditional hunting prey and valuable commodity (black bear *Ursus americanus* and its gall bladder).

Communicating the need for conservation also finds hurdles in the cases of less charismatic fauna, such as desert pupfish *Cyrinodon macularius*, prairie chickens *Tympanuchus cupido,* and snail darters *Percina tanasi,* whose value is not widely evident and whose use in litigation against development in the USA leads to cynicism and 'conservation fatigue' among the lay population.

These disparate examples speak to a more general problem: the inability to communicate technically or scientifically derived knowledge to a policy establishment or a local community in a way that converges with existing knowledge in those communities, or in a way that outcompetes anti-conservation interests on the ground (Goldschmidt, 1996). After all, there still is little consensus among the conservation community, much less the general public, on general notions of sustainability, preservation, conservation or 'wise use'. Even less can be expected from getting species populations, water levels, habitat or other structuring conditions for conservation 'right'. For the policy establishment, especially, information must be communicated with an eye toward political success. In local communities, scientific information must be made part of local knowlege, rather than its opposite.

TRAPS AND SNARES

In cases where conservation values are successfully agreed upon and communicated – that tropical forests should be left as much intact as possible, for example – a number of stereotypical methods of enhancing conservation prove problematic. Some well-established recent postulates of conservation make the case clear:

- *Postulate 1*: Conservation, like politics, is mainly local. So, conservation action plans must take place in local communities, where both local knowledge and mutually reinforcing behaviours are present (this is the simplest rendition of community-based conservation, which can be applied to a number of different project styles to promote conservation).
- *Postulate 2*: Secure tenure promotes conservation (the property rights postulate) (see des Clers (1998) on collective good vs. public goods).
- *Postulate 3*: Local peoples are conservationist by nature or by practice (the small is beautiful, ecologically noble savage, dwellers in the land postulate).
- *Postulate 4*: Commercial consumptive use can become conservation.

In the context of each of these postulates, field-based, science-oriented conservationists can make a difference in their own work and in allegiance with others. Some recent directions in the literature give us guidance to some principles of action that are, in fact, durable principles of politics. Returning to the postulates above, we can see that

- *Postulate 1*: Conservation, like politics, is mainly local. Several aspects of this plain statement invite refinement of the kind locally based conservationists can provide. First, it will be more apparent to people in the community than to outsiders that communities are highly differentiated, complicated environments (Marks, 1991; Agrawal, 1998), in which political actions must be carefully contrived, and in which local participation is critical to success. Conservation, unlike macroeconomic development, cannot be separated from place. That means that action must emanate from places where people live their lives and construct their political behaviours and institutions. In this regard, the macropolitical economy of the global environment (Pearce,

1997) does not provide good guidance for conservation action. (It goes without saying that in an epoch of global environmental change, local conservation may not be enough. For example, atmospheric transport of pollutants can change the species composition of vegetation communities, or cause oligotrophic bodies of water to become eutrophic, with all the attendant implications for cross-trophic dynamics.)

- *Postulate 2*: Secure tenure promotes conservation. This argument slips too easily into an argument for private land or marine tenure rights. The wide world of conservationists who have embraced property rights as a strong premise for conservation have missed some critical points: first, that property rights are extremely diverse in relation to land, wildlife and genetic material, all of which are subjects of political contestation (Naughton & Sanderson, 1995); secondly, that property systems are not commensurable across cultural divides (meaning that 'our' ideas of property are not universally held, and therefore are not neutral numeraries of conservation or development); and, thirdly, that after all the visibility given to property rights, nowhere in the literature can we find a causal relationship between secure tenure and preferred environmental outcomes. In fact, much evidence in the American public lands debate suggests that property rights are not an effective vehicle for promoting conservation, except against the extreme standards of open-access resource exploitation. In the Western lands case, ranchers eagerly try to mimic private land rights with grazing rights on public lands, but those rights hardly enhance conservation outcomes. Neither do the private forest concessions of the northwest USA, which have resulted in abusive deforestation at the expense of natural forest sytems region-wide. Outside the USA, the willingness of the development community to use property rights to advance sustainability is evidence of the ideological narrowing that impairs conservation enquiry (Lindblom, 1990). Needless to say, if conservationists were to suggest that the socialisation of property rights might prove superior in terms of conservation outcomes, the proposition would be unacceptable because of the same narrowing.
- *Postulate 3*: Local peoples are conservationist by nature or practice. This most remarkable debate continues, long after the essential point has been made (that low output producers/harvesters have complex approaches to resource management, and are not simple Utopians who live in harmony with nature). In fact, while this position has been taken partly to defend local practices against invasion from outside forces, it

puts poor local people in an impossible position. First, they are pressed by forces on all sides to increase their off-take or to degrade their land. Secondly, they are held up against all of this pressure as the only hope for sustainable use (Hutton & Dickson, Chapter 20). And, thirdly, they are inevitably condemned and their property rights challenged when they fail to meet the standards set for them by outsiders on both sides of a debate taking place outside their power. No such standards are applied to populations in fragile environments who are not poor.

- *Postulate 4*: Commercial consumptive use can become conservation. This postulate has a heritage that emanates from the beginnings of sustainable use, which at first emphasised the economic viability and relative innocence of harvesting such tropical commodities as Brazil nuts, rattan and other non-timber forest products. By now, most concede that such experiments have depended a great deal on subsidies of some kind, from price supports to monopsonies (sole consumers) such as the icecream sellers Ben and Jerry's. In fact, Freese (1999) argued that subsidies are an institutional answer to the problem of sustainable use, which presupposes that those who decide those subsidies (which are also taxes on others and prices set in non-market environments, which have failed elsewhere (Folke *et al.*, 1998)) will know how to manage an artificial price to best conservation benefit. But the real problem with commercial consumptive use is that the determination of the supply, demand, exchange and distribution of commodities will be set by agents with norms that are inconsistent with conservation. In the case of commercial consumptive use for trade, the market value of commodities is most often remote from the site of production. This invariably means less sensitivity to the long-term degradation of the site itself, especially when the commodity or exploitative practice in question (reef fishing, logging of tropical hardwoods) can be moved from site to site as the effects of resource depletion become apparent. This allows the argument for trade in general to be supported; at the same time one can sustain the argument against trade in specific instances.

In general, conservationists have adopted one of three strategies in politics: to remove the connection between conservation and human impacts, to argue instead that conservation must be sought for its own sake; to argue that conservation has its own referents and values, but can be done within the ambit of human use; or to denominate conservation as a function of, or in terms of, human use.

The first, though it is the most difficult to sustain, has its merits. If one can establish the value of species or ecosystems or whatever conservation 'target' independent of human impact or value, the terms and standards to be applied when dealing with the human side will be clearer. So, if a protected area or an area designed for restoration or an endangered species is removed analytically from its human surrounds, the ecological values can be determined independently of the human impact (parks, furry animals, and degraded ecosystems such as the Everglades are good examples). The same cannot be said of denominating conservation in terms of use. Once the value of a species or ecosystem is purely or even principally economic (Brazil nuts, game animals, or ecotourist landscapes), it is difficult in the extreme to disconnect the political discourse from the market.

WHAT'S THE STORY?

An advantage of empirically based, locally engaged conservation research and action is its added value in constructing plausible conservation experiments. Conservation, like development, is a 'narrative' set by the powers-that-be (Fairhead & Leach, 1996; Leach & Mearns, 1996; Roe, 1998). The tendency of international NGOs and development agencies alike is to globalise conservation successes, as if they represented successful templates that might be applied practically anywhere. Integrated Conservation and Development Projects, extractive reserves, communal fisheries and other similar ideas have been made 'portable' by international conservation and development agents. Therein lies the greatest potential trap: generalising the conservation programme beyond the specificities of place. As is rarely the case in market-driven development designs, in conservation, 'wherever you go, there you are', meaning that place does make a difference. Conservation designs are not portable, without respect to place. This is especially true in the politics of conserving endemic species or ecosystems: pygmy marmosets are not howlers; the Everglades is not the Pantanal. The stories of these species or ecosystems and their challenges are unique to place, ecosystem, community and organism.

The advantage this offers is the superiority of field experience over generalisation. If, in fact, local knowledge is important, and if the livelihoods of local resource managers determine the outcomes of sustainability experiments, and if field work in community-based conservation is participatory and collaborative, the community of conservationists who are engaged in local-scale projects has a great deal to contribute to current practice. It is particularly clear that local field biologists, hydrologists and the like can contribute performance measures to adaptive exercises in conservation politics. That power depends on telling the story effectively.

Such a potential contribution is vulnerable to two great dangers, though: first, to accept the history of local use as it has been written (which, in Africa and much of Asia, means written by recent colonial authority, and in Florida or the Chesapeake Bay by urban interests and industry), rather than as it is told locally; and, secondly, to fall prey to the development trap, which denominates conservation actions in terms of their economic contribution to the 'betterment' of local peoples. Development has been largely unsuccessful in terms of sustainability and in redistribution of income. It has succeeded in increasing the flow of modern services and in generating more economic production. The political arithmetic that developmentalists use to say that development is good does not have anything particular to say to conservationists. The conservationist needs to tell a separate story, not one of sustainable development.

THE SCALE LIMITS OF SUCCESSES

Related to the problem of interpreting local environmental histories over long stretches of time is the issue of scale. An abiding problem of international environmentalist efforts has been the poor organisational connectivity across scales of space, organisation, human environment and time. In many ways, international agreements have been among the most successful symbolic victories in the last three decades. The Convention on International Trade in Endangered Species of Wild Fauna and Flora (CITES), the International Whaling Convention, the Montreal Protocol, the International Ivory Ban, the Framework Convention on Climate Change (FCCC), and many others have changed global perceptions of the importance of environmental sustainability at some scale. Some successes may be mainly perceptual, whereas others substantively involve more accurate monitoring (especially CITES and the Whaling Convention), scientific cooperation (FCCC and the Antarctic Treaty), or private–public collaboration (Montreal Protocol on ozone depleting substances).

What characterises and limits all of these successes to some extent is their lack of real connection to local communities in which the subjects of their concern are harvested, and the inability of international agreements to break with two essential weaknesses of conservation politics: the dominance of international organisations, including international NGOs, in setting the international political agenda; and the related lack of a differentiated understanding of conservation purposes.

Added to this weakness – or lack of connectedness to the local 'story' – is the problem of open systems. Within this set, which describes most marine systems and many terrestrial systems, is the subset of ecosystems or social systems driven by exogenous forces: the Falklands squid fishery, driven by global or European Union (EU) fisheries policy; the upland Amazon, whose forests are threatened by relative prices in beef, government policy toward colonisation schemes, and the market for non-timber forest products; or the Florida Everglades, driven by competing jurisdictions of federal, state, local and tribal government, as well as by ornamental horticulturalists and freight forwarders who pollute the system with exotics, perhaps without giving it any thought whatsoever.

SLEEPING WITH THE ENEMY: THE PUBLIC CONFUSION OVER WILDLIFE SYMBOLS

In 1996 and 1997, the Humane Society USA (HSUS) began an international campaign to stop the culling of African elephants in southern Africa. Sadly, the campaign, which targeted USAID support for the CAMPFIRE programme in Zimbabwe, ignored the large literature available from the Africa Resources Trust and others on CAMPFIRE, along with most of the issues of importance to local peoples: self-government, income, pest management and the like. Instead, HSUS and its South African colleagues contended that programmes such as CAMPFIRE in Zimbabwe are actually a 'struggle for the soul of conservation', in which predatory sustainable use advocates battle those concerned with the rights of 'sentient beings' to live in peace (Barrit, 1996; Koch, 1996; Corn & Fletcher, 1997). This represents nothing less than the international alienation of resource management from its geographical and cultural context, replacing those values with generic calls for preservation of all life (see Hutton & Dickson, Chapter 20).

Essential to conservation's ability to counter such campaigns, or their analogues (pitting recreational and commercial near-shore fishers against each other at the expense of local small-scale fishers; large-scale agriculture against forest preservation in the tropics, with local settlers buffeted by both) is the willingness to form coalitions with local contingents who may not be conservationists per se. These partners may be near-coast shrimpers in Louisiana, or wildlife 'poachers' from traditional Florida. They may even extend to agriculturalists and hunters, as has been the case with migratory birds. To be associated with extreme organisations advocating the complete sanctity of all animal life is to fly in the face of human history and to give up far more in gains than could possibly result in productive alliances.

KILLING THE MESSENGER

An article in *Nature* (Masood, 1997) mentioned a British House of Lords report criticising scientists for being partly to blame for the depleted state of global fisheries, as they had issued cautious scientific advice that, in turn, had been used by fishers and managers to continue overfishing. The article goes on to recognise the many problems of fisheries models, including recruitment, global climate change, variable or unknown mortality from fishing, and the like (see Punt & Smith, Chapter 3). It is convenient in this case, and in others, to project the accusation of unsound management practices onto small-scale fisheries in the developing world, which apparently do not compare well with the EU, or the USA, for that matter. Such argument is remarkably disingenuous. As can be seen, for example, in the case of the Falkland Islands squid fishery (des Clers, 1998), missing knowledge about the biology of the squid *Loligo gahi*, or exogenous biophysical drivers, pale by comparison with the rampant growth in commercial fishing capacity and its relocation in the 1980s to new fishing grounds, including the Falklands. In fact, the EU had allowed its policy of capacity reduction in the fleet to result in a displacement of capacity to the Falklands. The short one-year cycle of the squid and the division of the fishery itself into two zones permits recovery, even in the face of interannual variability. But not without regard to fishing off-take. In the case of the Falklands, that harvest is exogenously determined, set in motion by EU policy, and politically beyond the Falklands.

The conservation community needs to have high profile responses to the 'blame the locals' innuendo that so characterises the conservation polemic today, and to be careful to avoid falling into any categorical political position, including the opposite, 'romanticise the locals' option. It is particularly difficult, but important, to stake out credible scientific positions that align conservation with local communities, but not to lay the burden of conservation entirely on their heads, for the reasons cited above.

CONCLUSIONS

Conservationists will always be better at conservation than politics, though it is clear the two roles are interwoven. The sense of this chapter is that two great political dangers continue to stalk good conservation practices: the implementation of policies that are too simplistic or wrong, or practices that are far more categorical than robust. Similarly, there should be a kind of Hippocratic oath for conservation, which would require that conservationists do no harm. The 'no regrets' policies that have been advocated in global environmental change certainly apply to conservation, and to conservationists as well as others on the political scene.

Herein lies the greatest political potential for getting the biology right: the careful, empirical elucidation of ecological dynamics in ways that allow policies to be 'micro-fitted' to both human and ecological variety and variability. Consider, for example, the relationship among primate populations, tropical forest exploitation, ecosystem diversity, and local human practices (for a review, see Fa & Peres, Chapter 10). Chapman & Onderdonk (1998) related the complex interaction of primates, other frugivores and interactants, kinds of human forest uses, and resulting plant and animal diversity. They show in their own work, along with other studies cited: the troubling connection between environmental 'solutions' such as extractive reserves and primate losses through hunting; the salience of hunting for loss of frugivores among other more apparently systemic human activities, such as logging and agriculture; and the importance of primate abundance to seed dispersal in tropical forests. This work not only suggests new research questions, but practically insists on cross-scale appreciation of ecological phenomena and attention to wildlife harvest as a central concern in overall tropical forest loss (Robinson *et al.*, 1999). But conservation will always be marginal to politics, however important it is to sustainability. The vocation of conservation should be science-based public policy at the local level, with careful efforts to scale up. To succumb to political opportunity or political time scales is to give up the long-term goals of conservation, which include the preservation of natural ecosystems with human impact, over the long time scales that evolution requires and politics abjures.

REFERENCES

Agrawal, A. (1998). Community in conservation: beyond enchantment and disenchantment. Unpublished Conservation and Development Forum Discussion Paper.

Ayensu, E. *et al.* (1999). International ecosystem assessment. *Science*, **286**, 685–689.

Barrit, D. (1996). The case against culling. *Mail & Guardian*, 1 March.

Chapman, C. A. & Onderdonk, D. A. (1998). 'Forests without primates: primate/plant codependency. *American Journal of Primatology*, **45**, 127–141.

Coles, R. (1989). *The Call of Stories: Teaching and the Moral Imagination.* Houghton-Mifflin, Boston, MA.

Corn, M. L. & Fletcher, S. R. (1997). African elephant issues: CITES and CAMPFIRE. Unpublished report from Congressional Research Service, Environmental and Natural Resources Division, 5 August.

Czech, B. & Krausman, P. R. (1997). Distribution and causation of species endangerment in the United States. *Science*, **277**, 1116–1117.

des Clers, S. (1998). The Falkland Islands squid fishery. In *Conservation of Biological Resources*, ed. E. J. Milner-Gulland & R. Mace, pp. 225–241. Blackwell, London.

Dobson, A.P., Rodriguez, J. P., Roberts, W. M. & Wilcove, D. S. (1997). Geographic distribution of endangered species in the United States. *Science*, **275**, 550–553.

Englund, H. (1996). Culture, environment and the enemies of complexity. *Review of African Political Economy*, **76**, 179–188.

Fairhead, J. & Leach, M. (1996). *Misreading the African Landscape: Society and Ecology in a Forest–Savanna Mosaic*. Cambridge University Press, Cambridge.

Folke, C., Kautsky, N., Berg, H., Jansson, A. & Troell, M. (1998). The ecological footprint concept for sustainable seafood production: a review. *Ecological Applications*, **8**(Supplement), 563–571.

Freehling, J. & Marks, S. A. (1998). A century of change in the central Luangwa Valley of Zambia. In *Conservation of Biological Resources*, ed. E. J. Milner-Gulland & R. Mace, pp. 261–278. London: Blackwell.

Freese, C. H. (1999). *Wild Species as Commodities: Managing Markets and Ecosystems for Sustainability*. Island Press, Washington, DC.

Goldschmidt, T. (1996). *Darwin's Dreampond: Drama in Lake Victoria*. Trans. S. Marx-Macdonald. MIT Press, Cambridge, MA.

Gray, T. S. (ed.) (1998). *The Politics of Fishing*. Macmillan, London.

Grumbine, E. (1992). *Ghost Bears: Exploring the Biodiversity Crisis*. Island Press, Washington, DC.

Holling, C. S. & Sanderson, S. E. (1996). 'The dynamics of (dis)harmony in ecological and social systems. In *Rights to Nature*, ed. S. Hannah, pp. 57–85. Island Press, Washington, DC.

Inamdar, A., de Jode, H., Lindsay, K. & Cobb, S. (1999). Capitalizing on nature: protected area management. *Science*, **283**, 1856–1859.

Kaplan, R. D. (1997). *The Ends of the Earth: A Journey at the Dawn of the 21st Century*. Papermac, London.

Karlsson, B. G. (1999). Ecodevelopment in practice: Buxa Tiger Reserve and forest people. *Economic and Political Weekly*, **34**, 2087–2094.

Koch, E. (1996). Who takes home the trophies? *Mail & Guardian*, 1 March.

Leach, M. & Mearns, R. (eds.) (1996). *The Lie of the Land: Challenging Received Wisdom on the African Environment*. International African Institute in cooperation with Heinemann and James Currey, London.

Lindblom, C. E. (1990). *Inquiry and Change: The Troubled Attempt to Understand and Shape Society*. Yale University Press, New Haven, CT.

Ludwig, D. (1993). Environmental sustainability: magic, science, and religion in natural resource management. *Ecological Applications*, **3**, 555–558.

Ludwig, D., Hilborn, R. & Walters, C. (1993). Uncertainty, resource exploitation, and conservation: lessons from history. *Science*, **260**, 17, 36.

Lugo, A. (1995). Management of tropical biodiversity. *Ecological Applications*, **5**, 956–961.

Mangel, M., Talbot, L. M., Meffe, G. K. *et al.* (1996). Principles for the conservation of wild living resources. *Ecological Applications*, **6**, 338–362.

Marks, S. (1983). *The Imperial Lion: Human Dimensions of Wildlife Management in Central Africa*. Westview Press, Boulder, CO.

Marks, S. (1991). *Southern Hunting in Black and White*. Princeton University Press, Princeton, NJ.

Masood, E. (1997). Fisheries science; all at sea when it comes to politics? *Nature*, **386**, 105–106.

McNeely, J. (1998). *Economics and Biological Diversity: Developing and Using Economic Incentives to Conserve Biological Resources*. IUCN, Gland, Switzerland.

McRae, M. (1998). Survival test for Kenya's wildlife. *Science*, **280**, 510.

Milner-Gulland, E. J. & Mace, R. (eds.) (1998). *Conservation of Biological Resources*. Blackwell, London.

National Research Council (1999). *Sustaining Marine Fisheries*. National Academy Press, Washington, DC.

Naughton, L. & Sanderson, S. (1995). Property, politics and wildlife conservation. *World Development*, **28**, 1265–1275.

Neumann, R. P. (1998). *Imposing Wilderness: Struggles over Livelihood and Nature Preservation in Africa*. University of California Press, Berkeley, CA.

Oates, J. F. (1999). *Myth and Reality in the Rain Forest: How Conservation Strategies are Failing in West Africa*. University of California Press, Berkeley, CA.

Oldfield, M. L. & Alcorn, J. B. (eds.) (1991). *Biodiversity: Culture, Conservation and Ecodevelopment*. Westview Press, Boulder, CO.

Pearce, D. (1997). The political economy of the global environment. *British Journal of Political Economy*, **44**, 462–481.

Redford, K. & Padoch, C. (1992). *Conservation of Neotropical Forests: Working from Traditional Resource Use*. Columbia University Press, New York.

Redford, K. & Sanderson, S. (1992). The brief barren marriage of biodiversity and sustainability. *Bulletin of the Ecological Society of America*, **73**, 36–39.

Robinson, J. & Redford, K. (1991). *Neotropical Wildlife Use and Conservation*. University of Chicago Press, Chicago.

Robinson, J., Redford, K. & Bennett, E. (1999). Wildlife harvest in logged tropical forests. *Science*, **284**, 595–596.

Roe, E. (1998). *Taking Complexity Seriously: Policy Analysis, Triangulation and Sustainable Development*. Kluwer Academic Publishers, Dordrecht.

Sanderson, S. E. (1997). The politics of natural and human systems. Presidential Plenary Lecture, Annual Meeting of the Ecological Society of America, Albuquerque, NM.

Sanderson, S. & Redford, K. (1996). Naming, claiming and distributing the world's biota: biodiversity politics and the contest for ownership of the world's biodiversity. In *Last Stand: Protected Areas and the Defense of Tropical Biodiversity*, ed. R. Kramer, J. Johnson & C. von Shaik, pp. 115–132. Oxford University Press, Oxford.

Shafer, C. L. (1999). National park and reserve planning to protect biological diversity: some basic elements. *Landscape and Urban Planning*, **44**, 123–153.

Soulé, M. F. & Sanjayan, M. A. (1998). Conservation targets: do they help? *Science*, **279**, 2060–2064.

Terborgh, J. (1999). *Requiem for Nature*. Island Press, Washington, DC.

Vitousek, P. M., Mooney, H. A., Lubchenco, J. & Mellilo, J. M. (1997). Human domination of earth's ecosystems. *Science*, **277**, 494–499.

PART VI

Final thoughts

22

Using 'sustainable use' approaches to conserve exploited populations

JOHN G. ROBINSON

Human society has always depended on the exploitation of wild species. With the advent of agriculture and industry, and the steady appropriation, modification and conversion of wild lands, that dependence has diminished. But people continue to harvest fish, fowl and forest, and human economy and well-being still depend on access to those wild resources (Eltringham, 1984; Johns, 1997; Pikitch *et al.*, 1997; Roth & Merz, 1997). Exploitation can, however, be of conservation concern: harvest can threaten directly the survival of exploited populations, compromise the integrity and diversity of biological communities and deplete resource stocks and stands.

The conservation community has addressed the issue of the conservation of exploited species in two ways. The first way has been to protect those species from exploitation or use. The most widely used mechanism has been to establish protected areas where wild populations cannot be exploited. The establishment of parks and reserves throughout the British Empire in the nineteenth and twentieth centuries, for example, was an attempt to protect previously exploited wildlife populations (MacKenzie, 1988). In a less permanent fashion, recent efforts to establish marine protected areas off the US coast (Schmidt, 1997; Jegalian, 1999) are geared towards protecting marine stocks from further exploitation until population numbers can rebound. Another mechanism has been to protect species by regulating their trade. The US Endangered Species Act of 1969 was enacted to protect species 'threatened with worldwide extinction' by banning their commercial import into the USA (Bean, 1983). The subsequent Convention on Trade in Endangered Species of Wild Fauna and Flora (CITES) controlled the importation of wild species into signatory countries. This international treaty prohibits trade of the most vulnerable species (those on Appendix I) and regulates the trade of other species who were judged to be threatened by harvest and international trade (those listed on Appendix II). The logic of this approach is that once exploited populations fall to a certain level when they are themselves threatened, or when their ecological role is threatened, then harvest has to be limited or stopped.

The second way to conserve exploited species is not to seek to stop all use. Instead, the approach has been to allow use to continue, but promote restraint in the harvest of wild populations so that populations never fall to the levels where the biological, social and economic consequences are unacceptable. This is the approach first promulgated at the Stockholm conference in 1980, promoted by the World Conservation Strategy (1980), developed further by the Brundtland Commission (1987), and advocated at the Rio Conference (1993). The common thread in all of these international accords is the promotion of national economic development based on natural resource use in a manner that (in the poetic words of the Brundtland Commission) 'seeks to meet the needs and aspiration of the present without compromising the ability to meet those of the future'. Wild living resources are to be used 'at rates within their capacity for renewal' (IUCN/UNEP/WWF, 1991). In other words, natural resources are to be used sustainably.

Neither approach can be universally applied. On one hand, the protection of populations from exploitation removes resources from people, often those that are underprivileged or socially marginalised and dependent on the wild resources (Hutton & Dickson, Chapter 20). Consequently such protection is difficult, often very expensive, and can be challenged on ethical grounds (Adams & McShane, 1992; Ostrom *et al.*, 1999). On the other hand, any and all significant uses of natural resources result in loss of biodiversity and dimunition of ecosystem functioning (Robinson, 1993). Human society and human behaviour are structured to maximise short-term resource acquisition, so managing people is a challenge (Ludwig *et al.*, 1993). And managing resources is extremely difficult because biological systems are very complex and the necessary information is rarely available (Ludwig *et al.*, 1993; Ludwig, Chapter 2). But where continued use of wild resources and conservation of wild species are both required, the only approach is to establish management systems that will allow 'sustainable use'.

SUSTAINABLE USE

If people are to continue to use or derive a benefit from wild populations, then one goal of 'sustainable use' is to use the resource efficiently (Mace & Hudson, 1999). If that use depletes the resource, threatening present or future use, or if use threatens wild populations or ecosystem functioning, then another goal is to promote restraint in the exploitation (Mace &

Hudson, 1999). These two goals, efficiency and restraint, are the most fundamental requirements of the concept of 'sustainable use' of wild, renewable, natural resources. With efficiency and restraint, the argument goes, use can occur while minimising the probability of species extinction, conversion of the habitat, loss of biodiversity, or degradation of the resource.

In this its simplest form, the concept of 'sustainable use' is not particularly controversial. However, the concept has evolved beyond being a mere balancing act to being an active conservation strategy. The argument is that use, if carried out with the appropriate efficiency and restraint, can actually promote conservation (e.g. Allen & Edwards, 1995; Hutton & Dickson, Chapter 20). According to this argument, promoting use, or allowing use to continue, allows wild resources to be valued by people, and if wild species and their habitats are valued, this discourages the conversion of natural habitat to other land uses. This strategy has been formally adopted by many elements within the conservation community. The eighteenth General Assembly of the World Conservation Union in Australia, for instance, passed a resolution (18.24) that states 'properly managed projects for the sustainable use of wildlife can enhance the conservation of wildlife populations and their ecosystems because of the economic and other benefits that such use provides'. This argument goes back to the very beginning of the International Union for the Conservation of Nature (IUCN, now World Conservation Union). In 1948, Julian Huxley, at the inauguration of the IUPN (International Union for the Protection of Nature, later IUCN), articulated this concept by stating (Holdgate, 1999) that, to be conserved, 'nature must be considered as a resource', otherwise nature areas will be converted for greater productivity for humans. In other words, use of wild species, if sustainable, should be actively promoted as a conservation strategy.

The correctness of this argument, as it applies to the use of exploited species, turns out to depend on the specific management goals (see also Mace & Reynolds, Chapter 1). It depends on what exactly is being sustained. Sustainability itself can be defined as 'simply the ability to maintain something undiminished over some period' (Lélé & Norgaard, 1996). In the case of 'sustainable use', 'use' by human consumers is to be sustained. To accomplish that, the 'somethings' that humans use also must be sustained and conserved. And it is in the definition of those 'somethings' that divergences in management goals become apparent. Some argue that it is the exploited species themselves on which people depend that need to be conserved. The management goal is therefore species conservation. Others argue that it is the ecosystems, of which the exploited species are a part, that need to be conserved. The management goal is therefore maintaining

ecosystem health, functioning or structure. Still others argue that it is resources in general that need to be conserved, and that the management
goal is sustaining human livelihoods.

These different management goals reflect the values and objectives of
different interest groups in human society. Consider the two following
understandings of 'sustainable use':

> Sustainable use means that the use of a species in a manner and at a level
> such that populations of the species are maintained at biologically viable
> levels for the long term and involves the determination of the productive
> capacity of the species and its ecosystem, in order to ensure that utilization
> does not exceed those capacities or the ability of the population to repro-
> duce, maintain itself, and perform its role or function in its ecosystem.
> (*US Wild Bird Conservation Act implementing regulations*)

> the use of components of biological diversity in a way and at a rate that does
> not lead to the long-term decline of biological diversity, thereby maintaining
> its potential to meet the needs and aspirations of present and future gener-
> ations. (*Convention on Biological Diversity, 1998*)

In the case of the US Wild Bird Conservation Act (WBCA), the ultimate
management goal of 'sustainable use' is the conservation of the specific
bird species being exploited, and the ecosystem in which it lives. The goal,
in the case of the Convention on Biological Diversity (CBD), is the conservation of the biological resource base for present and future human consumers. Both are concerned with the conservation of exploited species, but
their ultimate goals are not identical and might not even be compatible.

The choice of different management goals is the outcome of a
sociopolitical process and is not a scientific decision per se (Robinson,
1993; Lélé & Norgaard, 1996). Different interest groups have different
goals. A government agency charged with promoting rural development
might have a goal different from that of a grass roots conservation organisation. Management goals, where wild species are being exploited, can usefully be distinguished into those that seek to sustain (a) species
populations, (b) ecosystem health, or (c) human livelihoods.

In this book we are concerned with the conservation of exploited species. To what extent does meeting different management goals result in the
conservation of those species? To answer this question, I first examine the
indicators of 'sustainable use' that have been used to measure the achieve-
ment of different management goals. I then consider whether management approaches based on species, ecosystems or resources are most
effective at conserving exploited species.

Table 22.1. Indicators of sustainable use. Examples applicable to different management goals

Management goals	Indicators of sustainable use
Species conservation	1. Populations show no consistent decline
	2. Populations are not vulnerable to extinction
	3. Populations maintain ecological role
Ecosystem health	1. Species richness and diversity maintained
	2. Primary productivity maintained
	3. Nutrient cycling maintained
	4. Landscape patterns maintained
Human livelihoods	1. Total catch or harvest maintained
	2. Catch or harvest composition maintained
	3. Catch or harvest per unit effort maintained
	4. Wood and non-timber yields maintained

MANAGEMENT GOALS

Species conservation

Indicators of sustainability, where the management goal is the conservation of a specific species, are frequently measurable in a scientific and objective way (see Table 22.1). The most fully developed system for exploited species is the set of criteria for listing species in the CITES appendices, a system itself based on the IUCN criteria for threatened species (IUCN, 1996). These criteria are highly detailed, but generally have the following broad basis:

- *Use does not result in a consistent decline in population numbers of wild species.* The absence of a consistent decline in population numbers is a *sine qua non* of the sustainability of use when the goal is the conservation of species (Robinson, 1993). A consistent decline indicates that the removal of individuals from a population is greater than the annual production, after taking into account natural mortality. Such a decline is distinct from short-term declines such as is usually evident at the onset of harvesting, or in species whose numbers fluctuate over time.
- *Use does not reduce population numbers to where they are vulnerable to local extinction.* If populations are reduced to low numbers, they might be unable to recover, and be in danger of extirpation. The mechanisms of small population extinction are well understood, and there is an emerging consensus of when 'small is too small' (Soulé, 1987).

- *Use does not reduce population numbers to where the ecological role of the species in the ecosystem is impaired.* Species occur as part of biological communities, and declines in their numbers affect the probabilities of survival of those other species, and the biological integrity of the community as a whole (see Kaiser & Jennings, Chapter 16; Redford & Feinsinger, Chapter 19). However, even though this criterion is widely used in discussions of sustainability of use (see WBCA above), and indeed is codified in Article IV of the text of CITES, until it can be measured unambiguously, it can only be used in a general way.
- *Use does not reduce population numbers to where they cease to be a significant resource to human users.* This indicator is codified in the US Marine Mammal Protection Act of 1969 as revised in 1981, which states its management goal as attaining 'optimum sustainable population', one in which the resource for human consumers is not depleted (Bean, 1983). A resource is considered depleted if population numbers fall below the maximum productivity of the population or species, keeping in mind the carrying capacity of the habitat and the health of the ecosystem.

Ecosystem health

Species are components of ecosystems, so the conservation of exploited species can be accomplished, in theory, if the indicators of sustainable use (Table 22.1) measure ecosystem 'health' (Constanza *et al.*, 1992). Here the management goal is not to compromise key ecosystem structures and processes, though human exploitation of natural resources might compromise ecological integrity and result in some loss to particular species (Callicott & Mumford, 1997).

The establishment of indicators at the ecosystem level is less advanced than those at the species level, owing to the difficulty of identifying and measuring ecosystem traits and the processes that underlie them (Clark, 1999). Nevertheless, there is a general consensus that such traits are measurable, and could serve as indicators of sustainable use (Grumbine, 1994; Chapin *et al.*, 1996). Indicators that have been suggested include the following:

- *Use does not significantly reduce biological diversity of the ecosystem.* The management goal specified in a number of international treaties and policy documents is to maintain biological diversity of the ecosystem (CBD, 1998; IUCN/SUI, 1999). The problem with this goal is that biological diversity itself is not an easily defined or measured parameter

(Sanderson & Redford, 1997; Redford & Richter, 1999), and therefore very difficult to use as an indicator of sustainability. A frequently adopted intermediate indicator for biological diversity is amount of habitat conversion (Dobson *et al.*, 1997). While more easily measurable, there is no consensus on the amount of habitat conversion necessary to significantly reduce biological diversity. Noss (1992), for instance, suggested keeping 50% in protected areas within each ecosystem, and Soulé & Sanjayan (1998) indicated that even that might not be sufficient. Much depends on the geographical distribution of that biodiversity (Pimm & Raven, 2000).

• *Use does not significantly diminish ecosystem structure and functioning.* One working definition of an ecosystem that is sustained is one that maintains its characteristic diversity of major functional groups (groups of species with similar effects on ecosystem processes; Lawton & Brown, 1993; Walker, 1995), productivity, and rates of biogeochemical cycling (Chapin *et al.*, 1996, 1997). Ecosystems are dynamic, and species composition, productivity and nutrient cycling all change in response through time; the management goal is to keep those changes within specified bounds. Our understanding of those bounds, however, remains primitive (Chapin *et al.*, 1997), making it difficult to use ecosystem structure and function as a good measure of sustainability.

• *Use does not reduce the mosaic of habitats.* Ecosystems include mosaics of habitat types, and maintenance of the landscape pattern is frequently an indicator of sustainability (Harwell, 1997). While there is a broad consensus that conserving a representative set of habitats is one appropriate indicator, the field of landscape ecology is not sufficiently developed to allow the specification of an optimal 'mix' of habitats that would maximise biodiversity conservation and maintain ecosystem structure and functioning (see Sanderson & Harris, 2000).

Human livelihoods

Species are components of ecosystems, which in turn are embedded in the cultural, economic, and political context of the human-dominated landscape. Where the management goal is to sustain human livelihoods, exploited species are resources and their conservation can, in theory, be accomplished by managing the resource base for human consumers (Table 22.1).

• *Use should not decrease the total availability of resources.* Sustainable use would be indicated when resources levels, measured in nutritional, economic or social terms, are maintained. Sustaining use of natural resources in general would only conserve those exploited wild species if their conservation provided a net benefit to human users.

People do not live by bread alone, and the quality of human livelihoods is not defined by people's simple access to natural resources. Therefore, for those for whom the management goal is to improve human livelihoods, there has been a tendency to specify additional indicators of sustainability. For some, greater equity in the distribution of natural resources is linked to the availability of those resources. For others, a more traditional relationship between people and nature is linked to resource availability. For yet others, a free-market economy is essential to increase resource availability. As a result, proponents of sustainable use who are concerned with human livelihoods therefore frequently advocate these additional social and economic indicators.

The argument frequently is that effective conservation requires the adoption of these indicators. I have argued that sustainable use in general does not require this adoption, although it can in specific cases (see Robinson, 1998). Nevertheless, for the sake of completeness, I list some of these indicators:

- *Use should further local community involvement in resource management.* The social indicator here is the empowering of rural communities. For instance, IIED (1994, p. ix) stated that 'a community's right to ownership and tenure *must* be secured for sustainable wildlife management' (emphasis added).
- *Use should further the integration of wild species and people across the landscape.* The social indicator here is the spatial and social reintegration of people and nature by removing the 'hard-edged' division between wild areas and human-influenced areas. For instance, Kock (1996) made the case for allowing use of natural resources in protected areas in southern Africa, and moving beyond strictly protected parks and reserves (see Hutton & Dickson, Chapter 20).
- *Use should promote local economic activity.* The economic indicator here is to bring wild species into the marketplace, resulting in increasing economic benefits. Roth & Merz (1997) actually define sustainable use as economic use. Only in this way, some advocates argue, can natural resources be conserved. This idea has been popularised as the 'Use it or lose it' school of conservation. Authors such as Child & Child (1990) have argued that wild species 'must pay their own way' in the modern

Table 22.2. Suggested effectiveness of different management approaches for different management goals

Management goals	Management approaches		
	Species management	Ecosystem-based management	Resource management
Species conservation	XXX	XX	X
Ecosystem health	X	XXX	XX
Human livelihoods	XX	XX	XXX

XXX, more effective; XX, effective; X, less effective.

world. Detractors (e.g. Hoyt, 1994; Lavigne *et al.*, 1996) use this argument to attack use of natural resources in general: 'The concept of sustainable utilization of wild life has taken on new connotations in recent years, placing increased emphasis on trade in dead wild life in the marketplace' (Lavigne *et al.*, 1996).

MANAGEMENT APPROACHES

Specifying the management goal does not specify the management approach (see Table 22.2). For example, managing the population directly, the ecosystem as a whole, or the resource base can accomplish a management goal of species conservation. In the case where the goal is the conservation of exploited species, what is the effectiveness of different management approaches? Are species management approaches more effective than ecosystem-based approaches or vice versa? The answers to these questions depend on the compatibility of different indicators of sustainable use. Does management that maintains species richness in an ecosystem ensure that species populations will not show consistent declines in numbers? Does maintaining total catch ensure the same?

Species management
Conserving exploited species directly is the approach classically adopted in wildlife management (see e.g. Caughley, 1977; Beasom & Roberson, 1985) and fisheries (Larkin, 1977). The development of the concept of maximum sustainable yield (MSY) was an attempt to define a single indicator that met all the requirements of sustainability, an attempt that was not totally successful (Larkin, 1977; Punt & Smith, Chapter 3). While indicators of

sustainable use at the species level are relatively easy to measure (Table 22.1), population dynamics are not easily characterised or predicted (e.g. Lande *et al.*, Chapter 4) especially at low population densities (e.g. Petersen & Levitan, Chapter 13); population response to harvesting is frequently uncertain (e.g. Peters, Chapter 11); populations themselves are not just aggregations of individuals but are structured by age and sex (e.g. Kokko *et al.*, Chapter 14). The constant difficulty is that species populations are often strongly influenced by interactions with other species in the system (e.g. Kaiser & Jennings, Chapter 16; Redford & Feinsinger, Chapter 17). Nevertheless, where the goal is species conservation, and where a specific population has a distinct identity and can be managed directly, a species-based approach is the most effective (Table 2.2). This is often the case with wildlife (e.g. Grigg & Pople, Chapter 18).

Ecosystem-based management

Conserving exploited species based on ecosystem indicators (Table 22.1) has a history in both fisheries (NAS, 1999) and forestry (e.g. Bawa & Seidler, 1998). In wildlife, some similar success has been achieved, especially with US endangered species management (e.g. Tasse, 1993). A number of indicators of sustainable use at the ecosystem level, such as maintaining habitat heterogeneity, area modified by people, overall productivity and disturbance regimes, have use for species conservation (Grumbine, 1994; Kaiser & Jennings, Chapter 16).

The challenge to the use of ecosystem indicators to conserve exploited species is that sustaining the ecosystem as a whole does not require conservation of all of its specific elements (Table 22.2). Ecosystems are characterised by high functional and structural redundancy (Lawton & Brown, 1993; Walker, 1995; Chapin *et al.*, 1997), so that frequently the ecological role of one species can be substituted for by that of another (Kaiser & Jennings, Chapter 16). Only in the case of keystone species (Chapin *et al.*, 1997; Simberloff, 1998) or other focal species (Lambeck, 1997), which have unique and strong ecological roles (e.g. Redford & Feinsinger, Chapter 17), is there a strong overlap between species and ecosystem indicators.

Resource management

Conserving exploited species when the management approach is ensuring resource availability to support human livelihoods is even less likely to be successful (Table 22.2). The management approach of sustaining the natural resource base alone can result in loss of key ecosystem structures and processes, significant loss of biodiversity and extinction of particular wild species (see Hulme & Murphree, 1999). Sustainable use might be indicated even if species populations are lost, if this allows the natural resource extraction system as a whole to be conserved. For example, the loss of large predators might be acceptable in southern Africa grasslands if this allows private landowners to maintain high enough stocks of ungulates to be economically viable, and thus avoid conversion to other land uses (R. Martin, personal communication). Maintaining resource availability can result in increasing the production from valued species at the expense of those species of less concern, even those that have resource value. This increased specialisation onto certain species and homogenisation of the resource base is akin to the conversion of a natural landscape into an agroscape (Salwasser, 1994; Freese, 1998).

CONCLUSION: SUSTAINABLE USE AS A CONSERVATION STRATEGY FOR EXPLOITED SPECIES

When both use and conservation are required, making that use sustainable is the only strategy. However, requiring 'sustainable use' as a broad goal does not specify what elements of wild communities will be conserved. Much depends on more specific management goals. To examine the consequences of different goals, I identified three distinct classes of indicators of sustainability: (1) ecological indicators for a single species, (2) ecological indicators for an ecosystem health, and (3) socioeconomic indicators for human livelihoods (Dixon & Fallon, 1989; Robinson, 1993). I also identified three management approaches: (1) managing for the species, (2) ecosystem-based management, and (3) resource management.

While indicators of sustainability for different management goals are broadly compatible and redundant, they are not identical (Table 22.1). Management approaches are most effective when they are matched to the appropriate management goal (Table 22.2). Thus species management approaches are most effective where the goal is species conservation, because the indicator of sustainability is the exploited species itself. These indicators are also the most easily measured in general. Ecosystem-based management can also be effective for species conservation, especially where the indicators of species conservation are difficult to measure, as is frequently the case with large-scale commercial fisheries and forestry operations. Resource management approaches are less effective for species conservation. Even though socioeconomic indicators are the most systemic, considering as they do both the ecosystem and socioeconomic context, their compatibility with the more ecological indicators is less clear, and they are the most difficult to measure.

ACKNOWLEDGEMENTS

I am indebted to my colleagues in IUCN's Sustainable Use Specialist Group for their concerned and deeply felt debate on the issues surrounding the 'Sustainable Use' of natural resources. I would especially point to the arguments with Marshall Murphree, David Brackett, George Rabb, Steve Edwards, Rowan Martin and Grahame Webb, which have sharpened my own thinking. Kent Redford and Jon Hutton dissected earlier versions of this manuscript, and their surgery is deeply appreciated.

REFERENCES

Adams, J. S. & McShane, T. O. (1992). *The Myth of Wild Africa: Conservation without Illusion*. W. W. Norton, New York.

Allen, C. M. & Edwards, S. R. (1995). The sustainable-use debate: observations from IUCN. *Oryx*, **29**, 92–98.

Bawa, K. & Seidler, R. (1998). Natural forest management and conservation of biodiversity in tropical forests. *Conservation Biology*, **12**, 46–55.

Bean, M. J. (1983). *The Evolution of National Wildlife Law*. Praeger, New York.

Beasom, S. L. & Roberson, S. F. (eds.) (1985). *Game Harvest Management*. Ceasar Kleberg Wildlife Research Institute, Kingsville, TX.

Callicott, J. B. & Mumford, K. (1997). Ecological sustainability as a conservation concept. *Conservation Biology*, **11**, 32–40.

Caughley, G. (1977). *Analysis of Vertebrate Populations*. Wiley, New York.

CBD (Convention on Biological Diversity) (1998). Report of the workshop on the ecosystem approach, Lilongwe, Malawi. UNEP/CBD/COP4/Inf. 9 (20 March 1998).

Chapin, F.S., Torn, M. S. & Tateno, M. (1996). Principles of ecosystem sustainability. *American Naturalist*, **148**, 1016–1037.

Chapin, F. S., Walker, B. H., Hobbs, R. J., Hooper, D. U., Lawton, J. H., Sala, O. E. & Tilman, D. (1997). Biotic control over the functioning of ecosystems. *Science*, **277**, 500–503.

Child, G. & Child, B. (1990). A historical perspective of sustainable wildlife utilisation. Unpublished paper presented at 18th IUCN General Assembly, Perth, Australia.

Clark, J. R. (1999). The ecosystem approach from a practical point of view. *Conservation Biology*, **13**, 679–681.

Constanza, R., Norton, B. G. & Haskell, B. D. (1992). *Ecosystem Health: New Goals for Environmental Management*. Island Press, Washington, DC.

Dixon, J. A. & Fallon, L. A. (1989). The concept of sustainability: origins, extensions, and usefulness for policy. *Society and Natural Resources*, **2**, 73–84.

Dobson, A. P., Bradshaw, A. D. & Baker, A. J. M. (1997). Hopes for the future: restoration ecology and conservation biology. *Science*, **277**, 515–522.

Eltringham, S. K. (1984). *Wildlife Resources and Economic Development*. Wiley, Chichester.

Freese, C. H. (1998). *Wild Species as Commodities. Managing Markets and Ecosystems for Sustainability*. Island Press, Washington, DC.

Grumbine, R. E. (1994). What is ecosystem management? *Conservation Biology*, **8**, 27–38.

Harwell, M. A. (1997). Ecosystem management of south Florida. *BioScience*, **47**, 499–512.

Holdgate, M. (1999). *The Green Web. A Union for World Conservation*. Earthscan, London.

Hoyt, J. A. (1994). *Animals in Peril: How 'Sustainable Use' is Wiping out the World's Wildlife*. Avery, New York.

Hulme, D. & Murphree, M. (1999). Communities, wildlife and the 'new conservation' in Africa. *Journal of International Development*, **11**, 277–285.

IIED (International Institute for Environment and Development) (1994). *Whose Eden? An Overview of Community Approaches to Wildlife Management*. Russell Press, Nottingham.

IUCN (World Conservation Union) (1996). *1996 IUCN Red List of Threatened Animals*. IUCN, Gland, Switzerland.

IUCN (World Conservation Union)/SUI (Sustainable Use Initiative) (1999). The principles of sustainable use within an ecosystem approach. Report for the 5th Subsidiary Body for Scientific, Technical, and Technological Advice of the Convention on Biological Diversity.

IUCN (World Conservation Union)/UNEP (United Nations Environment Programme)/WWF (World Wide Fund for Nature) (1991). *Caring for the Earth: A Strategy for Sustainable Living*. IUCN, Gland, Switzerland.

Jegalian, K. (1999). Plan would protect New England coast. *Science*, **284**, 237.

Johns, A. G. (1997). *Timber Production and Biodiversity Conservation in Tropical Rain Forests*. Cambridge University Press, Cambridge.

Kock, M. D. (1996). Zimbabwe: a model for the sustainable use of wildlife and the development of innovative wildlife management practices. In *The Exploitation of Mammal Populations*, ed. V. J. Taylor & N. Dunstone, pp. 229–249. Chapman & Hall, London.

Lambeck, R. J. (1997). Focal species: a multi-species umbrella for nature conservation. *Conservation Biology*, **11**, 849–856.

Larkin, P. A. (1977). An epitaph for the concept of maximum sustained yield. *Transactions of the American Fisheries Society*, **106**, 1–11.

Lavigne, D. M., Callaghan, C. J. & Smith, R. J. (1996). Sustainable utilization: the lessons of history. In *The Exploitation of Mammal Populations*, ed. V. J. Taylor & N. Dunstone, pp. 250–264. Chapman & Hall, London.

Lawton, J. H. & Brown, V. K. (1993). Redundancy in ecosystems. In *Biodiversity and Ecosystem Function*, ed. E.-D. Schulze & H. A. Mooney, pp. 255–270. Springer-Verlag, Berlin.

Lélé, S. & Norgaard, R. B. (1996). Sustainability and the scientist's burden. *Conservation Biology*, **10**, 354–365.

Ludwig, D., Hilborn, R. & Walters, C. (1993). Uncertainty, resource exploitation, and conservation: lessons from history. *Science*, **260**, 17, 36.

Mace, G. M. & Hudson, E. J. (1999). Attitudes towards sustainability and extinction. *Conservation Biology*, **13**, 242–246.

MacKenzie, J. M. (1988). *The Empire of Nature*. Manchester University Press, Manchester.

NAS (National Academy of Sciences) (1999). *Sustaining Marine Fisheries*. National Academy of Sciences, Washington, DC.

Noss, R. F. (1992). The wildlands project: land conservation strategy. *Wild Earth* (Special Issue), **1**, 10–25.

Ostrom, E., Burger, J., Field, C. B., Norgaard, R. B. & Policansky, D. (1999). Revisiting the commons: local lessons, global challenges. *Science*, **284**, 278–282.

Pikitch, E. L., Huppert, D. D. & Sissenwine, M. P. (eds.) (1997). *Global Trends: Fisheries Management*. American Fisheries Society Symposium no. 20, Bethesda, MD.

Pimm, S. L. & Raven, P. (2000). Extinction by numbers. *Nature*, **403**, 843–845.

Redford, K. H. & Richter, B. D. (1999). Conservation of biodiversity in a world of use. *Conservation Biology*, **13**, 1246–1256.

Robinson, J. G. (1993). The limits to caring: sustainable living and the loss of biodiversity. *Conservation Biology*, **7**, 20–28.

Robinson, J. G. (1998). Evolving understanding of sustainable use. In *Enhancing Sustainability – Resources for our Future*, ed. H. A. van der Linde & M. H. Danskin, pp. 3–6. IUCN, Gland, Switzerland.

Roth, H. H. & Merz, G. (1997). *Wildlife Resources: A Global Account of Economic Use*. Springer-Verlag, Berlin.

Salwasser, H. (1994). Ecosystem management: can it sustain diversity and productivity? *Journal of Forestry*, August, 6–10.

Sanderson, J. & Harris, L. D. (2000). *Landscape Ecology. A Top-Down Approach*. Lewis, Boca Raton, FL.

Sanderson, S. E. & Redford, K. H. (1997). Biodiversity politics and the contest for ownership of the world's biota. In *Last Stand. Protected Areas and the Defense of Tropical Biodiversity*, ed. R. Kramer, C. van Schaik & J. Johnson, pp. 115–132. Oxford University Press, Oxford.

Schmidt, K. F. (1997). 'No-take' zones spark fisheries debate. *Science*, **277**, 489–491.

Simberloff, D. (1998). Flagships, umbrellas, and keystones: Is single species management passé in the landscape era? *Biological Conservation*, **83**, 247–257.

Soulé, M. E. (1987). *Viable Populations for Conservation*. Cambridge University Press, Cambridge.

Soulé, M. E. & Sanjayan, M.A. (1998). Conservation targets: Do they help? *Science*, **279**, 2060–2061.

Tasse, J. (1993). Exploring an ecosystem approach to endangered species conservation. *Endangered Species Update*, **10**, 1–62.

Walker, B. H. (1995). Conserving biological diversity through ecosystem resilience. *Conservation Biology*, **9**, 747–752.

Index

Note: page numbers in *italics* refer to figures and tables.